Visual Planned Giving:

An Introduction to the Law & Taxation of Charitable Gift Planning

Russell James III, J.D., Ph.D.
Professor & CH Foundation Chair in Personal Financial Planning
Texas Tech University
www.EncourageGenerosity.com

ISBN: 0615986277
ISBN-13: 978-0615986272

DEDICATION

To Vickie Hampton, Kay Sanford, and Linda Hoover for making the work possible

CONTENTS

	Preface	Pg. 1
1	Introduction: The Secret to Understanding Planned Giving	Pg. 3
	Basic Tax Concepts	
2	A Super Simple Introduction To Taxes	Pg. 19
3	Elements and Timing of a Charitable Gift	Pg. 31
4	How to Document Charitable Gifts	Pg. 49
5	Valuing Charitable Gifts of Property	Pg. 63
6	Income Limitations on Charitable Deductions	Pg. 89
	Give and Get Back	
7	Bargain Sale Gifts	Pg. 119
8	Introduction to Charitable Gift Annuities	Pg. 133
9	Taxation of Charitable Gift Annuities	Pg. 155
	Give Part and Keep Part	
10	Gifts of Partial Interest	Pg. 187
11	Remainder Interests in Homes & Farmland	Pg. 207
12	Charitable Remainder Trusts	Pg. 229
13	Charitable Lead Trusts	Pg. 269
	Special Techniques	
14	Life Insurance in Charitable Planning	Pg. 295
15	Donating Retirement Assets	Pg. 331
16	Private Foundations and Donor Advised Funds	Pg. 347
	Quiz Questions, Answers, and Explanations	
	Chapter 3 Questions	Pg. 381
	Chapter 4 Questions	Pg. 384
	Chapter 5 Questions	Pg. 387
	Chapter 6 Questions	Pg. 391
	Chapter 7 Questions	Pg. 394
	Chapter 8 Questions	Pg. 398
	Chapter 9 Questions	Pg. 401
	Chapter 10 Questions	Pg. 404
	Chapter 11 Questions	Pg. 409
	Chapter 12 Questions	Pg. 414
	Chapter 13 Questions	Pg. 419
	Chapter 14 Questions	Pg. 423
	Chapter 15 Questions	Pg. 427
About the Author		Pg. 432

PREFACE

This is not your father's law and tax book (Part I). The purpose of this text is to communicate to fundraisers and financial advisors the basic concepts of planned giving in a friendly, straightforward, and visually attractive format, while provided explanatory text that might be helpful where the visual elements are insufficient. The intended use is for the reader to flip through the images in the sections of interest until reaching an image that seems new or confusing, at which point the surrounding explanatory text may be helpful. The citations in the text are relatively sparse and for those desiring more technical texts with superior citations I recommend Thomas J. Ray, Jr.'s, *Charitable Gift Planning*, Catherine W. Wilkinson & Jean M. Baxley's, *Charitable Giving Answer Book*, Bruce R. Hopkins' *The Law of Fundraising*, and articles at the planned giving design center, www.pgdc.com.

This is not your father's law and tax book (Part II). This book is intentionally published in a print-on-demand format. This means that changes can be incorporated into the current version of the book within a matter of days. It also means that I would be most appreciative of any information related to errors, trivial or otherwise, because these are easily corrected. Please e-mail me at EncourageGenerosity@gmail.com if you happen to find such. Note, however, that some errors of omission are intentional as this is not intended to be an exhaustive treatment of every possible transaction type and option, but rather is intended to be a basic primer on charitable gift planning.

The slides used in this text are from the courses that I have taught for many years as part of the on-campus and online Graduate Certificate in Charitable Financial Planning and Masters of Science in Personal Financial Planning both in the Department of Personal Financial Planning at Texas Tech University, as well as in my course in Charitable Gift Planning at the Texas Tech University School of Law. Information on the online Graduate Certificate in Charitable Financial Planning is available at www.EncourageGenerosity.com. Additionally, the PowerPoint or pdf version of many of the slides contained herein and audio of some related lectures are also available, for free, at the website.

And now, on to the disclaimers. *This notice is made in order to comply with applicable Treasury Department and other regulations (including but not limited to Circular 230): This book is not intended to provide personal legal, tax or financial advice. Consequently we urge you to seek the advice of your own legal, tax, or financial professionals in connection with gift and planning matters. This text is not intended to be used and cannot be used, for the purpose of avoiding tax-related penalties.*

This document is for information and illustrative purposes only and does not purport to show actual transaction results applicable to your specific situation. It is not, and should not be regarded as investment, legal, or tax advice or as a recommendation regarding any particular transaction or course of action. Opinions expressed herein are current opinions as of the date appearing in this material only and are subject to change without notice. Reasonable people may disagree about the opinions expressed herein. All transaction and investments entail risks. There is no guarantee that investment or tax planning strategies

1 INTRODUCTION:
THE SECRET TO UNDERSTANDING PLANNED GIVING

Sophisticated planned giving can be intimidating for professional fundraisers, financial advisors, and donors. It seemingly offers complex terms, complex calculations, and the risk of serious penalties if done incorrectly. It is no wonder that many simply turn away from the field to stick to the easier approaches they already know. Yet, this fear leads to enormous lost opportunities for the donor, the fundraiser, and the financial advisor. This book is intended to make the concepts of planned giving friendlier and more intuitive. When advisors and fundraisers understand the core capabilities of planned giving, they are able to provide dramatically increased value to their clients, donors, and nonprofit organizations. That starts not with mastering the vast complexity possible in planned giving, but with understanding the underlying simplicity common to almost all of planned giving.

Planned giving and simplicity don't normally go together. The perception of planned giving is that it can be enormously complex. This perception is accurate. Planned giving transactions can be among the most complex transactions. They can involve Charitable Remainder Trusts, foundations, Charitable Lead Trusts, capital gains taxes, income taxes, estate taxes, gift taxes, special business entities, a four-tiered income accounting system, life insurance, arcane documentation requirements, and more. When facing this forest of rules and regulations, it makes perfect sense that many simply throw up their hands and retreat. Yes, planned giving can become quite complicated. Yet, amidst this forest of details, a core simplicity motivates nearly all planned giving transactions.

Behind all of the complexity lies this simplicity. Gift planning can do two things. Fundraisers should use it for two main reasons. Financial advisors should use it for two different main reasons. That's it. If you remember these sets of two, you will understand the basic what and why of planned giving.

It's not that complicated. Gift planning can do two things, lower taxes and trade a gift for income. Regardless of how massively complex a planned giving transaction can become, it will do only these two things. If you understand this simple reality, you understand what planned giving structures can accomplish.

So, if planned giving can only do these two things, why do we need an entire book – indeed many, many books most of which are far more complex than this one – to cover planned giving? It is true that planned giving can only do two things (lower taxes and trade a gift for income), but there are a wide variety of ways in which these two things can be accomplished.

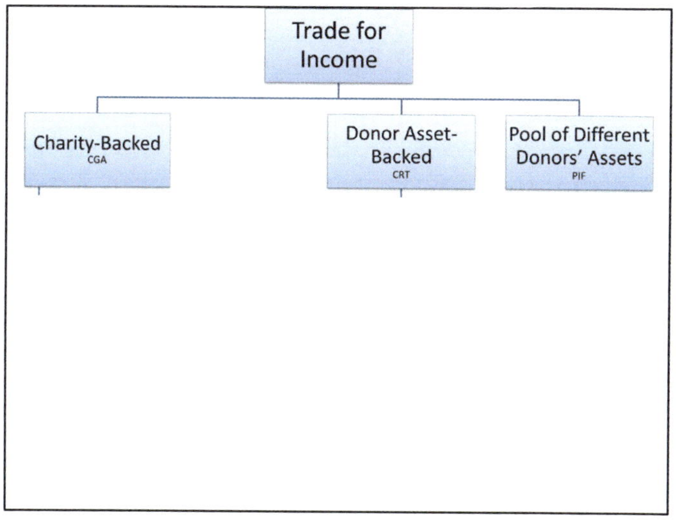

Let's begin with trading the gift for income. The first question to answer is, "Where should the income come from?" Does the donor want the income payments to come from, and be guaranteed by, the charity? If so, then she would consider a Charitable Gift Annuity (CGA). Does the donor instead want the income payments to come from, and be backed by, the assets contributed by the donor? If so, then she would consider a Charitable Remainder Trust (CRT). Perhaps the donor would prefer to have the income payments come from, and be backed by, a large pool of assets contributed by many donors. If so, then she might consider the, relatively rare, pooled income fund (PIF). Instead of having one option (trading a gift for income, yes or no), the donor now has three options. The menu of options does not stop with these three choices.

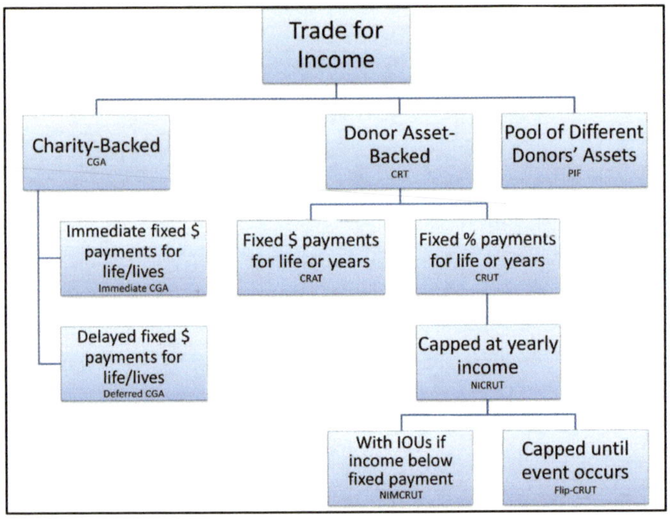

First, the donor can choose where the income payments should come from. Next, the donor can choose what kind of payments she would prefer. If the payments are coming from the charity, she can choose to take fixed dollar payments for one or two lives where the payments begin immediately following the gift. This is the standard Charitable Gift Annuity. The donor may instead prefer to delay the start of the payments until some future point, such as retirement. This is a deferred Charitable Gift Annuity.

If the payments are coming from a Charitable Remainder Trust holding the donors assets, there are even more options for the income. Just as with a Charitable Gift Annuity, a Charitable Remainder Trust can make fixed dollar payments for life or multiple lives. Alternatively, the Charitable Remainder Trust can make fixed dollar payments for a set period, up to 20 years. Or, the Charitable Remainder Trust can pay a fixed percentage of its assets, either for life or lives or for up to 20 years. This means that if the value of the assets in the Charitable Remainder Trust increases or decreases, so do the payments. This may be attractive as a way to combat the effects of inflation through investment performance, especially because the donor often can continue to manage or select the manager of the assets. In yet another variation (Net Income Charitable Remainder Unitrust) the payments coming out may be capped at the income received from the trust investments. This may be helpful to prevent a forced sale when the trust holds only an asset that generates no income. Even this alternative has two additional variations. In the Net Income with Make-up Charitable Remainder Unitrust, any payments reduced due to low income in one year can be made-up in later years when income is high. Finally, the flip-CRUT combines two types of Charitable Remainder Trusts, starting as a NIMCRUT or NICRUT and then "flipping" to a standard CRUT upon the occurrence of an event such as the donor reaching retirement age or the sale of a difficult-to-market asset. Through creative asset management, this can allow the assets to grow rapidly with no taxation or payouts until the donor desires to start receiving them at some later point.

Thus, what starts as a simple concept – trading a gift for income – quickly becomes cluttered due to the many options available. Instead of throwing up our hands when faced with the alphabet soup of CGA, deferred CGA, CRAT, CRUT, NICRUT, NIMCRUT, and flip-CRUT, the key is to remember that there is just one core idea – trading a gift for income. Everything beyond this is simply variations available to better match the desires of the donor.

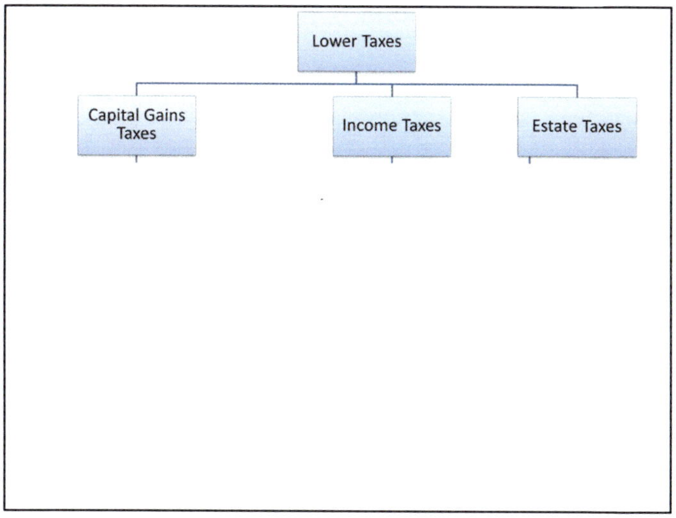

The second thing gift planning can do is lower taxes. Lowering taxes can be great for the donor (gifts are cheaper), great for the advisor (providing serious value to the client and reducing the tax bite on assets under management), and great for the charity (making bigger gifts more affordable). But, lowering taxes can be a complicated process. In fact, most of the complexity in planned giving comes from tax laws and, consequently, most of this book deals with tax law. Determining the best way to lower taxes first depends upon which type of taxes we are interested in lowering. Planned giving can lower capital gains taxes, income taxes, and estate taxes, but the techniques differ depending upon which tax is the focus.

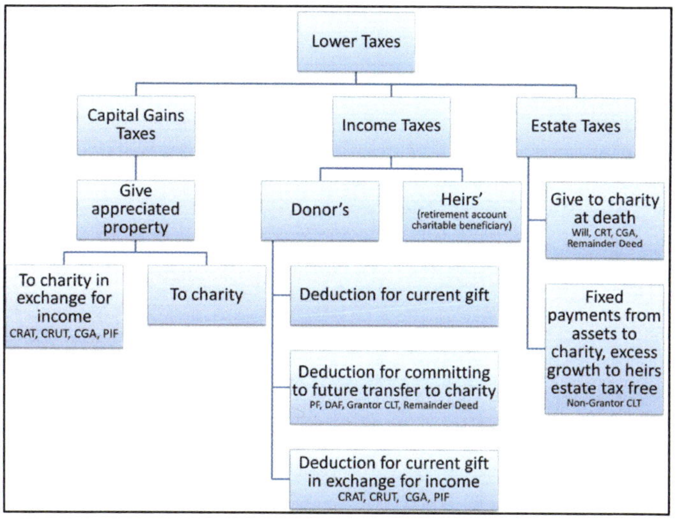

Lowering capital gains taxes occurs when the donor gives appreciated property, rather than cash, to the charity. Because the charity – and not the donor – sells the appreciated property, no taxes are paid. The donor can either give the property to the charity, or give the property to the charity in exchange for income – with all of the options available as discussed above.

Lowering income taxes can occur in a number of ways. In the simplest form, the donor can take an income tax deduction for making a charitable gift of money or property. Beyond this, there are several methods by which a donor can take an immediate income tax deduction in exchange for a transfer that will not be received by the charity for many years, often not until after the death of the donor. These strategies include the Charitable Remainder Trust, the remainder interest deed in a home or farmland, the private foundation, the donor advised fund, and the grantor Charitable Lead Trust. Additionally, the donor can still receive an income tax deduction when making a charitable gift in exchange for income, such as with a Charitable Remainder Annuity Trust (CRAT), Charitable Remainder Unitrust (CRUT), Charitable Gift Annuity (CGA), or Pooled Income Fund (PIF). Not only can charitable giving lower income taxes for the donor, it can also lower income taxes for the donor's heirs. When deciding which assets to leave to charity at death, the donor may choose to leave money in traditional retirement accounts (IRAs, 401-Ks) to charity. If the heirs receive these funds, they must pay income taxes when they withdraw the funds. Charities, in contrast, do not pay income taxes. Thus, wise planning leaves the tax-heavy assets to charity, reducing the income taxes that would otherwise be owed by the heirs without diminishing the charity's share.

Charitable planning can also lower estate taxes. Of course, money or property left to charity at death is not subject to estate taxes. Thus, money or property left to charity through a will, Charitable Remainder Trust, or remainder interest deed will escape estate taxes. The Charitable Remainder Trust may also be combined with an Irrevocable Life Insurance Trust structured in such a way as to avoid estate taxation in on

life insurance received by the heirs. A non-grantor Charitable Lead Trust allows the donor to pass any growth above the relatively low §7520 interest rate to heirs completely without taxation.

Of course, lowering taxes can be combined with the techniques of trading gifts for income. We can stack the methods into substantially complex transactions. For example, the donor could transfer highly appreciated corporate shares into a charitable remainder unitrust paying 6% of all trust assets per year to the donor and donor's spouse for life with payments limited to income (with makeup provisions) until the shares are sold, with part of the value of the income tax deduction and payments being used to fund an irrevocable life insurance trust to provide estate tax free inheritance to the children, where the Charitable Remainder Trust, at the death of the surviving spouse, transfers all remaining assets to the donor's private family foundation managed by the donor's children and grandchildren. Yes, it can get complicated. But, underneath this frightening mess of acronyms, trusts, foundations, and law, the basic concept is still the same. Planned giving can do two things – lower taxes and trade a gift for income. That's it.

Planned giving can do two things, lower taxes and trade a gift for income. That's nice, but it doesn't necessarily explain why a fundraiser should know about planned giving. Planned giving has a real impact on nonprofits only when it leads to larger gifts. These larger gifts don't come simply because a gift might be slightly cheaper due to a tax benefit. Instead, they come from two sources – asking for assets instead of cash, and addressing the donor's other financial concerns.

For the fundraiser, the simplest approach is to ask for money. Getting the donor to write a check is clean and quick. Beyond sending an appropriate gift receipt, it requires no knowledge of taxes, investment, finance or law. These gifts of cash are the big, red "easy" button for fundraiser and donors. So, why learn all of this planned giving stuff? Because when fundraisers ask for cash, they are asking small.

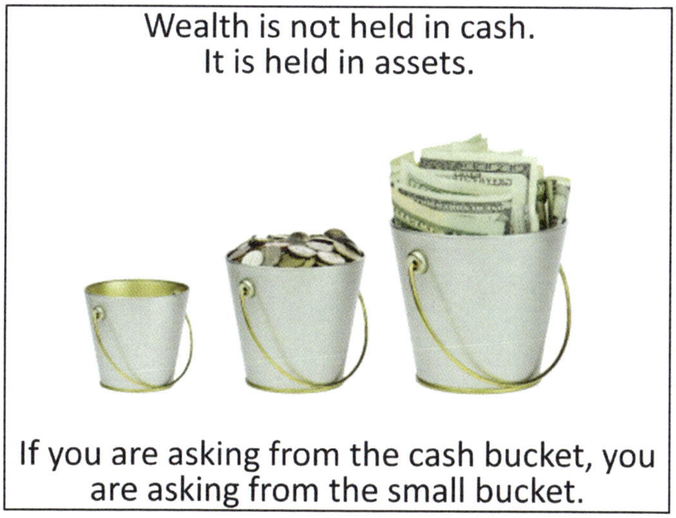

This doesn't mean that a fundraiser can't ask for a big check. It means that when the fundraiser asks for cash, regardless of the size of the request, he or she is asking for money out of the cash "bucket," and the cash bucket is the smallest bucket. Significant wealth is not held in cash, it is held in assets.

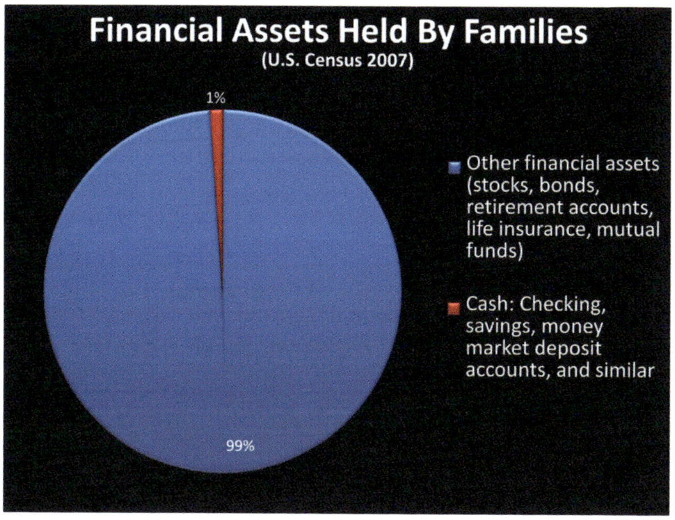

Only a tiny fraction of financial assets, not to mention real estate or tangible personal property, are held in a form that is accessible by simply writing a check. Wealth is held in other forms and these forms are much less accessible. This lack of access may come from the difficulty in easily selling all or part of the asset, from legal barriers, or from negative tax consequences resulting from a sale. It is certainly easier for the fundraiser to ignore this less accessible wealth and simply concentrate on the 1% of financial assets that are held in cash. Taking the easy route means that the fundraiser will always be asking from the small bucket. Without changing this perspective, neither the fundraiser nor the donor will be focused on the possibility of those truly transformational gifts that inevitably come from non-cash assets.

A more obvious way in which planned giving can generate more charitable gifts is by addressing the barriers that prevent donors from making larger gifts. In conversation, this is frequently phrased as, "I wish I could do more, but..." Whatever follows this introductory line often reveals the primary barrier preventing the donor from making the desired gift. Most commonly, these barriers to giving relate to other financial obligations. This is where planned giving's power to trade a gift for income becomes especially relevant.

The exact nature of the barrier to further giving will vary from donor to donor. Often the barrier will relate to the need for income. For example, the donor may feel pressed to save for retirement. In such cases, a deferred Charitable Gift Annuity or Charitable Remainder Trust might be of interest. A donor indicating the barrier of being on a fixed income may lead to the opportunity to suggest gifting assets in exchange for additional income, thus permitting a gift and addressing the financial limitation. Of course, a fundraiser who is asking only for cash would never think to consider asking for assets, much less asking for assets in a way that generates income for the donor. One of the most common concerns among older donors is the risk of outliving one's assets. The Charitable Gift Annuity is a solution directly intended to address this concern by trading a gift for guaranteed lifetime income.

Those with substantial wealth may also have limited cash due to the wealth being tied up in a farm or business. Such assets may appear inaccessible to the donor, given the substantial capital gains tax that would be due at their sale. The informed fundraiser can point out the variety of ways in which such assets can be sold without the need to pay capital gains taxes in a charitable transaction that generates income for the donor. Even if the donor is not immediately interested in such a transaction, simply making sure that the donor knows such options are possible *before* the sale of the business is an important first step.

A donor's concern for immediate income may lead them to postpone a gift and instead consider putting a gift in their will. Such a result is perfectly acceptable, but it may also bring up opportunities to discuss converting the gift at death from a revocable gift to an irrevocable one. This conversion not only secures the gift for the charity, but also can generate substantial tax benefits to the donor through methods such as a remainder interest gift in a home or farm, a Charitable Remainder Trust, or even a Charitable Gift Annuity.

For the well-informed fundraiser, the magical phrase beginning with, "I wish I could do more, but…" should spark a wide range of possible solutions and suggestions. Getting the opportunity to inform the donor about these can be as simple as asking; "What if there was a way you could do both? Would you like to hear about that?" This simple form of appreciative inquiry identifies when the donor might truly be interested in learning. This also avoids the sense that the fundraiser is aggressively pushing the donor. Instead, the fundraiser is simply serving in the role of an informed advisor, available whenever the donor so desires.

This book will review an wide variety of planned giving methods that involve transfers of assets rather than cash. Before diving into that complexity, let's look at a simple example of how a fundraiser can effectively shift from asking for cash to asking for assets. This doesn't involve trusts, annuities, foundations, or legal documents. Yet it allows the fundraiser to start asking for assets instead of cash in a way that can generate enormous benefit to the donor.

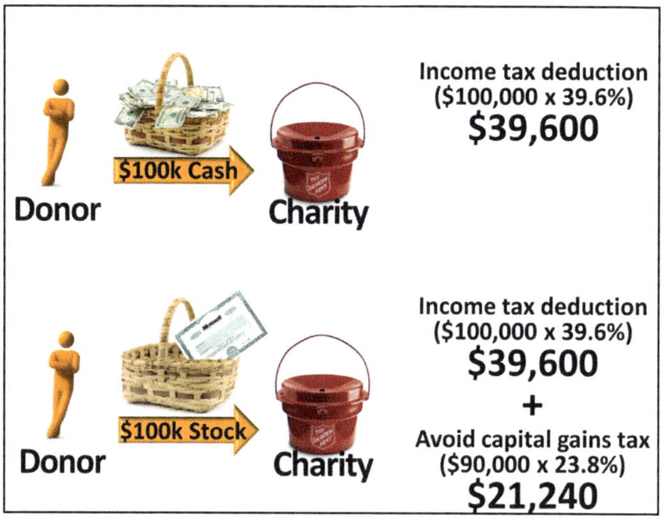

Suppose a donor is interested in giving $100,000 cash. (It could be any significant amount, but we will use this as a nice even dollar figure.) Of course, most fundraisers will respond to such a possibility by simply encouraging the cash gift and then thanking the donor. But, for the fundraiser who understands a little bit of planned giving, this offer opens up the possibility to both benefit the donor and shift the donor's mindset towards the concept of giving assets rather than cash. For the itemizing donor at the top tax rate without other restrictions, the cash gift could create a federal tax benefit of 39.6% of the value of the gift – in this case, $39,600. Suppose the donor also holds $100,000 of highly appreciated publicly traded stock. Maybe the donor purchased 10,000 shares at $1 and they are now worth $10. This appreciation is great for the donor, but it also carries with it a tax burden. At the moment he sells those shares, the donor will owe a tax bill of 23.8% on every dollar of appreciation. In other words, a sale of the shares will cost the donor 23.8% X $90,000 ($90,000 is the amount of increase in value from $10,000 to $100,000), or $21,240. There is no way for the donor to convert this $100,000 in appreciated stock into $100,000 of cash without paying the IRS $21,240.

Now there is. If the donor decides to give the shares of publicly traded stock to the charity and keep the $100,000 in cash, the donor ends up with $100,000 in cash and no tax liability. The charity receives the $100,000 in shares and immediately sells them. Because the charity is a nonprofit organization, it pays no taxes on this sale. After the sale, the charity ends up with the same amount of cash as it would have if it had simply accepted the check. Additionally, the donor is able to keep the $100,000 in cash he was initially going to give to the charity, thus converting the shares to cash without paying any taxes. In this case, the donor is still able to take the full $100,000 income tax deduction for the gift of stock. Thus, the donor gets the double benefit of a tax deduction plus avoidance of the capital gains tax.

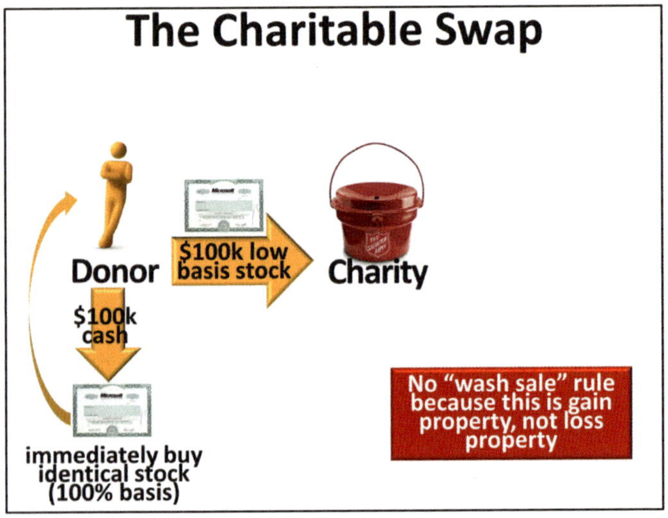

Although the tax consequences are beneficial, it appears to require the donor to have a simultaneous desire to make a gift and to change his investment portfolio. This is not true. The donor can maintain precisely the same portfolio before and after the transaction. In this case, instead of keeping the $100,000 in cash that the donor was going to give to the charity, the donor uses that cash to purchase new shares to replace those he just gave to the charity. Instead of giving $100,000 of cash, the donor gives $100,000 in appreciated stock and then immediately uses the cash to purchase $100,000 in new shares of the stock. As a result, the donor's investment portfolio doesn't change, except that the new shares were purchased for $100,000 instead of $10,000. This is a fantastic result for the donor because whenever the donor does decide to sell the shares, his capital gain (or loss) will now be based on this much higher purchase price. If the donor decides later to sell these new shares when the price was still $100,000, he will owe no capital gains taxes. If the donor had kept the original shares and then decided to sell them later when the price was $100,000, he would have owed $21,240 in capital gains taxes ($90,000 appreciated X 23.8%). This "charitable swap" of gifting shares and purchasing replacement shares can be completed on the same day. There is no rule requiring waiting as with the "wash sale" rule, because these shares are appreciated. The "wash sale" rule applies only to shares that have gone *down* in value. (The "wash sale" rule should never be a concern in a charitable transaction because depreciated investments should never be given to charity. Instead, they should be sold in order to get the tax benefit of the loss with sale the proceeds donated if desired.)

Some fundraisers may react to this highly beneficial transaction with indifference. If the fundraiser's job is simply to ask for cash, then alerting donors to these hidden tax benefits is just not in their job description. From this perspective, the donor's financial welfare is of no concern to the fundraiser. This cavalier attitude of intentional incompetence is not only bad for the donor; it is also bad for the nonprofit. A fundraiser who wants to encourage large, transformational gifts must shift the donor's perspective from giving cash ("giving from the little bucket") to giving assets ("giving from the big bucket"). On the surface, it may not seem like a tremendous win for the charity to convert a $100,000 cash gift into a $100,000 stock gift. Psychologically, it is a great achievement. Now, whenever the donor prepares to sell a highly appreciated asset this special tax benefit may arise in his mind. Gifting is no longer associated just with spare cash, but now it comes to mind whenever assets are moved. Understanding the tax benefits of gifting, rather than selling, appreciated assets opens up the entire world of sophisticated planned giving. This same technique will be employed repeatedly in various transactions involving Charitable Remainder Trusts and Charitable Gift Annuities where the donor not only avoids the capital gains tax but also receives income based on the full, untaxed amount of the gifted asset. This world of opportunity starts with an important shift in the donor's mindset from giving cash to giving assets.

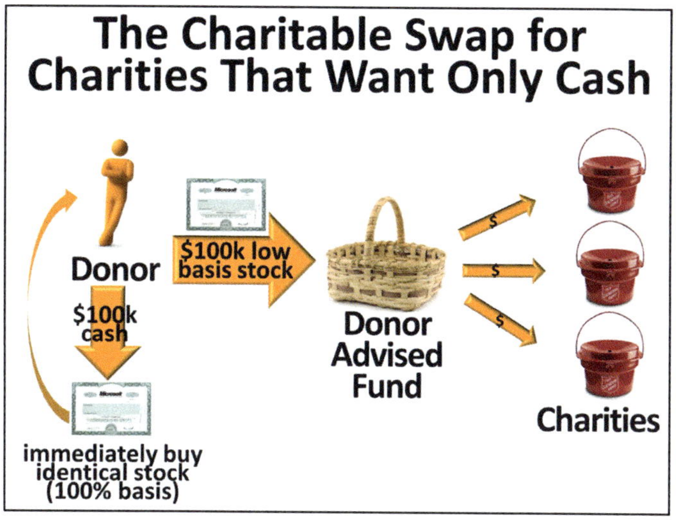

What about the donor who wants to give to a very small charity that doesn't accept shares of stock? Is this great tax advantage impossible? No. Even if the charity doesn't know how to deal with gifts of stock, the donor can complete this transaction using a donor advised fund. The donor gifts the shares to a donor advised fund such as those operated by various financial institutions (Fidelity, Vanguard, and Schwab). This transfer to a donor advised fund creates an immediate income tax deduction. The donor then directs the donor advised fund to sell the shares and write a check to the charity. The charity receives only the cash and never has to deal with the securities, but the donor still receives the tax benefit. The rest of the transaction can occur as before with the donor using the cash he would have gifted to the charity to purchase replacement shares of the stock.

To this point, we have been looking at planned giving from the perspective of the fundraiser and the nonprofit organization. However, planned giving can be useful not just for fundraisers, but also for financial advisors. Some financial advisors may sell life insurance products in which case the variety of transactions involving life insurance, discussed in later chapters, will be of direct interest. Even for those financial advisors who are compensated solely as a percentage of assets under management, understanding charitable planning can be an important proficiency. Well informed financial advisors can become more attractive to clients with significant charitable interests by providing dramatic planning benefits. Such clients are often those with substantial wealth, making them particularly attractive for the financial advisor. Additionally, a variety of charitable planning techniques, such as Charitable Remainder Trusts, private foundations, and donor advised funds, allow advisors to continue to manage the funds within the charitable instrument, sometimes for multiple generations. In many cases, these funds are undiminished by the otherwise common effects of capital gains taxes, income taxes on earnings, estate taxes and division among heirs, resulting in greater assets under management.

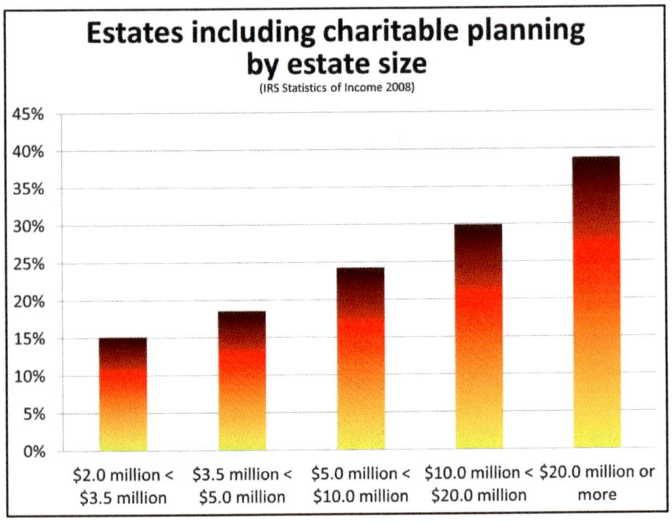

Charitable planning expertise can be particularly useful for financial advisors who wish to work with wealthier clients. As wealth increases, the tendency to engage in charitable planning also increases. Thus, this body of knowledge is particularly useful in attracting and benefitting the higher wealth clients that are so often sought after by financial advisors. A financial advisor might use this knowledge as a means of marketing his or her services. This can be done formally through the offering of seminars, perhaps to the significant donors or board members of a local charity. It can also be done informally through conversations. Simply learning that a person has made a significant gift (often easily identified by various donor recognition levels) can lead to a conversation over whether the gift was of cash or appreciated securities and an explanation of the relative benefits of gifting appreciated securities through the "charitable swap" technique. Providing such value to prospective clients can be a good first step to establishing a relationship as an advisor.

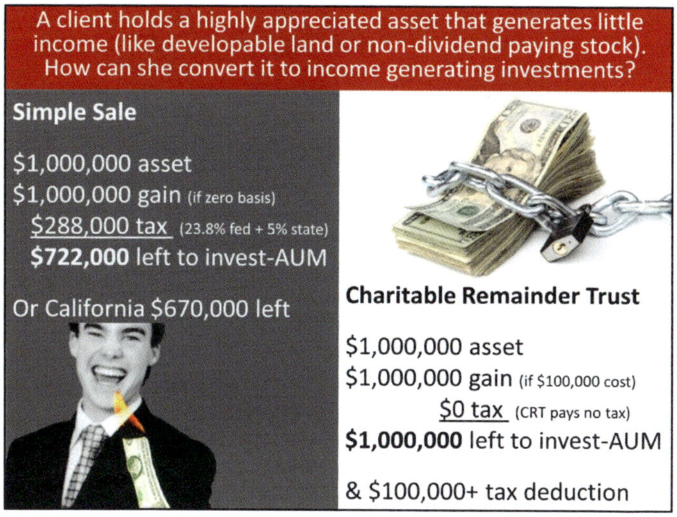

Helping clients to take advantage of the tax benefits available through charitable planning can benefit financial advisors not only by demonstrating the value of their advice to clients, but also by increasing the client's assets under management. Take the example of a client who holds a highly appreciated asset that generates little or no income. Such occurrences are quite frequent as those who build significant wealth often do so by owning relatively illiquid businesses or properties that appreciate and are undiminished by regular taxation. At some point, the client may wish to convert this non-income producing asset to an income-generating asset. The standard approach to such a conversion is to simply sell the asset and use the proceeds to purchase another asset that generates more income. However, if the client already has interest in leaving a charitable gift at death, this may not be the best approach. Instead of selling the asset and paying the resulting capital gains taxes, the client could transfer the asset to a Charitable Remainder Trust, allow the trust to sell the asset, and then receive income for life from the trust with the remainder going to a charity at death. This charitable approach not only avoids the capital gain taxes (the Charitable Remainder Trust is a charitable entity and thus pays no taxes upon the sale of the appreciated asset), but also generates an immediate income tax deduction. Such dual tax benefits can significantly increase the amount of funds available to be managed by the financial advisor. During the client's life, the financial advisor can manage the funds in the Charitable Remainder Trust, including those as assets under management subject to the advisors normal management fees.

Taking the example of a $1,000,000 asset with no basis, the traditional "sell and reinvest" strategy would net $722,000 in the typical state with a roughly 5% state capital gains tax. (The calculation is a little more complex than that shown here as state capital gain taxes are typically levied on the gain remaining after payment of federal taxes.) In a higher taxation state such as California, such a sale may result in only $670,000 left to invest. Contrast this with the Charitable Remainder Trust where the entire $1,000,000 remains after the sale, available to be invested and managed by the financial advisor. Additionally, such a transaction will generate an income tax deduction of at least $100,000 increasing the assets under management outside of the Charitable Remainder Trust by reducing tax payments. Depending upon the state income tax rates, this tax deduction may be worth $45,000 or more. Thus, charitable planning results in assets under management of $1,045,000 or more instead of only $722,000 or even $670,000. Clearly, this is no small difference for the client and the advisor.

In addition to the increase in assets under management resulting from avoidance of capital gains taxes and generation in income tax benefits, charitable planning can also increase assets under management by providing for tax-free growth environments. Over time, investments that grow without taxation will accumulate much more rapidly than their regularly taxed counterparts, leading to greater assets under management. A simple version of such tax-free growth is available with a donor advised fund. Money transferred to a donor advised fund must eventually be given to a charity – although at present there are no time restrictions on when this would occur. In the meantime, the financial advisor can take fees for managing the funds and the funds can grow without taxation because the account is a charitable account. Similarly, Charitable Remainder Trusts pay no taxes on investment income. Like to a traditional IRA, taxation occurs only when funds are removed from Charitable Remainder Trust. Assets within a private foundation do not grow entirely tax free, but the tax rate is only 1% or 2%, making them almost tax free.

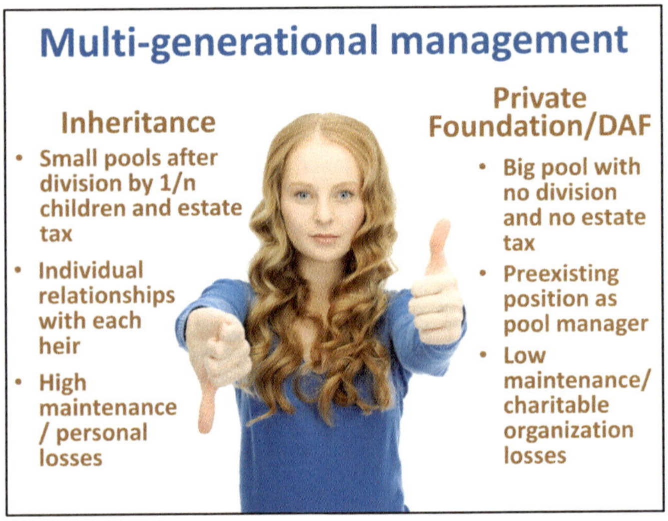

Creating multi-generational charitable entities, such as private foundations, can also increase the length of time that a particular financial advising firm will be able to manage the funds. In the typical estate scenario, the death of the client results in the loss of all assets under management. First, the wealth is reduced through estate taxation and then it is divided into smaller pools corresponding with the number of heirs. This creates a situation where the advisor either cannot or would prefer not to continue as the asset manager. Continuing to manage the assets would require having relationships with each of the heirs stronger than those of their other potential financial advisors. Even if such connections were possible, the advisor is faced with managing more relationships for smaller pools of money. At a minimum, the time commitment and hassle for the financial advisor is significantly multiplied. Realistically, the funds will likely leave the advisors management upon the death of the client.

However, if the client had established – during life and through estate planning – a multi-generational charitable entity, the advisor is in a much stronger position. The charitable pool of funds is undiminished by either estate taxation or division among heirs. The advisor's existing role as charitable asset manager places him or her in a strong position to continue in that role after the death of the client. Rather than having to be the top choice for each individual heir, the advisor need only be acceptable to the majority of those appointed by the deceased client. Further, managing charitable funds is often much easier than managing personal accounts. Losses to the charitable entity tend to be less personally distressing than losses from one's own investments. Such a dispassionate management scenario often reduces the amount of personal coaching and "hand-holding" necessary during inevitable market fluctuations, making the asset management that much easier for the financial advisor.

Throughout this book, we will explore a wide variety of charitable planning techniques. The tax and financial consequences of many of those techniques can become quite complex. There is no need to despair in the face of such seemingly unending minutia. Instead, remember the simple secrets to planned giving. Planned giving can do two things, reduce taxes and trade a gift for income. Fundraisers should use it for two main reasons, to ask from the big bucket of assets, rather than the small bucket of cash, and to work with donors who say the magic phrase, "I wish I could do more, but…" Financial advisors should use it for two different main reasons, to provide dramatic benefit to highly desirable clients, and to increase multi-generational assets under management.

2 A SUPER SIMPLE INTRODUCTION TO TAXES

At its core, gift planning can accomplish two things. It can trade a gift for income and it can reduce taxes. Most of the complexity in charitable planning comes from the desire to reduce taxes. Consequently, most of this text is focused on tax laws related to charitable giving. Before we jump into a review of the various charitable tax strategies, it may be useful to begin with a quick review of the fundamentals of the U.S. tax system.

We start with the most basic concept. Since 1913, the federal government has levied an income tax. For example, if a taxpayer earns a salary, he or she must pay a percentage of that earned income to the federal government in taxes. Taxes are also charged when a taxpayer sells an item at a profit (called a capital gain). Income from a capital gain is taxed at different rates than earned income, and so is calculated separately.

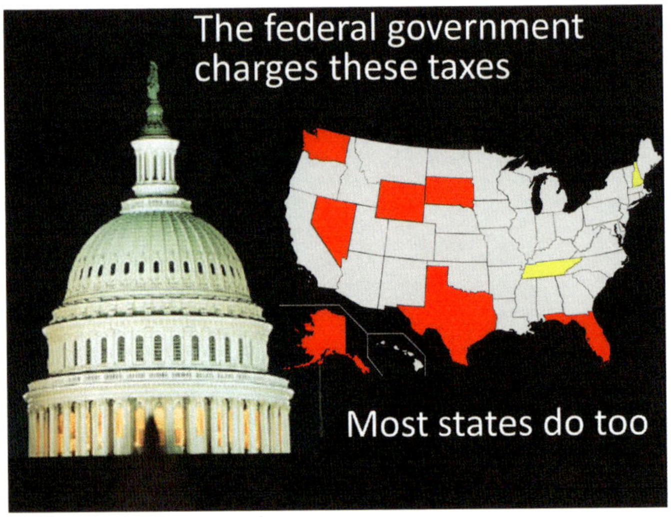

Not only does the federal government charge income and capital gains taxes, but most states do as well. Taxpayers in these states pay both federal and state taxes. In some of these states the state rules for charitable deductions are identical to the federal rules. Other states reduce this deductibility or provide special incentives for particular types of charities. Given the variety of these rules, we will not review the various rules for charitable deductions from state income taxes, but will instead concentrate on the federal tax system.

Income and capital gains taxes are not the only form of federal taxation, of course. The federal government charges taxes on the gratuitous transfer of money from one person to another, either at death (estate taxes) or during life (gift taxes).

A consistent feature of the federal tax systems is that the tax rates are not flat. As income increases, the income tax rate increases and the capital gains tax rate increases. As estate size increases, the estate tax rate increases. As total (non-charitable) gift size increases, the gift tax rate increases. These increasing tax rates mean that the tax effects from the same transaction may vary dramatically from person to person. In this text we will most commonly calculate the effects for a taxpayer at the highest federal tax brackets and ignore state taxes, but the actual results will differ depending upon the actual tax circumstances of the individual donor.

The 2014 federal income tax brackets for a single person serve as an example of increasing (a.k.a., "progressive") tax rates. As a taxpayer earns more money, he or she will tend to pay a larger and larger share of this earned income in federal income taxes. A "marginal" tax rate refers to the rate charged on the last dollar of earned income. Calculating taxes owed is not as simple as finding the marginal tax rate and multiplying it by the taxpayer's taxable income. Instead, each separate level of income is taxed at the rate indicated in the tax table.

At the lowest level of taxable income, calculations only require using one rate. For example, a single taxpayer with $5,000 of taxable income in 2014 would pays taxes at the 10% rate for all of his or her taxable income. This taxpayer would owe $500 in taxes ($5,000 x 10%). However, beyond this lowest bracket of taxable income, calculating taxes owed becomes a bit more complicated.

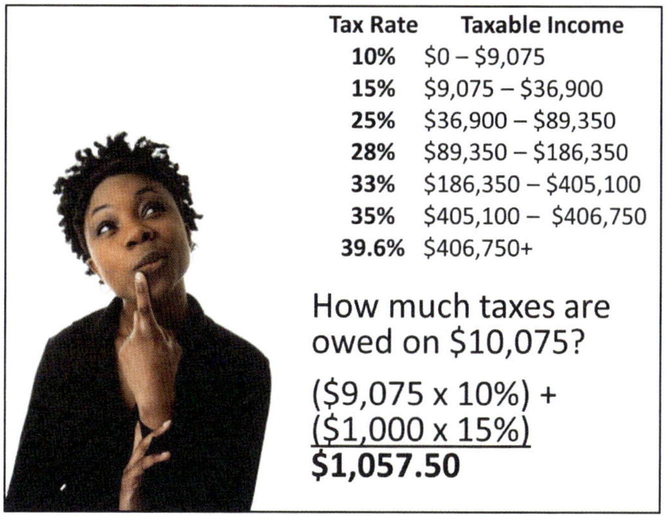

For example, if a single taxpayer had $10,075 of taxable income in 2014, then the first $9,075 would be taxed at 10%, and the remaining $1,000 would be taxed at 15%. It is incorrect to simply use the 15% rate for all of the taxpayer's taxable income. (I.e., do not simply multiply the total $10,075 of taxable income by 15%.) The 15% rate is the *marginal* tax rate, because it is the rate charged for the *last* dollar that the taxpayer earns. But, the 15% rate does not apply to *every* dollar the taxpayer earns.

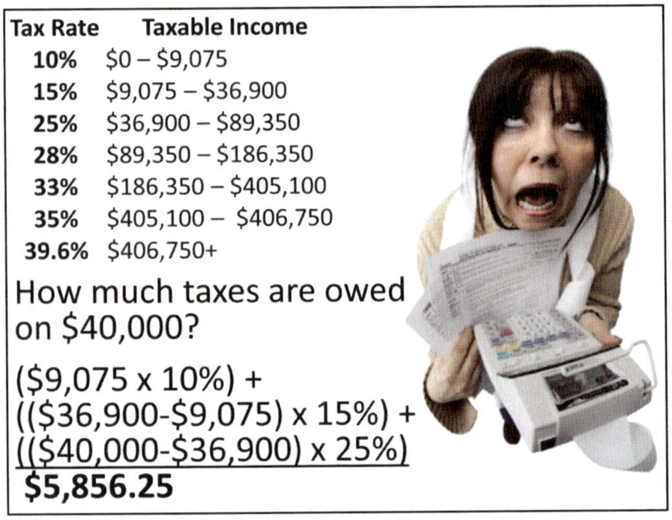

As a taxpayer earns more income and moves further up the tax brackets, calculating the income taxes owed requires more steps. For example, a single taxpayer with $40,000 of taxable income would pay a 10% rate on the first $9,075 of income earned, a 15% rate on the next $27,825 earned ($27,824 is the difference between the top of the 15% tax bracket, $36,900, and the bottom of the 15% tax bracket, $9,075), and a 25% rate on the final $3,100 earned ($3,100 is the amount of the $40,000 taxable income above the bottom of the 25% tax bracket which starts at $36,900).

Charitable gifts may generate charitable income tax deductions. Consequently, it is important to know how to calculate the effects of such deductions. An income tax deduction reduces taxable income. The value of a reduction in taxable income is the tax owed at the original taxable income less the tax owed at the reduced taxable income. Thus, understanding the value of a tax deduction (such as a charitable tax deduction) requires the ability to calculate taxes owed at various levels of taxable income, and this requires understanding how tax brackets apply to taxable income.

Tax deductions reduce taxable income. So, for example, a taxpayer with taxable income of $10,000 who then takes a $1,000 additional deduction will have $9,000 of taxable income.

A tax deduction has the same effect on taxable income regardless of the amount of taxable income earned by the taxpayer. Whether the taxpayer's taxable income is $10,000, $100,000 or $10,000,000, an additional $1,000 deduction will reduce the taxpayer's taxable income by exactly $1,000. However, the *value* of the $1,000 deduction may vary greatly depending upon the taxpayer's taxable income.

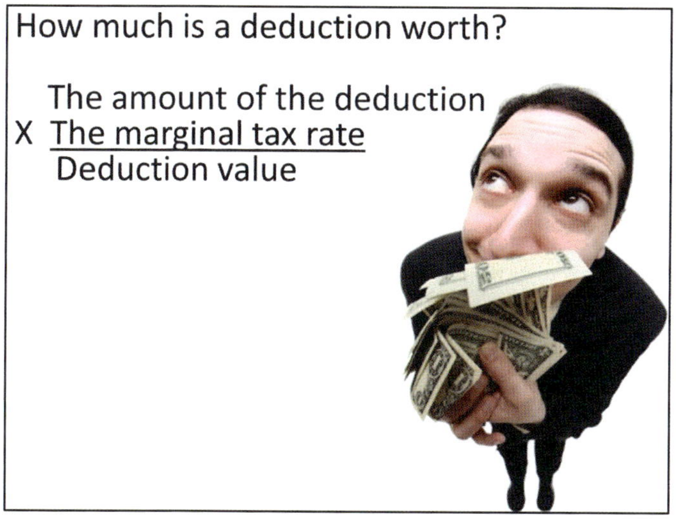

A $1,000 deduction is not worth $1,000. The deduction amount indicates the amount by which taxable income will be reduced, but its value depends upon the tax rate of the taxpayer. Just because a $1,000 deduction reduces taxable income by $1,000 at all income levels does not mean it is worth the same at all income levels. Often the value of the tax deduction is the amount of the tax deduction multiplied by the taxpayer's highest tax bracket. So, a $1,000 deduction is worth $100 to a taxpayer in the 10% tax bracket. That same tax deduction is usually worth $396 to a taxpayer in the 39.6% bracket. This difference in value helps to explain why charitable tax deductions may be more interesting to those with higher incomes.

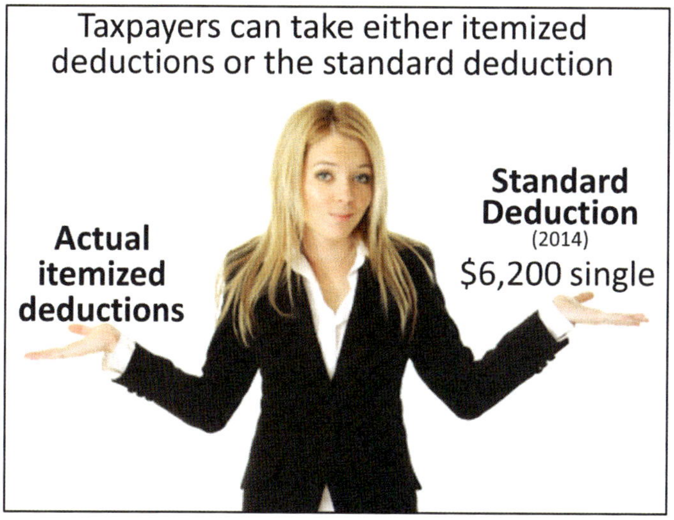

Charitable income tax deductions are an *itemized* income tax deduction. Other examples of itemized income tax deductions include the mortgage interest deduction, deductions for medical expenses greater than 10% of adjusted gross income, and deductions for state and local taxes. In order to use itemized deductions, a taxpayer must give up the standard deduction. So, a taxpayer who takes the standard deduction cannot use any charitable income tax deductions.

An itemized tax deduction such as a charitable tax deduction may, in fact, be worth nothing to a taxpayer. Consider the example of a single donor who made $4,000 of deductible charitable gifts in 2014, but had no other itemized deductions. This donor would face the choice of using either $4,000 of itemized deductions or using the $6,200 standard deduction. Obviously, the donor would be better off to take the standard deduction. Consequently, the $4,000 charitable income tax deduction has no value to this donor. This also helps to explain why charitable deductions tend to be of greater interest to higher income taxpayers. Such taxpayers are more likely to have other itemized deductions – principally the mortgage interest deduction – that are larger than the standard deduction. These "itemizers" can use the full value of any additional deductions because other deductions have already surpassed the value of the standard deduction.

Although the charitable income tax deduction is a common tax benefit of charitable transactions, it is not the only tax benefit. Thus, a good deal of charitable planning allows for positive tax consequences even for those taxpayers who cannot use the charitable income tax deduction. These tax benefits come not through deductions to reported income but by avoiding or postponing recognition of income in the first place. Thus, it is important to recognize that there is much charitable tax planning available even for donors who use the standard deduction.

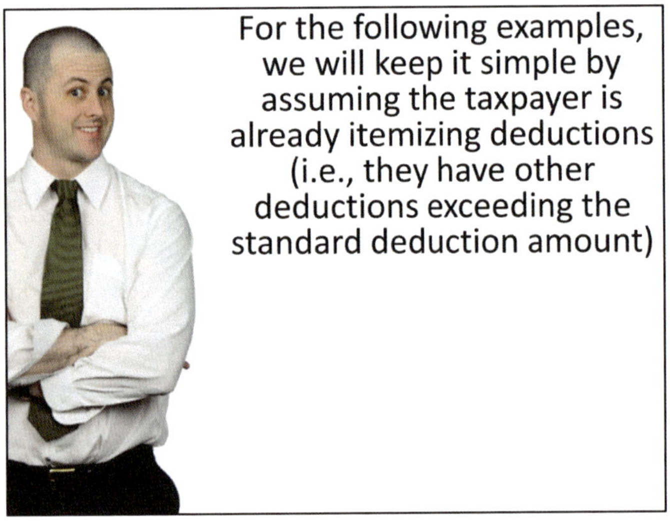

For the remainder of this text, the examples will assume that donors are already itemizers. In other words, due to other itemized deductions, the donors are assumed to be already foregoing the standard deduction. Consequently, the donors are assumed to use every dollar of any charitable deduction.

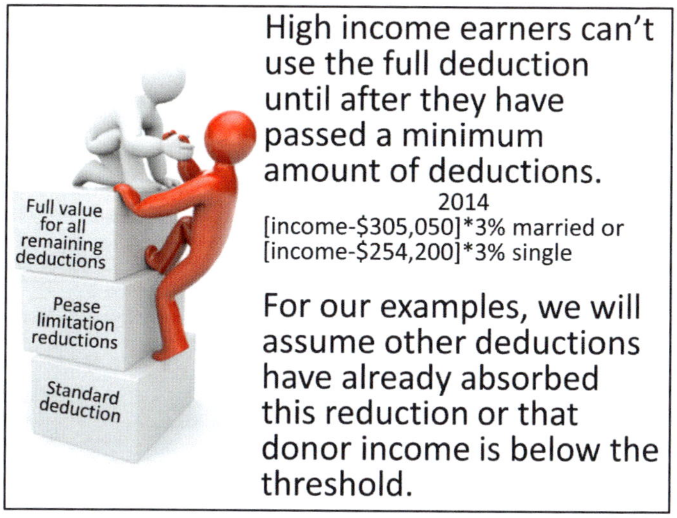

An additional limitation for itemized deductions, such as the charitable income tax deduction, is referred to as the Pease limitations. High income earners must reduce their itemized deductions either by 3% of the excess of their adjusted gross income (AGI) less the applicable threshold amount or by 80% of all itemized deductions except medical expenses. For example, a single itemizing taxpayer with $300,000 of income (AGI) and $15,000 of itemized deductions ($5,000 of which were medical expenses) in 2014 would have to reduce these deductions by the lesser of

1) ($300,000-254,200)x3%= $1,374 or
2) $10,000x80%=$8,000

For the remainder of this text, all examples will assume that this limitation does not affect additional charitable deductions either because the donor is below the income thresholds or because the donor's other itemized deductions exceed the 3% floor.

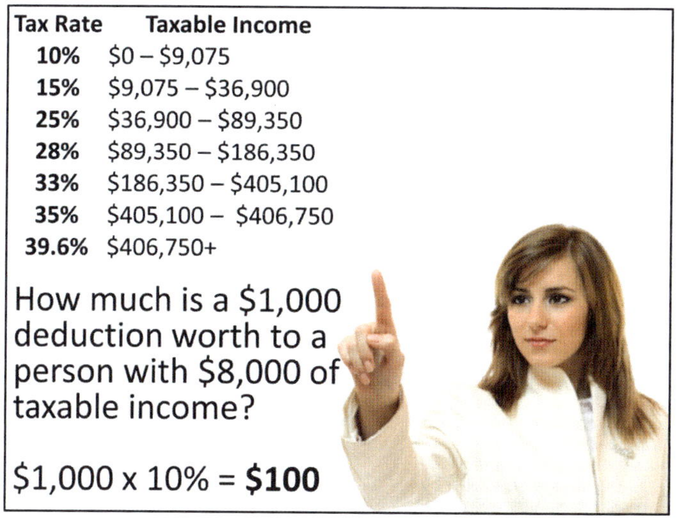

As mentioned previously, the value of a tax deduction depends upon the tax rate of the taxpayer. For example, a single taxpayer with $8,000 of taxable income in 2014 would pay $800 in taxes. If the taxpayer were to have received an additional $1,000 deduction, his or her taxable income would have fallen to $7,000 and he or she would have owed $700 in taxes. Thus, the $1,000 deduction would have caused the taxpayer's tax bill to drop by $100.

Tax Rate	Taxable Income
10%	$0 – $9,075
15%	$9,075 – $36,900
25%	$36,900 – $89,350
28%	$89,350 – $186,350
33%	$186,350 – $405,100
35%	$405,100 – $406,750
39.6%	$406,750+

How much is a $1,000 deduction worth to a person with $500,000 of taxable income?

$1,000 x 39.6% = **$396**

The same tax deduction is worth more to a higher income taxpayer. For example, a single taxpayer with $500,000 of taxable income in 2014 would pay $155,115.75 in taxes. If the taxpayer were to have received an additional $1,000 deduction, his or her taxable income would have fallen to $499,000 and he or she would have owed $154,719.75 in taxes. Thus, the $1,000 deduction would have caused the taxpayer's tax bill to drop by $396.

Tax Rate	Taxable Income
10%	$0 – $9,075
15%	$9,075 – $36,900
25%	$36,900 – $89,350
28%	$89,350 – $186,350
33%	$186,350 – $405,100
35%	$405,100 – $406,750
39.6%	$406,750+

How much is a $1,000 deduction worth to a person with $10,000 of taxable income?

($925 x 15%) +
($75 x 10%)
$146.25

In the prior two cases, the quick way to calculate the value of the deduction would have been to simply multiply the deduction by the taxpayer's marginal tax rate (e.g., $1,000 x 10% marginal tax rate = $100 in the first example and $1,000 x 39.6% marginal tax rate = $396 in the second example). However, this simple approach does not work if the deduction causes the taxpayer's marginal tax rate to change. If the deduction causes the taxpayer to change tax brackets, then part of the deduction will be valued at the higher tax rate and part will be valued at the lower tax rate.

As an example, consider the value of a $1,000 deduction to a single taxpayer with $10,000 of taxable income in 2014. The taxpayer begins at the 15% marginal tax rate. However, after applying the first $925 of the deduction, the taxpayer now has $9,075 of taxable income and drops into the lower tax bracket. Thus, any further deductions will reduce taxation not at the original 15% rate, but at the lower 10% rate. The first $925 of the deduction reduces taxes at a 15% rate, and the final $75 of the deduction reduces taxes at a 10% rate. The value of the deduction is thus, ($925x15%) + ($75x10%) = $146.25.

Put another way, a single taxpayer with $10,000 of taxable income in 2014 would pay $1,046.25 in taxes. If the taxpayer were to have received an additional $1,000 deduction, his or her taxable income would have fallen to $9,000 and he or she would have owed $900 in taxes. Thus, the $1,000 deduction would have caused the taxpayer's tax bill to drop by $146.25.

A separate set of tax rates applies to capital gains. A capital gain occurs when a taxpayer sells an investment for more than he or she paid for it (including the cost of improvements). This profit – the difference between the sale price and purchase price – is the amount of the capital gain.

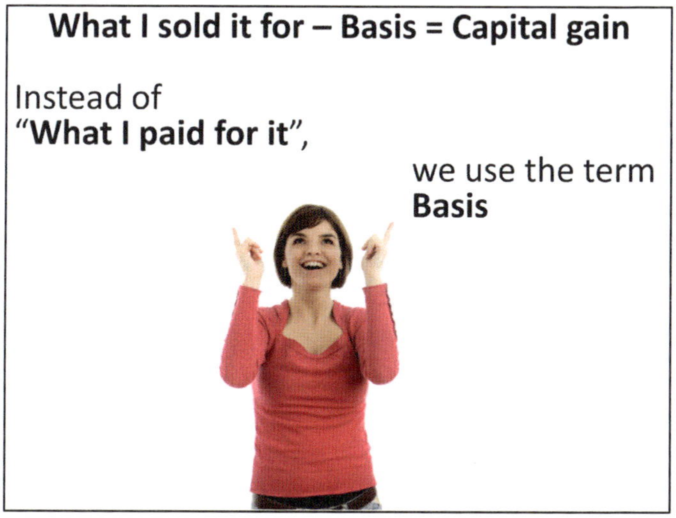

Capital gain is calculated as the sales price less the taxpayer's "basis" (or "adjusted basis") in the property. In most circumstances, the basis is simply the amount that the taxpayer paid for the investment. However, basis is not always identical with the original price.

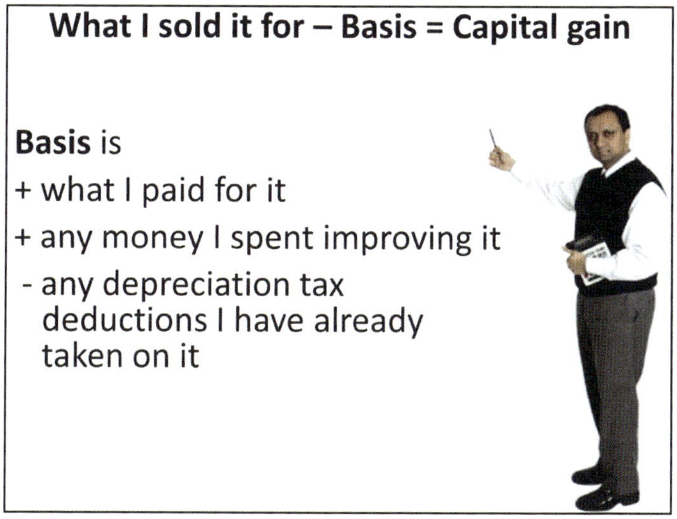

Basis always starts as the amount paid for the investment, but it can be adjusted later. For example, if an investor purchases an apartment building for $1,000,000 and then spends $250,000 making capital improvements and additions to the building, the investor's basis would increase to $1,250,000 (the $100,000,000 original purchase price plus the $250,000 of improvements). This makes sense intuitively because in order to get the new, improved building the investor had to spend a total of $1,250,000.

Less intuitive is the effect of depreciation tax deductions. The investor who purchased the apartment building is allowed to assume for tax purposes that the building is slowly wearing out (i.e., depreciating). Each year, the taxpayer is allowed to claim this wearing out process (depreciation) as a loss, offsetting gains or income from certain other sources. These depreciation deductions reduce the taxpayer's basis in the property. (If this were not the case, the taxpayer would be able to deduct the same dollar twice, first as a depreciation deduction and later as a reduction of the capital gain.) Depreciation deductions do not apply to financial instruments such as stocks or bonds or to raw land. Consequently, this text will not address depreciation unless the transaction specifically involves a gift of developed real estate.

If I owned the item for more than one year, it is a **long-term** capital gain

Taxable income bracket	Long-term capital gain + ACA
10% or 15%	0%
25%, 28%, 33%, or 35%	15%
25%, 28%, 33%, or 35% & modified AGI $200,000+ (single) or $250,000+ (married)	18.8% (15% + 3.8%)
39.6% + modified AGI $200,000+ (single) or $250,000+ (married)	23.8% (20% + 3.8%)

If the taxpayer owns the investment for more than one year, any gain is taxed as a long-term capital gain. Long-term capital gains tax rates are lower than those for ordinary income or short-term capital gains. The capital gains tax rates are 0%, 15%, and 20%. However, the Affordable Care Act imposes an additional 3.8% tax on net investment income of taxpayers over certain income thresholds (e.g., $200,000 of modified AGI for a single individual, $250,000 for a married couple filing jointly, not indexed for inflation). Net investment income includes capital gains as well as other types of investment income such as interest, dividends, rent, and royalty income. Consequently, depending upon the taxpayer's taxable income and modified adjusted gross income, capital gains are taxed at 0%, 15%, 18.3%, or 23.8%. These rates do not depend upon the amount of capital gain income, but rather depend upon the amount of overall taxable income and modified AGI. Consequently, all of the taxpayer's capital gains for a particular year will be taxed at the same rate. (I.e., there is no run up the rate schedule where some gains are taxed at 15%, then some at 20%, and so forth.)

As described previously, the federal government charges taxes on the gratuitous transfer of money from one person to another, either at death (estate taxes) or during life (gift taxes). Transfers to charitable organizations are not taxable. Thus, any part of the estate that is transferred to a charity will not generate estate taxes. Similarly, any gifts made during life to charity will not generate gift taxes. This simple reality can be leveraged to create substantial estate tax planning opportunities through the use of trusts such as a non-grantor Charitable Lead Trust or Charitable Remainder Trust.

Most people are not affected by estate and gift taxes because the exemption levels are quite high. For example, in 2014 there is no tax on estate and gift transfers that, when combined, do not exceed $5,340,000 for a single taxpayer or $10,680,000 for a married couple. Thus, estate tax and gift tax planning is now limited to the realm of the wealthy. However, estate planning can also affect other taxes, such as capital gains and income taxes, which are not limited to the wealthy. Thus, tax planning in estates can still be quite important even where estate taxes are not relevant.

An additional tax, referred to as the generation skipping transfer tax, can arise if the taxpayer makes transfers that "skip" a generation. For example, if a grandparent makes a gift (either during life or at death) to the child of his or her living child, this transfer skips a generation. The amount of these generation skipping transfers that, when combined, exceeds the exemption equivalent amount ($5,340,000 in 2014), will generate an additional 40% tax. This 40% generation skipping transfer tax is applied to the amount remaining after application of the 40% estate and gift tax. As with the estate tax, because of the high exemption amounts, these generation skipping transfer tax issues are a concern only for those taxpayers transferring substantial wealth. However, when they apply, the combined impact of these taxes can be dramatic.

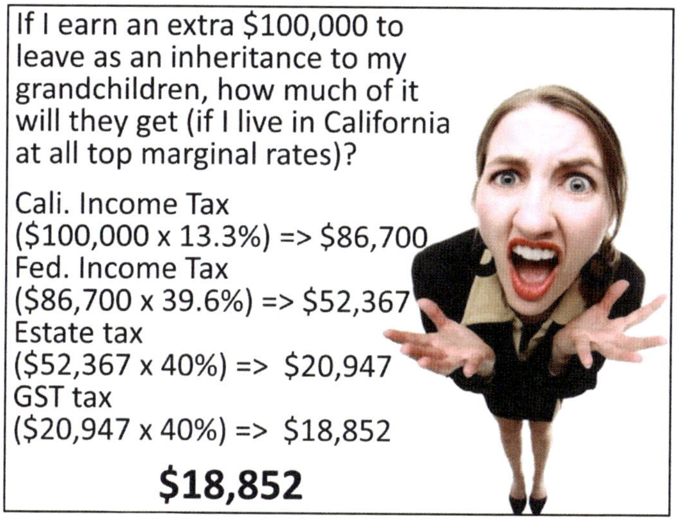

As an extreme example of how burdensome the various types of taxation can become, consider the case of a taxpayer who wishes to earn an additional $100,000 to leave as an inheritance to his or her grandchildren. If this person were living in the state of California and at all of the top marginal tax rates (e.g., in 2014 having income over $1,000,000 and having previously made over $5,340,000 of generation-skipping gifts), the tax consequences would be severe. The additional $100,000 of income would first be subject to California's 13.3% state income tax, costing $13,300. Assuming the taxpayer could successfully claim all of the 13.3% tax as a deduction against his or her federal taxes (e.g., no Pease limitations), the 39.6% federal tax would be applied only to the remaining amount of $86,700, generating a tax bill of $34,333.20. After paying the federal income tax, the remaining $52,366.80 could then be available to be inherited by the grandchildren. This transfer at death would generate a 40% estate tax costing $20,946.72 and leaving $31,420.08. However, if the grandchildren's parents were still alive, this estate transfer skips a generation and is thus also subject to the generation skipping transfer tax. This generation skipping transfer tax generates an additional 40% tax on the remaining $31,420.08 costing $12,568.03 and leaving $18,852.05 for the grandchildren. Although certainly not commonplace, this extreme example shows just how important tax planning can be in the face of such potentially extreme tax consequences. As taxation increases, the value of tax planning – including charitable tax planning – also increases. Consequently, charitably inclined individuals facing significant tax burdens are often excellent candidates for sophisticated charitable planning.

3 ELEMENTS AND TIMING OF A CHARITABLE GIFT

Understanding what a charitable gift is and when a charitable gift is made, seems like an obvious and simplistic task. What could be easier? As we will see in this chapter, what initially appears to be a simple concept can become quite complex. But, a fundamental competence required of anyone who will be advising donors about charitable gifts is to know what tax consequences such gifts will generate. We know that charitable gifts can generate income tax deductions. But, applying that knowledge requires that we know what constitutes a charitable gift for tax purposes. Regardless of its size or its benefit to a charity, any transfer that does not meet the definition of a charitable gift for tax purposes will generate no charitable deduction. So, let's begin by looking at what is a charitable gift for tax purposes and then consider examples of transfers that are not charitable gifts for tax purposes.

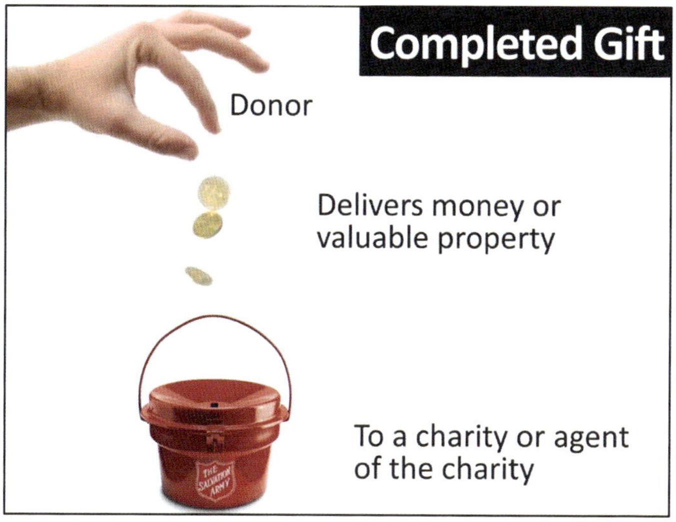

A deductible charitable gift occurs when the donor delivers money or valuable property to a charity or agent of the charity. That's it. There is nothing particularly complicated about the definition (except perhaps the phrase "agent of the charity" which simply means a representative of the charity). How then could things possibly become complicated when we start with such a simple definition?

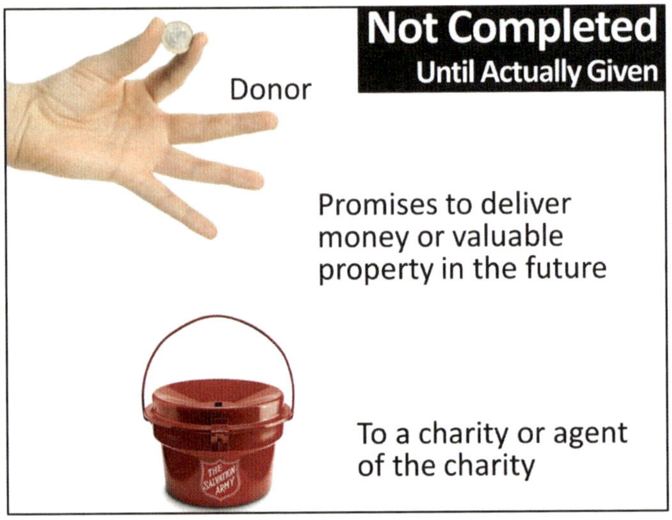

The first example of an action that is not a charitable gift for income tax purposes is a *promise* to deliver money or valuable property in the future. A promise is not a gift. Even if the promise is a legally enforceable written contract, it is still just a promise, so it is not a gift – at least not yet. Once the promise is fulfilled and the donor actually delivers money or valuable property to the charity (or agent of the charity), then – and only then – the definition for a gift is met.

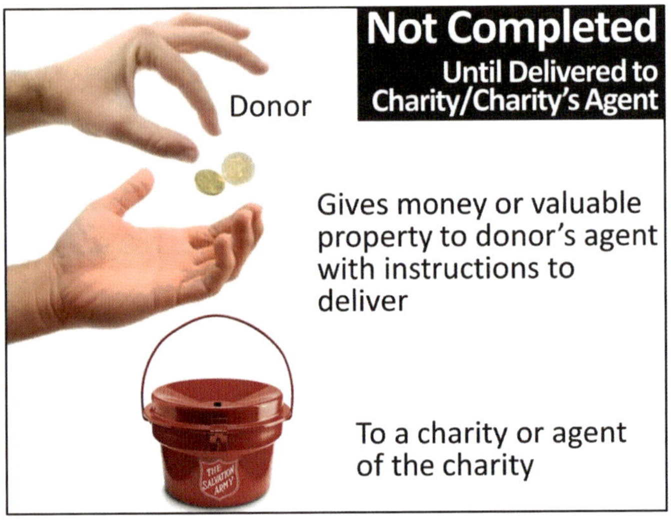

Another example of an action that is not a completed gift is when a donor gives money or valuable property to the donor's agent (i.e., the donor's representative) with instructions to deliver the gift to a charity or agent of the charity. Because the money or valuable property is still in the hands of the donor's representative, it has not yet become a completed gift. Once the money or valuable property is given to the charity (or the charity's representative/agent), then – and only then – is there a deductible charitable gift.

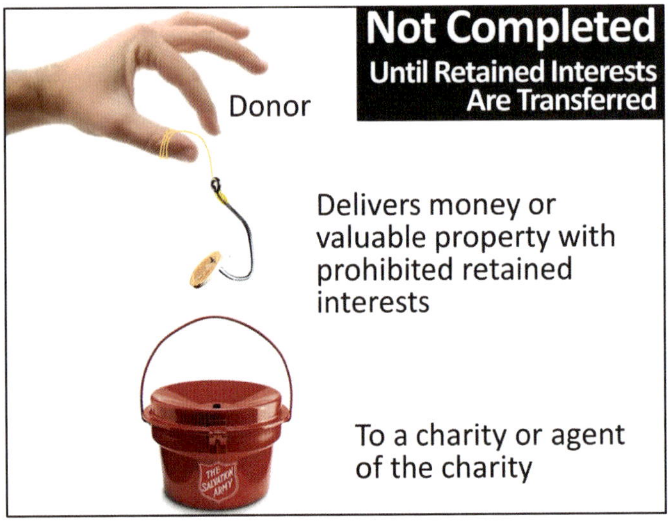

Another example that does not qualify as a charitable gift for tax purposes is when the donor delivers money or valuable property to the charity, but still retains prohibited control over the money, even after the transfer to charity. This retained control prevents the gift from being deductible until such time as the retained interests expire or are also given to the charity. This area is a bit more complicated because there are specific retained interests that are permitted by the tax code. Nevertheless, the general rule is that if a donor retains rights to control the money or get the money back, such a transfer is not (or, at least, not yet) a charitable gift.

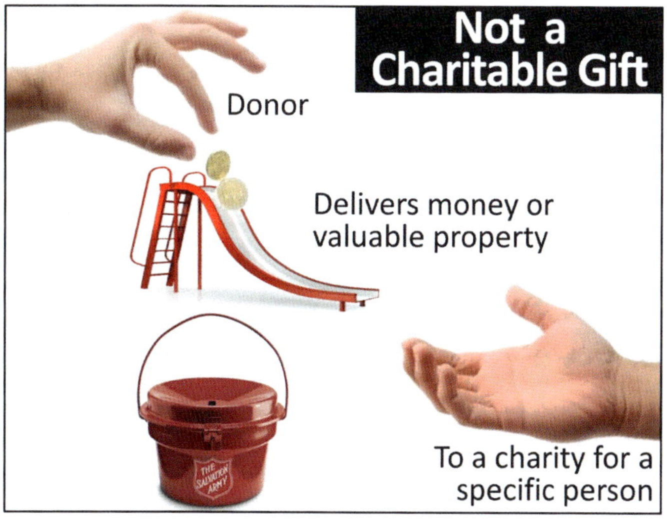

The last example of a transfer that is not a deductible gift is when a donor delivers money or valuable property to a charity for delivery to a *specific* person. A person is not a charity. Any person, even a person in serious financial or medical need, is not a charity. Giving money to a specific person is not a charitable gift for tax purposes. This fundamental rule cannot be avoided by simply giving money to a charity with the requirement that the money must then be delivered to a specific person. Such a transfer is treated as if it were a direct transfer to the person. And, since a person is not a charity, the transfer is not a deductible charitable gift.

To this point we have looked at the rules in their conceptual form. Let's now look at some examples applying these rules to actual gift scenarios. Beginning with a simple transaction, suppose a donor puts a cash gift in a stamped envelope addressed to the charity. The donor then puts the envelope into a mailbox at the local United States Post Office on day one. On day two, this cash arrives safely at the charity. When did this transaction become a completed gift for tax purposes?

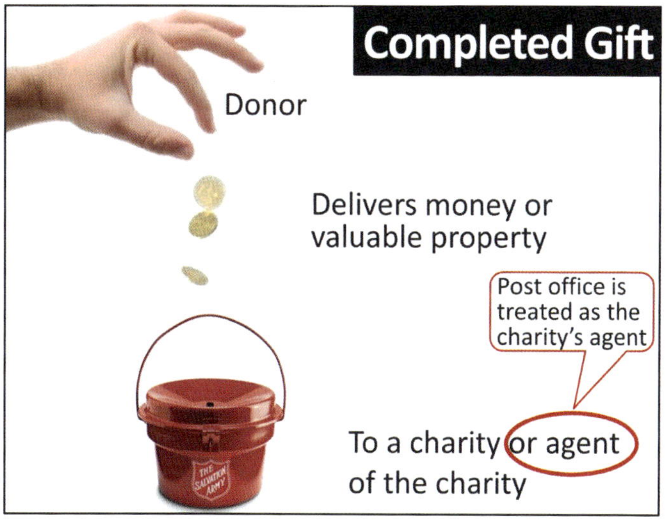

The answer, as always, is that the gift is complete when the donor delivers money or valuable property to the charity or agent of the charity. The tricky part is knowing that the United States Postal Service is considered to be an agent of the recipient. Even though the charity has not received the money on day one, the charity's agent has received the money. Consequently, the gift is a completed gift on day one. (Note that only the United States Postal Service is considered to be an agent of the recipient. If the gift had been delivered, for example, by FedEx or UPS, it would be considered as held by an agent of the donor until it arrived at the charity.)

Because the donor has delivered money to an agent of the charity (in this case, the United States Postal Service) on day one, the gift was a completed gift for income tax purposes on day one.

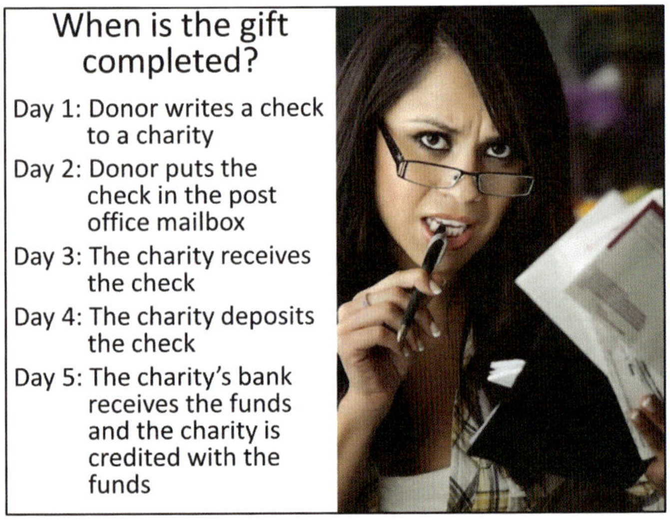

Next, let's examine another common situation. On day one, the donor writes a check to a charity. On day two the donor puts the check in the United States Postal Service mailbox and it is taken by the mail carrier. On day three, the charity receives the check in the mail. On day four, the charity deposits the check. Finally, on day five, the charity's bank receives the funds and the charity is credited with the funds. On which of these days was the gift completed for income tax purposes?

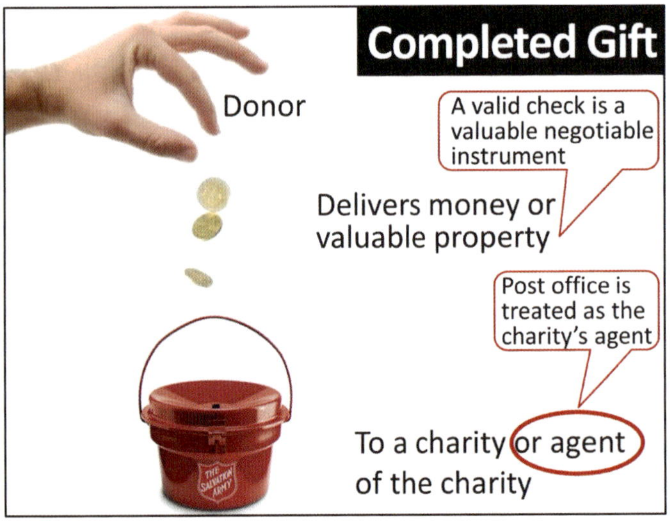

The answer, as always, is that the gift is complete when the donor delivers money or valuable property to the charity or agent of the charity. The tricky part in this situation is to understand that a valid check is valuable property. Conceptually, the idea is that a valid check is not just a promise to pay, but is a valuable negotiable instrument (sort of like a corporate bond) making it valuable property even prior to its deposit.

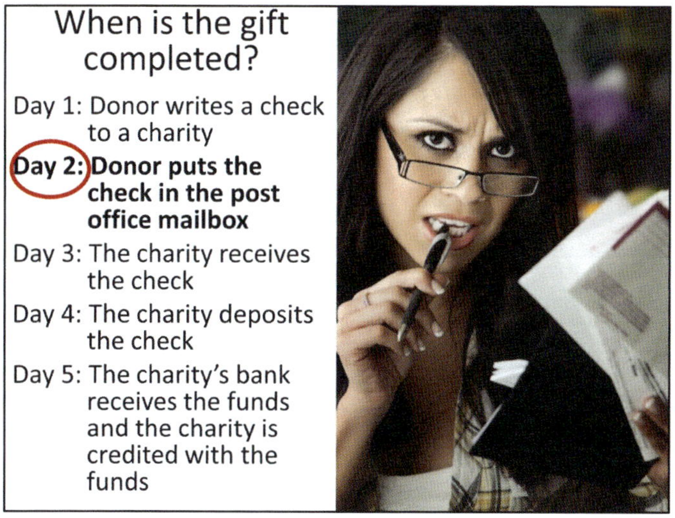

Because a valid check is considered to be valuable property, and because the post office is considered to be the agent of the charity, the charity's agent receives valuable property on day two. Thus, the gift is complete for income tax purposes on day two.

We have been examining questions of when, precisely, a transfer becomes a completed charitable gift for income tax purposes. Why do we care so much if the gift is complete on day one or day five? The first answer is that this is a learning tool to understand what is and what is not a deductible charitable gift. By understanding the moment at which the transfer becomes a deductible gift, it allows us to more precisely understand the definition of a charitable gift for income tax purposes. Beyond this educational purpose, however, knowing the exact day can itself be quite important. There can be a big difference between one day and the next for tax purposes.

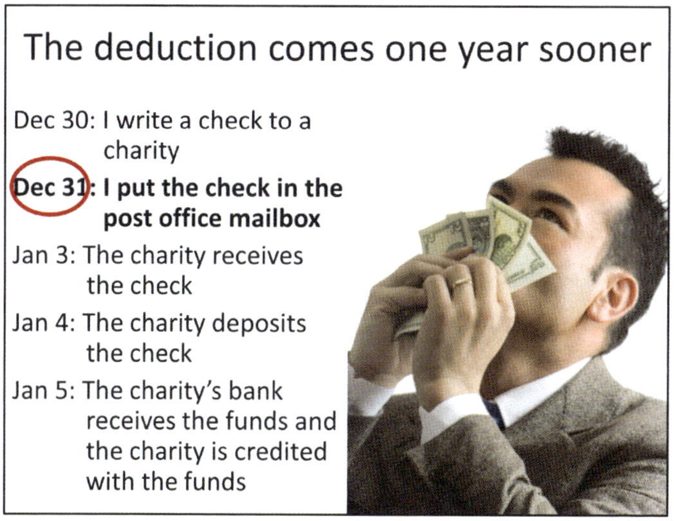

For example, a gift completed on December 31 can be deducted one year earlier than a gift completed the next day. Waiting for an additional year can be a substantial consequence of knowing precisely which day a gift becomes complete for income tax purposes.

Indeed, much more substantial consequences may result when the tax circumstances are different in the different years. The deductible gift may not be usable in the later year due to, for example, charitable deduction income limitations or use of the standard deduction. In such cases, knowing the exact date when the charitable gift is complete for income tax purposes can be the difference between a valuable deduction and a useless deduction.

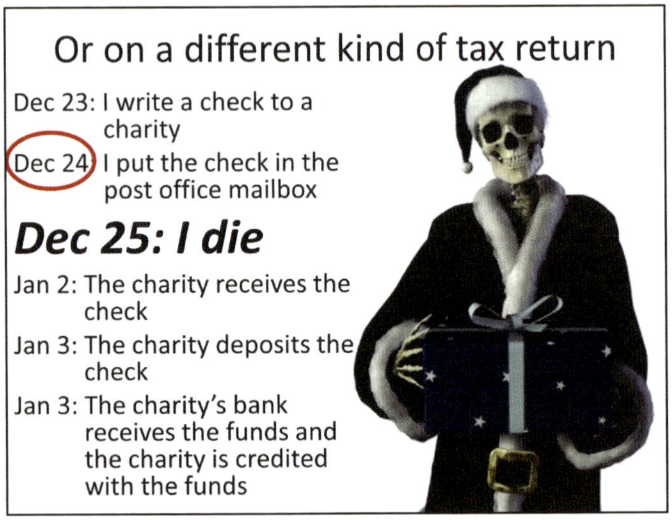

The difference in the date on which a charitable gift becomes complete for income tax purposes may also have significance if the donor happens to die during the process.

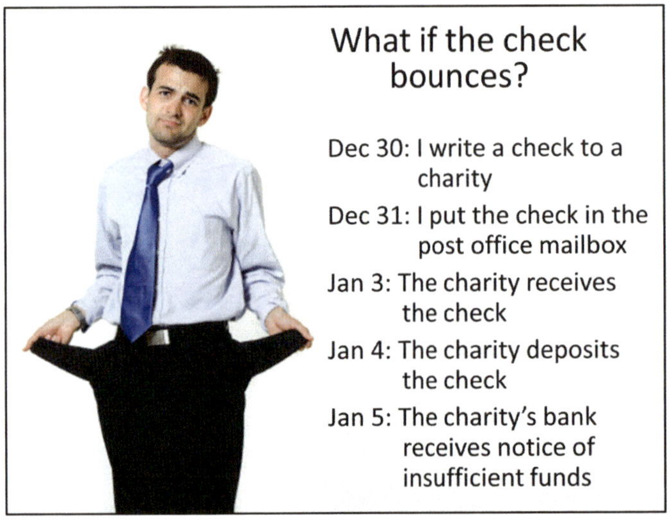

Let's now return to some additional examples demonstrating when a deductible charitable gift occurs. Suppose we have a scenario identical to the previous example of a check mailed to a charity. However, in this case, the check bounces. How is this scenario handled under the income tax charitable deduction rules?

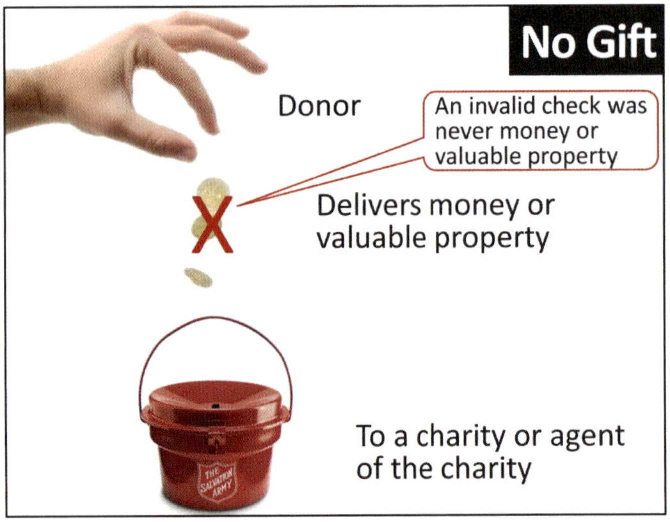

The answer, as always, is that the gift is complete when the donor delivers money or valuable property to the charity or agent of the charity. The key understanding in this case is that an invalid check was never considered to be valuable property. Because the donor never delivered valuable property to the charity, there was no charitable gift. (In a sense, the future knowledge that the check would bounce is attributed back to its date of origin, meaning that at no point was the check ever valuable property.)

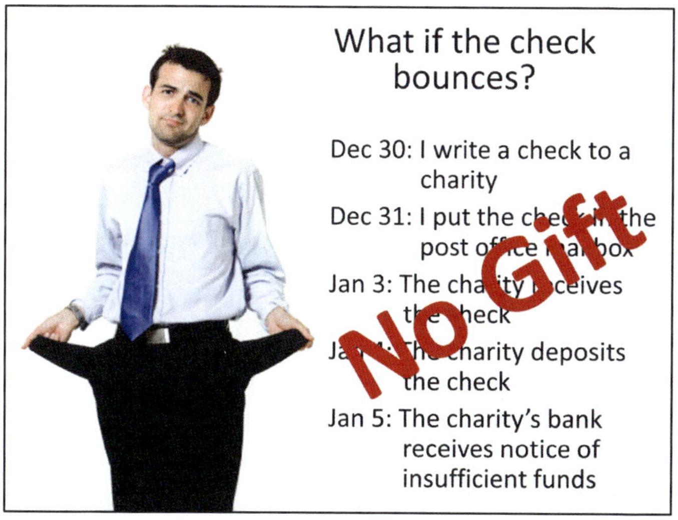

Because the donor never delivered valuable property to the charity, at no point did a charitable gift occur for income tax purposes.

How then would we treat a post-dated check? In this case, the post-dated check is delivered to the charity's agent (the United States Postal Service) on December 26. However, the check cannot be deposited prior to January 1, because it is post-dated to that day. So, when is the gift completed?

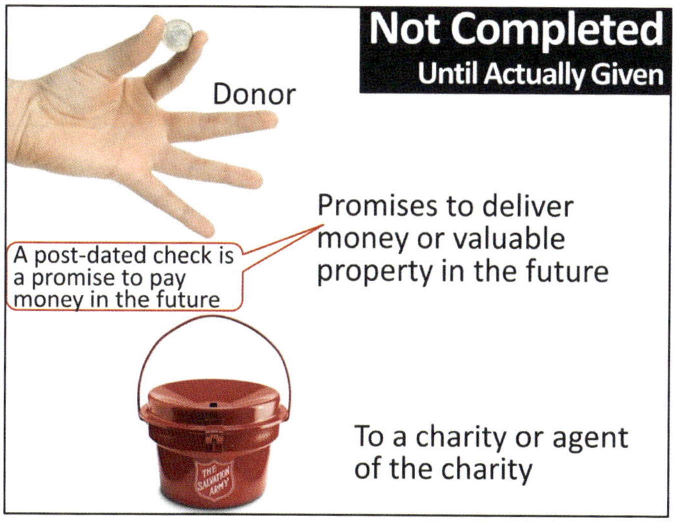

The critical piece of information in this scenario is to understand that a post-dated check is considered to be a promise to pay money in the future. So, unlike a normal check, which is immediately considered to be valuable property, a post-dated check is considered to be only a promise to pay in the future. A promise to give money or property to a charity in the future does not constitute a deductible gift. Thus, the post-dated check is not a completed gift when it is transferred to the charity or the charity's agent. Once, however, the date of the check arrives, it immediately becomes valuable property. If, at that time, it has been delivered to the charity or the charity's agent, then the gift is complete.

Thus, in this scenario, the gift is complete on January 1. That is the date on which the charity has received valuable property. On December 31, the charity did not have valuable property, but instead had only a promise to pay. On January 1, the promise to pay was converted to a valuable negotiable instrument, and thus the gift was complete.

What about a credit card gift? Suppose a donor makes a donation by credit card and the charity is credited with the funds. However, it is not until much later that the donor actually makes the payment on the credit card to pay for this transfer. At what point was the charitable gift completed?

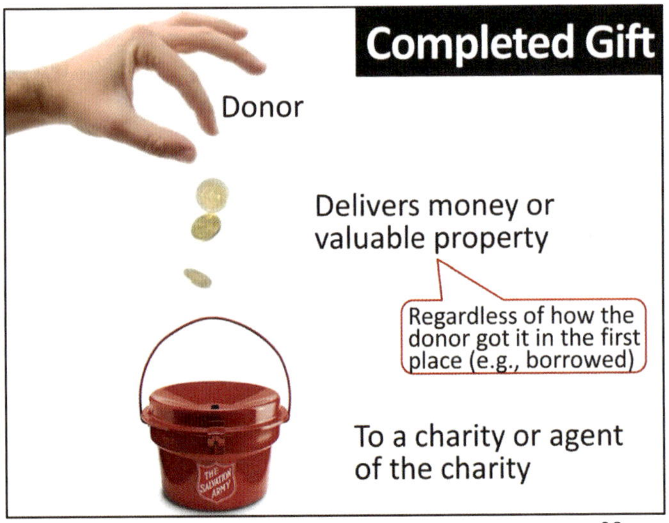

The answer, as always, is that the gift is complete when the donor delivers money or valuable property to the charity or agent of the charity. In this case, the donor delivered money to a charity on the date of the credit card transfer. The fact that the donor borrowed this money is irrelevant. The donor delivered money to a charity, meaning that the gift is a completed gift. This is true even if the donor never pays the loan used to make the gift to charity.

Consequently, the gift in this scenario is a completed charitable gift for income tax purposes on December 31. When, or if, the credit card bill is later paid is not relevant to the timing of the gift.

Let's now consider a slightly different example. In this case, the donor earns rebates from her credit card company. The donor clicks online to donate those rebates to a charity. Later, the credit card company mails a check to the charity. At what point is the gift complete?

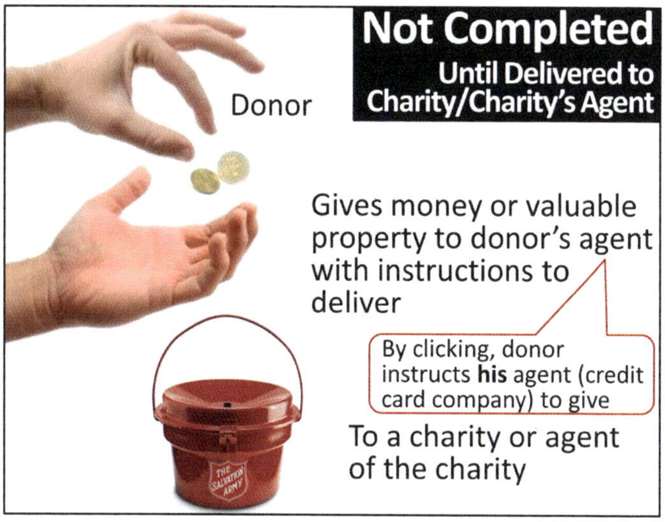

The answer, as always, is that the gift is complete when the donor delivers money or valuable property to the charity or agent of the charity. This does not occur when the donor clicks online to donate the rebates, because neither the charity nor the charity's agent has yet received any money or valuable property. Instead, what has happened is that the donor has instructed her agent (the credit card company) to deliver money to a charity. This instruction is not a completed gift until the donor's agent actually delivers the money to the charity or the charity's agent.

When the donor's agent (the credit card company) delivers a check to the United States Postal Service (the charity's agent), addressed to the charity, the gift is considered to be complete. Thus, on day nine, the donor's agent has delivered valuable property to the charity's agent, making the gift complete for income tax purposes.

What about a legally enforceable contract? In this case, the donor signs a legally enforceable contract (in the form of a pledge to donate). As is required by accounting rules, the charity books this legally enforceable contract as an asset in the charity's general ledger. The charity, in this case, then sells the right to collect on this pledge to an accounts receivable purchasing agency. As a result, the charity receives cash from the accounts receivable purchasing agency and then spends the cash. Only later, does the donor actually fulfill the pledge by making the agreed payment. Given that the charity has already received and spent money resulting from the pledge, when does the charitable gift actually occur for income tax purposes?

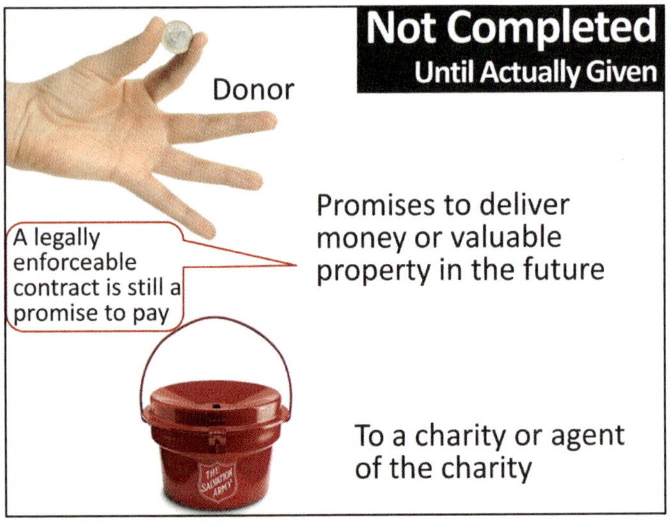

The answer, as always, is that the gift is complete when the donor delivers money or valuable property to the charity or agent of the charity. Prior to the donor fulfilling her pledge and actually transferring money to the charity, there is no gift. Although it is true that the charity has received money, the charity has not received money from the donor. The only thing the charity has received from the donor is a promise to pay money in the future. And, a promise to pay money in the future to a charity is not a completed gift until the money is actually given.

Consequently, there is no charitable gift until the donor actually pays the pledge by transferring money to the charity. Whatever the charity happens to do with the pledge in the meantime is irrelevant to the issue of when the charitable gift occurs.

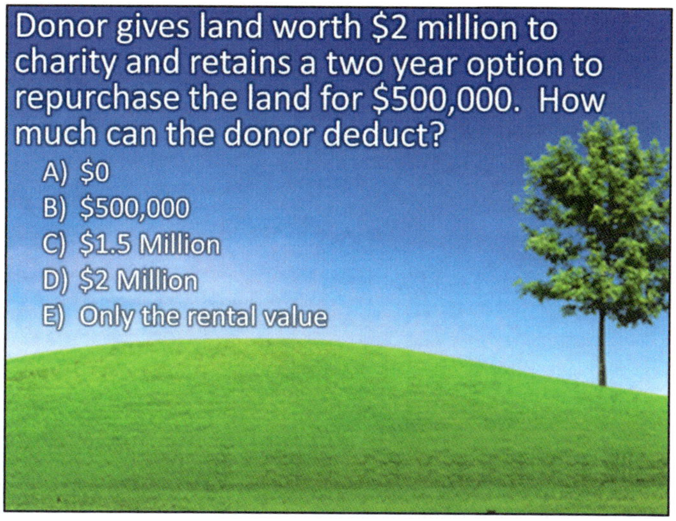

Suppose a donor gives land worth $2 million to a charity, but keeps the right to repurchase the land for $500,000 during the first two years after the gift. How much can the donor deduct immediately after making this transfer of land to the charity? Can the donor deduct $2 million (the value of the land given to the charity), $500,000 (the minimum payment the charity will receive regardless of what happens), nothing, or some other amount?

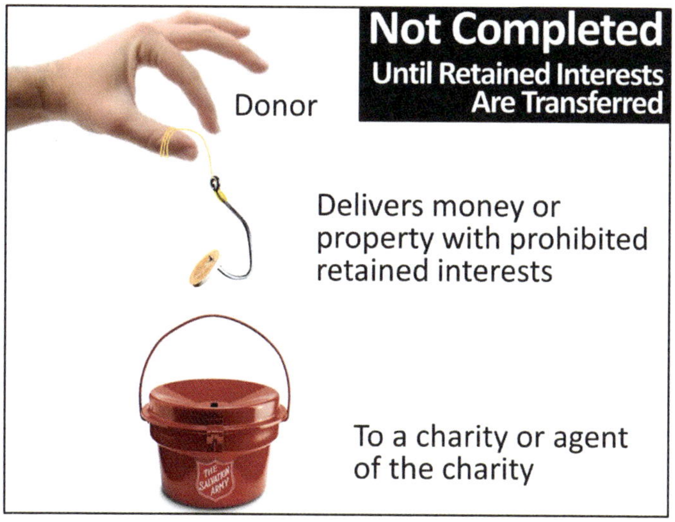

In this case, the donor has delivered valuable property to a charity, but has kept a prohibited "retained interest." The donor has made a transfer of the property, but the donor can get that property back, if the donor so chooses. The deduction for this type of retained interest transfer is not calculated based upon the difference between the value received by the charity and the value retained by the donor. Instead, there simply is no deduction so long as the prohibited retained interests remain. Thus, for tax purposes, the donor has made no gift at the point of the initial transfer due to the donor's retained interests in the property.

Because the donor has retained prohibited interests, there is no charitable deduction at the time of the initial transfer of the land to the charity.

Suppose we come back to that same scenario two years later. Assuming that the donor has not exercised the option to purchase the land, that option to purchase the land expires. Does this have any effect on the donor's ability to take a charitable deduction?

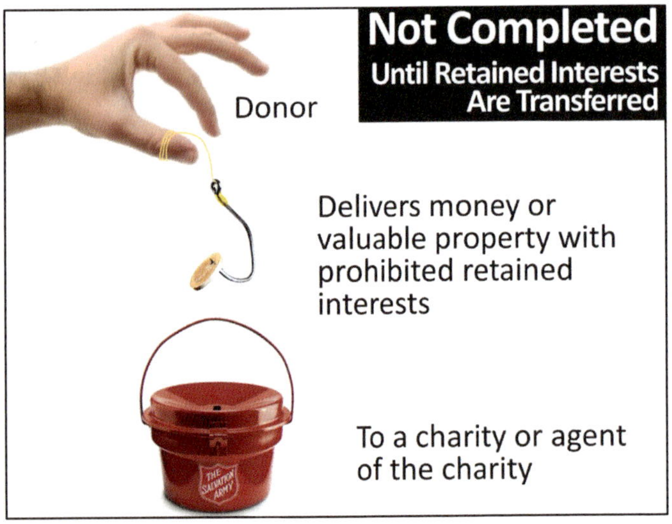

The donor initially delivered property to the charity with a prohibited retained interest. That transfer is not considered to be a charitable gift until all prohibited retained interests expire or are given to the charity. Two years later, the donor's prohibited retained interest expires. Thus, at that point, the donor has no retained interests in the property. This means that the gift is finally a completed charitable gift.

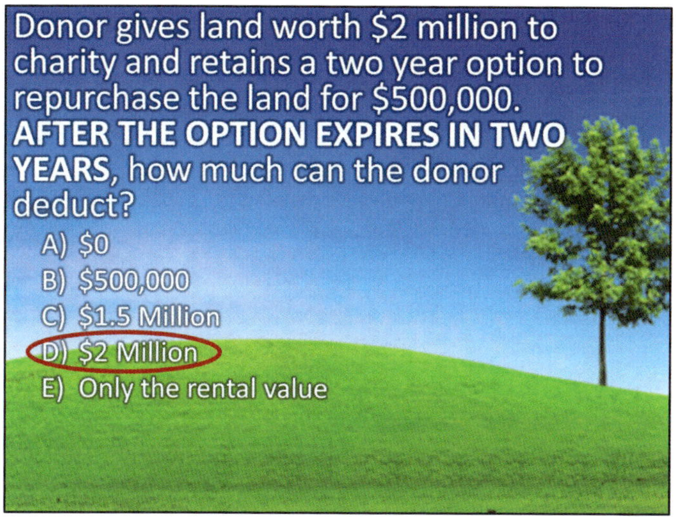

Because the donor no longer has any retained interests, the charity becomes the sole owner of the property. The value of that transfer is the value of the property, in this case $2 million. Thus, the donor may deduct a $2 million charitable gift, but not until all prohibited retained interests either expired or are transferred to the charity.

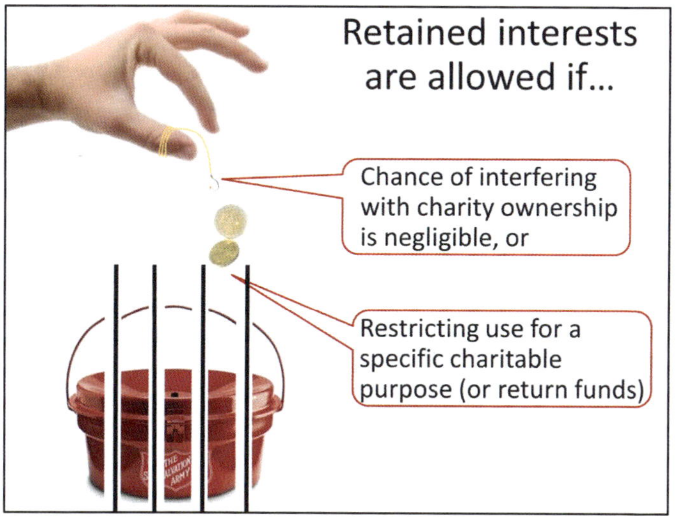

We have been examining prohibited retained interests. However, there are some types of restrictions on charitable gifts that do not interfere with the charitable deduction. These are restrictions where the chance of interfering with the charity ownership is negligible, or where the donor restricts the use of the charitable funds for a specific charitable purpose. The donor is allowed to restrict the use of funds for a specific charitable purpose and can even retain the right to receive the money back if the charity does not use the funds for that purpose. Indeed, this is the standard legal result of putting a restriction on a charitable gift. The charity's penalty for violating the restriction is that the donor then has the right to demand the return of his or her gift.

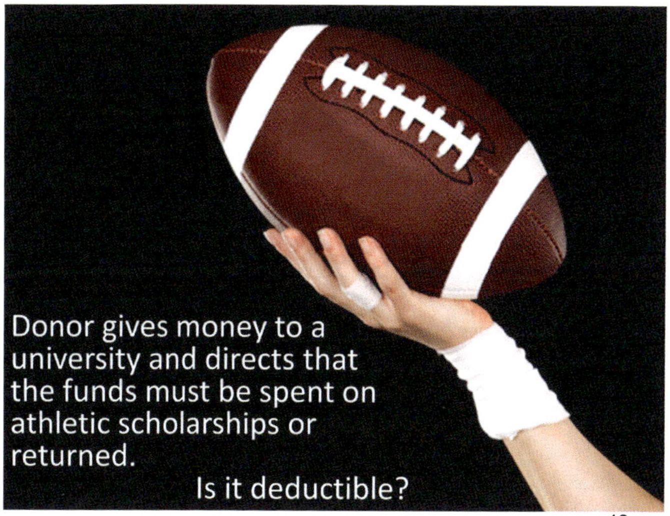

So, let's take a look at a common scenario. Suppose a donor gives money to a university and directs that the funds must be spent on athletic scholarships. This use is considered to be a charitable use of the funds. Under state law, if the university fails to use the funds for the designated charitable purpose, the donor has the right to demand the return of the funds. What is the effect on the charitable deduction given that the donor retains this level of control over the gift?

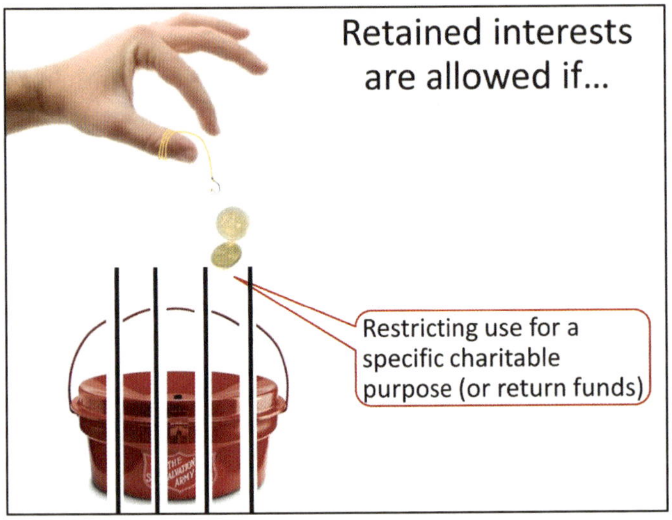

This retained control by the donor is perfectly acceptable because it is restricting the gift to be used for a specific charitable purpose. The retention of this right has no impact on the timing or amount of the charitable gift deduction. The gift is deducted just as it would be if the gift were given with no restrictions.

Suppose instead of limiting the use of the funds to athletic scholarships, the donor gave money to the university, and directed that the funds must be spent on a scholarship for a specific student.

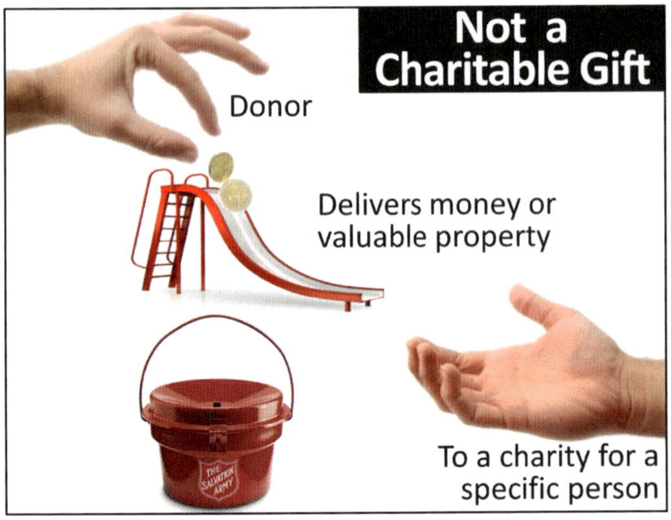

In this case, the transfer is not a charitable gift. A person is not a charity. A transfer to a specific person, even a financially needy person, is not a charitable gift. Requiring the charity to transfer the funds to a specific person makes this a transfer to a specific person, and therefore not a charitable gift.

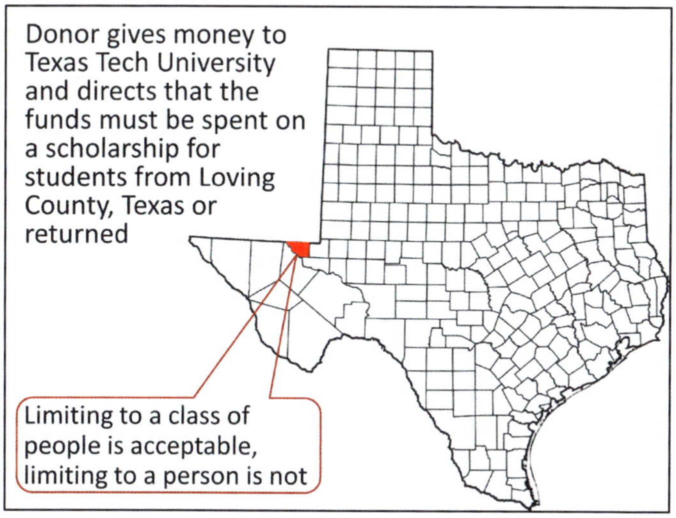

Note that the donor can restrict the beneficiaries to certain groups, but not to a specific individual. Thus, it is perfectly permissible for a donor to restrict his gift to funding scholarships for athletes, or even for students from a particular county. These are categories of people and not specific individuals. (Of course, if the donor restricted recipients using such categories that only one specific person could qualify, this cannot be used as a sneaky way to avoid the tax consequences of restricting the gift to a specific individual. This would still be, in reality, restricting the gift to be used for a specific person.)

Suppose that the donor intended to transfer the funds to benefit a specific individual, but did so in a more subtle manner than blatantly retaining a legally enforceable right. Could this softer approach result in both a transfer to a specific individual and a charitable deduction? This issue was addressed in a federal appeals court case where the donor to a university included the following note with his gift: "I am aware that a donation to a scholarship fund is only deductible if it is unspecified, however, if, in your opinion, and that of the authorities, it could be applied to the advantage of [specific named student], I think it would be constructive." The college received the gift and applied the money to the student's account. What was the tax result?

The donor's deduction was disallowed. Although not based upon mandatory legally enforceable rights, the court recognized this as a soft way to both take a charitable deduction and benefit a specific individual. Such a combination was not consistent with the goals of the charitable tax law, and thus the gift was not deductible.

This chapter ends by examining a special exception to the previous timing rules. The exception applies only to charitable gifts from C-corporations. (A C-corporations is the normal, standard corporation form, as contrasted with smaller closely-held S-corporations.)

This special rule for C-corporations allows them to make a charitable gift within 2 ½ months *after* the end of the tax year and treat the charitable gift as if it was made in the prior tax year. This exception is allowed only for C-corporations using accrual accounting and only where the board authorized the giving during the tax year.

The motivation for allowing this exception to the normal timing rules is that such corporations are limited to deducting a maximum of 10% of their net income for charitable gifts. Calculating the corporation's net income for the year (especially when on an accrual accounting basis) is a difficult process. This difficulty would otherwise prevent corporations from making deductible charitable gifts up to the maximum, because of the uncertainty in knowing the corporation's net income for the year prior to the end of the year. By giving C-corporations on an accrual accounting basis this extra 2 ½ months, the tax code permits sufficient time to both calculate the net income for the previous year, and make charitable transfers up to the 10% of net income limit. However, the board must have committed to making such gifts in the previous taxable year. So, the charitable transfer idea cannot have been a new one that occurred after the end of the tax year, but must have already been authorized.

This ends the section on elements and timing of a charitable gift. As in other areas of charitable planning, we start with a simple rule. In this case, the rule is that a deductible charitable gift occurs when the donor delivers money or valuable property to a charity or agent of the charity. However, when that rule is applied to a variety of complex scenarios its interpretation can become challenging. Nevertheless, understanding what is deductible and when it is deductible is a fundamentally necessary skill for anyone who will be advising donors about charitable transactions. Thus, there is practical value in understanding the intricacies of the elements and timing of a deductible charitable gift.

4 HOW TO DOCUMENT CHARITABLE GIFTS

In this chapter we will examine how to document charitable gifts in order to preserve the income tax deduction. Admittedly, this is one of the less fascinating topics related to charitable planning. There is little room for creativity or interesting combinations, as is possible in other areas of charitable planning. Nevertheless, successfully obtaining the appropriate charitable deduction should be a fundamental expectation when working with any planned giving advisor and part of obtaining that deduction requires appropriate documentation. So, despite the relatively dry nature of the material, it is essential material and, consequently, must be mastered.

To understand the importance of the documentation rules, it is useful to deal with a common misconception. There is an expectation that as long as the donor was not abusing the system, and was, in fact, taking the "correct" deduction, that a documentation error would be a minor and correctable problem. If honest mistakes did not lead to severe penalties, being intimately familiar with the documentation rules would not be essential. Unfortunately, this perception is absolutely false. The consequences for even minor documentation oversights are dramatic and subsequently uncorrectable. Even if the donor actually deducts what would otherwise be the correct amount, minor documentation errors can reduce or completely eliminate the deduction. This loss of deduction cannot be regained through later

correction of the documentation errors.

Let's take an example from a tax court case to illustrate the point. A donor made a charitable gift of $80,000 of non-publicly traded stock with a cost basis of $3,700. The valuation of the stock as being worth $80,000 was a correct valuation. However, the donor did not obtain a qualified appraisal prior to taking the deduction. (We will see later that such appraisals are required for gifts of nonpublicly-traded stock in this amount.) So, the donor correctly valued the gift and took the charitable deduction based upon that correct valuation. What, then, is the result of this oversight where the donor did not obtain a qualified appraisal in advance?

The result of the error in documentation was that the donor could not take the fair market value deduction (which was not adequately documented), but could only take the cost basis (which was documented). So, instead of having an $80,000 deduction, the donor had a $3,700 deduction. The loss of $76,300 of deduction could not be corrected by later obtaining a qualified appraisal. It was simply lost. (Translation: documentation is a big deal.)

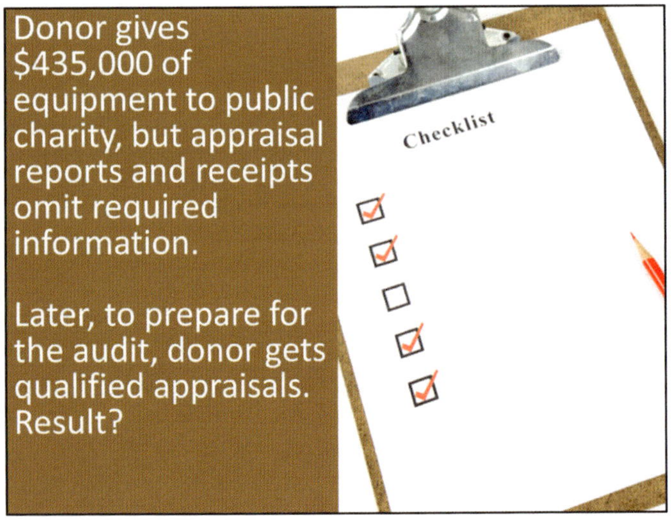

Let's now look at another example involving an even larger charitable transfer. In this case, the donor gave $435,000 of equipment to a public charity. As we will later see, such gifts require a qualified appraisal. The donor did get an appraisal. The appraisal was correct in valuing the transfer at $435,000. However, the appraisal report and accompanying receipts omitted some information that was required for qualified appraisals. After receiving notice of an audit, the donor corrected this problem by obtaining a new appraisal which met all of the qualifications for a qualified appraisal. Both the original appraisal and the new qualified appraisal correctly valued the equipment at $435,000.

What was the result of this initial oversight by the donor, followed by the corrected appraisal?

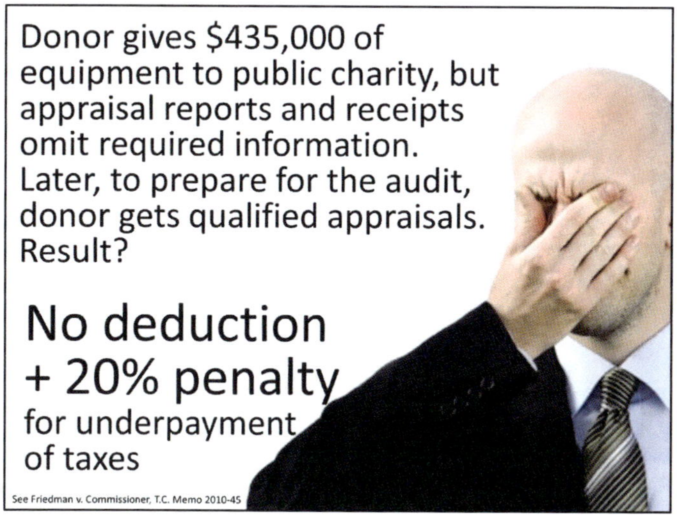

The donor's entire $435,000 deduction was disallowed. The donor had not followed the full requirements for documentation prior to taking the deduction. The lack of documentation meant that there would be no deduction. Attempting to fully document after the deduction was taken was irrelevant. As a result of losing this deduction, the taxpayer was required to pay the additional income taxes and make a 20% penalty payment for underpaying his taxes initially, along with accumulated interest since the original due date of the tax return. Thus, in this case, the donor ended with a tax result worse than if he had never made the charitable transfer in the first place. (Translation: documentation is a big deal.)

These examples show just how important it is to know and follow the documentation rules. Even if the material is a bit dry and uncreative, it is, nevertheless, absolutely essential for anyone involved with advising donors. So, having been properly motivated, let's now examine the documentation rules themselves.

We will be looking at seven different levels of documentation requirements based upon the type and amount of gift being made. As the complexity and amount of these gift types increase, so do the documentation requirements. The idea here is that documentation increases as the opportunity for abusing the tax deduction rules increases. There is, for example, relatively little potential for significant tax revenue loss from a deduction for a $50 cash contribution. Conversely, the opportunity to take a $500,000 deduction for the gift of a painting has a much greater potential for abuse.

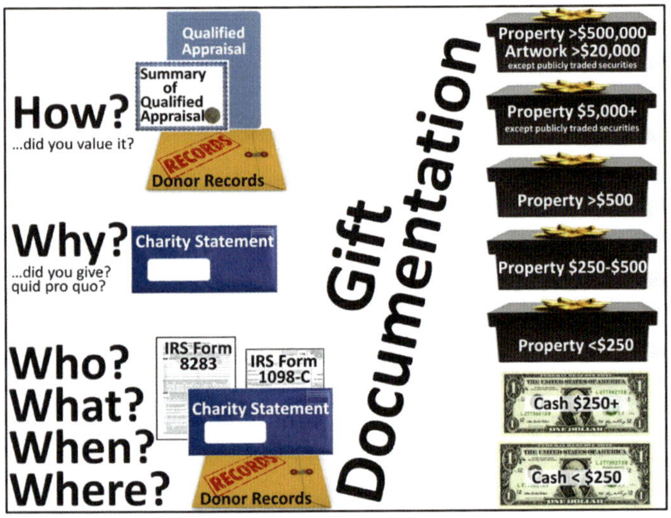

Different levels of documentation require answering different questions. All gifts must somehow document answers to the questions of, "Who made the gift?", "What was the gift?", "When was the gift made?", and "Where was the gift given?" Depending upon the level of documentation required, these questions may be answered by donor records, a statement from the charity, and/or completing IRS forms.

Some gifts must also document an answer to the question of whether or not the donor received any goods or services in return for the gift (i.e., this was part of the reason WHY the donor made the gift). The answer to this question can be documented only by a statement from the charity.

Finally, some larger gifts also require documentation of how the gift was valued. This "How?" question can be answered by donor records or a qualified appraisal. In some cases, the entire qualified appraisal must be submitted with the tax return and, in other cases, only a summary must be submitted. This is the general framework for how documentation levels increase as gift amounts and complexity increases. Let's now examine the rules in more detail, starting with the smallest gifts.

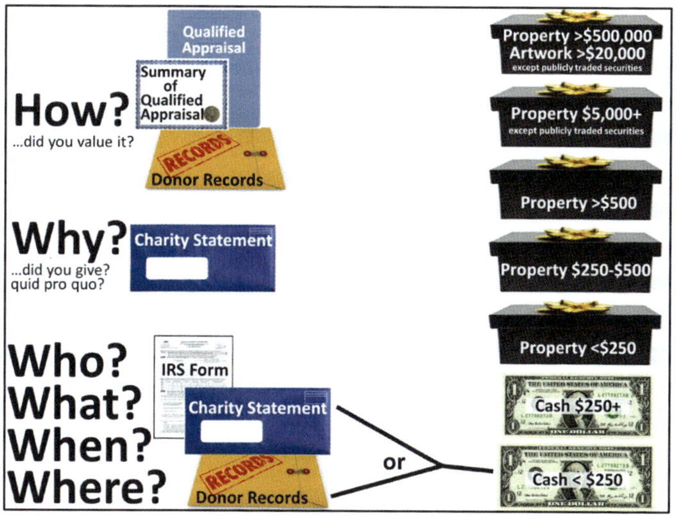

Gifts of cash under $250 require documentation of only the first block of questions (i.e., answers to the "Why?" and "How?" questions are not needed). For these small gifts, documentation can come from either donor records or a statement from the charity.

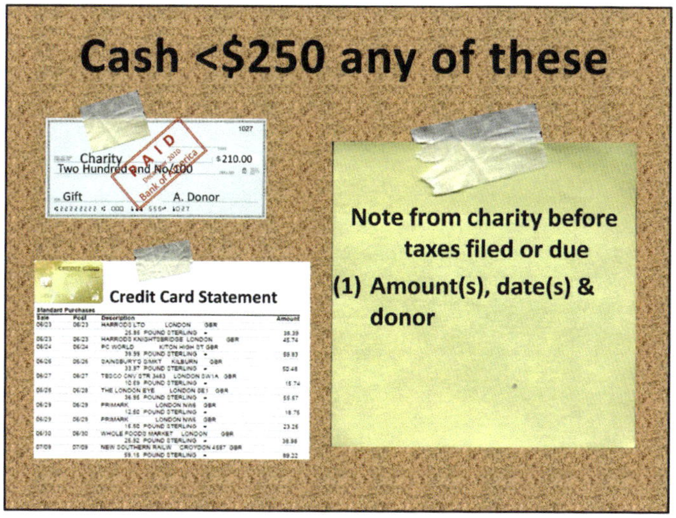

Specifically, cash gifts under $250 may be documented by a canceled check, a credit card statement, or a note from the charity indicating the amount, date, and the donor. As with other forms of documentation, this must be in place prior to taking the deduction. Thus, the note from the charity must have arrived by the time the tax return was filed, or if the taxes were filed late, then the note must arrive by the time that the taxes were due (including any extensions). No corrections are allowed for documentation created after taking the deduction (or after the tax return was due). Note that, because of these documentation requirements, deducting a gift of actual currency, no matter how small, requires a receipt from the charity indicating the amount, date and donor. Note also, that a "credit card statement" here refers generally to any type of statement from a bank or financial institution demonstrating the amount and date of the gift, the donor, and the recipient charity. So, for example, a statement from a check card or debit card would also be sufficient.

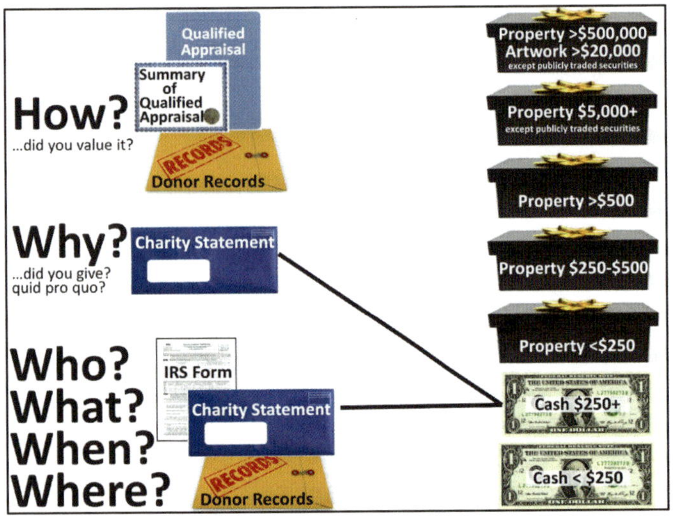

For gifts of cash of $250 or more, the documentation requirements are increased. Answers to the first block of questions can be documented only with a statement from the charity. In addition, the donor must have a statement from the charity indicating any *quid pro quo* related to the gift. *Quid pro quo* gifts refer to situations where a donor receives some item or service from the charity in direct exchange for the gift (such as, for example, a benefit dinner where the donor's ticket represents both a contribution and payment for a meal).

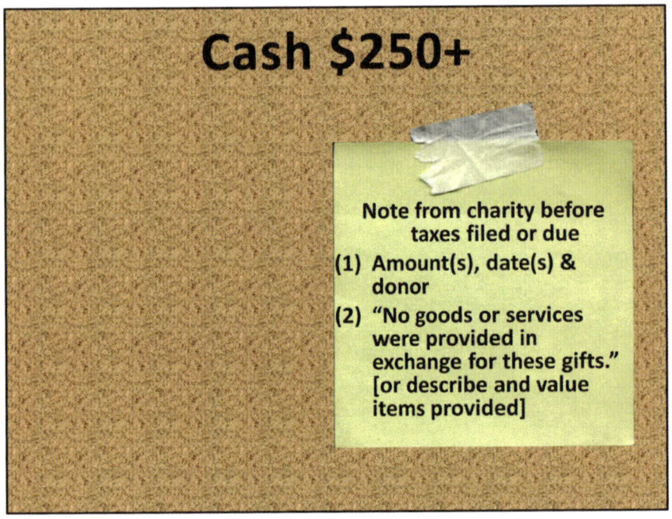

For gifts of cash of $250 or more, the only documentation permitted is a receipt from the charity indicating the amount, the date, the donor, and using the magic phrase, "no goods or services were provided in exchange for these gifts." (Of course, if the charity did provide goods or services in exchange for the gifts, the charity must describe and value the items.) A canceled check, for example, will not be sufficient to document gifts of $250 or more. Only a receipt from the charity with the previously mentioned elements will be sufficient.

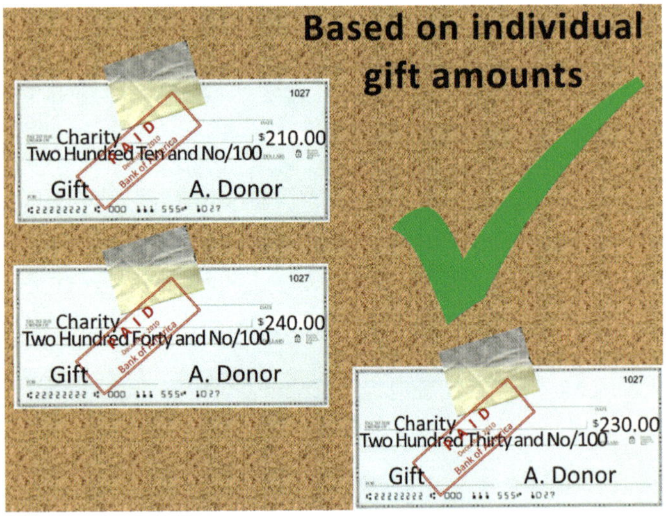

The documentation requirements are based upon each individual gift amount and not the total of all gifts made to the organization. So, for example, a donor could make $240 contributions every day of the year to a charity, and all of these gifts could be documented by the canceled checks. (However, in an extreme case, such as a donor simultaneously giving a stack of $240 checks to a charity, the IRS could collapse the transaction and treat it as a single transfer.)

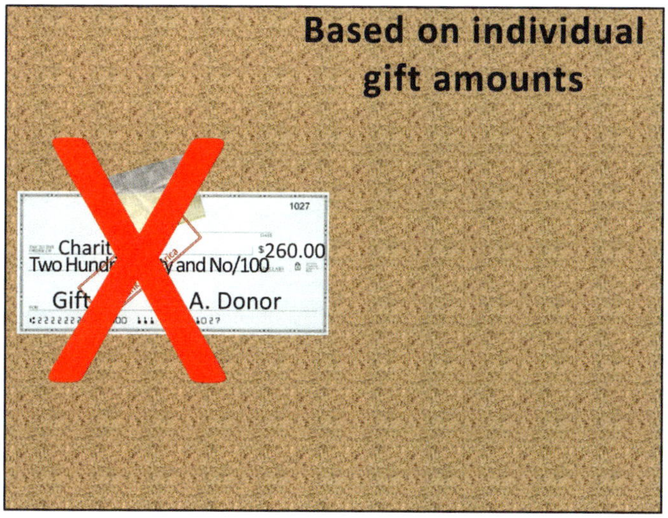

Even though a donor can document an unlimited number of charitable contributions under $250 with canceled checks, if any one contribution exceeded this amount, then a canceled check would not be appropriate documentation for that one contribution.

One exception to these documentation requirements for gifts of $250 or more applies to payroll deduction gifts made to a united appeal. Such gifts are problematic because there is no individual charity that could document the charitable transfer from a specific individual donor. Thus, it is not possible to comply with the typical substantiation rules.

Because of this difficulty, such gifts are exempted from the requirement for a receipt from a charity. Instead, donors can substantiate with evidence of a pledge card indicating that no goods or services were given in exchange for the gift and documenting the amounts by the W-2 or pay stub.

Gifts of money over $250 are all documented in the same way, regardless of the amount. Thus, at this point we have covered the rules for documenting gifts of money. However, much of the complexity in documentation, and much of the potential for abuse, comes from gifts of property. Let's now examine these rules.

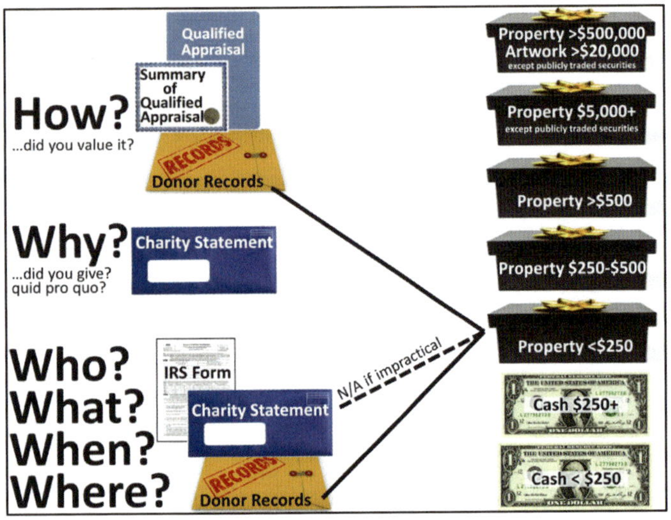

The smallest gifts of property (under $250) require donor records to answer the questions of "Who made the gift?", "What was the gift?", "When was the gift made?", "Where was the transfer made?", and "How was the gift valued?" Except where it is impractical, these donor records must include a receipt from the charity indicating what was given, when, where, and by whom.

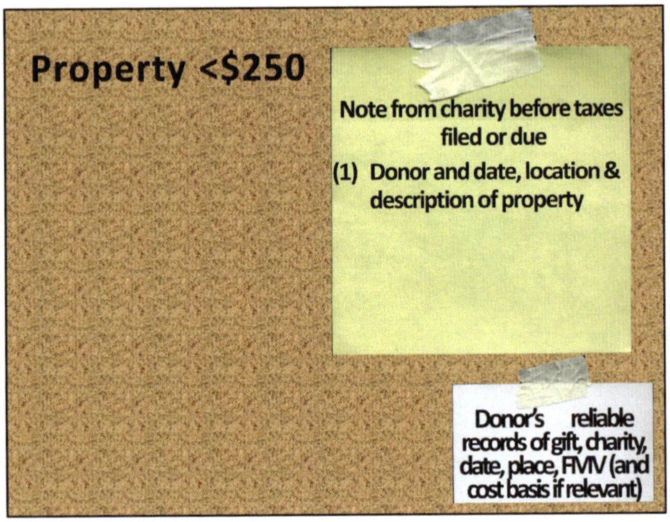

So, for gifts of property under $250, the donor must have a receipt from the charity indicating the donor, the date, the location, and the description of the property (except where obtaining such a note is impractical). The donor's own records should indicate these things as well (although these records may include the charity's receipt). However, in addition, the donor must have reliable records proving the fair market value of the property (and, if relevant, also proving the donors basis in the property). Note that the charity is never expected to provide a valuation of the property. Although some charities may choose to include this in a receipt, such valuation has no legal effect. The charity is not qualified to give an appraisal.

For small property gifts (under $250) an exception is made to the requirement of a receipt from the charity when such receipt is impractical. A typical example of a scenario in which such a receipt is impractical is where the donor gives clothing or property to an unattended drop box.

In such cases, no receipt is required from the charity.

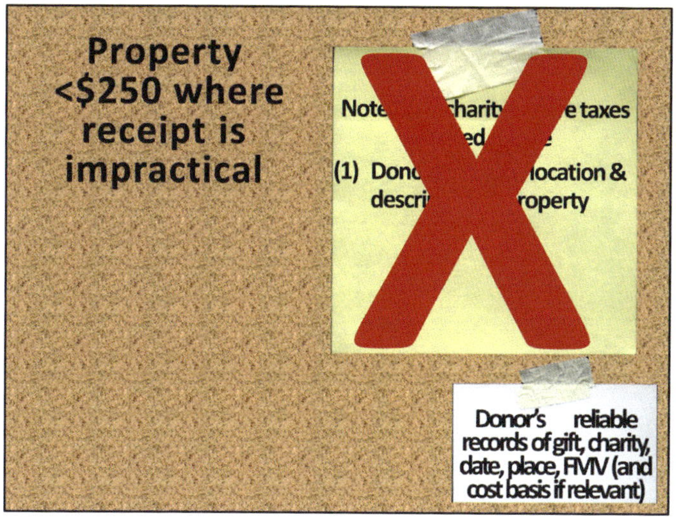

However, even when a receipt from the charity is not required, the donor must still provide reliable records documenting the gift, the charity receiving the gift, the date of the gift, the place of the gift, and the fair market value (and cost basis when relevant) of the property.

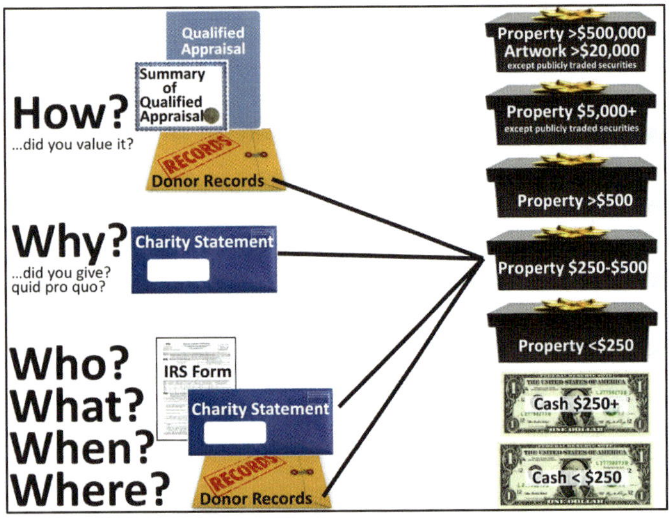

For gifts of property worth $250-$500, documentation must answer all of the potential questions (Who? What? When? Where? How? and Why?). In addition to the documentation required for smaller gifts of property, the donor now must provide a statement from the charity and there is no exception for impracticability. This statement must not only answer the basic questions ("Who? What? When? Where? Why?) but must also answer the *quid pro quo* question(i.e., How?).

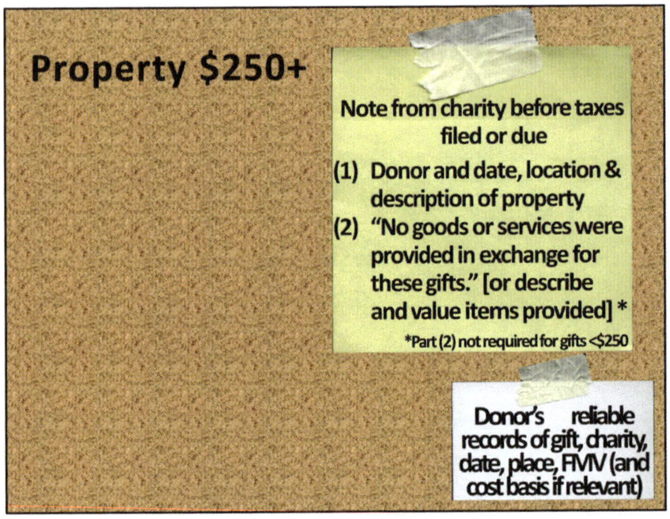

Thus, for gifts of property of $250 or more, the donor must have both a receipt from the charity indicating the donor, the date, the location, and a description of the property along with the phrase "no goods or services were provided in exchange for these gifts," as well as the donor's own reliable records indicating the fair market value of the property, (and cost basis if relevant).

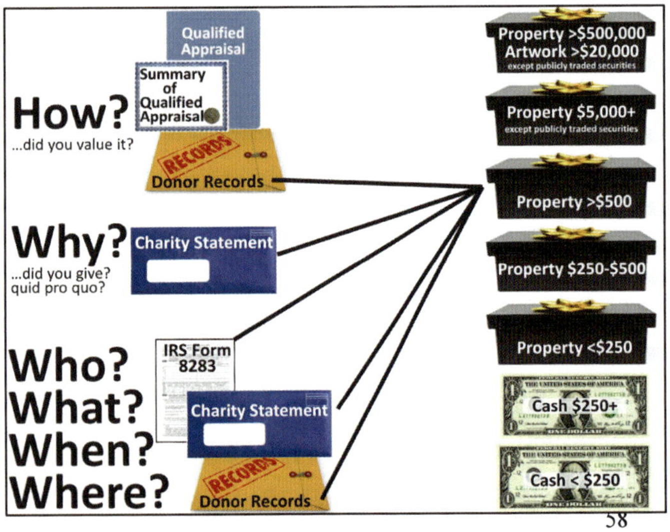

For gifts of property over $500, all of the previous documentation is required in addition to the filing of IRS form 8283.

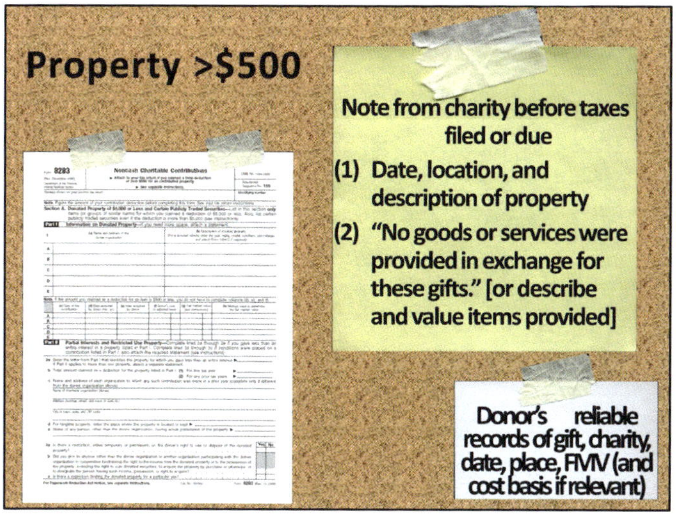

The IRS form 8283 filing is required for all property gifts valued at $500 or more. Note that for property gifts of $500 or more, all potential documentation items are required, excepting only a qualified appraisal, which is a requirement limited to specific types and amounts of property.

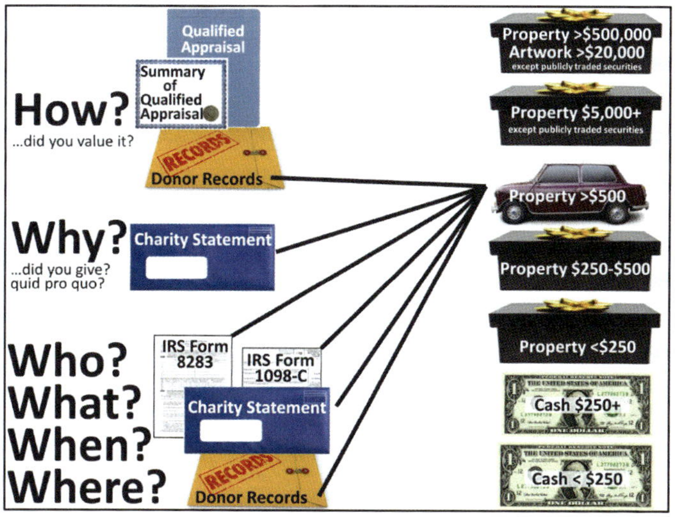

Additional IRS forms are required for gifts of property over $500 if the gift was of an automobile, boat or plane. Specifically, these gifts require the filing of IRS form 1098-C by the charity.

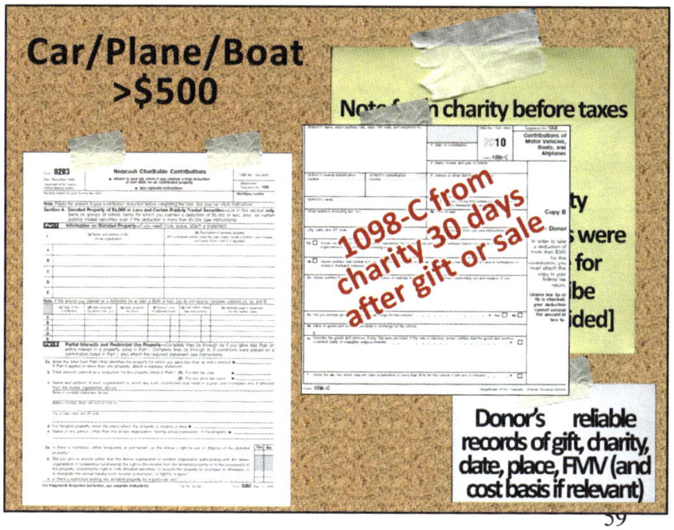

Form 1098-C must come from the charity within 30 days of the gift or the sale. Gifts of automobiles, boats, or planes that are intended to be sold by the charity cannot be valued (for tax deduction purposes) until after the charity has sold the item. This is because the deduction is limited to the amount the charity receives for the item in the subsequent sale. If, however, the charity intends not to sell the item, but to make use of it in its charitable purposes, then the charity may verify this intent by filing Form 1098-C within 30 days of receiving the gift. (In such cases, the valuation need not wait for the sale of the item.)

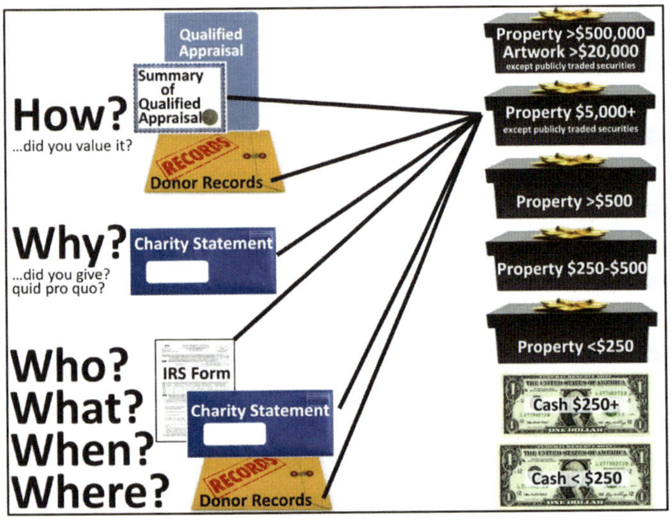

Finally, with gifts of property of $5,000 or more, the donor must obtain a qualified appraisal and must attach a summary of the qualified appraisal to his or her tax return. This qualified appraisal is not required for publicly traded securities. Publicly traded securities are very easy to value and there is relatively little dispute about their valuation at any one point in time because they can be immediately bought or sold at publicly available prices.

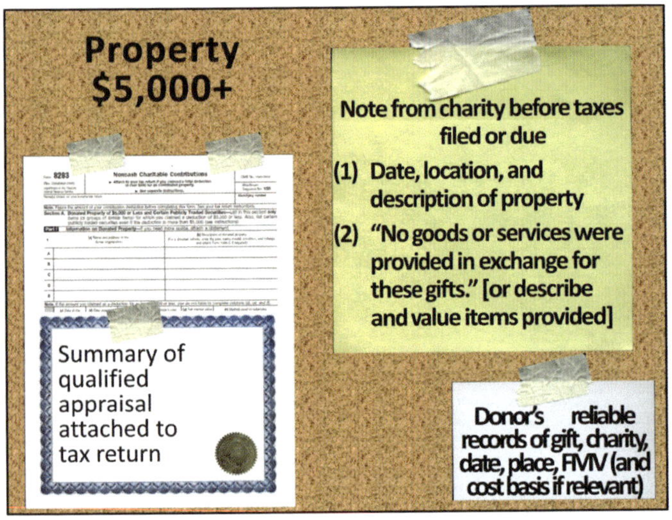

Thus, for gifts of property of $5000 or more, all of this documentation is required: Charity receipt with gift date, location, and description and *quid pro quo* statement, Donor records of gift, charity, date, location, fair market value and basis (if relevant), IRS Form 8283, and a summary of a qualified appraisal attached to the tax return. If any item is absent, no deduction is allowed.

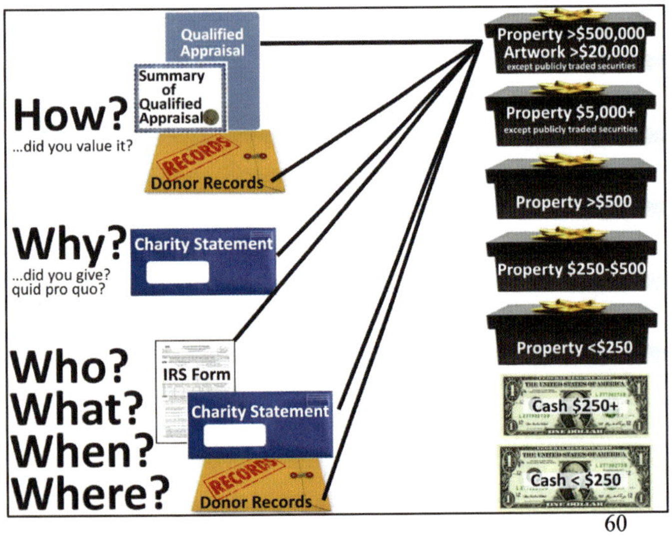

The highest level of documentation is reserved for gifts of property over $500,000 or gifts of artwork over $20,000. As before, publicly traded securities are exempted from the appraisal requirement because their valuation is relatively simple. Note that these are the gifts with the greatest potential for abuse. Gifts of property over $500,000 may be subject to a variety of interpretations of fair market value. And, given their value, such differences of opinion can have a dramatic difference on the payment of taxes. Thus, these large gifts warrant the most careful scrutiny by the IRS.

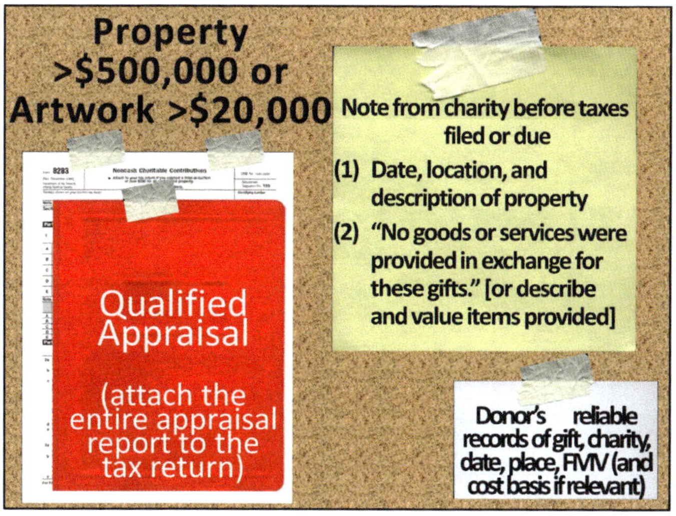

Because these type of gifts will be subject to the highest level of scrutiny, it makes sense that the entire qualified appraisal must be included with the tax return. Not only are very large property gifts included (over $500,000) in this highest documentation level, but even moderately size gifts of art are also included (over $20,000). This reflects the challenges in the valuation of artwork and the consequent opportunities for abuse. Remember that for some taxpayers combining both state and federal income taxes can make deductions worth $.50 on the dollar. Thus, if a valuation were made that was more than twice what the donor could actually sell the property for, it becomes more profitable to give rather than sell the property. This potential for over-valuation is much more likely with property, such as artwork, where intrinsic value is difficult to define.

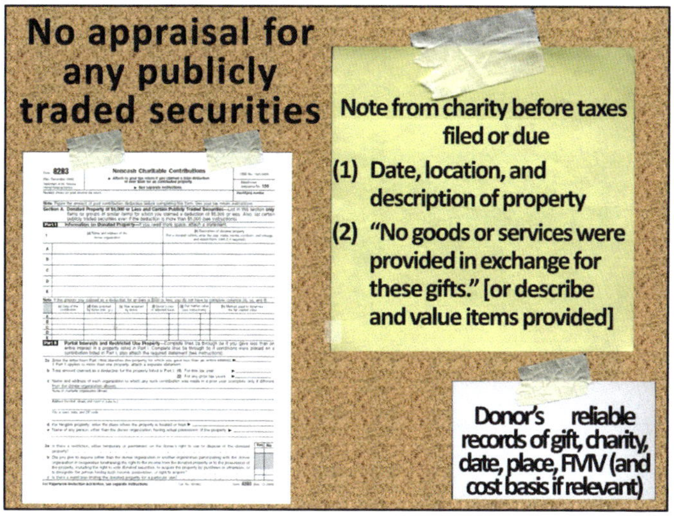

As a reminder, appraisals are not required for gifts of publicly traded securities, regardless of the size of the gift. Thus, a donor could deduct a $10 million gift of Microsoft shares with no appraisal.

Finally, there are *de minimus* exceptions to the normal rules for *quid pro quo* gifts. A *quid pro quo* gift is one where the donor makes a gift, but also receives something of value in return for the gift. Typically, these scenarios require both that the charity report the value of the item given to the donor and also that the donor reduce his or her deduction by the value of the item received from the charity. Although the charity is not a qualified appraiser, it is required to make a "good faith estimate" of the value of the item. IRS regulations indicate, "The organization may use any reasonable methodology in making a good faith estimate, provided it applies the methodology in good faith."

However, if the gift was $75 or less, the charity is not required to report the *quid pro quo* part of the transaction (i.e., they do not have to report the cost or value of the item given to the donor). The rule applies only to the charity's reporting requirement.

The donor must still reduce his or her deduction by the value of the item received in exchange for the gift. The donor can ignore the value of the item received by the charity in exchange for the gift only when one of two *de minimus* exceptions apply to the donor. First, the donor can ignore the value of the item received in exchange for the donation if its value does not exceed 2% of the value of the donation. This exception does not apply to items received that are worth more than $101. (Note that this $101 level is a 2013 inflation-adjusted number that changes every year.) Second, the donor need not consider the value of the item received in exchange for a gift if the cost of the item to the charity was equal to or less than $10.10 so long as the gift made in order to receive the item was at least $50.50. (As before, these are 2013 numbers that are adjusted annually for inflation.) These *de minimus* rules are intended to reduce reporting hassles for items of an inconsequential amount.

Although admittedly among some of the least interesting rules related to charitable gift planning, these documentation rules are nonetheless important. The penalties for violating the rules can be severe and typically there is no opportunity to correct documentation errors after a deduction has been erroneously taken.

5 VALUING CHARITABLE GIFTS OF PROPERTY

As we begin the topic of valuing charitable gifts of property, it is useful to consider why this topic is so important. As discussed previously, the vast majority of wealth in this country is not held in cash, savings accounts, checking accounts, or money market accounts. Consequently, if we wish to ask for gifts of wealth, then, by and large, we are asking for gifts of property. In other words, if we want to ask from the "big bucket" of wealth, then we need to ask for gifts of property, meaning any type of non-cash asset. A fundamental requirement of being able to ask for these property gifts from the "big bucket" is an understanding of how such gifts are valued for tax purposes. As we will see, this is no small issue. Different types of assets in different types of transactions may be valued dramatically differently, including a valuation of zero dollars. So, in order to be able to learn how to ask from the "big bucket", it is essential to have a basic understanding of how gifts of property are valued. Obviously, a fundraiser or advisor who suggests a charitable gift of property, while being unaware that the deduction in that particular case would be far less than the value of the property, is creating serious potential problems. This chapter is intended to eliminate that risk by reviewing the rules for valuing charitable gifts of property.

If you have been previously familiar only with cash gifts to charity, then this issue of valuation may be new to you. Cash gifts include all cash equivalent transactions such as checks, currency, or credit cards. Gifts of cash require no valuation. The value is simply the amount of the gift. Because the valuation is simple, calculating the deduction is also simple. Although cash gifts are simple, the bulk of a donor's wealth is rarely held in cash. Understanding gifts of non-cash assets opens up the possibility for many more sophisticated and beneficial conversations with donors.

The simplicity of valuation with cash or cash equivalent gifts contrasts with the complexity of valuing several kinds of property gifts. An initial cause of this complexity may come from the difficulty inherent in valuing certain types of property. Additionally, there are special tax rules for charitable gifts of certain kinds of property which can themselves alter the valuation of the property for tax purposes. These rules have at times been put in place to curb abuses of the charitable gift tax deduction. Because many of these rules were created in a reactive fashion – responding to particular individual abuses – it has resulted in a hodgepodge of rules that are not always consistent. Consequently, because so many specialized exceptions have arisen over the years, it is not always enough to know a single approach to valuation of charitable gifts of property. Nevertheless, there are some general principles that apply to most gifts of property.

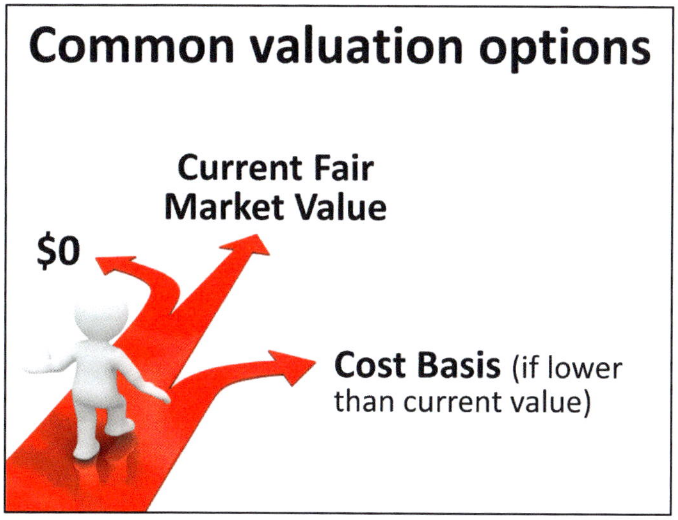

Despite the variety of rules and exceptions, we can sort the most typical valuations into three categories. With a few exceptions, the value for tax deduction purposes of a charitable gift of property will be (1) the fair market value of the property, (2) the cost basis of the property – only where such basis is less than the fair market value of the property, or (3) nothing. Notice that the most advantageous valuation that we can receive under any circumstances is the fair market value of property. This is an important fact because when working with donors, the almost universal expectation is that the charitable gift of property will generate a charitable deduction equivalent to the value of the property. Asking for property gifts that generate no deduction or a much reduced deduction without understanding that reality in advance places the fundraiser or advisor in a highly unfavorable position. Thus, as a prerequisite to suggesting charitable transactions involving property, the fundraiser or advisor must be familiar with the rules for deducting such property gifts in order to avoid embarrassment, financial loss, and broken relationships. So let's explore these three most common valuation options for property given to charity.

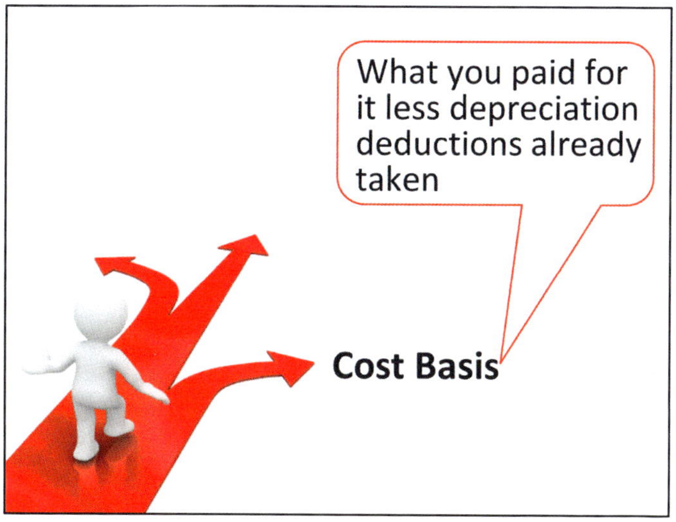

One of the common valuation options for charitable gifts of property is the property's "cost basis," or what is referred to more technically as "adjusted basis." I use the term cost basis here because, in most cases, the adjusted basis is simply the amount paid for the item by the donor (i.e., its cost to the donor). So, if a donor paid $100 for an item that is now worth $200, the deduction for giving that item to charity will be $100 if the gift is valued based on its cost basis. Note that the cost basis valuation of charitable gifts of property is never used when the cost basis is greater than the property's fair market value. Cost basis valuation of gifts of property can only lower the value of the gift compared with its fair market value, not raise it.

The cost basis of property can include other items besides the initial purchase price. For example, if I purchase a house for $100,000 and then spend $30,000 on an addition to the house, my basis in the home is $130,000. So, the basis of a property includes both its initial purchase price and any subsequent capital expenditures.

Calculating the basis of a property becomes more complex if we consider depreciation deductions. Not all property is subject to depreciation deductions. However, this is common with property that has been used for business purposes. Essentially a depreciation deduction allows a person to claim that the property has become less valuable because it is wearing out. So, for example, if I purchase a $5000 computer for my business, I can claim that after one year of use the computer is worth $4000. Consequently, I have a depreciation deduction of $1000. I can do this for each of the first five years that I use the computer in my business until, after five years, it is completely depreciated. If after five years, I have taken depreciation deductions of $5000, my basis is $0. I paid $5000 and then deducted $5000 of depreciation deductions, so $5000 -$5000 = $0.

Depreciation deductions affect charitable deductions for gifts of property because I can't deduct the same item twice. So, if my $5000 computer purchase has already generated $5000 of deductions (through depreciation), I cannot then give it to charity and generate another $2000 deduction (even if it is truly worth $2000). This would mean deducting the same item twice. As a result, the value of property for purposes of determining the charitable deduction is always reduced by any depreciation deductions that have already been taken. This is true both for gifts that are valued by their cost basis and for gifts that are valued at fair market value. Of course, not all property can be depreciated. In fact, depreciation is not a concern in most property gift transactions. But it is an important concept to keep in mind for those cases when it does arise (primarily physical items used in business operations).

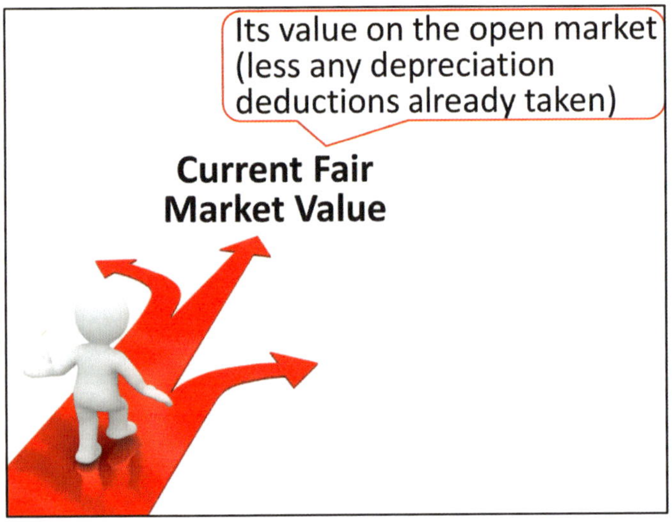

Charitable gifts of property can also be valued at their current "fair market value." This is, of course, the normal valuation. It simply answers the question, "How much is this item worth?" More technically, the IRS indicates that fair market value is the price that property would sell for on the open market. It is the price that would be agreed on between a willing buyer and a willing seller, with neither being required to act, and both having reasonable knowledge of the relevant facts. For our purposes, it is easiest to think of fair market value as simply the answer to the question, "What could you normally sell it for?" or, "What is it worth?" As mentioned above, even when property can be deducted at its fair market value, this deduction must be reduced by any previous depreciation deductions already taken on that property by the donor. (Because, again, deducting the same dollar more than once is not allowed.)

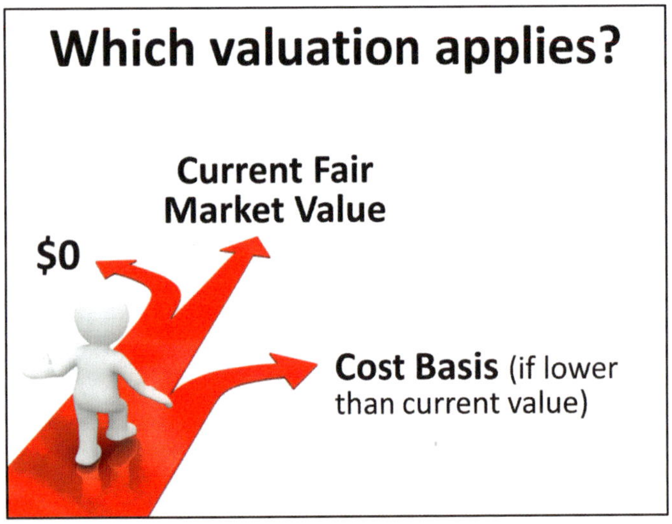

When valuing an item of property to be given as a charitable gift, the initial issue is, for almost all transactions, "Which of these 3 valuation approaches apply?" How will the item be valued for purposes of the charitable tax deduction? Will we be able to deduct its fair market value, its basis, or nothing at all? Let's now look at the basic framework that determines which of these deduction amounts we can use.

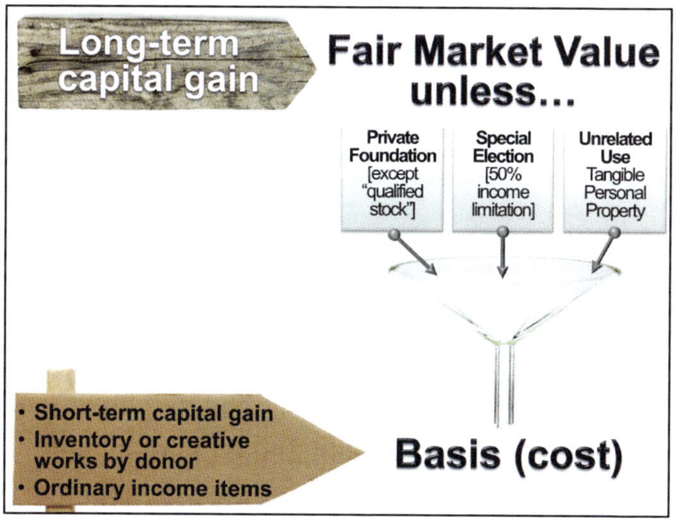

If proceeds from the sale of the property would have been considered ordinary income if the donor had sold the property, rather than given it to a charity, then the donor may deduct only his or her basis in the property. So, for example, if a cobbler received $100 for selling a pair of his shoes, this money is considered to be ordinary income. Selling shoes is his ordinary business. If the cobbler gave a pair of shoes that normally sells for $100 to a charity, his deduction would not be $100 (the fair market value). Instead his deduction would be limited to his cost basis in the shoes (i.e., his cost of materials in the shoes). Similarly, if an artist painted a painting and gave it to a charity, her deduction would be limited to the cost of the canvas and paint used in the painting. Just as with the cobbler selling shoes, if the artist had sold the painting, the money from the sale would have been taxed as ordinary income to the artist.

The cost basis valuation also applies to any property that has been held by the donor for one year or less. If this property had been sold for a profit, that profit would have been short-term capital gain. All such short-term capital gain property is valued at its basis for purposes of the charitable deduction. (Any property that would have generated a loss if sold would not be valued at its basis because, in that case, the basis would be higher than the fair market value. And, we are never allowed to use basis for valuation if it is higher than fair market value.)

The only type of non-cash property that has a *chance* of being valued at fair market value for a charitable deduction is long-term capital gain property. We begin with the assumption that long-term capital gain property can be valued at its fair market value for charitable tax deduction purposes. However, several circumstances can cause long-term capital gain property to drop out of fair market value valuation and be reduced to cost basis valuation.

The first scenario where long-term capital gain property can be dropped into cost basis valuation is if the property is given to a private foundation, rather than to a public charity. Although here we have an exception to the exception, because if the gift is "qualified stock" then it can still be deducted at fair market value. Another reason that long-term capital gain property may not be valued at fair market value for tax deduction purposes is if the donor has made a "special election" to accept the lower valuation in exchange for a higher charitable deduction income limitation. (This is discussed in the chapter on income limitations for charitable deductions.)

A third circumstance when long-term capital gain property will not be valued at its fair market value is when such property is "unrelated use" tangible personal property. It is easiest to think of tangible personal property as movable physical property. So, this would not include immovable real esate such as land or anything permanently attached to the land, like a building. This also would not include *intangible* personal property, such as shares of stock or bonds. (Stocks and bonds, physically, are just pieces of paper. They have value only because of the rights they represent, not because of the paper they are printed on.) "Unrelated use" tangible personal property is property that the charity does not intend to use in furtherance of its charitable purposes. If, for example, the charity intends to simply sell the gifted item, then the item is "unrelated use" property. (Note that this is true even though the cash from the sale of the item will be used to further the charitable purposes of the organization.)

We have been examining long-term and short-term capital gain property, but haven't mentioned capital loss property. Capital loss property is property that is worth LESS at its sale than the owner orginally paid for it. In that case, the fair market value would be less than the cost basis of the property. If fair market value is less than the cost basis of the property, then we must use the lower value regardless of what kind of property is being gifted. If we are dealing with loss property, short-term or long-term makes no difference for gift valuation.

Another reason we don't discuss gifts of capital loss property is because donors should never give capital loss property. Instead the loss should be realized and deducted upon the sale of the property. So, for example, if I bought a share of stock for $110 and it is now worth $10, it is better for me to sell the share and then give the proceeds to charity, rather than to give the share directly to the charity. If I sell the share, I will recognize a loss of $100 ($110 purchase price less the $10 sale price). This loss can offset other gains that I might otherwise have to pay taxes on. But if I give the share directly to a charity, I lose the ability to recognize that loss, and so I lose a valuable tax benefit. The charitable tax deduction is the same whether I give the share directly to the charity or sell the share and then give the proceeds to the charity (i.e., $10). This is why capital loss property should not be given directly to the charity, but instead should be sold and the proceeds given to the charity.

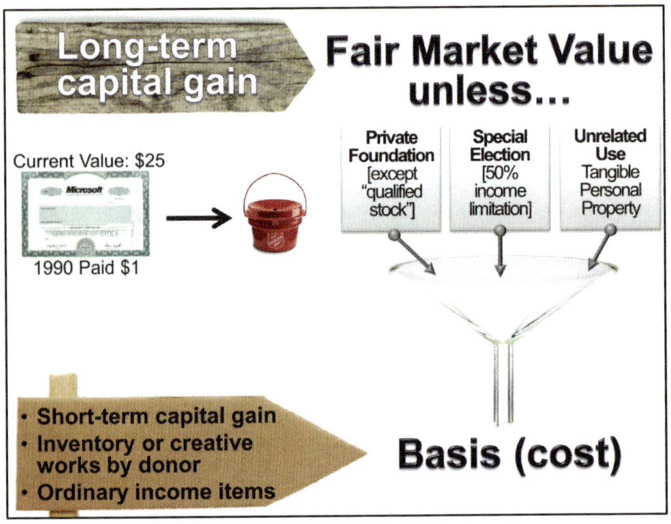

Let's now work through some examples that demonstrate how these rules function with specific gifts. Suppose that I own a share of stock that I paid one dollar for in 1990, which today is worth $25. I give that share of stock to a public charity. How much could I deduct for that charitable gift?

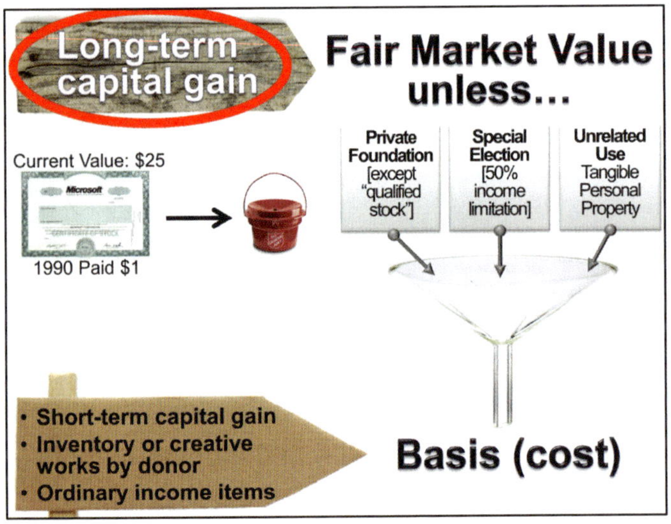

First, we see that the stock is long-term capital gain property. Why? First, it has gone up in value, therefore, it is gain property. Second, I have owned it since 1990. This means I have owned it for more than 12 months and, therefore, it is long-term capital property. Combining the fact that it is gain property with the fact that it is long-term property results in it being long-term capital gain property.

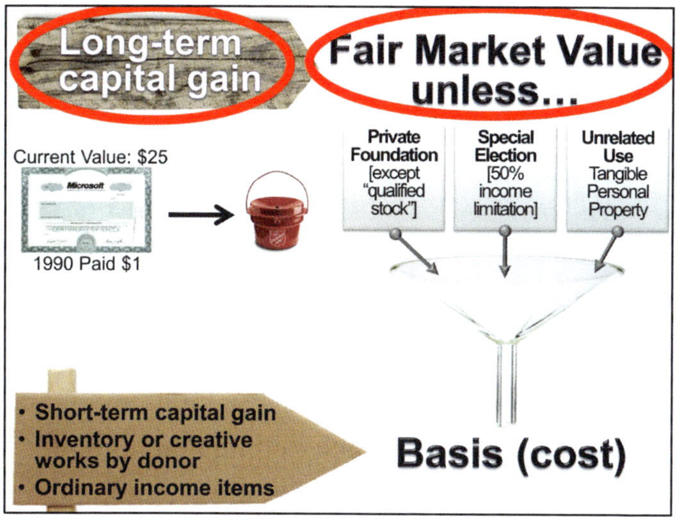

Because it is long-term capital gain property, this means that I can deduct its fair market value (in this case, $25), unless one of the three exceptions applies.

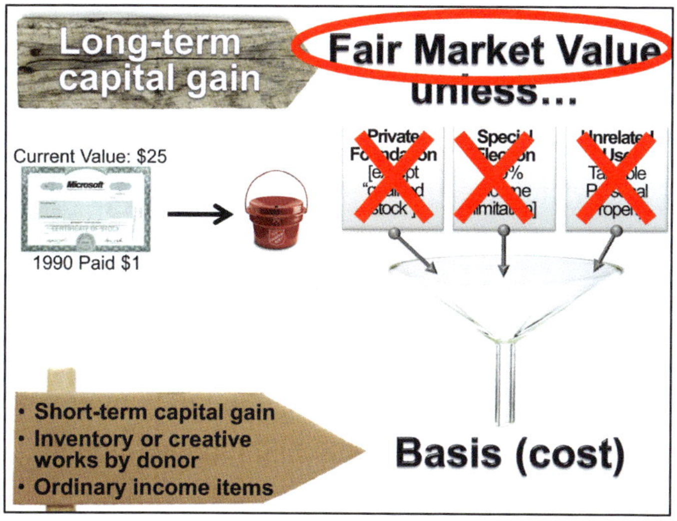

In this case, none of the three exceptions apply. I am not giving the property to a private foundation, but instead have given it to a public charity. I have not made a special election to reduce the valuation, so that exception does not apply. And finally, this is *intangible* personal property, therefore, the third exception, which relates to *tangible* personal property, does not apply. Because none of the three exceptions apply, I can deduct this gift at its fair market value of $25.

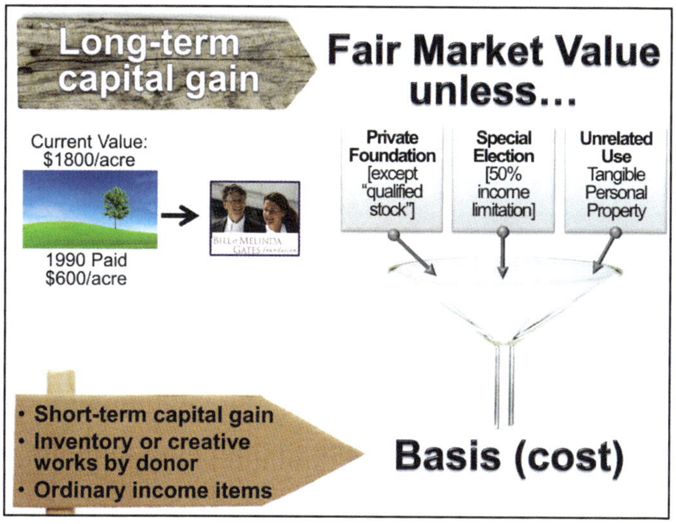

Now suppose I have farmland that I purchased for $600 an acre in 1990, which is now worth $1800 an acre. I contribute this farmland as a gift to a private foundation. How much per acre can I deduct for this gift?

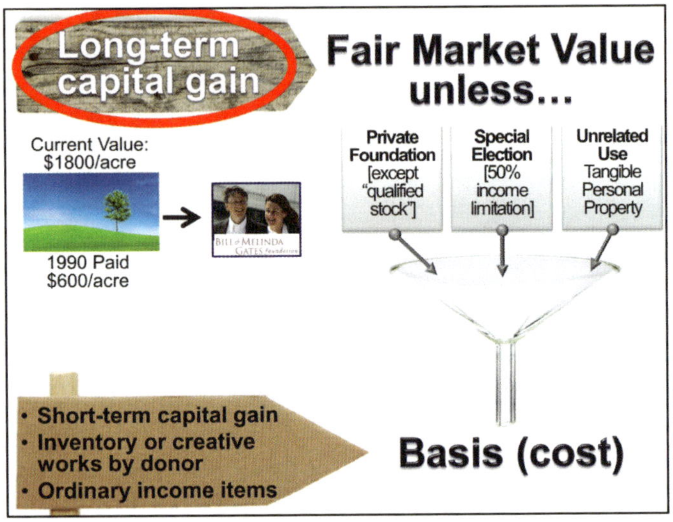

As before, we begin by recognizing that this is long-term capital gain property. First, it has gone up in value. And, second I have owned it for more than 12 months.

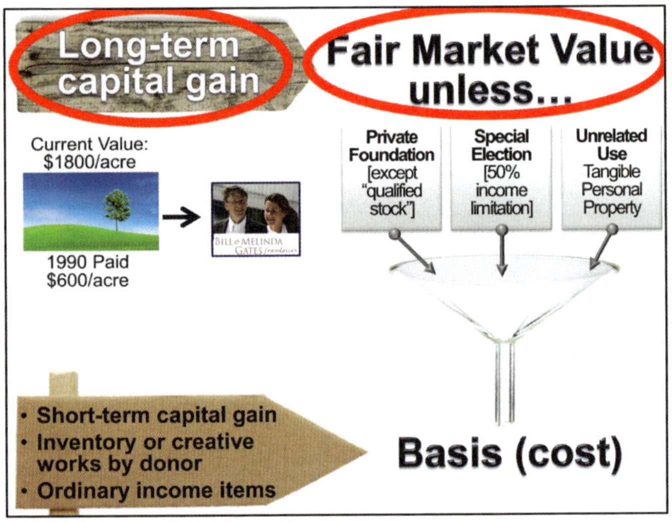

Because this is long-term capital gain property, we start with the possibility that I may be able to deduct its fair market value, unless one of the exceptions applies.

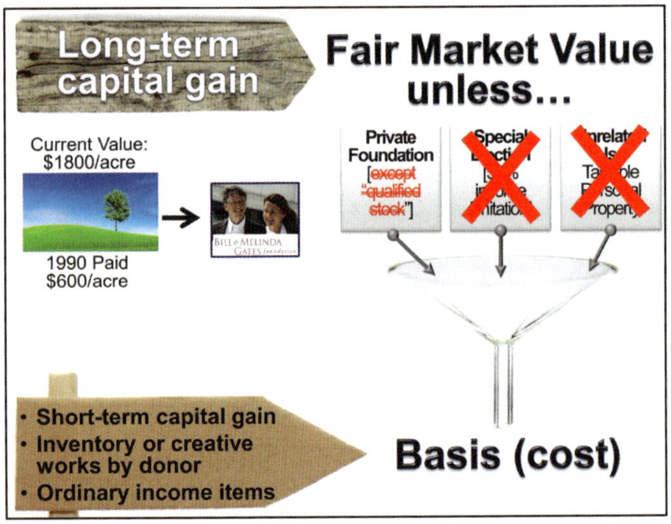

I have not made a special election to have my gift's valuation lowered, so that exception does not apply. Similarly, this is not tangible personal property. (It is real property.) Therefore, the tangible personal property exception does not apply either. However, I have made this gift to a private foundation. Consequently, I will not be able to deduct its fair market value, unless it is "qualified stock". Clearly, this is not any type of share of stock, because it is real property. So, this exception to the exception is not relevant.

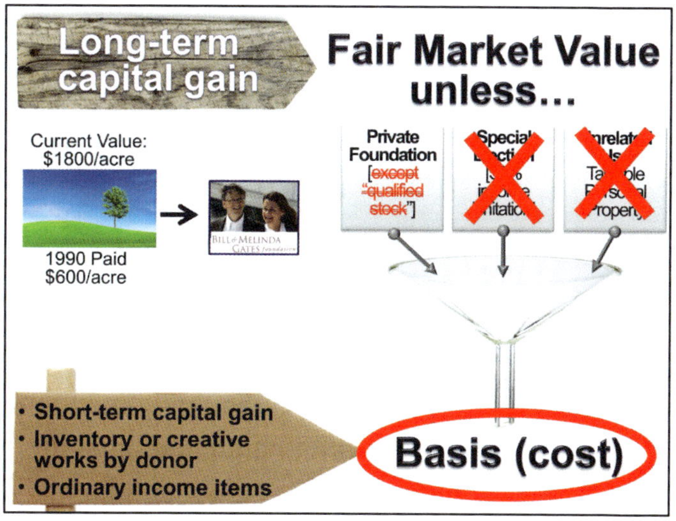

As a result of making this gift to a private foundation (since it is not "qualified stock"), my deduction for the charitable gift of land will be limited to its cost basis. In this case, that means that my deduction will be limited to $600 per acre.

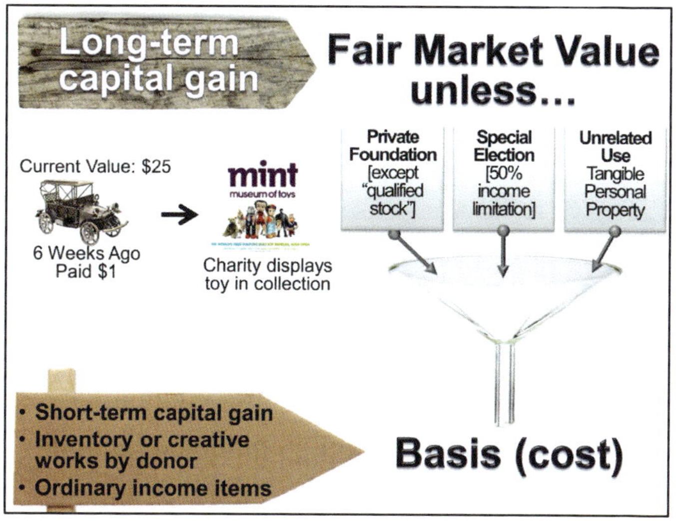

Next, let's look at an example involving a different kind of property. Suppose I purchased an antique toy car six weeks ago for $1. This was quite a good purchase, because today the value of the antique toy car is $25. My plan is to give the toy car to a museum of toys that is also a public charity. The charity is interested in the car for its historical value and intends to display the car in its museum collection. How much can I deduct for my gift of the antique toy car to the public charity?

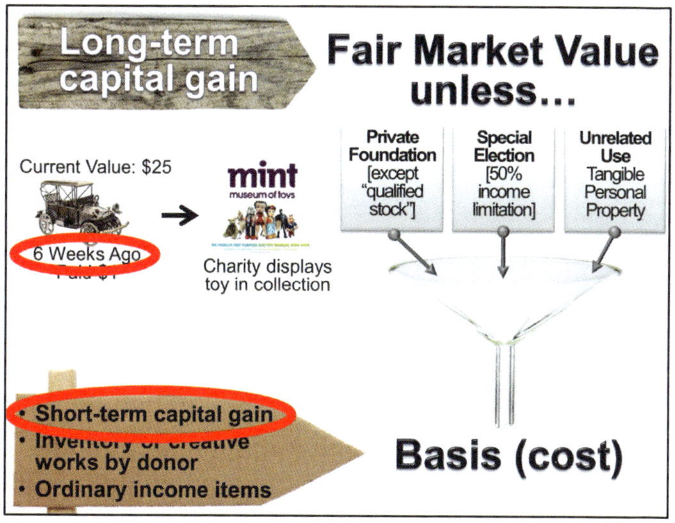

The answer to this question is actually simpler than it may seem at first. Because I have owned the antique toy car for only six weeks, it is short-term capital gain. Because it is short-term capital gain, I do not have to be concerned with any of the rules concerning "related use" or "unrelated use" tangible personal property.

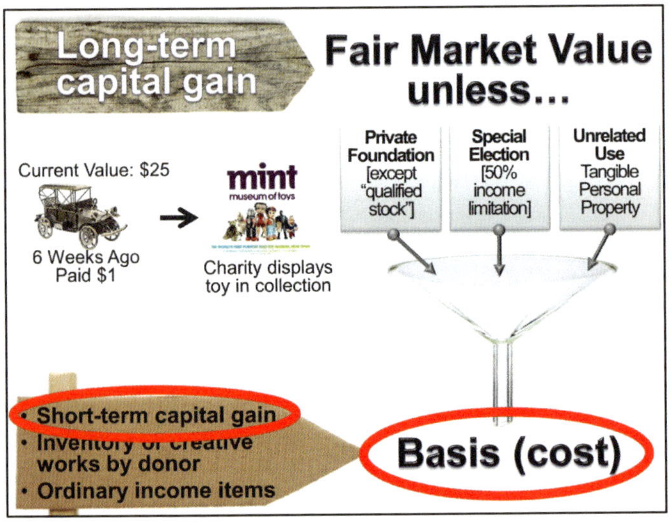

These exceptions are irrelevant because, as short-term capital gain property, this item may be valued only at cost basis. (As always, valuing at cost basis assumes that the cost basis is less than fair market value. Here, of course, it is, because the cost basis of $1 is less than the fair market value of $25.)

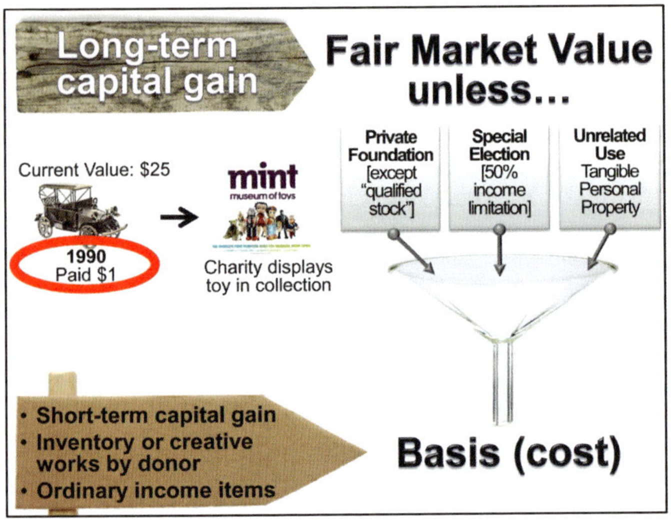

Now let's change the example only slightly. Now, let's assume that I purchased the antique toy car, not six weeks ago, but in 1990. How does this change the result?

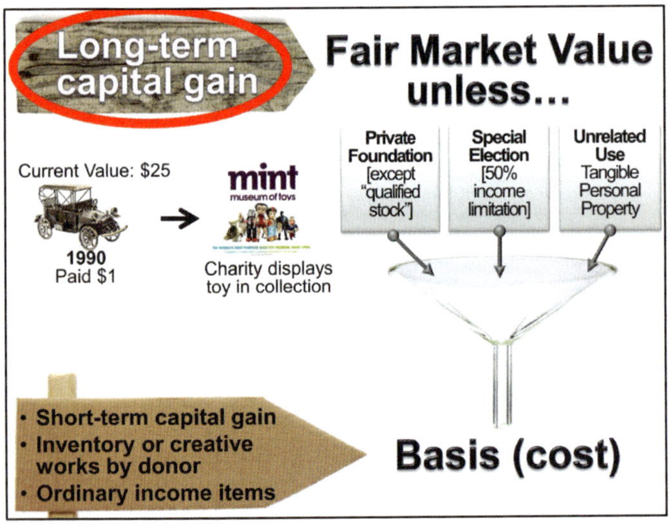

To begin with, since I have owned the property for more than 12 months and it has gone up in value, this property is long-term capital gain.

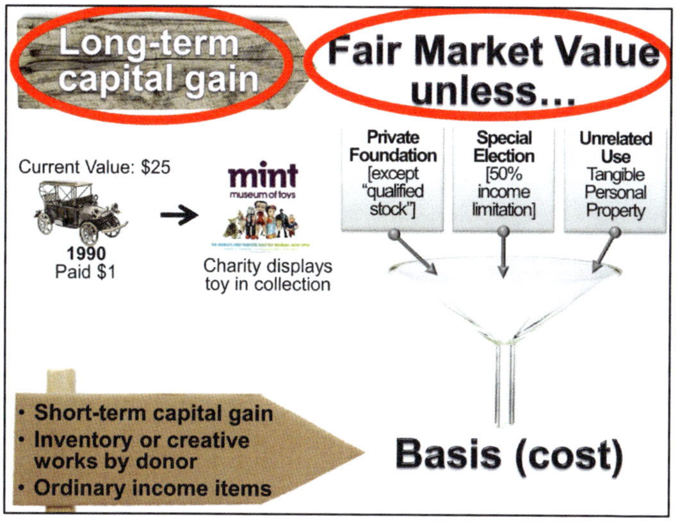

Because this is long-term capital gain property, there is the potential to deduct the full fair market value of the gifted property, rather than only its cost basis. Of course, this is only true if none of the exceptions apply.

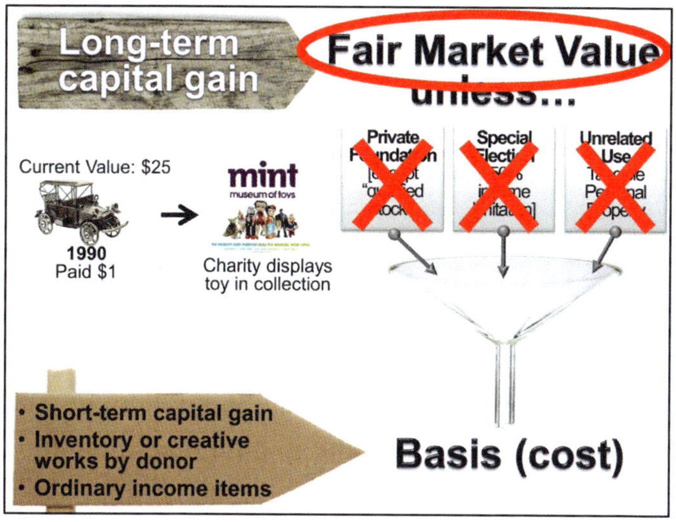

The first exception does not apply, because this is not a gift to a private foundation. It is a gift to a public charity, in this case a museum of toys. Next, I have made no mention of a special election, so this exception does not apply either. Finally, this is tangible personal property and consequently the unrelated use exception could apply. However, in this case, the charity will actually be using the gifted item in furtherance of its charitable purposes. Thus, this property is related use property, not unrelated use property. Consequently, none of the exceptions apply. Because none of the exceptions apply, we are allowed to deduct the full fair market value of the property donated to the charity. In this case, I mentioned that the charity "intended" to use the item in its charitable operations by displaying the toy in its collection. How can the IRS prevent abuse of this rule by charities that would say they "intend," to use gifts of property, but then simply sell the gifted property?

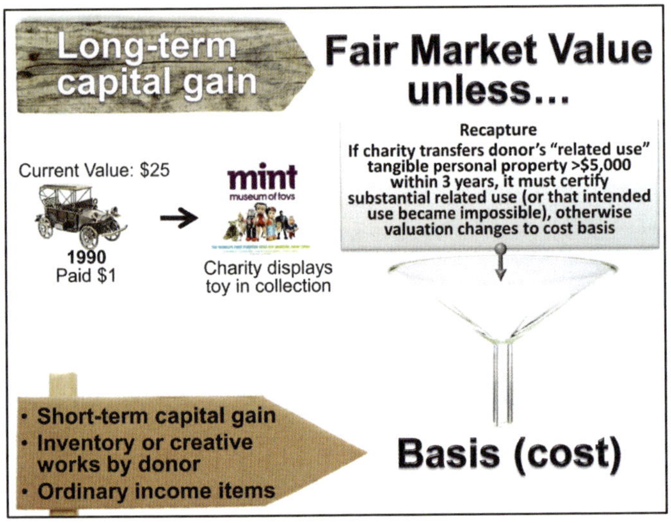

In this case, abuse is limited by the recapture rule. If a charity sells (or otherwise transfers) the property item within three years, the valuation could change from fair market value to cost basis. Such a change of valuation would require the donor to amend his or her tax returns to reflect the lower deduction. This recapture rule applies only to tangible personal property worth more than $5000. (The IRS does not want to hassle with recapture for small gifts.) For these larger gifts, a transfer or sale of the property by the charity within three years will lead to the reduced valuation for the charitable deduction. This occurs unless the charity certifies that it made substantial related use of the property prior to sale or that the intended use became impossible.

So, for example, if my toy car were worth $25,000 (instead of $25) and the charity sold the toy three months later, then my original deduction would be subject to recapture. However, if the reason the charity sold the car was because their museum location burnt down, making it impossible to display the car as originally intended, then no recapture would be required (assuming that the charity certified that the original intended use became impossible). Alternatively, if the charity had, for example, displayed the car for 2 ½ years in its collection prior to the sale of the item and it was willing to certify this substantial related use, this certification could also prevent recapture. Obviously, the simplest and cleanest way to avoid recapture is to make sure the charity does not sell the item for at least three years. If the charity does sell within three years, but it also certifies that one of these two exceptions applies, that will also avoid recapture. However, this certification must be accurate. The charity must sign under penalty of perjury, and there is a $10,000 fine if the charity provides false information.

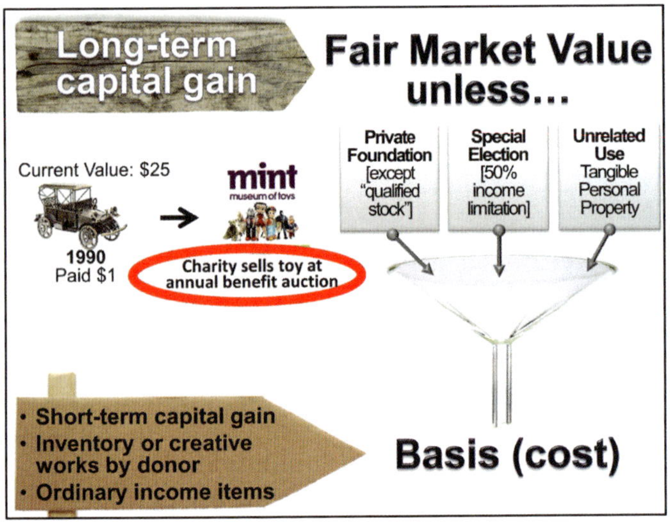

So, what happens if the charity does not use the item, but instead simply sells it soon after receiving it? In this case I give my antique toy car to a public charity that displays toys in its museum, but they don't want to display my toy. They just want to sell it. So, after I've given it to them, they sell the toy at their annual benefit auction. What happens then?

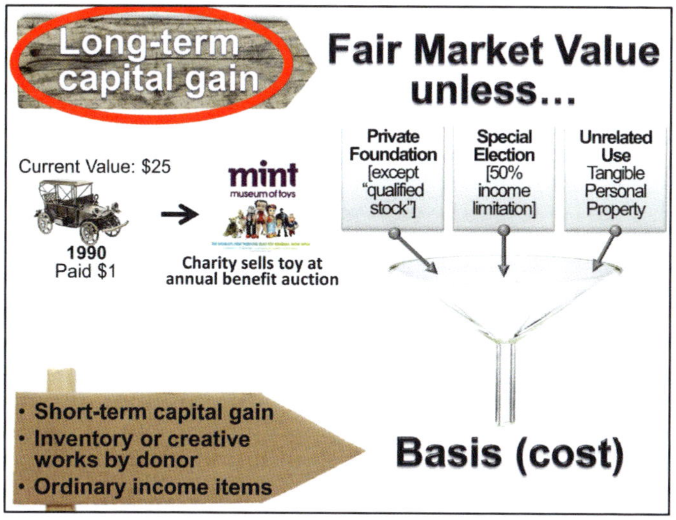

Once again, this is still long-term capital gain property because I have owned it since 1990 and it has gone up in value.

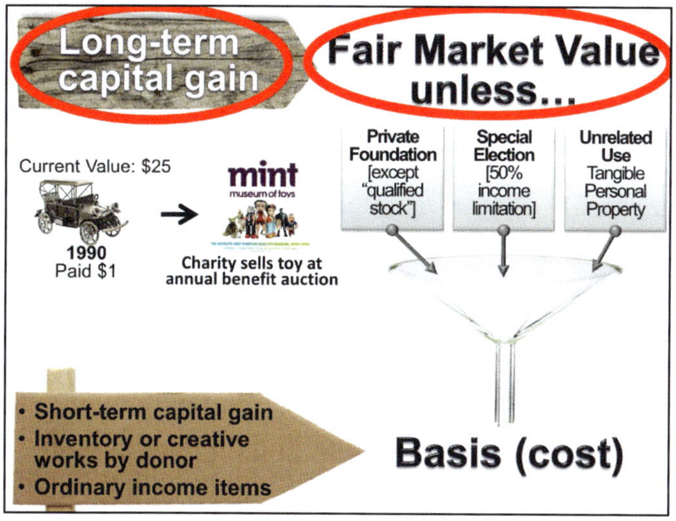

Because this is long-term capital gain property, we at least start with the possibility that it could be valued at fair market value (unless one of the exceptions applies).

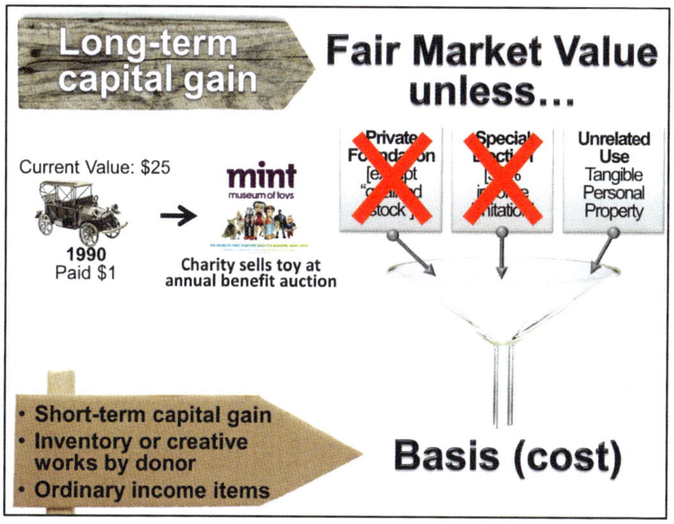

In this case, one of the exceptions does indeed apply, because this is *unrelated use* tangible personal property. It is unrelated use property, because the charity did not use it. Instead, they simply sold it for money. It is tangible personal property, because it is a toy car, a physical item that I can move. Thus, this tangible personal property is not being used by the charity, but is instead simply being sold, and the except to fair market valuation does apply.

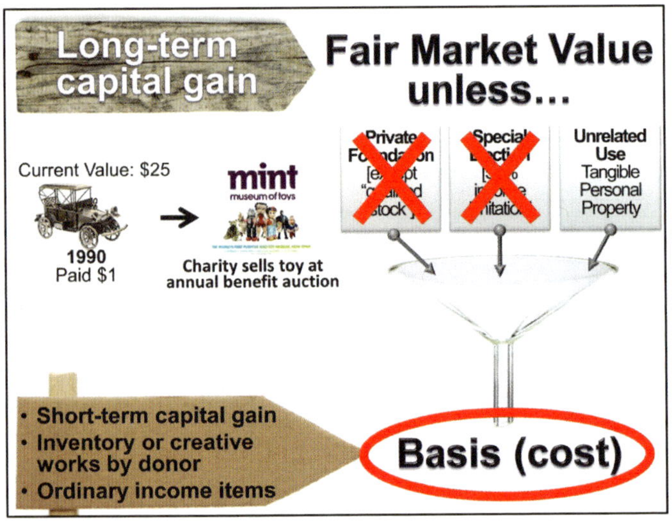

Because one of the exceptions applies, I am not allowed to use the fair market value for calculating the deduction. Instead, I must drop down to the cost basis valuation. So, my gift generates a deduction of only $1.

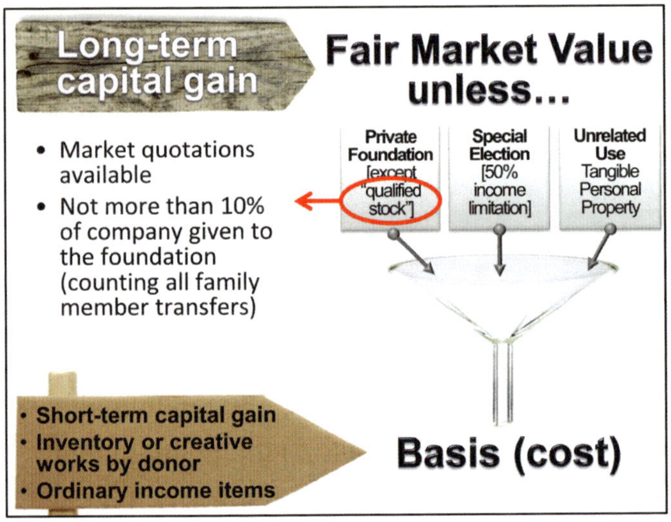

A final exception to the exception that we haven't yet discussed is the rule related to "qualified stock". Qualified stock is what we normally think of when we think of publicly traded stocks. That is, we are talking about stocks that are traded on an exchange such that market quotations are regularly available. So, for example, any stock traded on the New York Stock Exchange can be qualified stock. Also, the private foundation cannot have more than 10% of the entire company when counting all family member transfers together.

What is the thought behind this rule? The intent is to avoid giving special benefit to large, closely-held, insider transactions. Consider the case of a family owned business where family members transfer shares of the business to their own private family foundation. This is a transaction which has substantial potential for abuse. The family members controlled the asset before the gift. And now, as board members of the private family foundation, they control the asset after the gift. Determining the fair market value of the gift may be quite difficult. This is especially true for closely held corporations where other investors may be uninterested in owning a minority share when the family still controls all aspects of the business. This is a transaction that the tax law allows, but it does not give special favored status to the transaction. (In the area of gifts of property special, favored status means allowing fair market value deductions.) The concept here is to avoid giving special privilege to a transaction that can easily be abused. Because private family foundations are often controlled by the donor or the donor's family, these transfers are generally less desirable than gifts to traditional public charities

The exception is allowed for cases in which the property given is almost like cash. It is almost like cash, because the shares are regularly traded and have an easily identifiable value. It is also like cash because it is not a very large share of the total ownership of the corporation (even when considering all family members' transfers together. Given the cash-like nature of the transfer, there is less concern about inappropriate or abusive transactions, making a fair market value deduction more appropriate. Let's look at an example of the mechanics of this kind of transaction.

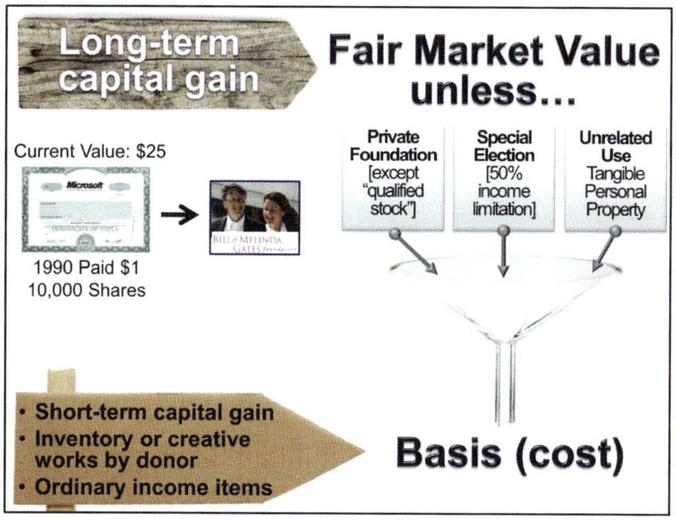

Suppose that I own 10,000 shares of Microsoft Corporation (a publicly traded corporation), which I originally paid $1 per share for and is today worth $25. I give these 10,000 shares to a private foundation. What is my deduction for this gift?

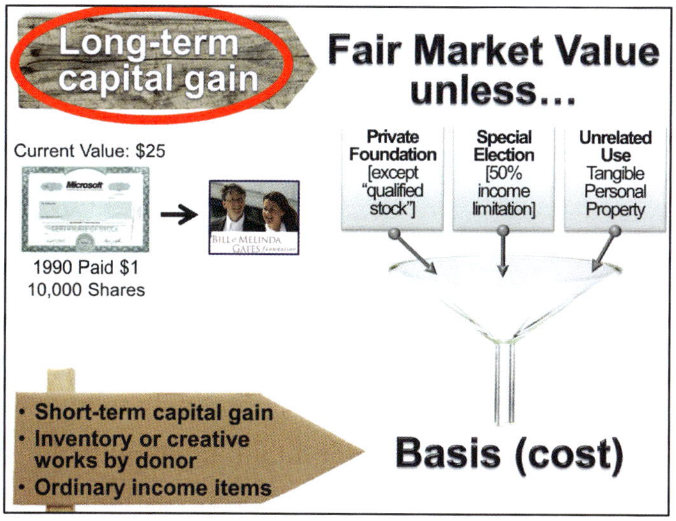

We begin with a recognition that this is long-term capital gain property. This is true because I have owned it for more than 12 months and it has gone up in value.

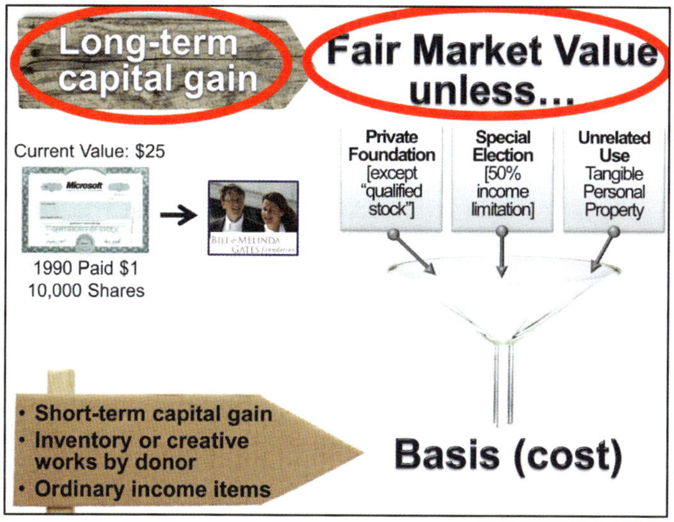

Because it is long-term capital gain, there is at least the potential that I can deduct its fair market value, unless one of the exceptions apply.

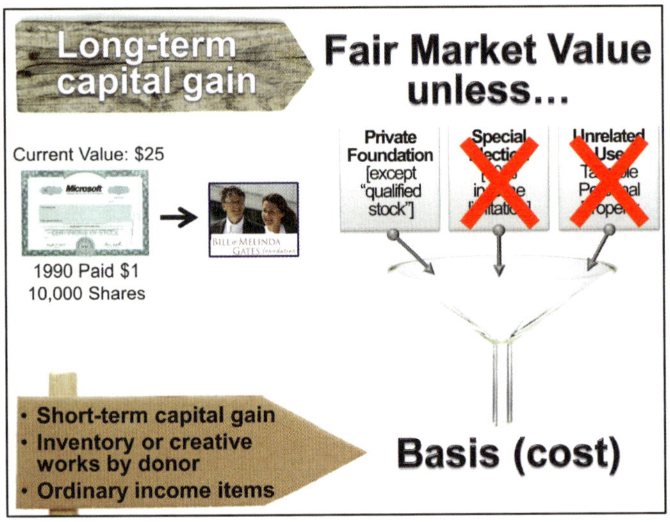

In this case, I am giving the property to a private foundation, so one of the exceptions to a fair market value deduction does apply, **unless** I qualify for the exception to the exception.

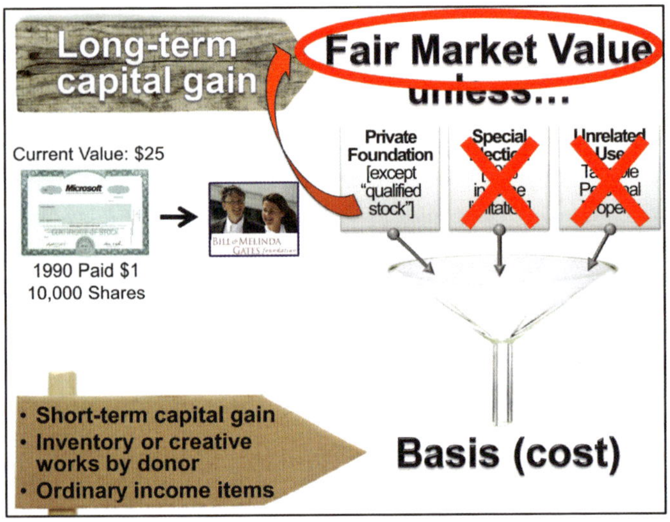

Because I am giving qualified stock, the normal rule for private foundations does not apply. As a result, I am allowed to deduct the fair market value of the shares of stock. Thus, my deduction is $25 per share ($250,000) rather than $1 per share ($10,000). The property is "qualified stock" because it was publicly traded (meaning that market quotations are available) and because 10,000 shares is nowhere close to a 10% ownership interest in the corporation (given that it has billions of shares).

What we have examined so far is the normal set of rules that apply to gifts of property. From time to time there have been special kinds of property that have created significant tax abuses. As a result, Congress has acted to create special rules that only apply to specific types of property, usually in response to these tax abuses. So now we turn to special kinds of property where our normal rules do not apply. We will look at the special charitable donation rules that apply to clothing, household items, cars, boats, airplanes, taxidermy, inventory, patents and other intellectual property.

Considering the complexity of the "standard" rules that we have already learned why would Congress add these special rules for specific assets? The answer is that Congress reacted to ongoing abuses that fit the technical rules, but were still considered to be inappropriate.

There is always a special potential for abuse in the area of deductions for gifts of property when ever the property has an uncertain valuation. Consider that if a taxpayer was at the top federal tax rate of 39.6%, and at the top state tax rate in a state like Oregon, where the top rate is 11%, that a deduction is worth over half of the value of the gifted property. When a property is difficult to value or difficult to sell, but can be immediately converted into a tax benefit worth more than $.50 of every appraised dollar, it can make such transfers highly attractive, even to those with little or no charitable intent. If a difficult to value item of property can be appraised for two or three times what it could actually be sold for in an immediate sale, it may be more profitable to donate the property, rather than to sell it. Such financial incentives make this area ripe for abuse.

What do these kinds of abuses that led to special rules look like? For example, a person might have old clothes that she would otherwise throw in the trash because they have little or no resale value. But instead of throwing them away the person could give them away and generate a charitable deduction. Perhaps the person may attempt to value the deduction based on the original cost of the clothing or some "estimated" value based on a percentage of the original cost, when in reality the poor quality clothing has little or no resale value.

Another abuse could result from gifts of automobiles where the automobile has some defect that reduces its value below the normal resale value for that model and year of car. Even though in reality the automobile may be worth nothing, except in a junkyard, taxpayers may be tempted to donate the vehicle and deduct the standard value for a vehicle of that age, make and model (i.e., the "blue book" value).

A particularly egregious abuse occurred in the area of donating stuffed animals to a wildlife Museum. In this scheme, the taxpayer would go on safari to hunt exotic animals, have the animals stuffed, and then donate the animals to a wildlife Museum. An appraisal firm would provide a high valuation for exotic stuffed animals (a valuation which might be difficult to disprove given the rarity of transactions and the high cost of acquiring new exotic stuffed animals). A few small wildlife Museums were willing to accept these donations (often taking in thousands of animals). The donor would then deduct his cost basis in the stuffed animal, including all of the costs of acquiring the animal, such as the entire expense of the safari travel. Thus, the IRS was essentially funding a substantial portion of safari tourism intended to kill exotic animals.

A different problem arose with copyrights and other intellectual property not simply because of the risk of fraud, but also because of the enormous difficulty in valuing such intellectual property in advance. If a best-selling author, like John Grisham, wrote a new book and immediately donated the copyright of the book to charity, such a donation would be enormously valuable. If a less well-known author did the same, the donation could be highly valuable and it could be worth nothing. The difficulty is that it may be impossible to tell at the time of the donation how much the gift is worth. No amount of sophistication, education, experience, or integrity of any appraiser will be able to correct that problem.

Because of the wide variety of problems and issues with these special kinds of property, each of them has their own special rule limited only to that specific kind of property.

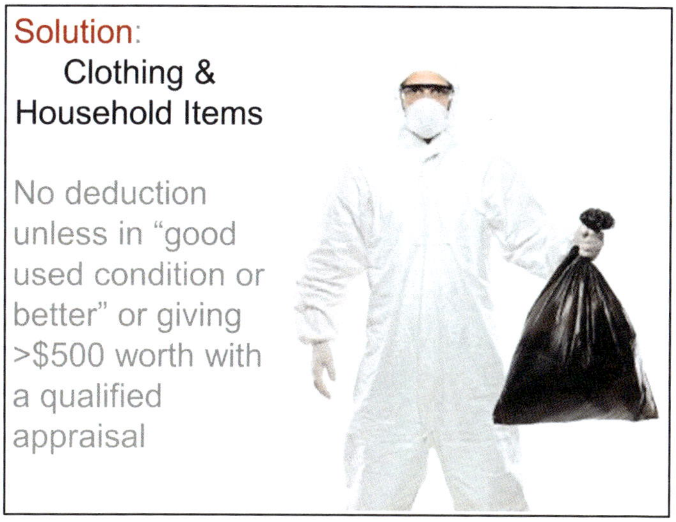

Clothing and household items cannot be deducted unless they are in "good used condition or better." Any deductions worth more than $500 must be accompained by a qualified appraisal. Requiring "good used condition" is intended to exclude worn out clothes. The $500 limit prevents financially significant abuse of the system without going through the detailed process of obtaining a qualified appraisal.

This same rule applies not only to clothing, but to other household items. Household items does not include art, antiques jewelry or collections. Instead, it refers to items like furniture, electronics, appliances, linens and the like

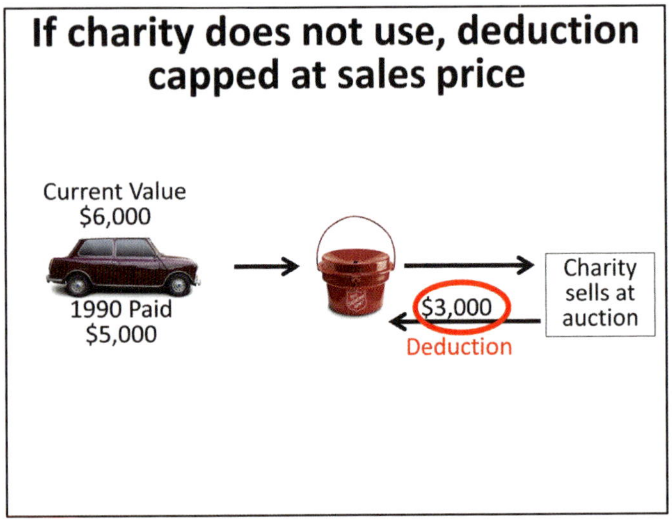

In order to prevent abuse with contributions of automobiles the special rule is that if the charity sells the automobile, the deduction may be no greater than sales price. For example, suppose I paid $5000 for a vehicle (i.e., basis) and it is currently worth $6000 (i.e., is fair market value). I give that vehicle to a charity, and it sells it. Unfortunately, in this case, let's suppose the charity did a poor job of pricing the vehicle. As a result, the vehicle sold for only $3000. In that case, I can only deduct $3000. This is true even though both my basis and the fair market value were higher than $3000. Note that this rule can only lower the charitable deduction from the amount that would normally result from the standard rules for gifts of property. So, if, for example, two benefactors of the charity ran the bid for the vehicle up so that it sold for $10,000, my deduction would not be $10,000. (In this case because this is personal property not used by the charity, my deduction would be the lower of fair market value or my basis, in this case $5000.)

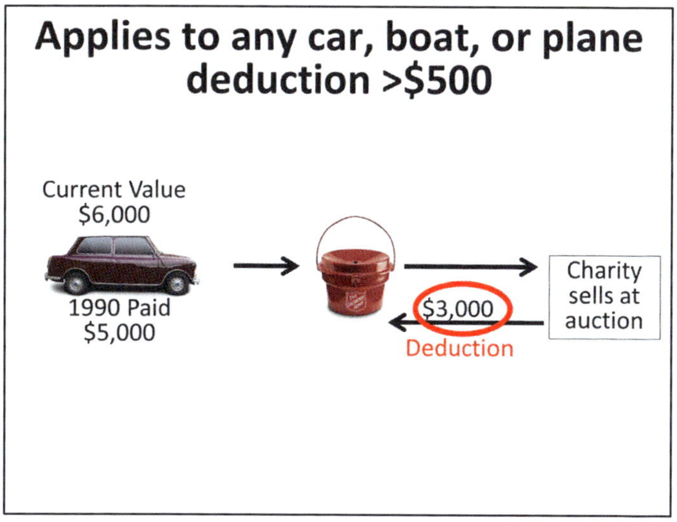

This same rule applies not only to automobiles, but also to boats and even planes. However, the IRS does not require this reduction if the charitable deduction was $500 or less. (Although it seems unlikely that automobiles, boats or planes would commonly be worth $500 or less.)

An exception to this rule applies if the charity will actually use the vehicle in furtherance of its charitable purposes, or intends to give the vehicle to a needy person rather than to sell it. If the charity is willing to certify this usage on Form 1098-C, then we can use the normal rules for valuing this gift of property (which in this case means either short-term or long-term related use personal property).

To address the problem of taxpayer financed safari trips, Congress limited deductions for taxidermy property to the cost of stuffing the animal only. Thus, none of the other costs of acquiring the animal may be deducted.

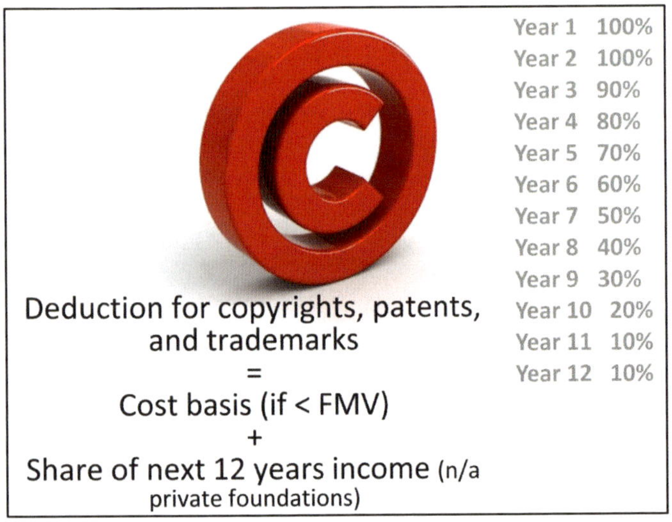

Deducting charitable gifts of copyright (or other intellectual property, such as patents and trademarks) is not simply a problem of fraud or abuse, but is fundamentally a problem of accurately valuing the property in advance. To resolve this issue, Congress allowed for the deduction of cost basis plus a share of the next 12 years of income from the intellectual property right. Thus, the full deduction does not come at the time of the initial transfer. Instead, the donor receives a stream of deductions over 12 years. In this way, the author giving a copyright to a charitable entity does not need to know its value in advance, but instead can simply deduct a share of the actual dollars that go to the charity as a result of the gift. This deduction of the income stream is only available for gifts to public charities and not to private foundations.

Note that, as in all other forms of charitable property deductions. The cost basis is deductible only if such basis is less than fair market value. Thus conceptually, it may still be necessary to estimate in advance, the fair market value of an intellectual property right. However, in practice, many such rights have little or no cost basis. For example, and authors cost basis would only include some paper and ink, but would take into account none of his or her time spent in producing the work. (Note that this is true with cost basis in other areas as well. For example, if I purchase a dirty car for $5000 and then spend three months cleaning and detailing it, my basis in the car is still only $5000.)

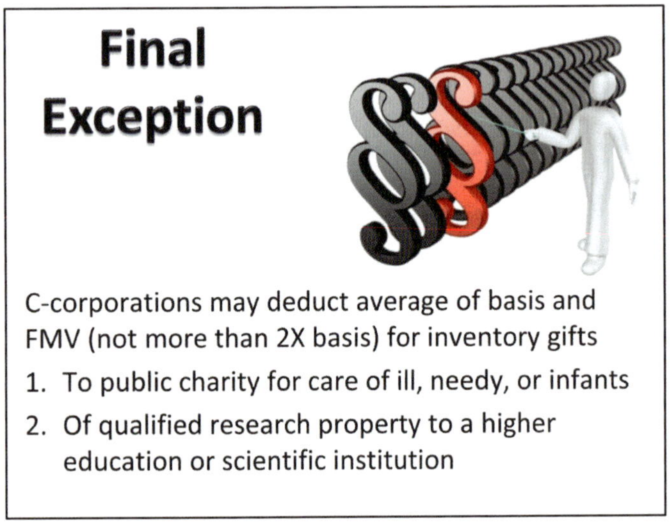

For the final exception to the standard valuation rules, we examine another unusual compromise on valuation. The normal rule for gifts of inventory is that only the cost basis of inventory is deductible. However, the tax code provides a special increase in the deduction for specific types of inventory gifts. If the donor is a standard corporation (known as a C corporation as opposed to the closely held or family business, S corporation), and it is giving inventory to a public charity for care of ill individuals needy individuals or infants or it is giving qualified research materials to a institution of higher education or other scientific institution, then it can receive a higher deduction. This higher deduction will be the average of basis and for fair market value. Thus, the Corporation receives not the most favored status (which would be fair market value.) Nor the less favored status (which would be cost basis), but instead receives something in the middle.

However, this deduction is still limited to no more than double the cost basis in the gifted items. This is to prevent a scenario where the deduction was worth more than the cost of manufacturing the property.

Although not exceptions to the general rule some items can be hard to value and consequently, the IRS requires a special kind of valuation for these items. So for example, in determining the fair market value of a used car taxpayers must use the private party value and not the amount for which it would sell on a dealer lot. For boats taxpayers may not estimate fair market value by simply looking at the generic price of similar size and ages of boats. Instead, boats require an individual appraisal. This is because there can be dramatic differences in the value and seaworthiness of boats of the same age and size making generic valuations less relevant. Again, remember that we need these rules to prevent scenarios where it is more profitable to give the item of property than to sell the item of property. So for example, if I had a boat that had significant issues with rotting and seaworthiness its actual value may be only a fraction of what a boat in good condition of a similar size and age would sell for. If I was allowed to deduct a gift of the boat based upon the typical value of such boats of the same age and size. It could create a situation where the deduction was worth more than what I could sell the boat for this is precisely the situation that the IRS wishes to avoid and hence the reason for requiring individual appraisals for boats. Similarly, when valuing gifts of clothing the valuation must be based upon what the used clothing would sell for in a consignment or thrift shop not based upon what it sells for new in a retail environment. Of course, the difference between what an Armani suit sells for in an upscale retail environment and what a used Armani suit would sell for in a thrift shop is dramatic.

Finally for gifts of large quantities of individual items valuation must be based upon the value of the entire lot of items. It is not permitted to estimate the value of a single item and multiply that by the total number of items gifted. For example, suppose I found a box of 1000 beanie babies on sale on eBay for $1000. If I purchased these then gave them to an orphanage over a year later for use in their charitable activities, I could be entitled to a deduction of fair market value (long-term capital gain related use personal property). However, even if the fair market value for a single beanie baby toy was $5, I could not claim a fair market value for my gift of $5000 ($5 X 1000). Instead, the fair market value would have to be based upon the value of the entire lot of 1000 such beanie babies.

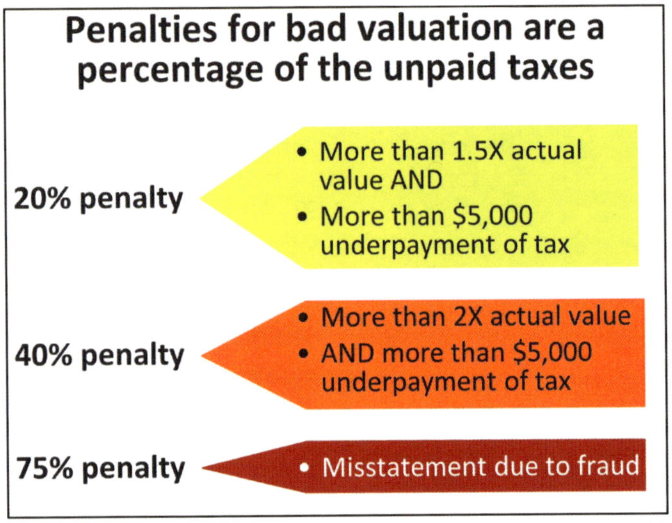

Of course, overvaluing a charitable gift if audited will results in the need to reduce the deduction to an appropriate value and the consequent need to pay for additional taxes and any interest accrued since the due date for those taxes. However, in addition to this repayment and interest. There can be penalties for overvaluing a charitable gift. Those penalties depend upon the amount of the gift and the degree of over valuation. If the gift was valued at greater than 50% of its true value, and as a result, there was more than $5000 in underpayment of tax, then the taxpayer must pay not only the taxes due, but also an additional 20% of the unpaid taxes. If in the previous case, the valuation was more than double the item's true value, then the penalty will be an additional 40% of the unpaid taxes. Finally, if the misstatement of value was due to fraud the penalty will be an additional 75% of the unpaid taxes, regardless of the amount of underpayment or the degree of over valuation. (Of course, tax fraud can lead to not only financial penalties, but also imprisonment.)

As discussed in the chapter on documenting charitable gifts, it is often a requirement to deduct gifts of property that the taxpayer must obtain an appraisal. Can the taxpayer avoid the penalties discussed above if the taxpayer had a qualified appraisal for the amounts reported? As with most things, the answer is: it depends.

There will be no tax payer penalty if the valuation was based upon a qualified appraisal and the donor made a good-faith investigation of value, and the valuation was less than double the actual value of the item. This exception would not apply if the appraisal was not a qualified appraisal based upon IRS guidelines. Even if the appraisal was a qualified appraisal the donor is still required to have made a good-faith investigation of the value of the item, besides simply relying upon the appraisal. But if both of those conditions apply, and the appraised value was not double or more, the actual value, then no penalty will apply. However, the unpaid tax resulting from the overvaluation and any interest must still be paid.

What are the penalties to the appraiser for making an excessive appraisal of an item of property gifted to a charity? If the valuation was more than 50% greater than the actual value of the item. The appraisers penalty will be the greater of $1000 or 10% of the tax underpayment. This penalty could be potentially catastrophic for appraisers who appraise items of extremely high value. Recognizing that such a rule would prevent even legitimate appraisers from functioning, the tax code limited the penalty for appraisers to 125% of the appraisers fee for making the appraisal. So if an appraiser charges $1,000 and values a piece of artwork at $10 million when it was actually worth only $5 million and this error results in a $1.5 million tax underpayment, the appraisers penalty will not be $150,000 (10% of the tax underpayment), but instead would be 125% of the appraisal fee, or $1250.

One interesting case that illustrates the sometimes unusual results from property valuation is that involving a work of art called "Canyon". This work of art was inherited by the heirs of an estate. The IRS appraised the value of the artwork at $65 million and charged $29.2 million in estate taxes on the item. This valuation was based upon the IRS definition of fair market value, which is the price that property would sell for on the open market. The problem in this case is that the artwork incorporated the use of a taxidermy eagle. The sale of such taxidermy eagle feathers or parts is prohibited by federal law. Consequently, the estate was required to pay a large tax on an item that could not be sold. The final resolution of this case has not yet been reached, but it is an interesting example of what could happen with items where the sale was restricted by law. But the valuation was based upon the price that the item would sell for on the open market. This could be one exception to the general principle that charitable planning should only be engaged in by people who have charitable interests. In this case, the heirs would have been much better off if the artwork have been gifted to a charity, rather than inherited by them.

6 INCOME LIMITATIONS ON CHARITABLE DEDUCTIONS

In this chapter we will look at income limits on charitable deductions. This is, unfortunately, a potentially confusing and challenging area of gift planning to understand. There are a variety of different limitations on charitable deductions, depending upon the nature of the gift and the recipient. Even more complex are the rules for how these different limitations interact in the current and future years. As much as possible, I will attempt to simplify, summarize, and visualize these rules in a way that makes them as understandable as possible. Nevertheless, the reader must recognize that this is a difficult area of charitable tax law that may require some effort.

So, before we begin to work through all of these complex rules and interactions, I think it is worthwhile to consider why all of this effort is necessary. Very little wealth in this country is held in the form of cash or cash equivalents like checking accounts, savings accounts, or money market accounts. If an advisor or fundraiser wants to be involved with large charitable transactions, he or she must understand how to work with gifts of assets rather than just cash. These income limitations rules are particularly critical issues for gifts of assets. A fundamental expectation for any advisor or fundraiser who is going to suggest the charitable transfer of an asset is, at the very least, to understand what charitable deduction that transfer will generate.

The first step in that process is to understand how the asset will be valued for purposes of the charitable deduction. (That topic is covered in the chapter on *valuation of charitable gifts of property*.) The second step in that process is to understand when those charitable deductions can be used, when they must be carried forward into the future years, and when they may be lost altogether. (This is the topic of the current chapter.) Although the process of understanding the rules for both steps can be a real challenge, this understanding is a clear prerequisite to intelligently recommending substantial gifts of assets. It is simply not appropriate to recommend a gift of substantial assets while having no understanding of the charitable deductions that will be generated or whether or not those deductions can even be used. Given the fundamental importance of this understanding as a prerequisite to encouraging large gifts of assets, let's move forward to examine the rules on income limitations for charitable deductions.

Although this topic will become complex, let's begin with the fundamentals. People in the United States usually pay taxes on income. People pay these taxes to the federal government. In most states, people also pay additional income taxes to the state government.

The next fundamental reality of interest to us is that charitable gifts can sometimes be deducted from income. These deductions are valuable to the extent that they reduce the taxes owed. Consequently, if we are going to recommend a charitable transfer, we should have an understanding of the deductions that will be created as a result of those transfers.

What is less well known is that charitable deductions may not be used to eliminate 100% of a person's taxable income. The total share of income that can be eliminated through charitable deductions in any one year may be 20%, 30%, or 50%, depending on the nature of the gift and the nature of the charitable recipient. Charitable deductions beyond these limitations cannot be used in the current year, but instead must be carried forward into future years. If the charitable deduction cannot be used within the following five years, it will expire. Consequently, it is possible for large charitable transactions to generate large charitable deductions that have *absolutely no value* because the income limitations are otherwise exceeded in the current and carry-forward years. Because we do not want to advise a donor about a large charitable gift without understanding when that gift will generate no (or limited) charitable tax deductions, it is important to understand these income limitation rules.

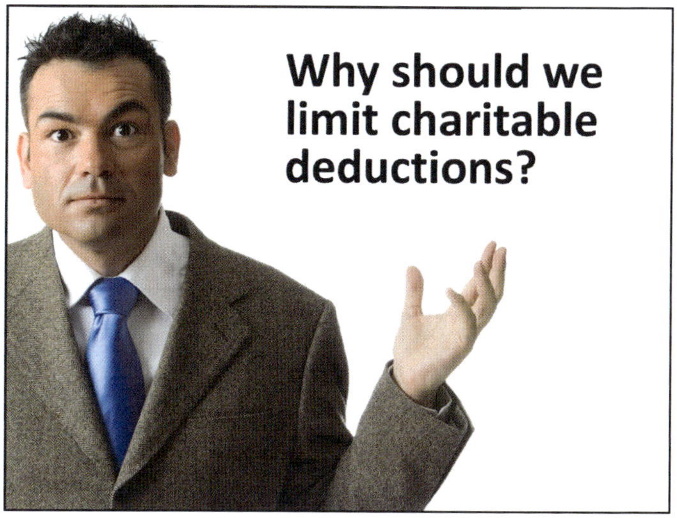

Before we review these rules in detail, let's consider why these rules exist. It would certainly be possible to have a tax code that placed no limitations on the total amount of charitable deductions that could be used in any year. The law could allow for donors to deduct up to 100% of their income. But it does not. Why not?

Encouraging charitable gifts is an important government policy objective, but it is not the only objective. If the law placed no limitations on the amount of charitable deductions, this could reduce the funds available for traditional government functions below an appropriate level. Charitable giving is useful, but at least some money must go to the government in taxes. The income limitations on charitable deductions ensure that this will occur.

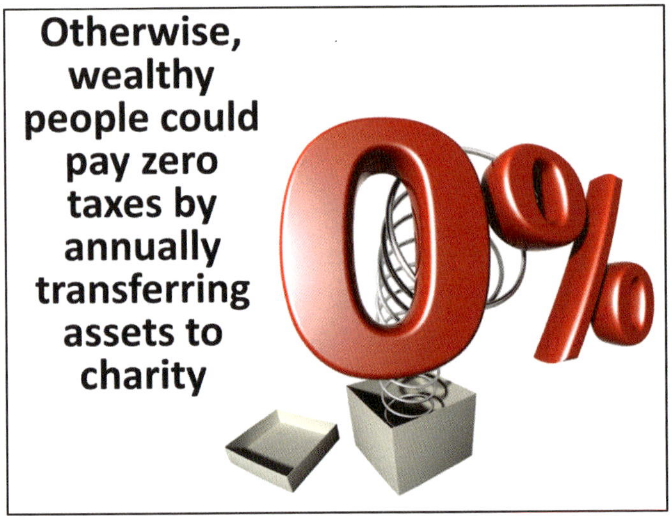

Aside from the concern with the overall level of revenue is the concern about who does and does not pay taxes. If there were no limits on charitable deductions, then those people with large assets relative to their taxable income (i.e., the wealthy) would be able to completely avoid income taxes by annually transferring assets to charity. This is especially concerning given that these transfers might very well go to private family foundations controlled by these wealthy donors. Those who did not have large assets relative to their income could not avoid taxation in this way. This could create a system where income taxes would be paid only by those who were not wealthy.

Such an outcome, where only wealthy people paid no income taxes, is potentially offensive. The income limitations on charitable deductions prevent this outcome. Regardless of how many assets are transferred to charity, a person cannot deduct more than half of his or her income. For transfers of less-favored assets or transfers to less-favored charitable entities (such as private family foundations) the share of income that can be deducted is even less.

There is sometimes confusion about the importance of the income limitation rules. If we are thinking of charitable gifts as gifts from income, rather than gifts of accumulated assets, it is difficult to imagine who would be making such large gifts of income.

We might think that these income limitations would apply only to some rare individuals who desired to spend just a tiny fraction of their income. If we think of charitable gifts as coming from income, then a person wishing to give away 80% or 90% of income must have taken some extreme vow of poverty! Since such individuals are rare, and, even when they do exist, are unlikely to be major donor prospects, this can make the income limitation rules seem almost irrelevant. This inaccurate perception arises from thinking of charitable gifts as coming out of income, rather than from assets.

In reality, the income limitation rules are far from irrelevant. Their significance is not from low wealth individuals giving away most of their income, but rather from high wealth individuals making substantial transfers of assets. The issue arises with high net worth individuals, not only because their assets are a very high multiple of their income, but also because charitable planning often involves large one-time transfers, rather than consistent transfers over many years.

For example, a person may wish to transfer a large block of low basis shares in a family owned corporation into a Charitable

Remainder Trust prior to contemplating the sale of the business. (This transaction can avoid the capital gains taxes that would otherwise have to be paid upon the sale of the business.) Such transactions usually envision a single large transfer of assets in one year. These large one-time transfers regularly come into conflict with the income limitation rules.

Income limitation rules are an issue not only for large transactions of the super-wealthy, but also for anyone with high assets relative to income. This is particularly common among retirees who have accumulated substantial assets, but may have little regular income. In fact, academic research has demonstrated that a large proportion of people in the United States giving 10% or more of their income to charity were relatively wealthy retirees with high assets and low income. (See James, R. N., III, & Jones, K. S. (2011). Tithing and religious charitable giving in America. *Applied Economics, 43*(19), 2441-2450.) In the same way, we would expect a substantial share of donors hitting the income giving limitations to also fall into this category.

Let's now begin examining the rules limiting charitable deductions based upon the donor's income. The highest amount of income that may be deducted using charitable deductions is a 50%. This highest limit is reserved for certain types of gifts going to a public charity, government, or *operating* private foundations. Because gifts to governments or *operating* private foundations are rare, I will simply refer to gifts to public charities.

Note that the typical private foundation is a *non-operating* private foundation. In other words, it simply holds assets and makes distributions to public charities, but it does not actually run nonprofit ventures such as schools, hospitals, or churches. In the remainder of this chapter, the term "private foundation" will refer, technically, to this most common type of private foundation, the *non-operating* private foundation. I will also refer generically to "income" in this chapter. Technically, the definition of income for charitable income limitation purposes is adjusted gross income for the year of the gift excluding any net operating loss carry back. But, no one wants to read "adjusted gross income for the year of the gift excluding any net operating loss carry back" 300 times, so I will simply write "income."

Different income limitations apply to different charitable transfers, depending upon the nature of the gift and the nature of the charity. The general rule is that deductions from charitable gifts made to a public charity can reduce one's income up to 50%. This highest 50% level is reserved for public charities and does not apply to gifts to, e.g., private foundations. The rule is written in such a way that the default income limitation for gifts to public charities is 50%. However, there is an exception for some types of long-term capital gain, in which case the percentage is 30%. Although not discussed in this text, there are also special rules for giving qualified conservation easements allowing farmers to have a 100% income limitation for such gifts.

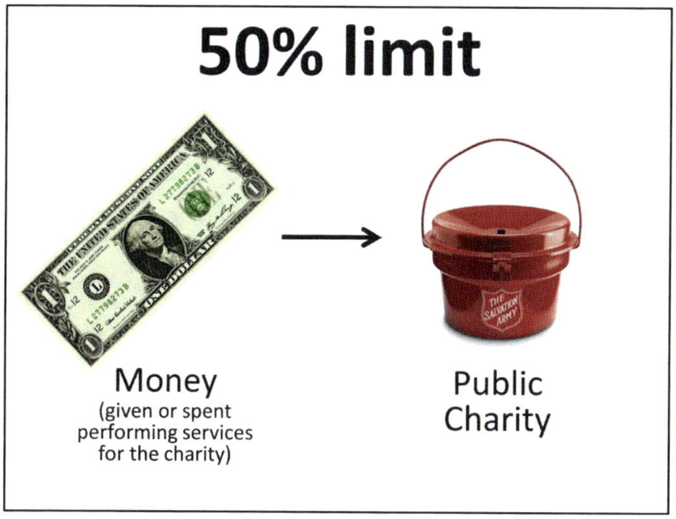

The simplest way to qualify for the 50% income limitation on charitable deductions is to simply give cash to a public charity. This is given the highest income limitation because it is a favored asset (not long-term capital gain) being given to a favored charitable entity (a public charity). There are no extra tax benefits from giving cash (e.g., no avoidance of capital gains taxes), so it is a favored asset. Public charities are generally favored in tax law as compared with private foundations. That general concept is applied here in that the 50% income limitation is available only for gifts to public charities, not for gifts to private foundations. As in other areas of charitable planning, the rules for gifts of cash here are relatively straightforward. So, let's now move forward into the complexity of gifts of property.

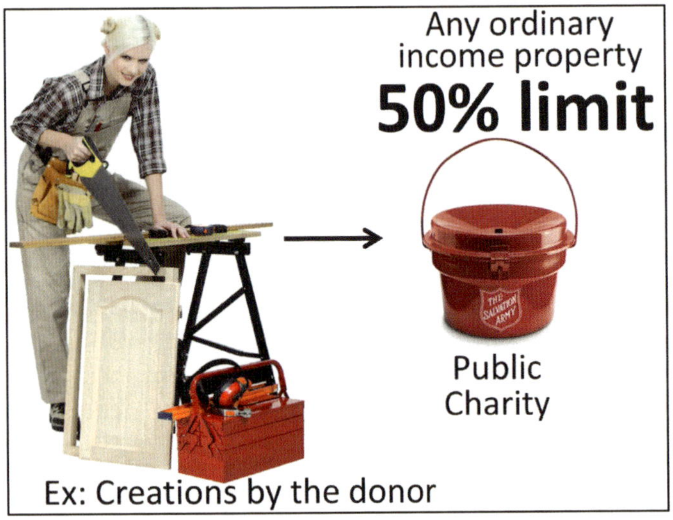

To begin with, any ordinary income property gifts to public charities also receive the 50% income limitation. As with gifts of cash, there are no extra tax benefits from giving ordinary income property, because it is valued at the lower of cost basis or fair market value. Thus, here we have a favored asset (ordinary income property is not long-term capital gain) being given to a favored organization (a public charity), resulting in the highest income limit of 50%.

There are a variety of types of property that will be treated as ordinary income if sold, and all will receive a 50% income limitation when given to a public charity. The first example of ordinary income property is creations by the donor. Thus, if a donor were to build cabinetry for the office of a public charity and donate that cabinetry to the charity, this type of gift would be subject to the 50% income limitation. (Of course, the deduction for this type of gift is limited to the cost of materials, even if fair market value is much higher.) Other gifts of creations by the donor could include examples such as artwork or a manuscript.

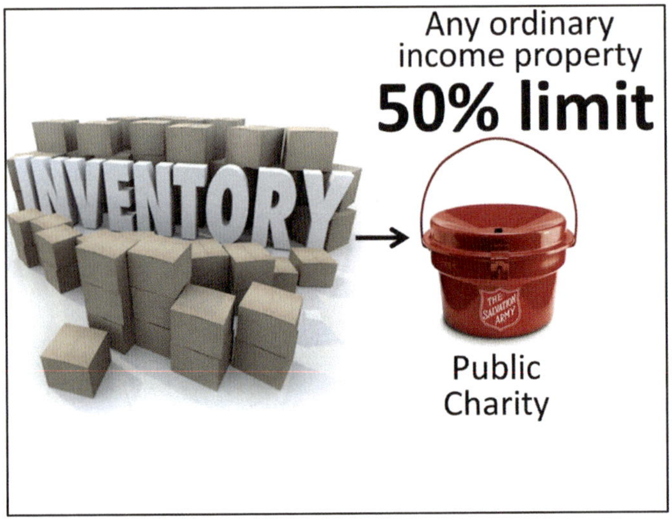

Inventory from a business is also ordinary income property. In cases where this inventory was given to a public charity, such gifts would be subject to the highest income limitation of 50%. So, for example, if a personally-owned local hardware store (sole proprietorship) were to donate cans of paint from its shelves to a public charity, the owner's deduction would be subject to the 50% income limitation. As before, the amount of the deduction would be the lower of the cost basis in the paint or its fair market value. This relatively lower valuation is somewhat offset by the ability to use the highest income limitation.

The final major category of property treated as ordinary income is short-term capital gain property. This is any capital gain property held for one year or less prior to its sale or transfer to the charity. As before, these type of assets are valued at their cost basis, rather than fair market value (assuming cost basis is lower). Given this less advantageous valuation, such gifts are limited only by the highest income limitation of 50%.

All of these different types of property, cash, works created by the donor, inventory, and short-term capital gain property, are all given the same income limitation of 50% when transferred to a public charity. They are all treated the same because they all fit the definition of not being long-term capital gain property.

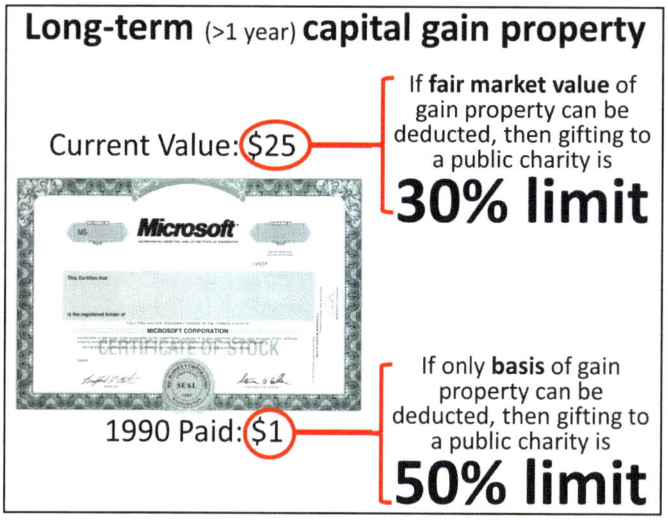

Why is long-term capital gain property treated differently than everything else? Gifts of long-term capital gain property come with a potential double tax advantage to the donor. First, the donor is allowed to deduct the full fair market value of the property transferred to charity. Second, the donor never had to pay any taxes on the appreciation (growth) of the property which generated a tax deduction. This combination of tax advantages does not apply to gifts of other assets such as cash or ordinary income property (which is valued at the *lower* of its basis or fair market value). Although the tax code allows this special benefit for gifts of long-term capital gain property, the income limitations lower the maximum amount of deductions that can be used from this type of transaction in any one year.

It might help to think of long-term capital gain property valued at fair market value as a "less-favored" asset. When a donor gives this less-favored asset to a favored recipient (public charity), the income limitation is lowered to 30%. The "favored" or "less-favored" terminology is not from the tax code, but I find it to be a useful concept to help understand intuitively why the rules are as they are. So, for example, in order to get the highest income limitation (50%), a donor must give a favored asset (e.g., cash or short-term capital gain property) to a favored charitable entity (e.g., a public charity). If a donor gives a less-favored asset (long-term capital gain property valued at fair market value) to a favored charitable entity (a public charity), the income limitation is lowered to 30%. Similarly, if a donor gives a favored asset to a less-favored charitable entity (a private foundation), the income limitation is also lowered to 30%. And, finally, if a donor gives a less-favored asset (long-term capital gain property) to a less-favored charitable entity (a private foundation), the income limitation is lowered to 20%. This concept reduces a range of complex rules to the simple equations of:

Favored + Favored = 50%

Favored + Less-favored = 30%

Less-favored + Less-favored = 20%

Within this context, long-term capital gain property is a less-favored asset. But, the reason it is less-favored is because it can be deducted at fair market value. So, in many cases where long-term capital gain property given to a public charity must be valued at cost basis, it is no longer a less-favored asset. This means that gifts of long-term capital gain property to a public charity may be subject to either a 50% limit (usually when valued at cost basis) or a 30% limit (usually when valued at fair market value).

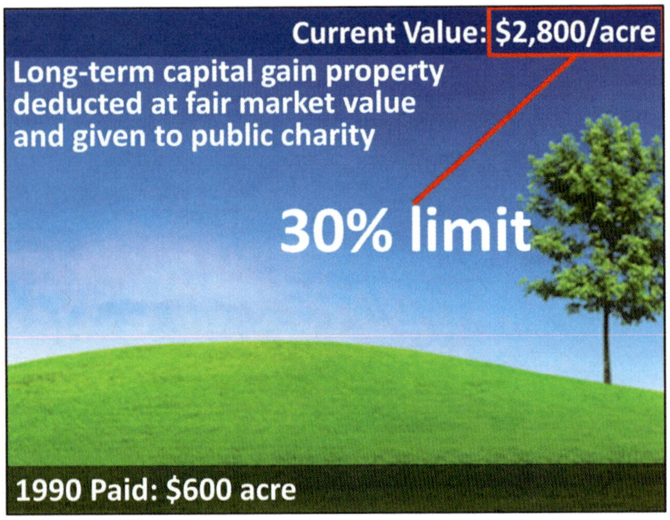

Let's consider the gift of an acre of investment land. The donor purchased the land in 1990 for $600, and today it is worth $2800. The gift of this land to a public charity would normally generate a charitable deduction of $2800. The donor receives the benefit of a large deduction and also avoids paying capital gains taxes on the $2200 of growth. (This is more beneficial than selling the land, paying the capital gains tax, and then transferring the net proceeds to the charity as cash.) Because the donor receives this special tax benefit, the tax code limits the amount of these deductions in any one year to 30% of the donor's income, requiring all additional such deductions to be carried forward into future tax years.

If, however, the donor is willing to give up this special tax advantage and only deduct the *basis* of all long-term capital gain property gifts, the donor is allowed to use such deductions up to 50% of his or her income. This "special election" applies to all long-term capital gain gifts made in a year. The donor may not select some gifts for this treatment and exclude others. In this case, the donor would be allowed to deduct only $600 for the gift of the acre of land to a public charity, rather than $2800. However, charitable deductions for these types of gifts to public charity could be used to reduce up to 50% of the donor's income. Obviously, this "special election" makes sense only for donors whose charitable deductions would otherwise be carried forward into future years. It may be particularly attractive in cases where donors are giving long-term capital gain property that has appreciated very little.

You may recall from the chapter on valuation of property gifts that tangible personal property has special rules for valuation. Tangible personal property includes all of those items that you can see and touch and move such as the items in your garage or home (but would not include the garage or house itself, because those are attached to the land, making them real property).

Tangible personal property also does not include financial instruments such as stocks or bonds. These are *intangible* personal property items. Physically, stock or bond certificates are simply pieces of paper. They do not have value from their physical properties, but instead have value only from their intangible legal properties. Although tangible personal property has special rules for valuation, the general concept used with other long-term capital gain property applies here as well. If the gift of long-term capital gain tangible personal property is valued at its basis, the deductions can be used up to 50% of income. If, instead, it is valued at fair market value, those deductions can be used up to only 30% of income.

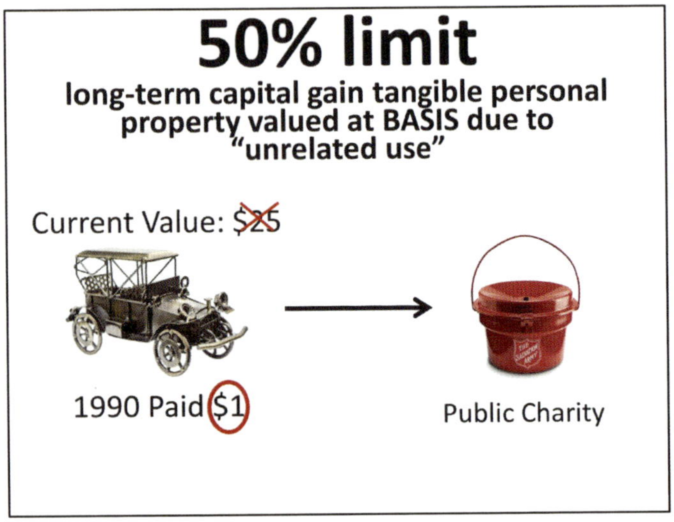

Suppose a donor purchased an antique toy car in 1990 for $1 and today it is worth $25. If the donor gives the toy to a charity that will immediately sell it, the deduction for the gift will be limited to its basis, in this case $1. The deduction is limited to basis because the charity is not using the property itself in its charitable function, but is instead selling the property, and using the proceeds. Although the donor receives a lower deduction, these deductions may be used to reduce up to 50% of the donor's income.

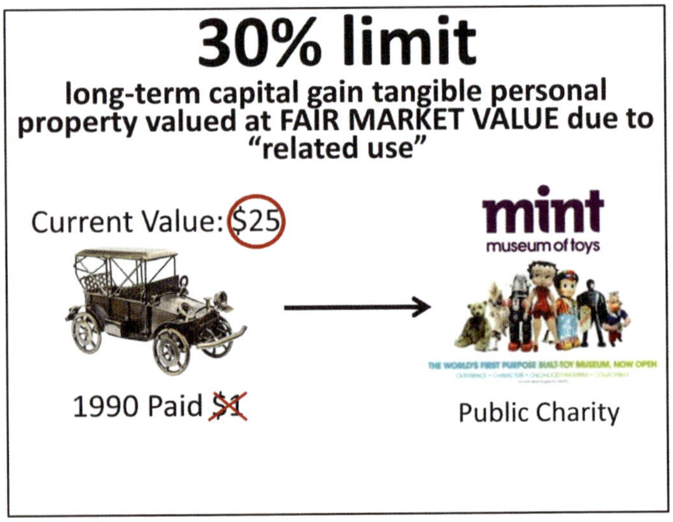

Conversely, if the donor were to give the antique toy to a nonprofit organization that displayed it in its museum as part of its nonprofit function, then the donor could deduct the fair market value of the gift. Thus, the donor would receive a charitable deduction of $25 rather than $1. Along with this greater deduction, however, comes the limitation that such deductions may reduce income by no more than 30% in any one year. (Note that this fair market value deduction is only available for long-term capital gain tangible personal property. Short-term capital gain tangible personal property is valued at the *lower* of its basis or fair market value, regardless of use by the charity.)

So, although the rules for long-term capital gain tangible personal property are different from those for other types of long-term capital gain property, the principle is similar. If a donor receives the higher (fair market value) deduction valuation then the donor receives the lower income limitation.

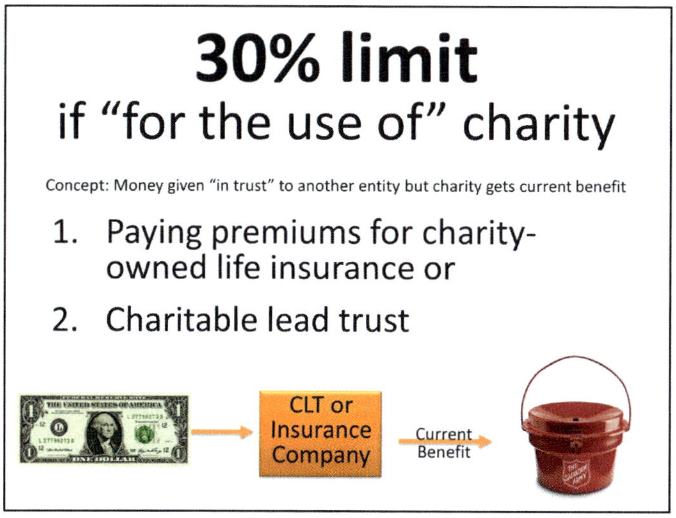

As mentioned previously, 50% is the default income limitation for deductions from charitable gifts to public charities. An exception to that rule is made for gifts of long-term capital gain which, in some cases, trigger a 30% income limitation. There are, however, some deductible gifts which are not considered to be made "to" a public charity, but still benefit a charity. These relatively rare transactions fall into the category of gifts made "for the use of" charity. Gifts, even gifts of cash, made not "to" a charity but "for the use of" a charity do not qualify for the 50% income limitation, but instead qualify for a 30% income limitation.

Although the general principle is that this term encompasses any money given "in trust" to another entity where the charity receives current benefits, there are really only two common scenarios where this issue arises. The first is paying premiums directly to a life insurance company for charity owned life insurance policies. The charity benefits from the transaction, because its life insurance policy premiums are paid. However, the money actually goes to the life insurance company, which is not a charitable entity. Similarly, a deductible gift can be made to a Charitable Lead Trust, where the trust pays a fixed amount of the gift to a charity each year for a period of years, with the remainder going to some non-charitable beneficiary. Again, the transfer to the Charitable Lead Trust benefits the charity, but the charity does not receive its share directly – only indirectly over time through the trust. [Note that this issue does not relate to Charitable Remainder Trusts, because they are themselves charitable entities whereas Charitable Lead Trusts are not.] Given that these are normally the only two applications of this special rule, it may be easier to simply note these two scenarios as exceptions rather than thinking of the general principle involved.

To this point we have been dealing only with public charities. These public charities are favored recipients in the income limitation rules. Consequently, they have the possibility of generating deductions for which donors can receive a 50% income limitation. In contrast, gifts to private foundations can never generate a 50% income limitation. Private foundations are somewhat less favored by the tax law. Typically, private foundations are family foundations that are controlled by the donor and the donor's friends and family. Although such private foundations do make annual distributions to public charities, they do not directly operate or manage charitable work. Being one step removed from charitable work and typically being controlled by the donor and the donor's family, these entities are given substantial tax benefits, but not to the same level as public charities. Let's now examine the rules for income limitations on charitable deductions for gifts to private foundations.

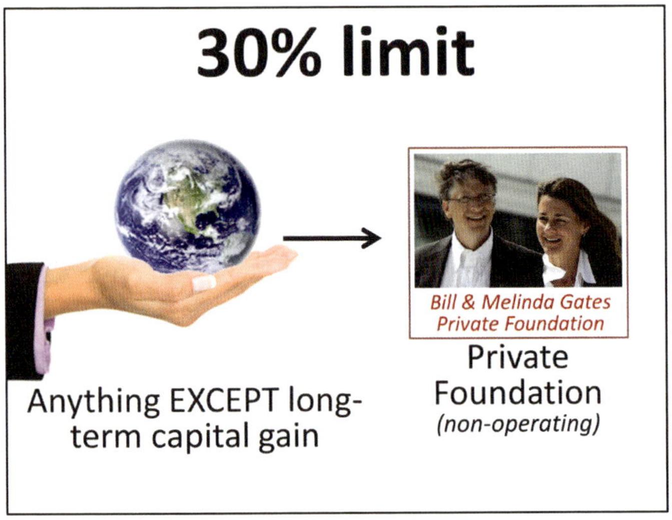

Just as with public charities, we begin with a similar concept in income limitations for private foundations. Any gifts, *except for long-term capital gain*, qualify for the highest income limitation for private foundations, which is 30%. Conceptually, this is a favored asset (i.e., not long-term capital gain) being given to a less-favored organization (i.e., a private foundation). Thus, the donor receives neither the highest income limitation of 50% (reserved for favored assets going to favored organizations) nor the lowest income limitation of 20% (reserved for less-favored assets going to less-favored organizations).

Here we will use the example of the Bill & Melinda Gates Foundation as a private non-operating foundation. Donors, however, rarely give to other people's private foundations, but instead create their own private family foundations, which, along with their friends or family members, they typically control and manage. Indeed, often one of the defining characteristics of a private foundation is that it does not receive substantial charitable gifts from the general public. Instead, private foundations are typically supported predominantly by gifts from one family.

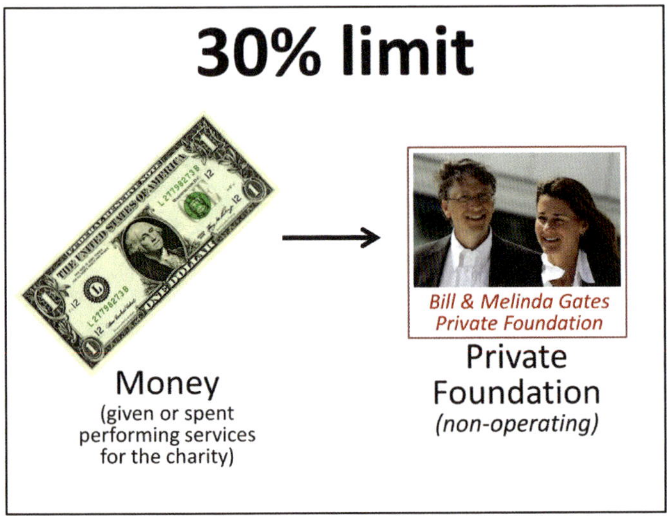

The same types of property gifts which qualified for the 50% income limitation when given to a public charity will also qualify for a 30% income limitation when given to a private foundation. The simplest example is, of course, a gift of cash. Note that gifts of cash include both cash given directly to a charity and cash spent performing services on behalf of a charity. (There is no deduction for time and effort spent on behalf of a charity.)

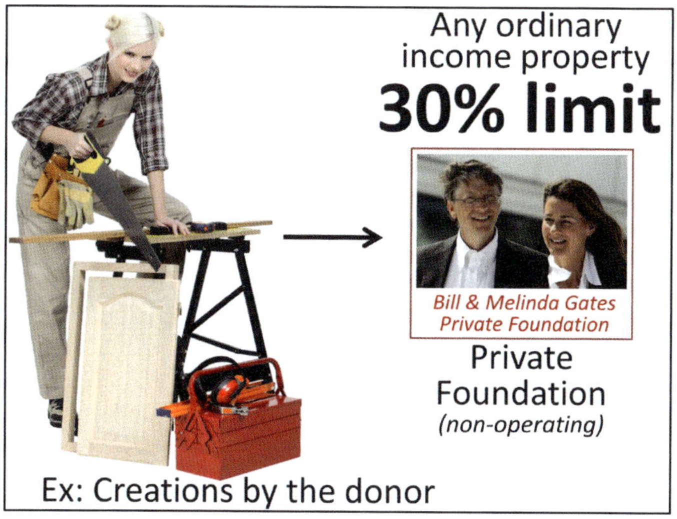

Also similar to the previous rules, gifts of ordinary income property qualify for the private foundation's highest income limitation of 30%. Ordinary income property includes any creations by the donor.

Ordinary income property also includes any inventory given to the private foundation. Such gifts also qualify for the highest income limitation available for gifts to private foundations of 30%.

And finally, also as before, short-term capital gain property (capital gain property held for one year or less) is treated as other forms of ordinary income property and also qualifies for the highest income limitation available for gifts to private foundations (30%).

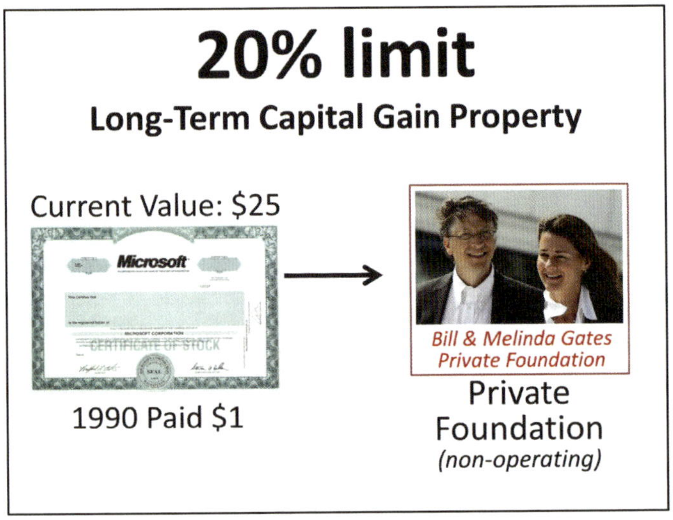

When donors give a less-favored asset (long-term capital gain property) to a less-favored organization (private foundation), this results in the lowest income limitation for individual donors of 20%. Note that this rule is simpler than that for public charities, because there are no exceptions that can increase the percentage, such as the "special election." Thus, the donor will receive the 20% income limitation, regardless of whether the long-term capital gain property was valued at fair market value (available only for "qualified stock") or basis.

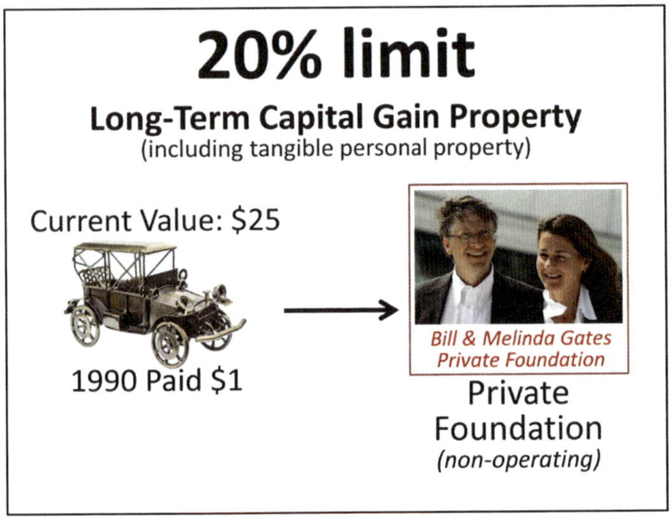

Just as the "special election" exception does not affect the income limitation for long-term capital gain property given to private foundations, so too the "unrelated use" exception for long-term capital gain tangible personal property does not affect the income limitations for gifts to private foundations. This happens to correspond with gift valuation rules; gifts of tangible personal property to a private foundation are always valued at the lower of basis or fair market value, regardless of the "related use" issue. In sum, the income limitation rules for gifts of long-term capital gain property are much simpler for private foundations. In such cases, the limitation is always 20%.

The previous income limitation rules apply to charitable deductions for individual taxpayers. Corporate giving for traditional C-corporations follows a single rule limiting deductions to 10% of taxable income. Just as with individual taxpayers, C-corporations can also carry forward excess charitable deductions for up to five years. S-corporations do not have separate income limitation rules, because all deductions simply pass through to become the personal deductions of the individual shareholders.

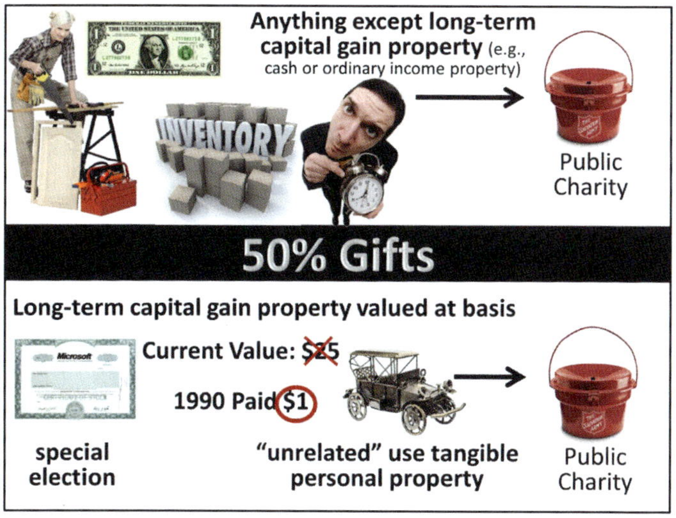

So, to summarize the income limitation rules: In order to receive the highest income limitation of 50%, a donor must give a public charity either something that is *not* long-term capital gain property, or is long-term capital gain property that is valued only at its basis and not its fair market value. (Such valuation can occur through a "special election" or a gift of "unrelated" use long-term capital gain tangible personal property.)

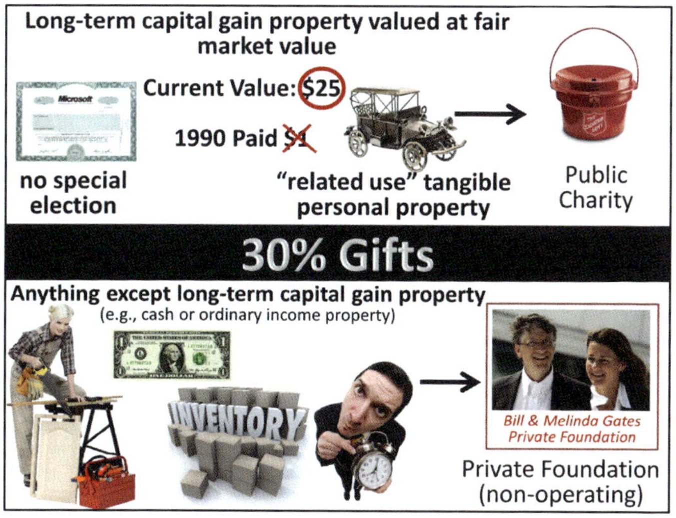

In order to receive the middle level income limitation of 30%, a donor must either give less-favored property (long-term capital gain valued at fair market value) to a favored charitable entity (e.g., a public charity), or give favored property (not long-term capital gain) to a less-favored charitable entity (e.g., a private foundation).

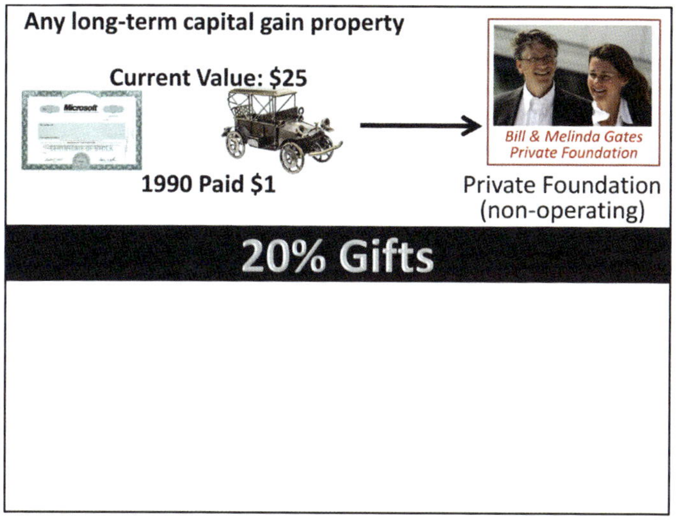

Finally, in order to receive the lowest level income limitation of 20%, a donor must give less-favored property (long-term capital gain) to a less-favored charitable entity (e.g., a private foundation).

So far, we have been considering the income limitations for charitable deductions from different types of gifts to different organizations. But, what happens when these income limitations are exceeded?

When income limitations are exceeded, the charitable deductions are not lost. Instead, the excess deductions must be carried over to future years. As soon as there is a year in which the income limitations are not exceeded for the type of charitable deduction carried over, those deductions may be used. However, the deductions must be used in one of the five years following the year of the gift. Otherwise the charitable deduction will expire.

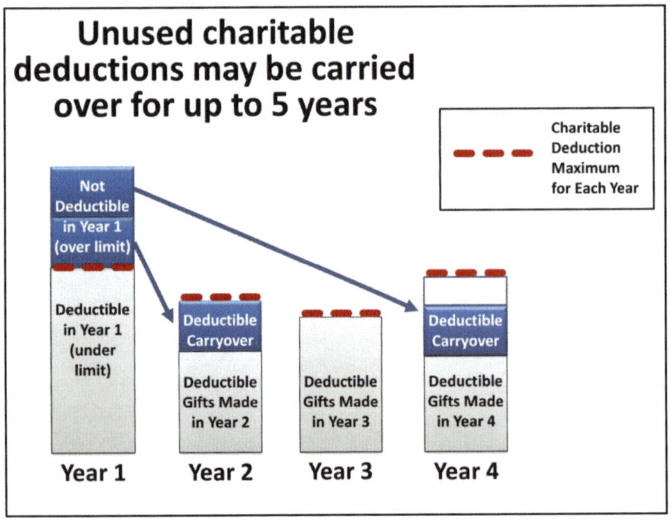

This chart is a visual demonstration of how unused charitable deductions may be carried forward. In each year, the dashed line represents the charitable deduction maximum dollar amount for this type of gift. In year one, the donor gives more than the charitable deduction maximum level. The portion given in year one up to the income limitation is shown below the dashed line and that part may be deducted in year one. The amount above the dashed line in year one must be carried over into future years. In year two the donor makes additional deductible gifts (designated in dark text). Note that gifts made during the year will be counted first, prior to counting any carryover deductions. After counting these gifts made in year two, there is still remaining space under the income limitation maximum for year two. Thus, part of the carryover deduction may be used in year two. In year three, the donor makes gifts up to the maximum income limitation. Consequently, no carryover deductions may be used in year three. Finally, in year four the donor again makes gifts, but there is still remaining space under the income limitation maximum for that year. Thus, the remainder of the carryover may be deducted in year four, leaving no additional carryover for future years.

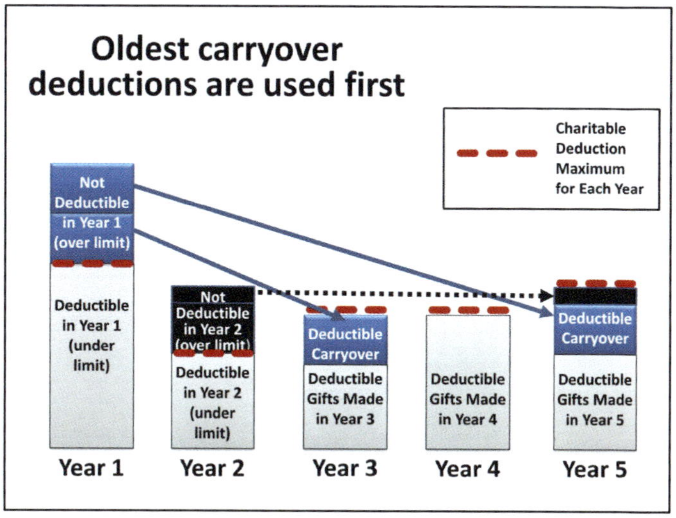

When a donor has carryover charitable deductions from multiple years, the oldest carryover deductions will be used first. This rule is advantageous to the donor because carryover deductions will expire after the fifth year following the year of the charitable gift. So, the donor would prefer to use the oldest carryover first to reduce the risk of the charitable deduction expiring. In the example in the chart, the donor gives more than the income limitation amount in both year one and year two. In year three, the donor gives less than the income limitation maximum, allowing for the use of carryover deductions. The carryover deductions from year one are used in year three, and not the carryover deductions from year two, because the carryover deductions from year one are older. In year four the donor makes gifts up to the income limitation and thus no carryover deductions may be used in that year. Finally, in year five, the donor again gives less than the income limitation maximum, allowing the remainder of the carryover deductions from year one to be used. After all of the year one deductions from this type of charitable gift are used, only then can the carryover deductions from year two begin to be used.

We have been examining scenarios in which the donor uses all of the charitable deductions generated in each year. But, what happens if a donor with carryover charitable deductions takes no itemized deductions for a year, and instead takes the standard deduction? (Note that taking the standard deduction is an *alternative* to taking individual itemized deductions such as the charitable deduction or mortgage interest deduction.)

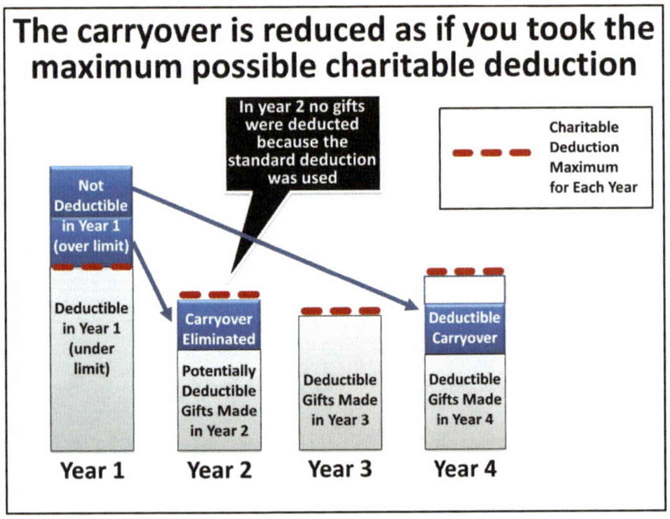

Even though the donor uses no itemized deductions in the year when he or she takes the standard deduction, the carryover charitable deductions will be eliminated as if the donor used as much of them as possible (i.e., up to the income limitations). In this example, the donor made excess charitable gifts in year one, generating carryover charitable deductions. In year two the donor made some deductible charitable gifts, but chose not to deduct those gifts in favor of taking the standard deduction. Even though the donor does not use any of the carryover deductions in year two, these carryover deductions will be eliminated as if the donor used as much as legally possible. Thus, the donor will lose carryover deductions in the amount of the difference between the income limitation in year two for this type of gift and the deductible gifts made in year two. This unpleasant result means that using the standard deduction is not an effective way of preserving carryover charitable deductions. Finally, in this example, the donor makes deductible gifts up to the income limitation for this type of gift in year three, meaning that no carryover can be used in year three. And finally in year four the donor makes additional gifts, but not up to the maximum level, thus leaving room for the remaining carryover deductions to be used in that year.

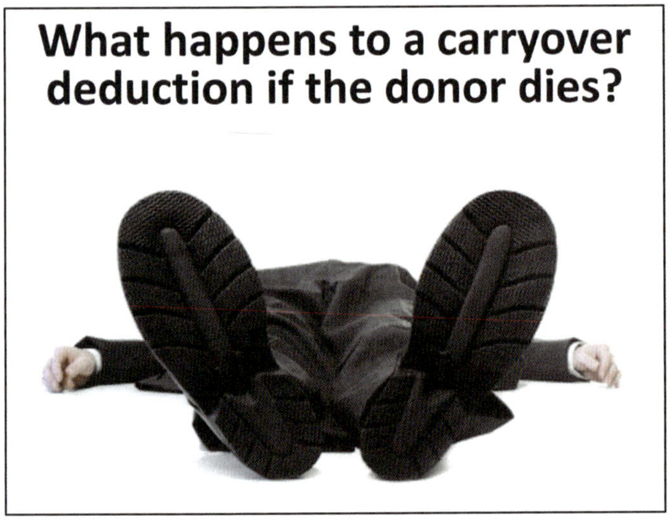

We have been considering how the donor can use these carryover deductions during the five years following the year of the gift. However, what happens if the donor dies with unused carryover deductions?

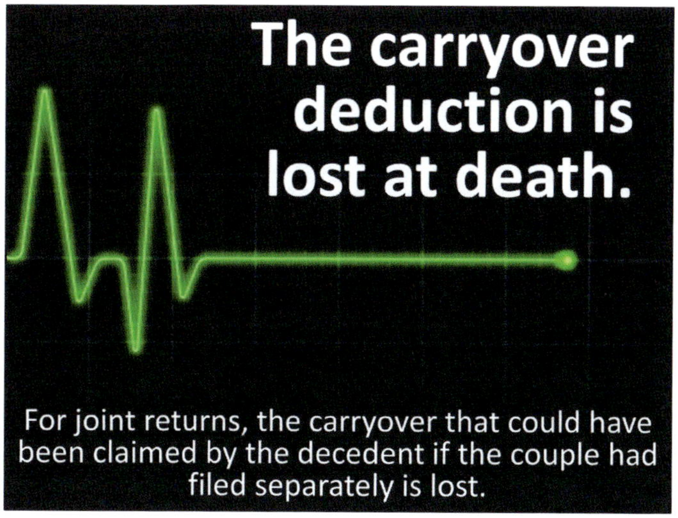

The answer, unfortunately, is that carryover charitable deductions are simply lost at death. For joint returns the amount of carryover lost is equal to the carryover that could have been claimed by the decedent, if the couple had filed separately. Thus, when a donor makes charitable gifts in excess of the income limitations, there is a risk that those carryover deductions may not ever be used. This could happen because the donor's subsequent income limitations (after absorbing current giving deductions in each year) are insufficient to absorb the carryover deductions, or because the donor dies prior to using the carryover deductions.

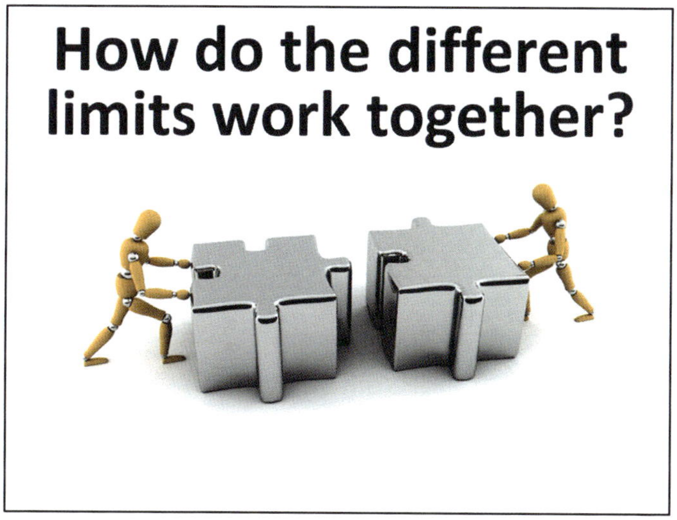

We have looked at which income limitations apply to which type of gifts. However, we have not examined how the different limits work together. This is a complicated but important question because we may be dealing with a variety of different limits that interact in different ways. (A donor cannot, for example, deduct up to 50% of his income with one type of gift and then deduct another 30% of his income with another type of gift and then deduct the final 20% of his income with a final type of gift.)

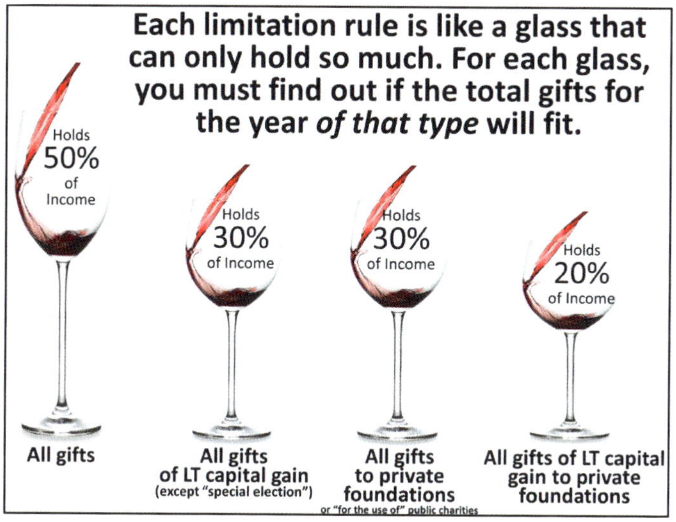

I think it is easiest to conceptualize the interaction of these rules by thinking of four different glasses. Each glass represents a specific income limitation rule for specific types of gifts. We then see if the total of each type of gift made during a year can "poured into" each type of glass. The first glass can hold up to 50% of income. All deductible charitable gifts for the entire year must be poured into this first glass. The second glass can hold up to 30% of income. Into this glass we must put all gifts of long-term capital gain (regardless of the recipient charity), excepting only capital gain for which a "special election" has been made. The third glass can also hold up to 30% of income.

Into this glass we must put all gifts to private foundations made during the year (as well as any gifts made "for the use of" public charities, meaning deductible gifts to a Charitable Lead Trust or to a life insurance company to pay for charity owned life insurance). The final glass can hold only 20% of income. Into this final glass we must put all gifts of long-term capital gain property made to private foundations during the year.

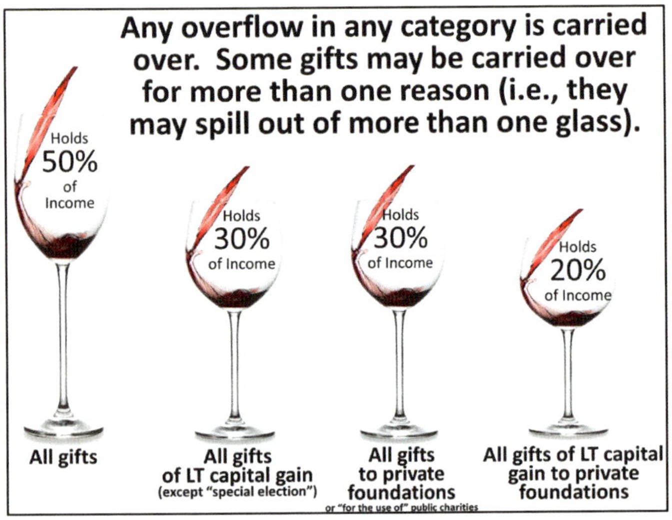

If the gifts of a particular type cannot all fit into the relevant glasses, there will be overflow. This overflow represents the amount of carryover deductions that cannot be used in the current year. Note that this spillage analogy works to calculate what deductions must be carried over. The amount that can be deducted is the total deductible charitable gifts for the year, minus what must be carried over. (Do not attempt to use the glass analogy to calculate the amount of deductions for a current year by thinking about how much *remains* in each glass, but instead focus only on the amount of *overflow* as representing deductible charitable gifts that must be carried forward into future years.)

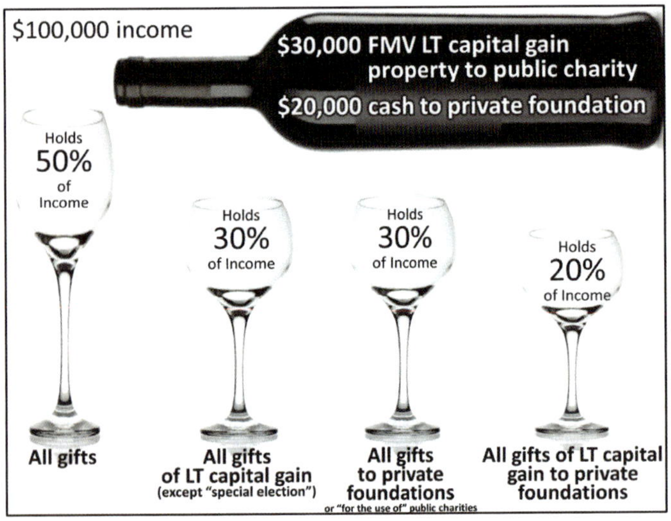

Let's look at the first example. The donor has $100,000 of income (as before, this means adjusted gross income excluding any net operating loss carry back). During the year, the donor has made a total of $30,000 of gifts of long-term capital gain property (valued at fair market value) to a public charity and $20,000 of cash gifts to a private foundation. Next we will attempt to "pour" these gifts into each glass.

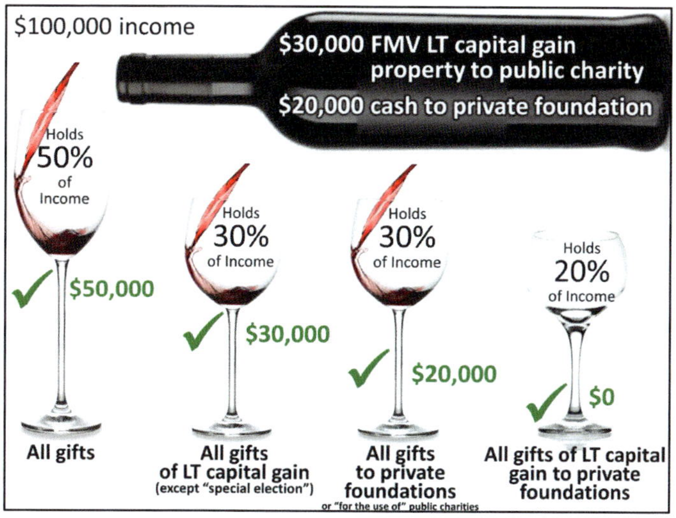

The first glass can hold up to 50% of income. All gifts must be able to fit into this first glass. In this case all gifts combined total $50,000. 50% of income also totals $50,000. Thus, there is no spillage with the first glass and therefore no carryover resulting from the first glass. The second glass can hold up to 30% of income. Thus, in this case, it can hold up to $30,000. Into this glass must be poured all gifts of long-term capital gain (except "special election" capital gain). The donor made a total of $30,000 of such gifts during the year and so, once again, there is no spillage. The third glass can also hold up to 30% of income. This third glass holds all gifts to private foundations, which in this case amount to $20,000. The $20,000 of gifts to private foundations easily fits into the $30,000 glass size and so, once again, there is no overflow. The final glass relates to gifts of long-term capital gain to private foundations and no such gifts were made during the year. So again, there is no spillage.

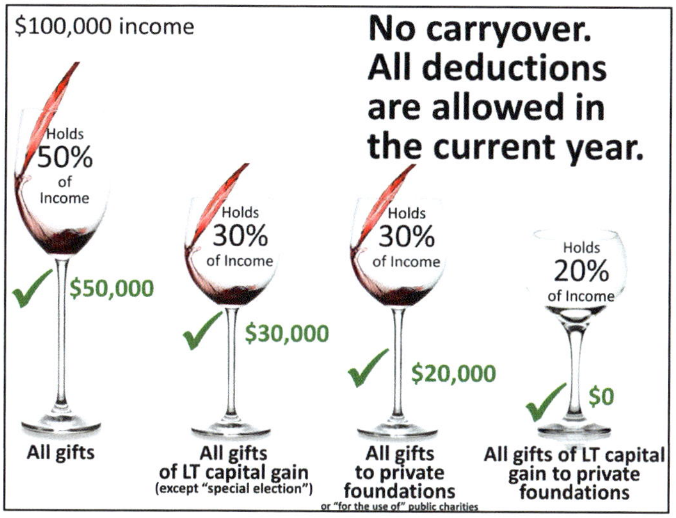

Because there was no spillage or overflow out of any of the four glasses there is no carryover. Thus, all charitable deductions will be allowed in the current year. (Remember that in this analogy the amount of charitable deductions allowed in the year is the total amount of deductible charitable gifts less any gifts that must be carried forward.)

We have not yet looked at an example in which there is spillage that generates carryover. However, before looking at one of these examples, we must first resolve the issue of which type of gifts gets deducted first and which type of gifts are carried forward first. For example, if we have spillage out of the first glass into which all gifts must be poured how do we know which gifts are carried forward? This is an important issue because the gifts carried forward retain their original identity and consequently must, in the future year in which they are used, be able to fit into each income limitation "glass" related to that type of gift.

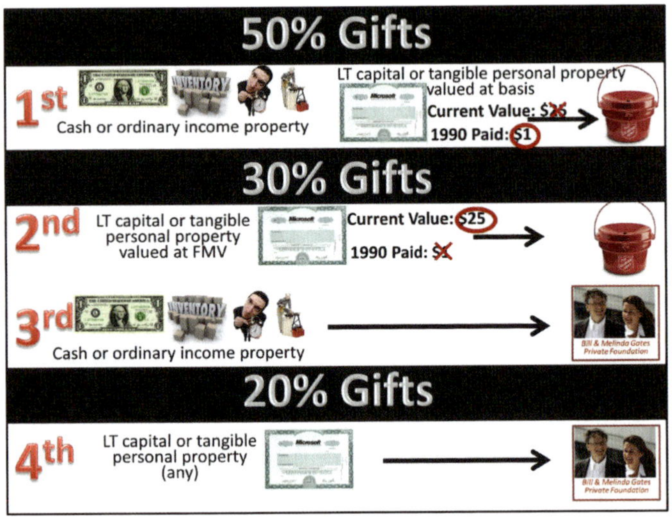

Fortunately, the question of which gifts are deducted first follows the same pattern of preference we have already seen with regard to which gifts have the highest income limitations. In other words, the more preferred gifts will be deducted first and the less preferred gifts will be carried over first. So, favored property (not long-term capital gain property valued at fair market value) given to a favored charitable recipient (e.g., a public charity), will be deducted first. Second, less-favored property (long-term capital gain property valued at fair market value) given to a favored charitable recipient (e.g., a public charity) will be deducted. Third, favored property (not long-term capital gain) given to a less-favored charitable recipient (e.g., a private foundation) will be deducted. Finally, the last type of gift to be deducted – and the first type of gift to be carried forward into future years – is less-favored property (long-term capital gain) given to a less-favored charitable recipient (e.g., a private foundation). This is the order that determines which type of gift will be counted first. So, if there is spillage out of a glass containing multiple types of gifts, such as the first glass which must contain all gifts, this ordering determines which type of gifts are deducted in the current year, and which type of gifts must be carried forward.

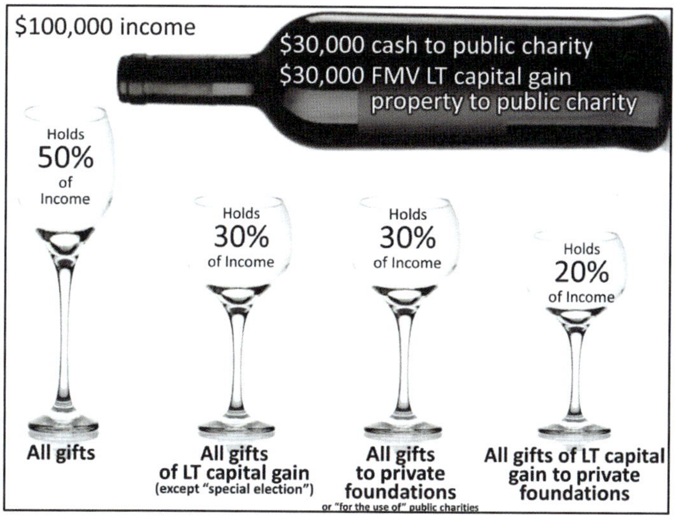

In this next example, the donor, once again, has $100,000 of income. During the course of the year, the donor has made a total of $30,000 of cash gifts to public charities and $30,000 of long-term capital gain property gifts (valued at fair market value) to public charities.

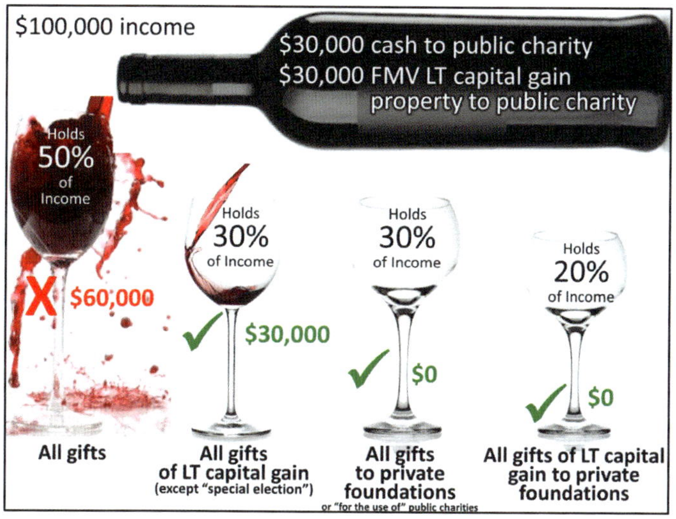

The first glass holds up to 50% of income (in this case $50,000) and must contain all deductible charitable gifts of any type. However, the donor has made a total of $60,000 of deductible charitable gifts during the year. This $60,000 cannot fit entirely into the $50,000 glass. Thus, we will have spillage and therefore carryover. We do not have similar problems with the second glass which can hold up to $30,000 of long-term capital gain gifts because only $30,000 of such gifts were made during the year. (We know these long-term capital gain gifts were not subject to the "special election" because they were valued at fair market value, i.e. "FMV"). No gifts were made to private foundations during the year, so nothing goes into glasses three or four. We have determined that there will be carryover due to the spillage in glass one. But, which gifts will have their deductions carried forward?

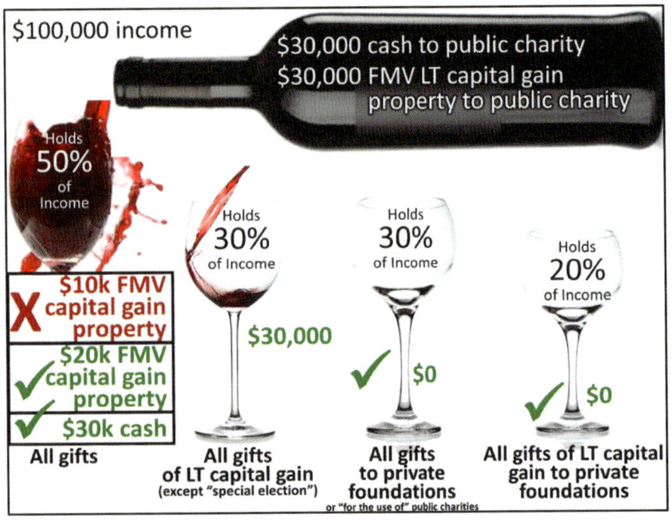

Because glass one cannot hold all $60,000 of deductible gifts made during the year, some gifts will have to be carried forward. The $30,000 of cash given to a public charity is the most favored kind of charitable transaction. Consequently, this gift will be deducted first. This means that the $10,000 of carryover will come entirely from the capital gain property gifts made to public charity.

One might ask, "What happens if we have different gifts within the same category?" For example, if we have gifts of short-term capital gain property to a public charity and also gifts of cash to a public charity, which one gets carried forward? The answer is that it doesn't matter, because both of these type of gifts are treated identically for tax deduction purposes.

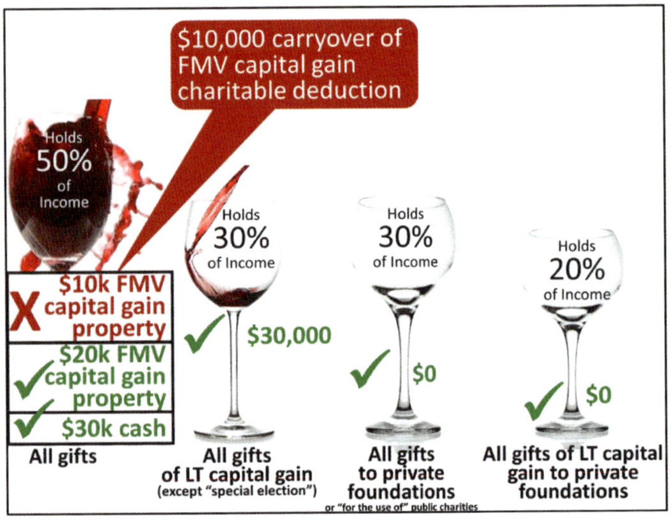

Thus, because we have $10,000 that cannot fit into the first glass this $10,000 of charitable deduction for fair market value capital gain property must be carried forward into future years.

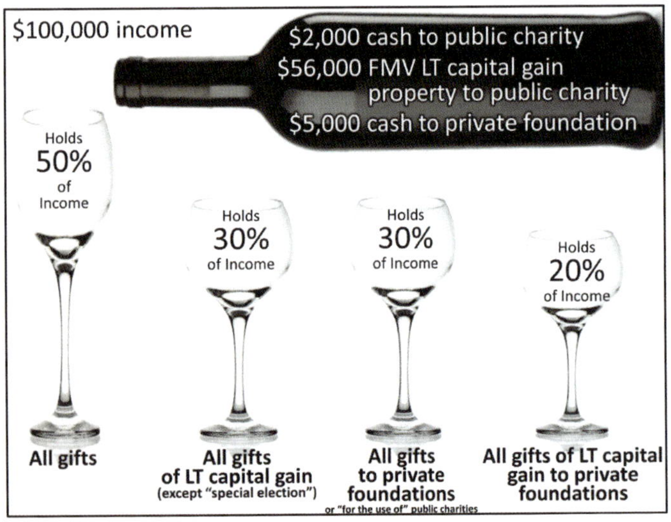

In this next example, our donor still has $100,000 of income. During the course of the year, the donor makes a total of $2000 of cash gifts to public charities, $56,000 of gifts of long-term capital gain property (valued at fair market value) to public charities, and $5000 of cash gifts to private foundations. Will this giving fit into the income limitation "glasses"?

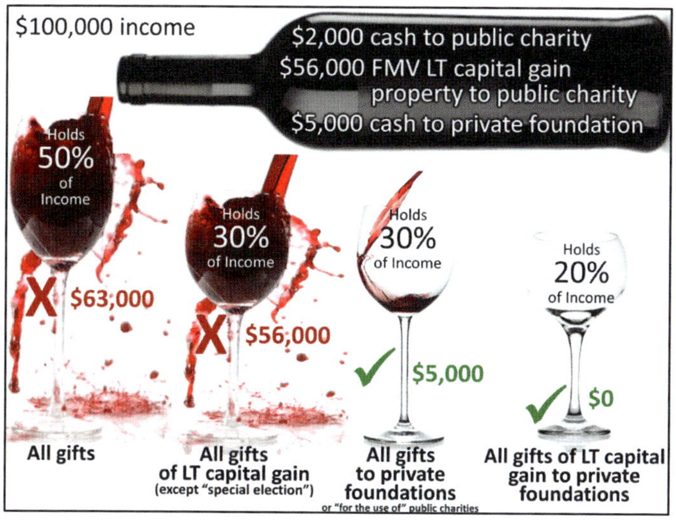

The first glass can hold up to $50,000 and includes all deductible charitable gifts made during the year. In this case, the donor has made a total of $63,000 of deductible charitable gifts. Consequently, we will have $13,000 of spillage out of this first glass. The second glass can hold up to $30,000 and includes all gifts of long-term capital gain (except "special election"). The donor, however, has made $56,000 of long-term capital gain property gifts (valued at fair market value, and therefore not "special election" property). Thus, there will be $26,000 of spillage out of the second glass. The third glass contains all gifts to private foundations and can hold up to 30% of income, which in this case means $30,000. The total gifts to private foundations were $5000, so there is no spillage out of this glass.

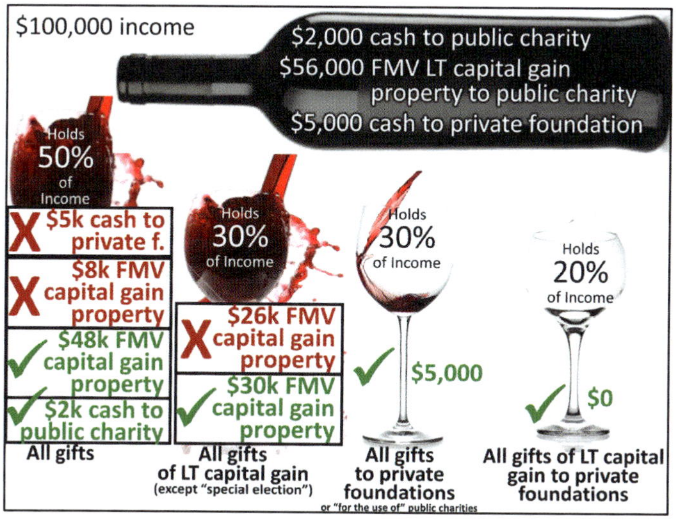

Which gifts are carried forward? The first glass will have $13,000 of spillage because there were a total of $63,000 of deductible charitable gifts and 50% of income is only $50,000. Gifts of cash to a public charity are the most favored type of gifts and so will be deducted first. Gifts of long-term capital gain to a public charity are deducted next. However, the cash to a public charity of $2000 and the long-term capital gain property to public charity of $56,000 exceeds the $50,000 holding capacity of this glass. Thus, $8000 of the long-term capital gain property gifts to public charity must be carried forward into future years, because it has spilled out of the class. Gifts of cash to a private foundation are deducted third (after gifts of cash to a public charity and gifts of long-term capital gain to a public charity). As a result, all of the $5000 in cash gifts to private foundations "spills out" of the first glass and must be carried forward into future years.

In this case we also have spillage out of the second glass, which makes things more complicated. The second glass can hold a total of $30,000 (30% of income). However, the donor made $56,000 of these types of long-term capital gain gifts. Thus, $26,000 of these long-term capital gain gifts spill out of the glass and must be carried forward into future years. $8000 of that $26,000 of long-term capital gain gifts were *already* being carried forward because of the spillage resulting from the *first* glass. However, this just means that this particular $8000 of long-term capital gain gifts will be carried forward for two different reasons (spillage out of glass one and spillage out of glass to).

Note that the gifts for the year must fit into each glass separately. The calculation for each individual glass is not affected by what happens in the other glasses. We do not, for example, say that only $30,000 of fair market value long-term capital gain property gifts must go into glass one, because the rest has spilled out of glass two already. Each glass is calculated without regard to the other glasses. This means that the same gift could be carried over for multiple reasons (i.e., the same gift spills out of multiple glasses), as we see here with the $8000 of long-term capital gain gifts that spilled out of both glasses one and two.

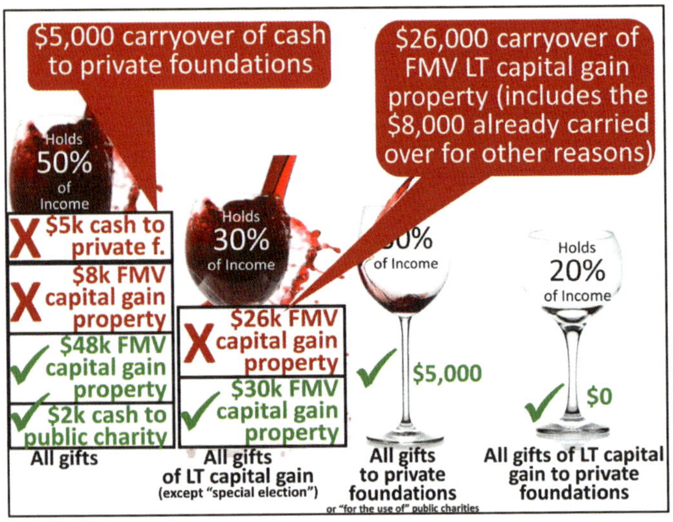

The result here is a carryover of both $26,000 of fair market value long-term capital gain property gifts to public charities and $5000 of cash gifts to private foundations. Thus, $31,000 of charitable deductions, in total, must be carried forward into future years. The donor made a total of $63,000 of deductible charitable gifts, and $31,000 must be carried forward into future years. As a result, only $32,000 may be deducted this year.

(Remember, the glass analogy is used to calculate the amount of *carryover*. To calculate the amount that can be deducted in the current year, simply subtract this total gifts carried over from the total deductible charitable gifts for the year. Do not attempt to calculate the deductible gifts for the year by using the dollar amounts with checkmarks by them in the accompanying image.)

Note that the $5000 in gifts to private foundations was well below the maximum for glass three, but this gift was still carried forward because of the spillage in glass one.

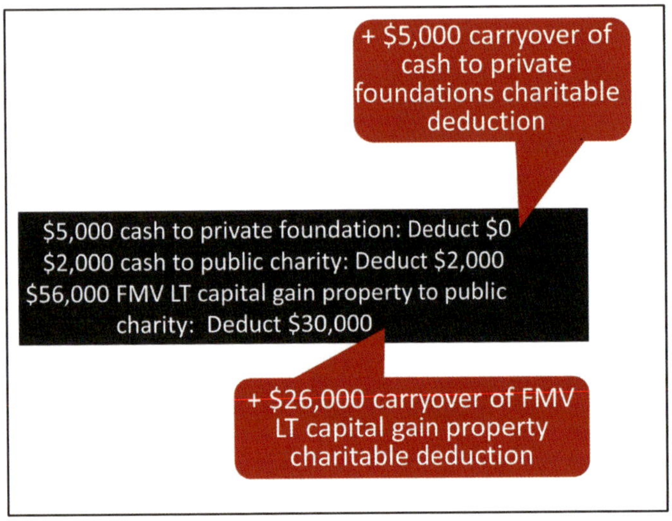

Returning to the three categories of gifts made by the donor during the year, the $5000 of cash given to private foundations generated no deduction for this year, but did generate $5000 of carryover deductions for future years. That $5000 of carryover deductions will, in future years, still be treated as deductions for gifts of cash to private foundations. Thus, in order to be used, these carryover deductions must be able to fit into the relevant income limitation glasses for the future years. The $2000 of cash gifts to public charities will all be deducted this year. Finally, the $56,000 of fair market value long-term capital gain property gifts to public charities resulted in a current year deduction of $30,000 and $26,000 of carryover. Again, this $26,000 of carryover will, in future years, still be characterized as fair market value long-term capital gain property gifts to public charities.

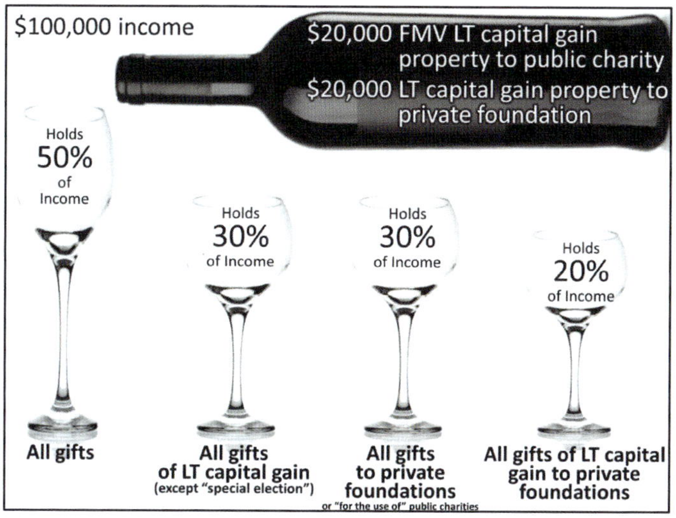

In this next example, the donor has given $20,000 of fair market value long-term capital gain property gifts to public charities and $20,000 of long-term capital gain property gifts to private foundations during the year.

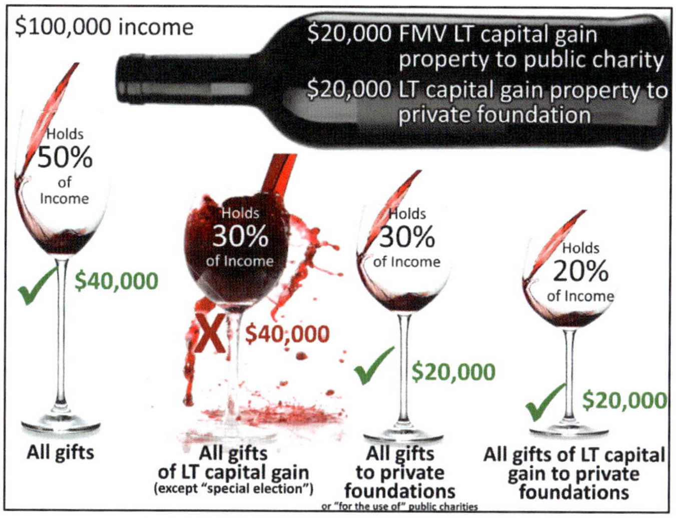

These gifts total $40,000 which fits into the first glass. However, all of these gifts are of long-term capital gain and all $40,000 will not fit into the second glass which holds only $30,000. Thus, there will be $10,000 of carryover. The third glass holds up to $30,000 in this case, and contains all gifts to private foundations. Only $20,000 of gifts were made to private foundations this year. Therefore, there is no carryover resulting from glass three. Glass four can hold up to $20,000 in this case, and contains all gifts of long-term capital gain property given to private foundations. Exactly $20,000 of this type of gift was given, and consequently there is no spillage from this fourth glass.

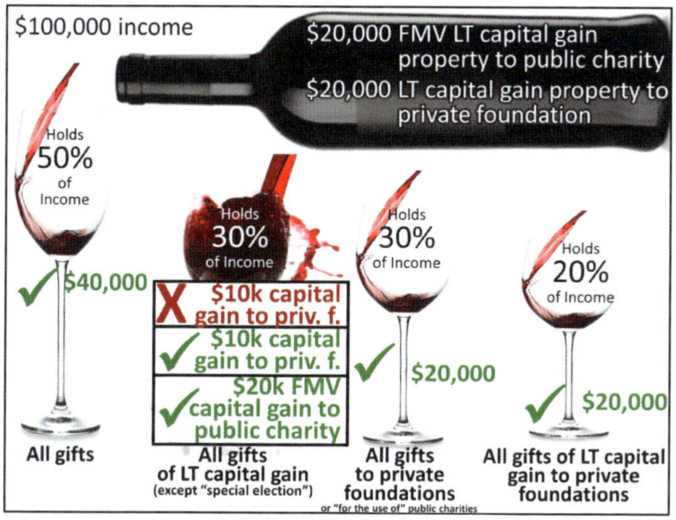

We know from the previous slide that $10,000 of deductible charitable gifts will have to be carried forward because of the spillage from glass two. But which type of gift is carried forward? Because long-term capital gain property gifts to public charities are deducted before long-term capital gain property gifts to private foundations, this means that all $10,000 carried forward will be gifts of long-term capital gain property given to private foundations.

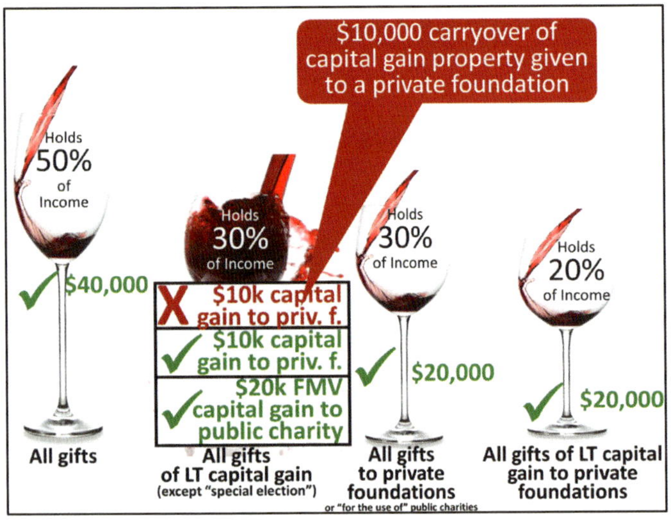

Thus, even though the entire capital gain property gift given to private foundations fits into glasses one, three, and four, $10,000 of this gift must still be carried forward into future years, because of the spillage from glass two.

As we end this examination of income limitations on charitable deductions, it is perhaps useful to recognize that this material is among the most complex in all of charitable gift planning. The analogies, explanations, and themes used in this chapter were intended to help the reader understand the rules intuitively. However, the comparisons made using spillage out of glasses and describing favored and less-favored property and favored and less-favored charitable entities are not examples or terms that come from the tax code or the IRS. These are put here only to be helpful to you. To the extent that they are not helpful ideas to help you internalize these rules then you may feel free to disregard them and focus more directly on the exact language of the internal revenue code.

7 BARGAIN SALE GIFTS

Bargain sale gifts are at once a relatively rare and quite common form of charitable planning. What does this mean? A traditional bargain sale gift, such as where a donor sells land worth $1 million to a charity for $500,000 is not a common occurrence for most charities. However, other forms of complex charitable planning involve the donor making a transfer and, in exchange, receiving back some benefit (such as a lifetime income stream resulting from a Charitable Gift Annuity). Although not referenced by this name, such transactions are, in fact, also bargain sales. Thus, it makes sense to first understand the rules for the simplest form of bargain sale transactions, because these same rules will apply later when we examine more complex charitable transactions. Let's begin with a definition.

A bargain sale is the sale of an asset to a charity at less than fair market value. A bargain sale is the same as a standard sale except that the sale price is intentionally lowered below fair market value for the purpose of making a gift to the purchasing charity. Alternatively, one may think of a bargain sale as a special form of charitable gift where the donor makes a gift of an asset, but also receives money or other valuable property back from the charity in exchange for the gift.

Calculating the charitable deduction for a typical bargain sale transaction can be relatively simple. The donor deducts the value of what she gave less the value of what she received from the charity in exchange for the gift. In this way, the rules for deducting bargain sale gifts are like the normal "quid pro quo" gifts. A donor who makes a $500 contribution and, in exchange, receives tickets to a charity dinner worth $100 may deduct $400 ($500 gift - $100 benefit). In both cases, the deduction is the value given less the value received. (This assumes that the donor is giving property which can be valued at fair market value for charitable income tax deduction purposes. If the donor gives property that can be valued only at the *lower* of basis or fair market value, then the charitable deduction rules are a bit more complex and will be reviewed later in this chapter.)

Following the same idea, suppose a charity wants land owned by the donor that is worth $1 million. The donor offers a lower price in order to benefit the charity and subsequently sells the land to the charity for $400,000. In this case, the donor has made a $600,000 charitable gift ($1,000,000 land given to charity - $400,000 payment received from charity).

A bargain sale can occur even where the charity does not directly transfer money to the donor. For example, a donor could make the gift of a $300,000 house to a charity where the house was subject to a $100,000 mortgage. The donor has exchanged property worth $300,000 for debt relief of $100,000, thus making a gift of $200,000. Such transactions may not be ideal, because the $100,000 of debt relief will count as income to the donor. This treatment of secured debt occurs regardless of the actual agreement for which party will ultimately make the debt payments. So, for example, if the donor donates a house with a mortgage, but agrees to make all subsequent mortgage payments, the transaction is still treated as if the donor received $100,000 of debt relief. Future mortgage payments made on the property owned by the charity will constitute charitable gifts at the time each is made, but the agreement to make future mortgage payments does not change the tax results of the initial transaction. The initial transaction is still treated as if the donor received a $100,000 benefit in exchange for transferring the property. Similarly, the donor is treated as receiving $100,000 of debt relief even if the donor is still legally liable to pay the remaining debt. For this reason, it is often disadvantageous to gift debt-encumbered property to charity.

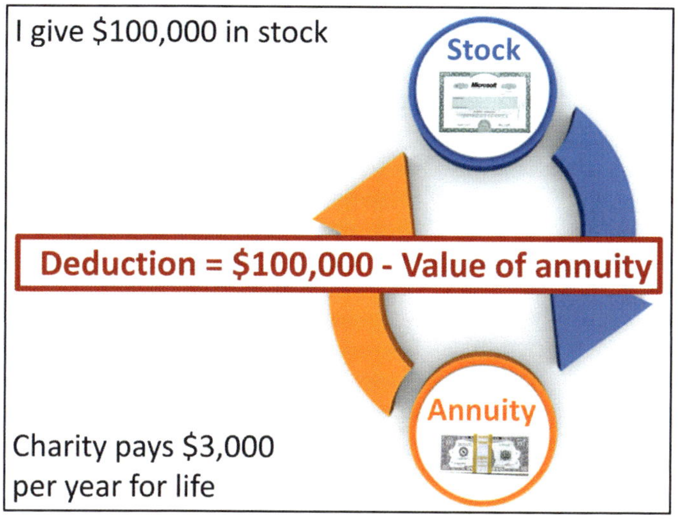

A Charitable Gift Annuity is another example of a bargain sale. Suppose, for example, a donor gives $100,000 of publicly-traded securities to a charity in exchange for lifetime payments of $3,000 per year for life from the charity. In this case, the donor has made a charitable gift of $100,000 less the value of the annuity. (We will postpone calculation of the value of such annuities for the chapter on taxation of Charitable Gift Annuities.) Although the ultimate calculations for such a charitable deduction are more complex, the fundamental principle of bargain sale transactions is the same. The donor deducts the value of what he gave less the value of what he received back in exchange from the charity.

The tax consequences resulting from bargain sales become more complex when we consider the results of bargain sales in recognizing capital gains. Let's first review how capital gains are calculated in normal transactions.

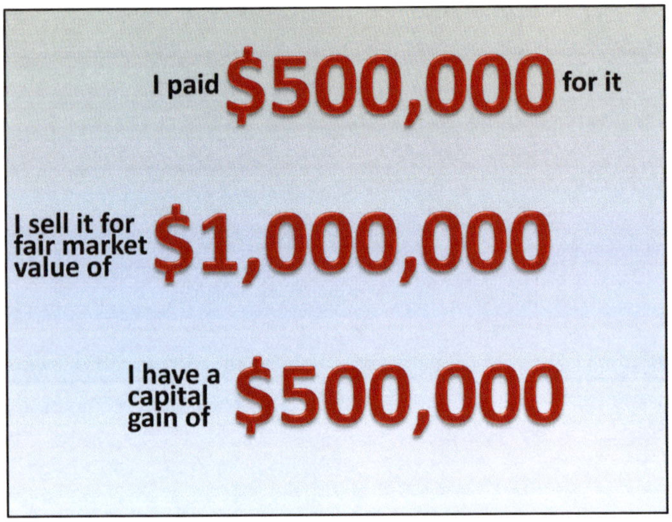

If an investor pays $500,000 for an item of property (such as shares of stock) and then later sells that property for $1 million, the investor has a capital gain of $500,000. The $500,000 paid for the property is referred to as "basis." The capital gain is simply the amount the investor received for the property less the amount the investor paid for the property or, in this case, $1,000,000 - $500,000. (We will pass over for the moment other potentially complicating factors that can alter the basis such as additional investments in improving the property or depreciation deductions previously taken, in order to focus on the basic concept of capital gain as the difference between the money received at sale and the money paid at purchase.)

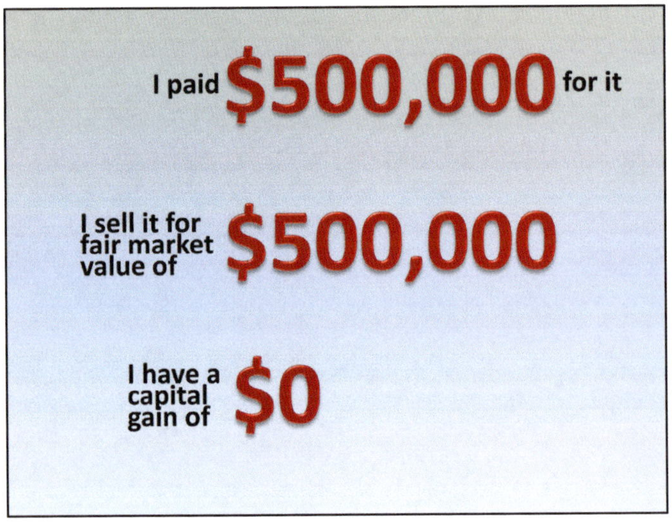

In another example, if the investor pays $500,000 for an item of property and then later sells the same item of property for $500,000, the investor has no capital gain. There is no profit to be taxed. These examples show the relative simplicity of calculating capital gain in a typical transaction. This simplicity changes dramatically, however, in the context of a bargain sale.

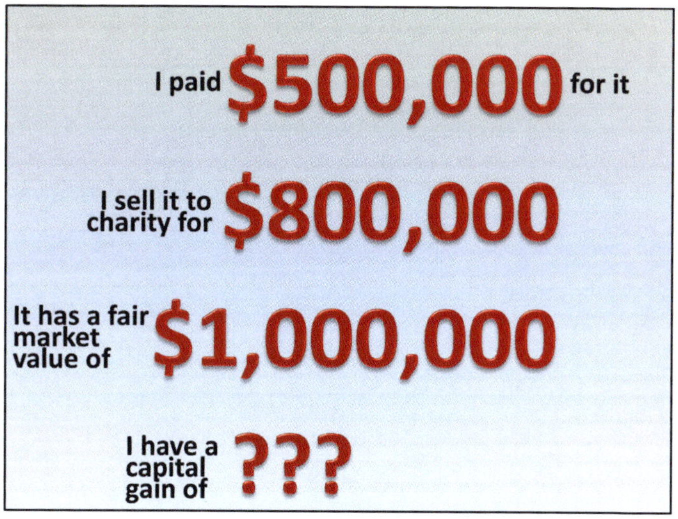

Suppose the donor pays $500,000 for property and the property grows in value to $1 million. However, instead of selling the property for $1 million, the donor wishes to benefit a charity, and so he sells the property to the charity for a bargain price of $800,000. What is the donor's capital gain on this type of transaction? The tempting, but *wrong* answer is to simply subtract the $500,000 purchase price from the $800,000 received from the charity. This is not the correct answer. The donor does indeed receive $800,000. However, because part of the value of the property was donated, part of the $500,000 basis in the property will apply to the "gift" portion of the transaction. Only the remaining share of the basis will be applied to the "sale" part of the transaction, and only this "sale" portion of the basis may be subtracted from the $800,000 received from the charity when calculating the capital gain. Let's walk through this calculation process step by step.

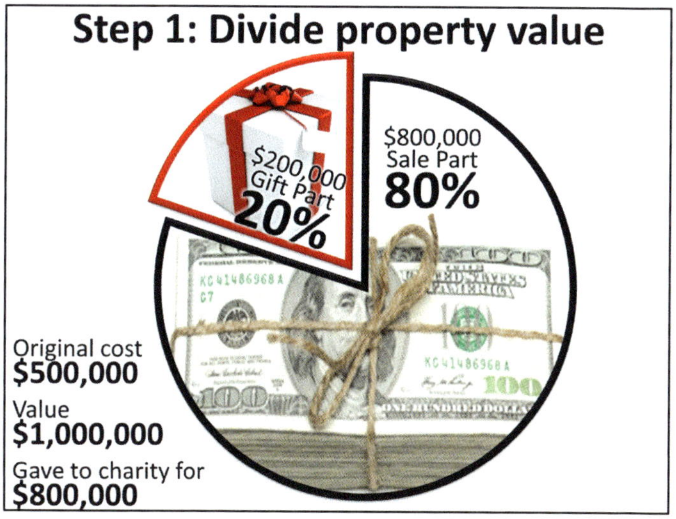

The first step in calculating the capital gain resulting from a bargain sale transaction is to divide the property value into the gift part and the sale part. In this case, the donor gave property worth $1 million to the charity in exchange for $800,000. Thus, $800,000 of the transaction was a sale (because the donor received full compensation for that share of the property). The remaining $200,000 of the transaction was a gift. Another way of thinking of this is that the donor sold 80% of the property and gifted 20% of the property.

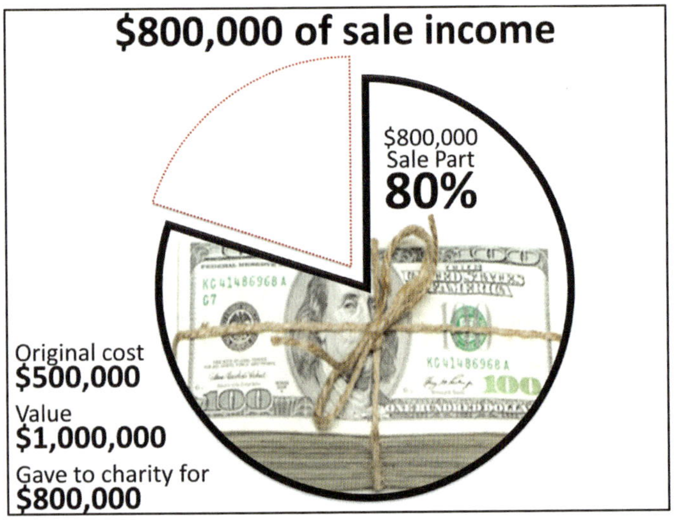

The donor received $800,000 from the "sale" part of the transaction. Thus, the donor will have $800,000 of capital gain income less the "sale" part of the donor's basis in the gifted property. In order to determine the "sale" part of the donor's basis, we must divide that basis between the "sale" part and the "gift" part.

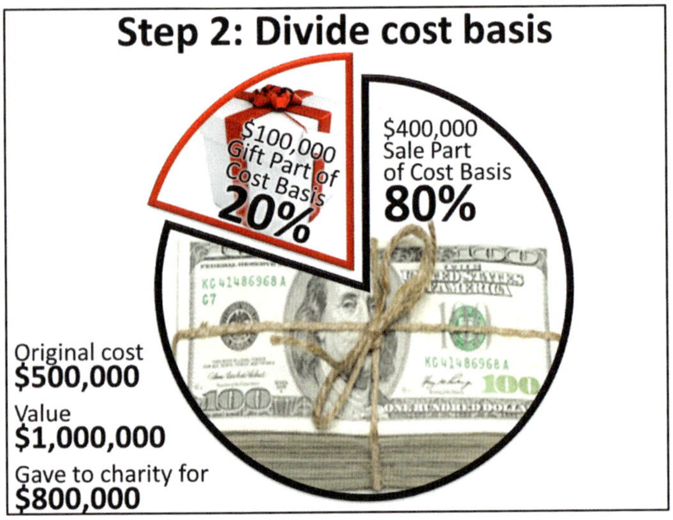

Because the donor is treated as having sold 80% of the property and gifted 20% of the property, 80% of the basis will apply to the "sale" part of the transaction and 20% of the basis will apply to the "gift" part of the transaction. Thus, the $500,000 original cost basis is divided between the "sale" part and the "gift" part of the transaction. Because 20% of the value of the property was gifted to the charity, 20% of the $500,000 original cost basis (i.e., $100,000) is applied to the "gift" part of the transaction. The remaining 80% of the value of the property was sold, i.e., the donor received full compensation for 80% of the value of the property. Thus, 80% of the $500,000 original cost basis (i.e., $400,000) is applied to the "sale" part of the transaction.

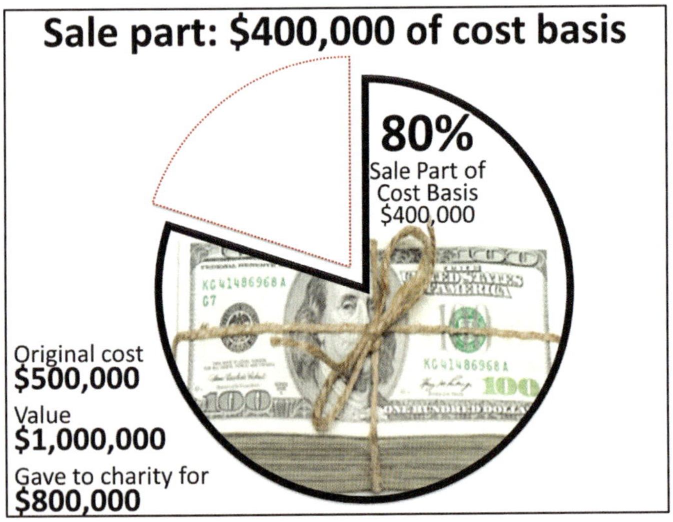

Because the donor received 80% of the value of the property, the donor can use 80% of the value of the cost basis when calculating capital gain. In this case, 80% of the cost basis is $400,000. This is the portion of the cost basis applied to the "sale" part of the transaction.

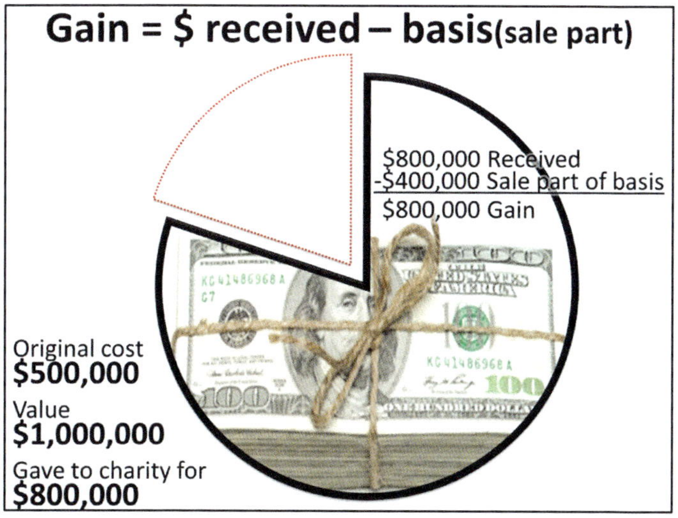

The donor's capital gain is the $800,000 he received from the bargain sale transaction less the $400,000 of basis that applies to the "sale" part of the transaction. Thus, the donor's capital gain is, in this case, $800,000-$400,000, or $400,000. It may seem disadvantageous to lose the ability to subtract the full $500,000 basis. Consider, however, the alternate transaction where the donor sold the property at a fair market value of $1,000,000 and then gifted $200,000 of the proceeds to the charity. The charity would receive the same $200,000 benefit in either transaction. However, if the donor sold the property he would pay tax on $500,000 of capital gain ($1,000,000 sale price - $500,000 basis). By using a bargain sale transaction, the donor has reduced his capital gain from $500,000 to $400,000. Considering that combined federal and state long-term capital gains tax rates (including affordable care act taxes) can be in excess of 33.3%, structuring this transaction as a bargain sale (rather than a sale then gift) can result in substantial tax savings for the donor.

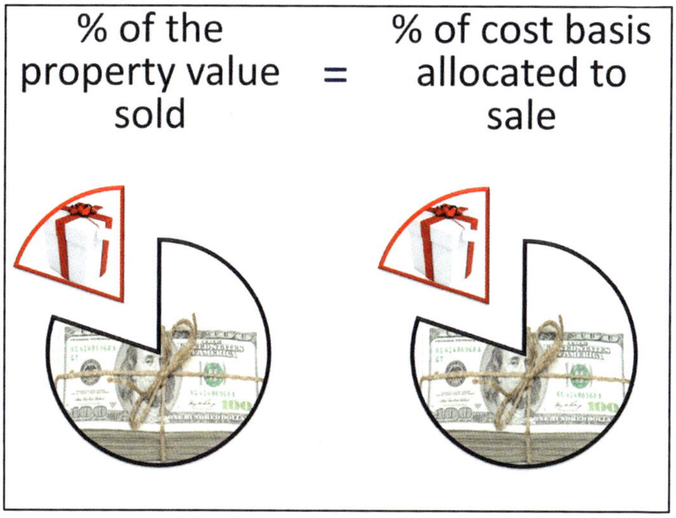

The basic principle of calculating capital gain in a bargain sale transaction is simply that the percentage of the property value that is sold (i.e., the percentage of the fair market value the donor receives in exchange for the property) is the percentage of the cost basis that can be used for calculating capital gains. The most important idea is to avoid the temptation of simply subtracting the amount paid for the property (basis) from the amount received for the property. Although this works for other types of capital gain calculations, it is not appropriate here because part of the basis is applied to the "gift" part of the transaction.

We have reviewed how the "sale" part of the basis is used to calculate the donor's capital gain. But, what happens to the "gift" part of the basis? When would we use this in a tax calculation?

The basis in gifted property is not relevant when the property can be deducted at its fair market value. In such cases, if an item of property were worth $100,000, the charitable deduction for gifting such property would be $100,000 regardless of the basis in the property. However, some types of property gifts to charity may be deducted only at the *lower* of basis or fair market value. For example, gifts of "unrelated use" tangible personal property are deducted at the lower of basis or fair market value. ("Unrelated use" here means that the charity will not be physically using the tangible personal property item in furtherance of its charitable mission, but most likely will instead be selling the item and using the proceeds.) In the case of a bargain sale involving such property, the deduction would be limited to the "gift" portion of the property's basis.

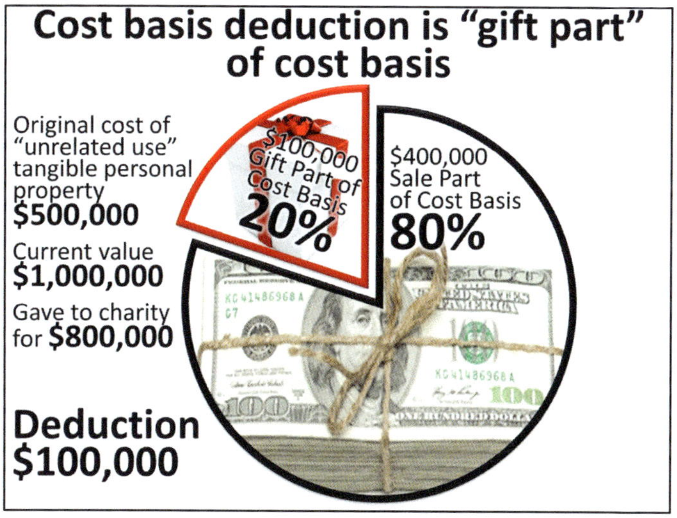

Let's return to our previous example, but now suppose that the gifted property was "unrelated use" tangible personal property. Because gifts of "unrelated use" tangible personal property can be deducted only at the *lower* of basis or fair market value, the donor in this case may deduct only the basis. However, the donor may not deduct the entire basis, because part of the basis was applied to the "sale" part of the transaction (and used in the donor's capital gain calculation). Instead, the donor may deduct only the "gift" portion of the basis, which, in this transaction, was $100,000 (i.e., 20% of the original $400,000 basis).

As mentioned previously, there are tax benefits to using bargain sales, especially when compared to the alternative transaction of selling an item of property for its fair market value and then donating a portion of the proceeds to charity.

The primary benefit of a bargain sale transaction as compared with selling the property at fair market value and then making a gift to charity out of the proceeds is the partial avoidance of capital gain tax. Using our original example (and assuming that the gifted property can be deducted at fair market value), the donor sells the $1,000,000 property to the charity for $800,000 and receives a $200,000 charitable income tax deduction. If instead, the donor sold the property for $1,000,000 and then gave the charity $200,000 out of the proceeds of the sale, the donor would also generate the same $200,000 charitable income tax deduction. However, the capital gain tax consequences of the two transactions differ. As calculated previously, the bargain sale results in a $400,000 capital gain (i.e., $800,000 received from the charity – 80% of the $500,000 basis). If instead the donor were to sell the property at its fair market value and then make a gift to charity out of the proceeds, the donor would recognize a $500,000 gain (i.e., $1,000,000 received from the sale - $500,000 basis). Both transactions result in the transfer of $200,000 of benefit to the charity. Both transactions result in the donor keeping $800,000 (pre-tax) from the sale. However, the bargain sale generates $400,000 of capital gain where the sale followed by a gift generates $500,000 of capital gain.

This benefit results from the same principle discussed in previous chapters; it is better to donate appreciated assets (when such assets can be deducted at fair market value) instead of cash. A gift of cash generates a single tax benefit: a charitable income tax deduction. A gift of appreciated property generates two tax benefits: a charitable income tax deduction and avoidance of capital gains tax. The bargain sale, when used with appreciated property, results in the same double tax benefit for the "gift" portion of the transaction.

A donor should not give depreciated property. Instead, the donor should sell the depreciated property, claim a loss for tax purposes, and then donate the proceeds of the sale to charity. The same principle applies to bargain sales. A donor should not make a bargain sale with the depreciated property, but should instead sell the depreciated property for its fair market value, claim a loss for tax purposes, and then donate some portion of the proceeds of the sale to charity. A tax loss is valuable. It can be used to offset other gains and thereby reduce the taxes owed. Giving depreciated property needlessly eliminates this tax benefit.

It is usually undesirable to give debt-encumbered property to charity because the donor will be treated as having received income from the charity in the amount of the debt attached to the gifted property. In some cases, it may be possible to shift the debt to other assets so that the property gifted given to charity will have no debt encumbrances. This produces a much more attractive tax result. Let's look at an example.

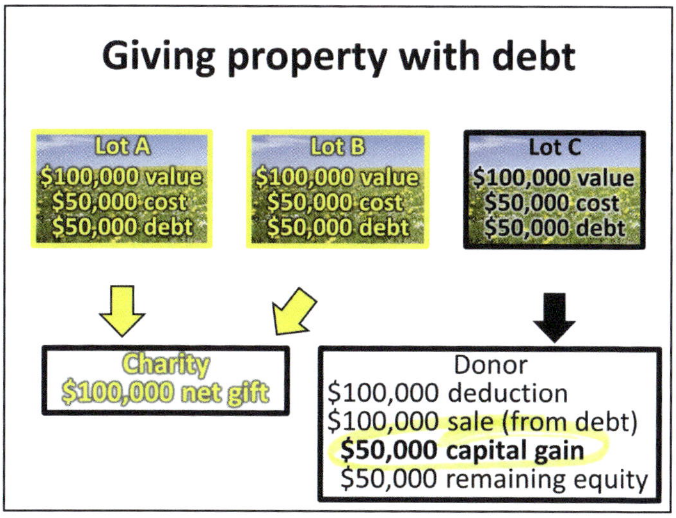

Suppose that a donor owned three pieces of land. Each property was worth $100,000, had been originally purchased for $50,000, and had a $50,000 mortgage. The donor could choose to give debt-encumbered property to the charity. However, giving debt-encumbered property to a charity is treated as a bargain sale where the donor receives debt relief in exchange for the gift. (This is true regardless of whether or not the donor actually remains liable for the debt.) Consequently, each gifted property would generate a $50,000 charitable income tax deduction ($100,000 property value - $50,000 "debt relief") and a $25,000 capital gain ($50,000 "debt relief" received – 50% of the $50,000 cost basis). In order to generate a $100,000 gift to charity, the donor would need to give two such properties, generating a $100,000 charitable income tax deduction and $50,000 of capital gain. There is, however, a much more advantageous way to make such a charitable gift if the debt attached to the properties could be shifted.

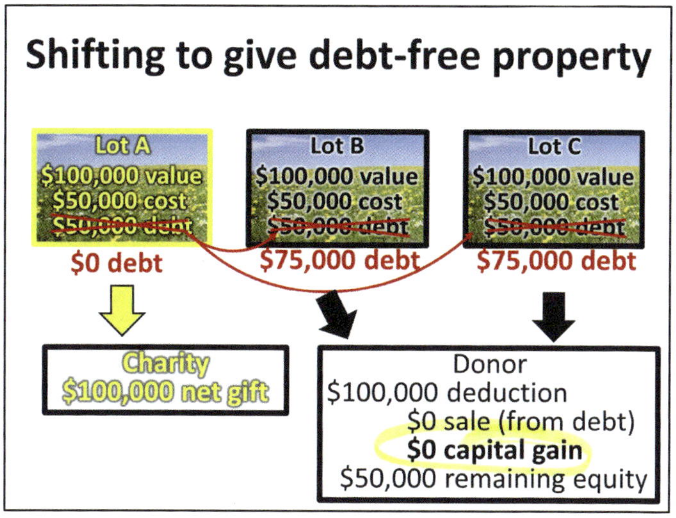

If the donor were able to transfer the debt from one property over to the remaining two properties, and then donate the single debt-free property to charity, the tax consequences are much better. (The likely process of such debt transference would be to refinance the remaining two properties to increase their debt from $50,000 to $75,000, using the proceeds from this refinancing to pay off the debt on the property to be gifted.) Gifting this debt-free property to charity results in the same $100,000 charitable income tax deduction as in the previous transaction involving the gifting of two debt-encumbered properties. It also leaves the donor with the identical $50,000 of remaining equity as in the previous transaction. The only difference is that instead of recognizing $50,000 of capital gain as in the previous transaction, the donor recognizes no capital gain from this alternative transaction. By simply altering the process for making the gift, the donor has received a substantially improved tax result.

Let's now examine a few interesting cases involving the bargain sale rules.

In the case of Browning v. Commissioner (109, T.C. 303, 1997), the taxpayer sold a conservation easement on his farm to the county for $309,000. A conservation easement prevents the land from being developed to its highest potential in order to maintain the natural or agricultural state of the land. Such conservation easements reduce the value of the land, and are, consequently, valuable property rights. The taxpayer indicated a desire to benefit the county and the county's conservation easement program in his decision to sell the conservation easement to the county for $309,000. The $309,000 sale price was based upon the standard rate at which the county agreed to pay for such conservation easements. The taxpayer obtained a qualified appraisal for his conservation easement rights of $518,000. The taxpayer claimed a charitable income tax deduction of $209,000 (i.e., $518,000 fair market value less the $309,000 sale price). The tax court ruled that this was an appropriate deduction because the donor sold a property right to the county for less than its fair market value with the intent of benefiting the county's program. (Charitable gifts include gifts to government entities as well as charitable organizations.) Note that this result happened even though the recipient organization did not necessarily believe that it was engaging in a bargain sale. The only requirements were that the donor sold the item for less than fair market value to the charity/government with the intent of benefitting the charity/government.

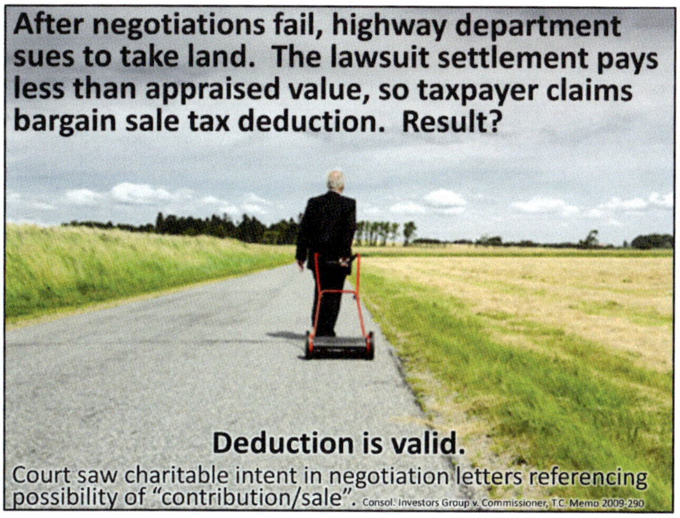

In a more extreme case (Consol. Investors Group v. Commissioner, T.C. Memo, 2009-290) a taxpayer was engaged in extended negotiations with the highway department over the sale of land to be used in the construction of a new road. These negotiations did not go well. The landowner believed the land to be worth far more than the highway department was willing to pay, and this belief was supported by an appraisal. As a result of the failure to reach an agreement, the highway department sued to take the land by force through eminent domain. In settlement of the contentious lawsuit, the taxpayer agreed to take an amount that was greater than the highway department's earlier offers but less than appraised amount. Throughout the process, the highway department strongly disagreed with the high appraisal valuation obtained by the taxpayer. Nevertheless, after settling the lawsuit, the taxpayer claimed a charitable income tax deduction for the difference between the appraised value and the amount ultimately received from the highway department. The tax court found that the taxpayer's appraisal was appropriate, meaning that the taxpayer received less than the fair market value in exchange for the land. Importantly, in the early negotiation period of this case the taxpayer had sent communication to the highway department referencing an interest in a sale or "contribution/sale". The court indicated that this communication established the donor's charitable intent in benefitting the highway department. Thus, despite the recipient's vociferous contention that they had paid fair market value and that there was no bargain sale, the taxpayer/donor was allowed to deduct the difference between the appraised value and the amount received from the government entity. This is an extreme case showing that it is not the charitable recipient's intent or belief that matters, but only that the donor sold property to the charity for less than fair market value with the intent of making a partial gift to the charitable entity.

As mentioned previously, understanding the tax consequences of bargain sale gifts serves two purposes. First, traditional bargain sales can be a useful charitable planning device. As contrasted with selling at fair market value and then making a gift out of the proceeds of the sale, a bargain sale gift can result in lower capital gain taxes. Second, other types of more complex charitable planning, such as Charitable Gift Annuities, are themselves forms of bargain sales. Thus, understanding the tax rules for bargain sales is helpful in understanding the tax consequences for these more complex transactions, because the same principles will continue to apply.

8 INTRODUCTION TO CHARITABLE GIFT ANNUITIES

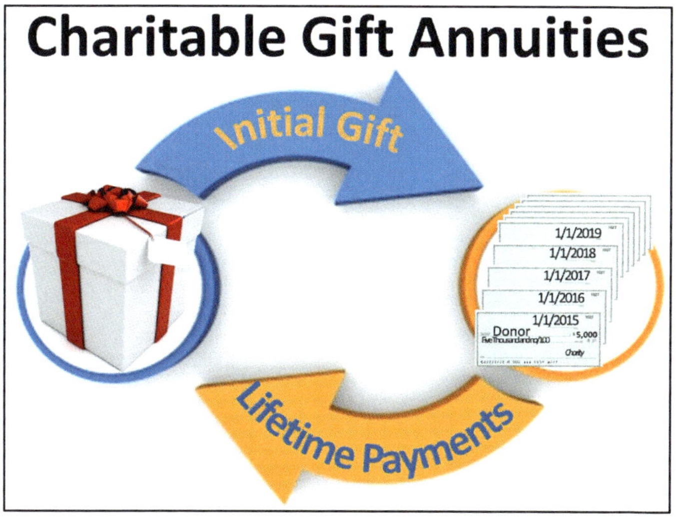

The essence of a Charitable Gift Annuity is that a donor makes a gift to a charity, and in return, the charity makes payments to the donor for life. Despite the simplicity of this concept, Charitable Gift Annuities are a powerful charitable planning vehicle that can be used in a variety of situations with donors from a wide range of economic circumstances. Like the more complex and expensive Charitable Remainder Trusts, Charitable Gift Annuities provide a source of regular payments to the donor. Also, Charitable Gift Annuities create an immediate tax deduction. Finally, when purchased with appreciated securities (or other assets), Charitable Gift Annuities provide the opportunity to defer capital gains taxes. This combination of tax advantages and income creation make Charitable Gift Annuities attractive for both donors and charities in a number of situations.

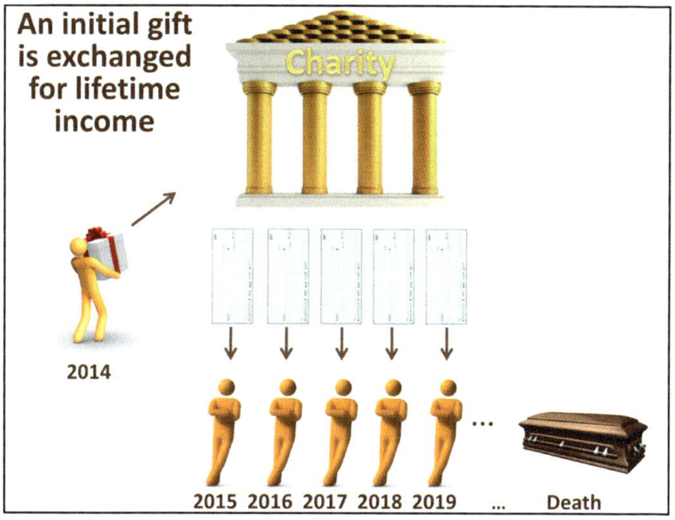

The most common form of a Charitable Gift Annuity transaction is where a donor makes a gift to a charity, and in exchange, the charity makes payments back to the donor for the donor's life. The payments can be annual, semi-annual, quarterly, monthly or even weekly. A Charitable Gift Annuity is an example of a bargain sale. A bargain sale occurs when the donor transfers a gift to a charity, and in return receives something worth less than the fair market value of the gift. In this case, the donor receives an annuity (i.e., a stream of payments for life) in exchange for a gift. The value of the annuity (as calculated by the IRS tables) must be less than 90 percent of the value of the gift. Thus, the donor makes a bargain sale, gifting money or property and in return receiving something worth less than the gift.

The lifetime payments resulting from a gift annuity are based upon the size of the gift and the age of the annuitant. (The "annuitant" is the person who receives payments for life. The annuitant is typically the donor. However, the donor could choose to purchase an annuity that pays to another person for the other person's life.) As seen in the table, an older annuitant will receive larger annual payments than a younger annuitant for the same gift. This difference exists because, on average, younger annuitants live longer and the charity will consequently have to make payments to younger annuitants for more years. The annuity payment is typically fixed for the life of the annuitant. So, for example, if a 55 year old purchased a $10,000 annuity, she would receive $400 per year for life. This $400 payment never changes. Thus, when the donor who had purchased the annuity at age 55 turned 85, she would still be receiving a $400 annual payment. (However, if she were to purchase a *new* gift annuity at age 85, it would pay a higher rate, because of her older age.) The higher payout rates at older ages helps explain why these gift annuities are most popular with older donors.

This table shows the suggested rates from the American Council on Gift Annuities for 2013. No charities are required to use these rates. However, most do. The intended goal of the American Council on Gift Annuities rates is to identify the payment level at which, on average, 50% of the face value of the initial transfer will remain with the charity at the annuitant's death. These suggested payout rates are based upon current interest rates and expected mortality. The rates can be changed every six months to reflect underlying interest rates.

This table reflects the remarkably low interest rates of 2013 when 1-year bank certificates of deposit paid about 1%. Why do gift annuities seemingly pay so much more than bank certificates of deposit? Because in a gift annuity, the donor loses the principal. A certificate of deposit generates income, but the principal is still owned by the depositor and can be withdrawn at any time. A gift annuity generates only lifetime payments. At death the payments end and there is no remaining asset in the donor's estate. Consequently, it is not appropriate to directly compare interest rates from a certificate of deposit with payout rates from a gift annuity. (Indeed, such comparisons are explicitly prohibited when marketing Charitable Gift Annuities.)

It is often wise for a charity to present more than one rate in a proposal to an individual donor. The suggested rate from the American Council on Gift Annuities could be termed the high rate (e.g., 4.0%) along with alternatives for a medium rate (e.g., 3.0%) and a low rate (e.g., 2.5%). Why would a donor voluntarily choose the medium or low rates? Because, fundamentally, the donor desires to benefit the charity and advance its cause. If the lower rate can meet the donor's income target it will generate a greater benefit for the charity (and a greater tax deduction for the donor). Many charities leave substantial gifts "on the table," by simply assuming that the donor will always want the highest rate from the charity, rather than presenting proposals that include three different rate options.

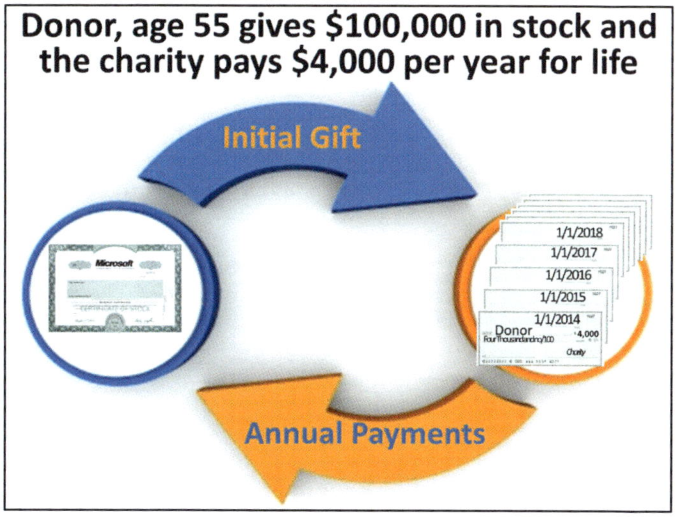

Using the previous rate table, if a donor aged 55 gave $100,000 in publicly traded securities to a charity in exchange for a Charitable Gift Annuity, the charity would make $4,000 annual payments back to the donor for the donor's life.

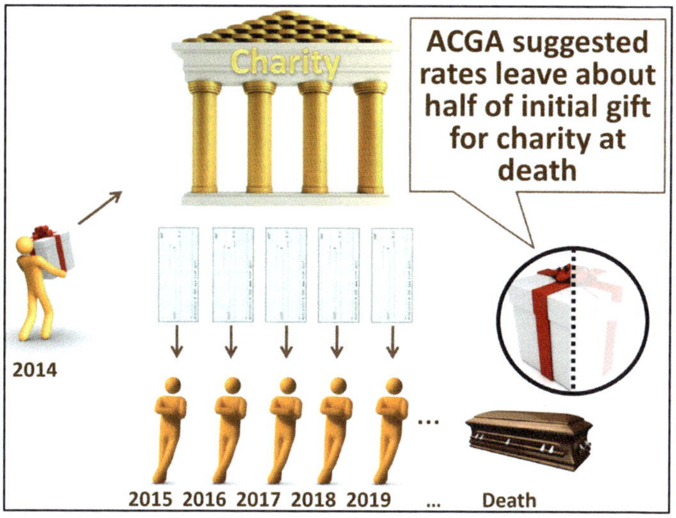

As mentioned previously, the American Council on Gift Annuities suggested rates are intended to leave half of the face value of the initial transfer available for the charity at the death of the annuitant (assuming that the charity makes the lifetime payments using interest and principle from the initial gift). This does not mean that the value of a Charitable Gift Annuity to a charity is half of the amount transferred by the donor. Although the charity is projected to receive half of the face value of the initial transfer, the charity must typically wait many years for this to occur. For example, a $10,000 gift annuity by a 30-year-old donor may be projected to ultimately result in a $5,000 residual going to the charity (after the lifetime of annuity payments are made to the donor); the charity must still wait an average of approximately 50 years to receive this $5,000 residual. The right to receive $5,000 in 50 years is worth far less than $5,000 today.

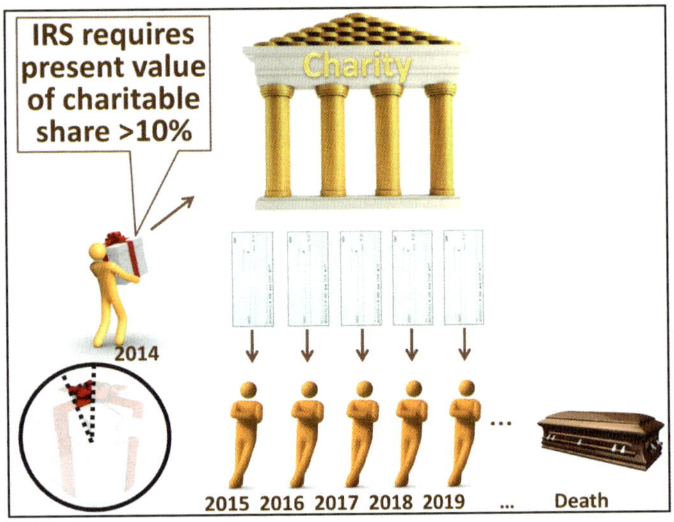

In order for a Charitable Gift Annuity to be considered a charitable arrangement for tax purposes, the annuity must be worth less than 90% of the value of the gift. This does not mean that the charity need only be projected to have a residual of more than 10% after making a lifetime of annuity payments. The projected residual amount comes to the charity only after years of waiting, so it is worth much less at the time the Charitable Gift Annuity is purchased. Returning to our previous example, the present value of an expectation of receiving $5,000 in 50 years is worth far less than $5,000 today.

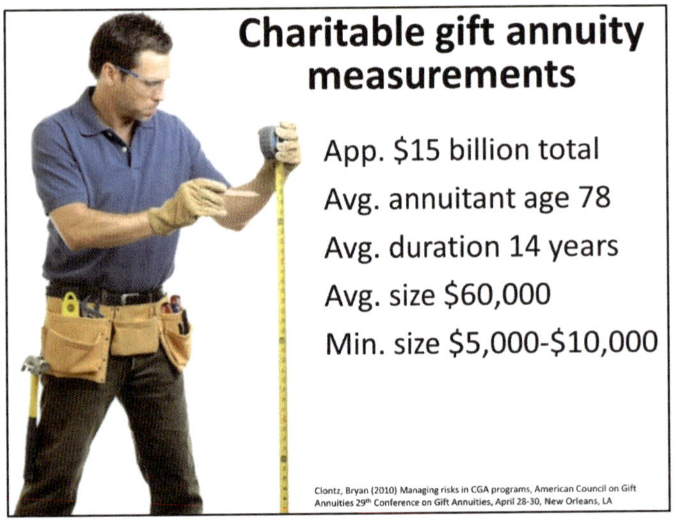

Although many Charitable Gift Annuities are relatively small, their usage is so common that, when combined, they constitute a $15 billion segment of charitable planning. The relatively small minimum size of Charitable Gift Annuities is part of the reason why they are so popular. Because gift annuities are issued by each individual charity, the minimum amounts depend upon the policies of each charity. However, it is not uncommon to find Charitable Gift Annuities available at the $5,000 or $10,000 level. This low entry level also allows hesitant donors to "experiment" with planned giving. It is not uncommon to see donors purchase a series of small Charitable Gift Annuities before increasing the size of gift annuity purchases. By giving donors experience with gifts that pay income, Charitable Gift Annuities can also serve as a gateway to more expensive and complex vehicles such as Charitable Remainder Trusts.

Data from the 2009 American Council on Gift Annuities survey of Charitable Gift Annuities shows that the average age of an annuitant at the time of making the gift was 78 years old. According to that survey, 81% of all Charitable Gift Annuities were purchased by donors aged 70 to 84. This attraction for older donors makes sense, both because of their post-retirement interest in secure lifetime payments and because of the sharp divergence between interest rates and lifetime payout rates available at older ages. In 2013, BNY Mellon Wealth Management reported that the majority of their more than 3,000 Charitable Remainder Trusts were established by donors aged 70 to 74 (See James, R. N. III & Franey, J., 2013, Trending forward: Emerging demographics driving planned giving. *National Conference on Philanthropic Planning*, Minneapolis, MN). This suggests that the peak age for Charitable Remainder Trust establishment is about five years younger than the peak age for Charitable Gift Annuity purchase. Other research suggests that the peak age for producing matured charitable bequest gift dollars is about 85 to 89 years of age (See James, R. N. III, 2013, *American Charitable Bequest Demographics, 1992-2012*). With upcoming increases in the population of older age groups, a demographic effect would be felt first in Charitable Remainder Trust establishment, second in Charitable Gift Annuity purchase, and last in matured charitable bequests.

The previous statistics establish that Charitable Gift Annuities are quite popular in charitable planning. Why? The reason for their popularity is that they are a simple way to fill a need for donors in a variety of circumstances. Let's examine some of those situations.

It can often be the case that older donors have substantial assets and would like to make major charitable contributions, but they worry that a major gift could leave them without enough assets for their lifetime needs. The worry is that he or she may outlive his or her assets. This concern can prevent the donor from making the substantial charitable gifts that he or she would like to make.

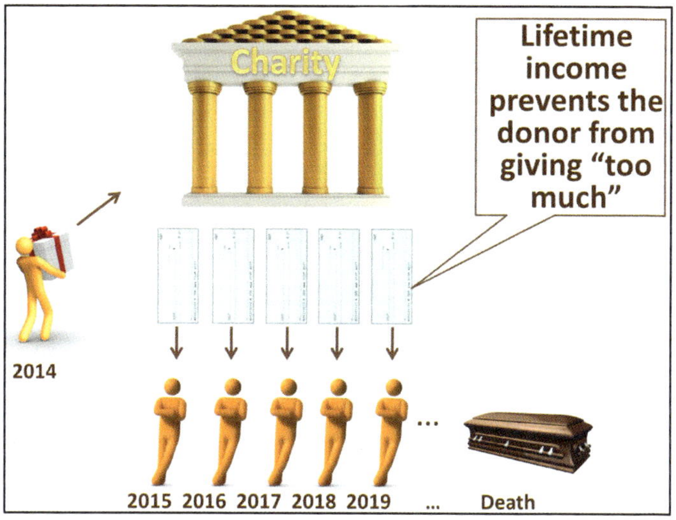

A Charitable Gift Annuity is designed to overcome this worry about outliving one's assets by providing a lifetime source of income. Where a donor might regret having made a major gift of assets if she later lived "too long" and needed those assets for regular lifetime spending, such concerns are alleviated by giving through a Charitable Gift Annuity.

The Charitable Gift Annuity may also be preferable to a simple charitable bequest because it generates immediate income tax deductions. Although understanding that annuity payment rates are not interest rates (because the donor loses the principal), if the donor is already planning to transfer the principal at death to the charity, then the Charitable Gift Annuity becomes exceptionally attractive. For example, if a donor owns a $10,000 certificate of deposit, which he has already designated a charity to receive at death, then his payments from a Charitable Gift Annuity would be more directly comparable with his interest earned on the certificate of deposit, because in either case, the charity will receive the principal at death. (Naturally, there are still differences that make this comparison inexact. For example, the donor can later choose to immediately spend the entire certificate of deposit, but with a gift annuity the donor has only a lifetime income stream.)

The Charitable Gift Annuity is also attractive for the charity because, unlike a charitable bequest, a Charitable Gift Annuity is an irrevocable gift. The charity need not worry about last minute changes to the donor's plan by the donor or nefarious heirs, because the transfer is already complete. Recent research shows that charitable plans become highly unstable in the years immediately prior to death (see James, R.N., 2013, *American Charitable Bequest Demographics: 1992-2012*). Thus, it is particularly beneficial to a charity to be able to convert revocable bequest intentions into irrevocable planned gifts, such as Charitable Gift Annuities.

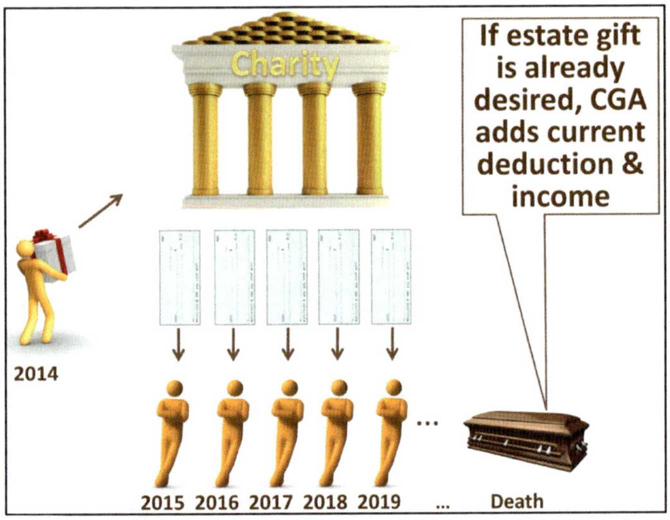

From a donor's perspective, a Charitable Gift Annuity can be preferable to leaving the same amount as a bequest gift because a bequest gift generates no income tax deduction and no lifetime payments. For a donor with the twin goals of generating lifetime income and making a post-mortem gift to a charity, the gift annuity works far better than alternative strategies such as investing and leaving a gift to the charity by will. Simply purchasing an immediate annuity from a life insurance company provides lifetime payments, but doesn't accomplish the donor's charitable goals. Similarly, writing a charity into one's will generates no income tax deductions. But, by converting that revocable bequest decision into an irrevocable Charitable Gift Annuity, the donor benefits the charity and generates immediate income tax benefits and lifetime income, making the gift annuity an attractive option.

Charitable Gift Annuities can also have advantages over more complex and expensive planned giving vehicles. If a donor is specifically concerned about having lifetime income that won't change or run out, the Charitable Gift Annuity can be an ideal charitable planning option. A charitable remainder unitrust can make payments for life, but the amount of each payment depends upon the return of the underlying investments. This risk could be diversified using a pooled income fund, but the payments will still vary with market fluctuations. A charitable remainder annuity trust makes fixed payments for life. However, if the investments in the charitable remainder annuity trust perform poorly, the trust can run out of money, causing the annual payments to stop.

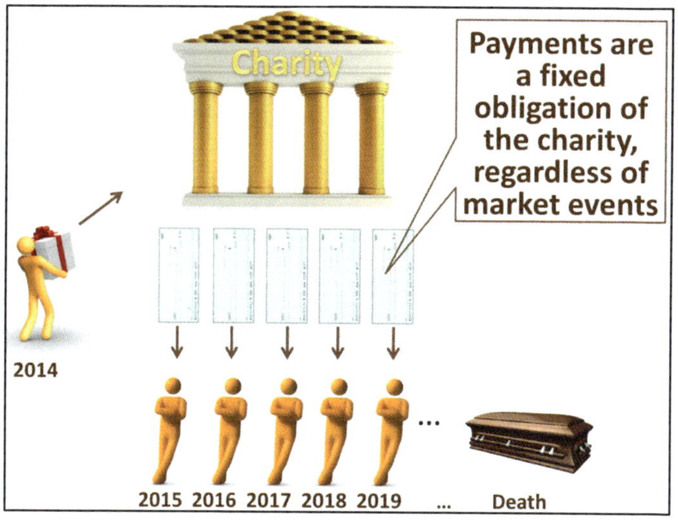

In contrast, the Charitable Gift Annuity payments are a fixed obligation of the charity, which must be paid regardless of investment returns or market events. So long as the charity continues to exist, the gift annuity payments must be made.

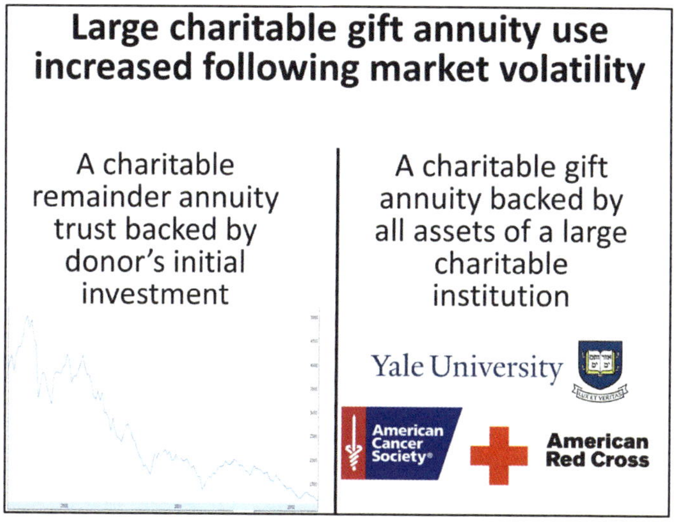

The security provided by Charitable Gift Annuities can be more attractive in times of market volatility. Traditionally, Charitable Gift Annuities have been considered primarily "small dollar" vehicles. However, following substantial market drops during the most recent financial crisis, the number of multimillion dollar Charitable Gift Annuities increased notably. The attraction of the Charitable Gift Annuity issued by a financially stable nonprofit is its ultimate security. Considering that, historically, major universities and churches have outlived successive generations of businesses and governments, some gift annuities may provide an exceptional level of security. Although other charitable planning vehicles, such as the Charitable Remainder Trust, provide opportunities for influencing investment choices, they are also exposed to investment risk. When attention to investment risk is high (such as following a market crash) the attraction of the guaranteed gift annuity payments increase as compared with the risk of a Charitable Remainder Trust.

Another reason Charitable Gift Annuities are so popular is that they are the simplest and easiest way to participate in charitable planning that produces both a tax deduction and income for the donor. Charitable Gift Annuities are the simplest way for fundraisers to respond to the common statement from donors that "I wish I could do more, but…" Charitable Gift Annuities offer a way for donors to make a gift and provide a payment stream for other needs, such as college tuition or retirement income. And yet the transaction can be as simple as writing a check and signing a one-page standard agreement from the charity.

If the enormous flexibility available with Charitable Remainder Trusts can be thought of as the paint palette of an artist, then the Charitable Gift Annuity is like the reliable number 2 pencil. Charitable Gift Annuities are simple and cheap for donors. There are no donor costs for setup or administration and the minimum investment amount is commonly only $5,000 or $10,000. Each Charitable Gift Annuity agreement with a particular charity is typically identical except for the donor's age, the payment rate and the amount of the gift. In contrast, Charitable Remainder Trusts are usually hand-crafted documents specifically designed for the individual donor and his or her particular desires. This enormous flexibility comes at a cost, both for the initial creation of the Charitable Remainder Trust and for annual administration. Because of these costs, the minimum feasible amount for a Charitable Remainder Trust is normally 10 times that of a Charitable Gift Annuity. Of course, there are significant potential advantages to using a Charitable Remainder Trust that are not available with Charitable Gift Annuities that can, in many cases, warrant the added expense for the donor. One solution is not universally better than the other; both can fit the specific needs in different circumstances.

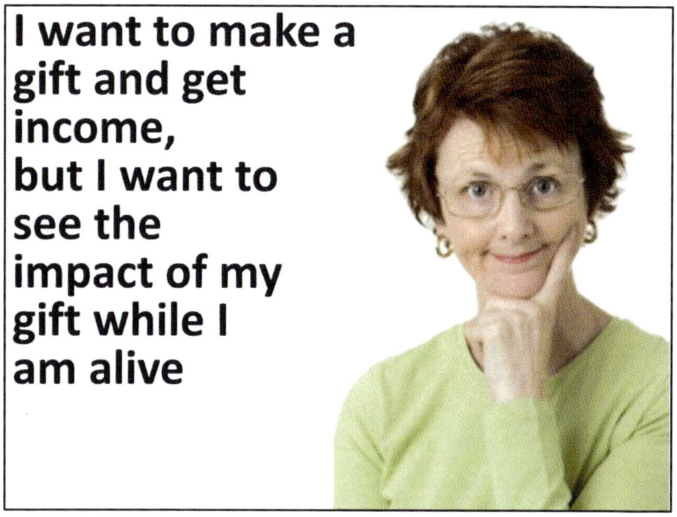

To this point we have been comparing Charitable Gift Annuities with leaving a charitable bequest. This anticipates a scenario in which the charity holds the initial gift amount, makes payments to the donor for life, and then only after the death of the donor takes the remaining amount of the gift to use for charitable purposes. However, the charity is not required to take this conservative approach (except in the State of New Hampshire). A charity could instead calculate the share of the gift that would normally be needed to make the lifetime payments and immediately spend the remaining amount. For a charity that chose to do this, the donor would be able to see the impact of his or her gift immediately. For some donors, this could be an especially attractive feature, especially when compared to a bequest gift where the donor would not be alive to see its impact.

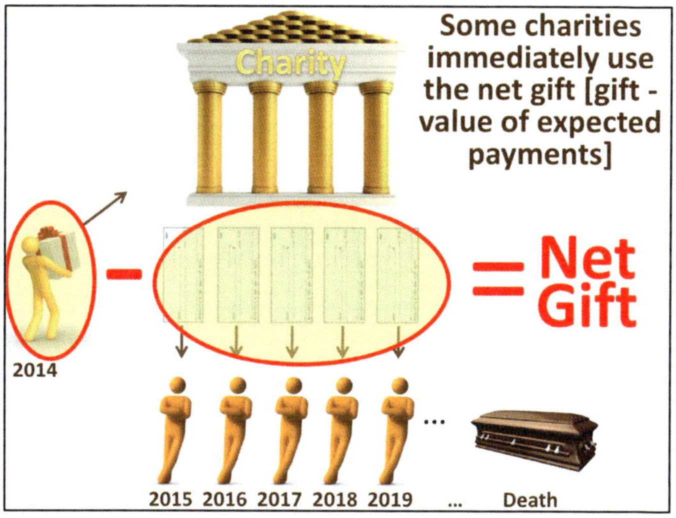

To make an immediate use of Charitable Gift Annuity funds, the charity spends the projected gift portion of the transaction. Calculating this projected gift portion involves estimating the donor's longevity and the charity's investment returns. Consequently, there is some risk involved if the projections are in error. This risk explains why not all charities engage in this practice of immediately using the projected gift portion of Charitable Gift Annuity funds. Nevertheless, it is an available option to charities in most states.

Note that in Florida, Tennessee, Washington, Hawaii, New Jersey, and Wisconsin the charity must hold the amount projected for the donor's payments plus a 10% cushion. In New York the cushion amount is at least 10%, and may be higher. Even in these jurisdictions, however, making immediate use of part of the Charitable Gift Annuity is permitted. In other jurisdictions, the charity could choose to immediately use even more than the projected "gift portion," although this creates a future net liability for the organization.

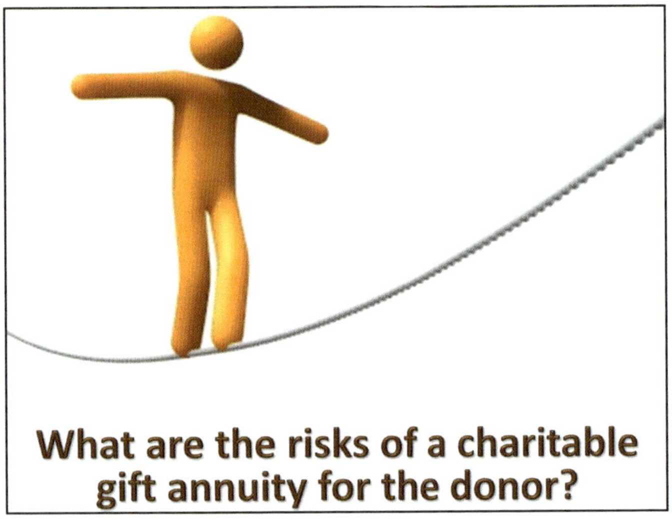

To this point we have been reviewing some of the features and benefits of the Charitable Gift Annuity. However, there are also some risks involved with the Charitable Gift Annuity. First, let's examine the risks for the donor.

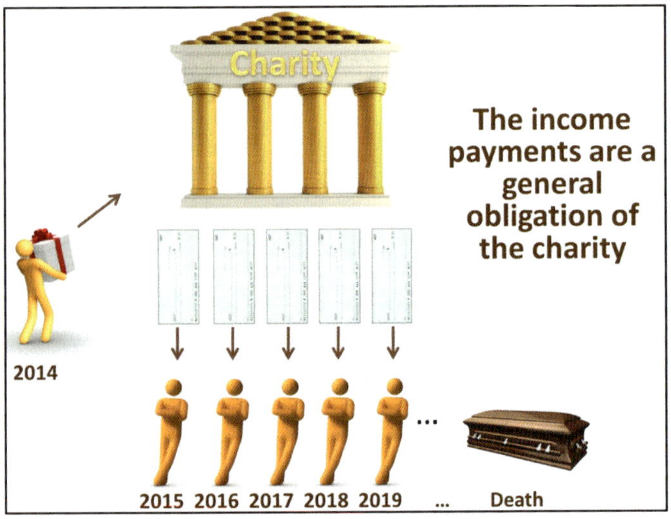

The annuity payments come from the charity. The charity is required to make these payments and they are a general obligation of the charity. So long as the charity survives, the donor need not be concerned with market crashes and other investment worries.

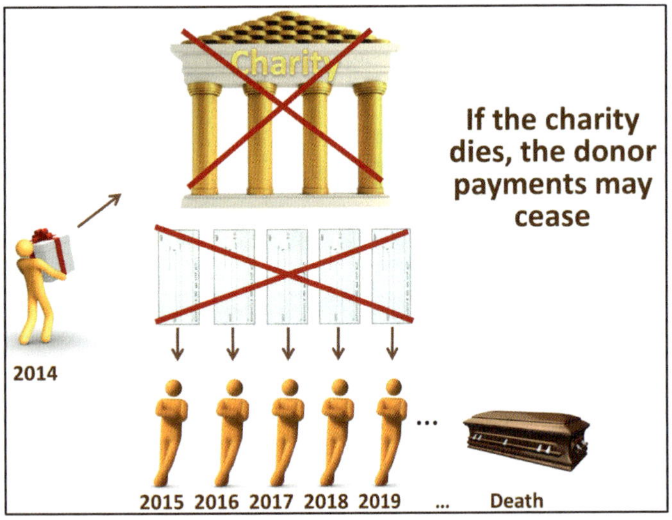

However, if the charity goes bankrupt, the donor payments may cease or be reduced. Thus, the primary risk for the donor is that the charity would be unable to make its payments in the future. As a general obligation of the charity there may be no specific assets that can be attached in the event of a bankruptcy. Although some charities have, and a few states require, segregated reserve funds, this segregation may not be sufficient to prevent other creditors from having a claim on the funds. Additionally, such segregated funds may also deplete due to poor investment decisions.

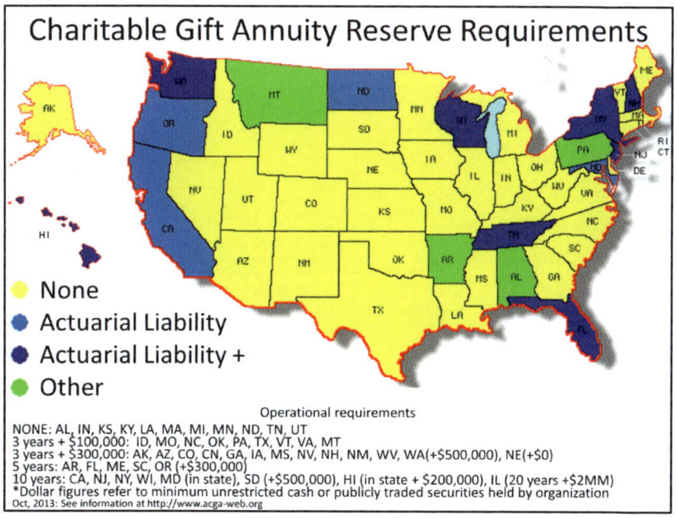

Compared with the field of commercial annuities issued by insurance companies, Charitable Gift Annuities are remarkably unregulated. As shown by this map, the majority of states have no reserve requirements for nonprofits issuing Charitable Gift Annuities. This means that a charity operating in one of the states working with a donor in one of these states could choose to immediately spend 100% of the amount given for the Charitable Gift Annuity and simply leave the payments as an unfunded obligation for the future. Several states have operating requirements such that a charity issuing Charitable Gift Annuities must have been in operation for a minimum number of years and have a minimum amount of unrestricted cash (or cash equivalents such as publicly-traded securities). Unrestricted cash, however, does not mean that there are no creditor obligations on the cash only that it is money that has not been temporarily or permanently restricted by a donor. Further, these requirements for unrestricted cash are fixed dollar amounts that do not vary, regardless of the number or amount of Charitable Gift Annuities being issued by the nonprofit. In essence, these operational requirements simply limit gift annuity issuance to charities that are not brand new and have at least a little money in the bank. Note that in states like Indiana, Kansas, Kentucky, Louisiana, Massachusetts, Michigan, and Minnesota, there are neither operational requirements nor reserve requirements. This means that a nonprofit could be created one day, start issuing Charitable Gift Annuities the next day, and then immediately spend 100% of the amount given for all Charitable Gift Annuities. Obviously, such a scenario entails substantial risk for the donor. At the same time, Charitable Gift Annuities issued by large stable nonprofits may be among the most secure lifetime payment streams available. However, the lack of regulation in some areas creates a "Wild West" scenario in which the donor must do some investigation to understand the risks involved.

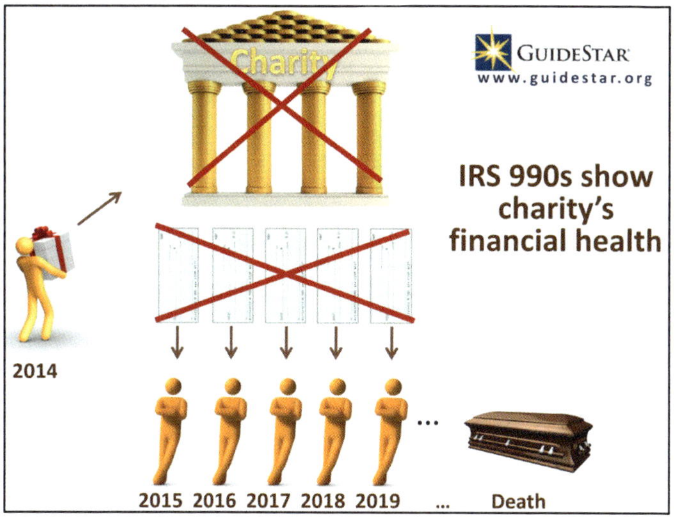

One way to investigate the financial condition of a charity is to examine the IRS form 990 for the charity. The IRS form 990 contains financial information about the charity, including assets, liabilities, income, and expenditures. Charities are required to provide these forms to anyone who requests them. Additionally, these forms are available from a number of websites for no charge. Some of the websites that currently post IRS form 990s are

- www.guidestar.org (free registration required)
- foundationcenter.org/findfunders/990finder/
- nccs.urban.org/ (click on "find an organization")
- www.eri-nonprofit-salaries.com/index.cfm (click on "Search Form 990s")

Given the complexity of reading and understanding financial statements, this is an area where a financial advisor could be particularly helpful to a donor.

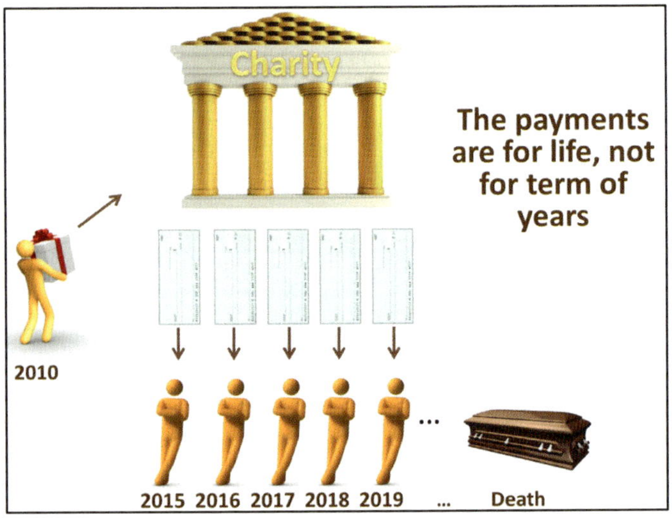

Unlike some commercial annuity products, Charitable Gift Annuities do not offer payments for a fixed term of years or a minimum guaranteed number of years. Instead, Charitable Gift Annuity payments are for life only. This is not due to the lack of willingness of charities, rather the IRS tax code penalizes charities for offering other varieties of gift annuities, even though these may be available from commercial annuity providers.

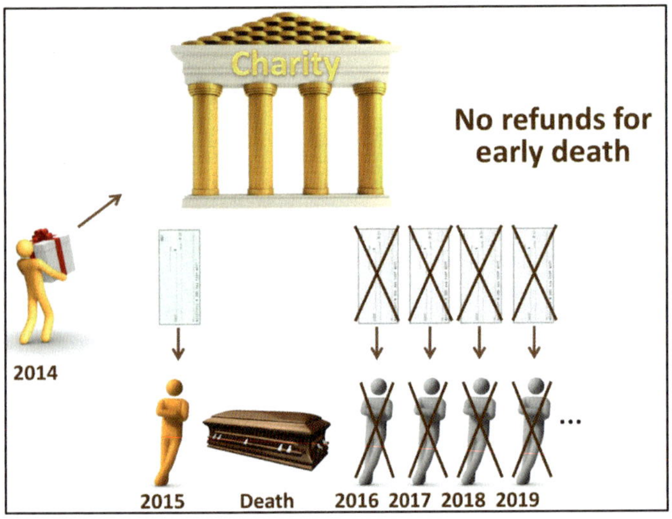

One risk in purchasing a gift annuity that makes payments for life is that the annuitant could die immediately after purchasing the annuity. Unfortunately for the annuitant, there are no refunds for early death, nor are charities allowed to offer gift annuities with guaranteed minimum payment amounts or with a fixed number of payment years. From a financial perspective, there is a clear risk in that the donor may receive very few benefits prior to death. However, if the donor's goal was to make a large gift to charity (but not risk outliving his or her assets), then the risk of receiving few payments is of less concern as the donor's goals will still be achieved.

To this point we have been considering the simplest and most common form of a gift annuity where the donor makes a gift and in return receives lifetime payments from the charity. Although a charity is not allowed to offer annuities with a guaranteed return in the event of premature death or annuities paying for a set number of years, the tax code does permit a few other gift annuities variations. (Note that if a charity were to offer gift annuities with terms outside of approved variations, the charity would be required to pay taxes on income earned from the gift annuities as unrelated business income tax, thus making them highly undesirable charitable giving vehicles.)

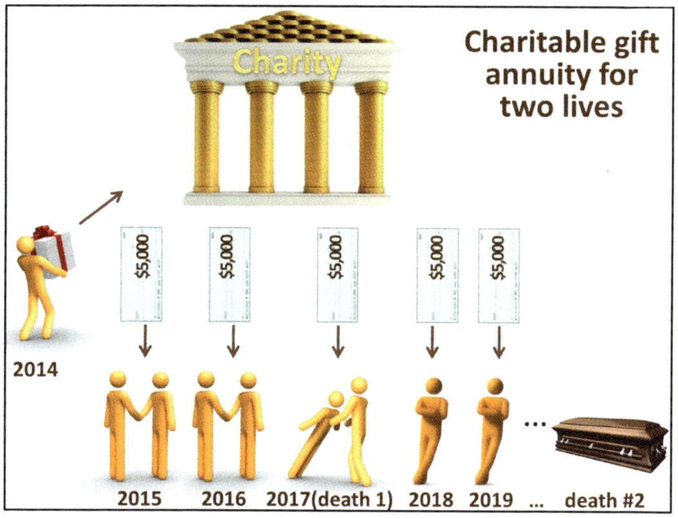

The most common variation on the traditional gift annuity is the gift annuity that pays for two lives. This means that the annuity payments will continue to be made until the death of the last of the two individuals to die. (The payment is not reduced at the death of the first to die of the two annuitants.) Most commonly, these gift annuities pay for the lives of the donor and the donor's spouse. However, there are no requirements that either annuitant be related to the donor. A gift annuity cannot, however, pay for more than two lives. Nor, can it pay for the life of someone who is not yet born (e.g., "pay for my life and the life of my first child if he or she is born before my death").

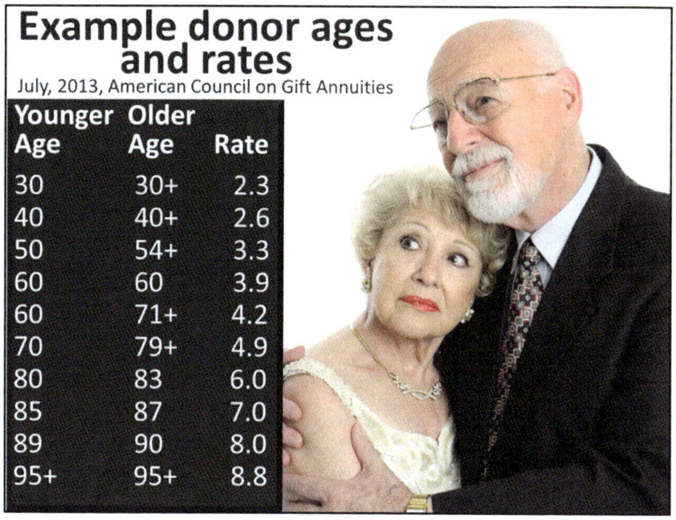

Younger Age	Older Age	Rate
30	30+	2.3
40	40+	2.6
50	54+	3.3
60	60	3.9
60	71+	4.2
70	79+	4.9
80	83	6.0
85	87	7.0
89	90	8.0
95+	95+	8.8

The American Council on Gift Annuities also issues suggested rates for these two-life annuities. As before, these rates vary depending upon prevailing interest rates and the ages of the two annuitants. The full table is much larger than for single life annuities, given the wider range of age combinations possible. This excerpt provides a few examples from that table.

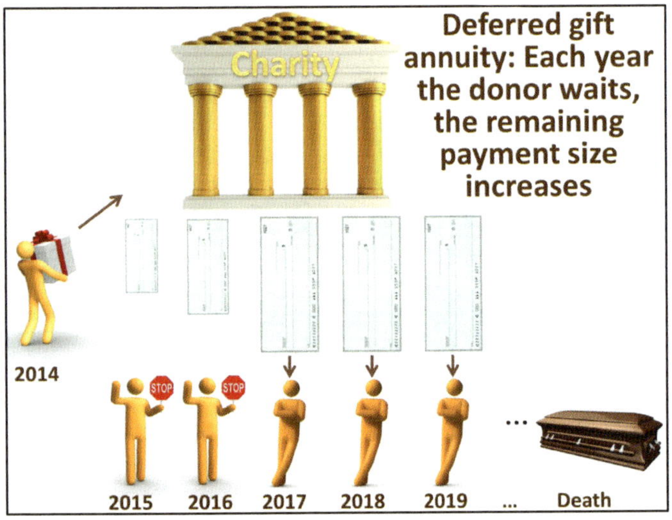

One particularly attractive variation of the standard gift annuity is the deferred gift annuity. If the donor does not need the income payments to begin immediately, the donor may choose to postpone the start of the annuity payments. Each year the donor postpones the start of the annuity payments will increase the size of the remaining payments. This may be helpful for donors who wish to make an immediate transfer, receive an immediate tax deduction, but postpone income until some future year, such as the start of retirement. The donor can either establish in advance when the annuity will begin or can decide each year whether or not to begin the annuity in that particular year (this is sometimes called a "flexible annuity", see PLR 9743054).

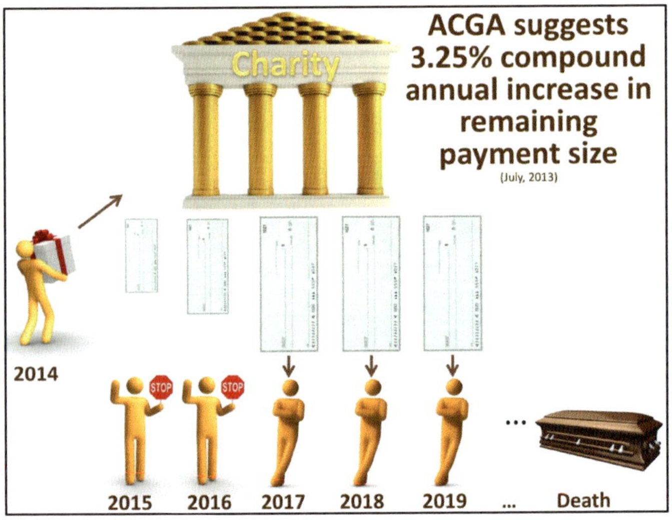

The essence of a deferred Charitable Gift Annuity is that if the donor postpones the start of the annuity payments, each remaining payment will become larger. The American Council on Gift Annuities suggests a compounding rate which incorporates current interest rates and the reduced longevity of the annuitant. If a compounding rate is so high that it increases the overall value of the annuity beyond the simple immediate annuity, it will reduce the available tax deduction.

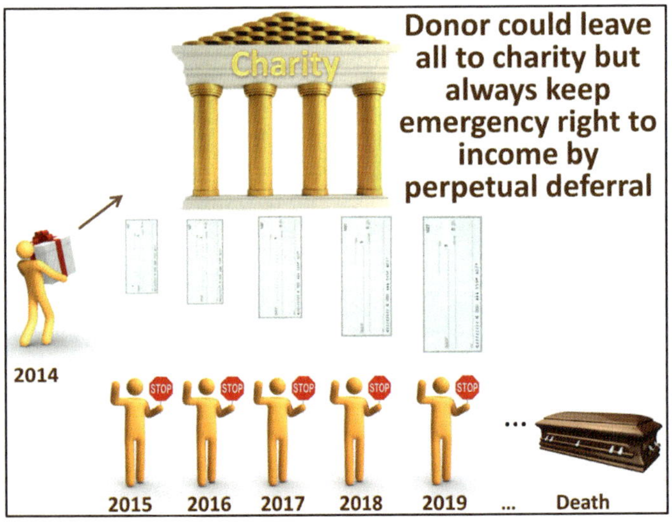

The deferred or flexible gift annuity also creates the opportunity for a donor to make a gift, but retain an "emergency" right to receive payments. This can be helpful with a donor who does not anticipate ever needing the payments, but who nevertheless feels insecure about making the gift because of unknown possibilities. The donor can choose to postpone the payments indefinitely and, at death, the charity would receive the entirety of the initial gift. Although the amount transferred to the charity is the same as could have been transferred through a bequest, this transaction allows for an immediate income tax deduction and also allows the charity to make immediate use of a portion of the initial gift.

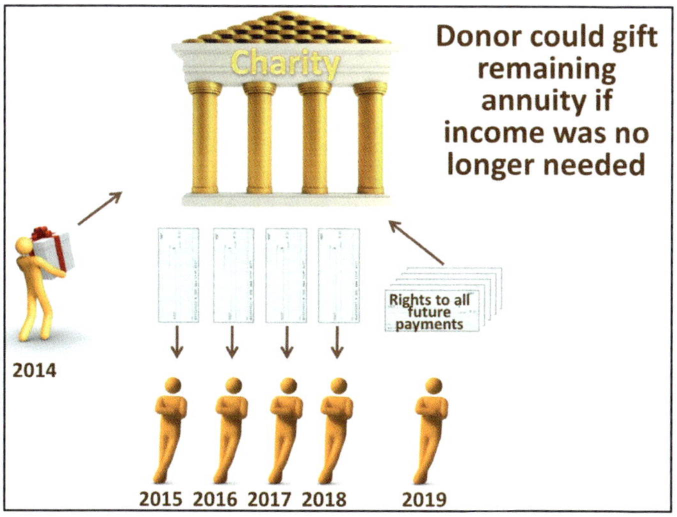

If a donor purchased a gift annuity and then later found that he or she no longer needed the annuity payments, the donor could gift the rights to all future payments to the charity and potentially receive an income tax deduction for that gift. This could be more tax efficient than receiving each check (which counts, at least in part, as income) and then gifting it back to the charity (which creates a deduction that may or may not completely offset the income, depending upon a variety of factors such as the amount of other itemized deductions, adjusted gross income level, and so forth).

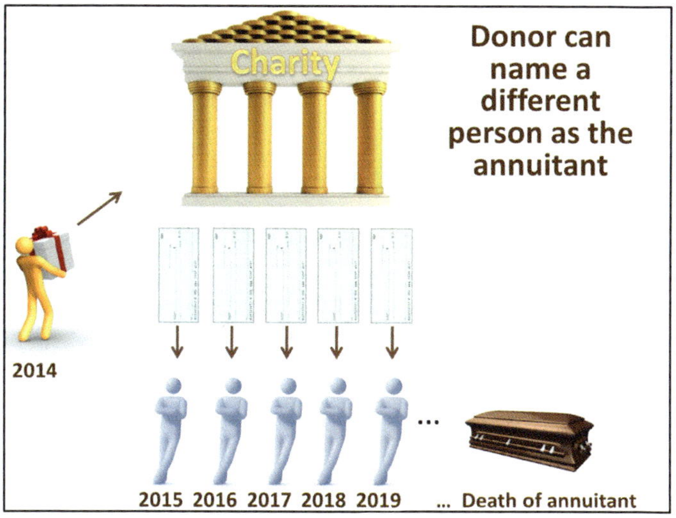

The typical Charitable Gift Annuity makes lifetime payments to the donor. However, the donor may instead select someone else to receive payments as the annuitant. This is a potentially taxable gift, so for a donor whose estate is large enough to be concerned with estate taxes, such gift tax considerations must be considered. (Although, as discussed later, such gift taxes can be reduced by the annual present interest exclusion because gifts of immediate annuities are considered to be gifts of present interests.)

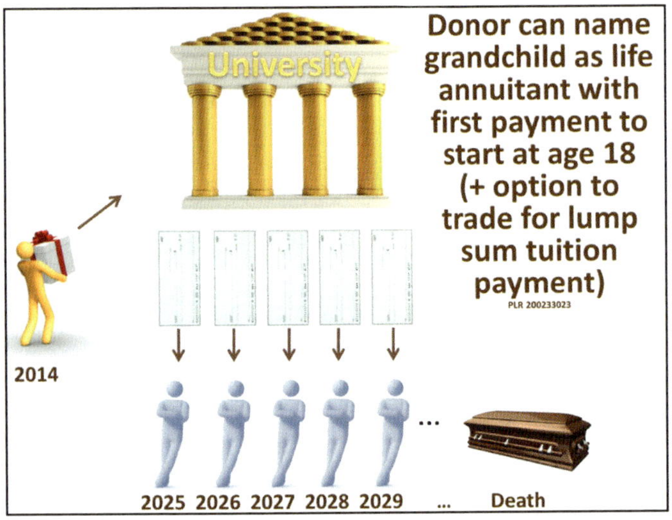

One creative variation on a Charitable Gift Annuity allowed a donor to name his grandchild as the life annuitant with the lifetime payments to begin at age 18. This particular annuity had an additional provision that allowed the grandchild to trade the lifetime income for an equivalent lump-sum tuition payment at the donor's alma mater. Because the annuity was issued by the donor's alma mater, this created an attractive incentive for the grandchild and a potential double benefit for the university.

We have discussed the risks for the donor in purchasing a Charitable Gift Annuity (consisting largely of the risk that the charity would go bankrupt or the annuitant would die too quickly). However, given the nature of the obligation to make lifetime payments, there are also substantial risks for charities that issue Charitable Gift Annuities.

A primary risk for the charity is that the annuitant may live much longer than projected. The charity is obligated to continue making payments for the life of the annuitant, regardless of how long the annuitant lives. A Charitable Gift Annuity that would have provided a substantial gift if the annuitant had lived to his life expectancy may instead generate a net loss for the charity if the annuitant lives far longer.

The primary protection for this type of risk is to have a large pool of annuitants with similar sized annuities. Although some will live many years beyond their life expectancy, others will

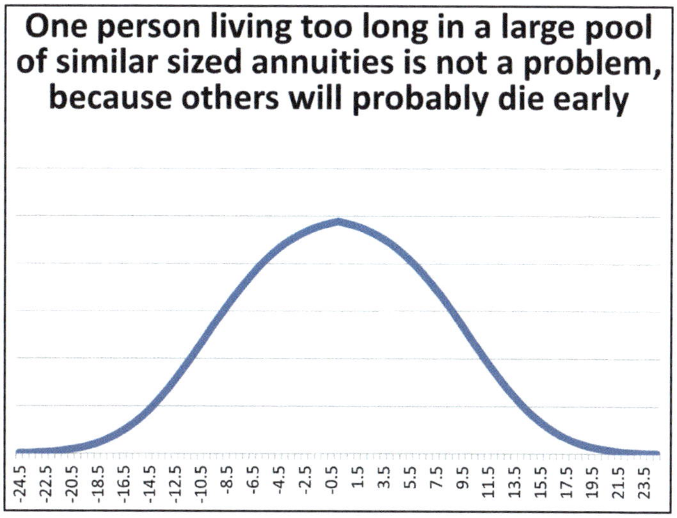

die sooner than their life expectancy and, on average, the lifetime payments should approximate life expectancies. The risk that one annuitant will outlive his life expectancy by 10 years is significant, but the risk that a pool of 10,000 annuitants will outlive their life expectancies by, on average, 10 years is very low.

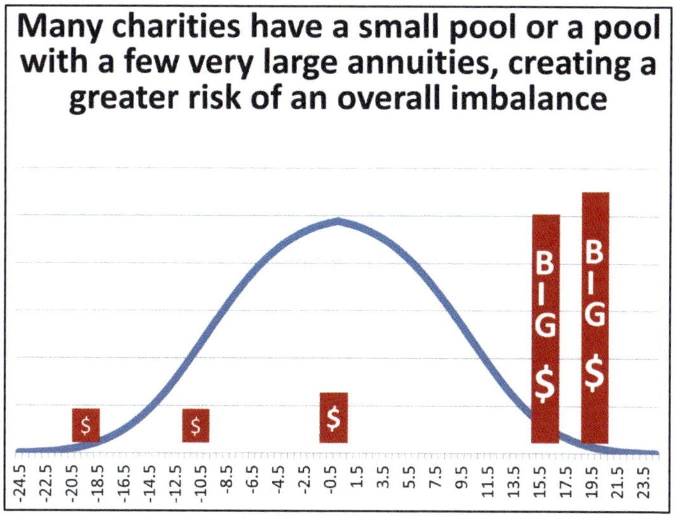

Many charities do not have the protection against longevity risk that comes from having a large pool of annuitants receiving similar sized annuities. This can occur either because the charity has a small pool of annuitants, or because the charity's pool contains a few very large annuities. A large pool of small annuities will not offset the risk of a few very large annuities. Suppose, for example, a charity has 1,000 annuities paying $1,000 per year and one annuity paying $1 million per year. The risk that the annuitant receiving $1 million per year will live longer than anticipated will not be offset by the early deaths of other annuitants because of the differential in the annuity sizes.

Longevity risk can also be influenced by the age of the donors when purchasing gift annuities. This is an area where the relative risk may be counterintuitive. Using standard payout rates, starting an annuity for an 80-year-old donor is actually riskier than starting one for a 40-year-old donor. This may seem odd, because of the expectation that the 80-year-old person will certainly not, on average, live as long as the 40-year-old. However, it is important to keep in mind that the payments to the 80-year-old are much larger than those for the 40-year-old. Keeping this in mind, why is the annuity for the older annuitant riskier?

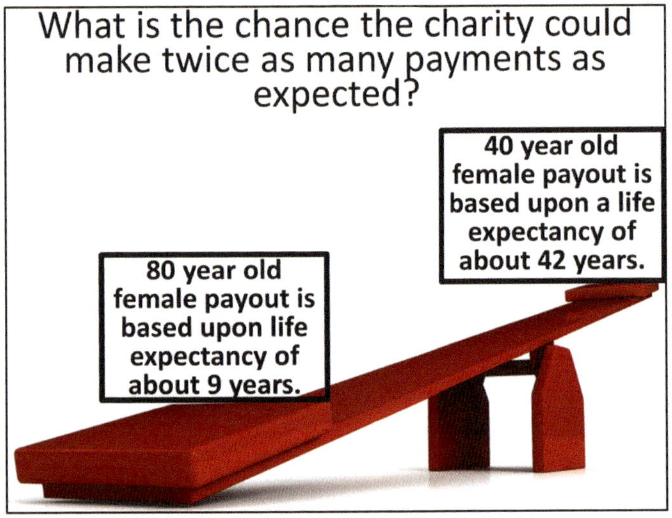

To understand why starting an annuity for the older annuitant is riskier (i.e., subject to greater variation), it helps to ask the question, "What is the chance the charity could make twice as many payments as initially projected?" The payout for an 80-year-old female is based upon a life expectancy of about nine years. If the 80-year-old female lived to the age of 98, the charity would make twice as many payments as projected. The potential for an 80-year-old to live to the age of 98 is quite significant. The payout for a 40-year-old female is based upon a life expectancy of 42 years. In order for the charity to make twice as many payments as projected, this annuitant would have to live to be 124 years old, which at present is essentially impossible. Thus, in comparison, the charity is far more likely to make twice as many payments as projected to the older annuitant, reflecting the greater risk (variance) with this annuity.

A charity can increase the risk that gift annuity obligations will ultimately siphon money from regular operating income by immediately using the projected gift portion of the Charitable Gift Annuity. This is inherently risky because the annuitants in the charity's pool will live longer than expected approximately half of the time, meaning that the charity has a 50% chance of having to make annuity payments from operating income in the future. This 50-50 chance is increased dramatically if the longevity tables used by the charity to calculate its payment obligations are inappropriate. For tax calculation purposes, the IRS requires the use of its tables based upon standard longevity expectations. However, these tables do not reflect the longevity expectations of people who buy annuities. First, people who are sick or know that they are approaching death do not buy annuities. By eliminating these people who are near death, the pool of individuals who purchase annuities will, on average, live longer than others of the same age. Second, people who are poor do not purchase annuities. Those who are poor do not, on average, live as long as those who are wealthy. Once again, this eliminates a group of individuals with relatively shorter life expectancies from the pool of individuals who purchase annuities. Finally, individuals who make charitable gifts tend to live longer than individuals who do not. Once again, the life expectancy of the pool of those who purchase Charitable Gift Annuities is much longer than the life expectancy of the population in general. Thus, a charity that removed the "gift portion" of a Charitable Gift Annuity as calculated by the IRS, should not expect to be able to cover the annuity payments from the remaining amount. (For a discussion of appropriate estimations of Charitable Gift Annuity life expectancies see Clontz, B. *The Methuselah effect: Longevity's impact on planned giving.* The National Conference on Philanthropic Planning, 2010.)

A charity can choose to issue a gift annuity in exchange for any type of valuable property. However, the gift

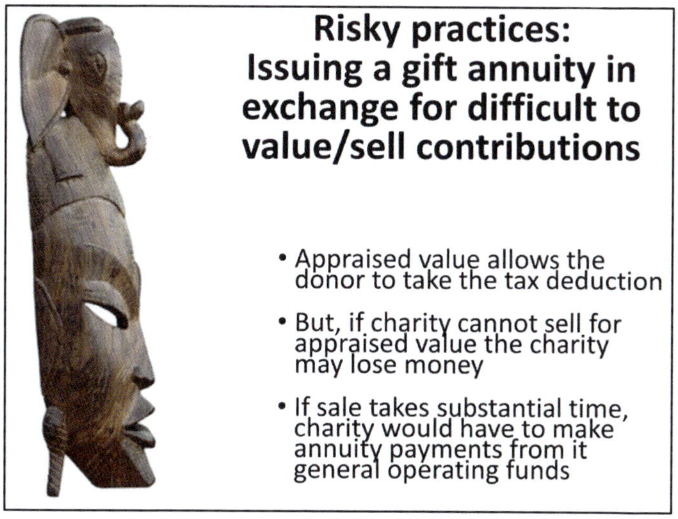

annuity is a risky proposition for the charity if the charity accepts difficult-to-value or difficult-to-sell property in exchange for the annuity. In the case of a simple gift of such property, the charity may get more or less than the appraised value, but the charity still gets some value. However, if the charity exchanges the property for a gift annuity, and later sells the property for less that its originally appraised value, then the charity may have given an annuity worth more than the gift. In other words, the charity can easily lose money on such transactions. Even if the charity is ultimately able to sell the property for its appraised value, if this sale takes some time, the charity will have to make annuity payments from its general operating income for some time. For these reasons, few charities will accept difficult-to-value or difficult-to-sell property in exchange for a gift annuity.

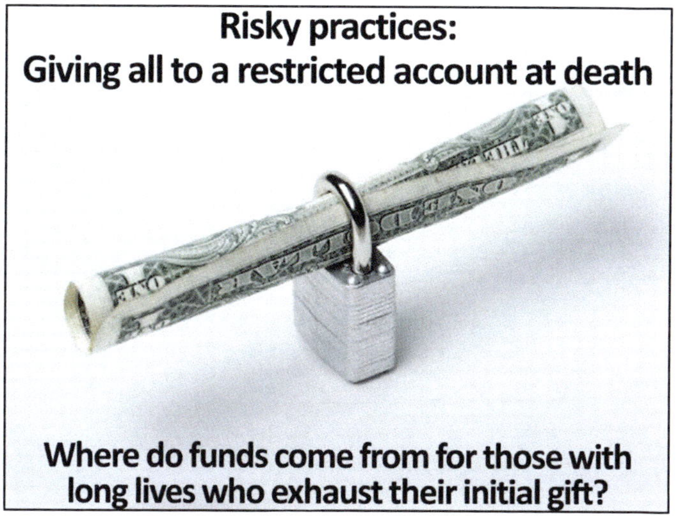

Another practice that increases the likelihood that a charity will ultimately have to make annuity payments from current income is allowing Charitable Gift Annuities to benefit a specific department or project within the charity. There is usually no problem with this practice if the charity holds the initial funds in the restricted account until the annuitant dies, but there can be. The question this raises is "Where do the funds come from for those annuities where the annuitant lives so long that the entire initial contribution is exhausted?" Will the targeted department or project have to make these payments from its operating income? If the payments come from the general annuity pool, then the general pool receives only the penalty from long lives (which are not paid for by the funds from the restricted purpose), but none of the benefit from shorter lives (which benefits the specific restricted purpose as required by accepting the donor's restrictions). Ultimately, this creates a net transfer from general unrestricted funds to the specific department or project funds over and above the donor's restriction. Although accepting such restricted purpose Charitable Gift Annuities may still be a wise fundraising strategy, the charity must recognize the potential for this secondary drain on funds available for unrestricted, general purposes.

To this point we have been discussing primarily the risk that a donor will live longer than expected. However, the charity may also have investment risk. When issuing a Charitable Gift Annuity, the charity takes a large sum of money upfront, and uses it to pay annual payments for a long period of time. This involves investing the upfront sum of money.

As the charity increases the risk for its investments, it increases the risk that those investments will perform poorly, ultimately requiring the charity to make annuity payments out of current operating income. To reduce investment risk to a minimum, a charity could invest in only secure fixed income investments of appropriate duration to closely match the payment obligations. Of course, as risk diminishes so too does the expected return and consequently the expected amount remaining at the death of the annuitant. Some charities invested their gift annuity pools heavily or entirely in equities during good times, and subsequently pulled out of equities following a market crash, resulting in gift annuity pools with net liabilities to the organization.

It is important to note that investment duration also plays a role in investment risk for annuity payments. For example, charities that issued gift annuities during a high interest rate environment, and then "conservatively" invested in secure *short-term* fixed income investments, were later faced with making these high annuity payments when interest rates for short-term fixed income investments had fallen dramatically. If instead the charity had invested in secure fixed income investments that matched the duration of the expected annuity payments, then subsequent changes in interest rates would not have caused problems. Essentially, the charity would have locked in the high interest rate investments at the same time the charity made the high interest rate commitment.

These sources of risk do not suggest that charities should avoid issuing gift annuities, because these risks are all manageable. An investment portfolio can be constructed to match the annuity payment obligations subject to the charity's risk/reward preferences.

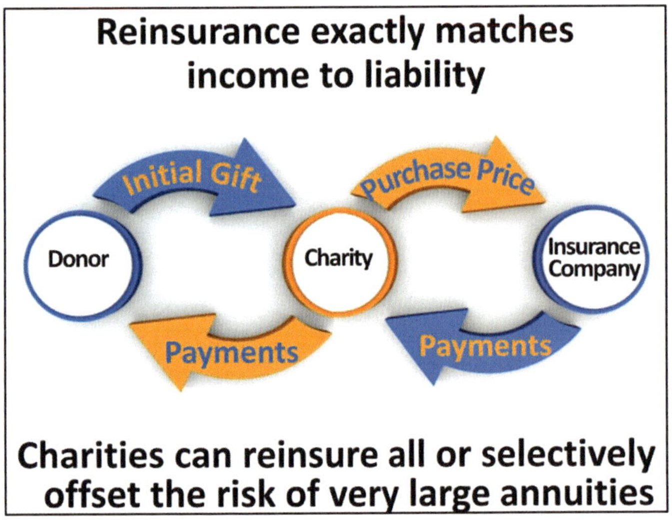

Of course, the "perfect match" for the annuity payment obligation is a commercial annuity. In this case, the charity simply purchases an annuity on the annuitant's life from an insurance company. Assuming the stability of the insurance company, the charity transfers all market risk, interest rate risk, and annuitant longevity risk. The charity simply becomes a conduit through which the insurance company annuity payments are made. Because the Charitable Gift Annuity includes a gift portion, there is enough money to purchase the commercial annuity and have funds remaining for charitable purposes. Additionally, by purchasing these commercial annuities the charity may immediately use the remaining funds. (This is true in all jurisdictions. Even those States with gift annuity reserve requirements recognize that there are no reserves needed where a commercial annuity substitute has been purchased.) The downside to this transaction is that the price of a commercial annuity includes not only the cost of making the payments, but also a profit for the issuing company. Thus, in theory, the charity could retain this profit margin by managing its own gift annuity pool. However, in practice, this may be difficult because managing a pool appropriately requires both expertise and a sufficiently large number of annuitants to reduce unexpected longevity risk. Even a charity that does not reinsure all of its gift annuities may appropriately consider reinsuring only its very large annuities. Remember that a large pool of small annuities will not be sufficient to offset the longevity risk for a small number of very large annuities. In this case, the only way for a charity to manage the risk that an annuitant with a very large annuity will live much longer than expected is to purchase a commercial annuity for that obligation, because there are simply not enough other large annuities in the charity's pool to offset the risk.

Financial advisors can become involved with Charitable Gift Annuities in a number of ways. As mentioned above, managing a gift annuity pool requires expertise to match the obligations with the investments and the charity's risk/reward preferences. This is precisely the kind of expertise that a financial advisor may bring to a charity. Additionally, a financial advisor can be helpful to a charity in managing its risk not only through appropriate investments, but also through the purchase of matching commercial annuities, either selectively for very large gift annuities, or universally for all gift annuities. Financial advisors can also be helpful to their clients who are considering gift annuities by examining the financial stability of the issuing nonprofit organization. Financial advisors may also be able to benefit the nonprofit organization (while simultaneously building a client base) by providing information to a nonprofit's donors about planned giving products such as Charitable Gift Annuities in cooperation with the charity.

A major benefit of Charitable Gift Annuities is that they are generally exempt from securities regulations. This is what permits nonprofit organizations to sell gift annuities in a largely unregulated environment. However, there are cases where the sale of a Charitable Gift Annuity will lose its exemption from securities regulation. This is a major issue because if the exemption is lost then the sale of these securities can result in criminal penalties (and, in fact, has resulted in jail time in previous cases). The sale of Charitable Gift Annuities will not be exempt from securities regulation where the annuities are primarily marketed as investments, rather than as a means to benefit the charity. An example of marketing a Charitable Gift Annuity as an investment is to compare the "yields" or "returns" with bank certificates of deposit, or other traditional investments. (As discussed previously an annuity payment rate is not a yield or a return, and thus, such comparisons are, prima facie, inappropriate.) The sale of Charitable Gift Annuities will also lose exempt from securities regulations if sales commissions are paid.

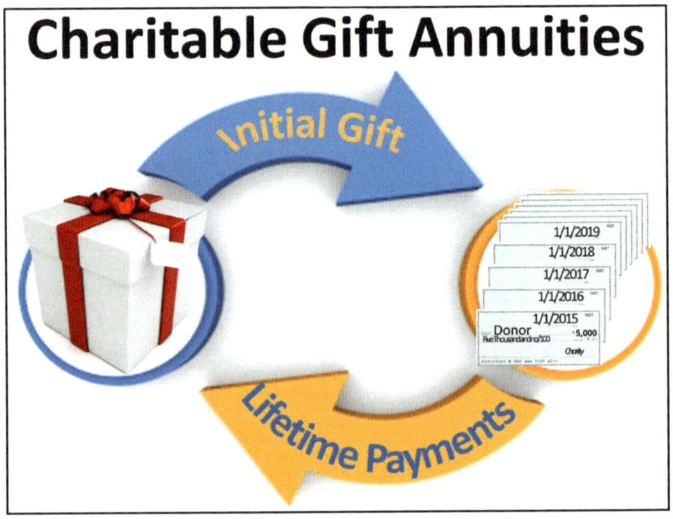

Charitable Gift Annuities are a handy and frequently used gift planning vehicle. Although simple in form and easy to complete, gift annuities do offer some flexibility in their structure. The simplicity in creating these agreements conceals a substantial complexity in understanding and managing the underlying risks. This complexity expands substantially when we consider the full tax implications of Charitable Gift Annuities. As such, these tax implications are discussed in their own separate chapter.

9 TAXATION OF CHARITABLE GIFT ANNUITIES

A donor makes a gift and in return receives annual payments for life from the charity. This is the basic concept of a Charitable Gift Annuity. Despite this underlying simplicity, understanding the tax implications of a Charitable Gift Annuity can be quite complex – so complex, in fact, as to warrant this separate chapter. What causes this complexity in tax consequences for Charitable Gift Annuities?

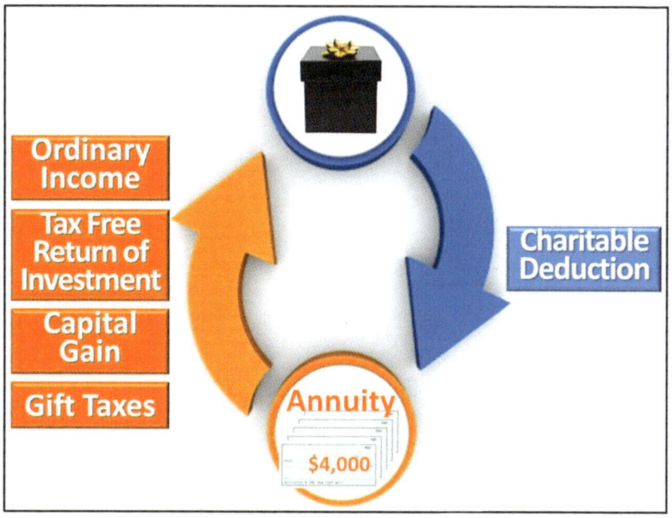

The complexity begins with the reality that Charitable Gift Annuities generate potential tax consequences in five different ways. The Charitable Gift Annuity is, at least in part, a charitable gift. Because it is a charitable gift, it generates a charitable income tax deduction for the donor. However, unlike other forms of charitable gifts, the Charitable Gift Annuity also generates a stream of payments to the annuitant. This lifetime stream of payments produces its own set of tax results. Some part of each payment will count as ordinary income to the recipient. Some part of some payments may also count as tax-free return of investment. If the gift given to the charity in exchange for the gift annuity was appreciated property, then some part of some payments may also be taxed as capital gain. Finally, if the donor decides not to take the payments for himself, but instead provides a lifetime income for someone else (other than the donor's spouse), then the donor has made a potentially taxable gift to the recipient. Thus, this single gift vehicle can result in capital gain income, ordinary income, an income tax deduction, tax-free return of capital, and a taxable gift. Let's begin with the calculation of the income tax deduction generated by the purchase of a Charitable Gift Annuity.

A Charitable Gift Annuity is a form of a bargain sale. As with other bargain sales, the charitable tax deduction is based on the value of what the donor contributed less the value of what the donor received. Determining the value of what the donor contributed is relatively easy. If the donor gave $10,000 in cash, then the value of the donor contribution is $10,000. Determining the value of what the donor receives in exchange for the gift (i.e., the value of the annuity) can be a bit more challenging.

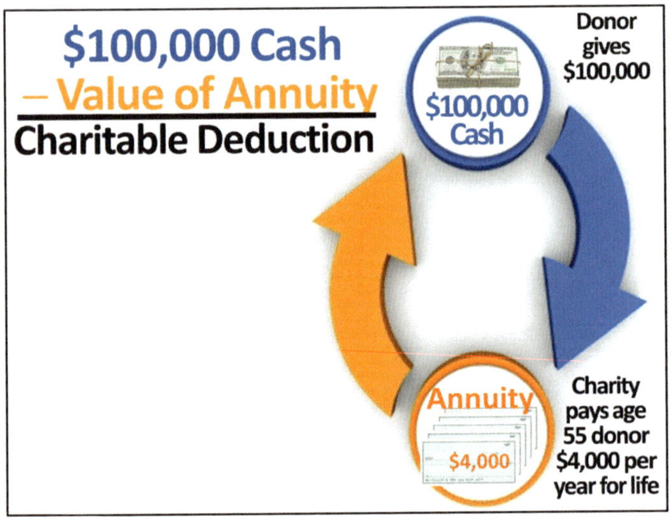

Let's look at a real example that we will return to throughout this section. Suppose that a donor, age 55, gives $100,000 in cash to a charity, and in exchange, the charity agrees to pay the donor $4,000 per year for his life. The charitable deduction will be the value of what the donor gave to the charity less the value of what the donor received from the charity. Determining the value of what the donor gave to the charity is simple. He gave $100,000.

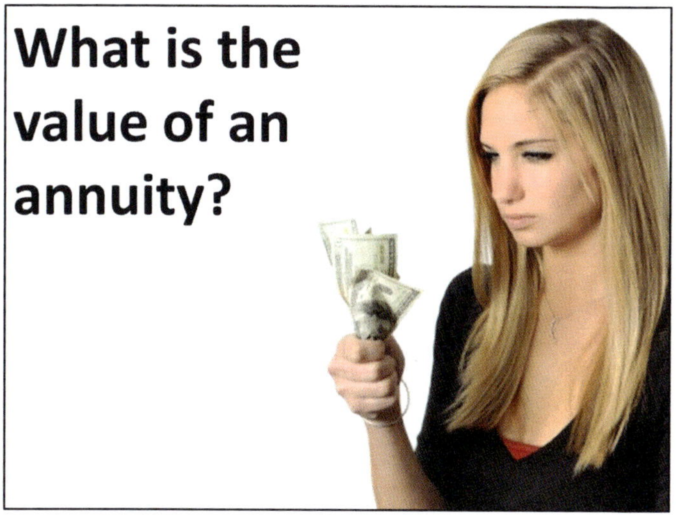

But, how do we determine the value of the annuity that the donor received in return for his gift? If the donor died immediately after making the contribution, then he would not have received any payments from the charity. On the other hand, if the donor lived for 50 more years, then the donor would receive 50 X $4,000 (i.e., $200,000) from the charity in exchange for his gift. Because it is impractical to wait 50 years to determine the donor's charitable deduction, we must instead *estimate* the *projected* value of the annuity at the time that the gift annuity was purchased. Thus, the value of the annuity will be based upon the idea that the annuitant will live to his projected life expectancy. The reality of whether or not the annuitant has a much longer or much shorter life will not affect either the initial valuation of the annuity or the charitable deduction. In our example, the value of the annuity is the value of receiving $4,000 each year for the life expectancy of a 55-year-old. The value of this payment stream will depend upon the prevailing interest rates. Why? Consider this. Generating $4,000 each year when interest rates paid 4% would require a $100,000 investment. If interest rates paid 1%, this would require a $400,000 investment. And if interest rates paid 16%, this would require only a $25,000 investment. Thus, the value of a $4,000 per year payment depends heavily on the prevailing interest rates. Fortunately, the IRS has a prescribed process for determining the appropriate interest rate and calculating the value of annuities. Let's now walk through that process step-by-step.

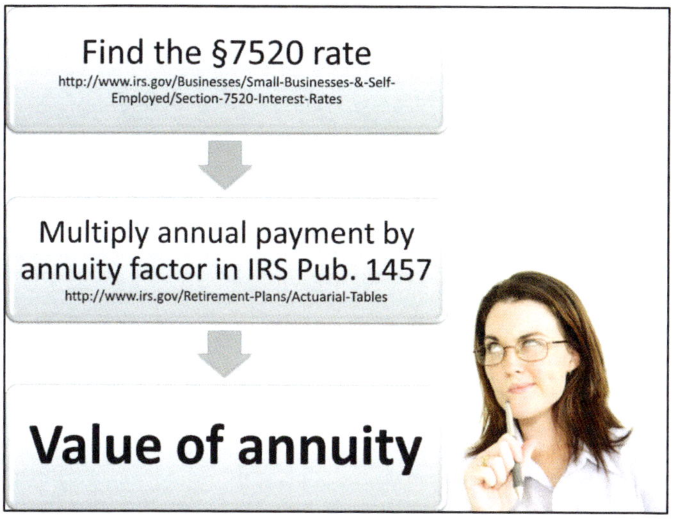

The first step in valuing an annuity is to determine the appropriate interest rate. For purposes of calculating the deduction for a Charitable Gift Annuity, the relevant interest rate is referred to as the §7520 rate. This rate is published on the IRS website at: http://www.irs.gov/Businesses/Small-Businesses-&-Self-Employed/Section-7520-Interest-Rates (It is also published on a variety of other planned giving websites.) Once we know the appropriate interest rate, we can find the appropriate annuity factor in the actuarial tables posted at http://www.irs.gov/Retirement-Plans/Actuarial-Tables Multiplying this annuity factor by the annual payment gives us the value of the annuity for purposes of our income tax deduction. Let's now walk through each step for our example Charitable Gift Annuity.

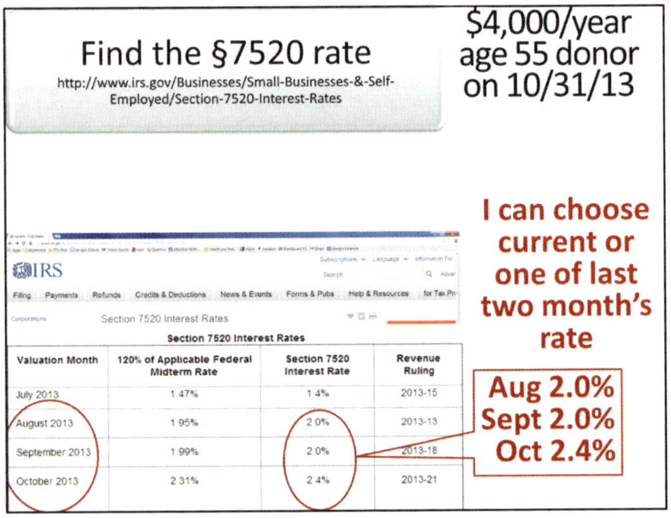

The first step in valuing the annuity is to determine the appropriate interest rate. Because the §7520 interest rates change each month, we will have to set a date for our hypothetical transaction. So, let's assume that our 55 year old donor gave $100,000 in exchange for a $4,000 per year annuity on October 15 of the year 2013. The IRS website for the §7520 interest rates shows that October had a 2.4% rate. However, tax law allows the donor to choose the current or either of the prior two month's §7520 interest rate for his calculation. (In fact the next month's rates are published several days early, so towards the end of the month, the donor also knows the interest rate for the upcoming month and could postpone the transaction in order to take advantage of a favorable rate change. In this case the November, 2013 rate was going to be 2.0%, so it would not have changed the donor's options.) For a transaction on this date, the donor could choose the 2.4% rate from October or the 2.0% rate from either August or September. Which rate should the donor choose?

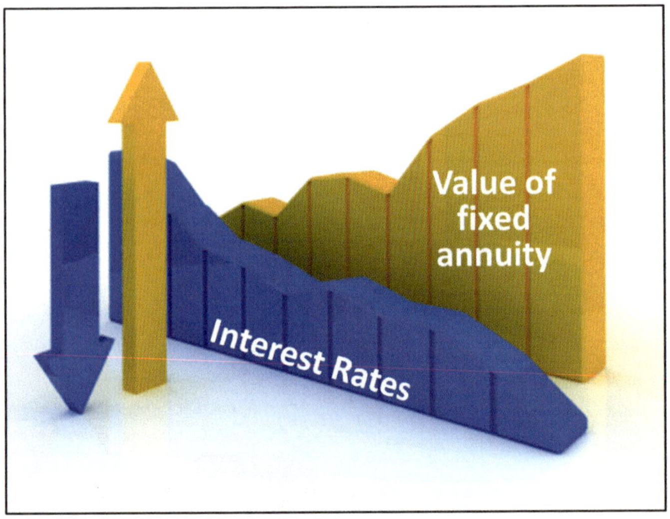

As discussed previously, the value of the annuity depends upon the current interest rates. As interest rates rise, it takes a smaller and smaller investment to generate $4,000 per year. Thus, the value of a $4,000 per year payment falls as interest rates rise. So, if the donor selects the higher interest rate (2.4%), the annuity the donor receives from the charity will be valued at less than if the donor selected the lower interest rate (2.0%). Does the donor want the annuity he receives to be valued higher or lower? In most cases, the donor is interested in having the highest charitable income tax deduction. Here, the donor's deduction will be $100,000 minus the value of the annuity. As the interest rate rises, the value of the annuity falls. As the value of the annuity falls, the value of the donor's deduction rises. Consequently, the donor will choose the higher interest rate (2.4%) in order to generate the highest charitable income tax deduction. (Choosing the higher interest rate is normally the "right" answer for a donor. However, if the donor cannot make use of the income tax deduction, then the lower rate is preferable because, as discussed later, it will increase the amount of each payment considered to be tax-free return of investment.)

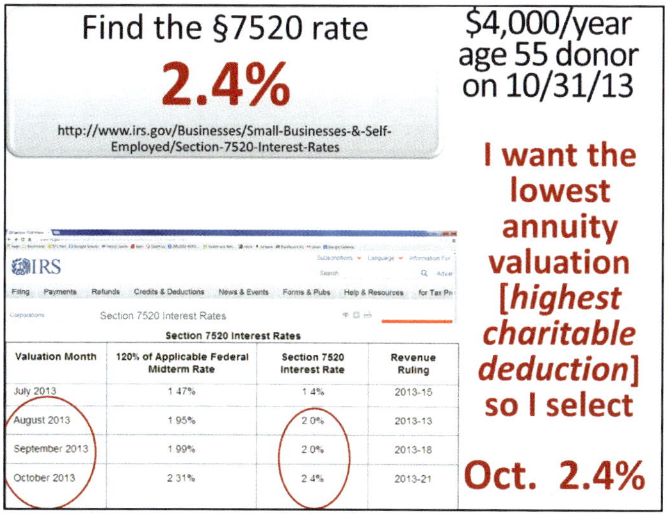

Because our donor wants the highest charitable deduction, he consequently wants the lowest valuation for his annuity. (Remember that the charitable deduction is the value of what the donor gives to the charity less the value of what the donor receives from the charity.) To get the lowest valuation for his annuity, the donor chooses the highest §7520 interest rate, in this case 2.4%.

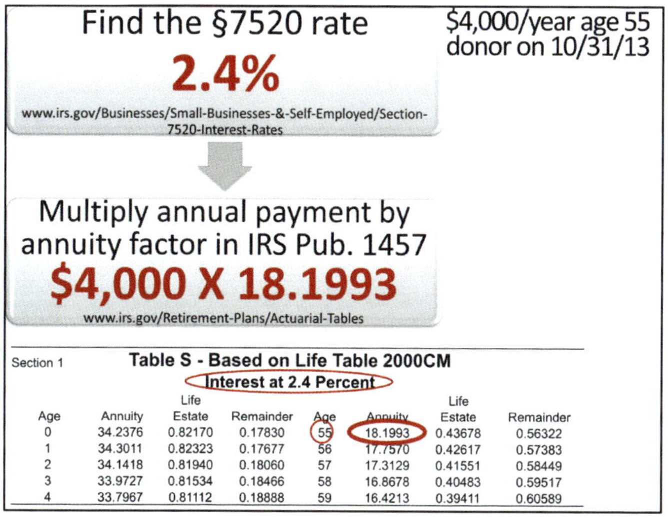

After identifying the appropriate section 7520 interest rate (2.4%), we next look at the relevant actuarial tables. Going to the IRS webpage (www.irs.gov/Retirement-Plans/Actuarial-Tables) provides links for tables of single life factors and last-to-die factors. In this case, the annuity pays for the life of the donor only and so we will use the table for single life factors (Table S). Scrolling down through this table until we reach the section for a 2.4% interest rate reveals the annuity factor for each age at this interest rate. Because our annuitant is age 55, we use the annuity factor of 18.1993. (Of course, if the annuitant were a different age or if the interest rate were different, then this annuity factor would also be different.) This annuity factor of 18.1993 is multiplied by the annual payment amount of $4,000 to generate the value of the annuity for purposes of calculating the income tax deduction.

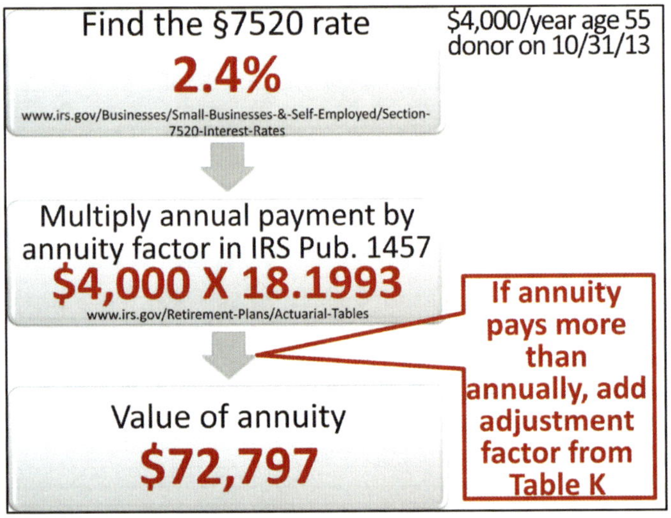

An annuity factor of 18.1993 multiplied by an annual payment of $4,000 generates a value for this annuity of $72,797.20. (As a point of comparison, if the donor had chosen the lower interest rate of 2.0%, then the annuity factor would have been 19.1825 and the annuity would have been valued at $76,730.00. The use of this lower interest rate would have reduced the donor's tax deduction by almost $4,000.)

Charities are allowed to make annuity payments more frequently than once per year. This slightly modifies the valuation of the annuity because the donor does not have to wait as long to receive his payment. (For example, if the annuitant is paid annually, he must wait 12 months to receive his first check, but if he is paid weekly he only waits 7 days. In either case, the total payments in each year still sum to $4,000. But, receiving the payments earlier in the year is more valuable than being required to wait until the end of the year.) This increase in value due to more frequent payments is calculated by multiplying the initial value by the frequency factor found in Table K. Table K is found at the same webpage with the other actuarial tables. The frequency factor for annual payments is simply 1.0, meaning that no valuation adjustments are made. The frequency factor for semi-annual, quarterly, monthly, and weekly payments will be greater than one and will depend upon the current §7520 interest rate. (The value of receiving the payment earlier depends upon how much interest that early payment could earn between the time it was received and the time the later payment would have been received.)

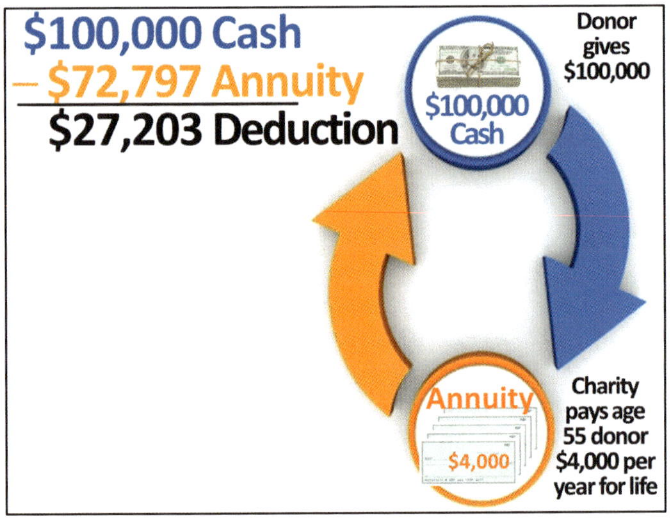

Having determined the value of the $4,000 per year lifetime payments to the donor, i.e., the value of the annuity, it is now easy to calculate the charitable deduction. As with any bargain sale, the charitable deduction is simply the value of what the donor gave to the charity (in this case cash worth $100,000) less the value of what the donor received from the charity (in this case an annuity worth $72,797.20). Thus, this transaction generates a $27,202.80 deduction for the donor.

Note that this calculation is based upon a $4,000 per year payout to a donor age 55 and corresponds with the suggested rates offered at the time of the transaction by the American Council on Gift Annuities. Charities are always open to paying a lower annuity than the suggested rates. It is good practice for charities to present a Charitable Gift Annuity proposal with three different payout rates, high (e.g., $4,000 per year as per the American Council on Gift Annuities suggested rate), medium (e.g., $3,000 per year), and low (e.g., $2,000 per year). Remembering that the goal of the donor is, in part, to benefit the charity, the lower rates may more closely match the donor's preferences and income needs while maximizing the benefit to the charity. If a donor chose one of the lower payout rates, the value of the resulting annuity would be less and, consequently, the charitable income tax deduction would be greater.

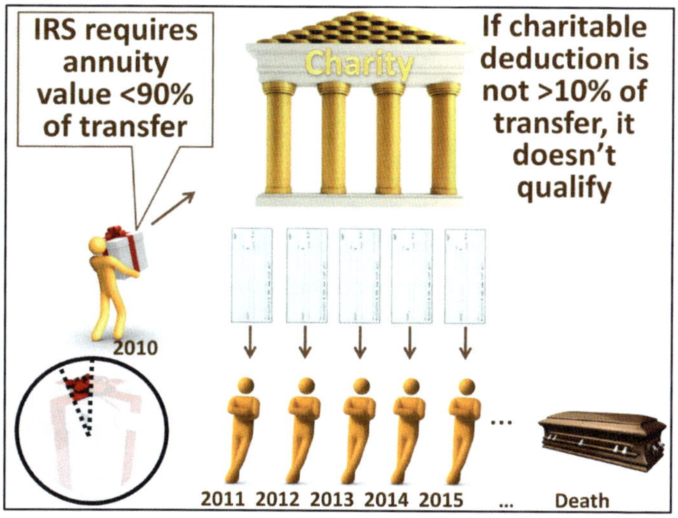

In our example, the charitable deduction was approximately 27.2% of the $100,000 given by the donor. Of course, if the charity had paid the donor more than $4,000 per year for life, then the charitable deduction would have been less. There is, however, a limit on how much the charity can pay to the donor. The IRS requires that the value of the annuity given to the donor must be less than 90% of the value of the gift the donor gives to the charity. A quick way to see that this requirement has been satisfied is to make sure that the charitable deduction is greater than 10% of the amount given to the charity by the donor. If this rule is violated the charity will be treated as if it is engaging in an unrelated (non-charitable) business and will be taxed accordingly. Consequently, charities do not normally offer gift annuities that violate this rule.

Our first example was the simplest Charitable Gift Annuity case where the donor gives cash in exchange for lifetime payments. However, married donors are frequently interested in payments that last for two lives, rather than just one. Two-life annuities are allowed and there is no requirement that the annuitants be related. (However, annuities for more than two lives are not permitted.) The actuarial tables used in the single life example will not work for a two-life annuity. Consequently, we must slightly alter the process for valuing such annuities.

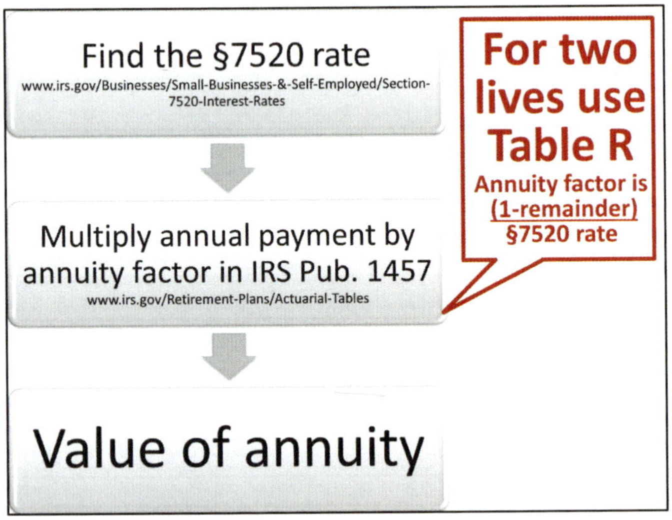

For two-life annuities, calculating the value of the annuity uses Table R, rather than Table S. However, Table R looks different from Table S. Where Table S has three numbers for each age (the annuity factor, the remainder interest, and the life estate), Table S has only one number for each age combination. This one number is the remainder interest factor. But, we don't want the remainder interest factor; instead, we want the annuity factor. Using Table S, requires knowing that the annuity factor is calculated by subtracting the remainder interest factor from one and then dividing this amount by the current §7520 rate. Thus, calculating the annuity factor for a two-life annuity will have one extra step.

As in the example for a single life annuity, once we know the value of the annuity given by the charity, we are able to calculate the tax deduction. The deduction is the amount given by the donor to the charity less the value of the annuity given by the charity to the donor.

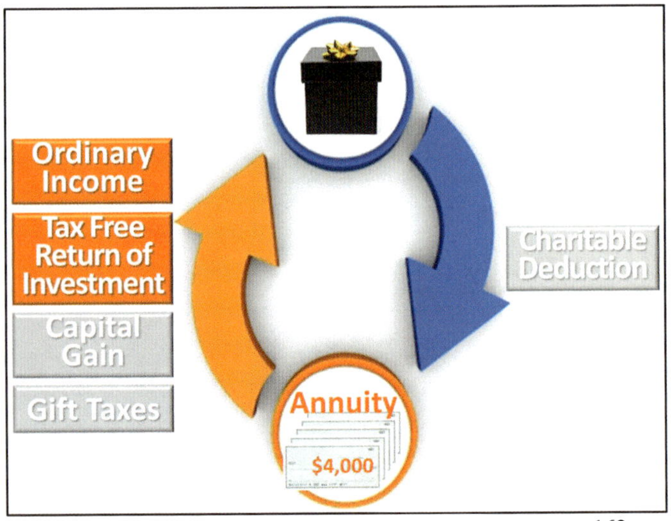

Knowing how to value the annuity allows us to calculate the charitable tax deduction resulting from purchasing the Charitable Gift Annuity. However, the tax implications of a Charitable Gift Annuity do not end there. Unlike other gifts, the Charitable Gift Annuity produces a lifetime income stream. Each year (or quarter, month, or week) the annuitant receives a check from the charity. How should the annuitant report this check to the IRS? Let's begin with the simple transaction where the Charitable Gift Annuity was purchased with cash. In that case, each check will be reported as some combination of ordinary income and tax-free return of investment.

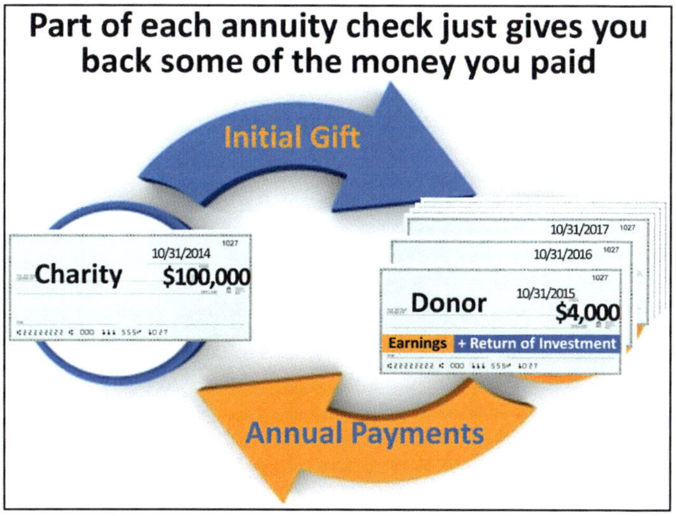

Some part of each annuity check given to a donor simply returns a part of the money paid for the Charitable Gift Annuity. This part is simply a return of the donor's original investment. There are no income taxes on this portion of the annuity check, because this is not "new" earned money coming to the donor. This is simply the donor's own money being returned to him. (Or, in the case of a gift annuity paid to someone other than the donor, this is simply a gift from the donor and is likewise not taxable income.)

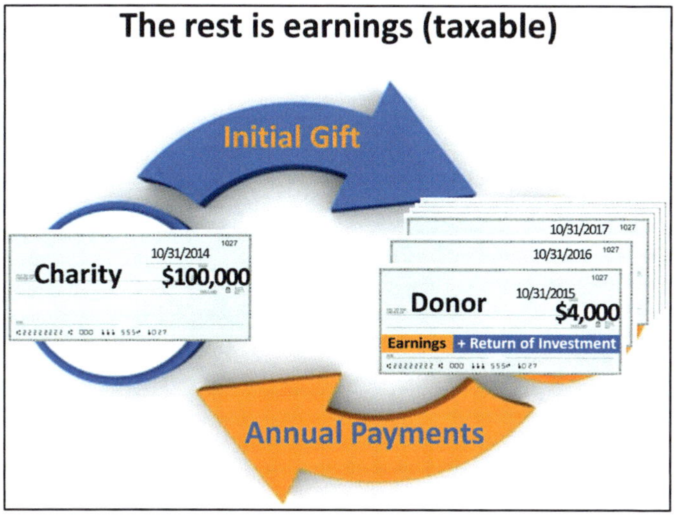

The remaining part of each annuity check is taxable. When the Charitable Gift Annuity is purchased for cash (i.e., not with appreciated property), this remaining part is taxed as ordinary income. In this case, everything that is not tax-free return of investment is taxable as ordinary income.

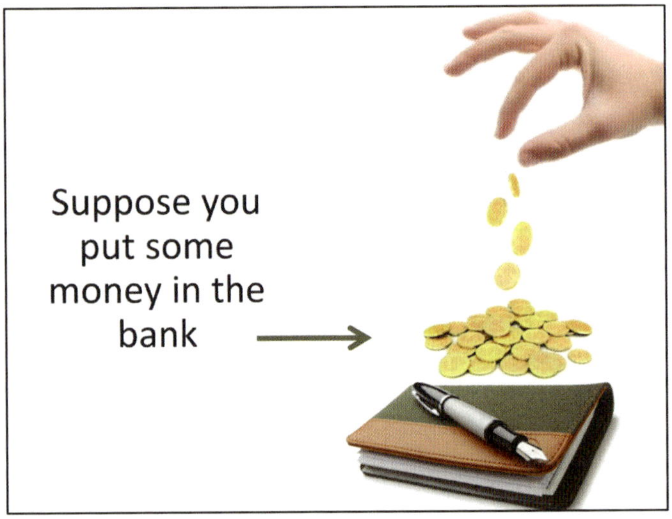

Let's look at an example that may help to explain the difference in tax treatment between earnings and tax-free return of investment. Suppose you open an interest-bearing bank account and put in $1,000.

Further, suppose that each year you withdraw all of the interest earned in the account and some of your original $1,000 deposit. So, for example, suppose that the bank account earns 5% interest per year. At the end of the first year you withdraw the $50 of interest earned on your $1,000 deposit and you withdraw $100 of your original deposit.

Do you pay more taxes because you withdrew $100 of your original deposit? Does removing $100 of your original deposit mean that you have $100 more of income this year? No. Removing money from an account does not cause you to have more income. It simply shifts the location of your money.

Putting money into an account and then removing the same money from the account is no different than burying money in the ground and then later digging it up and taking it out of the ground. This is tax-free return of investment. The money was yours before you put it in the ground and is still yours after you take it out of the ground. Neither of these actions changes your taxable income, even if they may change the amount of cash in your pocket.

Let's return to the example of the bank account where you earned $50 in interest (on the original $1,000 deposit) and withdrew $150. Do you pay taxes on the $50 of interest earned during the year? Yes. This $50 is not part of the $1,000 original deposit. It is new. This new money earned on the deposit is taxable income. The idea of taking all of the interest and some of the principal each year from a bank account is similar to receiving an annuity. Each annuity check represents all of the earnings during the year, plus some of the original investment. The portion of the annuity check that represents a return of the original investment is not taxed. The rest is treated as earnings and is taxed as ordinary income.

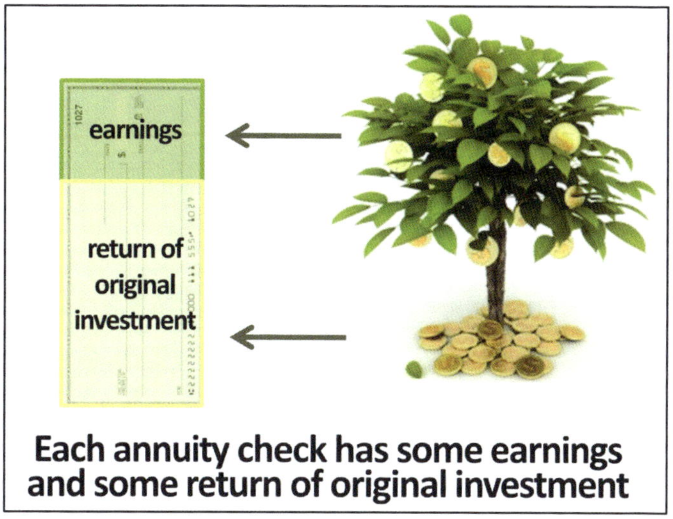

So long as the annuity was not purchased with appreciated property, each annuity check will consist of some combination of taxable earnings and non-taxable return of original investment. Using our analogy, the tax-free return of investment is like removing some of the original principle from a bank account, and the remainder of each annuity payment is like the taxable earnings from a bank account.

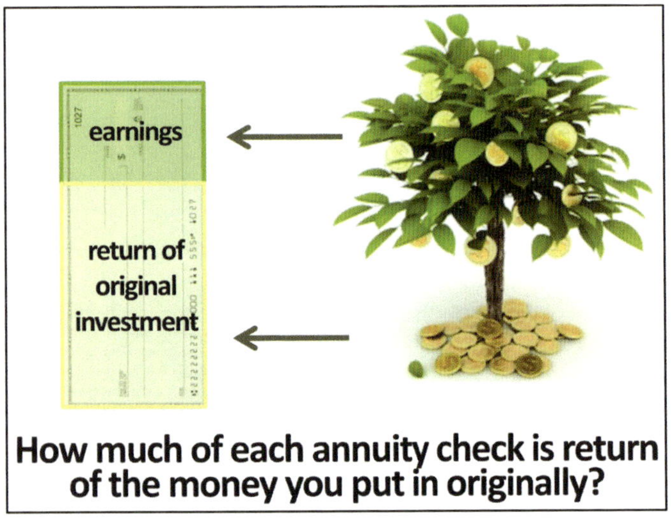

How much of each annuity check is taxable income? We calculate this indirectly by determining how much was simply a return of the money originally invested. The rest is taxable income.

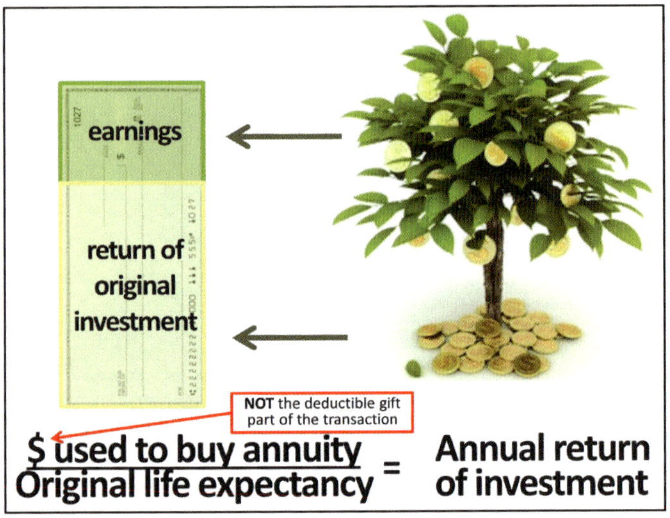

The formula for determining the amount of each annuity check that qualifies as tax-free return of investment is to divide the part of the transaction used to purchase the annuity by the annuitant's original life expectancy. Note that the part of the transaction used to purchase the annuity is not the entire cost of the Charitable Gift Annuity. Part of the cost of the Charitable Gift Annuity is a charitable gift. That is the part which generates the charitable income tax deduction. The *rest* of the money used to purchase the Charitable Gift Annuity (i.e., *not* the deductible gift part of the transaction) is the money used to purchase the annuity part. It is this part of the transaction that was the investment part (i.e., not a gift). Consequently, this is the part of the transaction that can become tax-free return of investment. The gift part of transaction cannot become tax-free return of investment, because it was given to the charity as a deductible charitable gift.

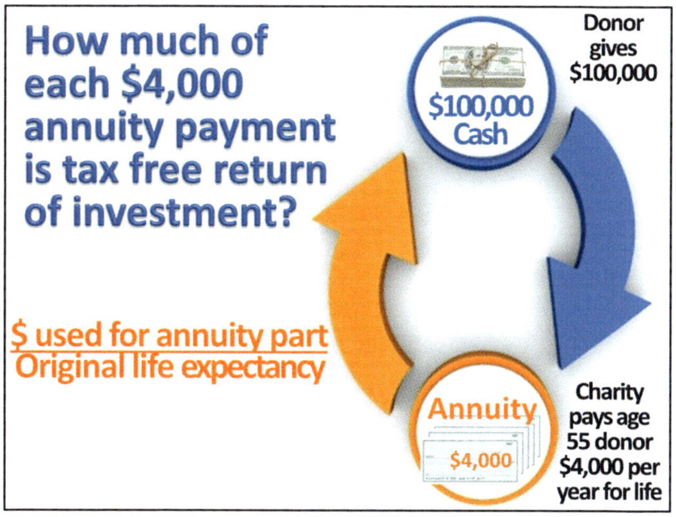

Let's return to our original example where a 55-year old donor gave $100,000 of cash to the charity and the charity, in return, agreed to pay the donor $4,000 per year for life. The amount of each annual $4,000 annuity check that is tax-free return of investment is determined by dividing the dollars used to purchase the annuity part by the annuitant's life expectancy when the Charitable Gift Annuity was purchased.

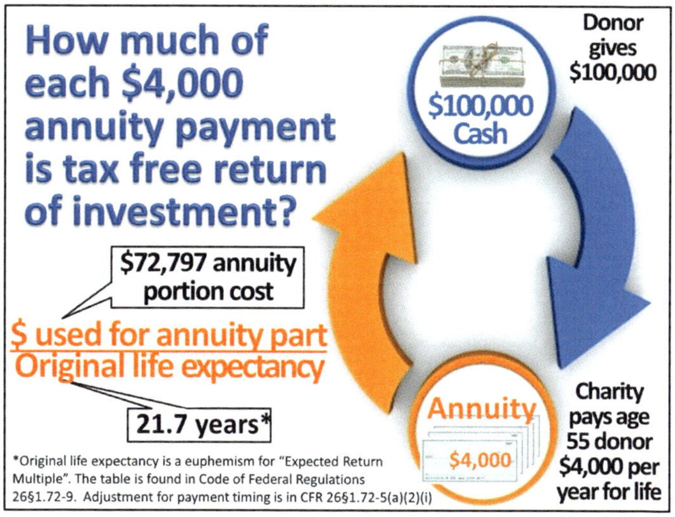

In this case we have previously calculated that the value of the annuity as $72,797.20. Thus, this is the portion of the $100,000 transfer that was used to purchase the annuity. The remaining amount from the $100,000 was not used to purchase the annuity. Instead, it was used to make a charitable gift (and was thus deductible as a charitable gift). Dividing this $72,797.20 annuity part by the annuitant's 21.7 year original life expectancy results in $3,354.71. Thus, $3,354.71 of each $4,000 annuity check will be tax-free return of investment until all of the donor's original investment has been returned. How do we find the annuitant's life expectancy? The life expectancy used for this calculation is called an "Expected return multiple" and is identified in the table found in the Code of Federal Regulations Title 26 §1.72-9. (Several free websites show the Code of Federal Regulation such as www.law.cornell.edu/cfr/) This factor is called an "Expected return multiple" because it is the period that payments are actuarially expected to be received. In this case, the "Expected return multiple" for a 55 year old male is 21.7 years.

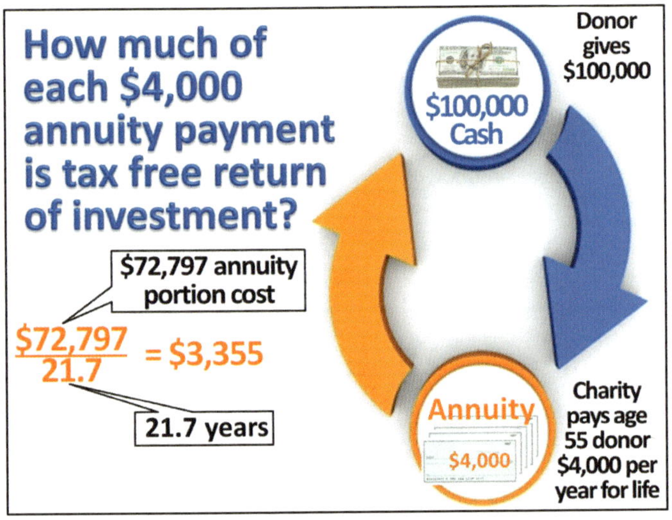

As a result of this calculation, we can now say that out of each $4,000 annuity payment, $3,354.71 will be treated as tax-free return of investment. This is how each annuity check will be treated until the entire $72,797.20 of the investment in the annuity portion has been returned. Note that the charity is required to send each annuitant an IRS Form 1099R which indicates what portion of each payment is tax-free return of investment, which part is taxable income, and (when the gift annuity was purchased with appreciated property) which part is capital gain.

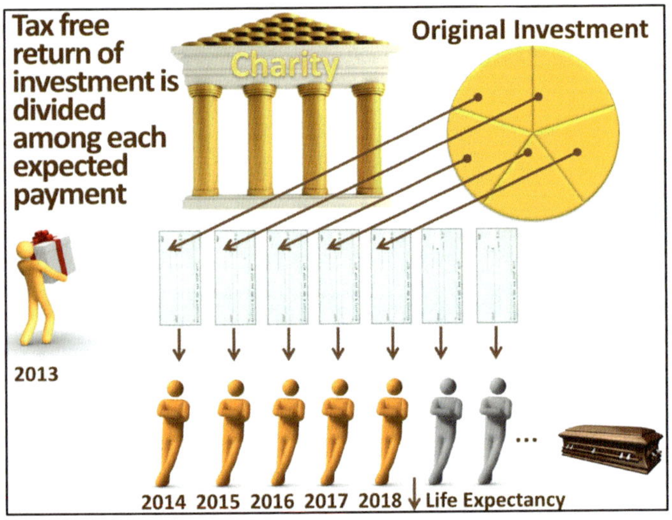

So, for example, if an older donor had a life expectancy ("expected return multiple") of five years, then each year for five years 1/5th of the donor's original investment in the annuity portion of the transaction would be returned to the donor. But what happens once the entire original annuity portion cost has been returned? (In other words, what happens if the annuitant outlives his or her "expected return multiple"?)

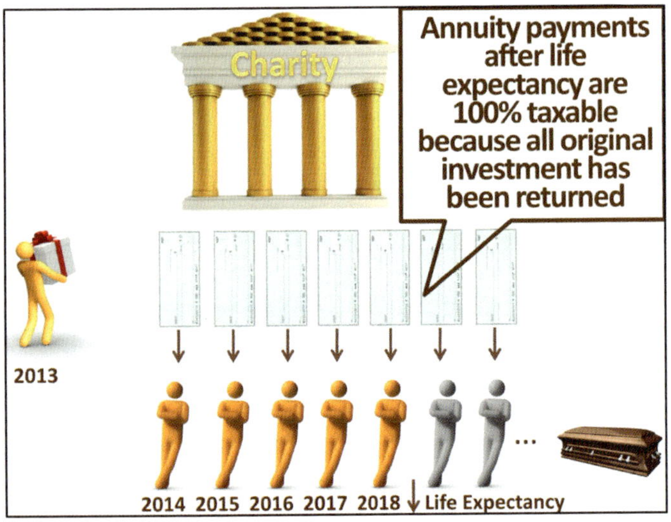

Once the entire original investment (in our example, $72,797.20) has been distributed to the annuitant, there is no part of the original investment left. Consequently, after that point, no part of the subsequent annuity payments will be tax-free return of investment. Thus, once an annuitant has lived past his or her life expectancy ("expected return multiple"), the entire annuity payment will be treated as ordinary income.

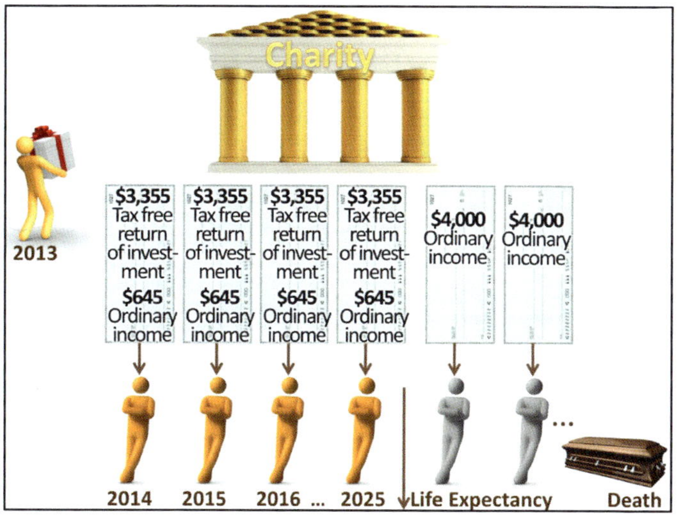

Returning to our example, $3,354.71 of each $4,000 annuity check will be treated as tax-free return of investment for 21.7 years. (For the check in the 22nd year, the tax-free return of investment would be $3,354.71 X .7, or $2,348.30.) After that point, however, every additional $4,000 check will be treated entirely as ordinary income.

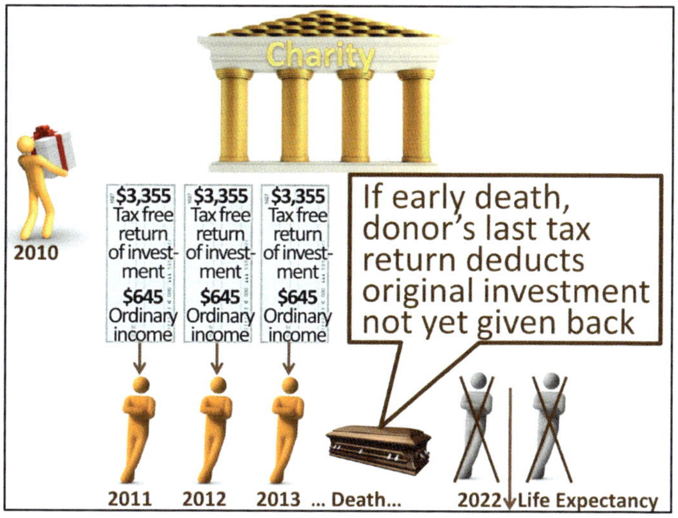

If the donor dies prior to reaching his original life expectancy ("expected return multiple"), then the donor fails to receive his entire original investment in the annuity portion of the transaction. In this case, the donor's last tax return can deduct the portion of the original investment not yet returned to the donor.

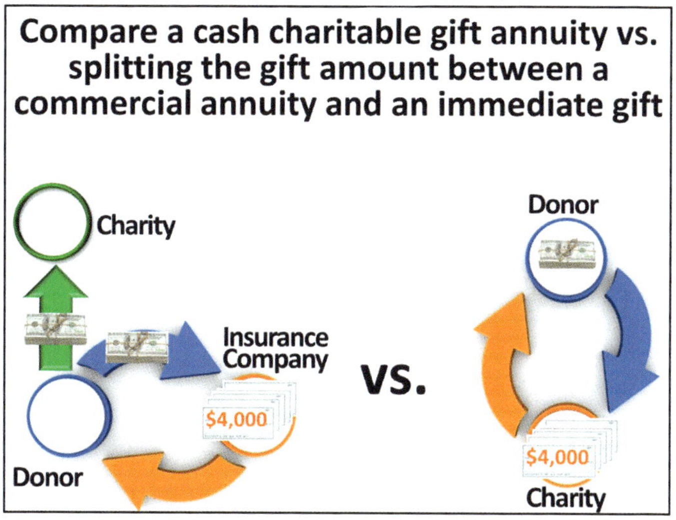

For a donor who wishes to benefit a charity that does not offer a Charitable Gift Annuity, a similar transaction would be to use part of the money to purchase a commercial immediate annuity from an insurance company and then simply donate the remaining amount to the charity. This accomplishes roughly the same goals as a Charitable Gift Annuity. However, there are two tax disadvantages that make this substitute transaction less advantageous.

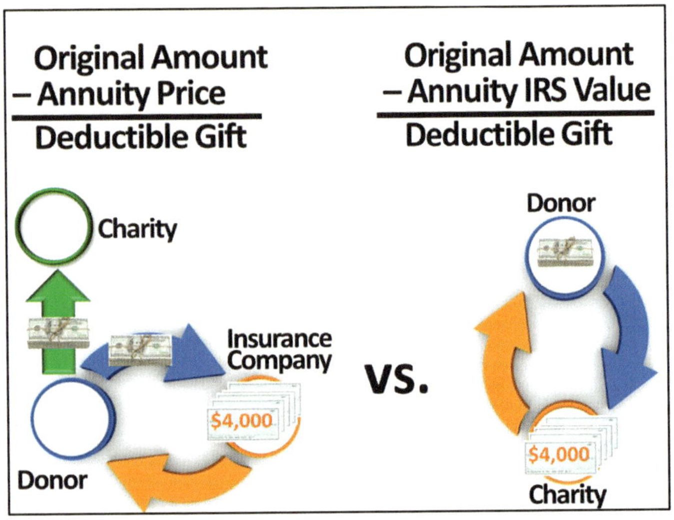

The deduction generated by the substitute transaction (purchasing a commercial annuity from the insurance company and donating the remaining cash to the charity) will be lower than the deduction generated by a comparable Charitable Gift Annuity. With a Charitable Gift Annuity, the charitable deduction is the amount transferred less the value of the annuity as determined by the IRS tables. In the substitute transaction the charitable deduction will be the amount given to charity, in other words, the total original amount less the price of the commercial annuity. However, a commercial annuity will inevitably be more expensive than the IRS valuation of a similar annuity from a charity. This occurs for two reasons. First, the commercial annuity product must incorporate the salaries and profit of the insurance company into its pricing. This margin must be above and beyond the value of the expected payout based upon current interest rates. Additionally, the IRS valuation for an annuity from a charity will be lower because the IRS uses standard life expectancy tables. However, people who buy annuities, on average, live longer than others of the same age. (As discussed in the previous chapter, this is because people who are sick or dying or poor do not purchase annuities. The exclusion of these groups means that those who purchase annuities will, on average, live longer than others of the same age.) Thus, the insurance company must price its annuity based upon the longer life expectancy of annuity purchasers, and not the generic life expectancy used by the IRS. This expectation of a longer life means that the insurance company must charge more for its annuities as compared with the IRS calculation.

The second tax disadvantage of the substitute transaction is that it cannot be used to shelter capital gains taxes when contributing appreciated property. Despite these disadvantages, if a donor wants to purchase a Charitable Gift Annuity with cash to benefit a charity that does not offer Charitable Gift Annuities (or perhaps does not offer them in the donor's state of residence), this substitute transaction might be suggested as a possible alternative. Having just mentioned that sheltering of capital gains as a potential advantage of Charitable Gift Annuities, let's now turn to a discussion of capital gains taxes.

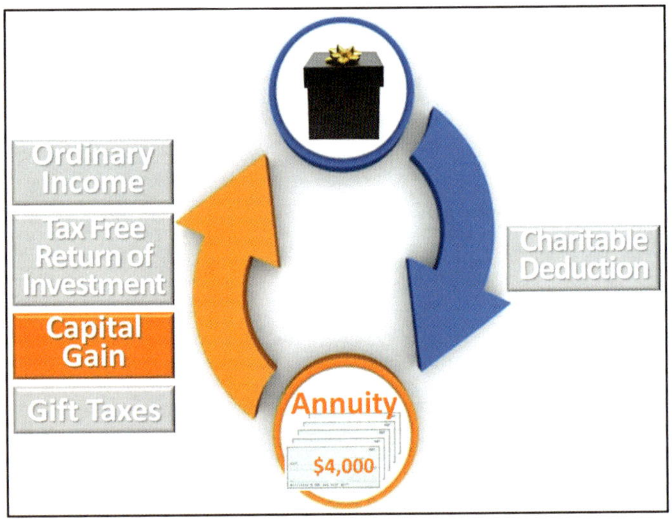

To this point, we have been looking at a Charitable Gift Annuity transaction where the gift annuity is purchased with cash. However, it is also possible to purchase a Charitable Gift Annuity with appreciated property. This complicates our tax scenario because when a gift annuity paying to the donor is purchased with appreciated property, some part of the annuity check given to the annuitant will be treated not as ordinary income, nor as tax-free return of investment, but rather as capital gain.

Let's first consider the straightforward rules that normally apply to capital gains. If a taxpayer buys an item (for example, shares of stock), for $500,000 and later sells the item for its fair market value of $1 million, then it is simple to calculate the capital gain. The capital gain is simply what the taxpayer sold the item for ($1,000,000) reduced by what the taxpayer originally paid for the item ($500,000). Thus, the taxpayer would have a capital gain of $500,000 (i.e., the profit from the sale would be $500,000).

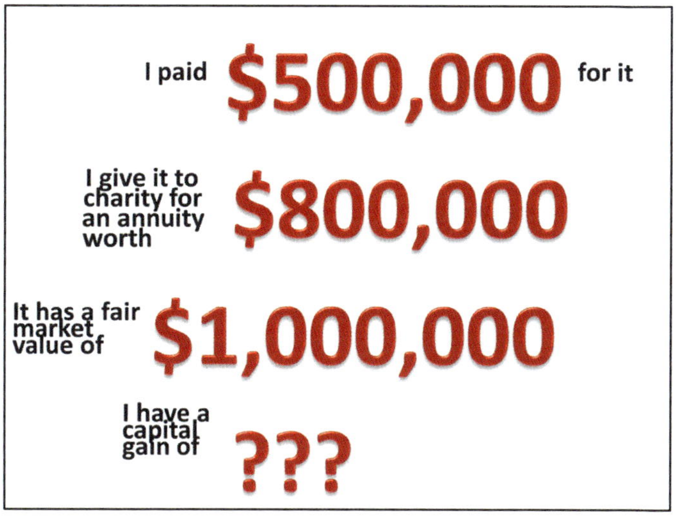

The capital gain calculation becomes more complicated in the context of a bargain sale. Suppose the taxpayer has the same asset which he purchased for $500,000 that now has the same fair market value of $1 million. But instead of selling the asset for $1 million, the taxpayer donates the asset to a charity, and in exchange for the donation receives an annuity worth $800,000. What is the capital gain resulting from that transaction? It is NOT simply the value of the annuity ($800,000) less the price of the property ($500,000). The calculation of capital gain for this transaction uses the same process for calculating capital gain in any type of bargain sale.

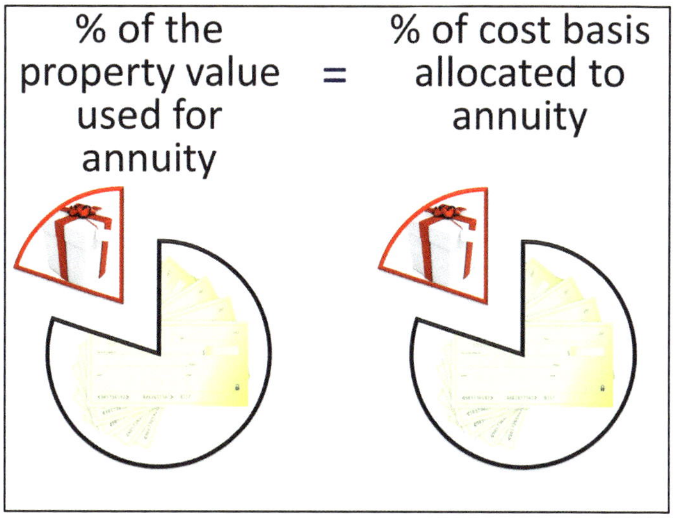

The reason that the capital gain on the previous transaction is not simply $800,000-$500,000 is because the donor may not use the entire $500,000 cost basis in the property for the annuity part of the transaction. Part of the cost basis is allocated to the gift portion and part is allocated to the annuity portion (a.k.a. the "sale" portion).

A simple way to think of a capital gain is "What I got for it" less "What I paid for it." In this case, it is easy to determine "What I got for it." The donor receives an annuity worth $800,000 (and also makes a charitable gift). Determining the "What I paid for it" is more tricky, because the donor paid for both the portion of the property that bought the annuity and the portion of the property that became a charitable gift. Only the basis from the share of the property that was used to purchase the annuity can be included in the capital gain calculation. (In some cases, the basis from the share of the property that became a charitable gift might also be important when, according to the rules on valuing charitable gifts of property, the value of the donation is limited to the basis.)

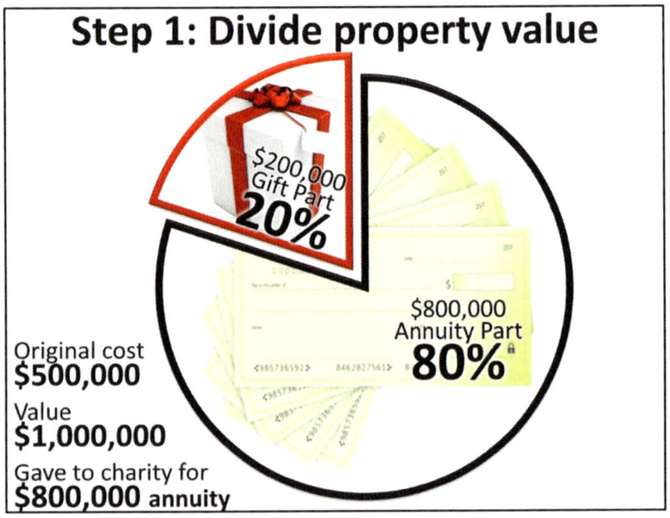

Let's apply this concept to our proposed transaction. The donor purchased property (perhaps intangible personal property like shares of stock) for $500,000 that grew in value to $1,000,000. He then gave that property to charity in exchange for a gift annuity worth $800,000. The first step is to divide the property into the part that was used to purchase the annuity (the "sale" part) and the part that was used to make a charitable gift (the "gift" part). In this case, $800,000 of the $1,000,000 property was used to purchase the $800,000 annuity. In other words, 80% of the property was used for the "sale" part of the bargain sale. The remaining 20% of the property was used to make a charitable gift (i.e., the "gift" part of the bargain sale)

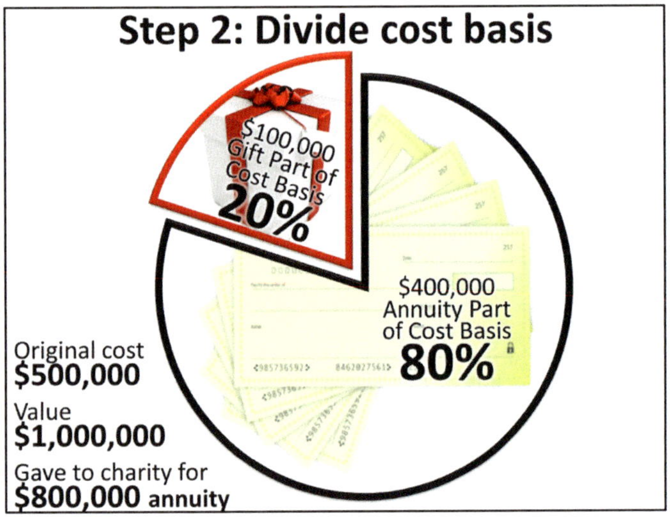

Next, we apply this same percentage division to the cost basis. The total cost basis was $500,000 (i.e., that was the purchase price of the transferred property). 80% of this $500,000 cost basis applies to the annuity purchase (i.e., $400,000 of basis applies to the "sale" part of the transaction). The remaining 20% ($100,000) of basis applies to the charitable gift. (And if the charitable deduction were, for some reason, limited to the basis in the property then the deduction would be for this $100,000 basis applying to the charitable gift, rather than for the full $200,000 difference between the transfer and the value of the annuity.)

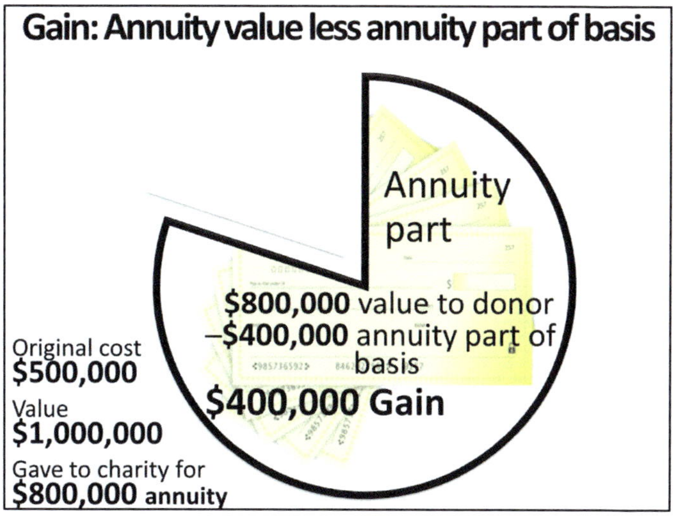

Now that we know both what the donor received for the property transfer (valued at $800,000) and the amount of the basis that applied to this annuity part (a.k.a. "sale part") of the transaction (i.e., $400,000), it is easy to calculate the capital gain. The capital gain is simply the value of the annuity ($800,000) less the amount of basis in the property applied to the annuity part of the transaction ($400,000), or $400,000.

When is the tax on this capital gain paid? The answer to this question depends upon who is receiving the annuity payments. If the donor purchases a gift annuity with appreciated property where the payments are made to another person (not the donor and donor's spouse), then the capital gain must be recognized immediately. This eliminates a substantial part of the tax advantage of purchasing a Charitable Gift Annuity with appreciated property. It also explains why such transactions are relatively rare. Nevertheless, the donor does still retain some advantage by giving appreciated property, rather than cash, to purchase the gift annuity, in that the capital gain attributed to the gift portion is avoided.

The preferable tax result occurs if the donor is receiving (or the donor and the donor's spouse jointly are receiving) the annuity payments. In this case, the capital gain is deferred over the life expectancy of the donor (or joint life expectancy of the donor and donor's spouse). The next best result to complete tax avoidance is tax deferral. In this case, the deferral is for an extraordinarily long period of time, making this a very attractive feature of purchasing gift annuities with appreciated property. In order to receive this treatment, the annuity must specify that it cannot be assigned to anyone (excepting the charity itself, the donor, and the donor's spouse). Even if the donor never uses the right to assign the annuity payments to someone else, simply having this right available will result in immediate recognition of all capital gain.

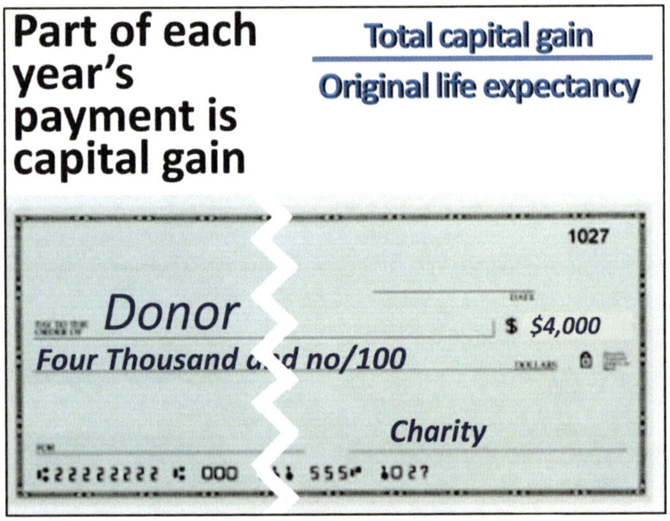

To calculate the share of each year's payment that will count as capital gain, the donor simply divides the total capital gain by his life expectancy (or the donor and donor's spouse's joint life expectancy if paid jointly). As before, this original life expectancy is called the "expected return multiple" and is identified in the table found in the Code of Federal Regulations Title 26 §1.72-9. The process for this calculation is identical to the previously discussed process for identifying how much of each year's payment will be tax-free return of investment.

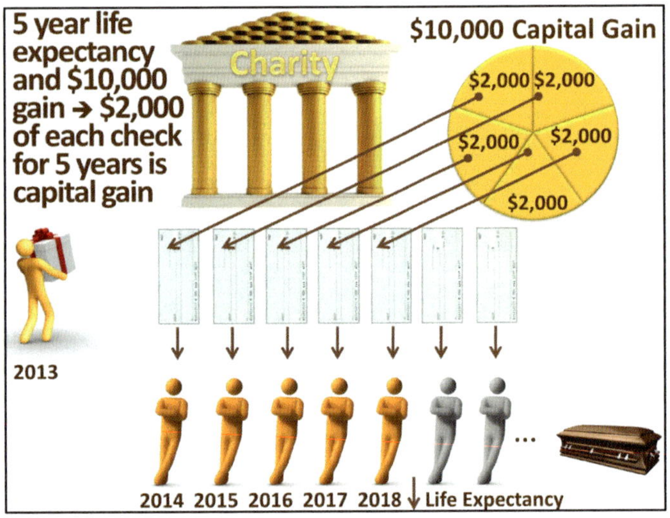

For example, if a donor had a five-year "expected return multiple" (i.e., life expectancy at the time of the purchase of the gift annuity) and a capital gain of $10,000 from the purchase of the gift annuity, then 1/5 of the capital gain would be recognized in each of the first five years. Thus, $2,000 of each annual payment check would count as capital gain for the first five years. After five years, the entire $10,000 in capital gain would have been recognized. Similar to the previous discussion of return of original investment, there is no additional capital gain to recognize if the donor outlives his "expected return multiple" (i.e., original life expectancy). Regardless of the price of the gift annuity or the use of appreciated property, after an annuitant outlives his or her "expected return multiple," all subsequent annuity payments will consist entirely of ordinary income.

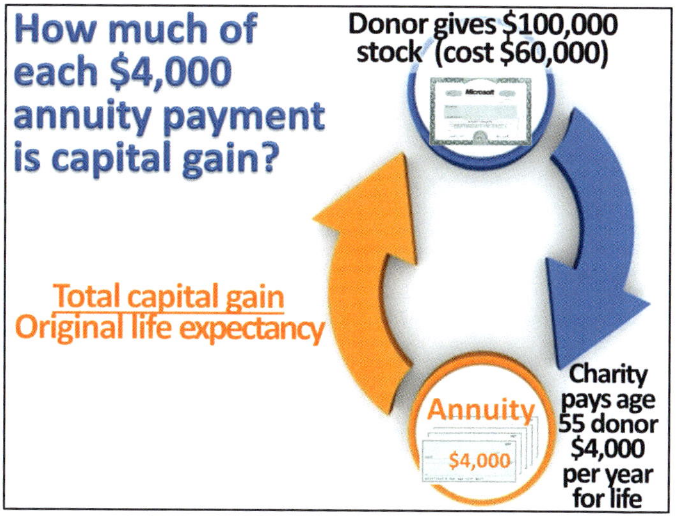

Let's now return to our previous example, with one modification. Rather than giving $100,000 in cash, the donor now gives publicly-traded stock worth $100,000. This is stock that the donor originally purchased for $60,000 (i.e., the basis of the stock is $60,000). In exchange for this stock, the charity agrees to pay the age 55 donor $4,000 per year for life. How much of each $4,000 annuity payment will count as capital gain? To calculate this, we simply divide the total capital gain by the original life expectancy (a.k.a., "expected return multiple").

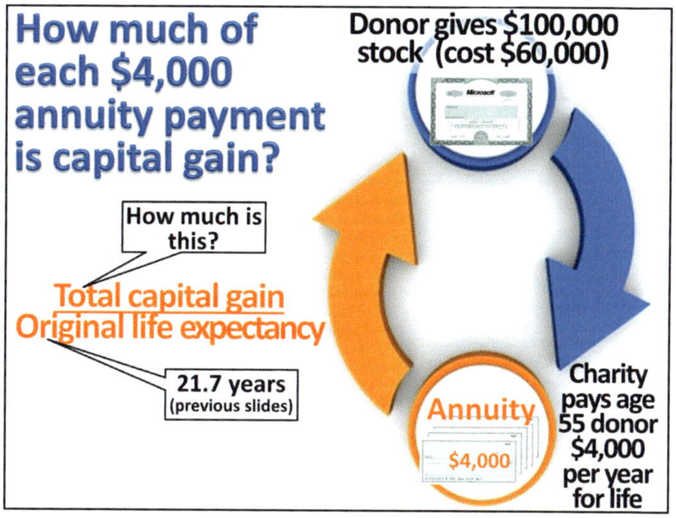

Determining the original life expectancy (a.k.a. expected return multiple) was already completed in the previous scenario. The table found in the Code of Federal Regulations Title 26 §1.72-9 indicates that for a 55-year-old male, the expected return multiple is 21.7 years. However, we have not yet calculated the total capital gain resulting from this transaction.

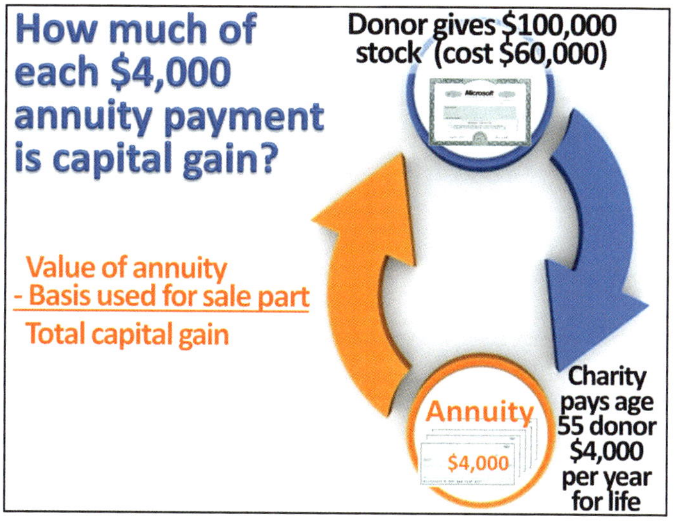

To calculate the total capital gain, we simply subtract the basis attributable to the sale part of the transaction from the value of the annuity. In other words, this is what the donor received (value of the annuity) less what the donor gave for the annuity (the non-charitable portion of the transaction).

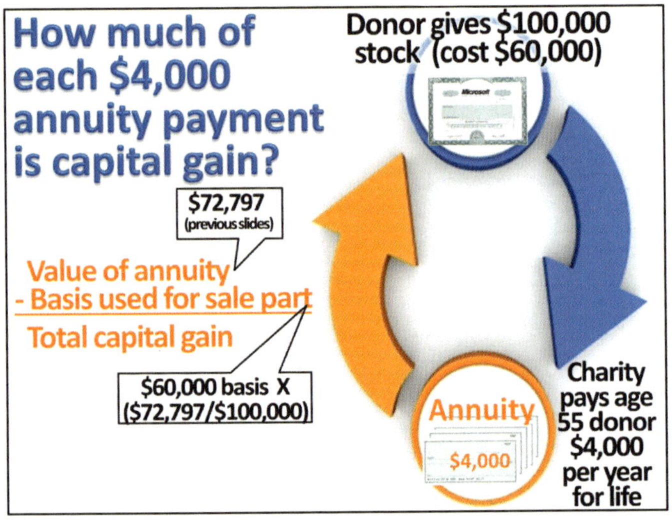

The value of the annuity is $72,797.20 as determined by the calculations from the previous example. (The fact that the annuity was, in this case, purchased with appreciated property has no effect on the value of the annuity being provided to the donor.) We do not simply subtract the entire $60,000 basis from the value of the annuity in order to calculate the capital gain because only part of the property was used to purchase the annuity and the remainder was used to make a deductible charitable gift. Thus, we can only use the share of the basis that represents the share of the property used to purchase the annuity (i.e., the "sale" part). In this case, the share of the $100,000 transaction used to purchase the annuity (i.e., the portion that is not a deductible charitable gift) was $72,797.20 Thus, 72.7972% of the property was used to purchase the annuity. Because 72.7972% of the property was used to purchase the annuity, 72.7972% of the basis may be applied to calculate the capital gain resulting from receiving the annuity. Thus, 72.7972% of the $60,000 basis (i.e., $43,668.32) may be used to calculate the capital gain.

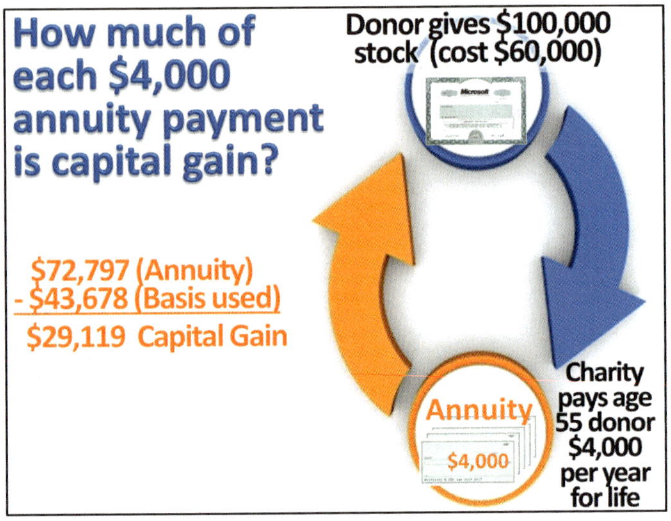

Subtracting this $43,668.32 (i.e., 72.7972% of the $60,000 basis) from the $72,797.20 value of the annuity results in a capital gain of $29,118.88. If this annuity were being paid to someone other than the donor (or donor and donor's spouse), then this capital gain would be recognized immediately. But, in this case, the annuity is being paid to the donor, so this capital gain can be spread out over the life expectancy of the donor as of the date of the transaction (a.k.a. "expected return multiple").

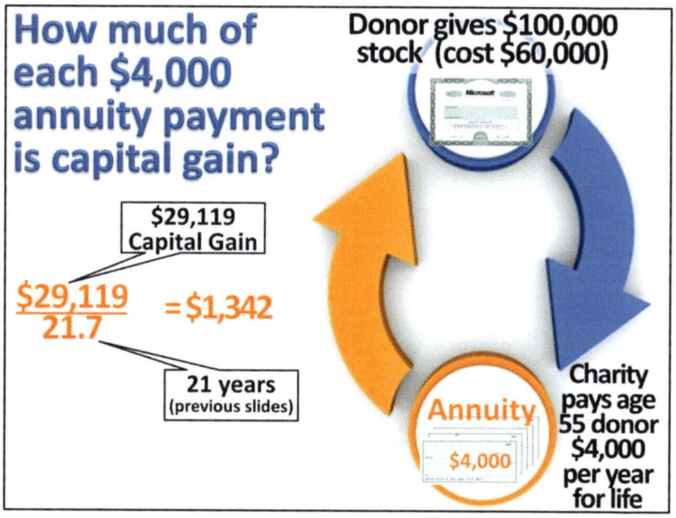

As a result, $1,341.88 of each check ($29,118.88/21.7) will be counted as capital gain until all of the capital gain ($29,118.88) is recognized.

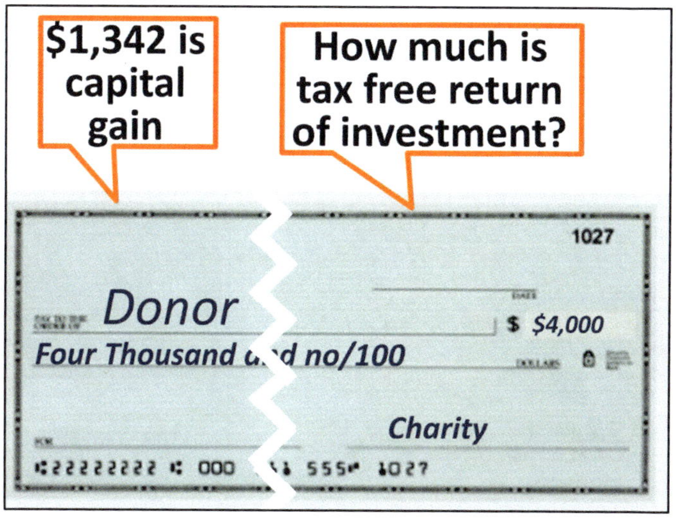

Now that we know that $1,341.88 of each $4,000 check will be counted as capital gain, this leaves open the question of the tax treatment for the remainder of each check. As before, part of each gift annuity check (received prior to the annuitant's outliving his or her expected return multiple) will be tax-free return of investment.

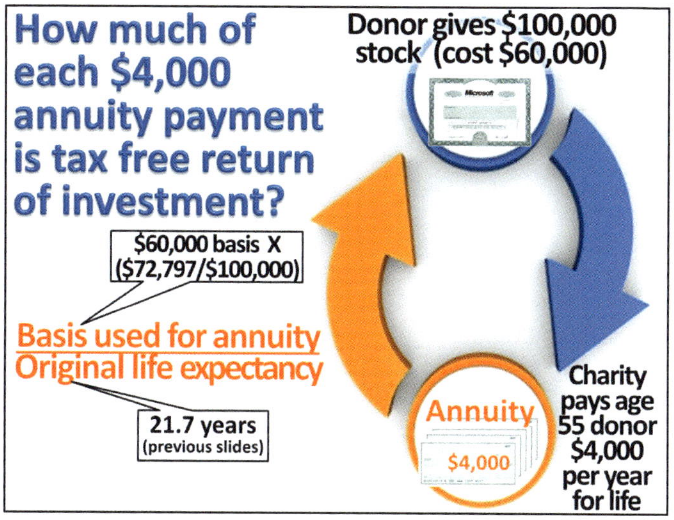

To calculate the amount of each $4,000 annuity payment that will qualify as tax-free return of investment, we divide the part of the basis used to purchase the annuity by the annuitant's expected return multiple (i.e., original life expectancy). In this case, 72.7972% of the property was used to purchase the annuity portion (with the remaining part of the property transferred as a deductible charitable gift), meaning that 72.7972% of the $60,000 basis may potentially be returned to the donor as tax-free return of investment.

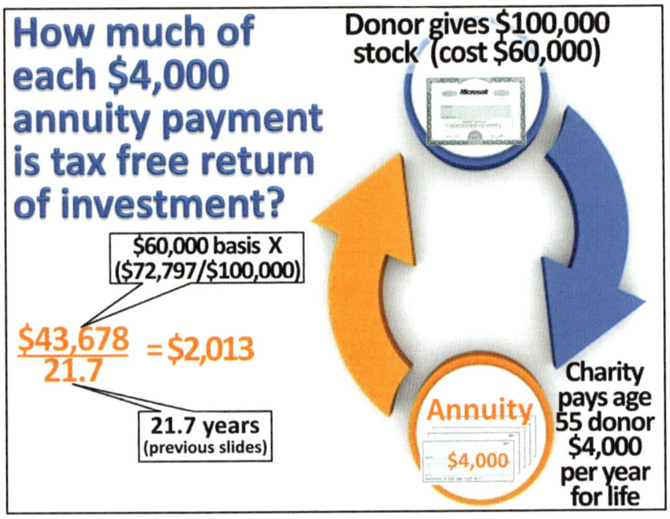

This $43,678.32 (72.7972% of the $60,000) of basis will be returned in equal shares over the first 21.7 years of the annuity payments, meaning that $2,012.83 of each annual $4,000 payment will be tax-free return of investment.

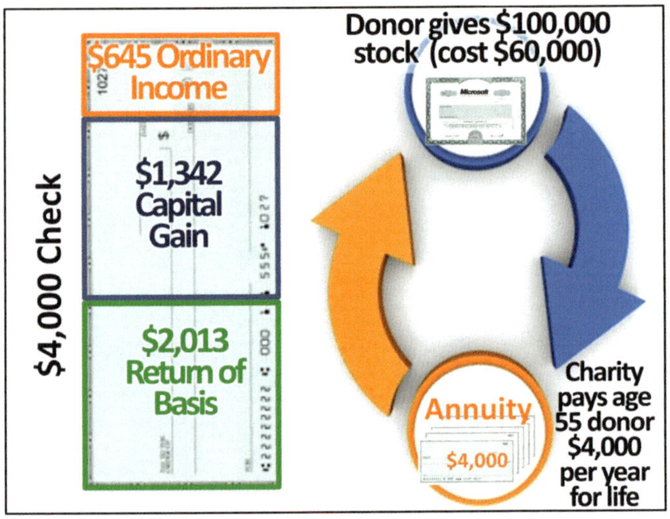

In addition to the $2,012.83 of each annual payment that will count as tax-free return of investment, part of each payment will be capital gain. As previously calculated, the capital gain portion of each check will be $1,341.88. Everything else, by definition, is ordinary income. Thus, in this case the ordinary income portion of each check will be the total check ($4,000) less the portion of each check that is tax-free return of investment ($2,012.83) and the portion of each check that is capital gain ($1,341.88), or $4,000-$2,012.83-$1,341.88=$645.29.

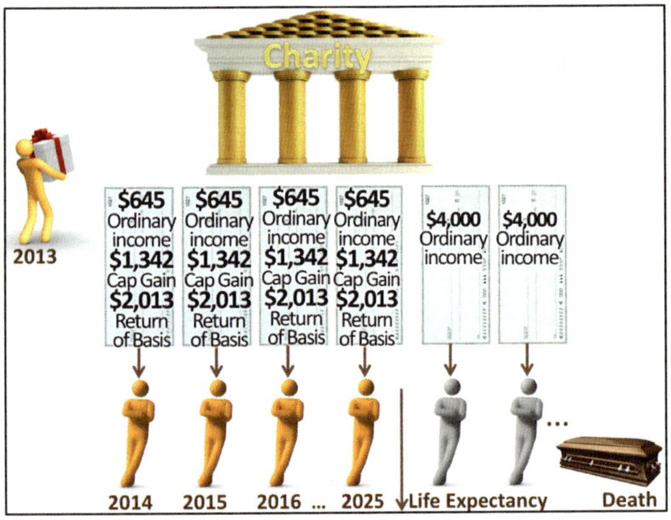

Until the donor/annuitant lives beyond his expected return multiple (i.e., original life expectancy) each $4,000 check will consist of $2,012.83 tax-free return of capital, $1,341.88 capital gain, with everything else ($645.29) treated as ordinary income. After the annuitant lives beyond his "expected return multiple" each $4,000 check will consist entirely of ordinary income.

As a side note, the tax treatment of the check in the 22nd year will be slightly different because of the 21.7 year "expected return multiple." In that year, all of the remaining capital will be returned ($2,012.83 X .7=$1,407.58), and all of the remaining capital gain will be recognized ($1,341.88 X

.7=$939.32), leaving the remaining amount of $1,653.10 ($4,000-$1,407.58-$939.32) as ordinary income.

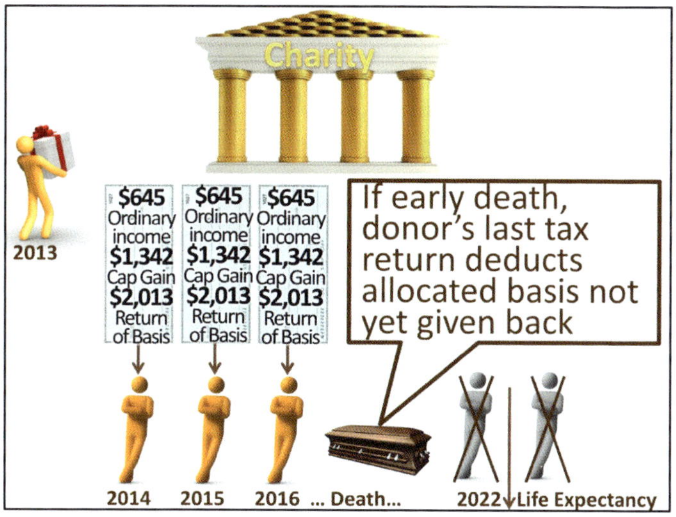

If the donor dies prior to reaching his original life expectancy ("expected return multiple"), then the donor fails to receive his entire original investment in the annuity portion of the transaction, i.e. the "sale" portion of the basis. In this case, the donor's last tax return can deduct the portion of the basis allocated to the annuity portion of the transaction not yet returned to the donor. No additional recognition of capital gain is made. (This makes sense because the donor, failing to live to his or her life expectancy, did not actually receive any further benefit.)

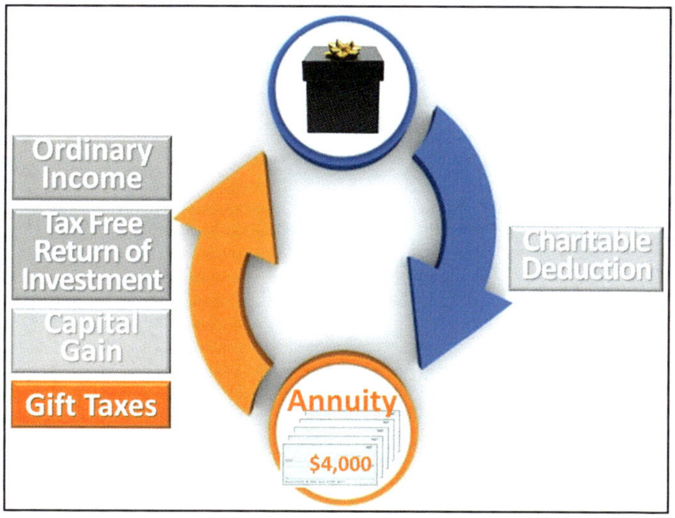

The final area of potential tax consequences for a Charitable Gift Annuity relates to gift taxation. When discussing gift taxation, we are not referring to any charitable gift or charitable gift portion of the annuity. Instead, we are considering gift transfers to non-charitable recipients. Gift transfers are taxed as part of the estate and gift taxation system. In 2013, the exemption amount for gift and estate taxes was $5.25 million (or $10.5 million for a married couple). Thus, for the vast majority of donors, estate and gift tax considerations will be irrelevant. But, for those where estate tax considerations are important, it is useful to understand the gift tax implications of purchasing a Charitable Gift Annuity that pays to someone other than the donor.

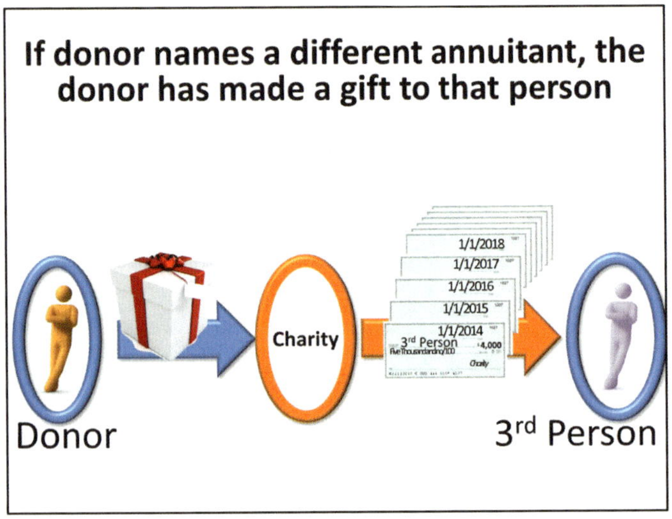

Simply put, if they'd donor names an annuitant other than himself, the donor has made a gift to that person. If that person is not the donor's spouse, then this gift is a taxable gift. The value of the gift is simply the value of the annuity as calculated previously.

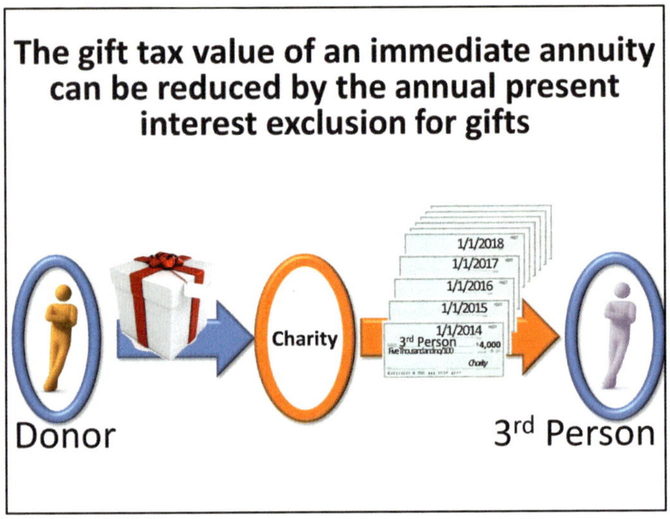

However, the value of the taxable gift made to the annuity recipient will be reduced by the annual present interest exclusion for gifts if the Charitable Gift Annuity if for the typical immediate annuity interest. For example, in 2013/14, the annual present interest exclusion for gifts was $14,000 per donor per donee. Thus, if a donor named another person as the beneficiary of a Charitable Gift Annuity where the annuity portion was valued at $100,000, the amount of the taxable gift would be $100,000-$14,000, or $86,000. This present interest exclusion would not apply if the gift annuity purchased was a deferred gift annuity, because the exclusion only applies for *present* interests. An *immediate* annuity is considered to be a present interest, but a deferred annuity is not.

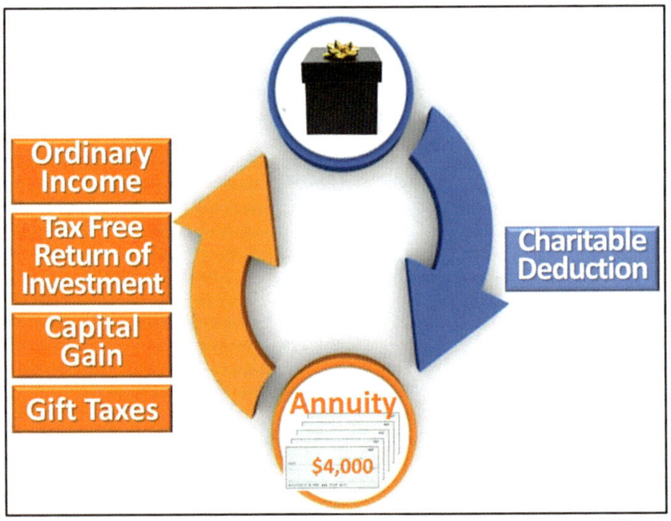

In sum, a transaction as straightforward as a Charitable Gift Annuity can result in a wide range of tax consequences, including a charitable income tax deduction, recognition of ordinary income, tax-free return of investment, recognition of capital gain (either immediate or deferred) and gift taxation. This same set of tax consequences also applies to other transactions such as a Charitable Remainder Trust, but in slightly different ways.

We have examined the taxation rules for Charitable Gift Annuities. However, certain scenarios can create unusual cases where the application of these rules may not be immediately obvious. So next we will turn to some of these tricky examples to see how the taxation rules operate in these circumstances.

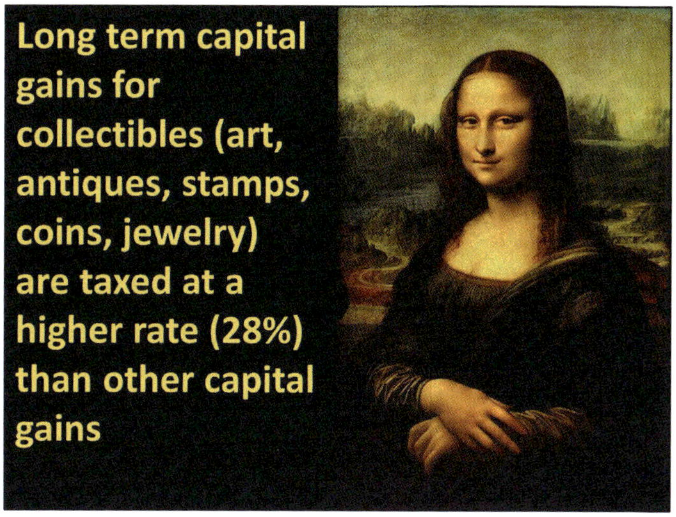

We have already examined the rules for capital gain resulting from purchasing a Charitable Gift Annuity with appreciated property. However, there is a separate tax rate for long-term capital gain for collectibles. Collectibles are items such as artwork, antiques, stamps, coins, and jewelry. Capital gain on these items is taxed at 28%. What taxation would result if a Charitable Gift Annuity were purchased in exchange for appreciated collectible items?

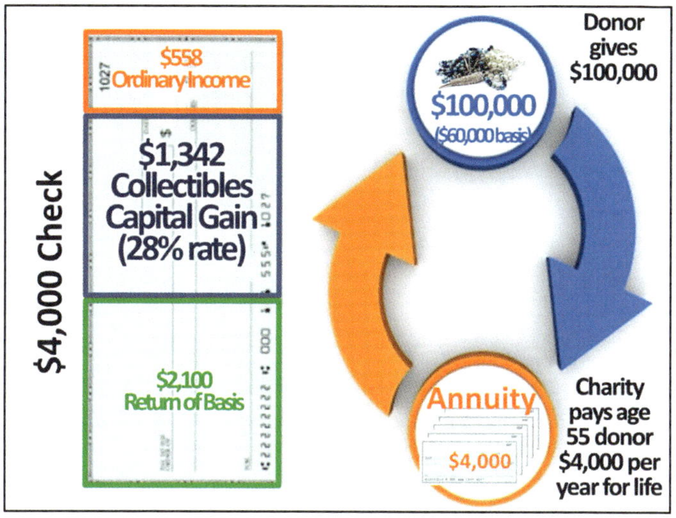

The initial calculations are identical to those used for any other item of capital gain property. Thus, the same amount of capital gain would be recognized from each check as in the previous example where the donor gave appreciated stock rather than appreciated collectibles. The only difference is that when the donor recognizes the capital gain, the donor must recognize the capital gain as capital gain for collectibles.

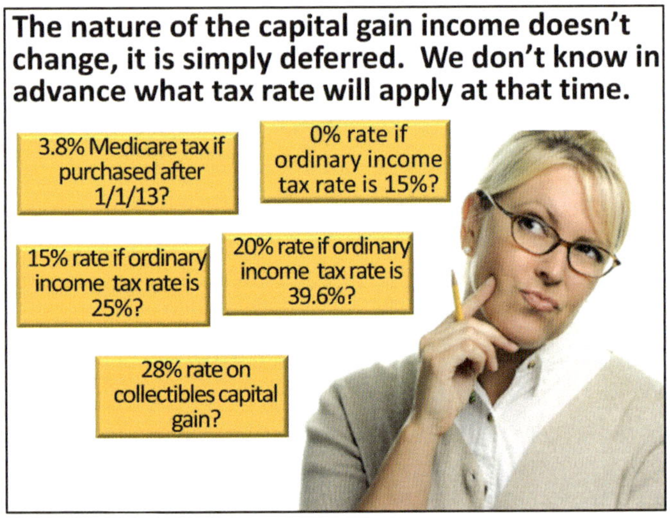

The general principle here applies to all forms of capital gain. The nature of the capital gain income does not change when it is later recognized by the donor. The result of the gift annuity transaction is to simply defer the recognition of the capital gain, but not to change the character of the capital gain. Although we know in advance how much and what type of capital gain will be recognized in future years, we cannot say with certainty what the tax rate will be for that type of capital gain in a future year. Even if current tax rules do not change, the donor's future income levels may change, which will cause the tax rate to change. Purchasing a Charitable Gift Annuity with appreciated property produces the clear advantage of paying capital gains taxes later, rather than today. However, if the donor is in a higher income bracket today, but will be in a lower income bracket in the future (e.g., after retirement), then the gift annuity transaction may result not only in tax deferral, but also in tax reduction (or even complete tax avoidance if the donor's future income is low enough). For the donor who is in a high income tax bracket today, but expects to be in a lower income tax bracket after retirement in the future, the Charitable Gift Annuity purchased with appreciated property generates the "double bonus" of an immediate income tax deduction today (when income and tax rates are high) and deferral of recognizing capital gain until future years (when income and tax rates will be low). The use of a deferred or flexible Charitable Gift Annuity which postpones the initial payments for some years can generate even longer tax deferral.

Given the higher tax rate (28%), the deferment of recognizing capital gains taxes with appreciated collectible items may be even more attractive than with the use of appreciated stocks. A key challenge in such transactions is that the charitable tax deduction may be limited to the share of basis applied to the "gift" portion of the transaction unless the charity plans to make use of the collectibles in its charitable purpose, rather than simply selling them. Let's examine how this might work using a different type of tangible personal property gift.

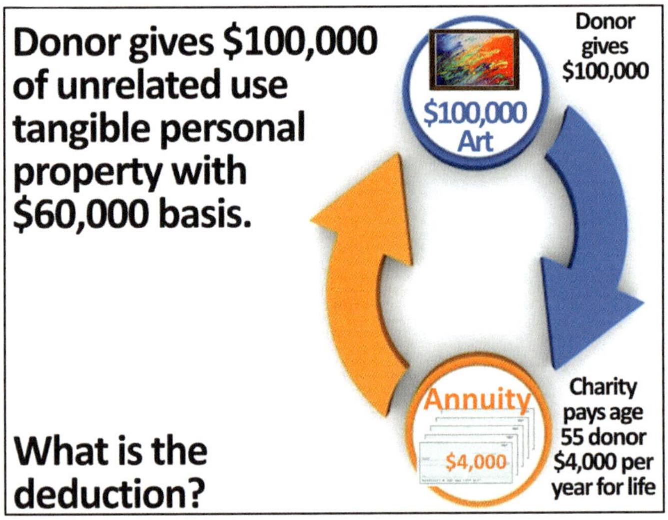

Suppose that a donor gives a work of art (or any other tangible personal property) to a charity in exchange for a gift annuity. The charity plans to immediately sell the art in order to provide funds for making the annuity payments. As in our previous examples, we will assume that the donor purchased the art for $60,000 more than one year ago, making this long-term capital gain, with a $60,000 basis. What is the charitable deduction for such a transaction? If we were giving $100,000 of cash, the deduction would be the difference between the $100,000 transfer and the value of the annuity (which we have previously calculated to be $72,797.20), or $27,202.80. The same deduction would apply if we were giving $100,000 of appreciated securities with the same $60,000 basis. However, in this case, the deduction will be lower. Why? The critical distinction here is that the gift is of "unrelated use" tangible personal property, because the charity intends to sell the artwork, rather than use it in its charitable purposes.

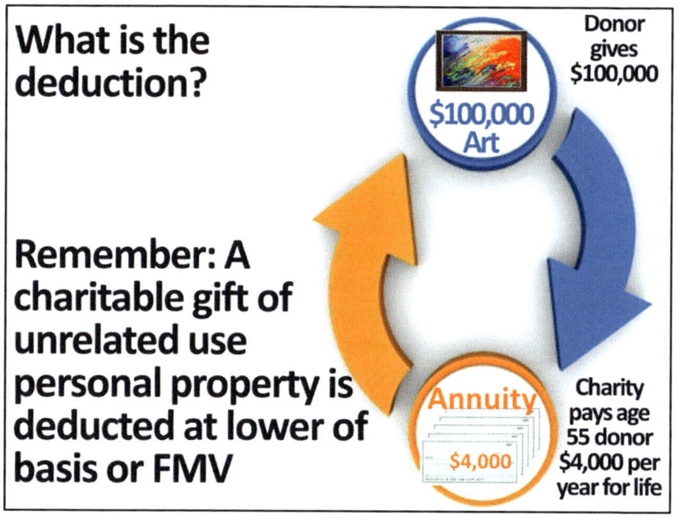

Because this is "unrelated use" tangible personal property, the deduction is limited to the *lower* of basis or fair market value. Of course, this rule applies to all gifts of "unrelated use" tangible personal property, regardless of whether or not those gifts are given in exchange for a gift annuity. Can we simply deduct the $60,000 basis as a gift? No. Because part of the basis is used to purchase the gift annuity (i.e., the "sale" part of this bargain sale), and only part of the basis applies to the charitable gift portion (i.e., the "gift" part of this bargain sale).

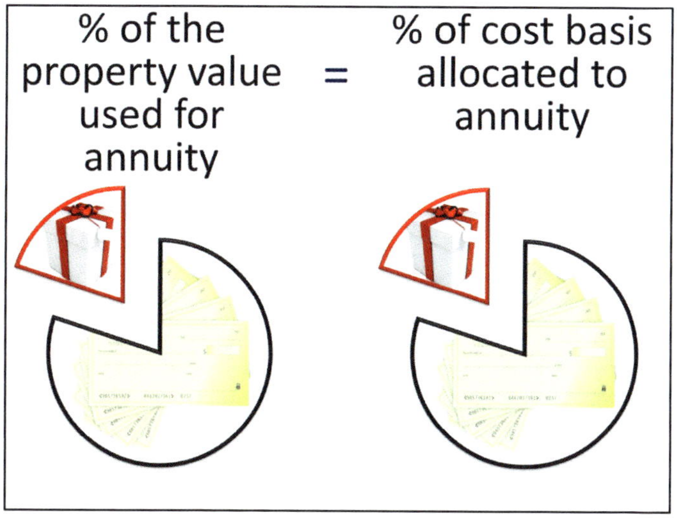

To calculate the share of cost basis used for the gift portion, we follow exactly the same process as before. The only difference here is that for this calculation we are interested in the gift portion of the basis, rather than the sale/annuity portion of the basis.

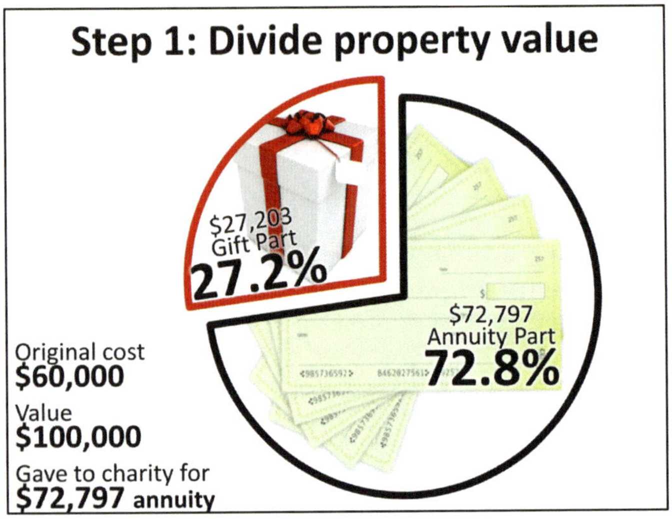

Just as before, the first step is to divide the property value into the gift portion and the annuity/sale portion. The annuity/sale portion is 72.7972%. This is because, as before, the IRS valuation of the annuity is $72,797.20. The remaining amount from the $100,000 transfer is the gift portion. Thus, the gift portion is 27.2028%, representing $27,202.80 of the $100,000 transfer. If the transfer from the donor was cash or appreciated securities held for more than one year, then this $27,202.80 would be the deductible gift. However, we cannot deducted this full amount, because for this type of property gift only the basis can be deducted, not the higher fair market value.

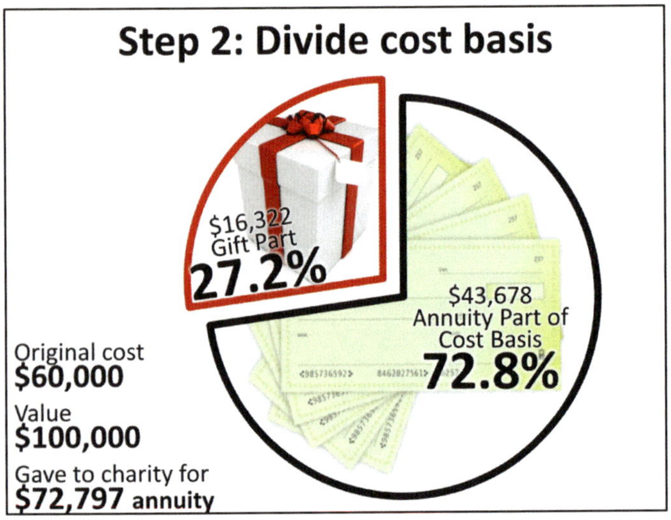

In order to calculate the deduction, we must divide the cost basis between the gift portion and the sale/annuity portion. The cost basis will be divided in exactly the same way that the property value (or total transaction amount) was divided. Thus, 27.2028% of the $60,000 basis (i.e., $16,321.68) will apply to the gift portion of the transaction.

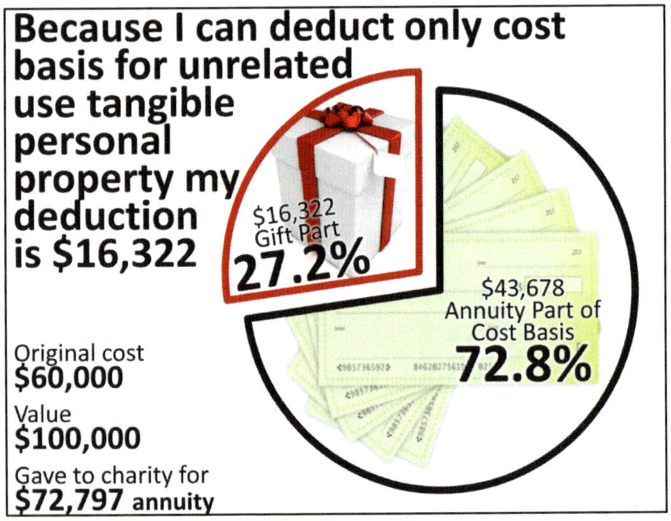

This $16,321.68 of the basis is the deductible charitable gift resulting from the transaction, because only basis may be deducted when giving "unrelated use" tangible personal property (such as artwork that the charity intends to sell).

Although the Charitable Gift Annuity is a relatively simple transaction (typically documented with a standard one or two page agreement used for all annuity sales from a particular charity), the tax results are as complex as those found in more advanced instruments such as the Charitable Remainder Trust. The taxation of Charitable Gift Annuities can become complicated, but it is often important to present them to prospective donors or clients in a simple, intuitive fashion, rather than burying the client with details. As with other forms of charitable planning, successful planning can generate a range of tax benefits, but should only be considered for clients who have a real charitable interest in advancing the work of the charity.

10 GIFTS OF PARTIAL INTERESTS

In this chapter we will examine charitable gifts of partial interests in property. The topic of this chapter may initially appear not as interesting or relevant as some of the chapters covering well-known specific techniques. However, gifts of partial interests (specifically retained partial interest gifts where the donor keeps some rights in property and gives other rights in the same property to the charity) are a fundamental concept that will be used again and again in advanced techniques. For example, Charitable Remainder Trusts, Charitable Lead Trusts, gifts of remainder interest in homes and farmland, and even qualified conservation easement gifts are all forms of partial interest gifts where the donor retains some rights in the property given to charity. Although this chapter does not address the specifics of such gifts (which are covered in their own chapters), this chapter provides a brief theoretical foundation of how and why partial interest gifts, such as these, are sometimes allowed and sometimes disallowed. Additionally, this chapter also covers some specific gifting techniques that, while relatively straightforward, may be useful in a variety of circumstances.

So, let's begin with a definition. What is a retained partial interest gift? A retained partial interest gift occurs when a donor gives a charity some rights to an item of property, but simultaneously keeps some other rights in the property. Notice that what is being divided here is not the property itself (such as taking the tire off of a car), but rather the legal rights to the property. In the law, property ownership represents a bundle of rights. These rights can be kept together where one person owns all of them, or these rights can be divided where different people own different rights. So, for example, the tenant in an apartment has certain rights, such as the right to use the property for residential purposes so long as the rent is paid. However, the owner of the apartment building also has rights in the apartment property, such as the right to take possession of the apartment at the end of the lease period. A retained partial interest gift occurs whenever a donor splits ownership rights apart and gives some of them to charity and while retaining others.

An example of splitting the rights between the donor and a charity would occur if the donor gives ownership of an automobile to a charity, but retains the right to use the automobile for one year. Given that the charity has received some rights (i.e., ownership in one year), is it reasonable to allow an immediate tax deduction for this transfer?

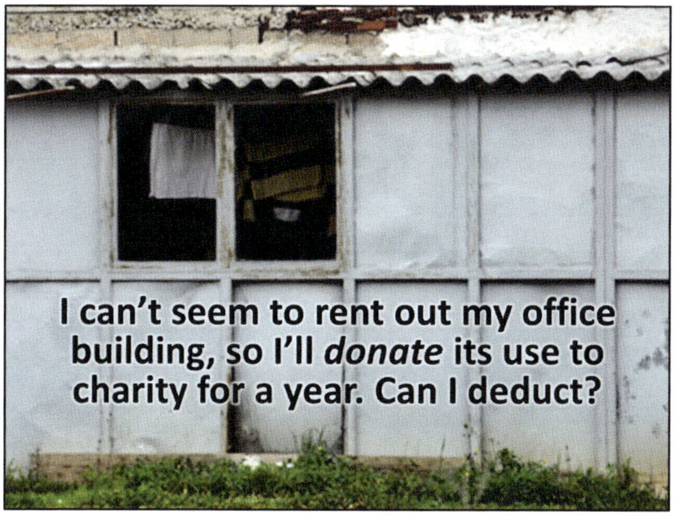

Another example of a partial interest gift reverses the previous situation by giving the charity the right to use the property for one year, after which the donor has full ownership rights. Given that the charity has received some rights (i.e., the right to use the property for one year), is it reasonable to allow an immediate tax deduction for this transfer?

Another example of a partial interest gift, would be a transfer of land to a charity where the donor keeps all rights to extract minerals from the land. Once again, the donor has retained some types of rights and the charity has received different types of rights in an item of property. Given that the charity has received some types of rights (i.e., the ownership of the land, except for mineral rights), should an immediate tax deduction be allowed for this transfer?

The general rule is that the donor cannot keep ownership rights in gifted property and still deduct the gifts. There are some very important specific exceptions to this general rule that we will examine in detail later. However, if none of these specific exceptions apply, the partial interest gift with retained rights will not generate a deduction.

So, for example, if the donor gives the title to his car to a charity, but retains the right to use it for one year, there is no immediate charitable income tax deduction. This is a partial interest gift with retained rights because the donor retains rights to the gifted property. This gift does not qualify for any of the special exceptions to the general rule against deductions for such partial interest gifts, so there is no immediate income tax deduction.

The emphasis is on there being no *immediate* tax deduction because the donor could later transfer the remaining rights to the charity or the donor's rights could expire. In either case, the transfer to charity would no longer be a retained partial interest gift because the donor would no longer have any retained rights. At that point, the transfer would become a completed gift not involving any retained interests and would therefore be deductible. So, in this example, after one year – when the donor's rights expire – then the gift of the vehicle is complete and could be deducted based upon its value at that time.

Similarly, allowing the charity to use property does not generate a deduction when the donor still retains underlying ownership of the property. Because the donor is retaining rights in the gifted property, this is a retained partial interest gift. Because none of the special exceptions apply to this partial interest gift it, therefore, will generate no deduction. Thus, allowing the charity the rent-free use of a building when the donor retains ownership rights to the building will generate no charitable tax deduction.

As a final example, transferring ownership of land to a charity, but retaining the mineral rights also generates no charitable income tax deductions for the donor. The donor has given some rights in the property, but retained some other types of rights in the same property, making this a retained partial interest gift. Because this transfer does not qualify for any of the special exceptions, the general rule (that partial interest gifts are not deductible) will apply.

These are all examples of the general rule (which has some very important exceptions) that donors may not keep some rights in the property and still deduct a transfer of other rights to a charity. Notice that this rule applies to retaining rights in the *same* property that was given to the charity. So, for example, it does not prevent a deduction for giving a specific 10-acre tract to charity from a 1,000 acre farm. In that case, the donor retains no rights to the 10-acre tract given to the charity, but retains rights only in the 990 acres not transferred to the charity. Similarly, a donor could give the steering wheel of an automobile to charity and keep the rest of the car. This would not be a partial interest gift because the donor retains no rights to the specific item of property (the steering wheel) given to the charity.

We have been examining cases where the general rule against deductions for partial interest charitable transfers applies. But, why do we have such a rule in the first place? Why not simply allow deductions for the fair market value of any partial interests transferred to the charity?

The problem with partial interest gifts is that the donor may be able to manipulate the property to get more value for the donor's share and less value for the charity's share. The charity may not complain about such manipulation because it is still getting some value, which is better than nothing. However, because the charity is getting less value than that assumed by the calculation of the tax deduction, this violates tax policy goals. How might a donor manipulate the property to reduce the charity's share if such partial interest gifts with retained interests were deductible? Let's look at a few examples.

Suppose a donor could transfer an automobile to charity, retain the right to use the automobile for one year, and still deduct the value of the automobile subtracting only one year of projected depreciation. Could the donor use the automobile in such a way that the charity would receive very little value at the end of the year? Yes. Thus, the donor would receive a tax deduction based upon a much higher value than that actually transferred to the charity. To avoid this problem, such partial interest gifts do not generate an immediate tax deduction.

Or, let's reverse the situation and give the charity the right to use the property while the donor retains ownership at the end of the use. Suppose a donor gives a charity the right to use his newly planted olive tree orchard for seven years. What if the donor was allowed to deduct the fair market rental value for farmland? In this case the land produces nothing for the first seven years. (Newly planted olive trees do not produce until after seven years.) A cooperative charity would not disturb the olive trees, allowing the owner to deduct the gift of a right which has no real value. Thus, once again, the donor would receive a tax deduction based upon a much higher value than that actually transferred to charity if this prohibition against partial interest deductions were not in place.

As a final example, let's suppose that a donor gave $2 million worth of stock in his corporation to a charity, but retained the right to repurchase the stock for $2 million any time in the next three years. This is a retained partial interest gift, because the donor is retaining some rights in the property gifted to charity. Were it not for the prohibition against deductions for such partial interest gifts, the donor could deduct $2 million. (This is logical because the charity receives $2 million of property and the right to repurchase the property must be accompanied by a $2 million transfer.) How could such a transaction be abusive of the tax code? Suppose that the corporation's only product was a new cancer drug that would be either approved or rejected by the FDA in three years. If approved the $2 million of stock would be worth $200 million. If rejected, the $2 million of stock would be worth zero dollars. If the partial interest charitable gift were deductible, the donor could guarantee a $2 million deduction – worth nearly $1 million in reduced tax payments depending upon the donor's income and state of residence – and still retain the repurchase rights to capture the potential $198 million gain. Even if the donor had no charitable interests, the charitable gift risk scenario (outcomes of $1 million benefit or $199 million benefit) could be preferable to the non-charitable risk scenario (outcomes of $0 benefit or $200 million benefit). Because of the partial interest rule this transaction would generate no *immediate* charitable deduction. (If the donor's right to repurchase expired, then, *at that point*, the gift would be completed, because the donor would have no retained rights in the stock. But, the deduction would be based upon the value of the stock at the time that the retained interests expired, not at the time of the initial transaction, thus eliminating the opportunity for changing the donor's risk scenario.)

These examples all serve to explain why the general rule prohibits donors from keeping some rights to a gift of property and still deducting the value of the partial interests gifted to charity. Understanding this underlying principle also helps to explain why the tax code allows for certain exceptions to the general rule. Specifically, these exceptions are cases in which the opportunities to abuse the charitable tax deduction have been largely eliminated.

One of the exceptions to the general rule against deducting gifts of partial interests is that the donor can deduct if he or she gives all or and "undivided portion" of his or her ownership interests. We will be exploring this exception in the rest of this chapter. Other notable exceptions to the general rule against deductions for partial interest gifts with retained interests include remainder interests in a personal residence or farmland, Charitable Remainder Trusts, Charitable Lead Trusts, pooled income funds, and qualified conservation easements. These other exceptions will be addressed in other chapters.

Why are partial interest gifts allowed if the donor gives all or an "undivided portion" of his or her interests? The underlying reason why partial interest gifts do not generally create a deduction is because of the potential for the donor to subsequently increase the value of his retained interests while reducing the value of the charity's interests. This type of behavior is not a risk when the donor gives all or an "undivided portion" of his or her interests.

If the donor gives away all of his interests, he has retained nothing which could be increased in value at the expense of the charity's interests. For example, if the donor owned only the mineral rights to a piece of land, he could deduct the gift of those mineral rights to a charity. In contrast, no deduction would be allowed if the donor retained ownership in the surface rights of the land, because the donor would not have given away all of his interests in the property. Thus, it is not the giving of partial interests to a charity that makes the gift nondeductible. Rather, it is the retention of some interests by the donor that makes the gift nondeductible.

However, the donor may retain rights to the property, if the donor gives an "undivided portion" of ALL of the rights owned by the donor. In this case, the donor gives a percentage (say, for example, 10%) of all of his rights in the property to the charity. There is no opportunity for the donor to increase the value of his rights while decreasing the value of the charity's rights, because the donor and the charity have identical rights (although perhaps with a different percentage ownership of those otherwise identical rights). Because the donor and the charity have identical types of rights, thus eliminating the risk of abuse, the retained interest by the donor will not prevent a charitable deduction. This difference between divided and undivided shares may be, at first, difficult to conceptualize. So, let's look at an analogy that may help to clarify this distinction.

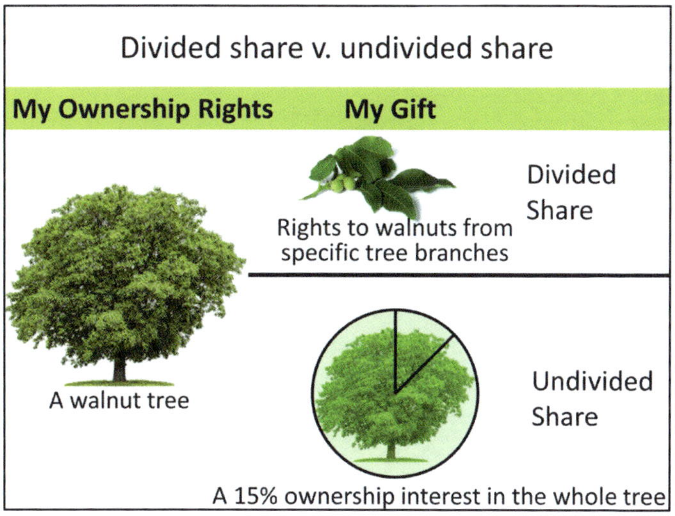

Suppose that a donor owns a walnut tree. Walnut trees are valuable both for their wood and for the walnuts that they produce each year. Suppose the donor wants to make a partial interest gift, giving something to the charity and keeping something for himself. The donor could designate a specific branch and give the charity the rights to collect the walnuts from that specific branch. This is a *divided* share gift (i.e., the donor is dividing the tree and giving the charity rights to the walnuts from a *specific* branch of the tree.) Alternatively, the donor could give a 15% ownership interest in the whole tree to the charity. This would give the charity the rights to 15% of any walnuts collected, 15% of the price of any wood sold from the tree, and the right to force the sale of the tree. This would be an "undivided share" gift, because the donor has shared a set share of *every* type of right he owns in the entire tree.

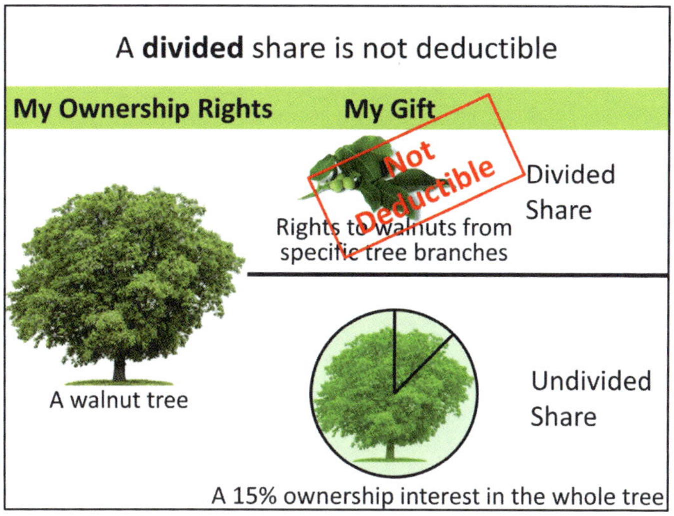

A "divided share" gift is not deductible. Divided share gifts provide the opportunity for the donor to subsequently reduce the value of the charity's share relative to the donor's share. For example, the donor might designate that the charity receives all of the walnuts from a particular branch. But, then at some later time the donor might cut off that branch so that it no longer produced walnuts. By doing this, the donor could increase production for the rest of the tree (which the donor still owns) by leaving the roots to more strongly support the donor's remaining portion of the tree. This opportunity for reducing the value of the charity's share relative to the donor's share is essentially the same logic that makes such divided share gifts non-deductible where no special exception applies.

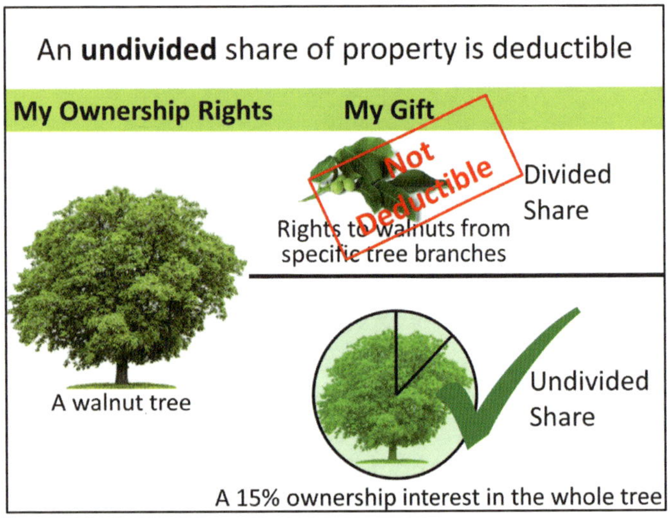

In contrast, an "undivided share" gift is deductible. When the donor gives a 15% ownership interest in the whole tree, this gives the charity the rights to 15% of any walnuts collected, 15% of the price of any wood sold from the tree, and the right to force the sale of the tree. There is no way for the donor to increase the value of his retained ownership rights relative to the rights given to the charity. If the donor cuts off a branch, both the donor (85%) and the charity (15%) own that branch as well as the remaining tree. Anything that decreases the value of the charity's interests also decreases the value of the donor's interest in exact proportion to their ownership percentages. Because there is no opportunity for abuse, this type of "undivided share" gift does generate a taxable deduction. Let's now examine some different examples of gifts to determine if they are divided share gifts (not deductible) or undivided share gifts (deductible).

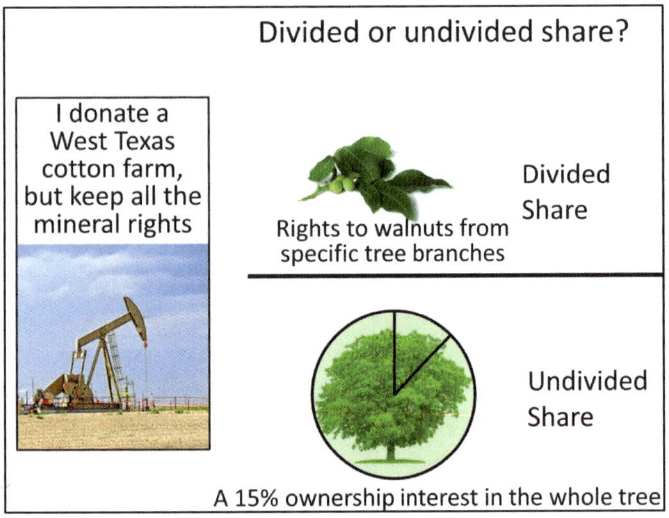

Suppose a donor gives a West Texas cotton farm to a charity, but keeps for himself all of the mineral rights to that farm. Is that a gift of an undivided share in all of the rights owned by the donor, or a gift of a divided share giving only specific kinds of rights to the charity? To use our original analogy, is this gift more similar to giving shared ownership in the whole tree (i.e., all types of rights) or more like giving rights only to specific branches (i.e., only specific types of rights, but keeping other types of rights entirely)?

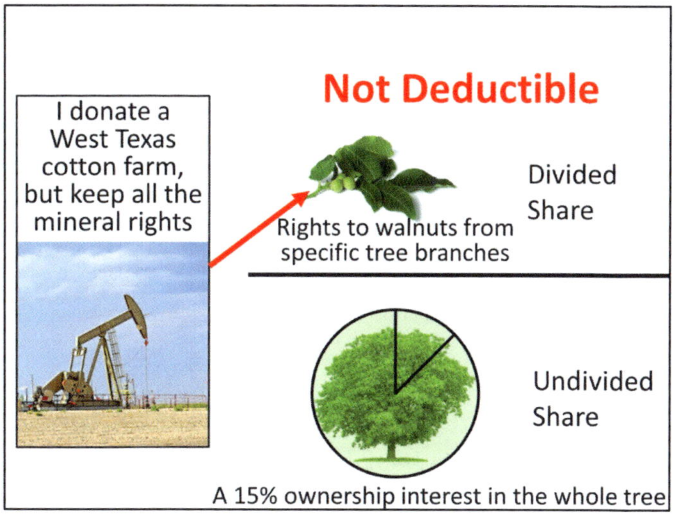

Here, the donor is making a charitable gift of a divided share. The donor is not sharing all of the different types of rights, but is instead keeping some types of rights entirely for himself. It may be that, to return to the tree analogy, the donor is giving rights to walnuts from a large majority of the tree branches. (In other words, the value of what the donor is giving may be worth more than the value of what the donor is keeping.) Nevertheless, this is still not sharing ownership in the entire tree (i.e., the charity is receiving an interest in only some types of rights, but is excluded from other types of rights which the donor is keeping).

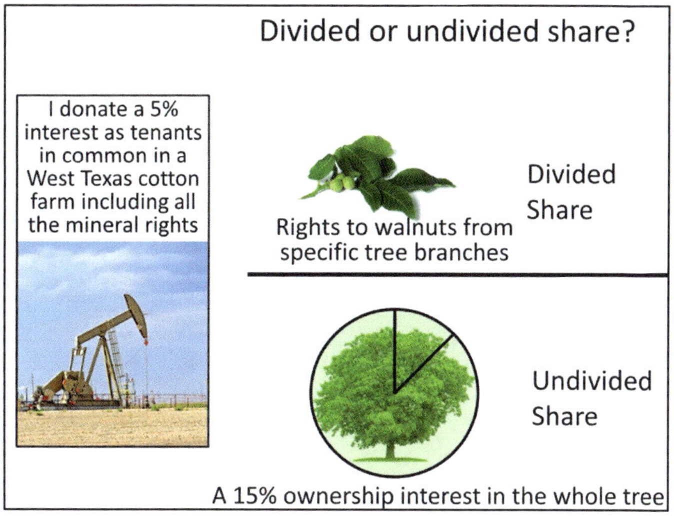

Suppose, however, a donor gives a 5% ownership interest, as tenants in common, in a West Texas cotton farm, including all mineral rights. (The "tenants in common" ownership form differs from the "joint tenants" ownership form in that if one "joint tenant" dies, the remaining "joint tenants" receive the deceased tenant's ownership share, whereas if one "tenant in common" dies, the other "tenants in common" have no inheritance rights.) Is this a gift of an undivided share in all of the rights owned by the donor, or a gift of a divided share giving only specific kinds of rights to the charity while keeping other types of rights for the donor?

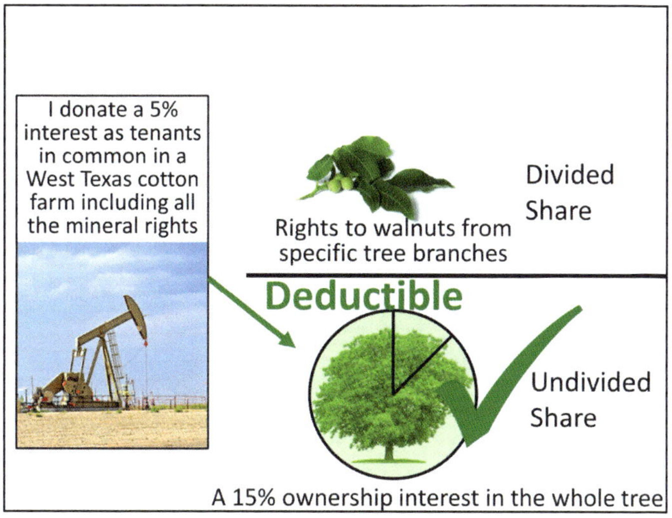

Here, the donor is sharing a portion of *all* types of rights owned in the property. Consequently, this is a gift of an undivided share (i.e., it is similar to giving a percentage ownership in the entire "tree"). Because it is a gift of an *undivided* share, it is a deductible gift.

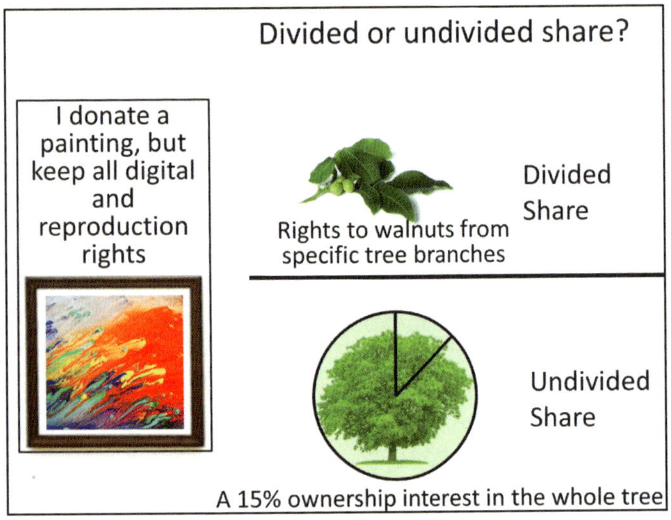

Suppose a donor gives a painting to a museum for it to own and hang in its gallery. However, the donor keeps for himself all of the digital and reproduction rights of the painting. (The donor plans to sell prints and online images of the painting even after the donation of the painting itself.) Is this a gift of a divided or an undivided share? In other words, does the charity receive only specific kinds of rights or a share of all rights owned by the donor?

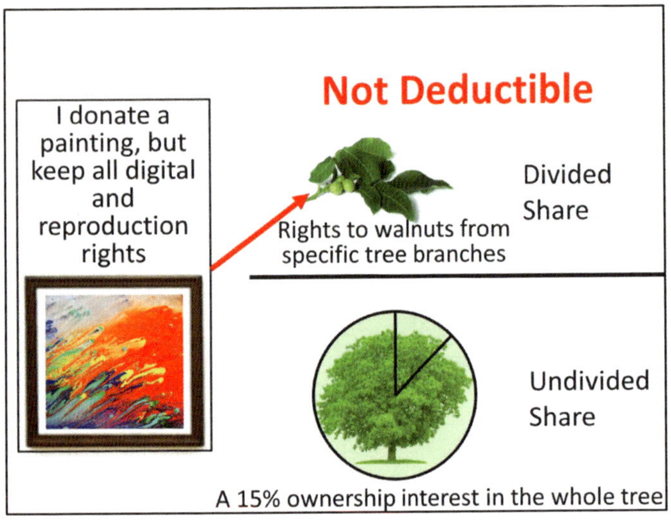

This gift is the gift of a divided share in the property and is therefore not deductible. The donor is keeping all of certain types of rights for himself. To return to the tree analogy, there are some "branches of the tree" in which the charity has rights and other "branches of the tree" in which the charity will have no rights.

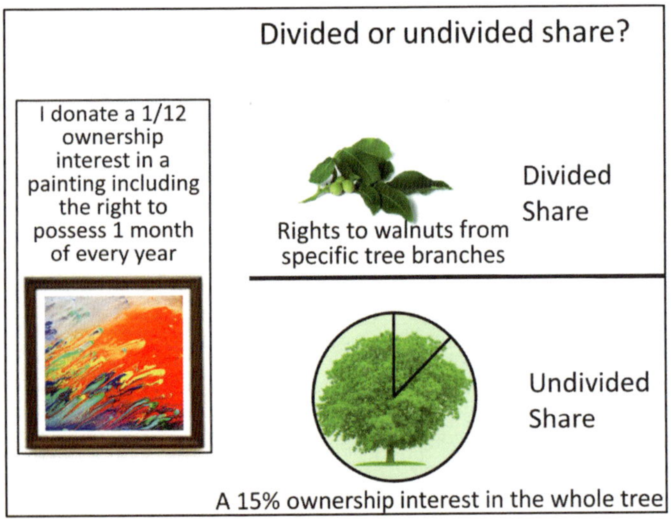

Now suppose that the donor gives a 1/12 ownership interest in all rights to a painting. This gift includes the right for the charity to possess the painting for one month out of every year. It also includes 1/12 of all other ownership rights owned by the donor in the painting. Is this a gift of a divided share (not deductible) or an undivided share (deductible)?

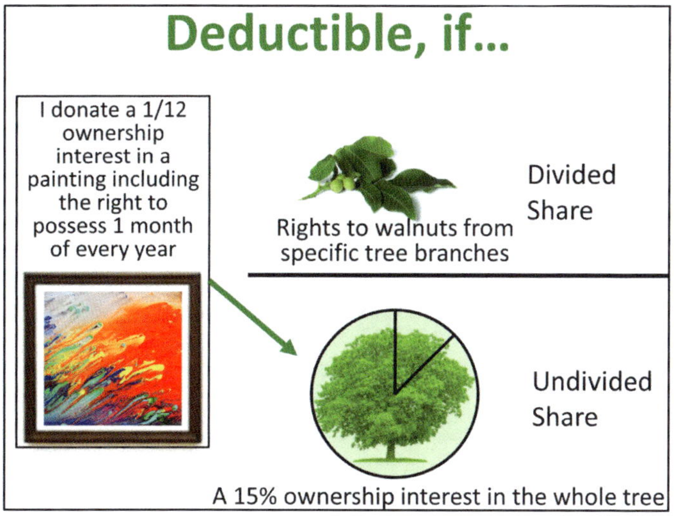

Because the charity receives a share of all of the rights owned by the donor, this is a gift of an undivided share. Such gifts of undivided shares are generally deductible. However, here we have a special rule that applies only to these kind of fractional shares in tangible personal property. The reason for this special rule was because of the popularity of these fractional interest undivided share gifts of artwork. A donor might have a large art collection, which he displays in his home on a rotating basis. Instead of rotating the artwork into his basement, the donor could rotate the artwork into an art museum by donating a fractional ownership interest. In this way, the donor's use of the property does not functionally change, yet, the donor can obtain a substantial charitable tax deduction. This type of gift clearly meets the general rules for a deductible gift of an undivided share of property. However, there was some concern about the overuse of this type of charitable deduction, which resulted in some special rules.

In order to deduct the gift of a fractional share in tangible personal property, the donor must be in the process of contributing the entire ownership of the tangible personal property to the charity. Specifically, all of the donor's rights must be given to charity within 10 years of the initial deduction for the first fractional share gift. Additionally, the donor must arrange his estate in such a way that if he dies prior to the end of the 10-year deadline then the charity will receive all remaining rights to the tangible personal property. Although we considered the example of artwork, this rule applies to all forms of tangible personal property, such as giving a fractional interest in an automobile, an antique, jewelry or other collectible item.

The amount of the deduction will be based upon the lesser of the value of the property during the year of transfer of a fractional interest or the value of the property during any previous year of transfer of a fractional interest. Thus, if the property increases in value after the initial gift of a fractional interest, the donor will not benefit from this increase in value.

Although these rules reduce the attractiveness of gifts of fractional shares in tangible personal property, they do still allow for the deduction under these special circumstances.

Given that these rules must be followed over a 10 year period of time, it is reasonable to ask what happens if the donor fails to transfer the rest of his interest to charity within the 10 year time? Or, similarly, what happens if the donor dies prior to the end of the 10 year period, and the estate does not give the remaining interest to the charity?

Violating the rules for gifts of fractional shares in tangible personal property results in recapture. Specifically, all previous deductions are now counted as ordinary income. The donor must pay the taxes on this ordinary income, plus interest, plus a 10% penalty on the taxes owed. The result of recapture is sufficiently unpleasant to deter taxpayers from taking this deduction without completing the ultimate transfer of all rights to the charity within 10 years.

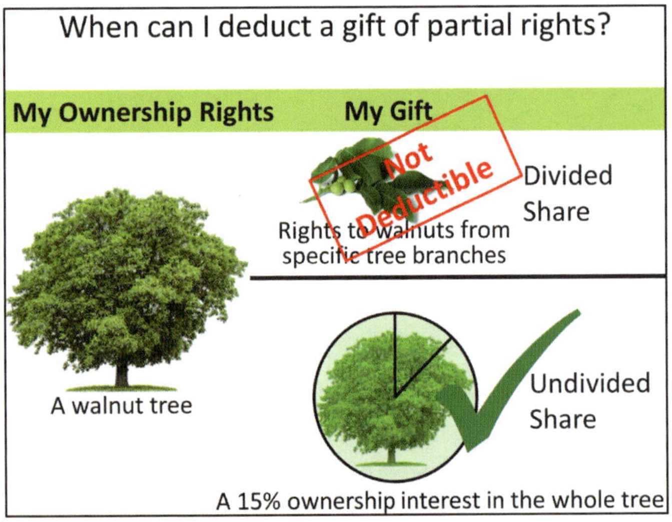

We have seen how a donor who retains specific types of interests in property and gives other types of interests to charity makes a nondeductible gift of a divided share in property. However, is there a case in which a donor may contribute less than the complete ownership rights (i.e., a partial interest) to the property and still deduct the gift?

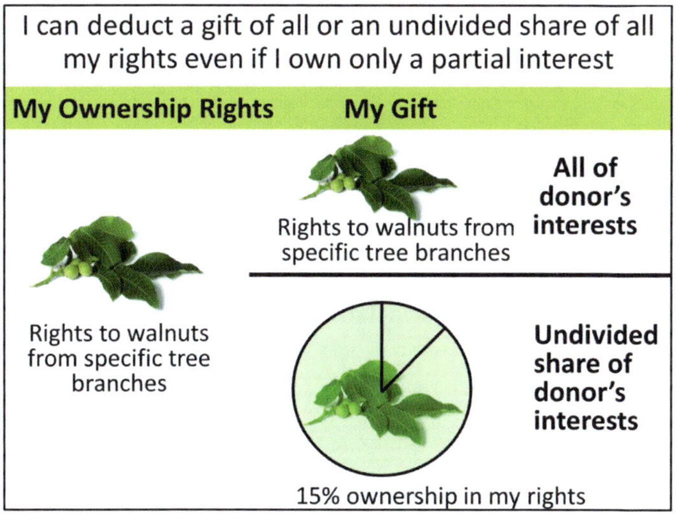

The donor is allowed to deduct the gift of a partial interest in property if the donor does not retain some other type of interest different from the type of interest given to the charity. So, to return to the walnut tree analogy, suppose that the donor does not own a walnut tree, but instead owns only the rights to walnuts from specific tree branches. The donor may contribute all of his rights to the specific tree branches to a charity and receive an income tax deduction.

Why is the donor allowed to deduct such a gift of partial interests to a charity? The reason for the prohibition against partial interest gifts to a charity where the donor retains some different type of right is to prevent the donor from increasing the value of his retained interest while decreasing the value of the interest held by the charity. In this case, if the donor gives everything that he owns (or a share of everything that he owns), then there is no risk of the donor increasing the value of the type of right that he has retained and simultaneously decreasing the value of the type of right that the charity owns. If the donor gives everything that he owns, he is retaining no rights in the property, thus eliminating the risk of this conflict. Similarly, if the donor gives a share of all of the interests he owns (even if he only owns partial interests), there is no way for the donor to increase the value of his interests while decreasing the value of the interests given to the charity. Consequently, these transfers are deductible.

Suppose a donor gives farmland to a charity. However, the donor never owned the mineral rights to the land. Thus, the donor is giving a partial interest in the land to a charity. Is this gift deductible?

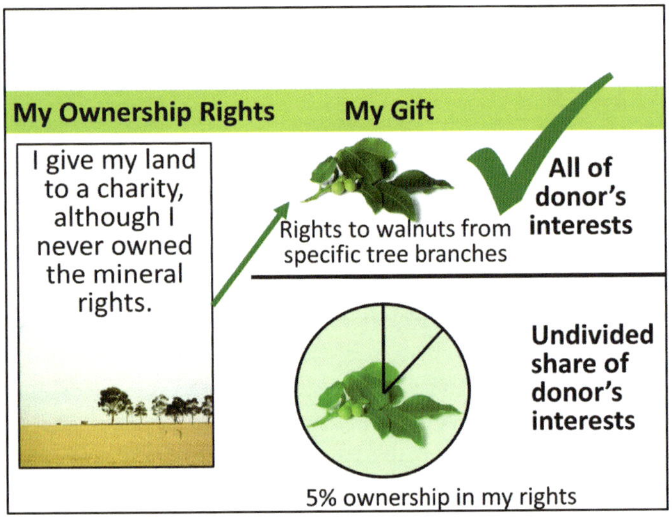

This gift is deductible because the donor is giving all of the rights he owns to the property. Whenever the donor gives all of the donor's interests in the property, there is no retained interest and consequently the gift may be deducted.

Suppose instead of giving the farmland to a charity, the donor gives a 5% interest in the farmland to the charity. As before, the donor never owned the mineral rights to the land. Is this a deductible gift?

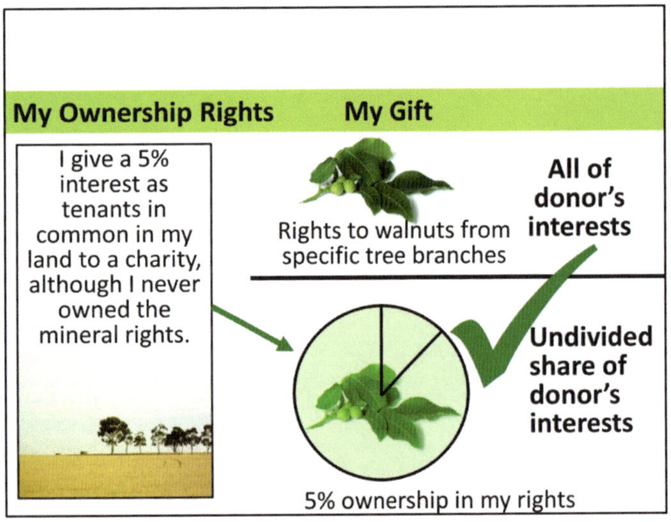

This is a transfer of an undivided share of all of the donor's interests in the property. Consequently, this is a deductible gift. The donor is not retaining any types of rights different from the types of rights given to the charity (although the exact ownership percentages differ).

This next transaction shows how these rules can be combined to generate creative and useful transactions. In this case, the donor begins by giving the charity the right to own his vacation home after he dies using a remainder deed (the remainder interest). The donor retains the right to use the property for the rest of his life (the life estate).

Although dealt with in a separate chapter, these types of remainder interest gifts are deductible as a specific exception to the general rule against deductions of partial interests where the donor retains different types of interests. The total ownership rights to a property consist of the life estate (right to use during life) and the remainder interest (right to own after death).

After this transaction, the donor's only remaining interest in the property is the right to use it for the remainder of his life. This right to use is called a life estate. The donor then gives an 11/12 interest in his life estate, keeping the right to use the property for one month out of the year. This gift is deductible because it is an undivided interest in all of the rights still owned by the donor. Through this series of transactions, the donor has been able to transfer and deduct all rights to the property, excepting only the lifetime right to use the vacation home for one month of the year. Depending upon the donor's age, this type of transaction could easily result in deductions of 95% or more of the value of the property. If the donor's use of the property had been to occupy it for only one month out of the year anyway, this massive deduction comes without changing the donor's lifetime use of the property.

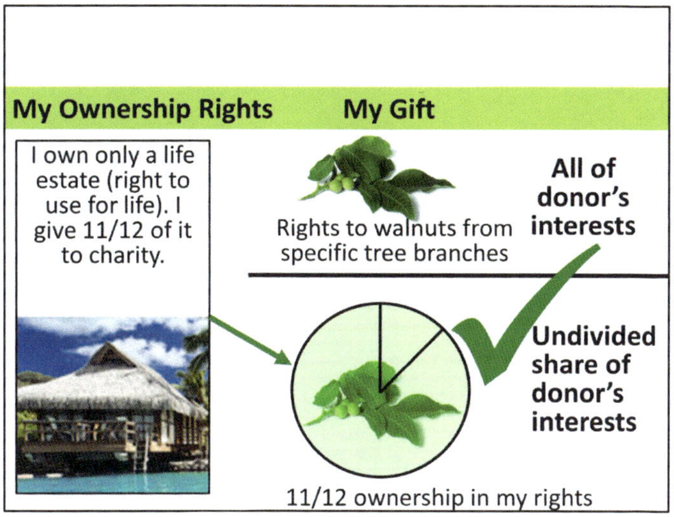

Note that if the donor had given an 11/12 interest in a life estate to the charity before giving the remainder interest, this would not have been a deductible gift. In that case, the donor would have been retaining a different type of right (the remainder interest), than the type of right given to the charity (a life estate). But, because the donor did not make the gift of the 11/12 interest in a life estate until after his only interest in the property was a life estate, the transfer is deductible. At that point, the donor is giving an undivided share of all of the donor's interests, because the donor's only remaining interest is a life estate in the property.

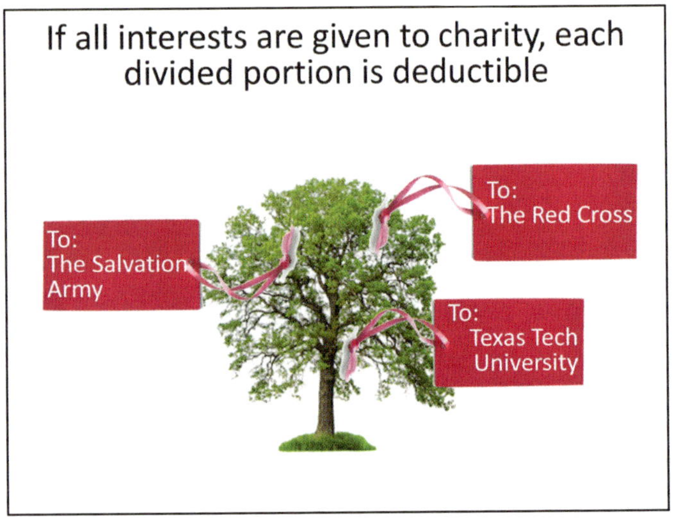

Partial interest gifts are also allowed if all of the donor's interests are transferred to different charities. As before, the concern is not with deducting the transfer of a partial interest to a charity, the concern is in allowing this deduction when the donor simultaneously retains different types of rights to the property. Such a concern does not apply here, because the donor keeps nothing for himself. It is thus perfectly acceptable to give a variety of different partial interest gifts to different charities.

As an example of this, if a donor were to give underlying ownership of farmland to the Red Cross, but give the mineral rights in the farmland to the Salvation Army and also give rent-free use of the property for 10 years to his local church, this would constitute a deductible gift of all the donor's interests in the farmland. Consequently, the donor could deduct the full value of the farmland, even though the ownership rights were split among multiple charities.

The bottom line result is that donors will get no deduction if they keep any type of rights that are different from the type of rights given to the charity. In other words, the donor must give or share all of his rights, or there is no deduction. The specific exceptions to this general rule (Charitable Remainder Trusts, Charitable Lead Trusts, pooled income funds, remainder interest in homes or farmland, qualified conservation easements) will be addressed in other chapters.

As we end this chapter, it might be useful to note that gifts of partial interests in property through the designated exceptions constitute the bulk of all planned giving structures. Allowing a donor to make a transfer to charity, but still keep some rights in the property is a technique which can allow the donor to make a charitable impact even in cases where he or she still has some needs from the property. This splitting of rights can create a fundamental benefit of planned giving: showing a donor who says, "I wish I could do more, but…" that it is possible to *both* benefit the charity *and* accomplish the donor's other financial goals, even when traditional outright gifts are not feasible.

11 REMAINDER INTERESTS IN HOMES AND FARMLAND

In this chapter, we will examine the somewhat-less-well-known charitable planning strategy of donating a remainder interest in a personal residence or farmland, often referred to as a "retained life estate" transaction. This topic is useful for two reasons. First, this strategy can be valuable for donors with an interest in leaving a bequest gift who would also like to receive an immediate income tax deduction for their commitment. The remainder interest gift instrument itself is relatively simple, and because few fundraisers or advisors are familiar with this option, it may prove to be a useful niche strategy that can lead to attractive opportunities.

Second, this is the simplest type of planned gift that generates an immediate tax deduction for a transfer that will usually benefit the charity only years later. Typically, the charity becomes the owner of the property only after one or more lifetimes (or sometimes after a fixed number of years). This same concept—a transaction that benefits a charity primarily in the distant future, but still generates an immediate income tax deduction—appears in a number of more complex contexts. This same idea appears again in charitable structures such as Charitable Remainder Trusts, grantor Charitable Lead Trusts, or Charitable Gift Annuities. But, in those cases the idea is combined with other financial benefits coming back to the donor from the trust or the charity. Before advancing to these more complex structures, it may benefit the reader to understand this relatively straightforward gift. In this way the remainder interest gift is not only an independently useful transaction, but serves an important conceptual building block for even more sophisticated planning.

As was addressed in depth in another chapter, a partial interest gift with retained interests occurs when a donor donates some types of rights to property, but keeps other types of rights in the gifted property. Remainder interest gifts are exactly this type of transaction. The donor gives a remainder interest (the right to own after death or after a period of years) in a home or farmland to charity, but keeps the right to use the property in the meantime (during life or for a period of years).

The general rule is that if a donor retains an interest in gifted property (giving the charity only a partial interest), the donor may not take a deduction for that type of transaction.

Gifts of remainder interests in a personal residence or farmland are a special exception to the general rule against deducting partial interest gifts where the donor retains other ownership interests in the gifted property. The other special exceptions to this general rule are Charitable Remainder Trusts, Charitable Lead Trusts, pooled income funds, and qualified conservation easements.

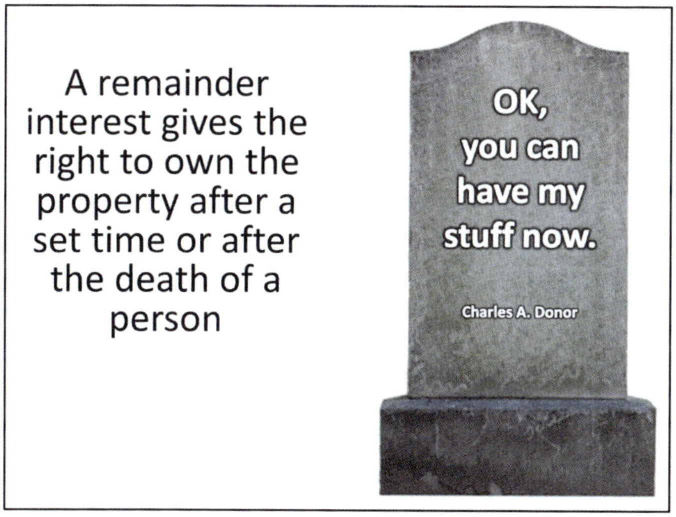

In many ways, a remainder interest is similar to a will. A remainder interest gives the right to someone else to become the owner of property after the death of the current owner (or another person) or after a certain number of years. Typically, the donor, who owns the property, gives a charity the right to own the property after the donor's death (or after the last to die of the donor and the donor's spouse). But, it is also possible to set up a remainder interest in a variety of different ways. Any person or persons can be used as the "measuring life" after which the property would go to the charity as the remainder interest holder. So, for example, a donor could gift a remainder interest to a charity that takes effect only after the death of the donor, the donor's spouse, and all currently living children and grandchildren of the donor. Although the charitable deduction for such a transfer might be relatively small—given the likely number of years the charity would have to wait to become the owner of the property—there would still be some charitable deduction. In another twist, a donor could give a charity the right to own the property after the death of, for example, the donor's sister and then donate the right to use the property for her life to the sister. Many such constructions are allowed, but they are also quite rare compared with the standard approach of the donor retaining a lifetime right to use the property and giving the remainder interest to the charity.

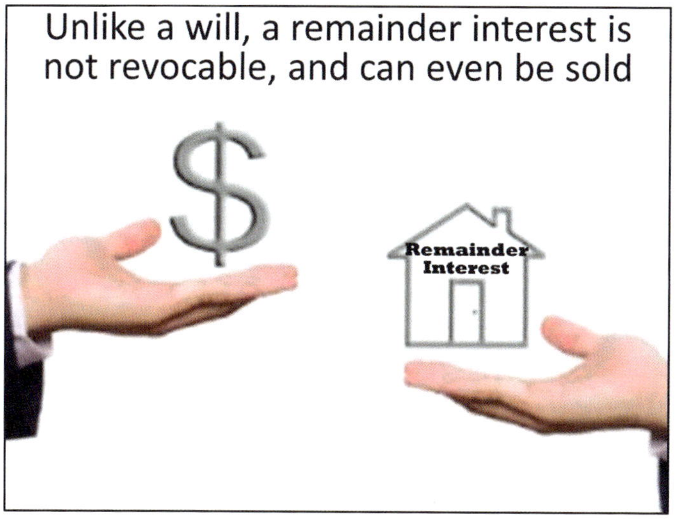

Although it transfers full ownership of property at death, the remainder interest differs from a will in important respects. Unlike a will, the decision to transfer a remainder interest in real estate is not revocable. Once the remainder interest is given, it is immediately owned by the recipient. This can be a tricky concept to understand. Even though a remainder interest might not result in the transfer of full ownership until after the death of the donor, that *right* to receive the property at death is *immediately* owned by holder of the remainder interest. Because this right is immediately owned by the remainder interest holder, it can even be sold.

For example, suppose a donor gives a remainder interest in his home to his favorite charity. This gives the charity ownership of the right to receive the home at the death of the donor. The charity could wait until the donor dies and then the charity would become the full owner of the home. However, the charity could instead immediately sell this right to an investor, in which case the investor would receive the home at the death of the donor. The home, at the death of the original owner, will be owned by whoever owns the remainder interest at that time. These later transfers have no effect on the charitable deduction. (In the same way, the charitable deduction for a donation of a share of stock is not affected by whether or not the charity later sells the stock to someone else). It is this irrevocable and transferable nature of the remainder gift that makes it immediately deductible.

Because the charity has received a valuable right today (one that can even be sold today), the donor can take a charitable deduction today. In contrast, no income tax deduction results from naming a charity in a will, because the charity has no rights prior to the donor's death. The charity can be removed from a will at any time, but giving a remainder interest deed is permanent.

Although the donor cannot prevent the future transfer of these rights from the charity to another buyer, it would be common for the charity to communicate with the donor in advance regarding its plans. In some cases, the donor may encourage the charity to sell the rights in advance, so that the donor may see the impact of his gift while he is still alive. For some donors, this is an attractive concept that would be impossible if using a will instead of a remainder interest deed.

This remainder interest gift must be transferred by means of a remainder interest *deed.* Even an otherwise identical arrangement created by a trust or a contract will not generate an income tax deduction. Only a deed will work. This makes the transaction documentation extraordinarily simple. Using a standard deed form with the transferee listed as "life estate to John A. Donor, remainder interest to XYZ charity" will usually be effective. (The simplicity of this transaction may, ironically, contribute to its underutilization as some attorneys may favor more complex arrangements that generate more billable hours.)

Taking a charitable deduction for the transfer of a remainder interest to charity is limited to specific types of property. Only two types of property are eligible: farmland and a donor's personal residence(s). Any land and improvements used to raise crops or livestock qualifies as farmland. The land will qualify as farmland even if the donor is not farming the land himself, so long as someone is using it to raise crops or livestock. Similarly, land being used to raise crops or livestock is farmland, even if its valuation is based upon its usefulness as commercial development property.

A donor need not transfer his entire farm, but can deduct a remainder interest gift in any part of a farm. (This is why I prefer to use the term "farmland" rather than "farm" in order to avoid the impression that the donor's entire farm must be given to charity at death in order to take this deduction.) For example, the donor who owns a 1,000 acre farm can take an immediate income tax deduction for giving a remainder interest in 10 acres of that farm.

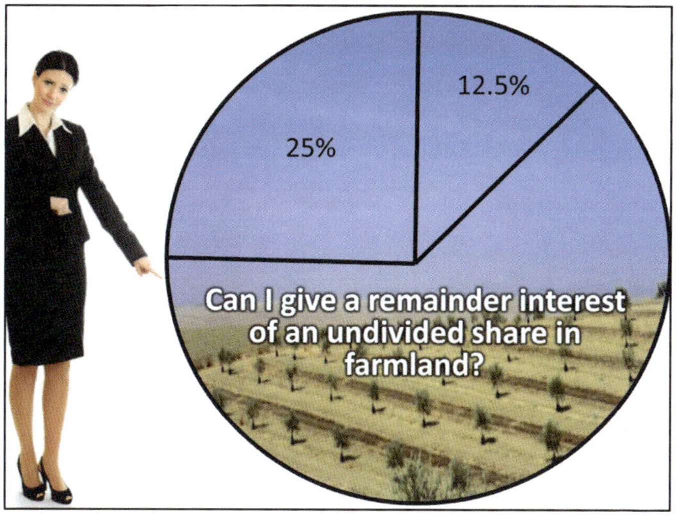

The donor can identify specific acreage within a farm to be gifted by a remainder interest deed. But, could the donor deduct a remainder interest gift of an undivided share in farmland? In other words, could a donor deduct the gift of a remainder interest in an undivided 10% interest in 100-acres of farmland, rather than a remainder interest in 10 specific acres?

The answer is, "Yes." Thus, a donor could make a remainder interest gift of 5% of his farmland. The donor could even choose to do this every year for 20 years until all of the remainder interest in the farmland was transferred. Such a spreading out of deductible gifts might be attractive to a donor, depending upon the donor's tax circumstances and the ongoing appreciation of the property. Appreciation is important because the value of each gift increases as the value of the underlying farmland also increases. Further, each gift may generate a greater deduction because the donor is one year older at each transfer, making the remainder interest more valuable due to the reduced life expectancy of the donor. (This is, of course, assuming the typical arrangement where the donor's life is the measuring life after which the property is transferred.) However, the deduction for such undivided interest gifts may be slightly reduced based upon the cost that a charity could incur to force a sale or division of the property (called "partitioning").

Can a donor deduct the transfer of a remainder interest in mineral rights? If the donor is transferring a remainder interest in only the mineral rights, this will not qualify for a charitable deduction. Mineral rights, by themselves, do not constitute farmland. Farmland is land used to raise crops or livestock and mineral rights, by themselves, cannot be used to raise crops or livestock. However, if the donor is transferring a remainder interest in farmland that includes both the farmland surface rights and mineral rights, this constitutes a deductible gift. Thus, the value of the gift will be based upon the total value of the land including both surface rights and mineral rights. But, this is only available if the mineral rights are transferred as part of the transfer of the farmland. It is, of course, also acceptable to deduct the transfer of a remainder interest in farmland where the donor does not own any mineral rights.

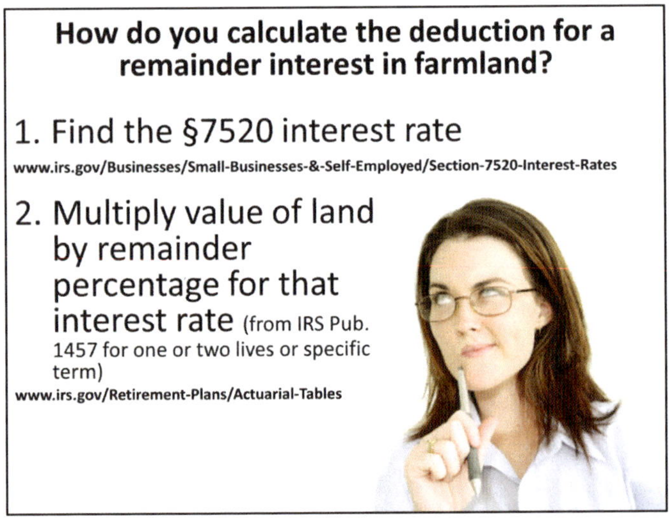

As mentioned above, transferring the remainder interest in farmland generates a charitable deduction. But, how much is this deduction? Certainly, the deduction will be less than if the donor immediately gave the land to the charity, but, how much less? The deduction will be the present value of the right to receive the land in the future. This present value depends upon the current value of the land, the interest rate, and how long the charity would likely wait to receive the land (i.e., the life expectancy of the donor if the donor is the measuring life).

As a practical matter, the calculation can be completed by identifying the interest rate (known as the §7520 rate) found at www.irs.gov/Businesses/Small-Businesses-&-Self-Employed/Section-7520-Interest-Rates and then using the interest rate to identify the correct remainder percentage for one or two lives or a specific term from the tables at www.irs.gov/Retirement-Plans/Actuarial-Tables Let's walk step-by-step through the process for completing such a calculation.

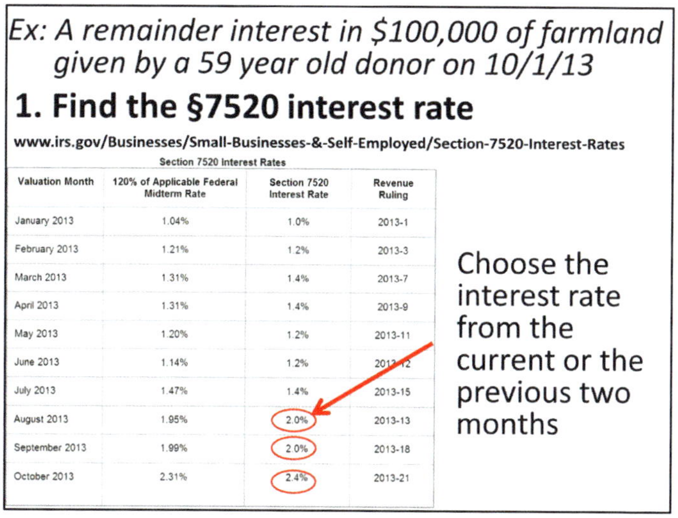

Valuation Month	120% of Applicable Federal Midterm Rate	Section 7520 Interest Rate	Revenue Ruling
January 2013	1.04%	1.0%	2013-1
February 2013	1.21%	1.2%	2013-3
March 2013	1.31%	1.4%	2013-7
April 2013	1.31%	1.4%	2013-9
May 2013	1.20%	1.2%	2013-11
June 2013	1.14%	1.2%	2013-12
July 2013	1.47%	1.4%	2013-15
August 2013	1.95%	2.0%	2013-13
September 2013	1.99%	2.0%	2013-18
October 2013	2.31%	2.4%	2013-21

Suppose we wish to calculate the charitable deduction for a remainder interest gift in $100,000 of farmland given by a 59-year-old donor on October 1 of 2013 where the charity receives the right to own the farmland upon the death of the donor. For this calculation, the age of the donor is the age at their nearest birthday on the date of the gift. First, we must identify the appropriate section 7520 interest rate. Following the link www.irs.gov/Businesses/Small-Businesses-&-Self-Employed/Section-7520-Interest-Rates on October 1 of 2013 displays the table containing the §7520 interest rate. The donor can choose the interest rate from the current month or the previous two months. In this case, the interest rate in the current month is 2.4% and the interest rate in the prior two months was 2.0%. Which interest rate should the donor choose?

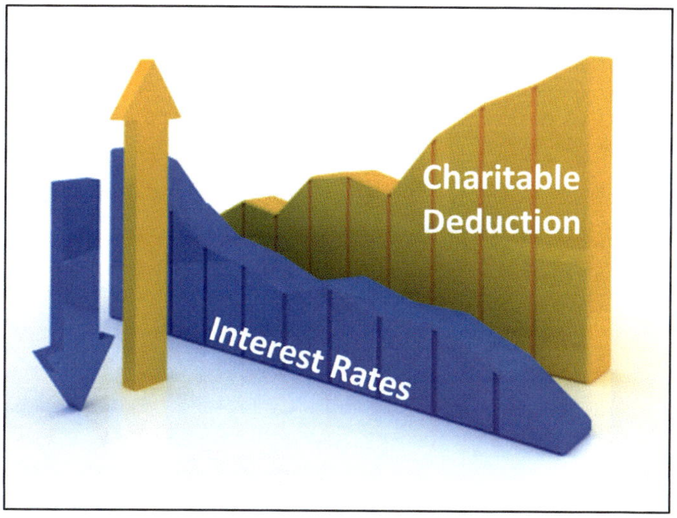

For gifts of remainder interests in homes and farmland the charitable deduction increases as the interest rate decreases. Consequently, the donor should always choose the lowest available interest rate. The gift to charity is calculated as the present value of receiving the farmland (at its current value) when the charity must first wait for the current life expectancy of the donor to expire. If interest rates are very low (e.g., 1%), then the cost of waiting is also very low. When the cost of waiting is low, the value of a gift requiring waiting will be relatively high. When the cost of waiting is high (e.g., a 10% interest rate), the value of a gift requiring waiting will be relatively low.

It may help to think about the present value of a remainder interest gift in these terms: How much money would a person have to put in the bank today such that it would be worth $100,000 at the end of the donor's current life expectancy? If the bank paid 1% interest on the account, then a larger initial deposit would be required than if the bank paid 10% interest on the account. Similarly, the present value of a remainder interest gift is higher if the prevailing interest rate (a.k.a. the §7520 rate) is lower, and vice-versa.

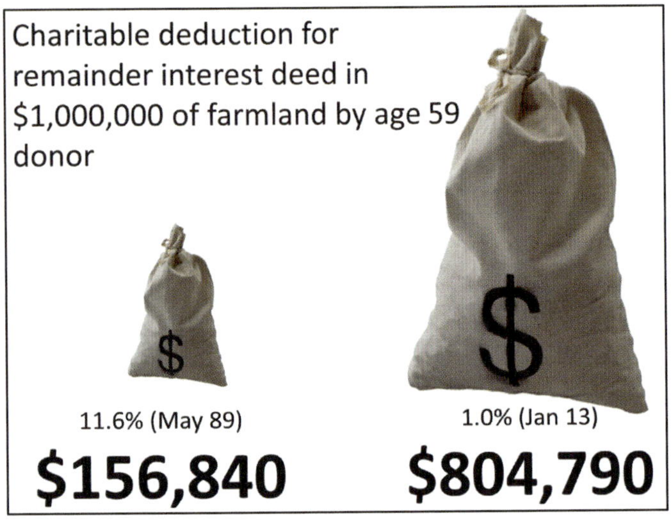

The impact of different interest rates on the charitable deduction for a remainder interest deed can be seen dramatically in this example. If the §7520 interest rate used is 11.6%, then the deduction for a gift of a remainder interest deed in $1 million of farmland by a donor aged 59 is $156,840. If the §7520 interest rate is 1.0% then deduction is $804,790. Since both of these interest rates were, at different times, the actual §7520 interest rate, this demonstrates real differences in the deduction of otherwise identical transactions. This is also why gifts of remainder interests in homes and farmland are so attractive during a low interest rate environment. This remainder interest giving technique is useful to keep in mind during such times because other more common techniques (such as Charitable Remainder Trusts) are often less attractive during a low interest rate environment.

Ex: A remainder interest in $100,000 of farmland given by a 59 year old donor on 10/1/13

1. Find the §7520 interest rate

www.irs.gov/Businesses/Small-Businesses-&-Self-Employed/Section-7520-Interest-Rates

Section 7520 Interest Rates

Valuation Month	120% of Applicable Federal Midterm Rate	Section 7520 Interest Rate	Revenue Ruling
January 2013	1.04%	1.0%	2013-1
February 2013	1.21%	1.2%	2013-3
March 2013	1.31%	1.4%	2013-7
April 2013	1.31%	1.4%	2013-9
May 2013	1.20%	1.2%	2013-11
June 2013	1.14%	1.2%	2013-12
July 2013	1.47%	1.4%	2013-15
August 2013	1.95%	2.0%	2013-13
September 2013	1.99%	2.0%	2013-18
October 2013	2.31%	2.4%	2013-21

Choosing the lowest rate creates the highest deduction, so here we select 2.0%

Understanding the relationship between interest rates and the charitable deduction for gifts of remainder interests results in selecting the lowest available interest rate from the §7520 table in the current or previous two months. In this example, the lowest interest rate is 2.0%. Consequently, we will use 2.0% as the interest rate for all subsequent calculations using this example.

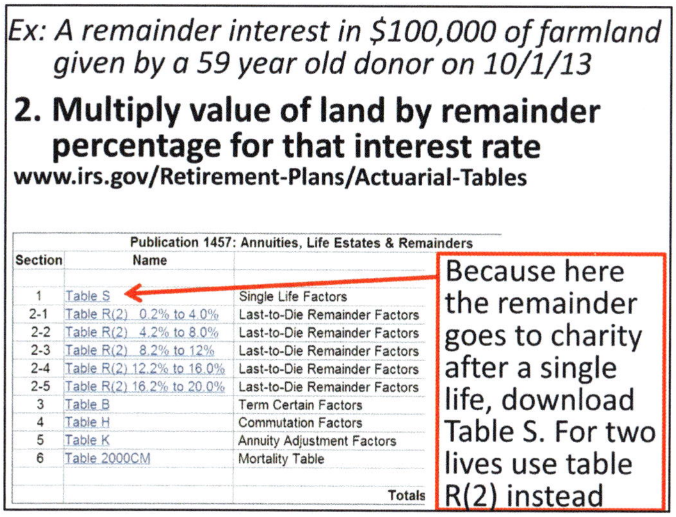

To find the percentage of the value of the land that will be deductible with a remainder interest gift, we must download the relevant table. (Links to these tables may be found at www.irs.gov/Retirement-Plans/Actuarial-Tables .) The tables provided allow calculations for a remainder interest when transferring at the death of one person, at the last to die of two people, or after a specific number of years (term certain). In the current example, we are calculating the deduction for a gift of a remainder interest in $100,000 of farmland given by a 59-year-old donor on October 1 of 2013 where the donor is the "measuring life" for the remainder interest. Consequently, we will click on Table S, which contains the single life factors. If the remainder interest would transfer to the charity at the death of the last to die of the donor and the donor's spouse, for example, then we would need to click on one of the table R(2) links (in this case, the first one, because it contains the remainder factors for a 2.0% interest rate).

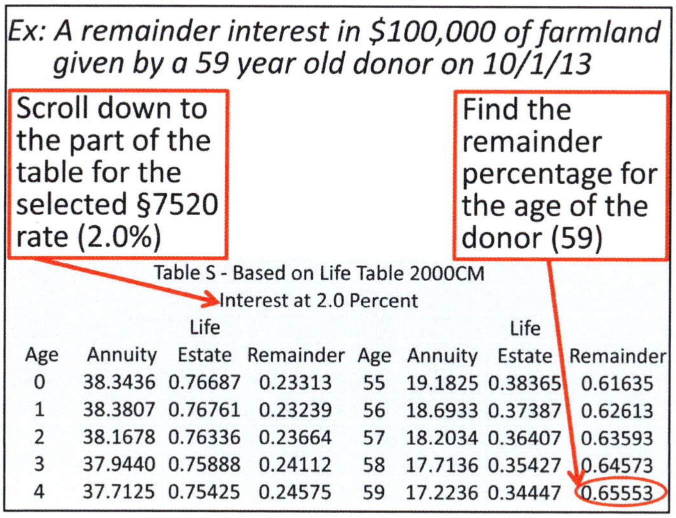

Clicking on the Table S link downloads an Excel file. The first task is to scroll down through the Excel file until reaching the portion of the table labeled as "Interest at 2.0 Percent," because this is the §7520 interest rate being used in this example. After this portion of the table is located, next finding the row associated with the age of our donor/measuring life shows a remainder interest factor of 0.65553. In simple terms, this factor means that this remainder interest gift will generate a charitable tax deduction of 65.553% of the value of farmland.

As you can see when scrolling through the table, the charitable deduction will be larger when the measuring life for the remainder interest is older. This makes sense because as age increases, life expectancy decreases, meaning that the charity will, on average, receive the property earlier.

Once the remainder interest factor has been correctly identified, the calculation for the deduction is simple. In this case, the donor can deduct 65.553% of the value of any land in which he makes a remainder interest gift subject to his lifetime right to use the property. Thus, the charitable income tax deduction for such a remainder interest gift in $100,000 of farmland is $65,553.

For a donor who has intent to leave a bequest gift to charity, a remainder interest gift may be particularly attractive. In both cases—whether through a will or through a remainder deed—the charity receives a gift at death. However, with a remainder interest deed, the donor receives an immediate income tax deduction that can often be very large. This does come at a cost. The primary cost is that the remainder interest gift, unlike a will, is irrevocable. The donor cannot later change his mind and decide to take back the remainder interest gift. Also, to be deductible, a remainder interest gift must be a gift of farmland or a home. Because of typical mortgage prohibitions against transfers, such a gift normally requires debt-free farmland or a debt-free house. Some donors may also be attracted by the reality that a charity can sell the remainder interest, and thereby generate immediate cash for current projects. The substantial tax deduction may also benefit the donor by increasing spendable assets (which now do not have to be spent on tax payments). This may be particularly attractive for a donor who does not wish to sell the home or farmland, but wishes to get an immediate monetary benefit from the property in order to supplement current income.

As discussed previously, remainder interests in farmland could be gifted in parts. This can be done either by gifting remainder interests in specific acreage in a farm or by gifting an undivided fractional share interest (e.g., 10.72%) in specific acreage. (Such undivided fractional share gifts are also available for gifts of remainder interests in personal residences.) This can provide the donor with tremendous flexibility. So, for example, the donor could make a remainder interest gift up to the point at which income giving limitations would result in further deductions being carried forward to future years. Making additional remainder interest gifts in future years may be preferable to carrying forward charitable deductions because (1) the deduction will, *ceteris paribus*, be larger as the donor/measuring life is one year older, (2) the deduction will be larger if the farmland has appreciated in value, and (3) the death of the donor, or donor's spouse if a joint gift, would not result in the loss of carryover deductions.

An additional reason for considering a series of remainder interest gifts would be to coordinate the receipt of tax benefits with the offsetting payment of life insurance premiums through an irrevocable life insurance trust (ILIT). Although dealt with in detail in another chapter, the basic idea is that the use of life insurance allows the heirs to receive money as a replacement for the value of the home or farmland they will no longer be inheriting. In some cases, the heirs may prefer the life insurance proceeds because life insurance purchased through an ILIT it is not subject to estate taxes. However, only a limited amount of money can be used each year to pay premiums of ILIT-owned policies without generating gift taxes (currently $14,000 annually per donee for each donor). Thus, spreading the deductions over a long period of time can help to match with the life insurance premiums paid over several years.

This combination of transactions, where a donor gives a remainder interest to a charity and then uses the value of the resulting tax deductions to purchase life insurance not subject to estate taxes, can be very attractive. The heirs lose the ability to inherit the property subject to the gifted remainder interest, but gain the opportunity to inherit life insurance proceeds. Because the home or farmland might have been subject to a 40% estate tax, estate tax-free life insurance proceeds could be particularly attractive. Let's examine the details comparing this type of transaction with less sophisticated charitable planning.

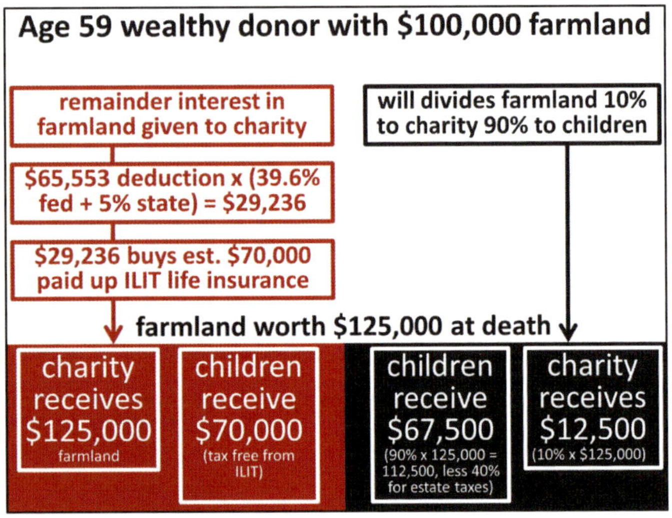

Let's return to our 59-year-old donor contemplating the disposition of $100,000 of farmland. In this case, let's suppose he is subject to a 40% marginal estate tax rate, a 39.6% federal income tax rate and a 5% state income tax rate. Further, suppose the donor wishes to benefit both the charity and his children at his death with the $100,000 of farmland. A simple, unsophisticated approach would be to draft a will in which part of the farmland (e.g., 10%) would go to the charity and the rest (e.g., 90%) would go to the children. Assuming that the property appreciates to $125,000 at the time of death, this would result in the charity receiving $12,500 (10% x $125,000). The children's share would be 90% (90% x $125,000 = $112,500), but their share is first subject to estate taxes of 40%, leaving a net inheritance of $67,500.

Let's compare the results from that simple planning with the use of a remainder interest deed and ILIT. As described above, a remainder interest gift in $100,000 of farmland by this age 59 donor generates an income tax deduction of $65,553. The value of a deduction depends upon the marginal income tax rate of the taxpayer. In this case, if we assume that the donor is at a 39.6% federal income tax rate and a 5% state income tax rate, this deduction would be worth $29,236. Using a rough estimate, let's suppose that this money could be used to purchase a $70,000 death benefit paid up life insurance policy. (As a side note, the amount of insurance that can be purchased from the remainder interest deduction may remain relatively stable in different interest rate environments. A low interest rate causes the deduction to be larger and the insurance to be more expensive, whereas a high interest rate causes the deduction to be smaller and the insurance to be less expensive.) At death, the children receive the $70,000 death benefit from the life insurance policy. However, this death benefit (because of the use of the ILIT) is not subject to estate taxes, so the children receive the entire $70,000. In this case, the children's inheritance is approximately the same with either charitable plan. However, with the use of the remainder interest, the charity receives the entire farmland, not just 10% of it. Thus, through sophisticated planning, the donor is able to give 10 times as much to charity at death without disadvantaging his children.

As a side note, it is still critical to engage in charitable planning only for those clients who have charitable interests. There are almost always sophisticated non-charitable estate planning strategies that are more effective at transferring wealth to heirs as compared with charitable strategies. But, for the client who wishes to have a charitable impact, these strategies are powerful. One simple approach to identifying a client's charitable interests is to draw a circle and explain, "You can leave your estate to three groups: people (family), charity, and government. Divide this circle into a pie chart showing how you would want your estate divided between these three groups." This conversation can quickly identify those who have charitable estate interests and those who do not. Additionally, of use to attorneys and financial advisors is the likelihood that the share assigned to government will be lower than that resulting from estates taxes, thus generating the motivation for exploring sophisticated estate tax planning.

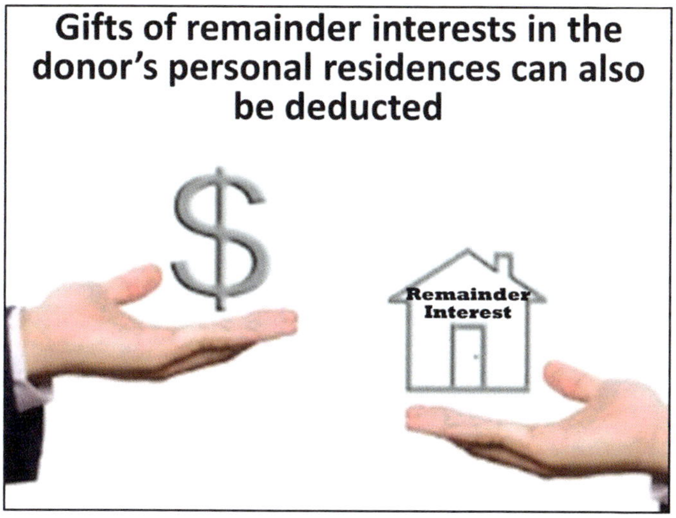

To this point we have been considering gifts of remainder interests in farmland. However, gifts of remainder interests in the donor's personal residence(s) can also be deducted, although the calculations are a bit more complex. The remainder interest must be in a personal residence of the donor, but it need not be the donor's primary residence. Thus, for example, the gift of a remainder interest in a donor's vacation home is deductible.

In fact, any home owned by the donor and used by the donor as one of his or her residences will qualify for a deductible remainder interest gift. This can even include a boat with bathroom, cooking, and sleeping facilities if it is actually used by the donor as a residence.

Calculating the deduction for a charitable gift of a remainder interest in a house is more complicated than calculating the deduction for a remainder interest in farmland. The deduction for a remainder interest in a house will be less than the deduction for a remainder interest in farmland of the same value. This is because farmland does not wear out or depreciate. In contrast, houses, over time, wear out. This expectation of the wearing out (depreciation) of the house must be incorporated in the estimation of the amount of value that the charity will receive at the end of the life of the donor/measuring life.

Returning to our previous example, suppose that the 59-year-old donor gave a remainder interest in a $100,000 personal residence, rather than a remainder interest in $100,000 of farmland. The deduction for the gift of the personal residence remainder interest would be less than for the farmland remainder interest ($65,553 for the farmland v. $44,843 for the home).

How is this deduction calculated? Part of the value of the personal residence is the value of the land on which the residence sits. The deduction for this part of the personal residence is calculated exactly like the deduction for the farmland. Thus, the remainder interest gift generates a deduction of 65.553% of the value of the *land* underlying the personal residence. (The 65.553% comes from the calculation process described previously for farmland.) There is also presumed to be an element of the house that does not depreciate, which is referred to as "salvage" value. Because this "salvage" value does not depreciate it is also deducted at the same percentage as the land (65.553%). The remaining value of the residence, however, is presumed to depreciate. Consequently, this portion of the value of the residence may not be deducted at the full 65.553% used for farmland, but must be reduced by a depreciation reduction factor. In this case, using the example described below, the depreciation reduction factor is .29586, or 29.586%. Thus, the depreciable part of the residence may be deducted at 35.950% (i.e., 65.553% less 29.603%). Combining the parts that can be deducted at 35.950% with the parts that can be deducted at 65.553% results in a total deduction of $44,831 for the $100,000 home.

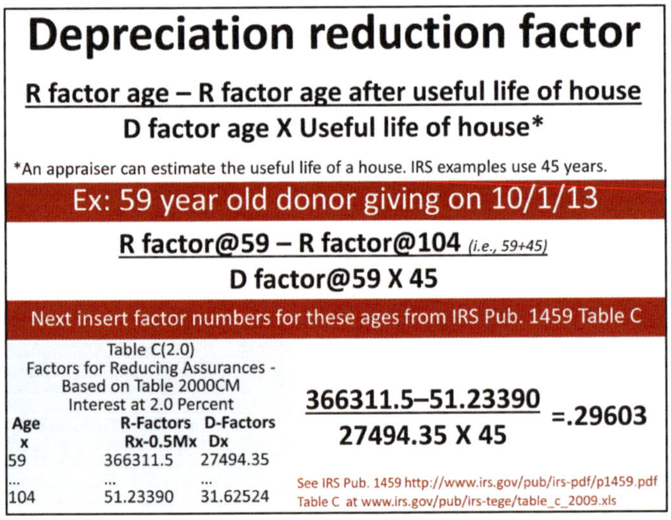

How is this depreciation reduction factor calculated? The calculation can at first seem to be complex or overwhelming. But, actually, it is simply a matter of copying the correct numbers into a division problem. Aside from the information located in the IRS table C of publication 1459 and the §7520 rate, the only additional information needed is the age of the donor/measuring life and the useful life of the house.

Unlike other areas of tax law where depreciation is incorporated into tax calculations, there are no set years for the depreciable life of a residence in this context. The useful life of the house should be estimated by an appraiser or engineer. The IRS examples use 45 years for the useful life of a house, and so this is often treated as a viable estimation depending upon the condition of the home.

We will take the cue from the IRS example for our situation, and assume that the residence will depreciate over 45 years. This, along with the §7520 interest rate and the donor's age, is the only information we need to use the IRS tables to complete the calculation. Following the instructions of IRS publication 1459 (www.irs.gov/pub/irs-pdf/p1459.pdf) we download table C (www.irs.gov/pub/irs-tege/table_c_2009.xls)

and scroll down to the segment titled with "Interest at 2.0 Percent". Here we find the numbers that plug into the formula to generate the depreciation reduction factor. The numerator of the depreciation reduction factor is the R factor at the donor's age minus the R factor at the donor's age after the useful life of the house (assuming the donor is the measuring life). So in this case, the numerator is the R factor at age 59 minus the R factor at age 104 (i.e., age 59+45 years). (If the life tenant's age plus the useful life of the house exceeded 109, which is the highest number on the table, we would simply use 0 for the R factor at the donor's age after the useful life of the house.) From table C with a 2.0% section 7520 rate, this makes the numerator 366311.5-51.2339 (or 366260.2661). The denominator of the depreciation reduction factor is the D factor at the donor's age multiplied times the useful life of the house. In this case, the denominator is the D factor at age 59 multiplied by 45, or 27494.35 X 45 = 1237245.75. Combining the numerator and denominator results in 366260.2661/1237245.75, or 0.29603. This is the depreciation reduction factor used in the previous calculation. In other words, this is how much less the percentage deduction for the constructed portion will be as compared with the land portion. In this example, the land portion can be deducted at 65.553%. The constructed portion must be deducted at 29.586% less (i.e., 35.967%).

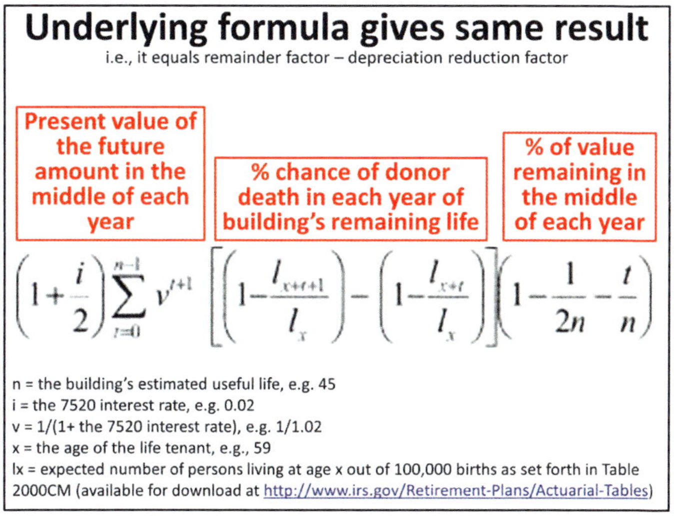

This process of plugging in the R-factor and D-factor numbers and then subtracting this result from the remainder interest factor in order to get the factor to apply to the depreciable part of the home is a shortcut to getting the result generated by the formula found in the IRS regulations. This formula is

$$\left(1+\frac{i}{2}\right)\sum_{t=0}^{n-1} v^{t+1}\left[\left(1-\frac{l_{x+t+1}}{l_x}\right)-\left(1-\frac{l_{x+t}}{l_x}\right)\right]\left(1-\frac{1}{2n}-\frac{t}{n}\right)$$

Where:
n = the building's estimated useful life, e.g. 45
i = the 7520 interest rate, e.g. 0.02
v = 1/(1+ the 7520 interest rate), e.g. 1/1.02
x = the age of the life tenant, e.g., 59
lx = expected number of persons living at age x out of 100,000 births as set forth in Table 2000CM (available for download at **http://www.irs.gov/Retirement-Plans/Actuarial-Tables**)

It is possible to calculate this formula directly. The result of calculating the formula directly is the remainder interest factor to be applied to the depreciable portions of the personal residence. The results should match those from using the shortcut method described above. Although the formula above looks quite intimidating, it can be explained descriptively. $\left(1-\frac{l_{x+t+1}}{l_x}\right)$ Starting inside the equation, this ratio uses the Lx numbers, representing the number of people, out of 100,000 births, expected to be alive at any given age. The ratio is the number of people, out of 100,000 births, alive at the donor's age+t+1 years over the number of people, out of 100,000 births, alive at the donor's age. For example, if the donor were 59 years of age, then the first calculation where t starts at zero would be the number of people projected to be alive, out of 100,000 births, at age 60 (87,595) divided by the number of people projected to be alive, out of 100,000 births, at age 59 (88,441). This ratio (87,595/88,411), or 99.08% is the likelihood that a person who is age 59 will live another year. Subtracting this ratio from 1 (in this case, 0.92%) gives the likelihood that a person who is age 59 will *not* live another year.

$$\left[\left(1-\frac{l_{x+t+1}}{l_x}\right)-\left(1-\frac{l_{x+t}}{l_x}\right)\right]$$

This bracketed part of the formula identifies the probability that the donor will die during a particular year for each year of the useful life of the home. We start with t=0, in which case the right hand parenthesis also equals zero. In our example of a 59 year old donor, the probability of death in the first year is, as calculated above, 0.92%. The probability of death occurring in the second year is the probability of death occuring within the first two years (left hand parentheses) minus the probability of death occurring in the first year (right hand parenthesis). The probability of death occurring in the third year is the probability of death occurring within the first three years (left hand parentheses) minus the probability of death occurring within the first two years (right hand parenthesis). This probability is thus calculated for each year of the useful life of the home (e.g., 45 years).

$$\left(1-\frac{1}{2n}-\frac{t}{n}\right)$$

This parenthetical calculation gives the percentage of value that will remain in each year, assuming straight line depreciation, for the depreciable parts of the house. For example, if the house is expected to have a 45 year useful life, then by year 20, it would be 44.4% depleted (20/45 = 44.4%), meaning that 66.6% (1-44.4%) of the value would remain. This explains the left and right portions of the parenthetical statement, but not the middle piece. Why would we also subtract 1/(2x the useful life of the house)? This simply reflects the additional depreciation (wear and tear) that occurs for the 6 months required to get to the middle of the year. This assumes that if the person dies during a year, they will die not at the beginning or the end, but in the middle of the year, so the depreciation will be ½ year. For example, the projected remaining share of the value if the donor died in the first year (t=0) would be 1-(1/90), or 98.89%, (the right hand ratio is zero), reflecting the idea that the donor is projected to die in the middle of the year. The projected remaining share of value if the donor died in the tenth year (t=9), would be 1-(1/90)-(10/45), reflecting the idea that the donor is projected to die in the middle of the year and the 1/90 depreciation that occurs during those six months must be substracted.

$$\left(1+\frac{i}{2}\right)\sum_{t=0}^{n-1} v^{t+1}$$

This final portion of the summation calculates the present value of the future amount. The v represents 1/(1+ the §7520 interest rate). If the §7520 interest rates were 2.0%, v would equal 1/1.02, or 98.04%. Thus, the present value of receiving the asset in year one is 98.04% of the projected value of the asset. The present value of receiving the asset in year two is 96.12% (from 98.04% X 98.04%) of its projected value in year two. The present value of receiving the asset in year three is 94.23% (from 98.04% X 98.04% X 98.04%) of its projected value in year three, and so on for each year of the projected life of the home. The final adjustment noted by the parenthetical component to the left of the summation symbol, increases the present value based upon the idea that the amount will be received not at the end of the year, but in the middle of the year. Thus, if interest rates are 2.0%, the final amount is increased by 1% (multiplied by 1.01 because 1+(.02/2)=1.01) to reflect the value of receiving the asset in the middle of the year, rather than at the end

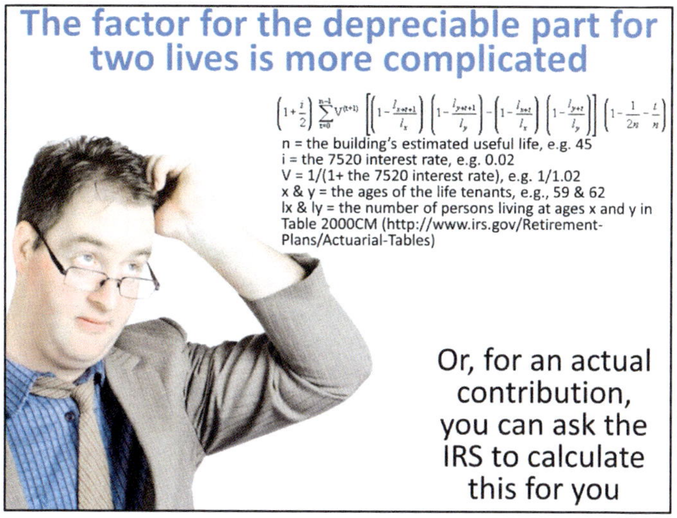

Unfortunately, there is no shortcut method for calculating the remainder interest factor to be applied to the depreciable portions of the personal residence if the life estate is for more than one life. For example, if the life estate will last for the lives of two people (e.g., a married couple ages 59 and 62), then the formula for the remainder interest factor to be applied to the depreciable portions of the personal residence is

$$\left(1+\frac{i}{2}\right)\sum_{t=0}^{n-1} V^{(t+1)}\left[\left(1-\frac{l_{x+t+1}}{l_x}\right)\left(1-\frac{l_{y+t+1}}{l_y}\right)-\left(1-\frac{l_{x+t}}{l_x}\right)\left(1-\frac{l_{y+t}}{l_y}\right)\right]\left(1-\frac{1}{2n}-\frac{t}{n}\right)$$

Where:
n = the building's estimated useful life, e.g. 45
i = the 7520 interest rate, e.g. 0.02
v = 1/(1+ the 7520 interest rate), e.g. 1/1.02
x and y=the ages of the life tenants, e.g., 59 & 62
lx and ly=the number of persons living at ages x and y as set forth in Table 2000CM (available for download at **http://www.irs.gov/Retirement-Plans/Actuarial-Tables**)

This can be calculated by hand, in this case requiring a summation of 45 different calculations, one for each year of the useful life of the property. However, it requires more steps than the short-cut method available for single life calculations. The parts of the equation represent the same idea as in the one-life example. The only difference in the equation is that the middle bracketed portion

$$\left[\left(1-\frac{l_{x+t+1}}{l_x}\right)\left(1-\frac{l_{y+t+1}}{l_y}\right)-\left(1-\frac{l_{x+t}}{l_x}\right)\left(1-\frac{l_{y+t}}{l_y}\right)\right]$$

now estimates the joint likelihood of the death of both life tenants, rather than just one.

If the calculation for the remainder interest factor to be applied to the depreciable portions of a two-life remainder interest gift appears too daunting, you may request the IRS to furnish this factor to you. To do so requires that you are dealing with an actual contribution (not simply a proposal), and that you forward the sex and date of birth of each life tenant, copies of the relevant instruments, and a statement of the estimated useful life of the depreciable property to the Commissioner of Internal Revenue, Attention: OP:E:EP:A:1, Washington, DC 20224.

A donor may also choose to give a remainder interest in a personal residence where the donor will retain the right to use the property (or give that right to someone else) for a fixed number of years. For example, the donor could deed a personal residence to a charity with the provision that the donor retains the right to use the property for 20 years. In this case, the deduction is based upon the value of the personal residence in 20 years. The current land and salvage value of the building are not depreciable, and so they are assumed to be worth the same amount in 20 years as they are today. The depreciable part of the personal residence will be reduced in value by the fixed number of years divided by the useful life of the building. For example, if a $100,000 residence was estimated to have a useful life of 45 years, with land value of $20,000 and salvage value of $10,000, then in 20 years the estimated value would be $20,000 land + $10,000 salvage + 70,000 depreciable building – [(20/45)x$70,000] depreciation, or a total of $61,111.11. Based on the idea that the charity will be receiving an item of property worth $61,111.11 in twenty years, the deduction for such a transfer would be $61,111.11 multiplied by the remainder interest factor for a term certain of 20 years. These remainder interest factors are published in Table B: Term Certain Factors available for download at http://www.irs.gov/Retirement-Plans/Actuarial-Tables. For a 20 year term when the §7520 rate were 2.0% at the time of the gift, the remainder factor would be 0.672971. Thus, the deduction for this transfer of this future interest in the personal residence would be $61,111.11 x 0.672971, or $41,125.93. Finally, if the value of the land may be reduced by depletion of its natural resources (e.g., valuable mineral rights), the expected depletion must be taken into consideration in estimating the value of the charity's remainder interest, although no specific methodology is mandated.

The remainder interest gift allows the donor to use the property for the rest of his or her life. (Actually, it is much more flexible than this, allowing for any period of years or the life or lives of any person or group of people, but such alternatives are rarely used.) What happens if the donor no longer wishes to use the property? Perhaps the property is a personal residence and the donor decides to move away to a warmer climate or to a nursing home. Or perhaps the property is a farmland and the donor becomes unable or uninterested in continuing to farm. Whatever the circumstances, either anticipated or unanticipated, the donor still has a variety of options available when he or she no longer wishes to personally use the property.

One easy solution is for the donor to simply rent out the property and take the income. If moving to a distant state, the donor will likely hire a property manager to manage the leasing and maintenance of a residence. It is also possible to sell the life estate to an investor who would then rent out the property, although such transactions are rare. If the charity owning the remainder interest is co-operative, both the life estate and remainder interest can be combined and the property can be sold with normal "fee simple" ownership. (The division of proceeds between the charity and donor must give the charity at least as much of a share of the proceeds as the IRS tables indicate the remainder interest is worth, based upon the donor's age at the time of the sale.) Most charities holding a remainder interest would be more than happy to agree to a sale and division of the proceeds.

Although less common, a charity could agree to issue a Charitable Gift Annuity (discussed in a separate chapter) in exchange for the donor gifting the life estate. The gift of the life estate would allow the charity to combine the life estate and remainder interest and sell the property whole. Proceeds from this sale could then fund the gift annuity payments. Of course, the same could be accomplished by a joint sale where the donor used the proceeds from his or her share of the sale to then purchase a gift annuity. However, this transaction would require the donor to immediately recognize any capital gain upon the sale of the property, whereas the gift annuity transaction would postpone such taxation. (Conceptually, the donor could even place her life estate interest into a Charitable Remainder Trust prior to a joint sale in order to avoid capital gains taxes. However, this is rarely done because the transaction amounts are not normally large enough to warrant the use of the more complex transaction and because the donor could not use, live in, or take rent from the property after it was transferred to the Charitable Remainder Trust.)

Finally, of course, if the donor were financially capable and charitably inclined, the donor could give his or her life estate to a charity. The gift could be to a charity holding the remainder interest or to any other charity. This is a deductible gift (even though it is the transfer of only a partial interest in property) because the donor would be retaining no interests in the gifted property.

One concern a charity may have about such transactions is whether or not the donor would choose to maintain the property. Of course, a charity could take the attitude that some gift is better than no gift and not concern itself about the risk of the property deteriorating or burning in the meantime. But, suppose the charity wished to maintain the value of its remainder interest – what are its options?

Although unfamiliar to most people, the life estate / remainder interest property division is a very old form of property ownership. Because of its long history, the rules for such ownership are well established in court cases (referred to as common law). These rules require that the owner of the life estate, referred to as the "life tenant," to pay for maintenance, insurance and taxes (a.k.a., MIT) on the property. Should a life tenant fail to pay for these, the holder of the remainder interest has the right to force payment through court action. Some charities like to avoid such legal actions, if at all possible. This is one reason why it is common for charities soliciting remainder interest gifts to require a written "MIT" contract (Maintenance-Insurance-Taxes). By requiring such an agreement, the charity can ensure that the donor understands his or her obligations. Even if the agreement places no more obligations on the donor than those provided for in common law, it can help to resolve conflicts by serving as a reference point for future conversations. This can be especially important in circumstances where the original donor is no longer managing the property due perhaps to incapacity or to death where the donor's life was not the measuring life. The typical scenario, where a donor is the life tenant, usually creates few problems because the donor wishes to benefit the charity. However, if the life tenant is hostile to the charity, problems are more likely to arise. For example, a donor could direct in his will that a personal residence could be used by his sister for life with the remainder interest going to the donor's favorite charity. In this case, the life tenant may have no interest in or connection with the charity. When there is no relationship and the life tenant fails to maintain, insure, or pay taxes on the property, the charity can take one of several strategies. Using a standard approach, the charity can simply enforce its legal rights through court action. Although this path is available, some charities might decide not to enforce their legal rights because of a risk of "bad press." In this case, it would probably be best for the charity to sell its rights to another investor, who would likely be far less concerned about such matters. If the charity is unwilling to enforce its rights or sell its rights to another investor, then the charity must be content with the land or salvage value of the property remaining at the life tenant's death. Note that, depending on state law, it may not be wise for a charity to intervene by paying taxes on the property. Unpaid taxes will ultimately result in the forced sale of the property, the proceeds of which will be subject to distribution, in part, to the charity as holder of the remainder interest.

The life tenant has the obligation, either under common law or under a written "MIT" contract, to maintain insure and pay taxes on the property. But, what about a life tenant who wishes to make improvements to the residence? Such improvements are certainly allowed by common law, although they must truly be improvements and not diminish the value of the property. What are the tax consequences of making improvements to property in which the remainder interest is owned by a charity?

The indication from IRS private letter rulings is that improvements made to property where the remainder interest is owned by a charity constitute additional charitable gifts. Improvements to a residence, such as the addition of a bedroom, increase the value of the property. The deduction would be based upon the increase in the value of the property multiplied by the percentage attributable to the remainder interest owned by the charity. This would be the same calculation process used previously, but updated for the donor/life tenant's current age. Thus, a donor who has given a remainder interest in his home to his favorite charity can generate additional tax deductions for any improvements made to his home.

The charitable gift of a remainder interests in a home or farmland is a relatively simple transaction that begins to demonstrate the power of sophisticated planning. Donors are able to take an immediate tax deduction without making any changes to the way they will use the property for the rest of their lives. Donors can use the value of this deduction to spend on themselves, invest in income producing assets, or even purchase tax-free life insurance for heirs through an ILIT. Although infrequently used, for the right donor and the right charity gifts of remainder interests in homes and farmland can be a powerful technique. As this simple strategy demonstrates, creative and powerful charitable planning is not just for the wealthy.

12 CHARITABLE REMAINDER TRUSTS

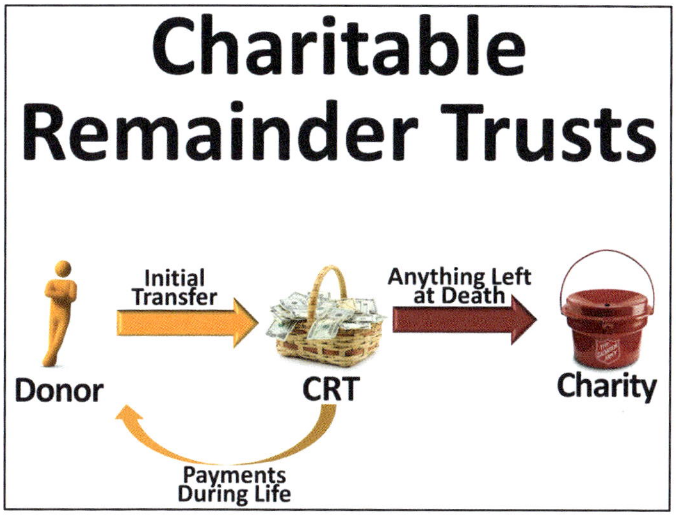

Charitable Remainder Trusts are the single most powerful and flexible charitable planning vehicle available to donors and charitable planners. These instruments offer enormous potential tax advantages along with enough freedom to address the needs of even the most exacting client with highly peculiar preferences. Unlike Charitable Gift Annuities, Charitable Remainder Trusts are typically individually created to precisely match the plans and preferences of the individual donor. This flexibility does come at a cost, specifically the cost of individually constructing and annually maintaining the trust. But, for large transactions these costs can be relatively inconsequential. Despite the unique nature of most individually-crafted Charitable Remainder Trusts, all must comply with the broad framework from the Internal Revenue Code.

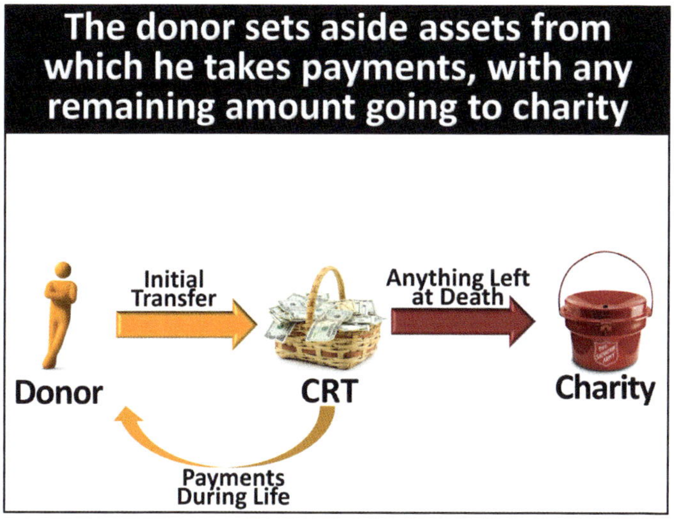

The most common form of a Charitable Remainder Trust is one where the donor places assets into a trust from which he receives payments for life, with any remainder going to charity at death. In the accompanying image, the Charitable Remainder Trust (CRT) is pictured as a basket holding cash. A trust is, essentially, a basket – with instructions – that holds money or other assets. The Charitable Remainder Trust is no exception. The Charitable Remainder Trust is a special kind of trust "basket," because it is itself a charitable entity. Consequently, the trust pays no taxes on income or capital gains from typical investments. The Charitable Remainder Trust differs from the Charitable Gift Annuity in that it is typically a donor-created vehicle. Whereas Charitable Gift Annuities are issued, administered and managed by the charity, the charitable beneficiary of a Charitable Remainder Trust may not even know of its existence until receiving the final distribution check.

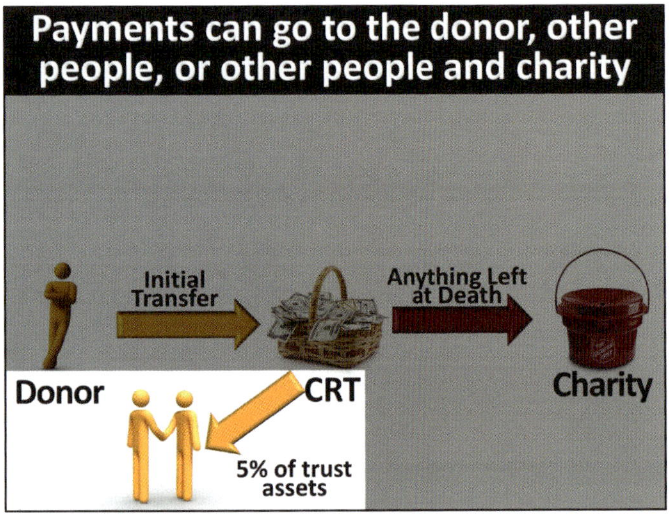

Although the most common form of the Charitable Remainder Trust is one where the donor sets aside assets from which he or she takes payments with any remaining amount going to charity at death, there are other varieties. For example, the payments need not go to the donor, but could instead go to someone else selected by the donor. The payment recipients (a.k.a., annuitants) could even be a combination of the donor, the donor's friends or family, or other charities. (However, at least one beneficiary must be non-charitable.)

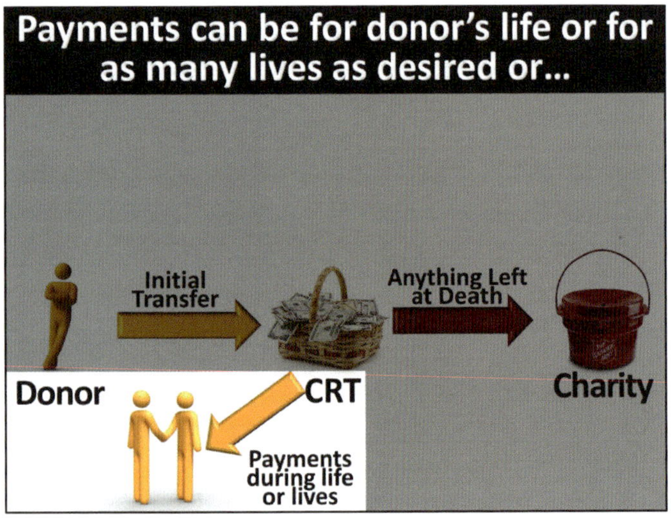

Although payments are typically made for the donor's life (or the joint lives of the donor and the donor's spouse), a Charitable Remainder Trust can pay for any number of lives. Where the Charitable Gift Annuity is limited to a maximum of two lives, no such limitation exists for Charitable Remainder Trusts. (The only requirement being that the individuals were alive at the creation of the Charitable Remainder Trust. This would prohibit a trust that would pay for the lives of "any of my grandchildren, whether currently living or born in the future.")

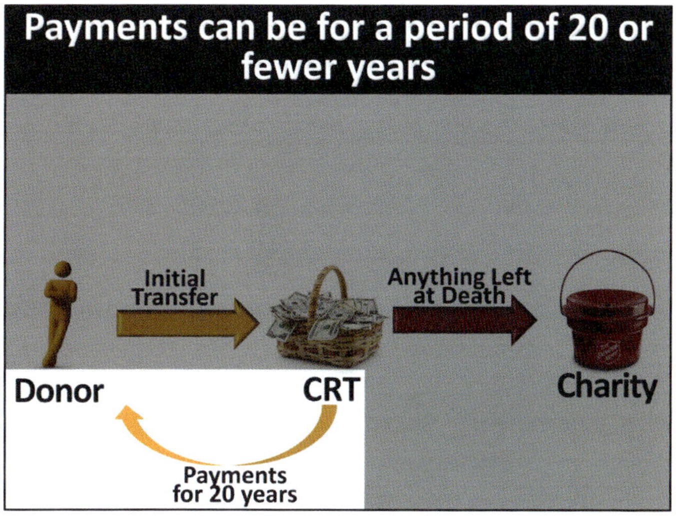

Alternatively, a Charitable Remainder Trust can pay for a fixed period of years. However, the fixed period of years cannot exceed 20 years. Thus, Charitable Remainder Trusts can be made to last much longer by selecting payments for a number of lives, rather than a fixed period of years.

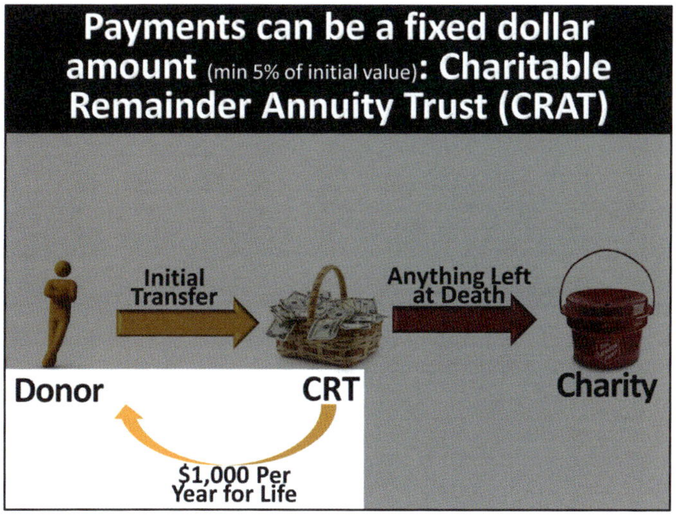

There are two types of Charitable Remainder Trusts. The first is a charitable remainder annuity trust (CRAT). The charitable remainder annuity trust pays a fixed dollar amount each year (or more frequently) for the life of the trust. In this way the charitable remainder annuity trust is very similar to a Charitable Gift Annuity. One difference is that the charitable remainder annuity trust is backed by the assets in the trust, where a Charitable Gift Annuity is backed by the issuing charity. If the assets in a charitable remainder annuity trust are exhausted (either due to poor investments or exceptional longevity of the annuitant) the annuity payments will cease. Similarly, if a charity becomes bankrupt, the Charitable Gift Annuity payments may be reduced or cease altogether, depending upon competing creditor claims and remaining assets. The relative security of annuity payments from a charitable remainder annuity trust as compared with a Charitable Gift Annuity depends upon the underlying investments in the trust or the financial strength of the issuing charity, respectively.

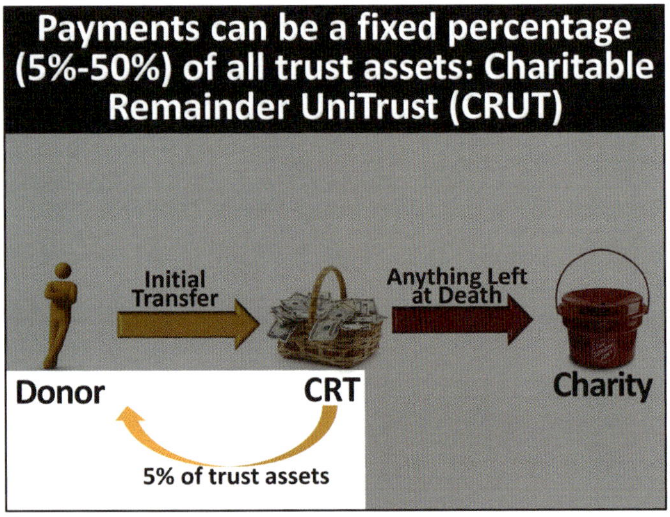

Alternatively, payments can be a fixed percentage (between 5% and 50%) of all trust assets. This type of Charitable Remainder Trust is referred to as a charitable remainder unitrust (CRUT). This is the more common type of Charitable Remainder Trust. Unlike the charitable remainder annuity trust, the charitable remainder unitrust allows the recipient to benefit from investment growth within the trust. The annuity payments in a CRAT are for a fixed dollar amount, but over time inflation can reduce the purchasing power of that fixed dollar amount. If inflation also results in higher interest rates for investments held by the CRUT, then its payments could increase over time, helping to maintain the purchasing power of the payments. Both the CRAT and CRUT are subject to investment risk. The risk in a CRAT is that the payments will cease due to exhaustion of all CRAT assets. The risk in a CRUT is that the payments will become smaller and smaller. The CRUT payment doesn't normally cease, because its payment is a percentage of the value of all assets currently in the trust. So, for example, if a 10% payout CRUT were established with $100,000 and the money was held in a non-interest bearing account, the first payment would be $10,000 ($100,000 x 10%), the second would be $9,000 ($90,000 x 10%), the third would be $8,100 ($81,000 x 10%), the forth would be $72,900 ($72,900 x 10%), and so forth. The payments would never actually cease, but would just become smaller and smaller over time. (Although after 132 years the payments would fall to less than one penny, so perhaps then the trust payments would necessarily cease.) A CRUT does not risk complete exhaustion like a CRAT unless the underlying investments became completely worthless due to market events.

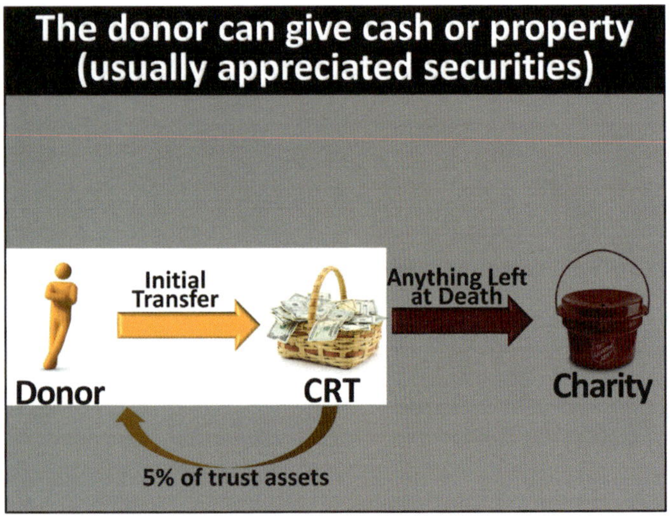

A donor can transfer cash or property to a Charitable Remainder Trust. Most commonly, this transfer is of appreciated property. As we will see later, the attraction for transferring appreciated property is that such transfers can avoid capital gains taxes, but still allow the donor to receive payments from the undiminished proceeds of the sale of the transferred property. Transfers to Charitable Remainder Trusts can include cash, shares of stock (other than subchapter S corporation shares), bonds, limited partnership interests, real estate, tangible personal property, and almost any other asset.

The donor creates the rules in a Charitable Remainder Trust, so long as those rules fit within the general guidelines for Charitable Remainder Trusts established by the Internal Revenue Code. This enormous flexibility, however, ends after the trust is created. A Charitable Remainder Trust is an *irrevocable* trust. Once the rules are created, the rules cannot normally be changed. This irrevocability is what allows the Charitable Remainder Trust to become a charitable entity (i.e., it cannot later be made less charitable). Irrevocability also allows the donor to take a tax deduction for his or her transfer to the trust.

The importance of irrevocability arises in other areas of charitable planning as well. A donor receives no income tax deduction for having a charitable beneficiary in his or her will because the donor could, at any point, remove all charitable beneficiaries. In contrast, when the donor transfers a remainder interest in a home or farm to a charity, the donor can take an immediate tax deduction, even though the charity will not become full owner of the property until the death of the donor. The key difference between a will and a remainder deed is that the will is revocable, and the transfer of a remainder deed is not.

Although the donor loses the ability to change the rules of the trust once it is created, the trust rules can still provide for ongoing donor influence in several areas.

In many cases the donor may act as trustee of the Charitable Remainder Trust and continue to manage the assets and investments. There are certainly guidelines that must be followed to ensure that the donor is not receiving any additional benefit from the trust or engaging in self-dealing, but there is no prohibition against a donor managing his or her own Charitable Remainder Trust. Alternatively, the donor may instead choose who the trustee will be and keep the ongoing power to appoint or remove trustees. The donor could select a friend, a family member, a trust company, or even a charity to serve as trustee of the trust.

However, some plans will require the use of an independent trustee. For example, the donor may not act as trustee if the trust allows for payments to be withheld or shifted amongst various non-charitable recipients. This keeps too much power with the donor, and causes the trust to be treated as simply the property of the donor.

Although the donor may not keep any rights to change which non-charitable beneficiaries receive payments (or the amount of those payments), the donor is permitted to decide which charity will receive the remainder interest at the termination of the Charitable Remainder Trust. The Internal Revenue Code requires only that the remainder interest ultimately goes to some charity. The donor could even choose for the remainder interest to go to a private foundation. Thus, the donor could establish a Charitable Remainder Trust payable to a university foundation, retain the right to change the charitable beneficiary, and later establish his own private family foundation and declare that foundation as the new charitable beneficiary. (If the donor keeps the right to name a private foundation as the charitable beneficiary, charitable deductions resulting from transfers to the trust will be subject to the income limitations for gifts to private foundations.)

This flexibility to change charities is available, but not required. It is perfectly acceptable to have a Charitable Remainder Trust where the remainder beneficiary cannot be changed (unless, for some reason, the remainder beneficiary no longer qualifies as a charity at the time of the termination of the trust). Indeed, most charities will not agree to act as trustee of a Charitable Remainder Trust unless they are named irrevocably as the remainder beneficiary.

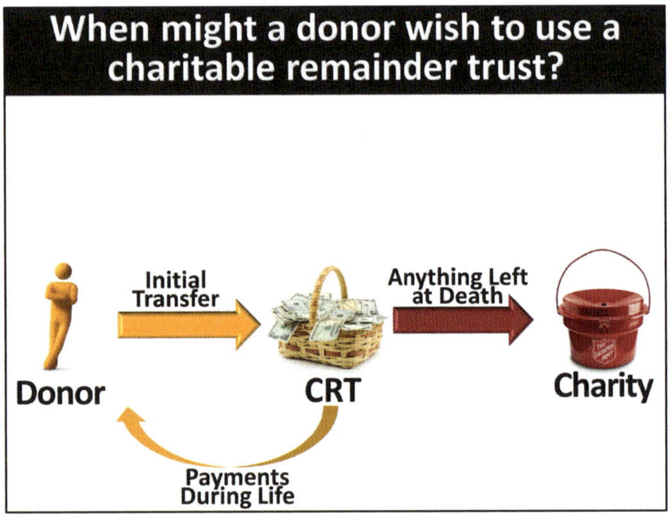

Given the flexibility of the Charitable Remainder Trust, it can be a useful tool for donors with a variety of financial goals and circumstances. The ability to take payments from the proceeds of highly appreciated assets – undiminished by capital gains taxes at their sale – accompanied by tax free growth of investments inside of the Charitable Remainder Trust along with receiving an immediate tax deduction for a post-mortem transfer make this an enormously attractive vehicle for the charitably-inclined donor with appreciated assets. Several common financial planning scenarios correspond almost exactly with the terms available in a Charitable Remainder Trust.

A donor who wants a fixed annual payment from investment assets and also wants to make a post-mortem gift to charity is an ideal candidate for a charitable remainder annuity trust. The charitable remainder annuity trust not only provides for fixed annual payments and an ultimate transfer to charity but, as compared with using a standard investment account and will, can produce enormous tax benefits.

The charitable remainder unitrust is well suited for the donor who wishes to retain control of his or her investments. Not only can the donor retain control, but with the charitable remainder unitrust, the donor also receives larger payments when assets grow in value. Where a wealthy client has a pre-existing desire to leave a bequest gift to charity at death, the use of a Charitable Remainder Trust will often be, by far, the most tax advantageous way to accomplish the client's other financial goals.

Although the most common form of Charitable Remainder Trusts pay for a life or lives, in some cases the fixed term trust can be ideal. If a client desires to make a substantial lifetime transfer to charity, but still has specific income needs for a fixed amount of time, the fixed term Charitable Remainder Trust can be an excellent solution. Such fixed-term payments can help to address a temporary income need due to early retirement or to a known obligation such as college tuition for a child or grandchild.

Although it is quite common for clients' to have financial planning needs that correspond with the allowable terms under a Charitable Remainder Trust, such needs could also be addressed without the use of the trust. For example, a donor could simply set aside money into a special account, withdraw annual sums from the account, and designate a charity as the "pay on death" designee. Functionally, this would work exactly like a Charitable Remainder Trust, except that the donor would retain 100% control and freedom. So, given this simple alternative, why would a donor choose to use a Charitable Remainder Trust? The answer is simple: tax benefits.

At its core, the Charitable Remainder Trust is attractive not just for its correspondence with the donor's pre-existing plans and goals, but rather for the special tax advantages that are otherwise unavailable. The wide range of tax benefits generated by the Charitable Remainder Trust are what drives its widespread use.

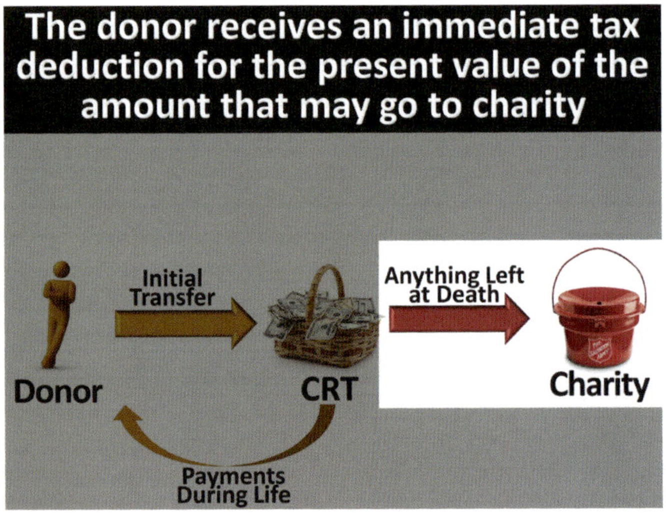

An initial and obvious benefit from using a Charitable Remainder Trust is that the donor receives an immediate income tax deduction for a transfer that will not go to charity for many years. Without using a Charitable Remainder Trust, the donor could still set aside an asset, take payments from the investment for 20 years, and donate whatever is left to the charity. But, the donor would have to wait 20 years before receiving a charitable income tax deduction. Even worse, if the donor wanted to take payments from the investment for life, donating the whatever remained to charity at death, then the donor would never receive any charitable income tax deduction. The Charitable

Remainder Trust allows a donor to *immediately* take a deduction in both of these scenarios even though the ultimate charitable beneficiary may not see funds for many years. This ability to create a large charitable income tax deduction where none would have existed before (or in some cases to pull forward those deductions by two decades) is very powerful. Additionally, as discussed later, the valuation of the deduction for post-mortem transfers is actually much higher than is actuarially appropriate given that wealthy donors, on average, live much longer than the typical person. Results from the Health and Retirement Study reported in *American Charitable Bequest Demographics* indicate that wealthy bequest donors live 5-7 years longer than poor non-donors do. Additionally, those who purchase lifetime annuities live longer than others of their age because the annuity-purchasing group typically excludes those who are seriously ill or known to be approaching death. Both of these factors point to the reality that Charitable Remainder Trust donors will, on average, live substantially longer than others of their same age. For tax deduction valuation purposes, this means donors will receive a deduction based upon their receiving payments for a much smaller number of years than will typically be the case (i.e., the tax deduction is greater than is actuarially appropriate).

Regardless of the actuarial discussion, there is no doubt that the income tax deduction available for making a post-mortem charitable transfer by a Charitable Remainder Trust is greater than that for making the same transfer by will. This is obvious because a charitable transfer by will generates no charitable income tax deduction. The Charitable Remainder Trust donor does give up some freedom in exchange for the tax deduction; he cannot later decide to give the charity's share to a non-charitable beneficiary. In contrast, a will – although generating no charitable income tax deduction – can be completely changed at any time.

One of the great sources of tax advantages available from a Charitable Remainder Trust relates to the postponement or avoidance of capital gains taxes. Critical to this advantage is the reality that donors may transfer highly appreciated assets to a Charitable Remainder Trust without triggering a recognition of capital gain. This is simply another application of the general principle that donors can give highly appreciated property to a charity, recognize no capital gain, and in many cases take a tax deduction based upon the full fair market value of the property. This fundamental tax benefit is why donors normally should give appreciated property, rather than cash (especially where the appreciated property is a fungible asset such as publicly traded stock that can be immediately repurchased with a higher cost basis). The Charitable Remainder Trust takes this basic advantage and applies it to a scenario where the donor not only makes a gift, but also receives a stream of payments from the gift.

The capital gains tax advantage from a Charitable Remainder Trust is not limited to the ability to transfer appreciated assets into the trust without generating capital gain. The Charitable Remainder Trust is itself a nonprofit entity. As such, the trust can recognize capital gains and earn income while paying no taxes. This creates two dramatic tax advantages. First, the donor can take payments from the full sale value of the highly appreciated asset, undiminished by capital gains taxes. (Whereas, a sale outside of the Charitable Remainder Trust would immediately cut the remaining amount available to invest.) Second, all future investment growth taking place inside the Charitable Remainder Trust occurs without taxation, excepting only potential taxation on the payments received by the donor. This makes the trust a perfect environment for the tax-free growth of assets, similar to a qualified retirement plan.

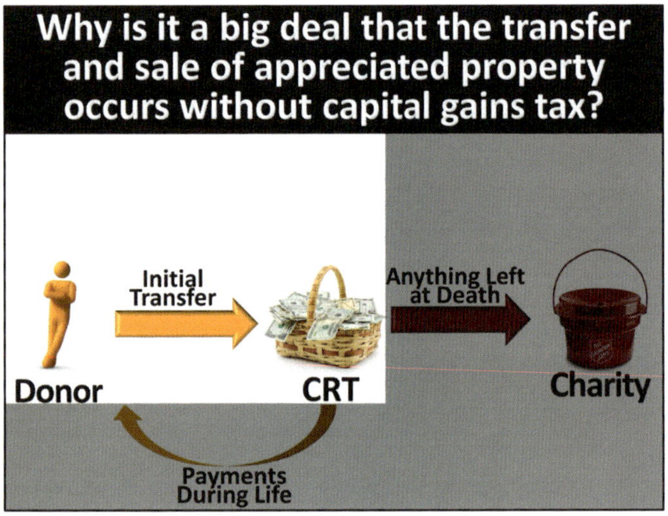

Without looking at the numbers in a few scenarios, it may not be immediately obvious why the ability to receive payments from the full sale amount of a highly appreciated asset can make such an enormous difference. So, let's turn to some examples to demonstrate this power.

We begin with a common financial planning dilemma. A client holds a low-basis, highly appreciated asset. Unfortunately, this asset generates little income. It is often the case that such an asset may be a substantial part of the client's wealth. Wealth is often built in the form of entrepreneurial and business-building activity. A client owning such a business may have a very valuable asset, but one which is difficult to convert into a reliable investment income stream. This may be true because the business is in a growth phase where it is important to reinvest earnings rather than pay out dividends. Or, this may be true because getting the business to reliably generate income requires the active participation of an owner who wishes to retire. Such entrepreneurial businesses have often been built over a long period of years such that the founder has little or no cost basis in the business.

Although business building is perhaps the most common scenario, there are others that can leave clients with low-basis assets the produce little or no income, such as owning farmland that has become developable land due to exurban growth, or highly appreciated artwork or collectibles, or investment property that has been fully depreciated out and is valuable for redevelopment purposes, but generates little current income. The natural reaction of most financial advisors seeing clients with income needs whose wealth is highly concentrated in such non-income producing assets is to convert them to diversified income-generating investments. But, such conversion requires a sale, and a sale creates capital gains tax liability. Such a sale can leave the client with much less wealth.

Suppose a client has a $1,000,000 asset with a zero basis. We will use a zero-basis scenario to show the most extreme case, but this is certainly not outside the realm of possibility. For example, a zero-basis asset may be a business built up by the owner over many years without significant up-front cash investment, a completely depreciated asset, or perhaps collectibles acquired or received as a gift where there is no documented purchase price. Although the owner wishes to convert this non-income producing asset into a diversified income-producing portfolio, that conversion process requires a sale. The capital gains taxes resulting from that sale significantly reduce the remaining assets available for investment. Thus, the usually good advice of diversifying investments and matching income needs with income production of investments is thwarted by the cost of selling the low-basis asset. This can keep the owner tied to undesirable investments because any sale would result in the loss of nearly a quarter of the value of the asset, just from the federal capital gains taxes alone. These federal taxes include the capital gains tax with a top rate of 20% and the 3.8% affordable care act surtax.

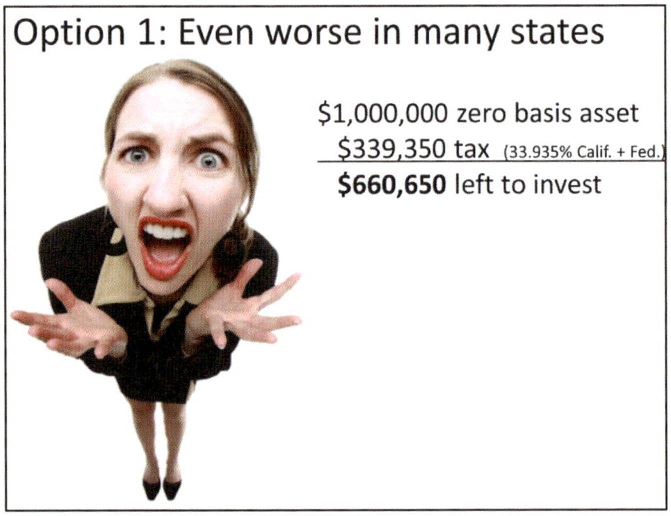

Of course, most owners live in states that also impose a state-level capital gains tax. (Currently, 42 of 50 states impose capital gains taxes.) Although state capital gains taxes may be deducted from the federal tax return, somewhat softening the impact, the addition of state capital gains taxes can make the prospect of a sale even more disheartening for owners. As an example, owners at the top tax rates in California will face, even with a full federal deduction, a blended rate of 33.935%. For the unfortunate owner who cannot tax full advantage of the Schedule A deduction for state taxes, this rate could increase to as much as 36.8%. When capital gains taxes are taking more than a third of the value of any gain, the option of selling even an underperforming highly appreciated asset can become unfeasible.

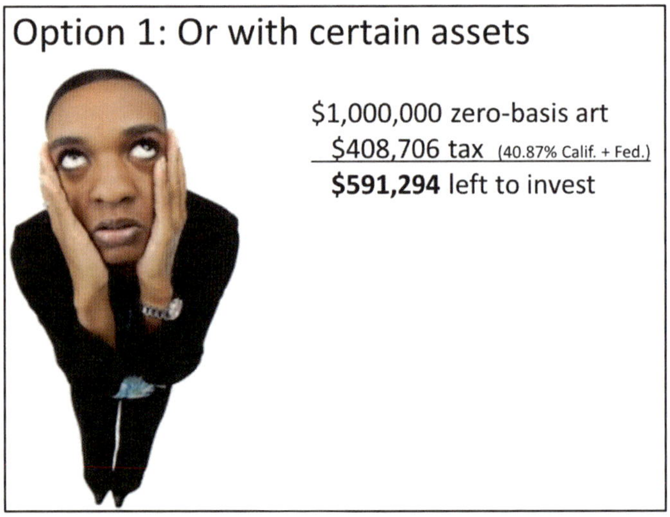

Beyond this, some assets are subject to even higher capital gains tax rates. For example, capital gain from the sale of collectibles – such as artwork – has a top federal tax rate of 28% in addition to the 3.8% affordable care act surtax, rising to 31.8%. Combining this with a 13% state tax in a state like California, if deductible, increase the top rate to 40.87% (or 44.8% if the Schedule A deduction for state taxes could not, for some reason, be used by the taxpayer).

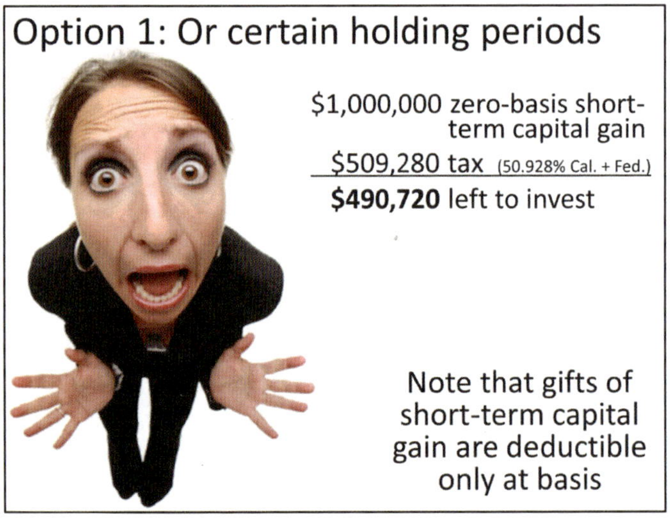

Perhaps the worst capital gains tax result comes from selling a short-term capital gain. A short-term capital gain results from the sale of an asset held for one year or less. This is taxed as ordinary income resulting in a top rate of 39.6% combined with the state income tax rate. For a taxpayer in California this results in a top combined rate of 50.928% assuming the ability to use the Schedule A deduction, or 52.6% otherwise. Although the prospect of losing more than half of the value of the asset due to a sale may be rare, it shows the potentially dramatic impact of capital gains taxes. In this particular example, because the underlying asset is short-term capital gain property any charitable gift would be valued based upon the lower of basis or fair market value. Thus, a zero-basis short-term capital gain asset would generate no deductible charitable gift. However, the ability to avoid losing more than half of the asset to taxation may be sufficiently attractive, even without the addition of a charitable income tax deduction.

The Charitable Remainder Trust provides an alternate path for an owner to be able to sell and earn payments from the highly appreciated asset. Critically, this path results in no reduction of the investment asset due to its sale. The ability to convert the asset into a diversified, income-producing portfolio while leaving the full value of the asset completely undiminished by capital gains taxes is potentially quite attractive.

Whether capital gains taxes would cause the owner to lose a quarter, a third, or more than half of the value of his or her asset, avoiding this reduction can result in a much higher level of investment income. The Charitable Remainder Trust offers the attractive option of being able to sell and reinvest a highly appreciated asset with no reduction by capital gains taxes. At a minimum, these capital gains taxes will be deferred to future years, often spreading across the lifetimes of one or more recipients. However, in many cases, the capital gains taxes are not simply deferred, but are completely avoided. Thus, the use of the Charitable Remainder Trust can, in many cases, produce a much higher level of income than would otherwise be available to the owner of a highly appreciated non-income producing asset.

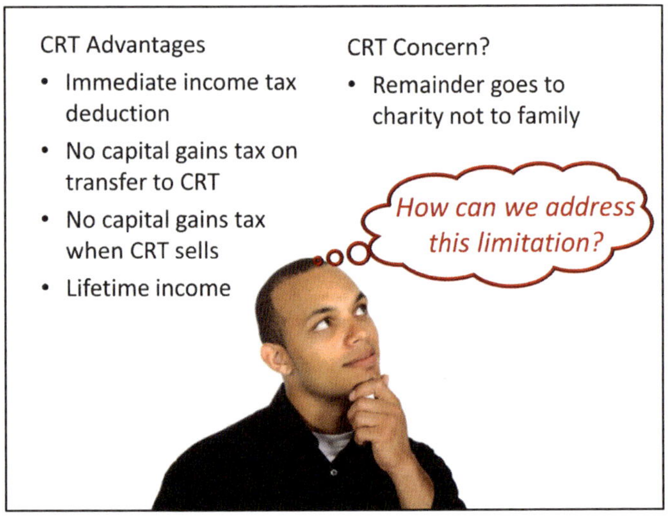

The advantages to using a Charitable Remainder Trust include receiving an immediate income tax deduction, avoiding capital gains taxes on the transfer or sale of underlying assets, and the enjoyment of lifetime payments based upon the full value of the investment asset, undiminished by initial capital gains taxes. These advantages do come with one primary cost. That cost is the requirement that any remainder amount is transferred to a charity. For a donor who already had the intention of leaving assets to charity at death, this result is perfectly appropriate. However, some donors may be particularly concerned about their surviving family members losing the ability to inherit the remainder interest. This might be addressed by giving heirs a lifetime payment stream from the Charitable Remainder Trust. Aside from this, there is another option that will provide the heirs with a lump sum inheritance to replace some or all of the asset that they will no longer be inheriting.

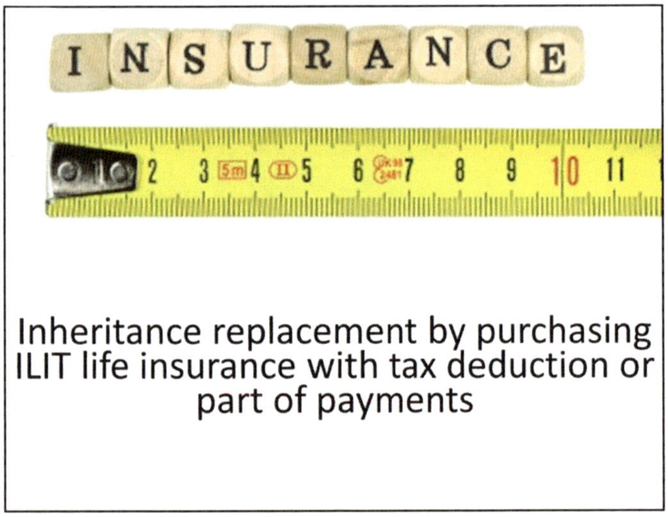

It is common to combine a Charitable Remainder Trust with an irrevocable life insurance trust as a means to replace the inheritance of the wealth being donated to the charity. The use of the irrevocable life insurance trust is a method to make the life insurance death benefit pass to the heirs with no estate taxes. In this way, the heirs may lose the rights to inherit an asset which would have been subject to estate taxes but in replacement they receive a tax-free life insurance benefit. Consequently, even a smaller life insurance benefit may be more attractive to the heirs because it passes free from estate taxes. The Charitable Remainder Trust transaction conveniently generates two potential sources to pay for the purchase of life insurance. First, the Charitable Remainder Trust creates an immediate income tax deduction. This allows the donor to take the value of this deduction (i.e., the taxes the donor would have had to pay but for the deduction) and use it to purchase life insurance. Additionally, the Charitable Remainder Trust creates a regular income stream, part of which can be dedicated by the recipient to pay for the purchase of life insurance. This method also allows the donor to transfer a much larger asset to charity, but then use proceeds from the Charitable Remainder Trust to satisfy the needs of heirs through "wealth replacement" by life insurance. Thus, even the primary disadvantage of Charitable Remainder Trusts to the heirs can be softened or eliminated through the use of a combination Charitable Remainder Trust – irrevocable life insurance trust (CRT-ILIT).

As with Charitable Gift Annuities, the taxation rules for Charitable Remainder Trusts can become complex. This is due to the multi-faceted tax dimensions of a Charitable Remainder Trust transaction. The Charitable Remainder Trust creates an immediate charitable income tax deduction as well as a stream of payments that can be treated as ordinary income, capital gain, and/or return of principal. With the exception of the valuation process for a fixed annuity, the tax treatment of a Charitable Remainder Trust is different than for an otherwise similar Charitable Gift Annuity. The Charitable Gift Annuity rules will not apply to payments received from the Charitable Remainder Trust.

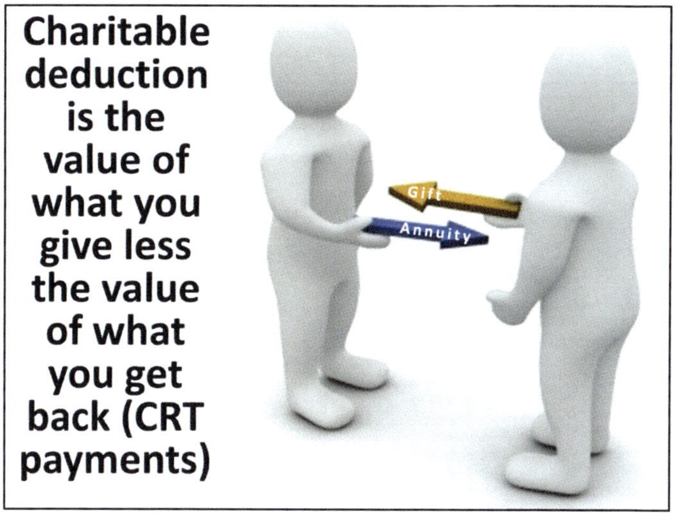

Just as with any bargain sale or *quid pro quo* transaction, the charitable deduction is simply the value of what the donor gave less the value of what the donor received back. In this case, what the donor receives back are the payments from the Charitable Remainder Trust. (Note that this is still the process for valuing the gift, even if the donor chooses to have the payments made to someone else.)

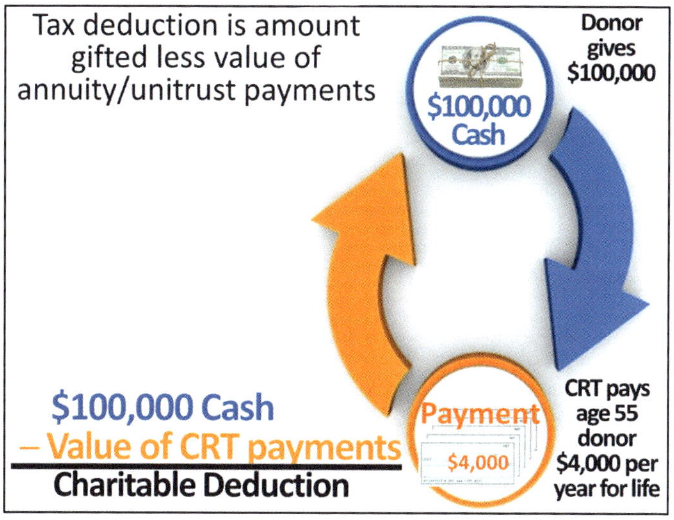

Let's take the simple example, borrowed identically from the numbers used with our Charitable Gift Annuity example, of a donor who gives $100,000 of cash to his Charitable Remainder Trust and, in exchange, receives the right to collect $4,000 per year for life from the trust. Just as with a Charitable Gift Annuity, the charitable income tax deduction is the amount gifted less the value of the annuity payments. In this case, we are dealing with a fixed annuity amount of $4,000 per year. However, the same concept applies if the donor were receiving a fixed percentage payment of, say, 5% of trust assets per year. The charitable income tax deduction is still the difference between what the donor gave and the value of what the donor received back. The only difference between the charitable remainder annuity trust and the charitable remainder unitrust is the calculation process for valuing the payments.

So how do we value the payments that are planned to come from the Charitable Remainder Trust? Naturally, we do not know in advance how long the annuitant might live. Nor do we know what the future returns of the Charitable Remainder Trust will be. But, we cannot wait until after the death of the donor (or some fixed period of years) before we calculate the value of the charitable income tax deduction. Consequently, the value of the payments are based upon the premise that the annuitant will live to his or her life expectancy as of the date of transfer, and that the investments in the Charitable Remainder Trust will always return exactly the §7520 interest rate as of the date of the transfer. Of course, if the annuitant lives longer than expected or the investment returns differ from the initial §7520 interest rate, the actual payments to the annuitant may vary widely. This ultimate reality does not affect the valuation of the payments for purposes of the charitable income tax deduction.

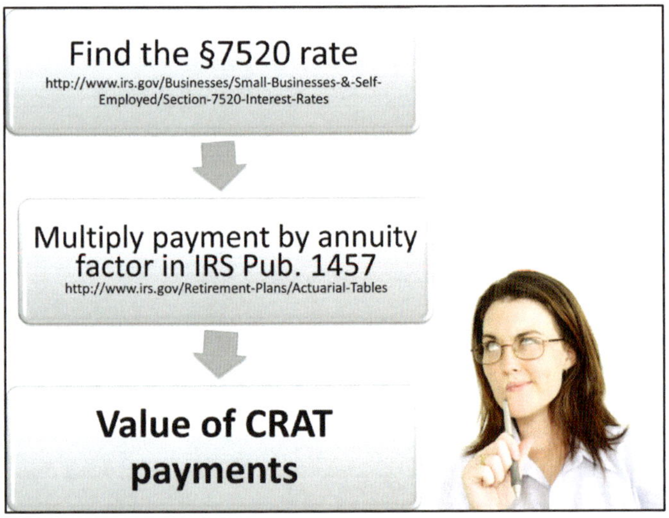

The process of valuing payments from a charitable remainder annuity trust is exactly identical to the process for valuing payments from a Charitable Gift Annuity. The first step is to find the §7520 rate, which is available at www.irs.gov/Businesses/Small-Businesses-&-Self-Employed/Section-7520-Interest-Rates and at a variety of other planned giving websites. With this rate, the one-life or two-life annuity tables can be used to identify the appropriate annuity factor (tables are located at www.irs.gov/Retirement-Plans/Actuarial-Tables). Multiplying this annuity factor times the payment (with a possible adjustment from Table K for payments starting earlier than, or given more frequently than 12 months) gives the valuation of the annuity for purposes of the charitable income tax deduction.

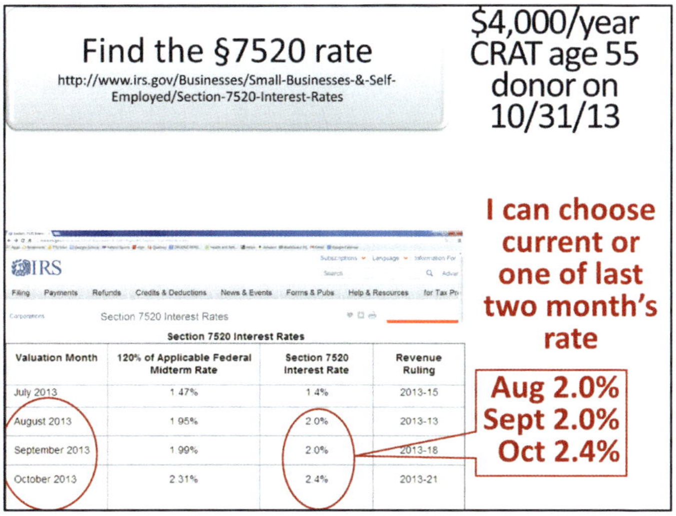

As with Charitable Gift Annuities, the donor is allowed to choose the current §7520 rate or either of the previous two months for the annuity calculation. Additionally, because the next month's §7520 rate is released towards the end of the previous month, the donor may have a choice among four different rates if the transaction can be briefly postponed. In our example of a charitable remainder annuity trust where the age 55 donor contributes $100,000 and receives a $4,000 per year annuity on October 31 of 2013, the three available rates were 2.0%, 2.0%, and 2.4%. On that date, the donor would also have known of the upcoming §7520 rate for November (which was 2.0%), and could have postponed the transaction if that rate had been more advantageous. In either case, the donor in this example has the choice of using the 2.0% or 2.4% §7520 rate. Which is preferable?

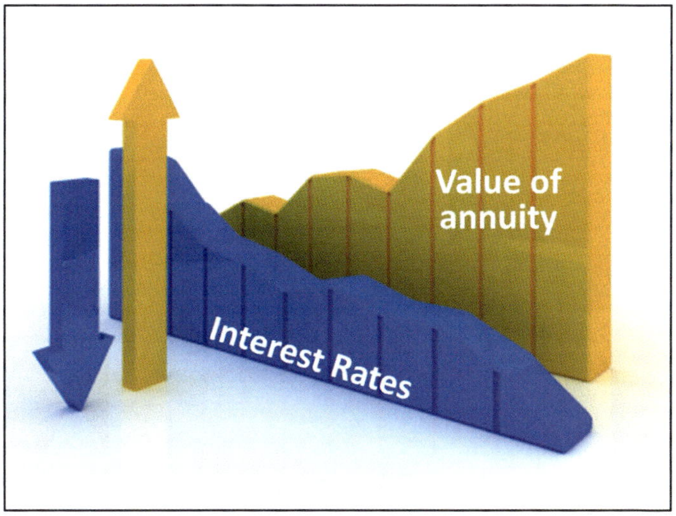

The theory is the same as that used with Charitable Gift Annuities. As interest rates increase the value of a fixed dollar annuity decreases. Because the charitable tax deduction is the difference between the $100,000 transfer amount and the value of the fixed dollar annuity, the donor will desire the use of the highest interest rate which produces the lowest calculated value for the annuity.

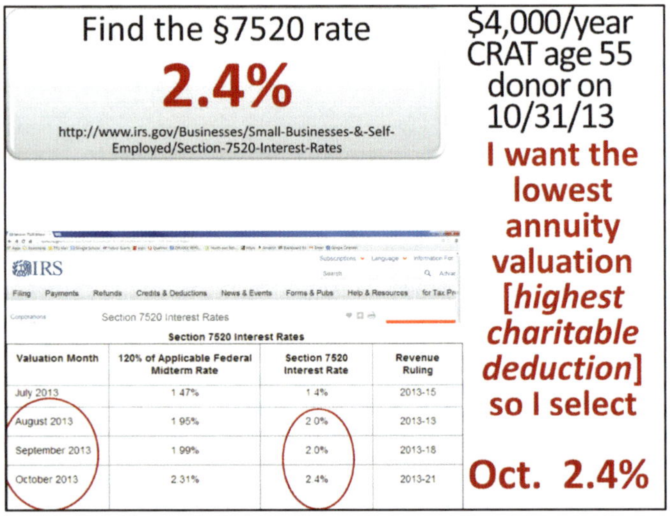

In this case, the donor is benefited by choosing the highest interest rate available, which is the 2.4% §7520 rate from October. This higher rate results in a relatively lower valuation of the annuity payment stream and consequently a relatively higher valuation of the charitable income tax deduction.

Although the higher interest rate results in a larger charitable income tax deduction it also results in a lower total investment portion, which will be counted as tax-free return of capital when returned. In cases where the charitable tax deduction could not be fully used, this could lead to a circumstance where the lower rate would be preferred. Such a scenario is much less likely with Charitable Remainder Trusts than with Charitable Gift Annuities. A Charitable Gift Annuity donor who lives to his or her life expectancy will receive all of his or her investment back as tax-free portions of the annual payments. In contrast, the tax characterization for payments from a Charitable Remainder Trust donor are quite different. It is quite possible for a donor not to receive back any of his or her investment back as tax-free repayment of principal in a Charitable Remainder Trust, which makes this strategy far less attractive for Charitable Remainder Trusts than for Charitable Gift Annuities. The rules for counting payments as return of investment will be discussed in more detail later in this chapter.

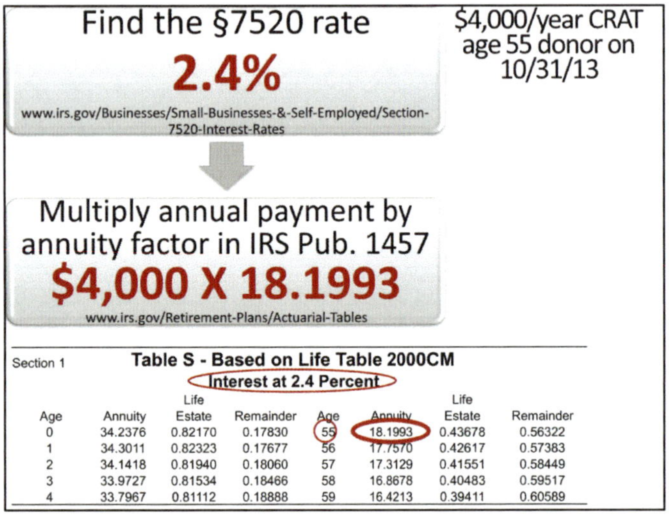

Once the §7520 rate has been selected, we can now move to the appropriate section of the single-life Table S. Once we are in the section of the single-life table S for a 2.4% interest rate, we see that the annuity factor for an age 55 donor is 18.1993. Multiplying this annuity factor times the $4,000 per year annuity payment gives the valuation for the annuity payments of $72,797.20.

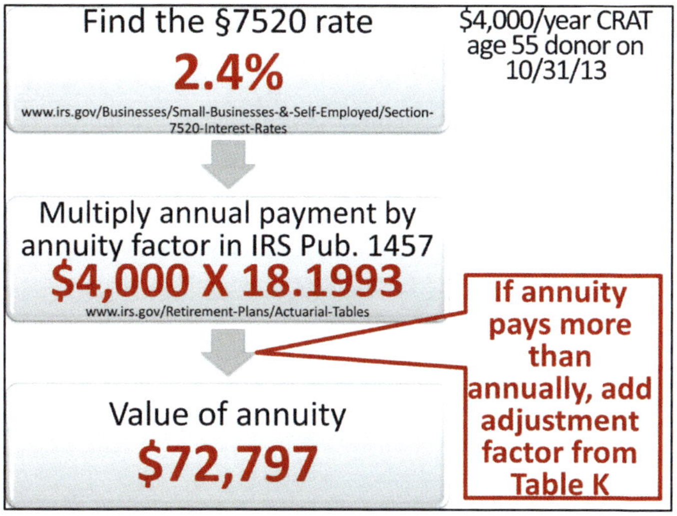

If this annuity payment were to be made annually on the anniversary of the initial transfer, the $72,797.20 valuation would be correct. If the annuity made its first payment prior to the anniversary of the initial transfer, or made payments more frequently than annually, the valuation would have to be increased by an adjustment factor taken from Table K from the same website. In that case, the annuity would be worth less (more) if the annuitant would receive the payments later (earlier) because payments received earlier could presumably be invested to earn additional interest.

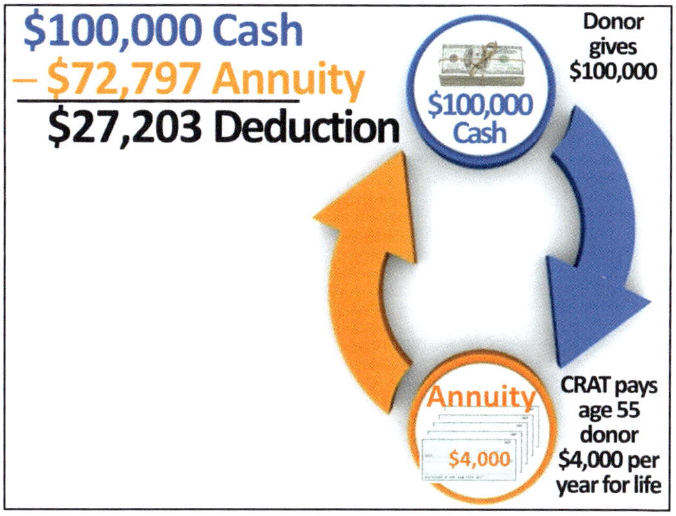

Just as with a Charitable Gift Annuity, the calculation of the charitable income tax deduction is simply the amount of the transfer, $100,000, less the value of the annuity, $72,797.20, for a total deduction of $27,202.80.

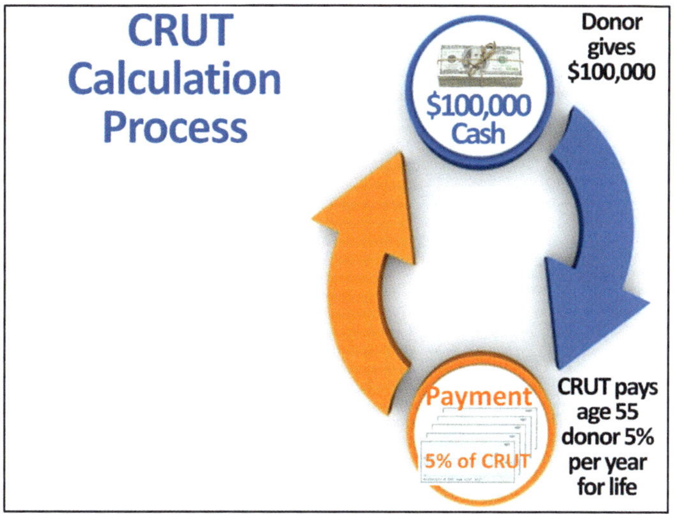

Now suppose the donor is receiving not a fixed dollar payment, but rather receiving 5% of all assets inside the Charitable Remainder Trust as of the anniversary date of the initial transfer. This is a unitrust, not an annuity trust. The process for calculating the charitable income tax deduction resulting from a transfer to a charitable remainder unitrust differs slightly from the calculation for a charitable remainder annuity trust. The concept, however, is identical in that the deductible gift is the difference between the transfer and the value of the payment stream promised to the annuitant.

CRUT Deduction Calculation

Multiply transfer by remainder interest factor in IRS Pub. 1458

$100,000 X .31450

www.irs.gov/Retirement-Plans/Actuarial-Tables

5% per year age 55 donor on 10/31/13 with annual payments on 10/31

Charitable deduction

$31,450

Section 1

Table U(1) - Based on Life Table 2000CM

	Adjusted Payout Rate									
Age	4.2%	4.4%	4.6%	4.8%	5.0%	5.2%	5.4%	5.6%	5.8%	6.0%
55	.37183	.35635	.34166	.32773	.31450	.30194	.29001	.27868	.26791	.25768
56	.38390	.36841	.35370	.33971	[illegible]	.31378	.30175	.29032	.27943	.26907
57	.39618	.38069	.36596	.35194	.33859	.32588	.31377	.30224	.29125	.28077

There are actually fewer steps for calculating the charitable deduction for a charitable remainder unitrust than for a charitable remainder annuity trust. To calculate the deduction for the age 55 donor receiving a 5.0% payout rate, we simply multiply the initial transfer amount by the remainder percentage found in table U of the same website (www.irs.gov/Retirement-Plans/Actuarial-Tables). This remainder interest is .31450 which, when multiplied by the $100,000 initial transfer, results in a charitable deduction of $31,450.

Notice that we did not use the §7520 interest rate in the calculation of the charitable income tax deduction for a charitable remainder unitrust. How is this possible? As interest rates rise, the amount remaining at the expiration of the annuitant's initial life expectancy would also rise. But, the present value discounting of that larger future value also increases due to the higher interest rate and this difference exactly offsets the increased remainder amount in present value terms. Let's look at an example. Suppose an annuitant had a 20 year life expectancy and received 5% of the value of the trust at the end of each year. If we used a 0% interest rate, then the amount remaining in 20 years would be $35,849. Because the interest rate was 0% the present value of that amount would also be $35,849. If instead we used a 10% interest rate, then the amount remaining in 20 years would be a much larger $241,171. But, the present value of $241,171 received in 20 years using a 10% interest rate is the same $35,849. Because the charitable income tax deduction is based on the *present* value of the predicted transfer to charity, changes in the interest rate have no effect on this deduction.

CRUT Calculation for differing payments

If payments other than annual given immediately after annual valuation, calculate adjusted payout rate (APR) as payout rate X table F (www.irs.gov/Retirement-Plans/Actuarial-Tables) reduction using appropriate §7520 rate. If factor for adjusted payout rate (APR) is not on unitrust table, use:

Factor above APR – [(factor below APR – factor above APR) X ((APR-rate below APR) /.002)]

The standard calculations for valuing the tax deduction for gifts to a charitable remainder unitrust are based on the assumption that payments to the annuitant will be made immediately each year after the annual valuation. When the payments are postponed, for example by being paid out monthly over the course of the following year, the annuitant receives a reduced benefit. For annuity trusts and Charitable Gift Annuities the valuation of this change in benefit due to intra-year timing of the distribution is calculated using table K. For unitrusts this adjustment is made using table F (linked at the same website at www.irs.gov/Retirement-Plans/Actuarial-Tables), which generates an adjusted payout rate. For example, a 6% payout rate, if paid quarterly beginning with the first payment immediately after the annual valuation when the §7520 rate is 2.4% generates an adjusted payout rate of 6% x .991168 or 5.947008%. This creates a problem because Table U contains remainder factors for 6.0% and 5.8%, but not for 5.947008%. Calculating the remainder factor (i.e., the charitable tax deduction) requires interpolating between the factor for 6.0% and the factor for 5.8%. The formula for this interpolation, where APR is the Adjusted Payout Rate is

Factor above APR – [(factor below APR – factor above APR) X (APR-rate below APR)/.002)].

So, if the annuitant were age 55 in the previous example (where the adjusted payout rate was 5.947008%) then the present value of the charity's remainder interest would be

.26791-[(.26791-.25768) X ((.05947008-.058)/.002)] = .26039.

As expected, this remainder interest factor (.26039) for the 5.947008% rate is between the factor for the 6% rate (.25768) and the 5.8% rate (.26791).

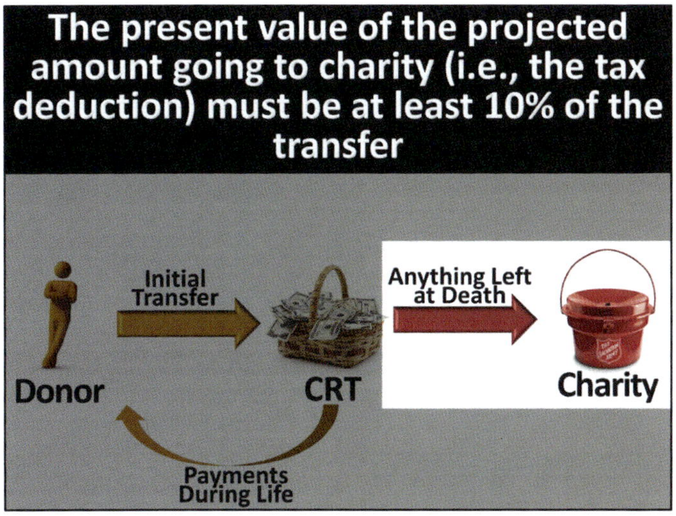

A contribution to a Charitable Remainder Trust is required to have a minimum of 10% of the present value projected to go to charity at the termination of the trust. This requires that an amount significantly larger than 10% of the original amount be projected to go to charity at termination, because the charity is required to wait a substantial amount of time before receiving any funds. In other words, in order to generate a *present* value of 10%, the *future* value projected to be given to the charity will necessarily be larger. Because the charitable income tax deduction resulting from a transfer to a Charitable Remainder Trust *is* the present value of the amount projected to go to charity, this means that the charitable income tax deduction for a transfer to charity must be at least 10%. If the amount projected to go to charity has a present value of less than 10%, the trust will not qualify as a Charitable Remainder Trust. This means that there will be *no* deductible gift. The general rule is that gifts where the donor keeps a retained interest of a different type than that given to charity are *not* deductible. The Charitable Remainder Trust is an exception to this rule. If a trust no longer qualifies as a Charitable Remainder Trust, then no exception applies and the gift is not deductible. Additionally, because the trust will no longer qualify as a charitable trust, it will be required to pay taxes on any realized capital gains or income resulting from trust investments. (In practice, such trusts can include language permitting the trustee to amend the trust – e.g., increasing the charitable share – for purposes of guaranteeing that the Charitable Remainder Trust rules are met.) Thus, it is essential that the trust is projected to give a large enough amount to charity to generate at least a 10% tax deduction. It is important to note that all of these calculations are based upon the amount *projected* to go to charity. The amount that is *actually* transferred to charity is irrelevant to the tax calculation. This amount can be greater or less depending upon the return on the underlying investments and, in cases where the trust payments continue for a life or lives, the longevity of the annuitant.

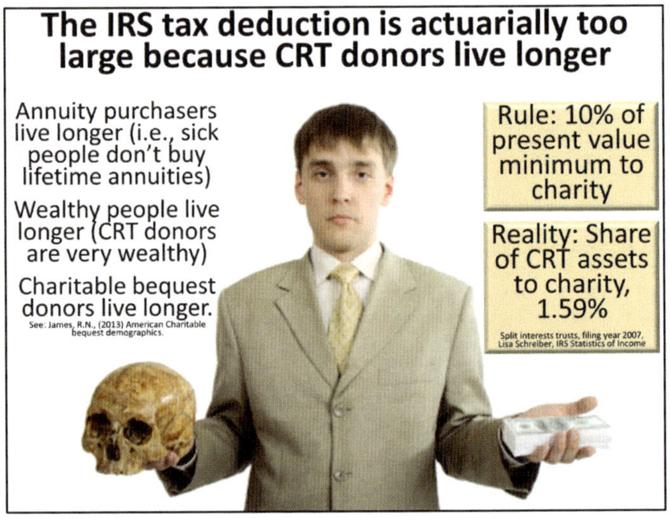

The amount projected to go to charity – and the tax deduction based on the *present value* of that amount – depend upon the longevity of the annuitant (who is typically the donor). The longer an annuitant lives, the longer a charity will have to wait to receive any funds. To the extent that the annual payments to annuitant(s) exceed the earnings of the trust, greater longevity will also result in a smaller nominal amount being left to the charity. (In the case of a charitable annuity trust, it is possible for the trust to completely exhaust, leaving no money for the charity, because the payments remain the same regardless of the funds remaining in the trust. Total exhaustion of a unitrust is less likely because payments become smaller as the trust amount becomes less.) The calculation used by the IRS to project the life expectancy of the annuitant systematically under-projects typical donor-annuitant life expectancy. Consequently, the tax deduction generated from transfers to Charitable Remainder Trusts is, actuarially, much larger than it should be. The source of this misprojection is that the IRS calculations are based upon *normal* life expectancy for a typical person of the annuitant's age. However, donor-annuitants, on average, live much longer than typical people of their same age. This is due to three reasons. First, annuitants self-select for health. In other words, people who know that they have a substantially greater risk of death generally don't purchase annuities. Clearly, it makes no financial sense for a person with a known terminal illness to purchase a lifetime stream of payments. Because this "sick" group is largely excluded, the resulting life expectancy of annuity purchasers is, on average, longer. (Unlike the IRS, commercial annuity companies use a special life expectancy table when pricing commercial annuities that reflects this selection bias.) Additionally, those who establish Charitable Remainder Trusts are typically quite wealthy. On average, wealthy people live longer than others of their same age. This may be due to factors such as the access to medical care and health promoting environments that money can purchase as well as physical and mental capabilities that help to both generate wealth and result in a longer life. Finally, recent evidence suggests that those with charitable bequest plans live even longer than those of their same wealth decile (see *American Charitable Bequest Demographics*). Charitable Remainder Trusts typically make a transfer of the donor's assets at the death of the donor, making them a form of general charitable bequest planning. The reason for this additional longevity among those with a charitable bequest plan has not been identified, but may relate to the importance of purpose and social connectedness in both giving and longevity. The net result of this combination of factors is that donor-annuitants will live, on average, much longer than IRS projections. Consequently, donors will receive a larger tax deduction than might be justified by reality. One potential indicator of this reality is the share of Charitable Remainder Trust assets actually distributed to charity. In 2011, for example, Charitable Remainder Trusts held over $99 billion in assets, but made charitable distributions of only $1.9 billion, or less than 2% (Rosenmerkel, L. S., 2013, *Split-Interest Trusts, Filing Year 2011*, IRS Statistics of Income). Arguably, this may be a "temporary" experience due to the relatively recent establishment of some Charitable Remainder Trusts. However, given that such trusts were authorized in the tax code in 1969, to have such a small portion of assets going to charities some 42 years later suggests the potential for additional causes of this result, such as actuarially inappropriate valuations.

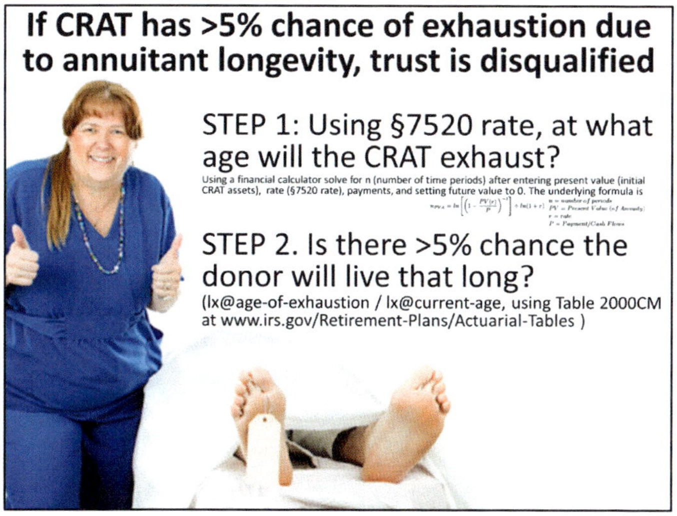

Both the charitable remainder unitrust and the charitable remainder annuity trust are required to project that an amount with a present value of at least 10% of the initial transfer should go to charity at termination. However, the charitable remainder annuity trust has an additional requirement. Unlike a charitable remainder unitrust, as the assets in a charitable remainder annuity trust grow smaller and smaller, the payment remains at its original dollar level. Because the payments do not become smaller as the assets in the charitable remainder annuity trust become smaller, there is a greater risk of total exhaustion of all funds in the charitable remainder annuity trust, especially where the annuitant lives much longer than expected. In the event of exhaustion, the donor would have enjoyed dramatic tax benefits with no actual charitable transfers ever taking place. This is a very bad result from the perspective of the goals of tax policy. To provide some protection against this disturbing outcome, a charitable remainder annuity trust will be disqualified if there is greater than a 5% chance of exhaustion due to annuitant longevity. As before, this calculation assumes that the trust will experience investment returns throughout its life equal to the §7520 rate at the creation of the trust.

There are two steps to determine whether or not there is a greater than 5% chance of exhaustion of a charitable remainder annuity trust due to the annuitant living much longer than expected. First, a standard time value of money calculation determines at what age the charitable remainder annuity trust would exhaust. Using a standard financial calculator this is done by solving for n (the number of time periods), after entering the interest rate (§7520 rate for the time period used), present value (the initial transfer amount), payments per time period (the charitable remainder annuity payment), and a future value of zero (the point of exhaustion). This amount of time (n time periods) is added to the annuitant's current age to identify the age at which the charitable remainder annuity trust would exhaust.

The next step is to determine if there is a greater than 5% chance that the annuitant will live to that age. This is determined simply by dividing the number of people alive at the annuitant's projected age of exhaustion by the number of people alive at the annuitant's current age, according to IRS Table 2000 CM. This table is located at www.irs.gov/Retirement-Plans/Actuarial-Tables, and the relevant numbers are labeled as Lx.

A trust intended to be a Charitable Remainder Trust can be disqualified for a number of reasons, such as being projected to leave too little to charity or having too great of a risk of exhaustion. But, what happens if the trust fails to qualify as a Charitable Remainder Trust under the tax code? A disqualified trust doesn't just disappear. Its failure to comply with the tax requirements for a Charitable Remainder Trust typically won't change the fact that the trust was created under state law, is irrevocable, and may be holding the assets transferred by the donor. So, what happens then?

Although the trust continues to exist as an irrevocable trust, it does not qualify for treatment as a Charitable Remainder Trust under federal tax law. Consequently all of the charitable tax benefits are lost. This means that the donor receives no tax deduction for transferring assets to the trust. Additionally, the trust itself is not a tax-exempt entity. Thus, whenever the trust sells an appreciated asset, the trust must pay capital gains taxes on that sale. This means that the donor loses the ability to defer recognition of capital gains taxes. Whenever the trust earns income of other types, it must also pay taxes on that income. This means the trust can no longer grow assets in a tax-free environment. In fact, trusts are subject to a "compressed" tax rate schedule, meaning that trusts pay the highest marginal income tax rate (39.6%) at a much lower level of income ($11,950 in 2013) than individual taxpayers do. As a result, the disqualification of a Charitable Remainder Trust would be a tax disaster for most donors. Because of this dramatically negative result, such trusts are typically drafted with language that allows the trustee to amend the terms of the otherwise irrevocable trust if such changes are required to allow the trust to qualify as a Charitable Remainder Trust under the federal tax law.

We have considered the charitable income tax deduction generated for the donor transferring funds to a Charitable Remainder Trust, and the tax treatment of gains recognized or income earned by the trust itself. There is one additional source of tax consequences for transfers to a Charitable Remainder Trust. This comes from the payments made from the Charitable Remainder Trust to the annuitant(s). When an annuitant receives a payment from the Charitable Remainder Trust, how should the annuitant report the payment on his or her taxes?

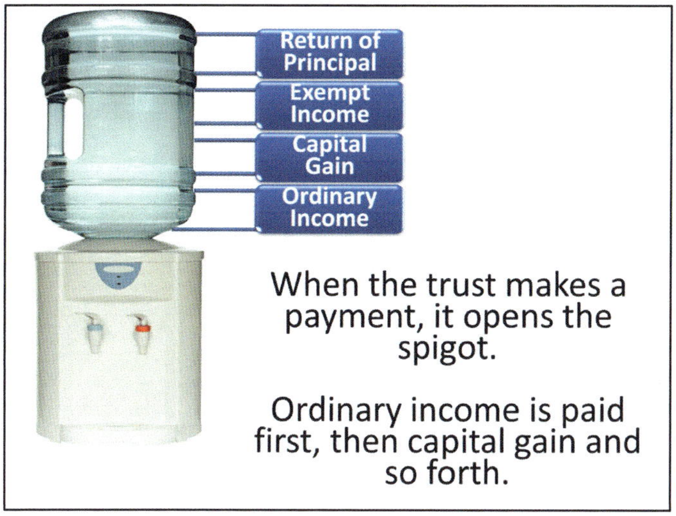

The tax treatment of payments coming to an annuitant depends in part on the tax characteristics of the money held by the Charitable Remainder Trust. The trust may be holding a variety of asset types including ordinary income, capital gain, exempt income, and initial principal (e.g., the basis in property initially transferred to the trust). So when a trust is holding all of these types of assets, how do we determine which asset type the annuitant receives? The fundamental rule is referred to as "worst in, first out" (WIFO). In other words, the annuitant receives the asset type that would normally generate the highest tax rates first. Assets with lower tax rates will be distributed only after there are no remaining assets with higher tax rates.

An easy way to visualize this rule is to think of the Charitable Remainder Trust assets as liquid inside a water cooler where the assets with the heaviest taxation are on the bottom and those with lighter taxation at progressively higher levels. When a payment is made from the trust, it is like opening the spigot at the bottom of the water cooler. The liquid with the heaviest taxation comes out first, and those with lighter taxation will come out only after those assets with heavier taxation have been completely drained. So, for example, all ordinary income will be paid out before any capital gain income. All capital gain income will be paid out before any tax exempt income. And distribution of tax-free return of principal will occur only when there are no other types of assets to distribute.

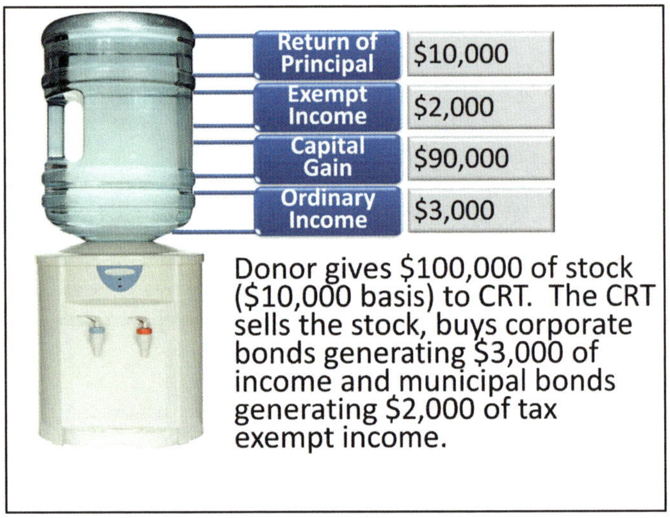

Let's consider an example to demonstrate how the WIFO (worst in, first out) rule works. Suppose a donor gives $100,000 of stock, which she initially purchased for $10,000, to a Charitable Remainder Trust. After receiving the stock, the trustee sells the stock for $100,000 and buys corporate and municipal bonds. During the first year of the trust, the corporate bonds generate $3,000 of income and the municipal bonds generate $2,000 of tax exempt income. Assuming that the Charitable Remainder Trust makes annual payments, what type of assets will be included in the trust at the end of the first year when the first payment is about to be made? The donor's $10,000 basis is included in the trust as an asset that could be paid to the annuitant as tax-free return of investment. At the next level, the trust has earned $2,000 of tax-exempt from its investments in municipal bonds. Next, the trust has $90,000 in capital gains from the sale of the stock for $100,000 (because the stock was purchased by the donor for $10,000). Finally, the trust has $3,000 of ordinary income earned from the corporate bond investments. The trust itself is a tax-exempt entity. Thus, the trust pays no taxes on any capital gain or income earned. However, if capital gain or ordinary income is distributed to an annuitant, then the annuitant will be taxed on that distribution based on the type of income/gain being distributed.

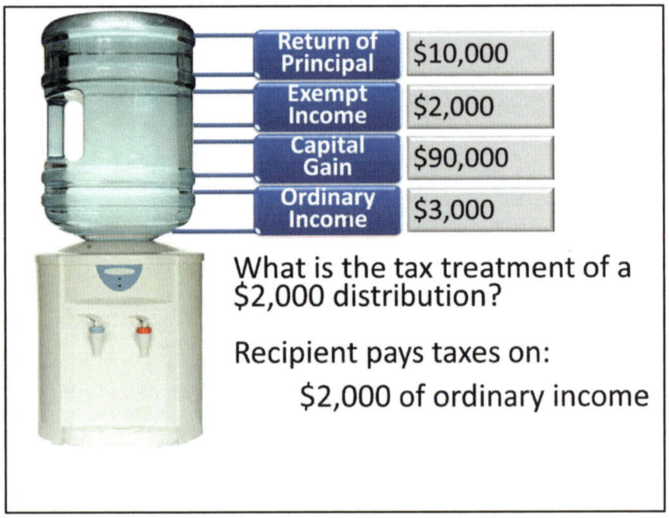

Suppose this Charitable Remainder Trust were required to pay $2,000 to the annuitant. How would the annuitant report this $2,000 payment on her taxes? In this case, the trust is holding $3,000 of ordinary income (earned from its investment in corporate bonds). Because all ordinary income must be paid out prior to the payment of other types of income, the entire $2,000 payment will count as ordinary income to the annuitant.

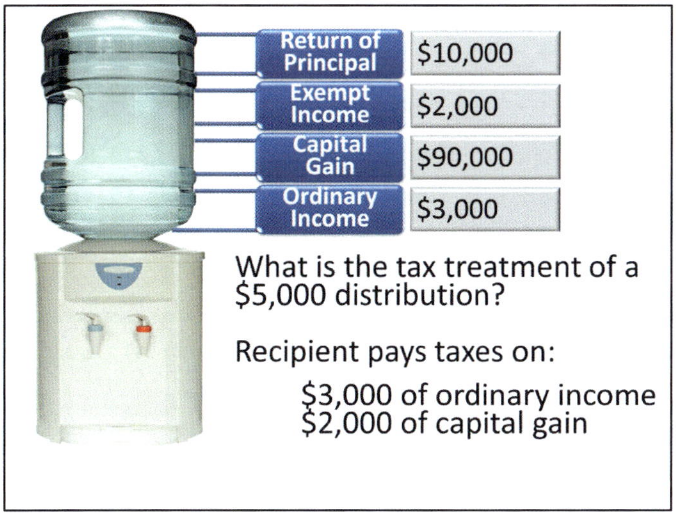

Suppose instead that the Charitable Remainder Trust were required to distribute $5,000 to the annuitant. How would the annuitant report this $5,000 on her tax return? Because the trust is holding $3,000 of ordinary income (earnings from the interest payments on corporate bonds), this amount must be paid out first. The remaining $2,000 would be paid from the $90,000 of capital gain held by the trust. The ordinary income is paid first because it receives the worst tax treatment (i.e., it generates the highest tax rates for the typical taxpayer). The capital gain is paid next because it is worse than either exempt income from the municipal bonds or tax-free return of investment from the donor's basis in the gifted property.

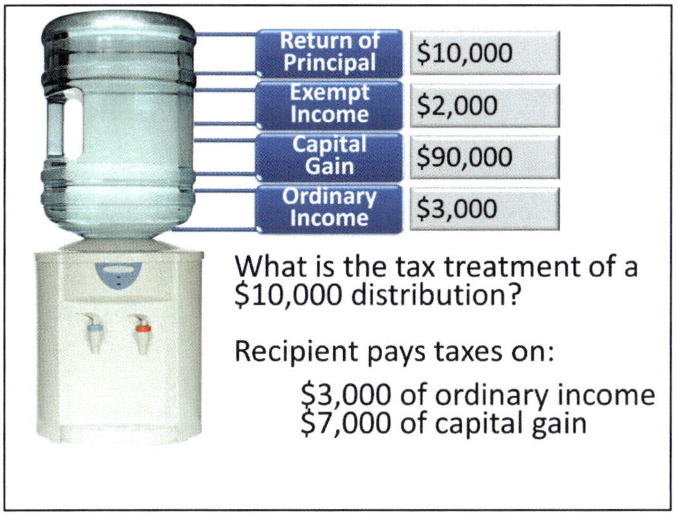

The WIFO concept (worst in, first out) dictates that all capital gain must be paid out before any payments are made from the exempt income or original basis. Thus, the distributions to annuitants would have to completely pay out all $90,000 of capital gain income to the annuitant before the annuitant could receive any form of exempt income or tax-free return of basis. Thus, it likely would make no sense for this particular Charitable Remainder Trust to invest in municipal bonds. The tax-exempt nature of municipal bonds does not affect the Charitable Remainder Trust itself, because the Charitable Remainder Trust is a tax-exempt entity and pays no tax on income earned. The tax-exempt nature of municipal bonds could benefit the annuitant if this tax-exempt income were paid to the annuitant, but such payments are highly unlikely, given the relatively large amount of capital gain yet to be distributed.

There are, of course, other more detailed distinctions in income type than those presented in this example. However, where the tax treatment of assets differs, the general WIFO rule typically applies. Thus, investment income recognized prior to December 31, 2012 – and thus not subject to the 3.8% healthcare surtax – would be paid out only after similar income earned after 2012. Similarly, a capital gain recognized after 2012 (and subject to the additional tax) would be paid out prior to any capital gain recognized in 2012 or earlier.

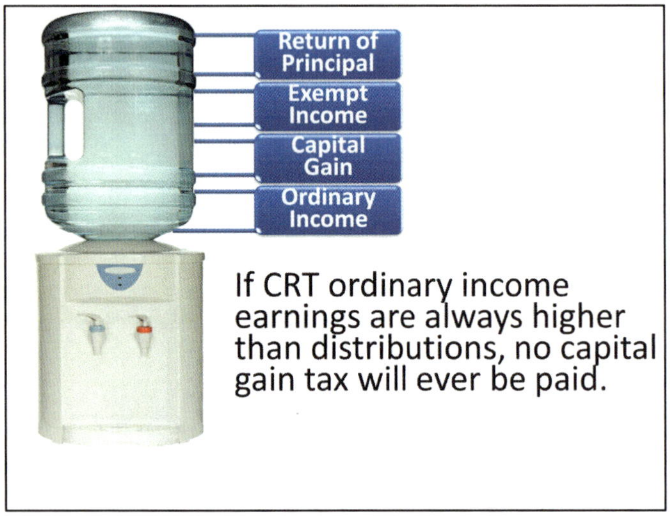

This tax treatment of distributions from Charitable Remainder Trusts means that capital gains taxes deferred through the use of a Charitable Remainder Trust might never be paid. If the trust's total ordinary income earnings are greater than its distributions, then no capital gains payments will ever be made. In this way the capital gains tax deferral can very often become complete capital gains tax avoidance.

In contrast, a Charitable Gift Annuity purchased with appreciated property can defer recognition of the capital gain, but will not avoid the tax. Conceptually, this could be phrased as a benefit of the Charitable Remainder Trust because the trust offers not just capital gains tax deferral but actual capital gains tax avoidance. But, in reality, the Charitable Remainder Trust annuitant avoids the capital gains tax only by paying the higher ordinary income tax. As compared with purchasing a Charitable Gift Annuity with appreciated property, the "advantage" of capital gains tax avoidance means paying higher ordinary income tax and never receiving tax-free return of investment.

To this point we have reviewed the standard Charitable Remainder Trust configurations. There are, however, a variety of different Charitable Remainder Trust structures that have received support from the IRS and tax courts. These special types of Charitable Remainder Trusts can be particularly attractive when dealing with special types of assets or specific income needs.

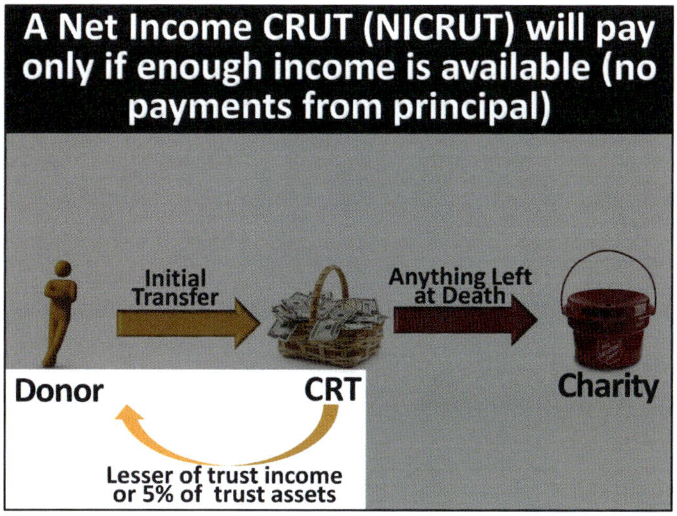

One of the earliest alternative forms of Charitable Remainder Trusts was the net income charitable remainder unitrust (NICRUT). This trust operates like a standard charitable remainder unitrust, with the exception that payments to the annuitant will be limited to the *lesser* of trust income or the unitrust percentage. This net income restriction can only reduce payments to the annuitant (and thus increase the charitable remainder) as compared with a charitable remainder unitrust. However, the addition of this net income restriction does not increase the charitable income tax deduction for contributing to the trust.

Given that a net income charitable remainder unitrust can only reduce payments to the annuitant, but does not increase the charitable income tax deduction, why would any donor voluntarily choose to accept such a limitation?

The attraction for including a net income limitation relates to the contribution of difficult-to-sell assets to the trust. A standard Charitable Remainder Trust requires that the payments must be made to the non-charitable beneficiary. But, if a trust was holding only a single, large, difficult-to-sell asset, this forced payment could mandate an immediate sale of the asset (or some part of it) in order to make the required payments to annuitants. For a trust established with, for example, valuable artwork, developable land, or closely-held stock, an immediate forced sale could dramatically diminish the sale price. In this case, the annuitant can be financially better off to forego his or her annual payments until the asset is sold at an appropriate price. This is not an option in the standard Charitable Remainder Trust, but can be achieved with the addition of a net income limitation on payments.

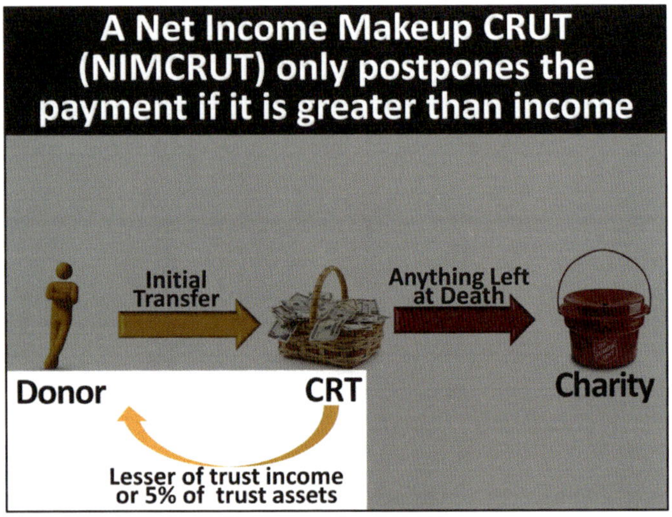

Today, use of the net income charitable remainder unitrust has fallen due to competition from newer alternatives that address the same basic problem of asset illiquidity. The net income makeup charitable remainder unitrust (NIMCRUT) has a similar provision limiting payments to net income, but also has the added provision that previously foregone payments (due to insufficient income) can later be made up whenever income is larger than the regular payments. Thus, although payments are still limited to net income, a payment in a particular year may be larger than the standard percentage amount in order to make up past payments that were missed.

Although the annuitant of a NIMCRUT may still receive less than in a standard charitable remainder unitrust, any missed payments come with an "IOU" from the trust promising to pay the missed payment to the extent that future net income exceeds the standard payment. The annuitant is still not entitled to any more payments than under a standard charitable remainder unitrust, but now any payments missed due to low income could conceivably be made up in some future year. Thus, the annuitant may receive more under a NIMCRUT than under a NICRUT, but would never receive more than if no net income provisions were included in the trust. Once again, the IRS support of this addition rests on the reality that the charitable remainder amount can be no less (and may be larger) than that of a standard charitable remainder unitrust. As with a NICRUT, the calculation of the charitable income tax deduction for a transfer to a NIMCRUT ignores the net income provision, despite the potential for the charity to receive a relatively larger amount.

Although the NIMCRUT represents an improvement from the NICRUT for the annuitant (because missed payments could be made up in the future), this improvement only applies where future income exceeds the standard payment amount. If future income never exceeds the standard payment amount, then the IOU from the trust will never be paid, and the NIMCRUT will be no better than a NICRUT. Further, it can easily be the case that the NIMCRUT pays less than the standard charitable remainder unitrust if future income is insufficient to make-up all previous underpayments due to the net income provision. This difficult reality led to the creation of the next generation of Charitable Remainder Trust variation, referred to as a "flip-CRUT."

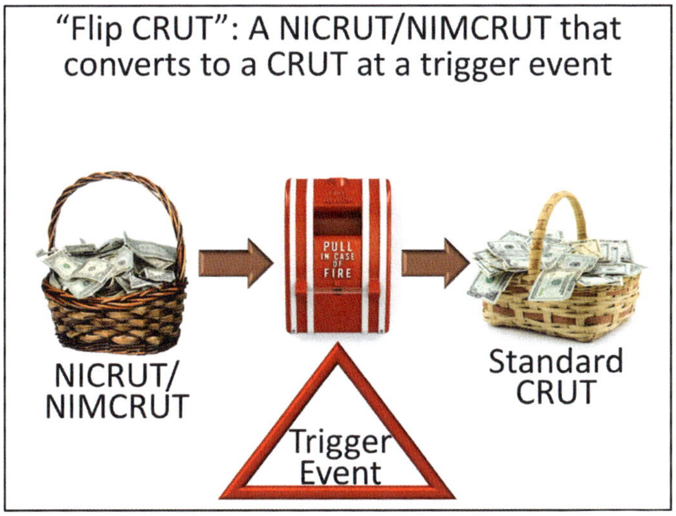

The flip-CRUT is a NICRUT or NIMCRUT that, upon the occurrence of a trigger event, converts to a standard charitable remainder unitrust for the remainder of the life of the trust. Once again, the charitable income tax deduction remains unchanged as compared with a standard charitable remainder unitrust. This combination allows for the trust to hold a difficult-to-sell item for any length of time without forcing a sale due to mandatory payments. But, once the item is sold, the trust can "flip" to a standard charitable remainder unitrust with no net income limitations.

Common trigger events permitted to generate such a "flip" from a NICRUT/NIMCRUT to a standard CRUT include the sale of a difficult-to-value asset or the annuitant's reaching a specific age. Thus, a flip-CRUT can be used both for difficult-to-sell assets and to address retirement planning needs where the annuitant may want to postpone receiving payments until reaching a retirement date.

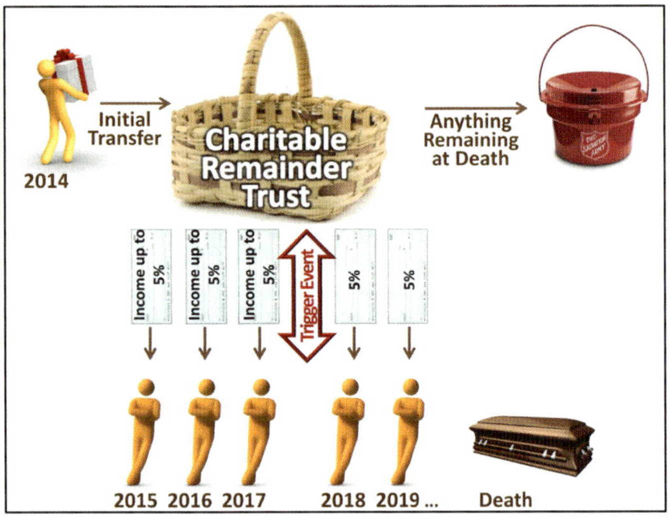

In a flip-CRUT, prior to the trigger event the annuitant receives the *lesser* of the fixed percentage of trust assets or income from the trust. Once the trigger event occurs, the annuitant receives a fixed percentage of trust assets for the remainder of the duration of the trust without regard to the trust's income. (Note that once a trust is converted to a standard CRUT as a result of the trigger event, there will be no "make-up" of any past missed payments. Prior to the trust flipping, a make-up payment could have been possible if the flip-CRUT were initially a NIMCRUT, but no make-up payments are allowed once the trust converts to a standard CRUT.)

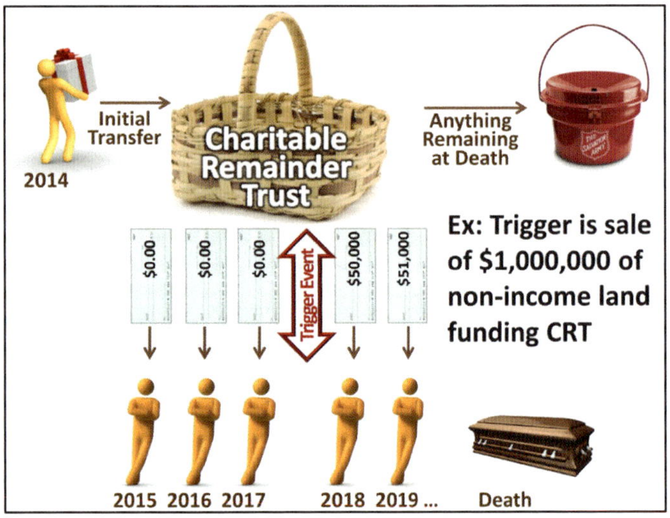

Suppose, for example, that the donor funded a 5% flip-CRUT with a non-income producing piece of land worth $1,000,000. Before the land was sold, the trust would receive no income, and thus would make no payments to the annuitant. However, once the land was sold, the trust would convert to a standard CRUT and the annuitant would receive 5% of the trust assets each year for the duration of the trust. This 5% is fixed and would not change regardless of how much income is earned in a particular year.

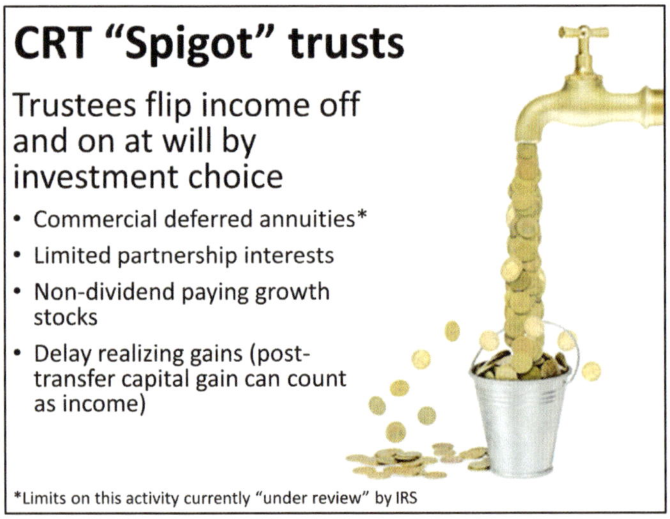

When Charitable Remainder Trust payments are limited to income (either permanently or for a time prior to "flipping" into a standard CRUT), the trustee can gain substantial control over the payment stream simply by changing the underlying investments. There are a variety of investments that offer opportunities for appreciation, but produce little or no income. Examples include non-dividend paying growth stock or limited partnership interests, artwork and collectibles, and developable land. When such investments held by a NICRUT or NIMCRUT generate no income, no payments would need to be made.

Why is this attractive? Consider a situation

where the donor wishes to create a source of retirement income for himself, but first wants the assets to accumulate in a tax-free environment for several years. The donor can create a flip-CRUT converting from a NIMCRUT to a standard CRUT upon the donor's reaching age 65. Prior to age 65, the donor/trustee can invest in non-income producing assets, insuring that he will receive no payments and recognize no income. Upon reaching age 65, the trust becomes a standard CRUT and the donor can immediately take a percentage of all assets, regardless of the income received by the trust. But what about all of the missed payments? One clever approach is to design the NIMCRUT phase where post-contribution capital gains are specifically defined as income. In the year prior to the retirement date (and "flipping" of the trust), the trustee could sell all of the investment assets, recognize large capital gains and use these gains to pay all outstanding IOUs (payment make-up provisions). The net effect can be to preserve all of the payments, but postpone their distribution until the desired ages. The distribution need not be so drastic as to make all sales and make-up payments in the final year. These sales and the resulting make-up distributions could be timed over several years to smooth the annuitant's receipt of income. Through the use of these techniques, however, the donor/annuitant can design an income stream that matches his or her retirement and tax planning goals.

Commercial deferred annuities are an investment which can be designed to generate no income recognition by the trust prior to a decision by the trustee to withdraw funds. This can be an ideal investment allowing the income "spigot" to be turned off and on at will. The annuity can accrue income that is not distributed to (or recognized by) the trust until payment is requested by the trustee. Once income is desired, the annuity can immediately be paid to the trust, creating a flood of income that can be used – in the case of a NIMCRUT – to make up past foregone payments. (This relies in part on a special provision in the income tax code which treats payments from an annuity contract as entirely ordinary income if the annuity is owned by a trust.) However, this particular approach generates more concerns than other investments. Specifically, there is a concern that the use of this investment may constitute "self-dealing". Although an early Technical Advice Memorandum provided some guidelines, since 1997 this practice has been under review by the IRS, and the IRS has specifically stated that it will not make any rulings related to the use of commercial deferred annuities in a NICRUT or NIMCRUT. Thus, the tax outcome for this particular arrangement is less secure, given the IRS concerns.

One creative approach to Charitable Remainder Trust planning is to design a flip-CRUT that converts on the sale of an economically insignificant, but difficult-to-value, asset. The traditional flip-CRUT is designed around the sale of a primary difficult-to-value (and hence, often difficult-to-sell) asset. However, the difficult-to-value asset need not be a substantial one. It can, in fact, be a single share of a closely-held company. In this case, the asset itself is economically insignificant, but allows the trustee to "flip" the trust from a NIMCRUT to a standard CRUT at will by selling the asset. Commentator Conrad Teitell labels this a "flex-CRUT" because it is so flexible.

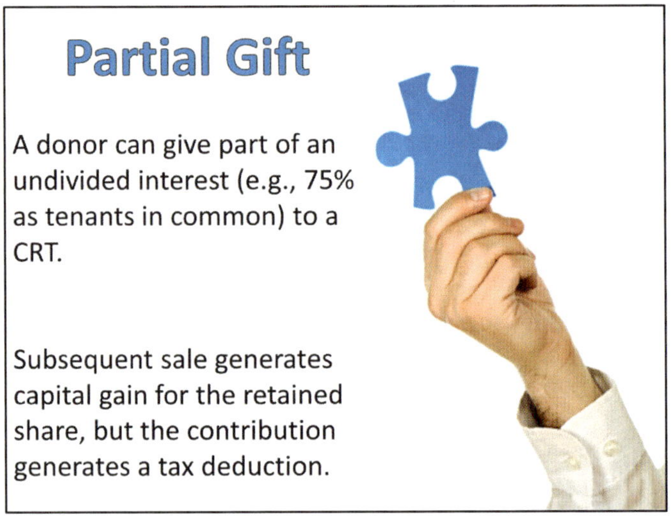

The typical Charitable Remainder Trust transaction involves the transfer of a substantial, highly appreciated asset to the trust. It may be the case that the donor's wealth is substantially tied to one property and the donor may not wish to contribute the entire property to a Charitable Remainder Trust. In such cases, a donor can choose to contribute an undivided share of the property to the Charitable Remainder Trust. Typically, this transfer would be made immediately prior to a sale in an effort to shelter some of the recognition of capital gain. Although the donor would still recognize capital gain on his share of the property at its sale, the share of the property owned by the Charitable Remainder Trust would not generate an immediate capital gains tax. Further, the donor might choose to make several contributions of undivided interests to a Charitable Remainder Trust in order to spread out the charitable income tax deductions over a longer period of time. For example, by donating 10% undivided interests each year for 10 years, the donor creates 10 years' worth of charitable income tax deductions rather than one large deduction in the first year. This may help to co-ordinate the charitable deductions with the income limitations on such deductions. Although charitable income tax deductions exceeding income limitations may be carried over for up to five years, spreading out the transfers may result in larger deductions due to the appreciation of the underlying property.

Comparing Charitable Remainder Trusts to Charitable Gift Annuities is much like comparing the artist's paint palette with a number 2 pencil. Charitable Gift Annuities are relatively simple, standardized agreements, often contained in a one or two page form document. For most charities, all of their Charitable Gift Annuity agreements are identical except for the payment amount and named annuitant. In contrast, Charitable Remainder Trusts are individually created to the specifications of the donor. Although Charitable Remainder Trusts must comply with the IRS guidelines, within those guidelines, there is enormous freedom and flexibility.

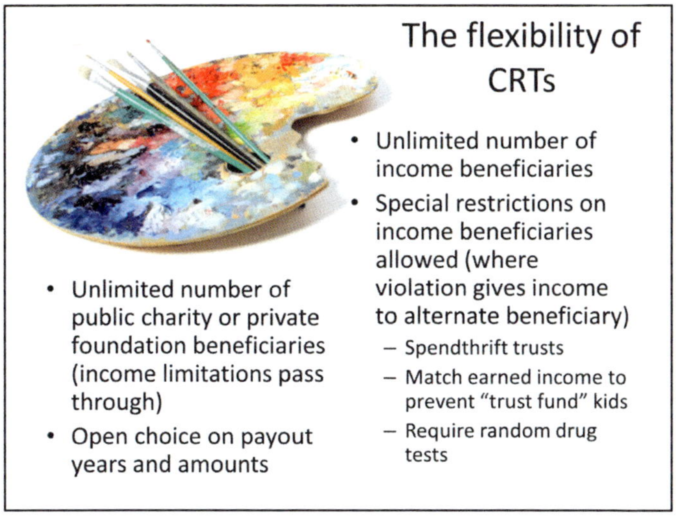

Some examples of the flexibility of Charitable Remainder Trusts (as contrasted with typical Charitable Gift Annuities) include the ability to name an unlimited number of public charity or private foundation beneficiaries and the ability to change the named charitable beneficiary at will. There are, of course, consequences of different choices. So, for example, gifts to a Charitable Remainder Trust where the remainder could possibly be paid to a private foundation will be subject to the income limitations and property valuation rules applicable to gifts to private foundations. The donor can create a Charitable Remainder Trust that will pay to any number of beneficiaries for any number of lives (where Charitable Gift Annuities are limited to a maximum of two lives). The donor can create a Charitable Remainder Trust that will pay for a fixed number of years, up to 20 (where Charitable Gift Annuities may not be paid for a fixed number of years). Where the Charitable Remainder Trust employs an independent trustee (i.e., not controlled by the donor), the trust can also create restrictions as to when certain annuitants will receive payments. Although the Charitable Remainder Trust must still make the required payments (of a fixed dollar or fixed percentage amount), the trust document may change the recipient of those payments. This "sprinkling" power (although it can be administered only by an independent trustee and not by a donor-trustee) can create amazing planning opportunities. For example, the payments can contain a "spendthrift" provision protecting them from being attached by creditors. Thus, for annuitants other than the donor, the payments can be protected from divorce, lawsuits, or bankruptcy. If the donor wishes to prevent his annuitant children (or grandchildren) from becoming lazy "trust fund" kids, he could limit the payments to a particular beneficiary to some multiple of their earned income. (Any un-claimed annuity payment would still need to be paid to other beneficiaries so that the total payment distributed was still fixed.) The donor could even require that annuitants pass a drug test in order to receive annuity payments. Almost any rules that can be imagined by the donor and administered by an independent trustee that are not against public policy can be included in a charitable trust document. Its flexibility is almost limitless.

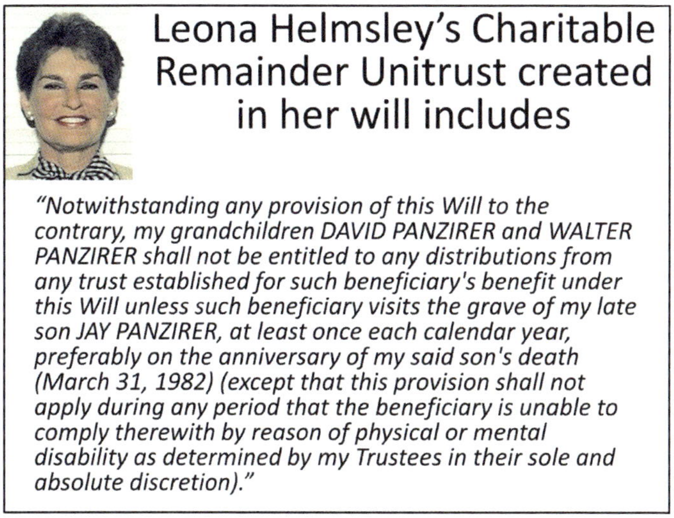

As a famous example of such flexibility, we can examine the Charitable Remainder Trust from the estate of hotelier Leona Helmsley. Typically, the provisions of Charitable Remainder Trusts are not publicly available, because these are private documents. However, in this case, the Charitable Remainder Trust was a testamentary trust (i.e., created in the will). Because the will is a public document, the provisions of this testamentary trust also became public. This trust required that the grandchildren beneficiaries must visit the grave of their father at least once each calendar year in order to receive their annuity payment. Because this trust was to be administered by an independent trustee (and not the donor herself), such "sprinkling" powers are acceptable. In the event that a beneficiary did not comply with the rules, *that* beneficiary would lose his payment and the payment would go to another named beneficiary.

Any trust, including a Charitable Remainder Trust, can be thought of as a basket. Like a basket, a trust holds things. In particular, trusts hold title to valuable assets and administer those assets in accordance with the instructions found in the trust document. However, certain types of assets can create problems when owned by a Charitable Remainder Trust.

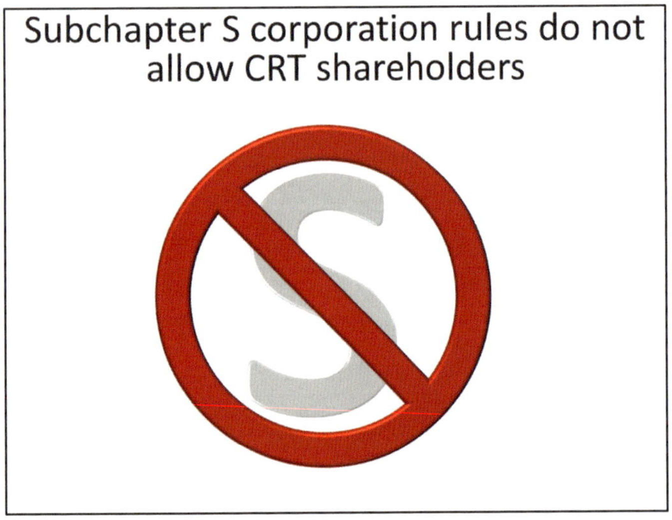

Subchapter S corporations are closely held (100 or fewer shareholders) corporations that are taxed is ways similar to partnerships. A Charitable Remainder Trust cannot hold subchapter S Corporation shares. This is not due to any restriction from the rules of Charitable Remainder Trusts, but rather due to the shareholder requirements of subchapter S corporations. Shareholders in such corporations must normally be natural persons. Although there are exceptions to this rule, a Charitable Remainder Trust is not one of them. (One exception allows public charities to hold subchapter S stock, thus allowing a Charitable Gift Annuity in exchange for such shares.)

What options are available for the donor who wishes to transfer the ownership of a business to a Charitable Remainder Trust, when the business is a subchapter S corporation? The corporation itself can contribute appreciated assets to a Charitable Remainder Trust and receive income for up to 20 years (lifetime income is not available for non-persons). Both the charitable income tax deduction and subsequent income payments pass through to the shareholders, and no capital gain is immediately recognized upon the sale of the asset. This is not a perfect solution, however, because it cannot be used to transfer "substantially all" corporate assets to a Charitable Remainder Trust, and payments cannot be made for annuitant lifetimes. Of course, a donor who controls the corporation could change its corporate form to a C-corporation by ceasing to make the S-corporation election, but such conversion has its own tax consequences that may be independently unattractive.

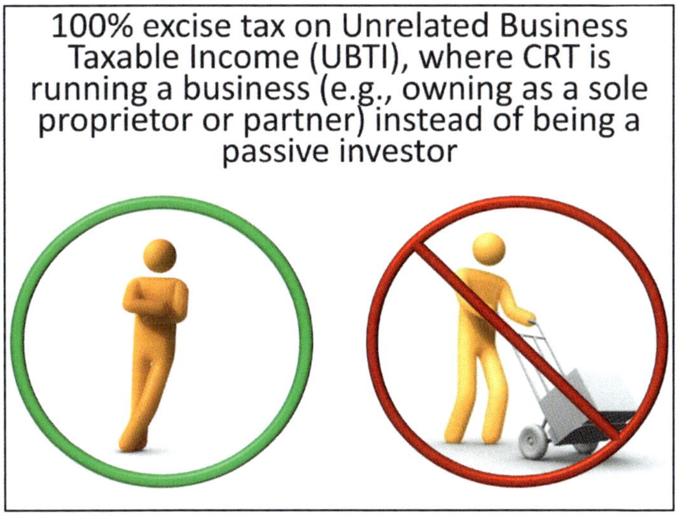

One of the most extreme forms of taxation comes when a Charitable Remainder Trust receives unrelated business taxable income (UBTI). Unrelated business taxable income is generated when the trust earns money by engaging in the operation of a business rather than simply being a passive investor. Such income is taxed at a 100% rate. Simply put, the IRS takes all of it.

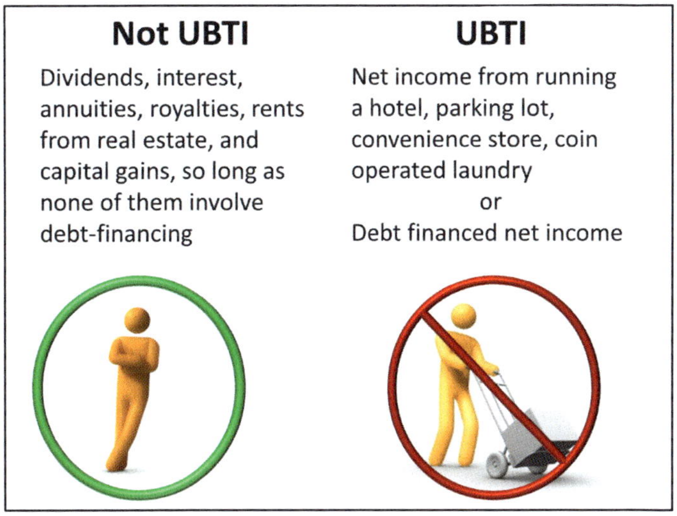

Typical investments do not generate unrelated business taxable income, because they are passive. Dividends, interest, annuities, royalties, rents from real estate, and capital gains are not unrelated business taxable income, so long as none of them involve debt financing. Conversely, if any of these sources of income are generated from debt-financed investments, then the income does qualify as unrelated business taxable income. Although rents from real estate will not be unrelated business taxable income – so long as there is no debt on the real estate – active management of businesses involving real estate, such as running a hotel, parking lot, convenience store, or coin-operated laundry, will create unrelated business taxable income. The key distinction is that when the trust is actively participating in the operation of the business, the resulting income is unrelated business taxable income. (Of course, the trust can be a shareholder in a corporation that engages in such activities, because then the trust is simply a passive investor rather than a manager.)

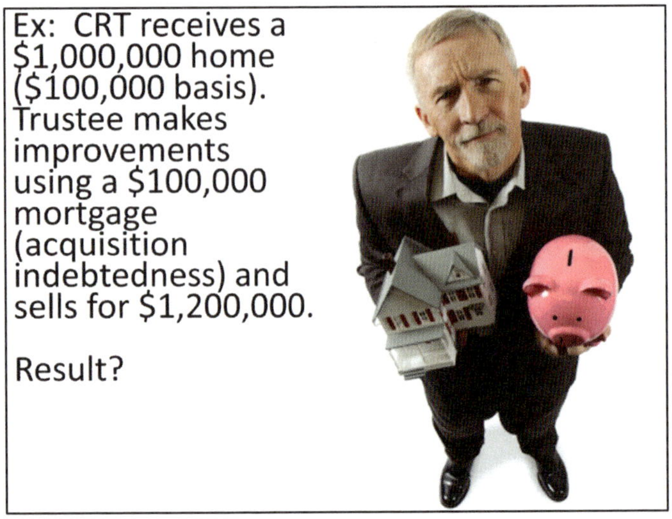

The extreme taxation of unrelated business taxable income in Charitable Remainder Trusts can produce surprising results. Consider a situation where a Charitable Remainder Trust receives a gift of a $1 million house transferred from a donor who had a $100,000 basis in the house. The trustee decides to authorize $100,000 of improvements to the house in order to get it in top condition to sell. Because the trustee has no other assets, he obtains the $100,000 by taking out a mortgage on the house. As a result of making the improvements, the house is later sold for $1.2 million and the mortgage is paid off at the sale. Clearly, the $100,000 investment was a good idea because it increased the value of the home by $200,000, right? Unfortunately, no.

Remember that dividends, interest, annuities, royalties, rents from real estate, and capital gains are not unrelated business taxable income, so long as none of them come from debt financing. However, in this case we have a capital gain from debt-financed property (due to the $100,000 mortgage). Thus, the capital gain becomes unrelated business taxable income. Unrelated business taxable income in a Charitable Remainder Trust is taxed at 100%. Consequently, the entire capital gain must be forfeited as a tax payment. Although an extreme example, this shows the importance of avoiding unrelated business taxable income in a Charitable Remainder Trust.

The Charitable Remainder Trust, like a private foundation, has strict rules against engaging in transactions with disqualified persons. Rather than reviewing these transactions to determine if they were beneficial to the charity or the Charitable Remainder Trust, all such transactions are simply prohibited. As a result, the Charitable Remainder Trust is not permitted to sell, lease, loan, or allow any use of assets by the trust's creator, contributor, trustee or their ancestors, descendants, or spouses. So, for example, a donor could not contribute a house to a Charitable Remainder Trust and allow his daughter to live in the residence prior to its sale. This would be a use of assets by a descendent of a contributor to the Charitable Remainder Trust and would thus be a prohibited act of self-dealing. Self-dealing can result in disqualification of the Charitable Remainder Trust.

One of the defining characteristics of a Charitable Remainder Trust is that it is an irrevocable trust. However, in some cases exceptions to this irrevocability have been allowed. For example, the IRS has previously allowed for the premature termination of a Charitable Remainder Trust, with a distribution of the assets based upon the present value of all interests. Note that this has been allowed previously, but is not a universally guaranteed option. For example, the IRS would not want to authorize such divisions where the lifetime annuitant was aware of some health condition that substantially shortened his or her life expectancy. In that case the calculated present value of the annuitant's interest, based on normal life expectancies, would substantially overstate the value of the annuitant's share. Nevertheless, if both the annuitant and remainder beneficiary agree, such division might be possible. The actual termination and distribution would likely require the intervention of a state court in order to circumvent the irrevocable nature of the trust agreement, because the trust itself is an entity created by state law. Federal law establishes only the federal tax treatment of the trust, but cannot create or dissolve the trust.

Another example of creativity that received approval by the IRS in a private letter ruling dealt with the charity's immediate need for funds to construct a building. Normally, a Charitable Remainder Trust would not be useful for such needs. The Charitable Remainder Trust typically pays nothing to the charity for many years or a lifetime. As a creative way around this limitation, the Charitable Remainder Trust was authorized to segregate funds and pledge them as collateral for a loan taken out by the charity. The lender was protected by the ability to seize the funds in the event of non-payment. The charity was able to immediately build the building while planning to pay off the loan with the charitable gift received from the Charitable Remainder Trust at its termination. In this way, the donor was able to see the impact of his gift immediately.

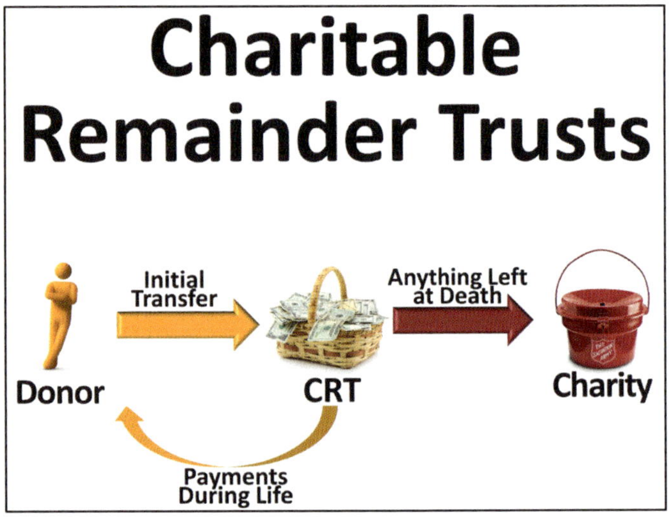

Charitable Remainder Trusts are, fundamentally, the most powerful complex tool available to gift planners. Charitable Remainder Trusts can be part of even more powerful, and more complex, planning when combined with other trusts. For example, a Charitable Remainder Trust can pay its remainder interest to a private family foundation with some part of the value of the charitable income tax deduction and annual payments used to purchase estate-tax-free life insurance through an irrevocable life insurance trust. The flexibility and possibilities from Charitable Remainder Trusts are almost limitless. This chapter simply paints the broad outlines for what is possible. As complex as these arrangements can become, fundamentally, their purpose is to (1) trade a charitable gift for income and (2) reduce taxes. Consequently, investigating the use of these instruments is warranted whenever a donor would like to make a substantial gift, receive income, and avoid income and capital gains taxes.

13 CHARITABLE LEAD TRUSTS

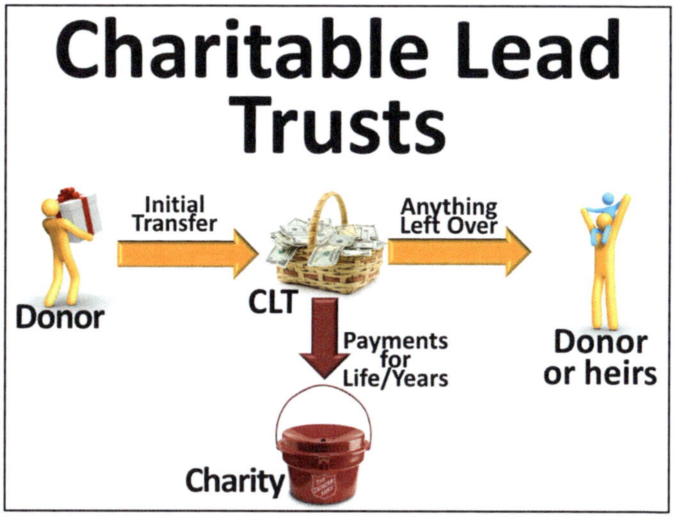

In both Charitable Remainder Trusts and Charitable Lead Trusts the donor makes a gift to the trust which then holds the asset, makes regular payments, and finally distributes the remaining amount at the end of the term of the trust. Unlike Charitable Remainder Trusts which provide payments to the donor or another person followed by the remaining amount going to charity, the Charitable Lead Trust provides payments to charity followed by the remaining amount going to the donor or another person.

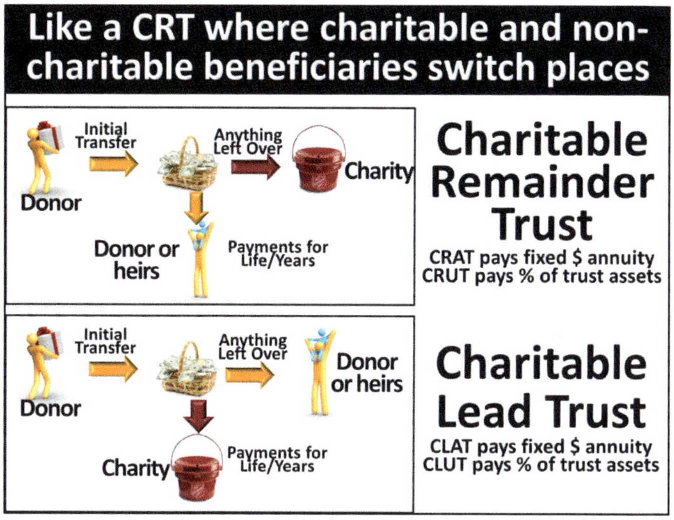

The Charitable Lead Trust is a mirror image of the Charitable Remainder Trust where the charitable and non-charitable beneficiaries change places. Just as with a Charitable Remainder Trust there are two types of permitted payments from a Charitable Lead Trust, the fixed dollar annuity and the fixed percentage unitrust. If the Charitable Lead Trust pays a preset dollar amount to charity each year, it is a Charitable Lead Annuity Trust (CLAT). If the Charitable Lead Trust pays a set percentage of all trust assets each year, it is a Charitable Lead Unitrust (CLUT). The Charitable Remainder Trust also permitted variations that could lower the ongoing payments, such as a Net Income Charitable

Remainder Trust (NICRUT), Net Income with Makeup Charitable Remainder Trust (NIMCRUT), or flip-charitable remainder unitrust (flip-CRUT). None of these options are available with a Charitable Lead Trust, because the ongoing payments in a Charitable Lead Trust go to the charity, and therefore may not be reduced.

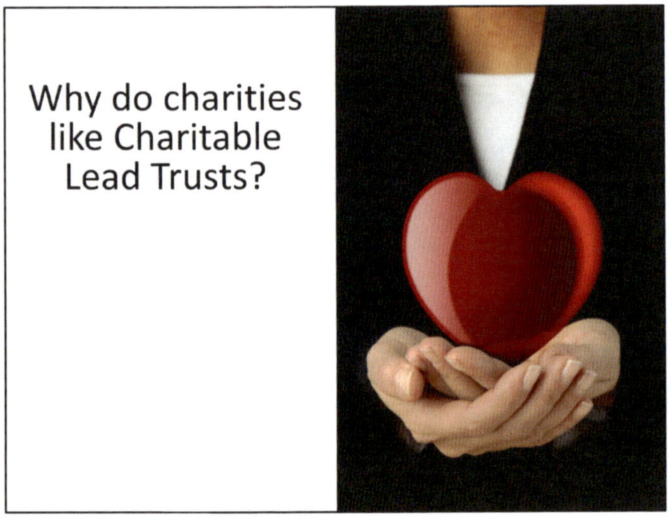

As a sophisticated charitable planning instrument, Charitable Lead Trusts can provide benefits to charities and to donors and their families. In general, charities like charitable planning because, ultimately, these plans are expected to benefit charities. Charitable Lead Trusts are particularly attractive to charities because they immediately generate income for the charity. In contrast, Charitable Remainder Trusts generate future benefit for charity, where that future may be delayed by many decades and, depending upon the longevity of the donor, may be significantly diminished compared with initial expectations.

Not only do Charitable Lead Trusts begin generating income for the charity immediately, but that stream of gift income is secured. At least annually, payments must be made to the charity for the duration of the Charitable Lead Trust. Better still for the charity – and unlike a Charitable Remainder Trust – the donor typically may not retain the right to change the named charity in the most common form of the Charitable Lead Trust (called a non-grantor Charitable Lead Trust). Although it is possible for a trustee who is not the donor to decide how the ongoing payments will be divided among several listed charities (PLR 200240027), this is a rare provision. Thus, in the great majority of cases the charity is assured of receiving its ongoing payments, even if the relationship with the donor subsequently changes.

Charities enjoy Charitable Lead Trusts because of the immediate, secured payments coming to the charity. However, aside from tax benefits, there are no obvious reasons for donors to use a Charitable Lead Trust. Charitable Lead Trusts do not provide income to the donor, or donor's family, as Charitable Remainder Trusts or Charitable Gift Annuities can. Thus, they don't fit into planning for retirement or for planned educational expenses.

Instead, the use of Charitable Lead Trusts is primarily motivated by tax benefits. The most common type of Charitable Lead Trust, called a *non-grantor* Charitable Lead Trust, is used predominantly as a method for reducing gift and estate transfers. However, there are some circumstances where this trust can also be used for income tax benefits as well. The less common *grantor* Charitable Lead Trust is used to capture income tax benefits, but not gift and estate tax benefits.

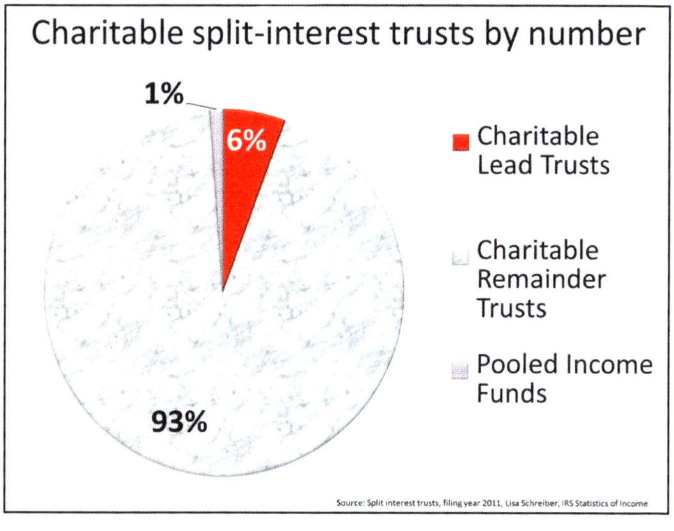

Charitable planners are more likely to work with Charitable Remainder Trusts than Charitable Lead Trusts simply because Charitable Remainder Trusts are much more common. Charitable Lead Trusts account for only 6% of all split-interest charitable trusts. (Split interest charitable trusts are Charitable Remainder Trusts, Charitable Lead Trusts, and pooled income funds.) Seeing what a small fraction of total split interest charitable trusts that Charitable Lead Trusts represent might lead one to believe that Charitable Lead Trusts are insignificant in charitable planning. However, this idea is mistaken.

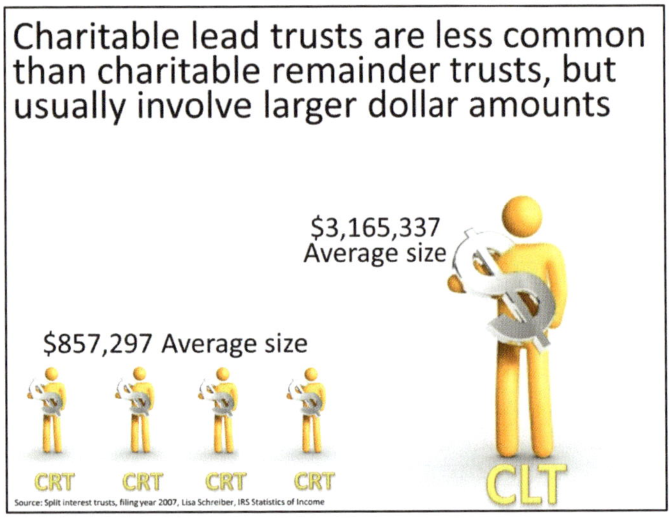

Although Charitable Lead Trusts are less numerous that Charitable Remainder Trusts, they are much larger. The typical Charitable Lead Trust holds more than 3½ times the assets of the typical Charitable Remainder Trust. Thus, although their numbers are relatively small, when they arise Charitable Lead Trusts often represent significant wealth.

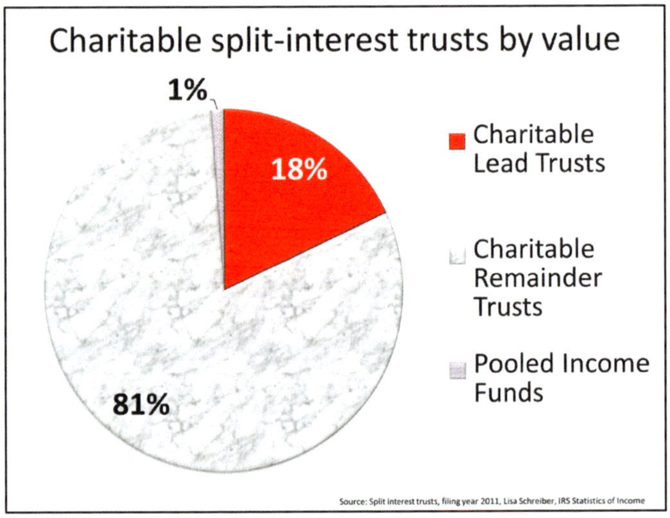

As a result of their larger size, Charitable Lead Trusts hold 18% of all assets amongst split interest charitable trusts, even though they constitute only 6% of such trusts. Thus, while Charitable Lead Trusts are less common, they do represent an important segment of charitable planning.

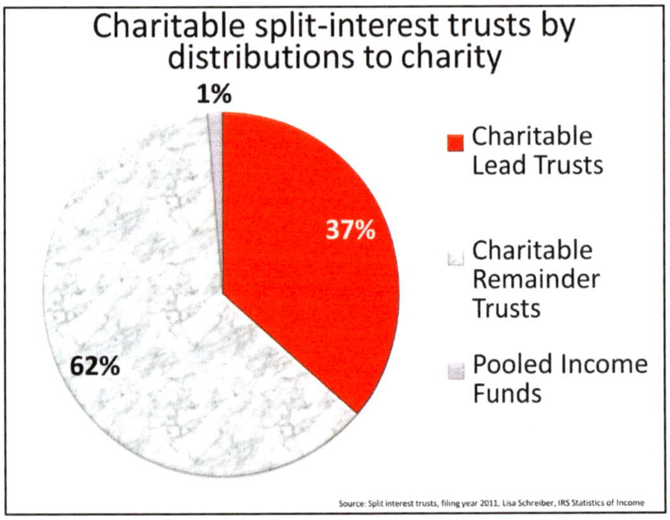

For those who represent charities, the most important figure may be not the frequency of the trusts, or even the assets held, but the actual dollars transferred to charity. In this category, Charitable Lead Trusts are quite significant, generating 37% of all transfers to charity. So, this infrequently used charitable planning vehicle, accounting for only 6% of all charitable split interest vehicles, results in charitable transfers of more than half the size of all Charitable Remainder Trusts. What accounts for this massive difference in actual charitable payouts? Where Charitable Remainder Trusts are annually paying out only 2% of all their assets, Charitable Lead Trusts pay out more than 5.3%. As discussed in the chapter on Charitable Remainder Trusts, those charitable vehicles typically transfer assets to charity only after the death of the donor. The charitable deductions for Charitable Remainder Trusts are based upon donors living to their actuarial life expectancy. However, Charitable Remainder Trust donors, on average, live much longer than their actuarial life expectancy. This occurs for three reasons. First, those known to have shortened life expectancies for medical reasons do not typically establish new Charitable Remainder Trusts, or otherwise convert assets into annuity payments. Thus, one tail of the life expectancy distribution is essentially cut off. (This is why, for example, the insurance industry uses a different life expectancy table for those who purchase annuities than for the general population.) Next, greater wealth is associated with a longer life span. Those who establish Charitable Remainder Trusts tend to be at the highest end of the wealth spectrum, and thus live longer than their actuarial expectations. Finally, those with a charitable estate plan tend to live longer than others of their same wealth category (see James, R.N., III (2012) *American Charitable Bequest Demographics* for evidence on this). Taken together, these all point to Charitable Remainder Trust donors living far longer than the standard actuarial expectations would predict. When these donors serve as the measuring life prior to the charitable remainder payout, as is typically the case, this will result in far more non-charitable payments – and a much later and smaller charitable distribution – at the end. Charitable distributions from Charitable Lead Trusts do not suffer from these same longevity issues. The typical Charitable Lead Trust pays out to charity for a fixed number of years, beginning immediately. These fixed term trusts are not affected by longevity expectations. Those Charitable Lead Trusts that do exist for a donor's lifetime generate *more* charitable transfers when the donor lives beyond life expectancy, not less.

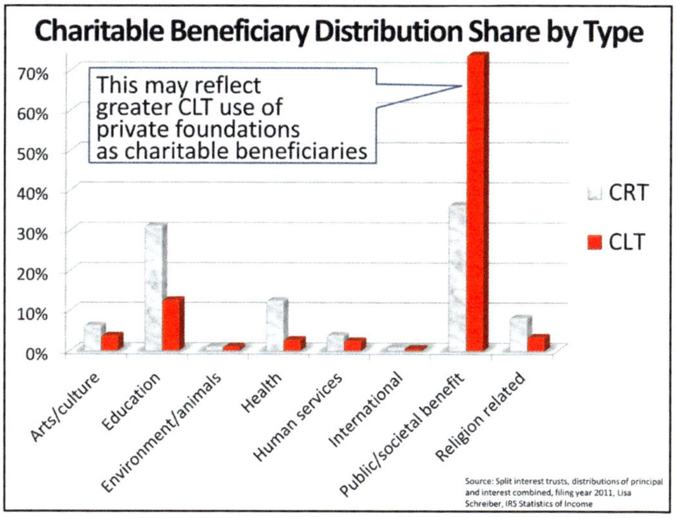

As shown in the accompanying chart, Charitable Remainder Trusts tend to most frequently benefit nonprofit organizations classified as "public/societal benefit," with substantial amounts also going to education and health related organizations. Charitable Lead Trusts have the same first and second most common beneficiary types. However, Charitable Lead Trusts are much more heavily concentrated in giving to nonprofit organizations classified as "public/societal benefit," as these receive over 70% of all charitable transfers from Charitable Lead Trusts. This might reflect a greater tendency for Charitable Lead Trusts to pay into private family foundations, which are most commonly classified as general "public/societal benefit" organizations rather than as topic-specific nonprofit organizations. As estate size increases among charitable estates, the tendency to leave money not to public charities but to private family foundations grows dramatically. Charitable Lead Trusts are predominantly used as an estate tax avoidance technique for the wealthy, making the association between Charitable Lead Trusts and private foundation beneficiaries plausible. Charitable Remainder Trusts, in contrast, hold fewer assets on average and may be used for a variety of tax and financial reasons by those whose estates are too small to generate estate taxation.

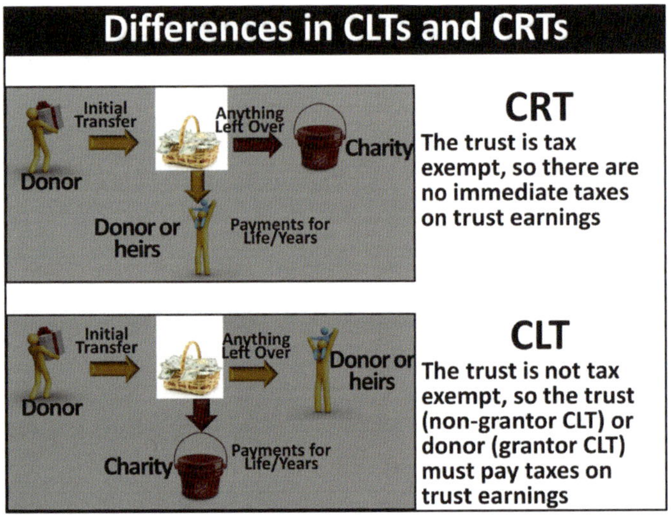

Although it is convenient to think of Charitable Lead Trusts as simply a mirror image of Charitable Remainder Trusts where the charitable and non-charitable beneficiaries switch places, there are other differences. Unlike the Charitable Remainder Trust, the Charitable Lead Trust is *not* a tax-exempt entity. If a Charitable Remainder Trust sells a highly appreciated asset, it pays no capital gains tax, because it is a tax-exempt entity. If a Charitable Lead Trust sells the same asset, it must pay capital gains tax, because it is *not* a tax-exempt entity. However, just as with other taxpayers, the Charitable Lead Trust may reduce its taxable income by making transfers to charity which results in a charitable deduction. And, unlike other taxpayers, the Charitable Lead Trust can typically deduct up to 100% of its income (other than unrelated business income) if it makes sufficient charitable gifts.

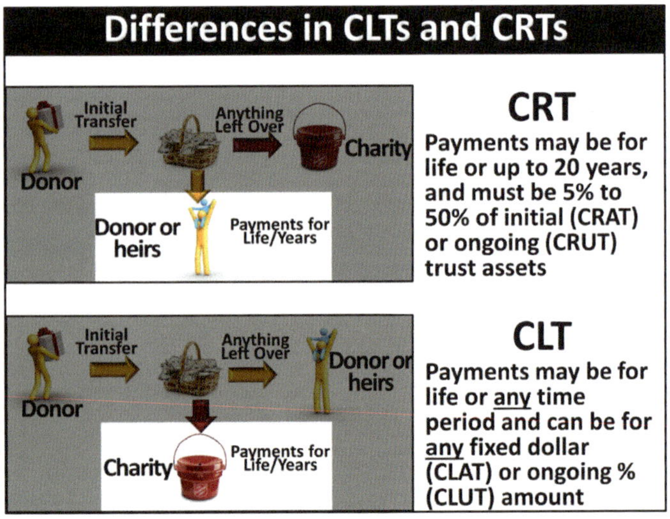

Because the Charitable Lead Trust is not a tax-exempt entity, some guidelines are more flexible than with a Charitable Remainder Trust. For example, Charitable Remainder Trusts can make payments for life or for up to 20 years. In contrast, Charitable Lead Trusts can make payments for life or for up to an unlimited number of years. The annual payments in a charitable remainder annuity trust must be between 5% and 50% of the initial trust assets. Annual payments in a Charitable Lead Annuity Trust can be as small or as large as desired. Further, Charitable Lead Annuity Trusts, unlike charitable remainder annuity trusts, do not have to be concerned with the risk of exhaustion being greater than 5%. The charitable remainder unitrust must pay between 5% and 50% of all trust assets each year, whereas the Charitable Lead Unitrust can payout any desired percentage. There is no requirement for a minimum of a 10% charitable deduction (present value of projected amount going to charity) as with Charitable Remainder Trusts. In fact, the most common type of Charitable Lead Trust (the non-grantor Charitable Lead Trust) generates no charitable income tax deduction to the grantor regardless of its terms. This freedom in options comes because the Charitable Lead Trust, unlike a Charitable Remainder Trust, is not a tax-exempt entity.

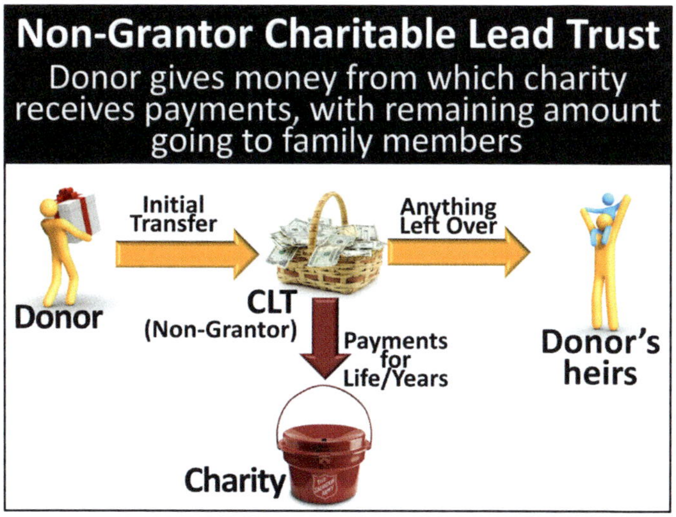

The most common type of Charitable Lead Trust is the *non-grantor* Charitable Lead Trust. The term *non-grantor* means that the Charitable Lead Trust is not owned or controlled by the donor (a.k.a., the grantor). Although the donor typically establishes all of the rules for the Charitable Lead Trust, once established the trust is irrevocable. Because this trust is usually an estate tax avoidance mechanism, it is critical for the intended tax results that transfers to the non-grantor Charitable Lead Trust stay outside of the donor's estate. Once these assets are outside of the donor's estate, none of them should return to – or be controlled by – the donor, so that the trust and all its assets stay outside of the donor's estate. The assets in the Charitable Lead Trust fund annual payments to a charity and then, at the end of the term of the trust, are paid to the heirs or other beneficiaries selected by the donor. The payments to charity (either predetermined dollar amounts or a predetermined percentage of trust assets) typically occur for a fixed number of years, but can continue for a life or multiple lives.

The primary purpose of non-grantor Charitable Lead Trusts is to reduce gift and estate taxes. Anything placed into a non-grantor Charitable Lead Trust is no longer owned or controlled by the donor. Although the donor typically creates the rules for the trust, the donor cannot change those rules once the trust is created. Unlike the Charitable Remainder Trust, the donor should not directly manage or control the assets of the non-grantor Charitable Lead Trust. This is avoided in order to ensure that all assets are excluded from the donor's estate. This focus on excluding the assets from the donor's estate is not typically a concern with standard Charitable Remainder Trusts. Why not? If a donor receives income from a Charitable Remainder Trust for her for life with the remainder going to charity at her death, the fact that the remaining assets are going to charity means that the inclusion of the assets in her estate is irrelevant. The assets come into the estate and then the assets are exempted from taxation because they are transferred to a charity. This is not the case with the non-grantor Charitable Lead Trust. Here the assets are distributed to family members, or other non-charitable beneficiaries, at the termination of the trust. If any assets are *included* in the donor's estate, perhaps because the donor exercised too much control over the assets, then the assets are *taxed* in the donor's estate.

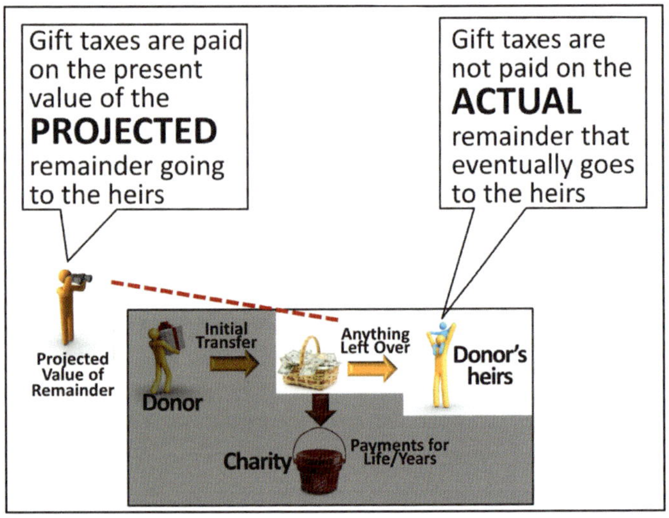

The fundamental tax advantage gained from the non-grantor Charitable Lead Trust is that when the donor makes transfers to the trust he or she pays gift taxes on the *projected* amount of the ultimate transfer to the heirs (i.e., any non-charitable beneficiaries), not on the *actual* amount of the transfer to heirs. The actual amount transferred to heirs at the termination of the trust is not subject to gift or estate taxation. This difference between the projected amount and the actual amount transferred to heirs creates an opportunity for tax efficient transfers.

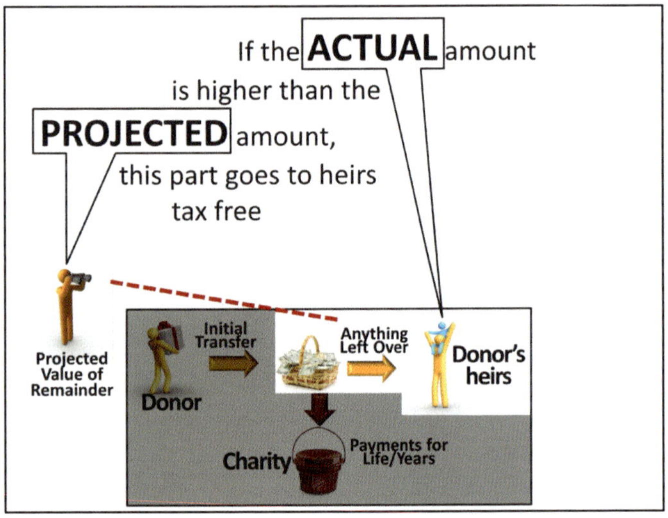

The key benefit for gift and estate tax planning purposes is that if the actual amount transferred to family members is higher than the projected amount, the difference between these two numbers is transferred without any additional gift or estate taxation. This part of the transfer to children, or others, is made free of estate and gift taxation.

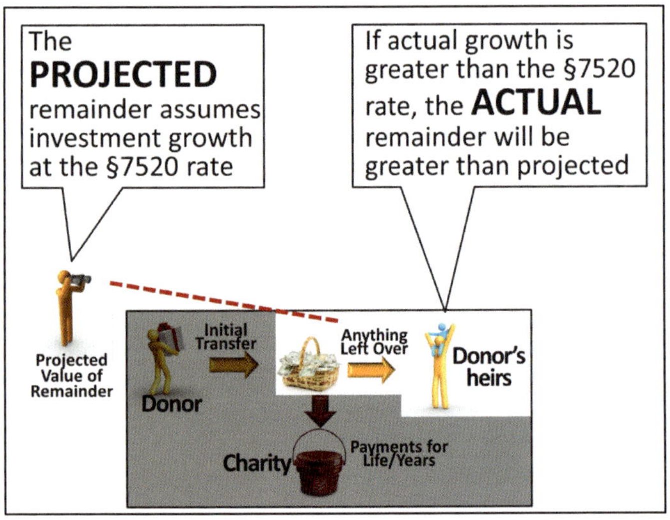

Gift taxes must be paid on the projected remainder that will be transferred to heirs (i.e., any non-charitable beneficiaries). This projection is based on the assumption that the assets in the Charitable Lead Trust will grow at the initial §7520 interest rate for the life of the trust. Any growth that occurs above the §7520 interest rate is therefore transferred free from gift or estate taxes. Of course, if the investments in the trust return less than the §7520 interest rate, then this advantage becomes a disadvantage because the initial gift tax would have been based upon a projected transfer larger than the actual transfer ultimately made to the heirs.

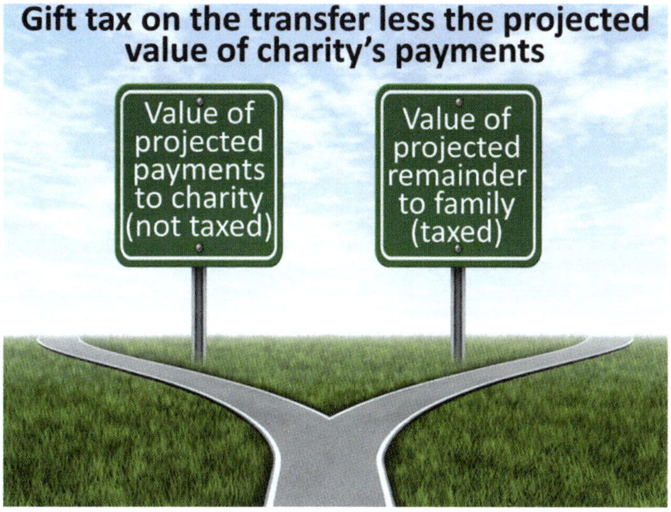

At the time of the transfer to the non-grantor Charitable Lead Trust, the donor must pay gift taxes on the value of the transfer less the present value of the payments projected to go to charity. The projected value of the amount going to charity is not taxed. The rest, which is the present value of the projected amount going to heirs, is taxed. Thus, calculating the taxable part of the transfer can be determined by estimating the non-taxable part of the transfer, i.e., the present value of the projected payments to charity.

What is the process for estimating the present value of the projected payments to charity? It is identical to the process for estimating the present value of the projected payments to the non-charitable beneficiaries in a Charitable Remainder Trust. This makes sense because the charitable and non-charitable beneficiaries switch places in a Charitable Lead Trust as compared with a Charitable Remainder Trust. The value of an annuity (or unitrust payment) in a Charitable Remainder Trust is the same as the value of the same annuity (or unitrust payment) in a Charitable Lead Trust.

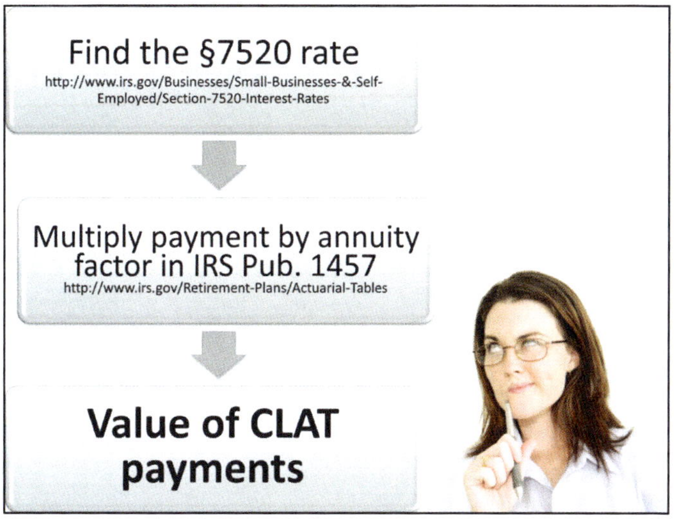

Determining the value of the annuity payments in a Charitable Lead Annuity Trust (i.e., the part not subject to gift or estate taxes) requires (1) finding the §7520 interest rate and (2) multiplying the annuity payment by the annuity factor in IRS Publication 1457 for that §7520 interest rate.

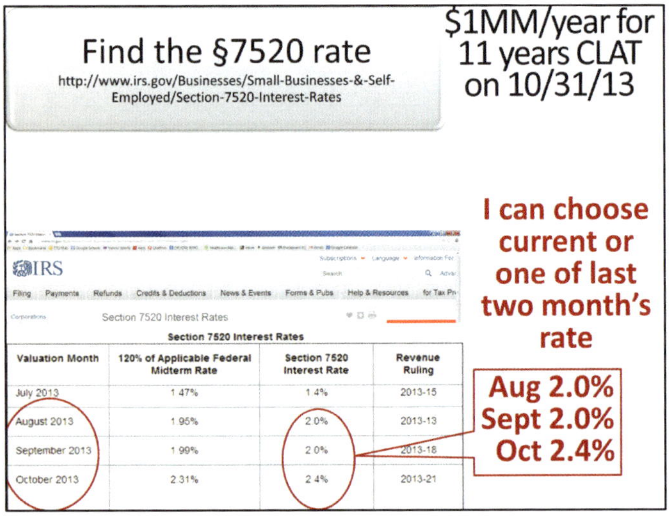

Consider the example of a non-grantor Charitable Lead Annuity Trust created on October 31, 2013 paying $1 million per year to charity for 11 years. What is the present value of these charitable annuity payments (i.e., the part not subject to gift taxes)? Calculating this first requires finding the §7520 interest rate. These rates are issued monthly and can be found on the IRS website at http://www.irs.gov/Businesses/Small-Businesses-&-Self-Employed/Section-7520-Interest-Rates, or on other planned giving websites. The donor may use the §7520 interest rate for the month of the transaction or either of the two previous months. Thus, the donor in this case may use the interest rates for October, September, or August of 2013. (Of course, by late in October the future rates for November would also have been posted so the donor could have delayed the transaction into November in order to take advantage of the November rates if desired.) For a transaction completed on October 31, 2013, the donor would need to choose between a 2.4% and a 2.0% §7520 interest rate. Which one is better for the donor?

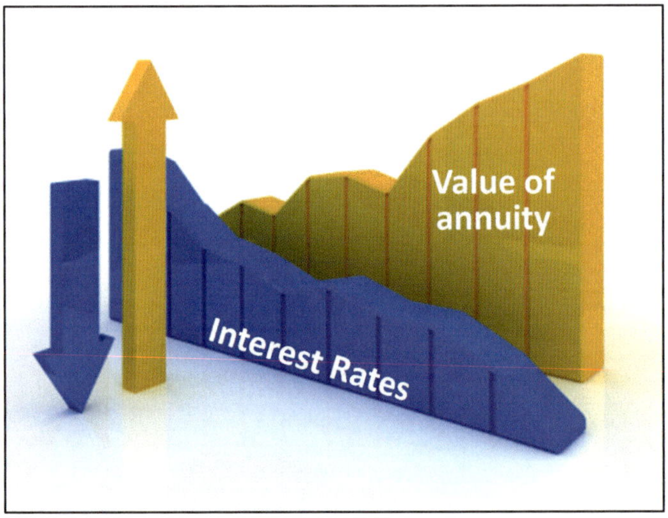

As interest rates rise, the value of a fixed dollar annuity decreases. Consider the value of an annuity that paid $1,000 per year when interest rates were 1%. An investor would have to invest $100,000 to generate that same income stream at 1%. However, if interest rates were 10% an investor would have to invest only $10,000 to generate that same income stream. Thus, the value of the income stream (the annuity) is much higher when interest rates are low and lower when interest rate are high.

Is the donor better off having the annuity valued higher or lower? In a Charitable Lead Annuity Trust, the annuity is the part that goes to charity. The value of the portion that goes to charity is *not* subject to gift or estate taxes in a non-grantor Charitable Lead Trust. So, the donor is better off having a higher valuation for this charitable portion (meaning a higher valuation for the annuity).

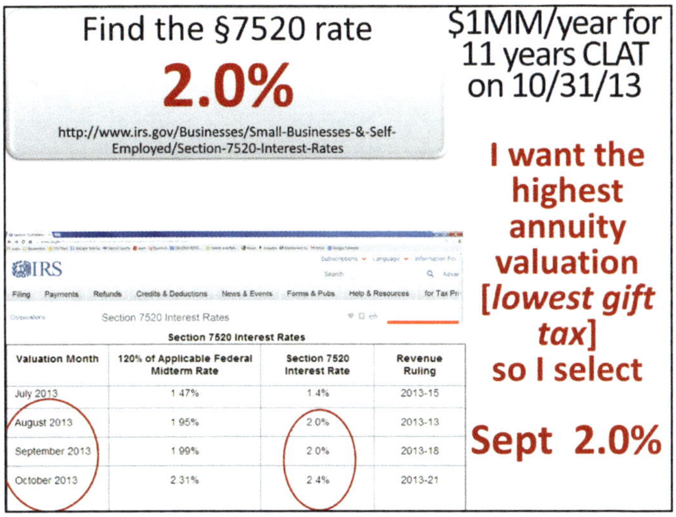

Returning to the three options for the §7520 interest rate of 2.0%, 2.0%, and 2.4%, the donor is better off choosing the lowest rate. Thus, for this calculation the donor should choose the 2.0% rate in order to get the highest annuity valuation, and therefore the lowest gift tax. This 2.0% interest rate will be used for all calculations for this transaction even though during the life of the trust the interest rates may fluctuate greatly. Only the initial §7520 interest rate is relevant to the tax calculation.

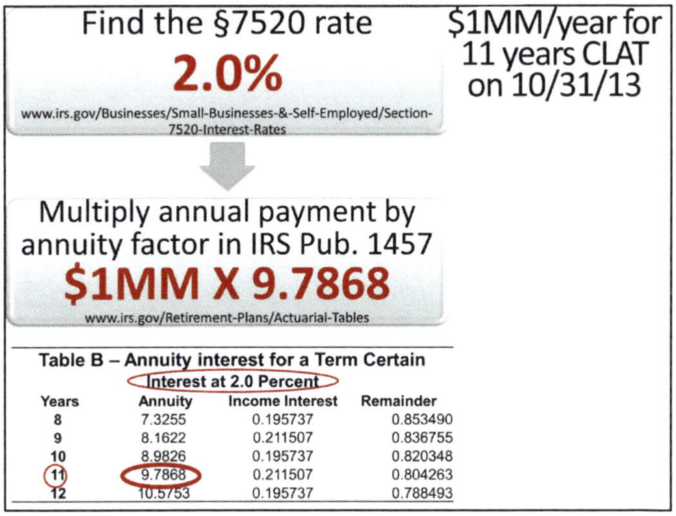

Once the appropriate §7520 interest rate is identified, the value of the annuity can be determined from the table associated with IRS Publication 1457 which can be found on the web at http://www.irs.gov/Retirement-Plans/Actuarial-Tables. In this case, the annuity will be paid for a fixed number of years, so we select Table B "Term Certain Factors." If instead the annuity was to be paid for life, we would select Table S for a single life or Table R(2) for two lives. These tables are also found on the same webpage. Examining Table B under the 2.0 percent interest rate heading shows that the annuity factor for an 11-year fixed term at that interest rate is 9.7868.

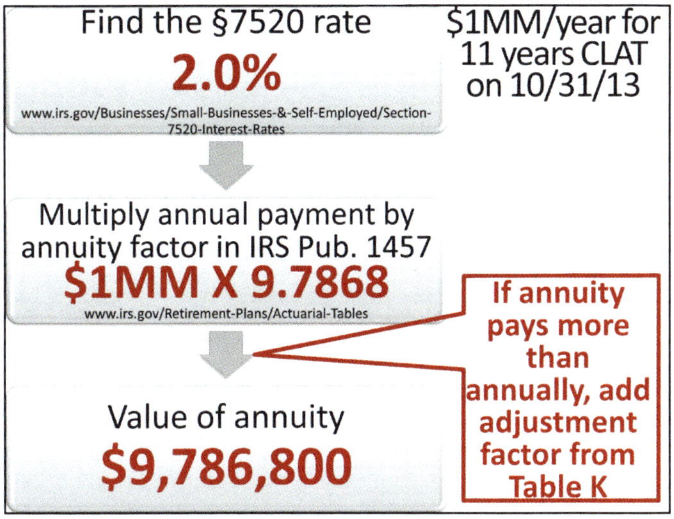

Assuming that the annuity pays annually, the value of the annuity is simply this annuity factor (9.7868) multiplied by the annual annuity payment ($1 million). Thus, the value of this annuity is $9,786,800. If the annuity paid more frequently than at the end of each year, then it would be slightly more valuable. (It is more valuable because the recipient gets the money slightly earlier.) For example, if the annuity were paid monthly (still with an initial §7520 interest rate of 2.0%) the value of the annuity would be $9,786,800 X 1.0091, or $9,875,859.88.

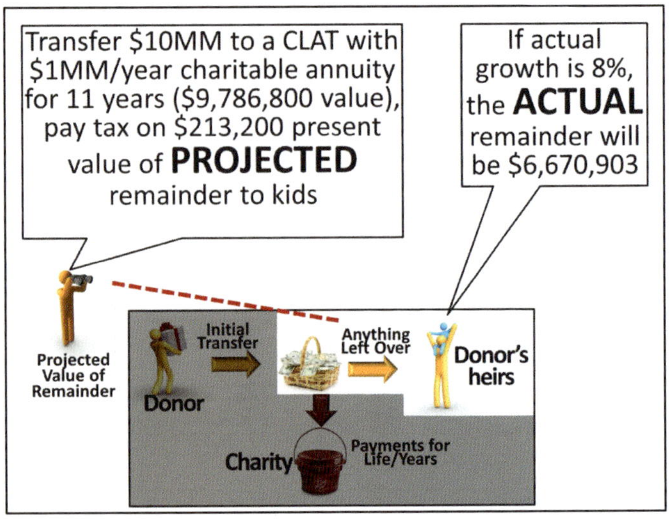

Suppose that the donor transferred $10 million to this non-grantor Charitable Lead Annuity Trust on October 31, 2013. The projected value of the charitable share, based upon 11 years of $1 million payments would be $9,786,800 as described above. This leaves a projected gift to the donor's heirs (or whomever the donor names to receive the remaining amount) with a present value of $10,000,000 less $9,786,800. Thus, the present value of the projected taxable gift to the heirs would be $213,200. If, during the life of the trust, the assets in the trust grow at a rate of 2.0% (equal to the initial §7520 interest rate) this projection will be accurate. However, if the assets in the trust grow at a rate faster than 2.0% this *extra* growth will go to the heirs without additional gift or estate taxation. For example, if the assets in the trust grew at a rate of 8%, the actual amount transferred to the heirs would be $6,670,902.51. This demonstrates the power of the non-grantor Charitable Lead Trust. The donor transfers over $6.6 million in value to heirs, but pays taxes on only $213,200.

In the previous example, the present value of the amount projected to go to heirs based on the §7520 interest rate was only $213,200. However, the donor could easily set the payments to charity such that the projected amount going to the heirs would be $0. This zeroed-out non-grantor Charitable Lead Trust results in no gift or estate taxation, regardless of the size of the *actual* transfer going to the heirs. Using a zeroed-out Charitable Lead Trust also eliminates the risk of paying unnecessary taxes if the trust assets *underperform* the initial §7520 interest rate. If the trust assets ultimately grew at a rate lower than the initial §7520 interest rate, then the trust would simply exhaust earlier than its intended term with no payments to non-charitable beneficiaries. But, since not taxes were paid, the donor has not lost any benefits due to the underperformance.

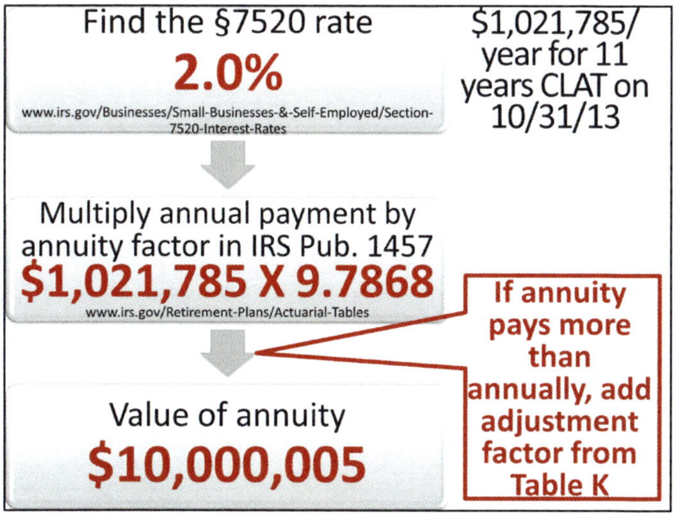

The calculation process for a zeroed-out Charitable Lead Annuity Trust is the same as before. In this case, the donor transfers $10 million into a non-grantor Charitable Lead Annuity Trust which pays $1,021,785 per year to charity for 11 years. The present value of this series of annual payments, at a 2.0% §7520 interest rate, is $10,000,005. This exceeds the value of the trust assets of $10,000,000. Thus, if the trust assets return exactly 2.0% during the life of the trust, there will be nothing left after the final charitable payment is made. If, however, the trust assets grow faster than 2.0%, any excess growth is transferred to the heirs (or other non-charitable beneficiaries). This transfer of extra growth occurs without any gift or estate taxation.

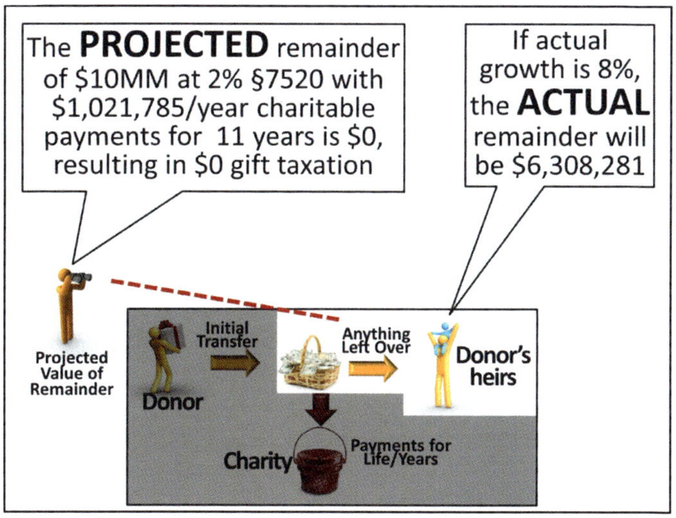

As before, the donor must pay gift taxes on the present value of the amount *projected* to go to the heirs. But, because $0 is *projected* to go to the heirs, there are no gift taxes. Any amount that *actually* goes to heirs – due to growth above the initial §7520 rate – also avoids taxation because the gift tax (of $0) has already been paid.

Conceptually, this might seem to be a lot of effort to go through just to be able to transfer the "extra" growth above the §7520 rate. But, consider that in the previous example if the $10 million transfer grew at 8% instead of the §7520 rate of 2%, this transaction results in $6,308, 281 being transferred to heirs with no gift taxes. For a donor at top tax rates, gifting that much after-tax money to heirs would otherwise have come at a cost of over $2.5 million in gift taxes or $4.2 million in estate taxes. (The estate tax cost of transferring this much after-tax money is higher than the gift tax cost because estate taxes also apply to the money used to pay for the estate tax, i.e., estate taxes are tax "inclusive.") For those subject to estate and gift taxes, this benefit is well worth the planning, even for smaller transactions. For example, a $500,000 zeroed-out non-grantor Charitable Lead Annuity Trust earning 8% could transfer $315,414 to heirs after tax, which otherwise would have cost $210,276 in estate taxes.

This tax savings is especially attractive to a donor who was already planning to make these charitable transfers. In that case the ability to gift the extra growth to heirs with no gift or estate tax is a "free" benefit available simply by using the non-grantor Charitable Lead Trust as the gifting mechanism. This is one of the reasons why *testamentary* zeroed-out non-grantor Charitable Lead Trusts are so attractive. For any taxable estate where the donor has already planned a substantial charitable estate gift, transferring the gift in the form of a testamentary zeroed-out non-grantor Charitable Lead Trust provides the opportunity for tax-free transfers to heirs with no downside risk to the heirs.

Because the non-grantor Charitable Lead Trust provides the opportunity to transfer extra growth, above the §7520 rate, free from estate and gift taxes, the value of this technique depends upon the growth rate of assets in the trust. Thus if clients have assets that they anticipate will grow more rapidly in future years these are the assets most suited for a non-grantor Charitable Lead Trust.

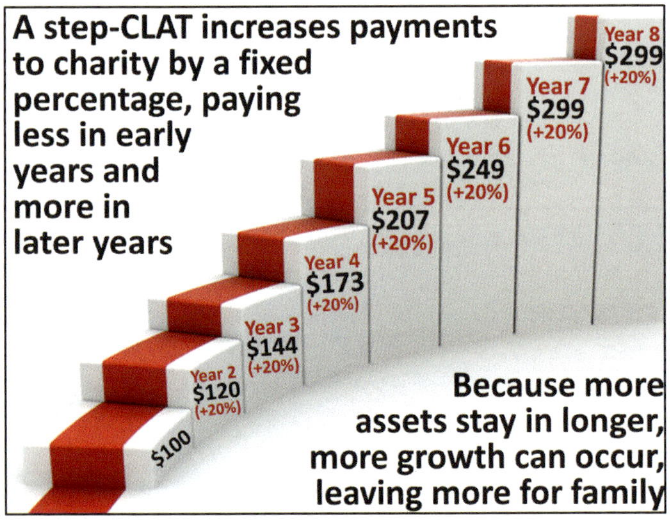

A step-CLAT (non-grantor Charitable Lead Annuity Trust) provides for steadily increasing payments to the charity during the fixed term of the trust. The payments are not flat, but they are known in advance. The motivation for pushing more of the charitable payments to the later stages of the trust term is that this allows more assets to stay in the trust longer. For assets that outperform the initial §7520 rate, the longer they stay in the trust the more excess growth they will generate. For example, the IRS has approved using annual 20% increases in the charitable payment amounts. Returning to our previous example, a zeroed out Charitable Lead Annuity Trust with a $10 million initial transfer could be generated by 11 annual payments starting at $362,000 and increasing by 20% each year. Taking this approach instead of paying the flat annuity rate (i.e., $1,021,785 per year) means that the charity receives lower payments at the start of the trust, but larger payments at the end of the trust. For instance, the first annual payment would be $362,000, but the final annual payment would be $2,241,409. If trust assets grew at 8% annually (instead of the 2.0% initial §7520 rate) the standard flat payout annuity in a zeroed-out non-grantor Charitable Lead Trust would leave $6,308,281 for the heirs. But, the 20% annual increasing step annuity in a zeroed-out non-grantor Charitable Lead Trust would leave $7,936,082. This extra $1.6 million in tax-free transfer results from keeping the faster growing assets in the trust longer. If, however, the assets underperformed the 2.0% initial §7520 rate both the traditional annuity and the step annuity would exhaust the trust and the heirs would receive nothing.

The more extreme version of keeping assets inside the Charitable Lead Annuity Trust is known as a "shark fin" Charitable Lead Annuity Trust. The name comes from a visualization of the payment amounts on a graph where the large charitable payments all come in the last year or two of the trust, forming a steep shark-fin like graph. The benefit to such a payout scheme is the same as with a step-CLAT (Charitable Lead Annuity Trust). The longer the assets are kept inside Charitable Lead Trust, the more excess growth they will be able to generate, assuming that they outperform the §7520 rate. Using these more extreme payouts is a more aggressive approach because it has not been approved (or disapproved) by the IRS. Some argue that 20% annual increases, which are allowed, should be treated as a maximum. The argument is that 20% increasing annuities is the maximum allowed for Grantor Retained Annuity Trusts, and so perhaps the IRS will dispute Charitable Lead Annuity Trusts that exceed this level.

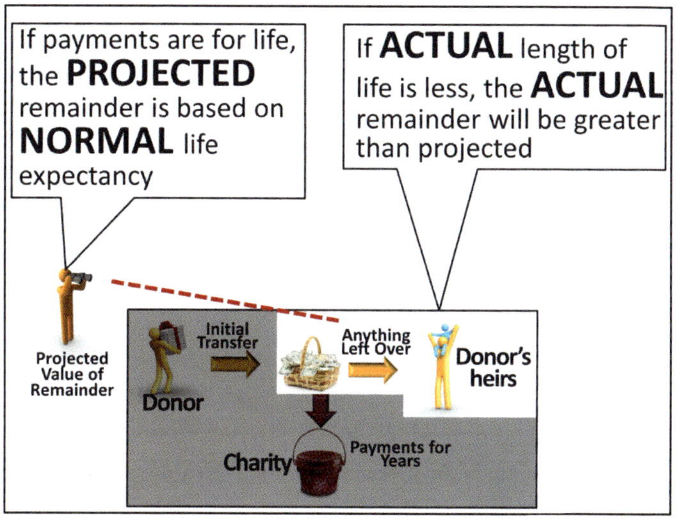

For Charitable Lead Trusts paying to a charity for a lifetime, the actual amount left for the non-charitable beneficiary depends not only on the rate of growth of the assets, but also on the length of the measuring life. For example, if a Charitable Lead Trust pays $100,000 per year for the life of a person whose age suggests a life expectancy of 30 years, the present value of that charitable payment would be $100,000 x 22.3965, or $2,239,650 (at a 2.0% §7520 rate). However, if the person only lived for two years, the actual payment to charity would be only $200,000. Just as before, gift tax is paid based upon the *projected* transfer to the non-charitable beneficiaries, not the *actual* transfer. Consequently, if a donor transferred $2.2 million to the previous Charitable Lead Trust with projected distributions to charity having a present value over $2.2 million, there would be no gift or estate tax on the transfer. This remains true even though the shortened life, in reality, would have resulted in $2 million being transferred to the heirs with no gift or estate taxes. Recognizing this reality led to the practice of creating "viatical" Charitable Lead Trusts (a.k.a., "vulture" Charitable Lead Trusts), where the measuring life for the charity's payments would be a younger person with a terminal disease. In response, the law was changed to limit the people who can be named as the measuring life for a Charitable Lead Trust.

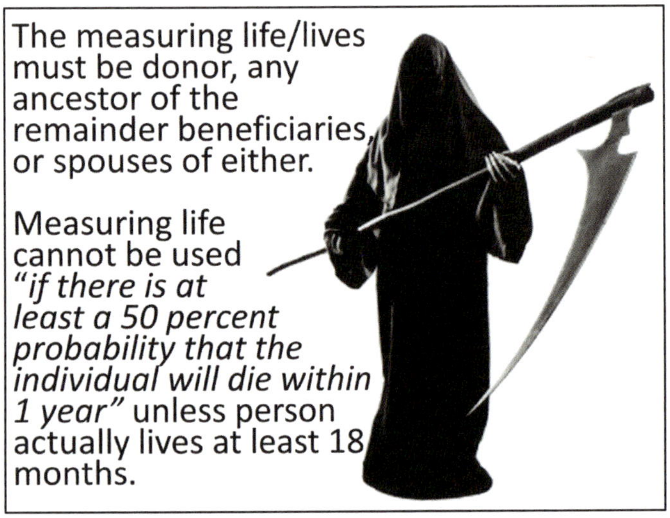

To prevent widespread viatical shopping, the measuring life for a Charitable Lead Trust is now limited to the donor, any ancestor of the remainder beneficiaries, or the spouse of either of these. Thus, taking advantage of a terminal diagnosis for tax planning purposes is still theoretically possible, but only within the much smaller close family group. Additionally, even one of these family members may not be used as the measuring life for a Charitable Lead Trust if there is at least a 50% probability that the individual will die within one year. Such a probability would be an issue of fact and subject to expert testimony. However, if the person who is the measuring life actually lives for at least 18 months after being named, then there is no requirement to meet the 50% probability test.

In Charitable Remainder Trusts it is quite common for the donor to retain the right to change the charitable beneficiary of the trust. So long as the trust requires that some charity will ultimately receive the funds, this retention of power creates no problems. In contrast, if the donor retains this power in a non-grantor Charitable Lead Trust the gift and estate tax advantages of the trust will be lost. Why? Retaining the power to change charitable beneficiaries causes the assets to remain in the donor's estate. Because the assets have not left the donor's estate, they are still subject to estate taxes at the donor's death. This same reality does not create tax problems for the Charitable Remainder Trust. The Charitable Remainder Trust assets may be included in the donor's estate, but when those assets are all transferred to charity at death they are not subject to estate taxation because of the unlimited charitable estate tax deduction. In contrast, the Charitable Lead Trust passes its assets to non-charitable beneficiaries at termination. Thus, inclusion of the Charitable Lead Trust assets in the donor's estate at death can result in estate taxation. Although the donor may not have this power, it is acceptable for the donor's spouse or some other family member to have the power to change charitable beneficiaries. Because it is not the donor who holds the power, this will not result in the trust assets being included in the donor's estate. (Note, however, that if the Charitable Lead Trust will pay to a "skip person" such as a grandchild with living parents, it is important that no one retains the right to change the charitable beneficiary. This is discussed briefly below in the section on generation skipping transfer taxes.)

It is also acceptable if the donor has the power to "request but not direct" an independent trustee to change the charitable beneficiary. Because the donor does not have the legal right to change the charitable beneficiary, keeping this right does not create estate tax problems. Along the same lines, it is perfectly acceptable for the Charitable Lead Trust to pay to a donor advised fund, even if the donor has the right to advise the charity regarding the timing and recipients of subsequent charitable transfers (see PLR 9633027). This right is only the right to give "advice." It is not a legal right to force a particular charitable transfer. Because it is not an enforceable legal right, it does not result in inclusion of the assets in the donor's estate.

The non-grantor Charitable Lead Trust may name the donor's donor advised fund as the charitable beneficiary because the donor has no legal right to control the distributions out of those funds (only a right to "advise" regarding distributions). Similarly, if the donor's private family foundation is named as a charitable beneficiary, it is important to show that the donor has no legal right to control the ultimate charitable grant recipients through his control of the private foundation. If the donor had this right, then the Charitable Lead Trust assets would still be included in the donor's estate. In order to prove that the donor has no ability to direct the ultimate distribution of those assets paid to the donor's private foundation, the terms of the gift should prohibit the donor from acting with regard to funds coming from Charitable Lead Trust. Further, such funds should be maintained in a separate account. There are no problems with inclusion in the donor's estate if the donor's spouse, children, or friends can control these separate funds in their role as foundation trustees, but the donor must be excluded. (Allowing another person to change the charitable beneficiary of the non-grantor Charitable Lead Trust itself creates negative consequence for purposes of generation skipping transfer taxes, but allowing others to keep the right to control distributions made from the private foundation that is the recipient of Charitable Lead Trust funds does not create any such problems.)

The IRS has allowed early termination of a fixed term Charitable Lead Annuity Trust. However, it has not allowed the division to be based upon the present value of the relative income and remainder rights (as has sometimes been allowed with a Charitable Remainder Trust). Instead, the charity must be paid all of the scheduled payments at the time of termination, without discounting for receiving the payments early. Thus, if 10 years remained in a fixed term Charitable Lead Trust where the charity received $1,000,000 per year, an early termination would require the immediate payment to the charity of $10,000,000, rather than the present value of the right to receive these payments over the next ten years. Charitable Lead Unitrusts, in contrast, may not be terminated early.

The primary estate and gift tax advantage to be gained through the use of a non-grantor Charitable Lead Trust comes from the taxation of the *projected* transfer to heirs rather than the *actual* transfer to heirs. This same advantage arises for generation skipping transfer taxes only with a Charitable Lead Unitrust (CLUT), but not with a Charitable Lead Annuity Trust (CLAT). With a Charitable Lead Annuity Trust, the generation skipping transfer tax is based upon both the *projected* and the *actual* transfers to the "skip person" (e.g., a grandchild whose parents are still alive). For both Charitable Lead Trust types, the donor can initially allocate generation skipping transfer tax exemption equal to the present value of the projected transfer to be made to "skip persons", just as with the gift tax. However, if the Charitable Lead Annuity Trust grows faster than the §7520 rate, then additional Generation Skipping Transfer Tax will be due at the termination of the Charitable Lead Annuity Trust. Worse, if the Charitable Lead Annuity Trust grows slower than the §7520 rate, ultimately leaving less to the "skip person" than projected, there is no refund of the allocated generation skipping transfer tax exemption. In contrast, the ultimate amount of the transfer is irrelevant to the calculation of generation skipping transfer tax for a Charitable Lead Unitrust. However, the Charitable Lead Unitrust is not an ideal mechanism for transferring the growth above the §7520, because such growth must be shared with the charity. The Charitable Lead Unitrust pays a fixed percentage of trust assets to charity each year, thus more rapid growth results in higher payments to charity.

As discussed above, the donor may not retain the right to change the charitable beneficiary of the Charitable Lead Trust. Otherwise, the assets of the Charitable Lead Trust will still be included, and taxed, in the donor's estate. However, allowing another person, such as a family member, to have this right to change charities does not create estate tax problems for the donor. It does, however, create a potential negative result for generation skipping transfer tax if the trust will be paid to a "skip person." In that case, leaving open the option to change the charitable beneficiary means that the transfer to the skip person is a "taxable distribution" rather than a "taxable termination." Under the generation skipping transfer tax rules, taxes from a "taxable distribution" are owed by the recipient "skip person" (I.R.C. § 2603(a)(1)), but taxes from a "taxable termination" are owed by the trust itself (I.R.C. § 2603(a)). For example, if $1,000,000 in generation skipping transfer taxes were due in a "taxable termination" the trust could pay those taxes with no negative consequences to the recipient. But, if the trust paid the $1,000,000 in generation skipping transfer taxes in a "taxable distribution," the trust would be paying the obligation of the recipient, meaning that the recipient would have received an additional $1,000,000 gift that would itself be subject to the generation skipping transfer tax.

Although the non-grantor Charitable Lead Trust can create significant potential tax advantages, as with other charitable planning techniques it is important to limit those techniques to clients with charitable interests. There are other ways to reduce estate taxes that do not involve making gifts to charity. For the non-charitable client, these techniques will inevitably be more appropriate. For example, a client may transfer excess growth to the next generation with similar results using a grantor retained annuity trust. Although this is not a perfect match for a Charitable Lead Trust (e.g., the client must outlive the term of the grantor retained annuity trust in order for the estate to receive the tax benefit), such techniques will typically be more appropriate than charitable strategies for the client who does not desire to make gifts to charity.

The primary role of non-grantor Charitable Lead Trusts is to aid in reducing gift and estate taxation. However, there is also a less well known role for these trusts in reducing income taxation. This opportunity arises when a donor's gifts no longer generate income tax deductions because of the income limitations on charitable deductions. In this scenario a donor might earn, e.g., $1,000,000 in interest and dividends on certain assets, donate the entire $1,000,000 to charity, but still be required to pay income taxes on the $1,000,000 with no useable charitable income tax deduction. The non-grantor Charitable Lead Trust can provide a solution to this income tax problem.

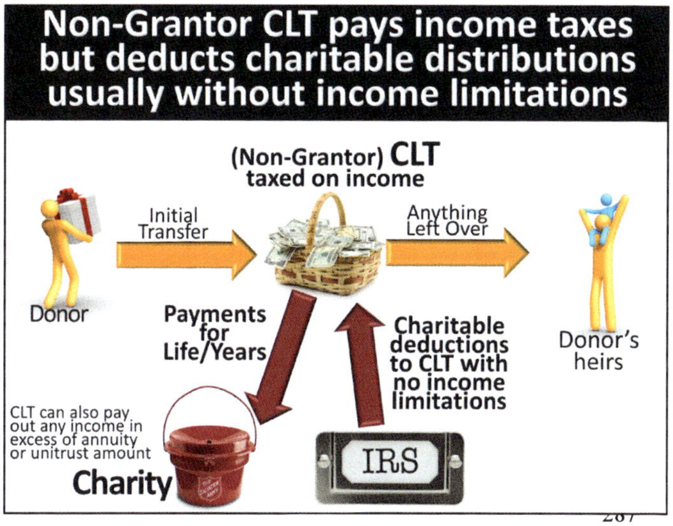

By transferring the income earning assets to a non-grantor Charitable Lead Trust, the donor no longer reports future earnings as income. Instead the trust itself reports these earnings, and pays taxes on them. Normally, this would not be considered a tax benefit because trusts have a compressed tax schedule (i.e., they pay the highest tax rate at a much lower level of income). However, non-grantor Charitable Lead Trusts can normally deduct payments to charity with no income limitations. Returning to the previous example, the donor owns assets generating $1,000,000 in interest and dividends annually. The donor would still have to pay taxes on that income even if she donated the entire amount to charity because the donor's other (or previous) gifts have already exceeded the income limitations on charitable deductions. However, if the donor transferred these assets to a non-grantor Charitable Lead Trust, the trust could deduct all gifts, up to 100% of income. Additionally, a Charitable Lead Trust may be written to allow distributions of any income in excess of the required annuity or unitrust amount, so that the trust would pay no income taxes. This plan works well when the donor wishes to make gifts out of income earned from assets, has no plans to consume the assets personally, but does desire to keep the underlying assets in the family.

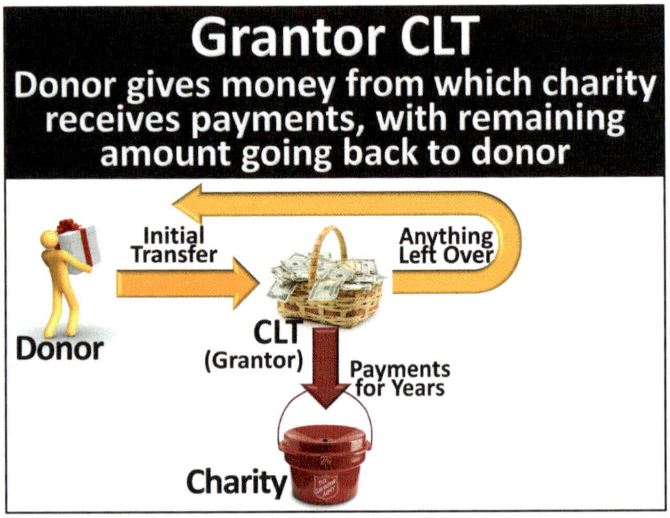

To this point the focus of the chapter has been on non-grantor Charitable Lead Trusts. A less common type of Charitable Lead Trust is the grantor Charitable Lead Trust. In the typical grantor Charitable Lead Trust the donor receives the remaining interest at the termination of the trust. Because of this, the trust is always considered to be owned by the donor. The grantor Charitable Lead Trust is not even a separate tax paying entity; it is simply an extension of the donor. If the trust earns income, the donor is treated as having earned the income. This trust is not used for estate and gift tax planning because the donor hasn't transferred anything out of his or her estate.

Instead, this trust is used for income tax planning purposes. Specifically, the donor is allowed to immediately deduct the present value of the future charitable gifts funded by the trust assets. This allows the donor to "pull forward" future charitable gifts and deduct them today (so long as the donor transfers sufficient assets into the trust to fund these gifts).

The tax deduction for transfers to grantor Charitable Lead Trusts is limited to 30% of adjusted gross income, or 20% if funded with long-term capital gain property, because the gift is considered to be "for the use of" charity rather than "to" charity. This is because the Charitable Lead Trust itself is not a tax-exempt entity (unlike the Charitable Remainder Trust). Additionally, the IRS has argued in a private letter ruling (8824039) that there should be no carry-over of unused deduction if the beneficiary of the Charitable Lead Trust is a private foundation.

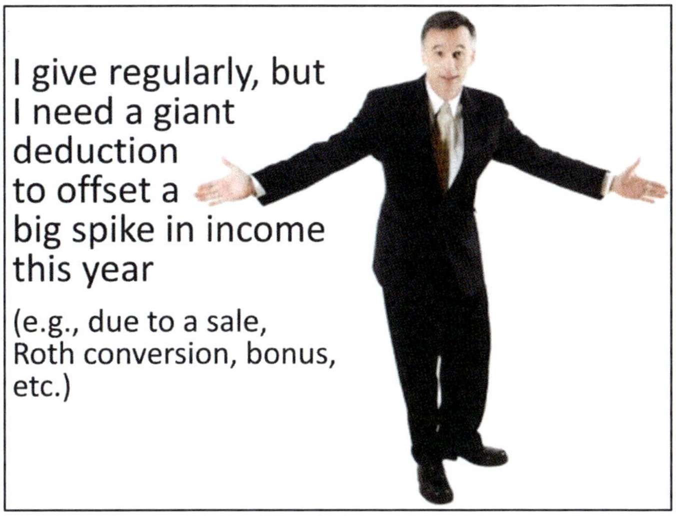

Pulling forward tax deductions for future charitable gifts is particularly useful when the donor's tax rates are high now, but will be lower later. The grantor Charitable Lead Trust allows the donor to take the deductions now, when they are more valuable, rather than later. This temporarily higher tax rate may result from a spike in income, perhaps due to the sale of an appreciated asset, a Roth conversion, or some other temporary income. Additionally, this difference in tax rates may occur as the result of a planned retirement where future income, and thus future tax rates, will be substantially lower after the retirement date.

Of course, the donor could simply make a large charitable gift during the year when income is high. Or, if the donor wishes to spread out the transfers to charity over many years, he or she could make a large transfer to a donor advised fund. Both of these approaches would also generate a large immediate income tax deduction. However, the non-grantor Charitable Lead Trust allows the donor to get the asset back after the expiration of the trust (or at least what remains of the asset after making the required payments to charity). Suppose the donor owns a large income-producing investment which generates $100,000 per year. Using a non-grantor Charitable Lead Trust, the donor could transfer the asset, use the income to pay for $100,000 annual charitable gifts, take an immediate tax deduction for all of the future $100,000 annual gifts, and then receive the asset back at the close of the trust. This could work especially well if the asset was desired to produce income in the future, for example in retirement planning, but would be better used to generate charitable tax deductions today. The other methods do not allow the donor to both keep the underlying asset and also take an immediate deduction for the future years of gifting.

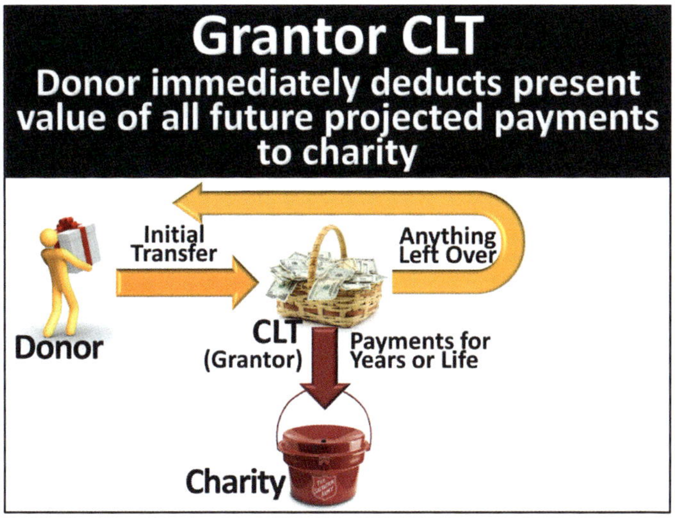

The typical grantor Charitable Lead Trust follows the plan of the accompanying diagram because the donor retains the reversion rights. There are other rights that will also trigger this grantor trust treatment, but many violate other Charitable Lead Trust rules (such as rules against self-dealing) and therefore eliminate Charitable Lead Trust treatment and the tax deduction.

In rare cases the grantor Charitable Lead Trust may continue to exist beyond the death of the donor. (This might occur where the trust is set to run for, say, 10 years, but the donor dies before the end of the 10 year period.) This creates a problem because the donor can no longer be treated as the owner of the trust and taxed with the trust's income. In such cases the grantor Charitable Lead Trust becomes its own separate tax paying entity (i.e., a complex trust) just like the non-grantor Charitable Lead Trust. This means that the trust is taxed with any income earned, but it can also deduct subsequent transfers to charity. However, to offset the fact that these anticipated gifts were *already* deducted by the donor, the deductions are recaptured on the donor's final income tax return. In other words the donor's original deduction, less the value of the amounts already paid to charity discounted to the year of the deduction, is treated as income in the year of recapture. This same result also occurs if the donor gives up his or her reversion rights (although the recapture will occur on the donor's tax return in the year that the rights were given up rather than on the donor's final tax return).

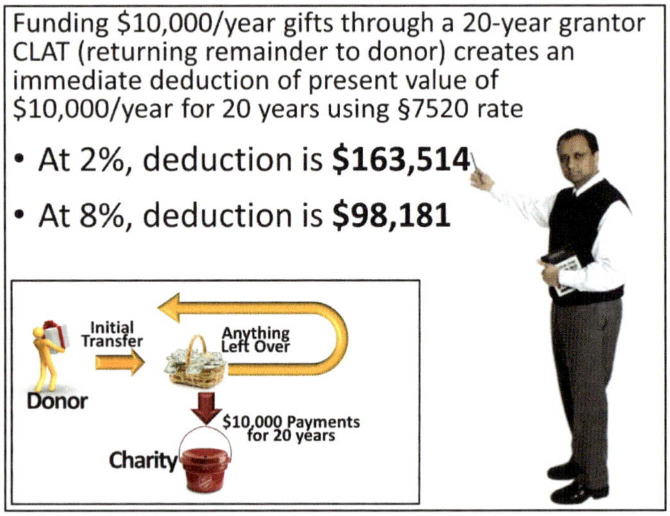

Because the non-grantor Charitable Lead Trust allows for a deduction today for transfers to be made to charity in the future, the value of the deduction depends upon the prevailing §7520 interest rate. The size of the deduction is much larger during lower interest rate periods than during higher interest rate periods. For example, a Charitable Lead Trust funded to support $10,000 annual charitable gifts for the subsequent 20 years will generate a $163,514 deduction if the §7520 rate is 2.0%. (The annuity factor for a 20-year term certain annuity at a 2.0% interest rate on Table B "Term Certain Factors" found on the web at http://www.irs.gov/Retirement-Plans/Actuarial-Tables is 16.3514.) But, if the §7520 rate is 8.0%, the same transaction generates a deduction of only $98,181.

Grantor Charitable Lead Trusts and non-grantor Charitable Lead Trusts have opposing tax characteristics. The grantor Charitable Lead Trust is treated as if it is still owned by the donor. Thus the donor receives the charitable income tax deductions, but is also taxed with the income earned by the trust, and the assets in the trust are considered to be owned by the donor for gift and estate tax purposes. In contrast, the non-grantor Charitable Lead Trust is treated as a separate tax payer. Transfers to the non-grantor Charitable Lead Trust do not generate income tax deductions. The trust pays taxes on any income it earns and it takes deductions for any transfers it makes to charity. Most importantly for gift and estate tax planning purposes, any assets in the non-grantor Charitable Lead Trust trust are outside of the donor's estate. Thus, the choice of the trust type will depend upon the tax goals of the donor.

There is, however, a type of Charitable Lead Trust that proposes to combine the characteristics of the grantor and non-grantor trust. The "defective grantor trust" or "super grantor trust" or "super trust" purports to create a Charitable Lead Trust where the donor may take an immediate tax deduction for future charitable gifts from the trust, pay taxes on any income earned by the trust, but the trust assets will not be included in the donor's estate. Thus, the estate and gift tax results are the same as with any other non-grantor Charitable Lead Trust, but the donor is actually able to take a personal income tax deduction as if it were a grantor Charitable Lead Trust.

The explanation behind this type of trust results from a slight inconsistency in the tax code. The income tax rules defining grantor and non-grantor trusts are *almost* identical to the gift and estate tax rules defining grantor and non-grantor trusts. But, they are not perfectly identical. If a donor keeps the right to get trust property by substituting other property of equal value this will trigger grantor treatment for the trust for income tax purposes. However, it does not trigger grantor treatment for the trust for gift and estate tax purposes. Thus an otherwise normal non-grantor Charitable Lead Trust can be converted into a "super grantor trust" by simply inserting this one right. This hybrid trust has not received clear approval from the IRS, but does appear to comply with the language of the tax code.

Charitable Lead Trusts are commonly funded with simple assets such as cash and publicly traded stocks and bonds. However, some assets can create complications or difficulties when transferred to a Charitable Lead Trust.

Although Charitable Lead Trusts are not private foundations, they are required to follow the private foundation rules against self-dealing, taxable expenditures, jeopardizing investments, and excess business holdings. Failing to follow these rules will result in the trust being disqualified as a Charitable Lead Trust. For example, the trust may not indefinitely hold too much ownership in a single business entity (no more than 20% ownership by the trust and all disqualified persons combined unless trust ownership is 2% or less). However, the trust may hold unlimited ownership in a business gifted to the trust for up to 5 years before it must sell the asset. Consequently, if the Charitable Lead Trust is established for a term of 5 years or less, it will not violate this rule. Another rule is that the donor may not transfer property to the trust with debt that is less than 10 years old because such transfer constitutes self-dealing. Also, the trust may not hold assets that are so risky as to jeopardize the charitable purposes of the trust. These rules are covered in detail in the chapter on private foundations.

Unrelated business income arises when a trust owns business interests in a form that generates ordinary income such as a sole proprietorship, a partnership, or a limited partnership interest where the limited partnership is actively managing a business operation and not simply collecting passive income from investments. In a Charitable Remainder Trust, unrelated business income results in a harsh 100% excise tax. No such excise tax applies to Charitable Lead Trusts, allowing them to receive unrelated business income. When the trust is a non-grantor Charitable Lead Trust any such income is simply attributed to the donor and treated as if it had been received directly by the donor. However, special rules apply if a *non-grantor* Charitable Lead Trust receives unrelated business income. In this case, the non-grantor Charitable Lead Trust may deduct only 50% of this income when it is given to a public charity, or 30% when it is given to a private foundation. This means that the trust cannot escape paying at least 50% or 70% of the unrelated business income tax, regardless of its charitable distributions.

Why should such a rule exist? The idea of having an unrelated business income tax is that nonprofits should not be able to outcompete for-profits in non-charitable commercial enterprises simply because the nonprofits pay no taxes. This would be unfair for regular businesses and would have a negative effect on tax revenues based upon regular commercial activity. If a non-grantor Charitable Lead Trust were allowed to operate a business and pay no tax on the earnings (because earnings were 100% distributed to a charity and resulted in a 100% tax deduction), the result would be the same as charging no unrelated business income tax. To avoid this result, contributions of unrelated business income are not fully deductible. As a result, a non-grantor Charitable Lead Trusts must pay some unrelated business income tax, even if all unrelated business income is donated to charity. (Note that the trust's ownership of a limited partnership interest will not generate unrelated business income if the limited partnership does not engage in the active management of a business, but simply holds passive investments and collects income from them. Thus, if a donor was using a limited partnership holding passive investments for the purpose of obtaining a valuation discount for estate tax purposes, such interests could be gifted to a Charitable Lead Trust.)

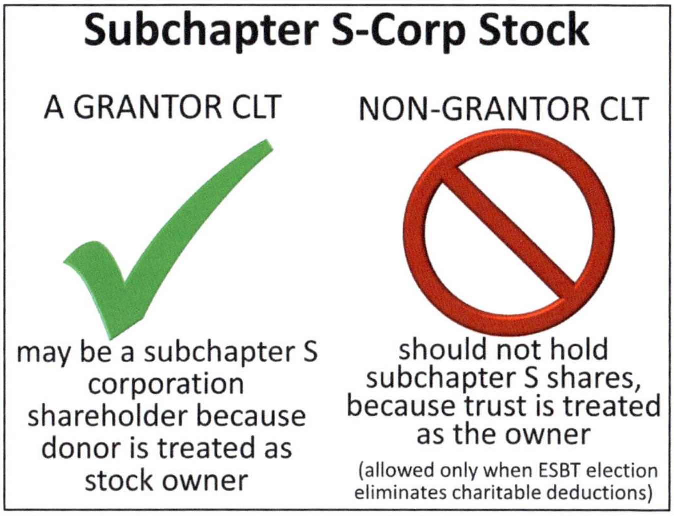

Subchapter S-corporation shares are most commonly held be people. These shares may not be held by another corporation, a partnership, or a Charitable Remainder Trust. (Doing so will cause the corporation to lose its subchapter S status and instead become a subchapter C-corporation.)

It is perfectly acceptable for a grantor Charitable Lead Trust to hold such shares because the trust is treated, for tax purposes, as being owned by the donor. Similarly the hybrid "super grantor" trust is also treated as a grantor trust for income tax purposes and could also hold subchapter S corporation shares. This is not the case, however, if the shares are held by a non-grantor Charitable Lead Trust. The non-grantor Charitable Lead Trust is a separate taxpayer from the donor. Because the trust is not a person, its ownership of subchapter S-corporation shares is not permitted under the subchapter S-corporation rules. There is one exception that permits a non-grantor Charitable Lead Trust to own such shares. This arises if the trust choses to make an ESBT (Electing Small Business Trusts) election. Such an election is usually undesirable for the non-grantor Charitable Lead Trust as any income earned from the shares may not be deducted as a charitable gift when transferred to charity.

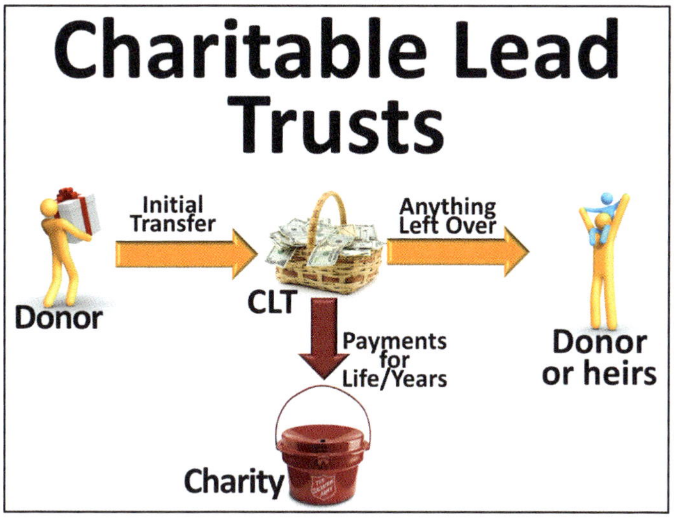

Charitable Lead Trusts can be complex vehicles (certainly much more complex than presented in this brief chapter), but this complexity should not prevent advisors and fundraiser from being familiar with their, potentially dramatic, tax benefits. Although relatively rare, these trusts represent a significant share of assets held in split interest charitable trusts and an even larger share of actual charitable distributions made from such trusts.

14 LIFE INSURANCE IN CHARITABLE PLANNING

Planning with life insurance creates many potentially positive opportunities for donors, advisors, and charities. Yet, there can be negative consequences from using life insurance as well. Some tax rules create negative consequences in certain cases. Some charities have had bad experiences and bad results working with life insurance professionals who promised more than they delivered. These potential pitfalls are no reason to ignore the benefits of life insurance, but rather should be a motivation to become more acquainted with the details of using life insurance in charitable planning in order to produce the best outcomes.

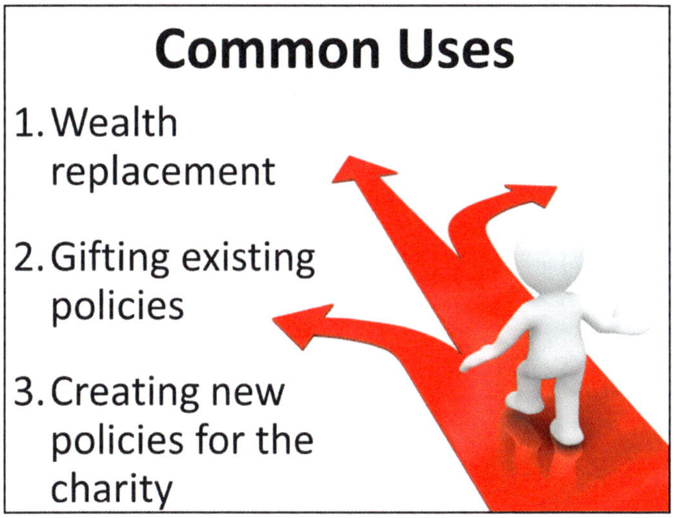

Many sophisticated charitable planning techniques, Charitable Gift Annuities, Charitable Remainder Trusts, Charitable Lead Trusts, gifts of remainder interests in homes or farms, bequest gifts in wills or trusts, all directly impact estate planning, typically reducing the heirs inheritance. It is not surprising then that another common estate planning tool, life insurance, can frequently be useful as a means to replace some or all of the heirs' inheritance lost due to charitable planning. Further, existing life insurance policies may have accumulated substantial value over time, making them a potential candidate for a charitable gift of property. Finally, some donors may desire to fund a large posthumous gift for charity by creating and making premium payments on a new charity-owned life insurance policy. Thus, charitable planning commonly employs life insurance in three different ways: wealth replacement, gifting existing policies, and creating new policies for charity. These three uses for life insurance involve dramatically different tax and planning issues. Consequently, each type of application will be reviewed separately.

Potentially the most powerful use of life insurance in charitable planning is as a "wealth replacement" for heirs or other non-charitable beneficiaries. Life insurance generates a pool of money (wealth) at the death of the insured. For younger families this wealth can be especially important as a way to replace the income (or services) lost by the unexpected death of a family member. In charitable planning, life insurance does not replace income, but instead replaces wealth. Charitable planning often involves the transfer of substantial assets (wealth) to charity either during life or at death. Life insurance provides a mechanism to replace all or part of the wealth gifted to charity for the heirs or beneficiaries who might otherwise have inherited that wealth. Importantly, life insurance can replace wealth in a tax-advantaged way after charitable planning has removed the wealth in a tax-advantaged way, resulting in the possibility of multiple layers of tax benefits.

The most powerful layer of tax benefits in these multi-layered charitable plans comes from the charitable instruments themselves. As reviewed in other chapters, charitable planning devices such as Charitable Gift Annuities, Charitable Remainder Trusts, or gifts of remainder interests in homes and farms can generate wonderful tax benefits in income, capital gain, estate, and generation skipping taxes. Despite these enormous tax benefits, advanced charitable planning techniques all have one thing in common; ultimately, they transfer assets to charity. Clearly, this means that such techniques should be limited to those who truly have charitable desires. Yet even among the charitable, these philanthropic desires are often not the only goal in a donor's plan.

Donors must often balance their charitable desires in estate planning against the desire to benefit family members or other non-charitable beneficiaries. The donor's desires to benefit his or her family may set the limit for any potential charitable estate gifts (or charitable planning techniques that diminish the remaining estate such as Charitable Gift Annuities). Life insurance can help balance these competing desires in a way that can increase both the gift to charity and the inheritance for other beneficiaries.

Not only can life insurance provide an alternative or supplemental inheritance to substitute for part or all of the wealth transferred to charity, but also, with certain types of planning, it can provide an inheritance that is not subject to estate taxes or generation skipping transfer taxes. For estates subject to the 40% estate tax rate and/or the 40% generation skipping transfer tax rate, the ability to receive tax-free inherited dollars is understandably attractive. Thus, the heirs may do well to trade a smaller amount of tax-free insurance in exchange for giving up a larger inheritance when the larger inheritance would have been taxable. Combining this with the tax advantages of charitable planning can create a win-win scenario where the donor is able to provide more for both charity and heirs through creative planning.

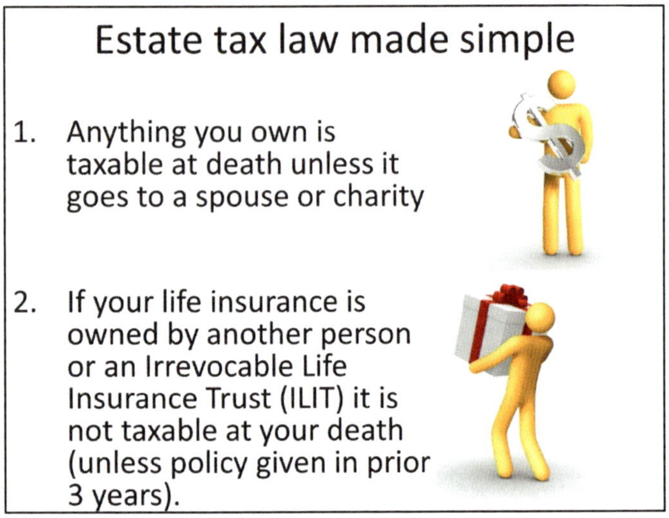

How is it possible for life insurance proceeds to avoid estate taxation? In simple terms, the estate tax applies to everything owned by the decedent at death except assets transferred to a spouse or a charity. Thus, proceeds from life insurance owned by the decedent will be subject to estate taxation (as well as generation skipping transfer taxation where applicable). However, if the decedent does not own the life insurance, then it is not normally subject to estate taxes (or generation skipping transfer taxes) at the decedent's death. This is true whether the life insurance is owned by another person, such as another family member, or by an artificially-created legal entity, such as an irrevocable trust. The exception to this rule is that if the decedent first owned the life insurance policy and then transferred it to another person (or legal entity), the policy will still be included in the decedent's estate for up to three years after the transfer. However, if the other person (or legal entity) originally purchased the policy then this waiting period does not apply.

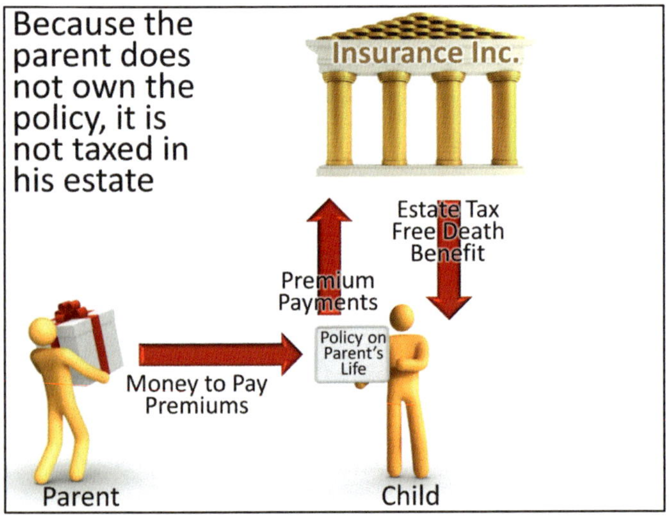

How would this work if another family member, such as a child of the insured, purchased the policy? The parent gives money to the child in order to allow the child to purchase a life insurance policy on the parent's life. Because the parent has not transferred the life insurance policy to the child, but instead simply given funds to allow the child to purchase the policy, the parent has never owned the life insurance policy. Since the parent has never owned the policy, it will not be included in the parent's estate. (If the parent had owned the policy and then given it to the child, the policy will still be in the parent's estate for three years after the date of transfer.) Upon the parent's death, the life insurance policy then pays its death benefit to the child. The child receives these life insurance proceeds free from estate taxation, because the life insurance policy was never in the parent's estate.

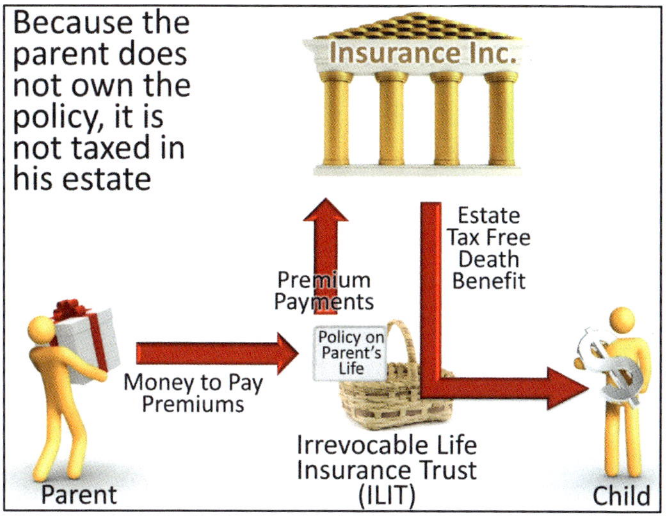

The same concept applies if the policy is owned, not by a child, but by a separate tax-paying legal entity not controlled by the parent, such as an irrevocable trust. Trusts designed for this purpose are referred to as ILITs (Irrevocable Life Insurance Trusts). The ILIT is, for tax purposes, a separate person. Thus, when the parent dies, the life insurance policy and its death benefit are not included in the parent's estate because another "person," the ILIT, owns the policy. The ILIT then receives the policy proceeds and distributes them to the child (or to whomever the ILIT document names as beneficiary).

An ILIT allows for distribution to multiple beneficiaries and ensures that money given for premium payments will be used for premium payments. By using an ILIT, the parent can establish rules for precisely where and how the money will be distributed. Because the child does not own the ILIT, the child's creditors, lawsuits, or divorce often cannot reach the ILIT assets. Although the parent cannot continue to directly control the ILIT after its creation, the parent can establish all rules that the ILIT trustee must follow in purchasing, paying for, and distributing the proceeds from the life insurance policy. This high level of control, without risk from potentially interfering family conflicts, is often attractive to those planning their estates.

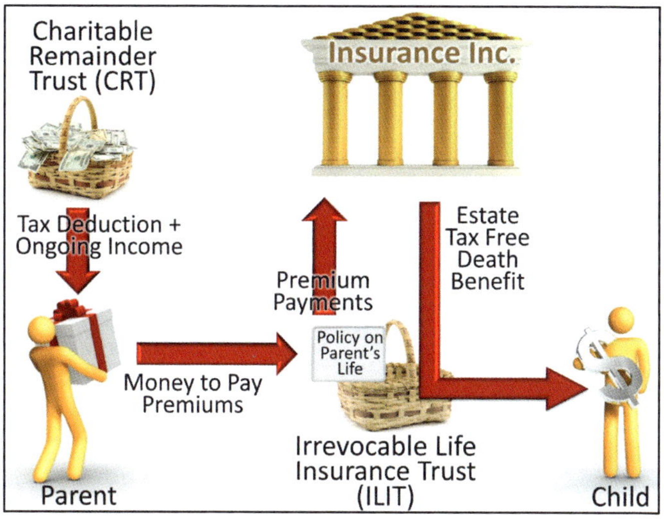

The ILIT is not, by itself, a charitable planning technique. Instead, the ILIT often serves as an attractive addition to charitable planning. The immediate tax deductions and lifetime income typically generated by Charitable Gift Annuities and Charitable Remainder Trusts provide a natural source of funding for this type of life insurance planning. At the same time, these gifts also reduce the remaining estate for heirs, increasing the potential interest in using life insurance as a means of replacing this donated wealth. Other charitable planning techniques, such a gifting a remainder interest in a home or farmland, do not generate ongoing income, but do generate an immediate tax deduction. In this case, the donor may consider using the money saved from the reduced tax liability to purchase life insurance.

Although the Charitable Remainder Trust, Charitable Gift Annuity, or gift of a remainder interest in a home or farmland reduces donor assets, the heirs may prefer to receive proceeds from an ILIT owned life insurance policy. The estate tax may have cut the value of other assets by up to 40%. Worse, the estate tax combined with the generation skipping transfer tax may have cut up to 64% from the value of other assets, if left to a grandchild with living parents or other "skip persons". The ILIT-owned life insurance policy generates a tax-free death benefit. In this way, the donor gives the taxable inheritance to charity and replaces it with a non-taxable inheritance funded by the increased income and tax benefits generated through the planned charitable gift.

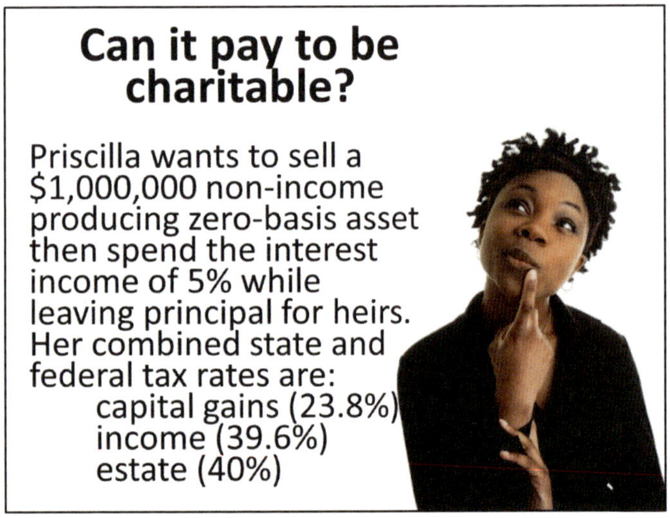

Combining charitable planning with life insurance planning can generate a range of tax benefits. The value of these benefits depends upon the tax circumstances of the donor. To see the potential power of these strategies, consider the case of a donor with a highly appreciated asset who is at the top federal tax rates for capital gains, income, and estate taxes. The donor has a $1,000,000 non-income producing zero-basis asset that she would like to sell, reinvest, and spend the interest income of 5% per year. (Low basis assets are a common financial planning challenge, especially with family businesses that started without a large initial cash investment.) She would like to leave the principal for heirs, but also has charitable interests. How can charitable planning make a charitable gift more affordable?

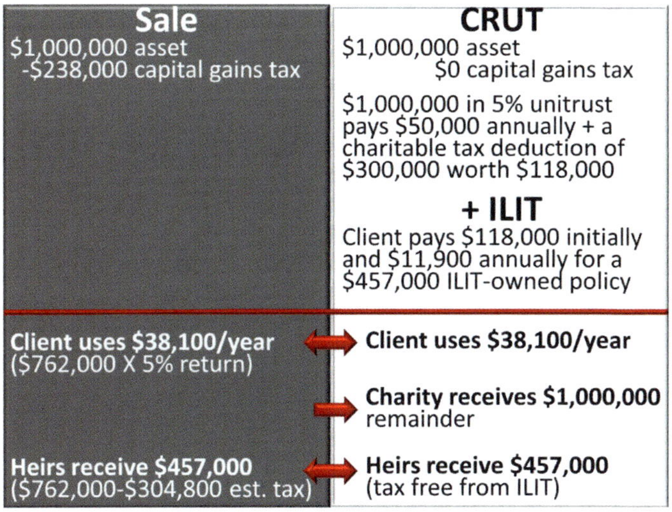

The traditional approach to the client's goals would be to sell the non-income producing asset, invest it, spend the interest earned, and leave the principal to the donor's heirs. This results in no charitable gift and substantial taxation. First, the sale of the appreciated asset generates a $238,000 federal capital gain tax (including ACA tax). Instead of having $1,000,000 to invest, only $762,000 remains after the taxes are paid. Earning 5% per year on this remaining amount generates $38,100 each year for the client to spend. The heirs inherit the entire principal, but due to a 40% estate tax on the principal, the heirs receive only $457,000 of the $762,000 principal.

As an alternative, the client could transfer the $1,000,000 asset to a charitable remainder unitrust paying her 5% of the trust assets for the remainder of her life. In this case, the Charitable Remainder Trust sells the $1,000,000 asset. As a non-profit entity, the trust pays no capital gains tax. This leaves the entire $1,000,000 available to generate income for the client. The payments from the trust, earning 5% annually, will be $50,000 per year as compared with $38,100 in the non-charitable approach. In addition to the higher payments, the transfer to the Charitable Remainder Trust generates a tax deduction. The exact amount of the deduction will depend upon the prevailing interest rates and age of the donor, but suppose the deduction is 30% of the transfer, i.e., $300,000. This $300,000 deduction can lower the donor's federal income taxes by $118,000.

Although the donor receives a large income tax deduction and greater income than with the first plan, the donor has partially disinherited her children who now have no claim on asset. This is great for the charity which will receive the $1,000,000 at the donor's death, but not as attractive for the heirs. To address this problem, the donor could purchase insurance using the value of the tax deduction and all or part of the increase in income. Although the amount of life insurance this will purchase depends upon prevailing interest rates and the donor's age and health, it is possible that an $118,000 initial premium plus an annual premium of $11,900 would purchase a $457,000 life insurance policy. (Note that as interest rates rise, the charitable deduction may decrease, but the cost of the insurance also decreases.) Because an ILIT owns the life insurance policy, the heirs receive the $457,000 tax free. This is identical to the after-tax benefit received from the $1,000,000 asset, which, after paying for capital gains taxes and estate taxes, left only $457,000 for the heirs. In other words, in the charitable planning scenario, the charity receives a $1,000,000 gift without any net cost to the donor or the donor's heirs. Of course, this is an extreme scenario in that the donor has a highly appreciated zero-basis asset and faces the highest federal tax rates. However, the charitable scenario actually becomes even more attractive if the donor lives in a state that charges taxes on capital gains in addition to the federal taxes on capital gain. Nevertheless, this example shows the potential power of combining charitable planning with life insurance planning as a way to benefit all parties.

Life insurance can also be used in less complex transactions. As an example, suppose a potential donor owns $100,000 of farmland that he would like to use for the rest of his life. At his death, he would like to leave the property to his favorite charity, but he is concerned about reducing his heirs' inheritance too much. How might charitable planning help in this situation?

Pairing life insurance with income-producing charitable planning vehicles like Charitable Remainder Trusts or Charitable Gift Annuities is a common combination, because these gifts generate income that can be used to pay premiums. However, life insurance can also be combined with other charitable planning techniques that produce valuable tax deductions. For example, gifts of remainder interests in homes or farmland generate charitable income tax deductions but require no cash. The value of these deductions can be used to purchase insurance to help offset the heirs' loss of the inheritance of the home or farmland. If estate taxes are a concern, the donor is able to use the value of the tax deduction from the IRS to purchase a tax-free inheritance (using an ILIT) for heirs in partial replacement of the taxable inheritance donated to a charity.

By giving the remainder interest in his farmland to charity today, the donor generates an immediate income tax deduction. If the donor is age 59 and the AFR is 1%, this gift would create an immediate deduction of $80,479. Assuming the donor could use this deduction at the top federal tax rate, it would lower his tax bill by $32,869. Depending on the donor's health, this amount might purchase a $50,000 single premium life insurance policy. Other donors would be in different situations, but many would be roughly similar. If the AFR were higher, the deduction would be lower, but the cost of life insurance would also be lower. If the donor were older, the deduction would be greater, but so would the cost of life insurance. With charitable planning, the donor is able to make the gift to charity, but also provide a substantial inheritance to his heirs. Here, the tax benefits from charitable planning fund the entire replacement inheritance. A simple will with a gift to charity would leave nothing from this asset for heirs. Of course, if the estate would be subject to estate taxes and the donor purchased the life insurance through an ILIT, the heirs are that much better off. In that case, rather than netting $60,000 from inheriting a $100,000 piece of farmland, the heirs could receive $50,000 tax-free from life insurance. This difference would change over time depending upon the growth of the value of the farmland. This growth in asset value also points out that the same transaction could be structured without life insurance. A donor could transfer the value of the tax deduction as a gift to an irrevocable trust for the benefit of the heirs (still using "Crummey" powers). Through investment of these funds, $50,000 or more would be available for heirs *if* the donor lived to his life expectancy. The primary advantage of life insurance is that is removes the risk of an unexpectedly early death, guaranteeing the larger amount. Along with this, however, it also removes the potential benefit of an unexpectedly long life where the asset could have grown in value for several more years.

Ultimately, charitable planning can generate income and tax benefits that would not otherwise be available. The ILIT provides a mechanism to convert these additional income and tax benefits into estate tax-free wealth for heirs. The use of the benefits in this way can help to balance a donor's competing desires for charitable and family estate transfers.

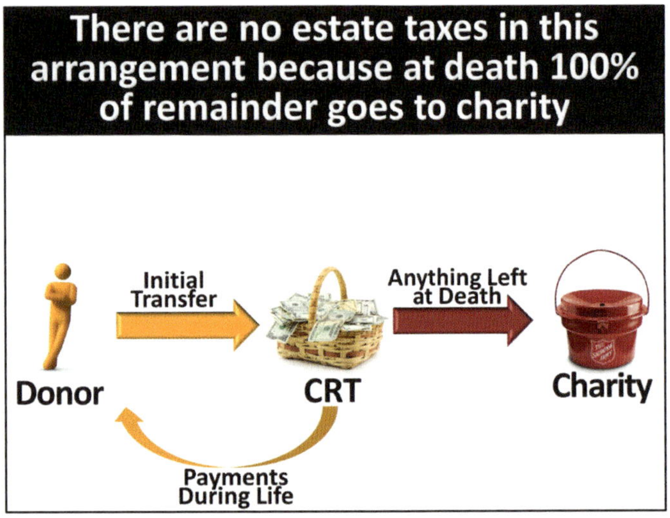

No gift or estate taxes result from the typical Charitable Remainder Trust arrangement. The donor receives an income for life and then at death any amount remaining in the trust goes to charity. Although the assets in the trust are included in the donor's estate, they generate no taxation because these assets go to charity. However, there are other Charitable Remainder Trust arrangements that can have different tax consequences.

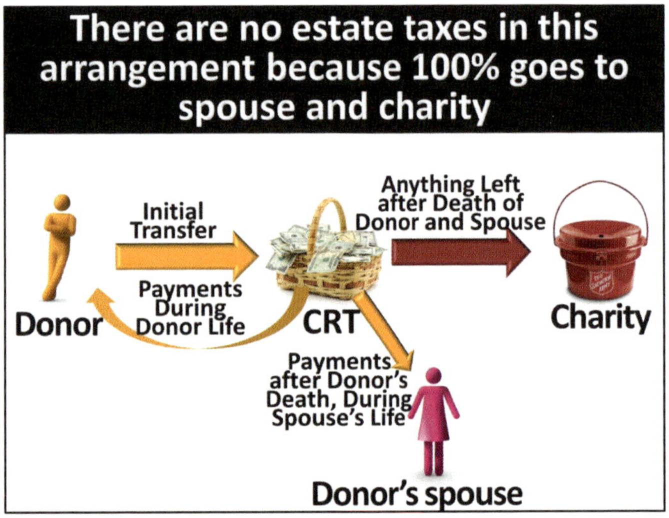

A donor may also establish a Charitable Remainder Trust that makes payments not only for the donor's life, but also for the life of the donor's spouse if the spouse outlives the donor. This is also a common arrangement for Charitable Remainder Trusts. It also generates no estate taxation because all interests go to the charity and the spouse, both of which are non-taxable recipients due to the unlimited marital and charitable estate tax deductions.

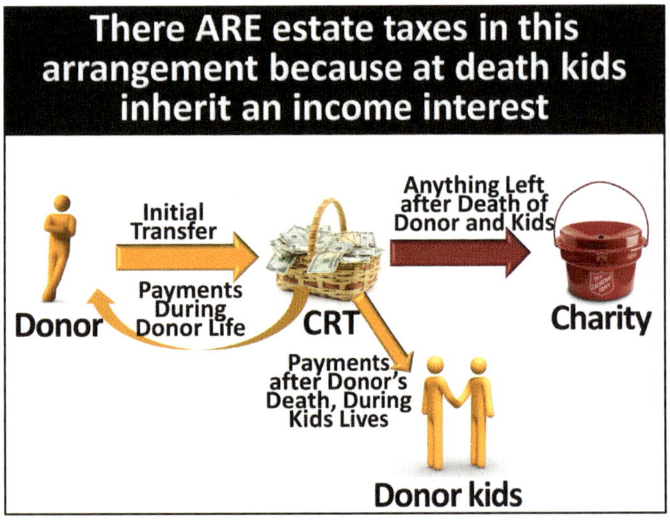

In contrast to the previous examples, if the donor chooses to make his children (or any other non-spouse) beneficiaries of the trust after his death this arrangement will generate estate taxation. At the donor's death, the estate must pay taxes on the present value of the children's annuity or unitrust interest. As before, the Charitable Remainder Trust assets are included in the donor's estate. However, in this case not all of those assets are going towards marital or charitable gifts. The children inherit this benefit and, consequently, it is subject to estate taxation.

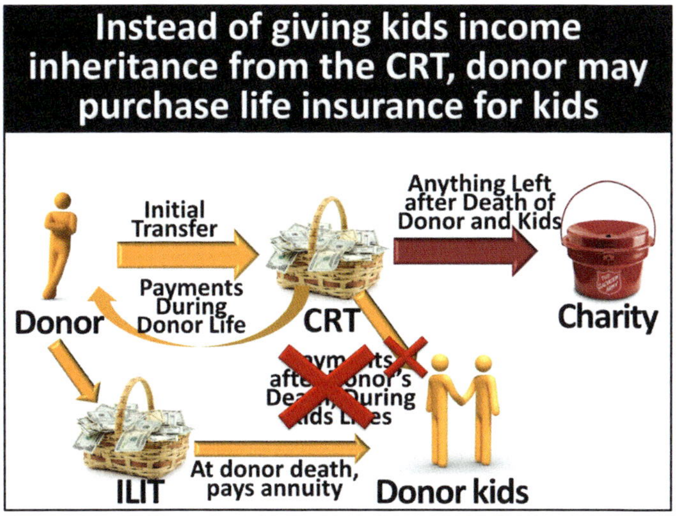

Because of the estate tax results from simply naming the children as secondary beneficiaries of the Charitable Remainder Trust, it may make sense to consider using an ILIT to accomplish the same purposes. In this case, the Charitable Remainder Trust provides no payments to the children. Instead, the ILIT purchases life insurance on the donor's life and then receives the death benefit at the donor's death. The ILIT then purchases annuities for the children that pay income to them for their lives. The net result to the children is the same – receipt of lifetime income. However, in the ILIT arrangement the value of the income interest is not subject to estate taxation.

.

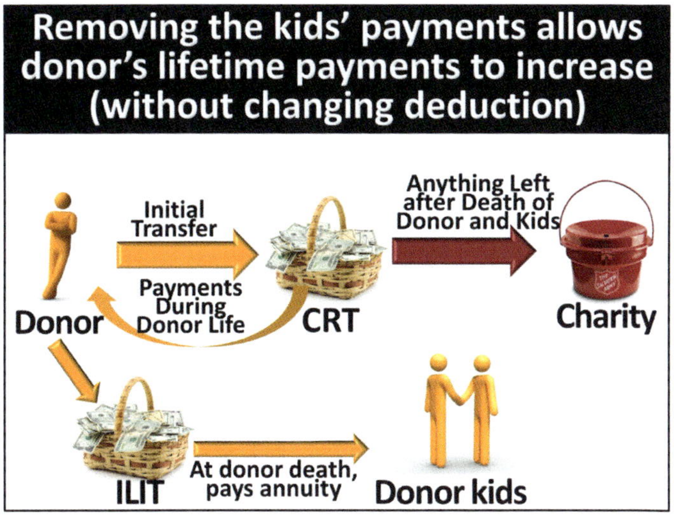

By removing the children as secondary beneficiaries of the Charitable Remainder Trust, the payments to the donor can substantially increase without altering either the tax deduction or the ultimate charitable gift. The amount of this increase in payments can pay premiums on ILIT-owned life insurance throughout the donor's life. This primary motivation for this substitution is to reduce estate taxes. However, if the donor's estate is not subject to estate taxation, then this substitution may be undesirable because the increased income during the donor's life will likely be subject to taxation (depending upon the tax characteristics of the underlying assets in the Charitable Remainder Trust). Donors should weigh the trade-off between income taxation and estate taxation in each case to find the most advantageous approach.

The previous examples presented a simplified process for using an ILIT. However, it can be helpful to understand a bit more about the different steps in creating and operating an ILIT and their potential consequences.

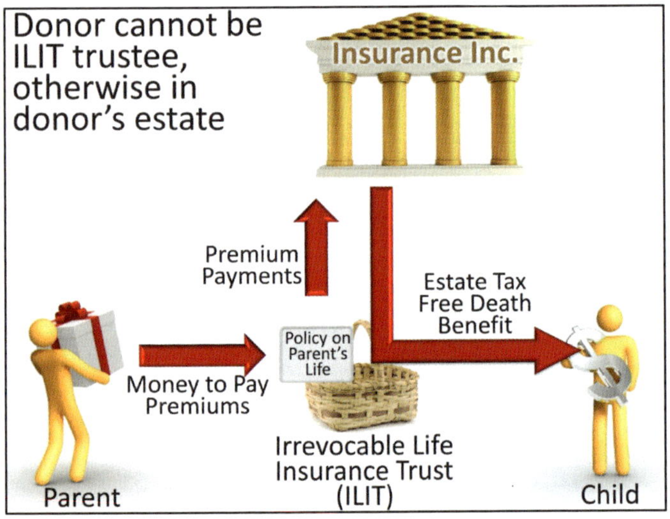

Although the donor can create the rules of the ILIT, even determining the exact wording of the trust document, the donor may not continue to directly control the assets in the ILIT once it is created. Thus, unlike, for example, a Charitable Remainder Trust, the donor may not continue to act as trustee of the ILIT. Doing so gives enough ongoing control to the donor that the ILIT will be included in the donor's estate which would eliminate the estate tax benefits.

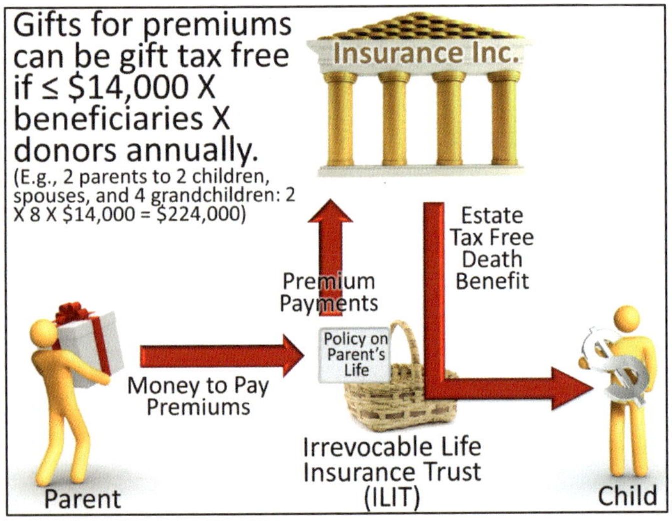

The amount a donor may transfer to another person without gift tax consequences is limited. Each year, a donor can make present interest gifts to other people up to this limit (e.g., $14,000 per donee in 2014) without any gift tax consequences. The amount applies to each donee and each donor. For example, a married couple with two married children each with two children of their own would have eight natural donees. Because both spouses have their own separate annual exclusions, this would allow the transfer of $224,000 (8x2x$14,000) each year without gift tax consequences.

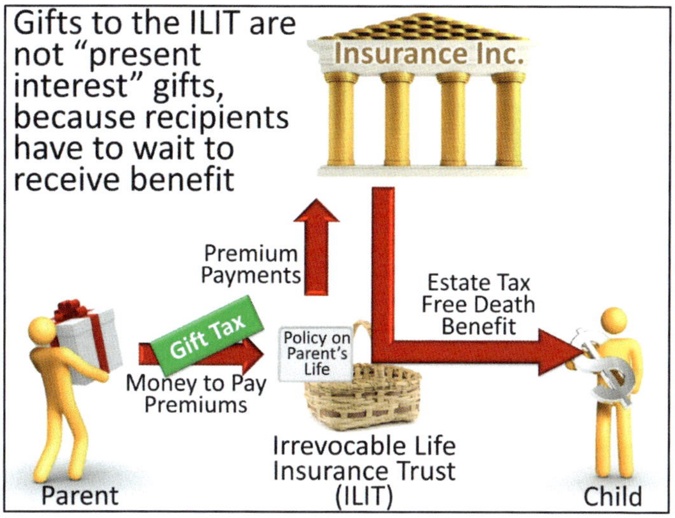

Unfortunately, direct gifts to an ILIT do not qualify for the annual present interest gift exclusion. Thus, direct transfers to the ILIT will have gift tax consequences. Specifically, any direct transfers will reduce the donor's available estate tax exemption. This would eliminate the benefit for the donor who ultimately gifted more dollars to pay premiums than the death benefit paid by the insurance policy. Every dollar of direct gifting to the ILIT will reduce the estate tax credit because gifts to the ILIT are not "present interest" gifts. Direct gifts to an ILIT do not qualify as "present interest" gifts because the beneficiaries of the ILIT do not receive any funds until sometime in the future. One extra step is required to avoid this bad result.

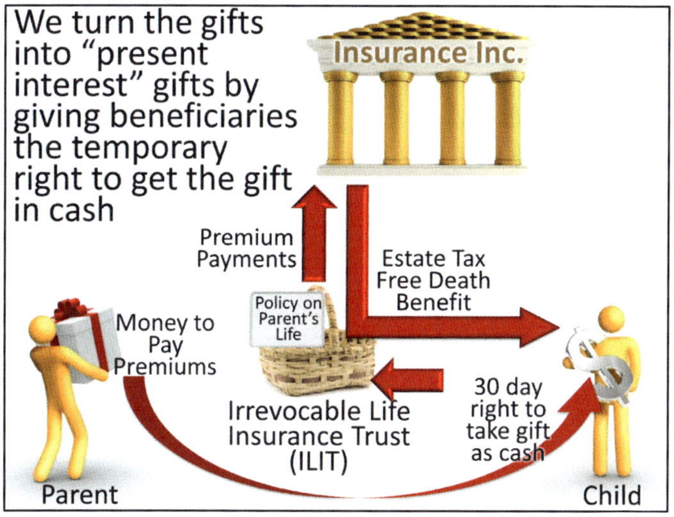

Instead of making transfers directly to the ILIT, the donor makes transfers to the ILIT but with the provision that some individuals (such as the donor's children) have, and are notified in writing of, a 30 day right to take the transfer as an immediate cash gift to them. Because the beneficiaries have a right to take the gift immediately as a cash gift, the gift from the donor becomes a "present interest" gift. This "present interest" gift then qualifies for the gift tax annual exclusion. For example, in 2014, each donee could receive a right to claim up to $14,000 of the transfer from each donor as immediate cash. This $14,000 transfer would generate no gift or estate tax consequences for the donor. The appellate court case that authorized this type of temporary power as a way to claim the present interest gift tax exclusion involved a taxpayer by the name of Crummey. Hence, these are known as "Crummey" powers.

The assumption in this planning is that the recipient of the Crummey powers will not take advantage of their right to an immediate cash withdrawal and will instead allow the money to go to the ILIT. Otherwise, the tax advantages of the planning process would be defeated. This is one reason why such rights are typically given in a family situation where the donor has sufficient influence over the recipient to prevent the cash withdraws.

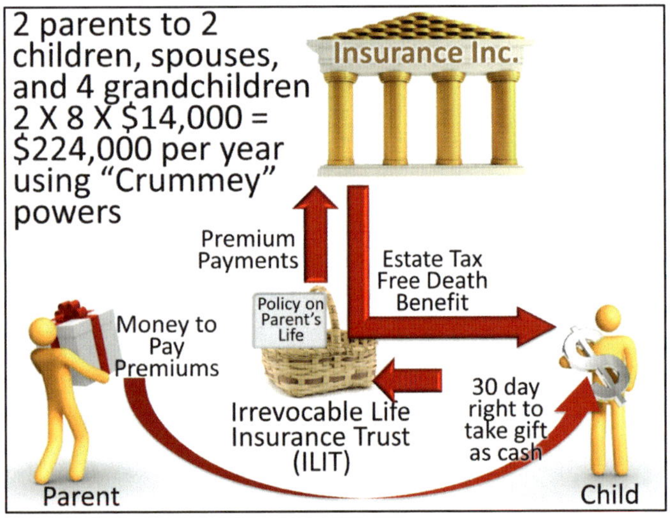

Although the present interest annual gift tax exclusion is relatively small (e.g., $14,000 in 2014), these can be used for every donor and every donee. When combined together for a larger number of donees, these add up to substantial annual transfers. For example if a married couple were making transfers with "Crummey" powers given to their two children, the children's two spouses, and four grandchildren, this would allow for the use of 8 separate annual present interest gift tax exclusions for each donor spouse (e.g., $14,000 X 8 X 2, or $224,000).

When this much money is used for premium payments, it can purchase a significant amount of life insurance – especially for younger and healthier donors. The annual present interest gift tax exclusion is also indexed for inflation (although changes occur only in $1,000 increments), allowing for potential funding increases over time.

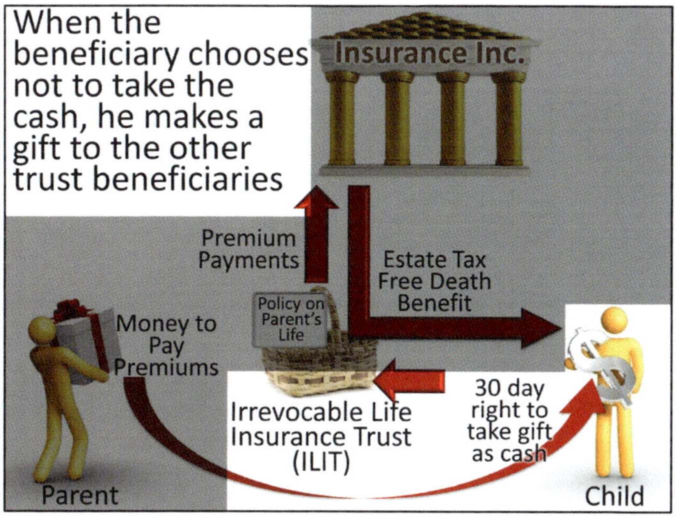

The use of "Crummey" powers solves one problem by converting the transfers into "present interest" gifts for the donors. At the same time, it creates a new problem. The new problem is that when the holder of the "Crummey" power chooses *not* to use his or her rights, he, in effect, makes a gift to the beneficiaries of the ILIT. If the power holder were the only beneficiary of the ILIT, then this would not be a problem. No gift would have occurred because the ILIT would benefit no one other than the "Crummey" power holder. But, the typical ILIT has more than one beneficiary. This means that failing to exercise the right to immediately withdraw the money results in a gift benefitting others. Once again, the same problem arises here, because the gift to the other ILIT beneficiaries is not a present interest gift. (As before, these beneficiaries must wait until the death of the insured to receive benefits from the expired withdrawal rights.) Because the choice not to use these powers is not a present interest gift, the annual present interest gift tax exclusion will not apply, causing the gift to reduce the "Crummey" power holder's gift and estate tax exemption.

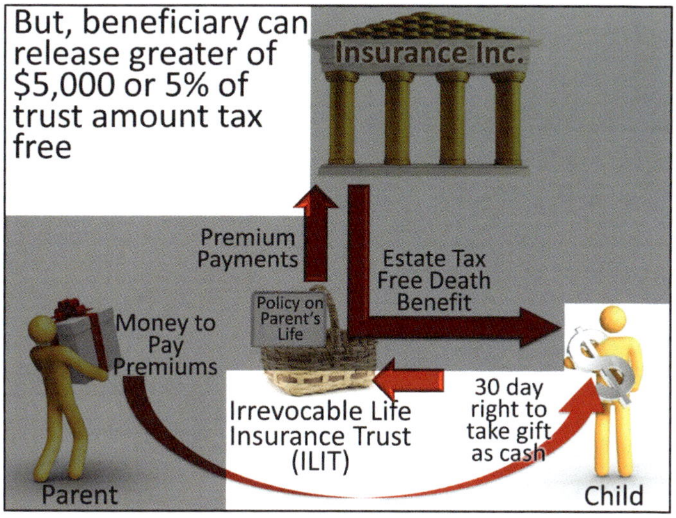

However, the beneficiary may release this type of power up to the greater of 5% or $5,000 each year without gift or estate tax consequences. This does not normally allow for the release of the full annual present interest gift tax exclusion ($5,000 is less than $14,000). One approach is to allow the beneficiaries' gift and estate tax exemption to absorb the difference, thus dispersing and postponing the tax effects to the next generation. There is also another potential alternative.

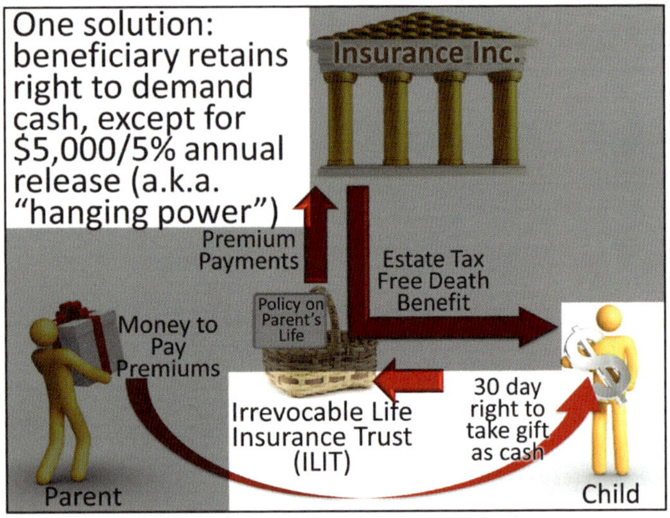

The "Crummey" powers may allow each beneficiary to keep the right to demand his or her share of the cash transferred to the ILIT indefinitely, with this right expiring only at the rate of the greater of $5,000 or 5% of the value of the ILIT per year. This type of provision is called a "hanging power" because the recipient hangs on to the right to demand the cash for a long time. With this drafting, the beneficiary never gives up more than the gift-tax-free amount of his or her right to receive cash (i.e., $5,000 or 5% of trust assets), preventing the beneficiary from making a taxable non-present-interest gift to the ILIT.

The use of hanging powers prevents the beneficiary from using up her own gift and estate tax exclusion amount, but can create problems of its own. The ability of the "5 and 5" powers to eliminate the accumulation of such hanging powers is limited. In fact, each beneficiary can use only one "5 and 5" exemption each year, regardless of how many ILITs or other trusts for which they have such powers. Over time, these hanging powers can continue to accumulate, meaning that the beneficiary has an increasingly large right to receive immediate cash. Creditors could take this right, and the beneficiary's estate will include any unexpired rights for estate tax purposes. Eventually, the "5 and 5" powers can begin to reduce the total hanging powers if, for example, "Crummey" gifts cease to be made. This could occur if the life insurance policy becomes fully-funded at some future point. Additionally, after the death of the insured, the ILIT will hold the entire death benefit. At this point, 5% of the trust assets may be worth far more than $5,000. Because the greater of these two amounts can be lapsed, this would allow for a rapid reduction in the total hanging powers for as long as the ILIT holds such substantial assets.

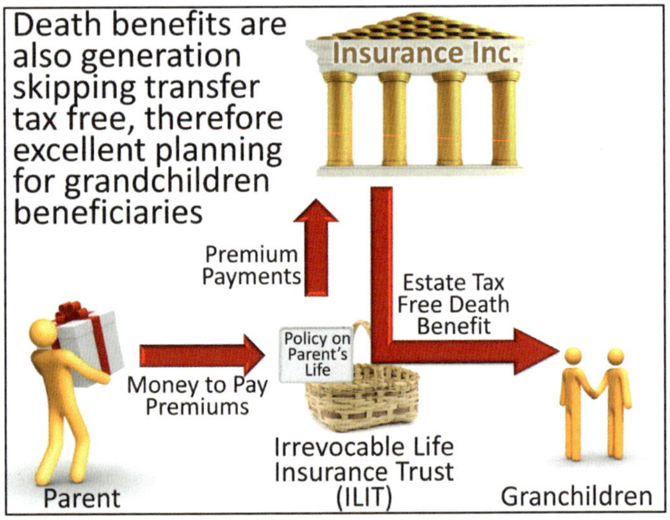

Because the donor does not own the life insurance, it is not included in the donor's estate. This not only avoids estate taxation on the death benefit, but also avoids generation skipping transfer taxation. A generation skipping transfer tax can apply when the donor makes a gift (or estate transfer) to a "skip person," such as a grandchild. A skip person is anyone two or more generations below the donor. However, if the skip person's parent (who is also the donor's descendent) has died, the skip person is treated as being one generation older. Transfers to such skip persons are subject to a generation skipping transfer tax of 40% *in addition to* the estate tax of 40%. The theory here is that normally, every generation must pay estate taxes on its transfer to the next generation. Giving wealth to a grandchild or great-grandchild "skips" out on taxation that would have been collected at the death of the previous generation. There is an exemption for generation skipping transfers, which is the same size as the estate tax exemption amount. For those transferring more than this exemption amount the potential application of both the 40% estate or gift tax and the 40% generation skipping transfer tax is disturbing. (Because the 40%

generation skipping transfer tax is applied to the amount left *after* payment of estate tax, the net result is a combined tax rate of 64%, rather than 80%.) By removing the life insurance from the donor's estate, the ILIT avoids both the estate tax and the generation skipping transfer tax.

Charitable giving with a life insurance policy can be simple. The owner of a life insurance policy can just name a charity as the beneficiary of the policy. At the death of the insured, the charity will receive a check for the death benefit. Although this transfer generates no estate taxation, it also – like other revocable gifts taking effect at death – generates no charitable income tax deduction. In order to generate a charitable income tax deduction, the donor must make a completed gift during life. Giving a policy to charity may constitute a substantial charitable gift, especially where the life insurance policy combines a death benefit (i.e., simple term insurance) with investment features. These policies can become valuable assets over time. Such policies may be particularly attractive candidates for donation when the original purpose for the life insurance no longer applies. Despite this attractiveness, the rules for tax deductions, the policies themselves, and the proper post-gift management of the policies by the charity can be complicated.

Life insurance can address needs in a variety of circumstances. As circumstances change, the original need for the life insurance may disappear. This lack of need for an existing policy is a common motivation for a donor's decision to donate the policy to charity. A donor may have purchased life insurance to replace his or her income in the event of death as a way to protect his or her minor children. Once the children are grown and independent, the original need for the policy no longer exists. An insurance policy may have been purchased for a business buy-sell agreement. For example, two partners in a business partnership may agree that at the death of one of them, the other will purchase the deceased partner's ownership for an agreed price. Each partner purchases life insurance on the life of the other so that, in the event of one partner's death, the surviving partner will have the cash to purchase the deceased partner's interest. This provides cash for the heirs and prevents the difficulties inherent in sharing forced ownership in an operating business with a group of heirs unfamiliar with the business. However, if the business relationship changes – perhaps due to the business closing or being sold – the need for the life insurance also changes. These are just two examples of the variety of ways in which a policy owner may find that he or she has too much life insurance for current needs. If, in combination with this lack of need for death benefits, the owner also wishes to forego the cash value of the policy in order to benefit charity, a gift of the life insurance policy may make sense.

When a donor gives a life insurance policy to charity it is important that the donor give up all rights to and benefits from the policy. This means, for example, that the donor may not keep any rights to change beneficiaries, surrender, assign or cancel the policy, pledge the policy for a loan, make withdrawals or loans from the cash surrender value, or hold any other reversionary interests. Attempting to retain any rights will result in no completed gift. This also extends to prohibit keeping indirect benefits for the donor, the donor's family, or anyone else designated by the donor. Not only does keeping some rights mean there is no charitable income tax deduction, but it also means that the life insurance policy will still be included in the donor's estate, and thus subject to estate taxation. Further, any additional premiums paid by the donor would not generate deductible gifts.

If the donor were to cash in a life insurance policy, any income generated would be treated as ordinary income, rather than as a capital gain. The donation of an ordinary income property item is valued at the *lower* of fair market value or the donor's basis. (In contrast, some long-term capital gain property items can be valued at fair market value, even when such value is higher than basis.) However, determining fair market value and even basis in a life insurance policy can be challenging.

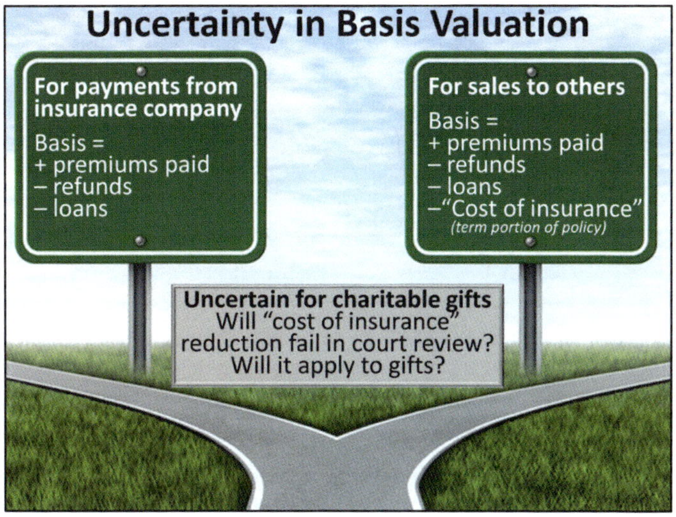

What is the basis in a life insurance policy gifted to charity? This is currently an unsettled question. Basis clearly includes all premiums paid for the policy. Clearly, any refunds or loans taken from the policy will reduce the basis. The uncertainty surrounds the issue of whether or not the basis should be reduced by the "cost of insurance." The IRS argument for considering "cost of insurance" is that the policy owner has invested premiums, but in return has received the advantage of coverage in the event of death. Thus, because the owner has already received this "peace of mind" benefit, his or her basis should be reduced by the value of this benefit. This value received is what it would have cost the owner to purchase just the death benefit itself (i.e., the term policy) from the company.

At present, it is clear that the basis is *not* reduced for this "cost of insurance" (a.k.a. "mortality charges") when money is received from the insurance company, e.g., through withdrawals, distributions, or surrendering the policy for cash value. (This is specified by statute in Internal Revenue Code §72.) The IRS has taken the, somewhat controversial, position that basis *is* reduced by this "cost of insurance" when a policy owner *sells* the policy to someone else (Rev. Rul. 2009-13 & 2009-14). There are no IRS examples specifically for calculating basis for a charitable deduction from a gift of a life insurance policy. However, charitable gifts to third parties, just like sales to third parties, are not covered by Internal Revenue Code §72, which addresses only payments coming back from the insurance company. It seems unlikely that calculating basis as reduced by the "cost of insurance" would apply to sales of policies, but not gifts of policies. (Such inconsistency would certainly lead to an interesting calculation in the case of a bargain sale to charity.) The most likely IRS position – absent any actual information at this point – appears to be that the basis rule for sales would also be the basis rule for gifts.

There is some question whether or not the courts will support this IRS position. Why? There is no statute directing this approach and this approach is not used in other contexts. For example, if a taxpayer buys a car for $25,000 and sells it a year later for $25,000 she does not report a gain of $5,000 because it would have cost her $5,000 to rent a similar car for a year and she was able to enjoy the benefits of the car while she owned it. The decision regarding whether or not to reduce the basis in a gift by the "cost of insurance" depends upon how aggressive the taxpayer wishes to be in this area of uncertainty.

For a taxpayer who wishes to reduce basis by the "cost of insurance," determining this number may be a challenge. Universal life policies typically report the "cost of insurance" component to policyholders, making this number easily accessible. For term insurance, the "cost of insurance" is simply the premium. However, for traditional whole life policies, the "cost of insurance" may not be reported or easily determined. Death benefit coverage expenses can vary depending upon the age and health of the insured, interest rates, and the quality and rating of the company issuing the policy. Consequently, determining what portion of a whole life policy represents "cost of insurance" can be complex.

Determining the fair market value of a gifted policy can also be a complicated procedure. Of course, all property gifts of $5,000 or more require a qualified appraisal. Consequently, the donor will not be the one to determine this valuation. For a newly issued policy, the valuation can be determined by the premium paid for the policy. For a paid-up policy (i.e., one in which no further premiums need be paid to keep the life insurance in force), the cost of a replacement policy for an insured of that age can be used as a basis for estimating fair market value. Most policies, however, are neither newly issued nor paid-up. For these policies where premiums payments are still required, valuation can be quite complex. The approved valuation methods often approximate the cash surrender value of the policy. A donor can use the greater of valuation allowed by the ITR or PERC methods. The ITR method is based on the "Interpolated Terminal Reserve" plus any unearned premiums and a pro rata share of estimated dividends to be paid for the year. There are, in fact, multiple possible methods to calculate the "Interpolated Terminal Reserve," but the life insurance company will typically provide their estimation of this number to the policy holder. However, this number – and, hence, this valuation approach – is not available for universal life or variable life policies. An alternative valuation is to use the PERC method. PERC comes from Premiums plus Earnings from the policy (such as interest, dividends, and withdrawals) minus Reasonable Charges (such as mortality charges). The PERC number is often roughly equal to the cash value for universal life policies. This PERC number is then multiplied by an "Average Surrender Factor," approximating the charge incurred in surrendering the policy for its cash value.

These traditional valuation approaches do not apply in cases where they are not an appropriate estimation of the value of a life insurance policy. This occurs when the insured has a terminal illness. IRS gift tax regulations specifically prohibit using standard valuation approaches when the insured has a terminal illness. In such cases, the "life settlement" market may provide a more appropriate, and much higher, valuation. This market purchases life insurance policies on the lives of terminally ill individuals. These policies are more valuable because the risk of death, and thus the likelihood of receiving the death benefit in the near future, is dramatically higher than for a typical insured. These valuations, however, can be more costly to obtain given the requirement to evaluate the health of a terminally ill individual.

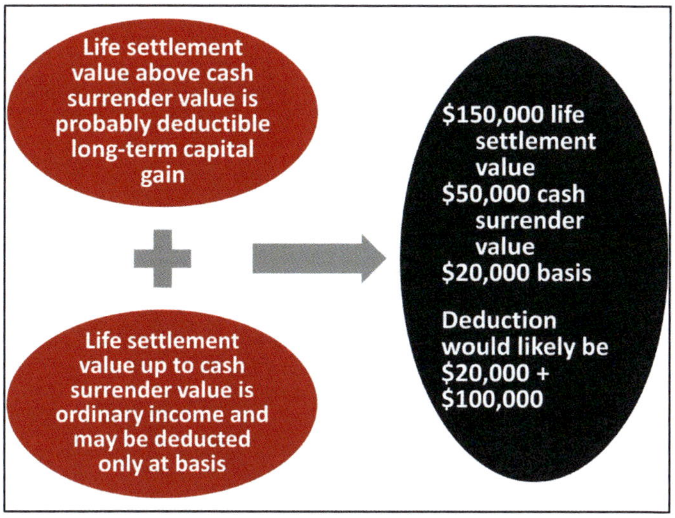

Valuing a donated policy based upon its higher value in the life settlement market creates a more complex calculation for the charitable income tax deduction. As mentioned previously, the typical tax treatment for a donated life insurance policy is to deduct the lesser of basis or fair market value. This is because if the donor were to cash in a life insurance policy, any income generated would be treated as ordinary income rather than capital gain. Ordinary income property is deducted at the lower of basis or fair market value. This picture becomes more complex when selling a policy in the life settlement market. In that case, the value received up to the cash surrender value would generate ordinary income, but the value above cash surrender value would generate capital gain income. (This capital gain treatment is the most likely result although this is not settled law.) This means the life insurance policy is in part ordinary income property and in part long-term capital gain property. The gift of the ordinary income portion of the life insurance policy (i.e., the amount up to the policy's cash surrender value) is valued at the lower of basis or fair market value. However, the gift of any long-term capital gain portion of the life insurance policy (i.e., the amount above the policy's cash surrender value) is valued at the *greater* of basis or fair market value. This leads to different treatment depending on the relative value of the basis, the cash surrender value, and the life settlement value. Consider the example of a policy with a $150,000 value in the life settlement market, a $50,000 cash surrender value, and a $20,000 basis. Gifting this policy would generate a $20,000 deduction for the ordinary income part (i.e., the part represented by the cash surrender value of the policy), and a $100,000 deduction for the long-term capital gain part (i.e., the part represented by the value over and above the cash surrender value). This, of course, assumes that the donor has not made a special election to value all long-term capital gain gifts during the year at the lower of basis and fair market value. If the life settlement value were not greater than the basis, then the gift would be valued at the lower of its fair market value or basis as with a typical policy. For example, if the basis was $200,000, the cash surrender value was $50,000, and the life settlement value was $150,000, then the deduction would be $150,000 (the lower of basis or fair market value). If the life settlement was lower than the cash value, then the life settlement value would be irrelevant and the policy would be valued as normal.

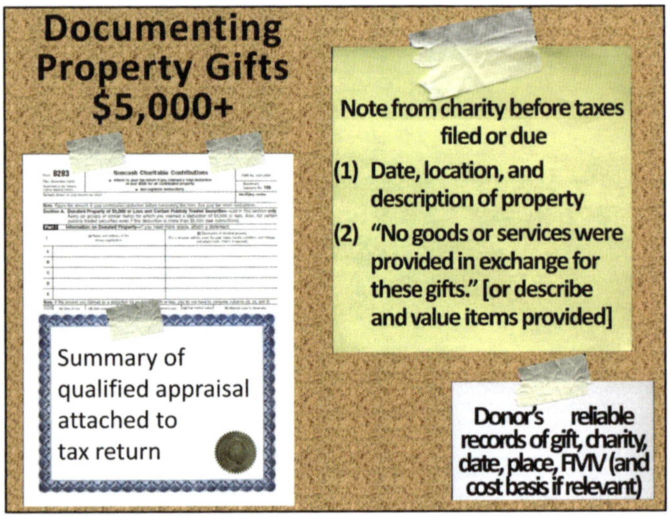

As with all charitable property gifts of $5,000 or more, documenting the life insurance policy gift of this size will require a qualified appraisal. In addition, the donor must complete IRS Form 8283, have reliable records of the gift, date, place, fair market value, and cost basis, and receive a note from the charity indicating the date of the gift with a description of the property and the magic phrase, "No goods or services were provided in exchange for these gifts."

The required appraisal for documenting the charitable gift of a life insurance policy cannot come from the insurance agent or the insurance company. They are parties to the transaction and are therefore disqualified. Consequently, gifting a substantial life insurance policy will require the employment of a qualified outside appraiser. Without such appraisal, the IRS will allow no deduction.

The typical result for donating property with an outstanding loan is that the donor is treated as having received income in the amount of the loan and having made a charitable gift of the remaining value of the property. The first part of this typical result still holds in the case of life insurance. The donor is treated as having received ordinary income in the amount of the loan, reduced by the applicable basis. The applicable basis is the amount of the loan multiplied by the ratio of the policy basis to the policy fair market value. For example, if a donor gifts a policy with a $100,000 fair market value, a $50,000 basis, and $10,000 of existing loans, the transaction will generate $5,000 of ordinary income for the donor ($10,000 loan x ($50,000 basis/$100,000 fair market value)).

However, because of special rules put in place to eliminate charitable split dollar transactions, the presence of a loan eliminates the tax deduction. Thus, as the result of gifting a policy with outstanding loans the donor receives no charitable income tax deduction, but still reports ordinary income.

The bottom line is that gifting policies subject to loans is an unwise approach. It would be better for the donor to pay off the loan first. Then, the donor can gift the policy without loss of the charitable deduction due to the charitable split interest rules. If this is not possible, then the donor may be better off to sell or cash in the policy, pay taxes on the gain, and then make an offsetting deductible charitable gift with the proceeds. At a minimum, it is likely that there will be more tax advantageous assets for the donor to consider gifting instead of a life insurance policy with outstanding loans.

Upon receiving the policy, the charity may do anything with it that any other policy owner could do. This includes surrendering the policy for its cash value, holding the policy until the death of the donor (if the policy is not paid up this will require the payment of premiums either by the charity or, if available, by the original donor), or selling the policy in the life settlement market. Selling the policy in the life settlement market is rare because such markets require extraordinarily high rates of returns for investors. Thus, if the charity is not in a desperate financial position, it is more appropriate for the charity to hold the policy and collect the death benefit. Charities sometimes have an inappropriate tendency to automatically cash out any life insurance policies received, rather than considering the possibility of continuing to hold the policy until the death of the donor. In many cases, the cash surrender value is well below the actuarial value of the policy. By automatically taking the cash surrender value of policies, charities may often be making poor financial choices as compared with continuing to hold the policy, even if holding the policy may require payment of additional premiums. Rather than immediately taking the cash surrender value, it would be more appropriate for charities to work with a life insurance professional to consider the relative financial value of continuing to hold the policy.

A donor may gift an annuity contract to a charity, but such gifts are usually not tax advantageous. Gifting an annuity contract will cause all gain in the contract to be immediately taxed to the donor as ordinary income. In contrast, continuing to hold the annuity, would allow the annuity owner to recognize that income over many years, rather than immediately. The donor may offset this immediate recognition of gain by the charitable deduction for the value the annuity contract (except for annuity contracts issued before April 23, 1987 that have not yet matured where the deduction is limited to the donor's basis in the contract). However, an alternative source for a charitable gift will often be more tax appropriate. For example, gifts of long-term capital gain will generate no recognition of taxable gain. Even gifts from cash may be better if they prevent the immediate recognition of gain resulting from giving an annuity contract. Gifting an annuity at death does not create these same income tax problems, although this requires an annuity that still has value after the death of the donor.

A third use of life insurance in charitable planning is to create a new policy specifically intended to benefit the charity at the death of the donor. In this way, the donor may provide for a large posthumous charitable gift, perhaps funding a significant charitable project. Without the use of life insurance, a donor could fund such a posthumous gift by simply saving up money in a donor advised fund and leaving it at death to the charity. However, this plan would fail if the donor did not live long enough to allow him or her to build up enough savings to fund the gift. The use of life insurance eliminates this risk. Through life insurance, the donor can guarantee that the project will be funded, even if he or she does not live long enough to fund the project through the normal means of savings or regular donations.

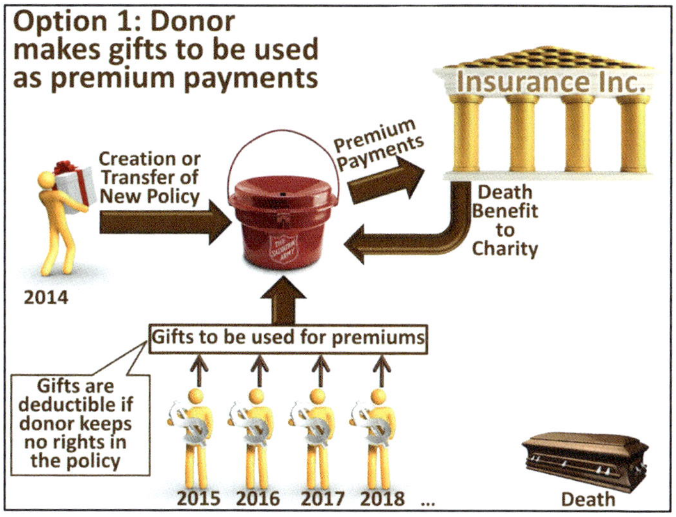

A donor could achieve the transfer of a large charitable gift at death by simply purchasing and owning a life insurance policy and naming the charity as the beneficiary of the policy. However, this approach would generate no charitable income tax deduction. No deduction is allowed in part because the donor could, at any time, change the name of the beneficiary to someone else. In order to generate a tax deduction, the donor must first donate the policy to the charity. Once the charity owns the policy, then the donor could continue to fund the premium payments by making gifts to the charity for that purpose. Although the donor does not retain a legal right to force the charity to use the gifts for premium payments, this is rarely needed as the threat of stopping future giving is usually sufficient to cause the charity to following the donor's preferences. In order for the transfer of the policy (and any subsequent payments of gifts to be used for premium payments) to generate a charitable gift, the donor must give up all rights to the policy as well as any direct or indirect benefits from the policy.

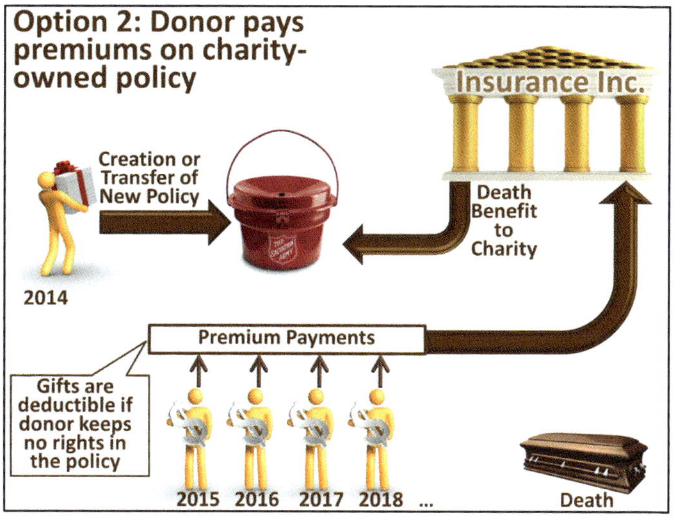

In an alternative arrangement, the donor may gift the policy to the charity (or the charity may create the policy) and then the donor can make premium payments directly to the insurance company. These premium payments are deductible gifts, assuming that the charity owns all rights to the policy. Some charities and insurance agents may prefer this arrangement as it could allow the insurance company to send premium notices directly to the donor, rather than burdening the fundraising staff with continued requests. There are, however, some differences in the treatment of premium payments made directly to the life insurance company and those made to charity.

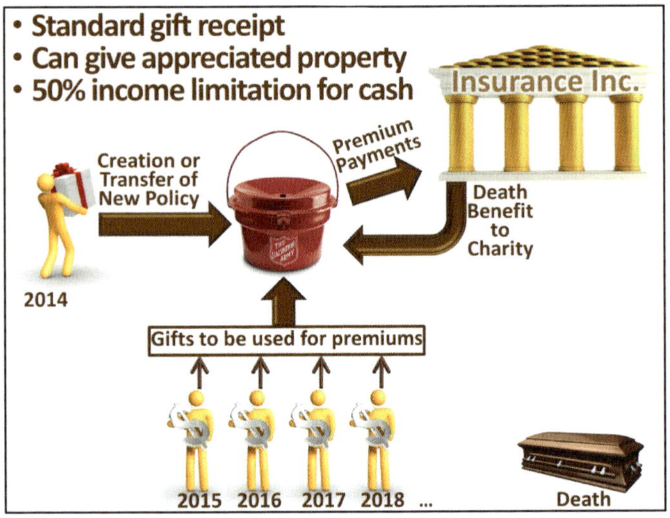

Gifts made directly to the charity for the purpose of funding premium payments are treated as any other gifts made to charity. The charity will issue receipts for the gifts just as with any other gift. Assuming that the donor is making cash gifts to a public charity, these are deductible up to 50% of the donor's adjusted gross income, just as with any other cash gift. The donor could give cash, but could also give appreciated property, which the charity could then sell in order to generate the cash needed to make premium payments. Giving appreciated property may provide the added benefit to the donor of avoiding long-term capital gain taxation.

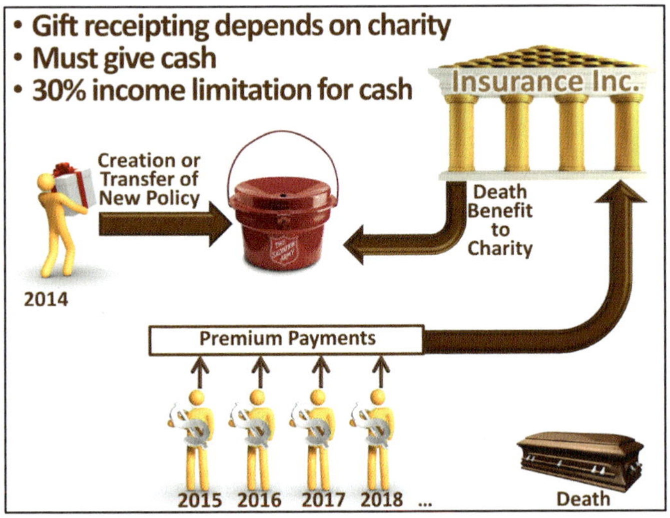

When the donor makes premium payments directly to the life insurance company, the results may differ slightly. Some charities will issue receipts for premium payments made directly to a charity owned life insurance policy, but some may not. Insurance companies will not accept appreciated property for premium payments, so the donor must use cash transfers. Finally, deductions for such transfers to life insurance companies may be limited to 30% of the donor's adjusted gross income, even where the policy owner is a public charity. This is based upon the idea that the cash is not being provide "to" the charity (which results in a 50% income limitation), but instead is being provided "for the use of" the charity (which results in a 30% income limitation). Some recent cases suggest the possibility of applying the 50% limitation to these transactions as well, but that issue is not currently settled.

Encouraging donors to create and pay premiums on charity owned life insurance policies comes with both potential advantages and potential problems for the charity. Thus, it does not make sense for charities to either universally accept or universally reject this approach. Instead, it is useful to consider the specifics of each scenario and the relevant needs of the donor and charity.

One potentially attractive feature of using life insurance is that donors of relatively modest means can fund large posthumous projects. For example, a healthy 40 year old donor might be able to purchase a $1,000,000 life insurance policy for premium payments of only $1,500 per year for the first 30 years of coverage (with premiums rising thereafter). Or, the donor could pay $20,000 for only 20 years, with no additional payments due after that point. Thus, a donor who would never anticipate the ability to make a $1,000,000 gift to the charity could fund that gift by using life insurance.

It is important to note, however, that unless the donor dies earlier than expected, the use of life insurance does *not* generate a larger gift than would have been possible by simply gifting the premium payment amounts to the charity and allowing them to grow until the death of the donor. The use of life insurance only provides protection against the early death of a donor who had otherwise intended to save or give enough to fund a large project. Further, the apparent ability of life insurance to generate a "big" gift may also rely on the natural misperception of future values. For a typical 40 year old donor, a $1,000,000 gift is a big gift. But, that donor is likely to live for approximately 40 years. If future inflation is similar to the past, then the future $1,000,000 gift received in 40 years will have the same purchasing power as a $190,000 gift today. Waiting 40 years to receive $190,000 of purchasing power in today's dollars does not feel quite as impressive as the large $1,000,000 figure. Additionally, recent evidence suggests that donors with planned posthumous gifts to charity live longer than others (see James, R. N., III (2013) *American Charitable Bequest Demographics*), meaning that the charity will have to wait even longer than normal to receive a death benefit from donors.

Some charities like the idea that subsequent gifts occur without ongoing fundraising efforts from the charity. For example, where the donor is making premium payments directly to the insurance company, the bill may come directly from the insurance company, and the donor may pay this as a matter of course along with other bills.

Because the use of life insurance typically involves the employment of insurance agents, these transactions create a natural sales force interested in proposing these planned giving transactions to clients. The proposition of having an agent advocating for the charity without the costs associated with hiring a traditional fundraiser may be attractive to charities. Having such a "free" sales force may be especially interesting to charities with limited resources to hire and train their own fundraising staff. In an ideal situation, both the charity and agent can benefit from these potentially symbiotic relationships.

There are, of course, potential downsides to the inability of charities to control or manage those who are proposing charitable transactions. The charity that gives access to its donor base may risk negative reactions from donors, depending upon the characteristics of the selling agent. The agent may focus primarily on making an immediate sale, whereas the charity may be hoping to foster a long-term relationship. Further, the agent may have little downside risk in offending those who are not interested in purchasing the product, whereas the charity may suffer long-term financial effects from damaged relationships with supporting donors.

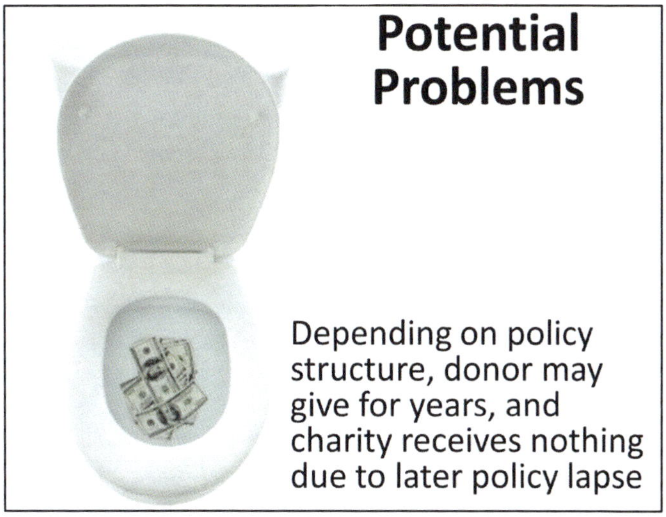

Another potential problem is the risk that donors will cease providing premiums for the insurance policies. Depending on the type of insurance, keeping the death benefit may require paying premiums for 10, 20, or 30 years or for the rest of the donor's life. It is difficult enough to maintain donor giving from one year to the next – the likelihood that a donor will be consistently committed over many decades or a lifetime is even smaller. For policies that do not reach "paid up" status, there is also a risk of lapse in advancing age. Often health or cognitive problems arise prior to death and these may increase the risk of financial oversight, such as failing to pay policy premiums. Further, such conditions also increase the likelihood that other family members may take over financial management. They may be less likely to have any commitment to the charity. Taken together, these factors reduce the likelihood that the premium payments will continue indefinitely and, thus, that the charity will ultimately receive any benefit.

Another risk in using life insurance is that the structure of the policy may, ultimately, provide more benefit to the insurance companies and insurance agents than to the charity. This is especially true where the risk for later lapse of the policy is high and such lapse would result in the charity receiving no death benefit. Thus, the donor may be regularly committing funds strictly for charitable purposes, but ultimately providing little or no benefit for charity. This does not mean that such gifting arrangements are inherently disadvantageous to charity, only that careful examination is appropriate.

An additional potential problem relates to the requirement of insurable interest. Taking out a life insurance policy on the life of another requires that the policy owner have an insurable interest in the insured. In other words, you cannot take out a life insurance policy on someone, just because you think the person will die soon. Allowing such speculation could even create financial incentives for murder. Thus, taking out a life insurance policy on another person normally requires some family or business relationship providing a reason for hedging against the personal or financial loss that would occur in the event of the death of the insured. If a charity takes out a life insurance policy on a major donor, with the goal of protecting against the loss of income that might occur in the event of the death of the donor, then the charity likely has a valid insurable interest. However, if the person had never been a donor, or perhaps had made only a few $20 gifts and the charity then takes out a $10,000,000 policy on the life of the donor – there may be serious questions about the presence of an insurable interest. Fortunately, almost all states have settled this matter by legislation. In these states, charity is granted an explicit insurable interest in any person (or in some cases any donor) who consents to becoming an insured life. To give you a feel for the specific requirements in your state, below are excerpts from different state statutes related to this topic (please check for any changes or other issues with local counsel before engaging in a transaction)

ALABAMA CODE § 27-14-3

Any provision of this section and chapter to the contrary notwithstanding, a charitable organization that meets the requirements of Section 501(c)(3) of the Internal Revenue Code of 1986, as amended, may own or purchase life insurance on an individual who consents to the ownership of purchase of that insurance.

ALASKA STAT. § 21.42.020

Notwithstanding the other provisions of this section, a charitable organization may obtain, by procurement, assignment, or otherwise, life or health insurance on an insured who consents to the issuance of the insurance.

ARIZONA REV. STAT. ANN. § 20-1104

A charitable organization as provided in section 43-1201, paragraph 4, which has a policy ownership interest has an insurable interest in the life of each proposed insured who joins with the charitable organization in applying for a life insurance policy naming the charitable organization as owner and irrevocable beneficiary.

ARKANSAS CODE ANN. § 23-79-103

Notwithstanding any other law or regulation to the contrary, any religious, educational, charitable, or benevolent institution, organization, corporation, association, or trust, including, but not limited to, Charitable Remainder Trusts, may be named beneficiary or owner, or both, of the policy or contract by any applicant for insurance upon his or her own life in any policy of life insurance issued by any life insurance company authorized to do business in this state or in the state of domicile of the applicant for insurance.

CALIFORNIA INS. CODE § 10110.1(f)

a charitable organization that meets the requirements of Section 214 or 23701d of the Revenue and Taxation Code may effectuate life or disability insurance on an insured who consents to the issuance of that insurance

COLORADO. REV. STAT. § 10-7-115

Notwithstanding any other provision of law, any organization that meets the requirements of section 170 (c) of the federal "Internal Revenue Code of 1986", as amended, may own or purchase life insurance on an insured who gives written consent to the ownership or purchase of that insurance.

CONNECTICUT GEN. STAT. § 38a-450

Any life insurance company doing business within the state may issue policies of insurance predicated upon the life or lives of any person or persons, payable at maturity to any educational, ecclesiastical, benevolent, charitable or eleemosynary corporation which can legally take and receive testamentary legacies, irrespective of a financial interest on the part of such corporation in the life of the person or persons insured.

DELEWARE CODE ANN. tit. 18, § 2705

Life insurance contracts may be entered into in which the person paying the consideration for the insurance has no insurable interest in the life of the individual insured, where charitable, benevolent, educational or religious institutions, or their agencies, are designated irrevocably as the beneficiaries thereof

D.C. CODE ANN. § 31-4716

A charitable, benevolent, educational, governmental, or religious institution that is described in § 501(c)(3) or § 170(b)(1)(A) of the Internal Revenue Code or a trust for the benefit of the institution that is qualified as a Charitable Remainder Trust under § 664 or a pooled income fund under § 642(c)(5) of the Internal Revenue Code may acquire an insurable interest in the life of an individual if: (1) The institution or trust is designated irrevocably as the beneficiary of the insurance proceeds or designated as the owner of the life insurance policy, or both; (2) The application for the insurance contract is procured and signed by the individual whose life is to be insured; and (3) Notwithstanding paragraph (1) of this subsection, the insured pays the premiums for the insurance policy for at least 3 years following the issuance of the policy.

FLORIDA STAT. § 627.404(2)b(7)

A charitable organization meeting the requirements of s. 501(c)(3) of the United States Internal Revenue Code, as amended, has an insurable interest in the life of any person who consents in writing to the organization's ownership or purchase of that insurance.

GEORGIA CODE ANN. § 33-24-3(j)

A charitable institution as defined under Sections 501(c)(3), 501(c)(6), 501(c)(8), and 501(c)(9) of the Internal Revenue Code of 1986 shall have an insurable interest in the life of any donor.

HAWAII REV. STAT. § 431:10-202(4)

A charitable organization as defined in section 467B-1 has an insurable interest in the life of each proposed insured who joins with said organization in applying for a life insurance policy naming said organization as owner and irrevocable beneficiary.

IDAHO CODE ANN. § 41-1805

Contracts of life insurance may be made and entered into in which the person paying the consideration for such insurance has no insurable interest in the life of the person insured, where charitable, benevolent, educational, or religious institutions are designated irrevocably as the beneficiaries thereof.

215 ILLINOIS COMP. STAT. § 5/245.2

Members of not-for-profit organizations that are exempt from taxation as described in paragraph (3), (4), (5), (9), or (10) of subsection (c) of Section 501 of the Internal Revenue Code or either past or present individual or family donors to a not-for-profit organization may obtain life insurance policies naming the not-for-profit organization as the irrevocable sole beneficiary of the policy. The not-for-profit organization, as the sole beneficiary of the policy, may continue to pay the premiums to the issuing insurance company where the donor discontinues the premium payments and continuance of the policy is a prudent investment.

INDIANA CODE §§ 27-8-18-4

A charitable entity that purchases or is transferred ownership of a life insurance policy under subsection (a) has an insurable interest in the life of the individual who consents to the charitable entity's purchase or ownership of the policy.

IOWA CODE § 511.39

A charitable organization described in section 501(c)(3) of the Internal Revenue Code, as defined in section 422.3, has an insurable interest in the life of a person who, when purchasing a life insurance policy, makes a donation to the charitable organization or makes the charitable organization the beneficiary of all or a part of the proceeds of the policy or joins with a charitable organization in applying for an insurance policy which when issued will insure that person's life and name the organization as owner or beneficiary of all or any portion of the benefits of the life insurance policy.

KANSAS STAT. ANN. § 40-450(b)

A charitable, benevolent, educational and religious institution qualified under section 501(c) of the internal revenue code shall be deemed to have an insurable interest in the life of an individual insured who has executed a written consent to the assignment of the insurance contract to such institution if such institutional assignee is named as the irrevocable beneficiary thereof.

KENTUCKY REV. STAT. ANN. § 304.14-050

(1)Life insurance contracts may be entered into in which the person paying the consideration for the insurance has no insurable interest in the life of the individual insured, where charitable, benevolent, educational, or religious institutions, or their agencies, are designated irrevocably as the beneficiaries thereof.

(2) In making such contracts the person paying the premium shall make and sign the application therefor as owner, and shall designate a charitable, benevolent, educational or religious institution, or an agency thereof, irrevocably as the beneficiary or beneficiaries of such contract. The application shall be signed also by the individual whose life is to be insured

LOUSIANA REV. STAT. ANN. § 22.902

Notwithstanding any other law or regulation to the contrary, any religious, educational, eleemosynary, charitable, or benevolent institution or undertaking may be named beneficiary in or owner of any policy of life insurance issued by any life insurance company upon the life of any individual. The beneficiaries or owners named shall have an insurable interest for the full face of the policy and shall be entitled to collect same.

MAINE REV. STAT. ANN. tit. 24-A, §2405

1. Life insurance contracts may be entered into in which the person, trust or trustee paying the consideration for the insurance has no insurable interest in the life of the individual insured, where charitable, benevolent, educational or religious institutions, or their agencies, are designated irrevocably as the beneficiaries thereof.

2. In making such contracts, the person paying the premium shall make and sign the application therefor as owner or as settlor of a trust, and shall designate a charitable, benevolent, educational or religious institution, or any agency thereof, irrevocably as the beneficiary or beneficiaries of such contract. The application must be signed also by the individual whose life is to be insured.

MARYLAND CODE ANN., INS. § 12-201(c)

(1) This subsection applies only to a charitable, benevolent, educational, governmental, or religious institution that is described in § 170(b)(1)(A) or § 501(c)(3) of the Internal Revenue Code, or a trust for the benefit of that institution that is qualified as a pooled income fund under § 642(c)(5) or a Charitable Remainder Trust under § 664 of the Internal Revenue Code.

(2) An institution or trust described in paragraph (1) of this subsection may procure or cause to be procured an insurance policy on the life of an individual if: (i) the institution or trust is designated irrevocably as the beneficiary of the insurance policy; and (ii) the application for the insurance policy is signed by the individual whose life is to be insured or the individual's legal guardian.

MASSACHUSETTS GEN. LAWS ch. 175, § 123A(2)

A charitable institution as defined under section 501 (c)(3), (c)(6), (c)(8), and (c)(9) of the Internal Revenue Code shall be deemed to have an insurable interest, without limitation, in the life of any donor.

MICHIGAN COMP. LAWS § 500.2212

Notwithstanding any other section of this act, an organization described in and qualified under section 501(c)(3) of the internal revenue code of 1986, 26 U.S.C. 501, has an insurable interest in the life of an individual who gives written consent to the ownership or purchase of a policy on his or her life.

MINNESOTA STAT. § 60A.0783(2)f

An organization in section 170(c) of the United States Internal Revenue Code of 1986, as amended through December 31, 2008, has an insurable interest in the life of any person who consents in writing to the organization's ownership or purchase of that insurance.

MISSISSIPPI CODE ANN. § 83-5-251

Any religious, educational, eleemosynary, charitable or benevolent institution or its agency may be named beneficiary in any policy of life insurance issued by any insurance company upon the life of any individual. A religious, educational, eleemosynary, charitable or benevolent institution or its agency designated as a beneficiary has an insurable interest for the full face of the policy and is entitled to collect the full face of the policy.

MISSOURI REV. STAT. § 377.080

A charitable, benevolent, educational or religious institution qualified pursuant to section 501(c)(3) of the federal Internal Revenue Code, as amended, shall be deemed to have an insurable interest in the life of an insured individual if, in the absence of any fraud or coercion: (1) The individual has designated the institution as a beneficiary; (2) The individual has made a gift or an assignment of an interest in life insurance on the life of such insured individual; or (3) The life insurance is owned by such charitable, benevolent, educational or religious institution and such institution has obtained the consent of the person whose life is being insured, as required by section 376.531.

MONTANA CODE ANN. § 33-15-201(5)

A charitable institution has an insurable interest in an individual if: (a) the individual authorizes the charitable institution to purchase insurance naming the charitable institution as an irrevocable beneficiary; and (b) the insurance is purchased with contributions made by the individual.

NEBRASKA REV. STAT. § 44-704(4)

Nothing in Chapter 44 shall prohibit an organization or entity described in section 501(c)(3) of the Internal Revenue Code or to whom a charitable contribution could be made under section 170(c) of the code or a trust all of whose beneficiaries are organizations or entities described in section 501(c)(3) of the code or to whom a charitable contribution could be made under section 170(c) of the code from procuring, effectuating, or causing to be procured or effectuated the ownership of any life insurance policy or annuity contract upon the life of an individual if such individual gives written consent to the issuance of such policy or contract when such organization, entity, or trust is the owner of such policy or contract. Nothing in Chapter 44 shall require such organization, entity, or trust to have an insurable interest as defined in section 44-103 in the life of such individual in order for a policy or contract to be procured or effectuated pursuant to this subsection.

NEVADA REV. STAT. § 687B.050

1. Life insurance contracts may be entered into in which the person paying the consideration for the insurance has no insurable interest in the life of the individual insured, where charitable, benevolent, educational or religious institutions or their agencies are designated irrevocably as the beneficiaries thereof.

2. In making such contracts the person paying the premium shall make and sign the application therefor as owner, and shall designate irrevocably a charitable, benevolent, educational or religious institution or an agency thereof as the beneficiary or beneficiaries of such contract. The application shall be signed also by the individual whose life is to be insured.

NEW HAMPSHIRE REV. STAT. ANN. § 408:2-a

I. A life insurance policy may be issued with the person paying the premiums for such insurance having no insurable interest in the life of the insured, providing a charitable, benevolent, educational, or religious institution or any other organization which qualifies for a charitable deduction under the Internal Revenue Code is designated irrevocably as the owner and beneficiary of the policy. II. A life insurance policy may be issued with the person paying the premiums designated in the application as owner and insuring the premium payer's own life and designating a charitable, benevolent, educational, or religious institution or any other organization which qualifies for a charitable deduction under the Internal Revenue Code as the irrevocable beneficiary of the policy. III. Nothing in this section shall affect the right of any person to effectuate life insurance on such person's own life, or by a person or any business entity on another life if there exists any reasonable expectation of pecuniary benefit or advantage, direct or indirect, in the continued life of the other person. IV. No life insurance policy may be issued under this section unless the insured has consented in writing to the issuance of such policy.

NEW JERSEY STAT. ANN. § 17B:24-1.1(5)

A nonprofit or charitable entity qualified pursuant to section 501 (c) (3) of the Internal Revenue Code of 1986 (26 U.S.C. s.501(c)(3)), or a government entity has an insurable interest in the life or physical or mental ability of its directors, officers, employees, supporters or their designees or others to whom it may look for counsel, guidance, fundraising or assistance in the execution of its legally established purpose, who either: (a) join with the entity in signing the application for insurance, which application names the entity as the owner and irrevocable beneficiary of the policy; or (b) after having been listed as owner, subsequently transfer ownership of the insurance to the entity and name the entity as the irrevocable beneficiary of the policy.

NEW MEXICO STAT. ANN. § 59A-18-5

A. Life insurance contracts may be entered into in which the person paying the consideration for the insurance has no insurable interest in the life of the individual insured, where charitable, benevolent, educational or religious institutions or their agencies are designated irrevocably as the beneficiaries thereof.

B. In making such contracts the person paying the premium shall make and sign the application therefor as owner, and shall designate irrevocably a charitable, benevolent, educational or religious institution or an agency thereof as the beneficiary or beneficiaries of such contract. The application shall be signed also by the individual whose life is to be insured.

NEW YORK INS. LAW § 3205

(3) Notwithstanding the provisions of paragraphs one and two of this subsection, a Type B charitable, educational or religious corporation formed pursuant to paragraph (b) of section two hundred one of the not-for-profit corporation law, or its agent, may procure or cause to be procured, directly or by assignment or otherwise, a contract of life insurance upon the person of another and may designate itself or cause to have itself designated as the beneficiary of such contract.

NORTH CAROLINA GEN. STAT. §§ 58-58-86

If an organization described in section 501(c)(3) of the Internal Revenue Code purchases or receives by assignment, before, on, or after the effective date of this section, life insurance on an insured who consents to the purchase or assignment, the organization is deemed to have an insurable interest in the insured person's life.

NORTH DAKOTA CENT. CODE § 26.1-29-09.1(3)d

In the case of religious, educational, eleemosynary, charitable, or benevolent organizations, a lawful interest in the life of the individual insured if that individual has executed a written consent to the insurance contract.

OHIO REV. CODE ANN § 3911.09

Any religious, charitable, scientific, literary, educational, or other institution or entity that is described in section 170, 501(c)(3), 2055, or 2522 of the "Internal Revenue Code of 1986," 100 Stat. 2085, 26 U.S.C.A. 170 , 501 , 2055 , 2522 , as amended, may be the owner of, or may be designated beneficiary in, any policy of life insurance issued upon the life or lives of one or more individuals. Any such institution or entity has an insurable interest in the life of each insured and is entitled to enforce all rights and collect all benefits to which it is entitled pursuant to the policy.

OKLA.HOMA STAT. tit. 36, § 3604

Life insurance contracts may be entered into in which the person paying the consideration for the insurance has no insurable interest in the life of the individual insured, where charitable, benevolent, educational or religious institutions, or their agencies, are designated as the beneficiaries thereof. In no event shall an individual be named as a beneficiary. In making these contracts, the person paying the premium shall make and sign the application therefor as owner and shall designate a charitable, benevolent, educational, or religious institution, or an agency thereof, as the beneficiary or beneficiaries of the contract. The application or any subsequent change of beneficiary designation shall be signed by the individual whose life is to be insured. These contracts shall be valid and binding among the parties, notwithstanding the absence otherwise of an insurable interest in the life of the individual insured.

OREGON REV. STAT. §§ 743.030

Life insurance policies may be effected although the person paying the consideration has no insurable interest in the life of the person insured if a charitable, benevolent, educational or religious institution is designated irrevocably as the beneficiary.

(2) In making such policies the person paying the premium shall make and sign the application therefor as owner. The application also must be signed by the person whose life is to be insured. Such a policy shall be valid and binding between and among all of the parties thereto.

PENNSYLVANIA 40 P. S. § 512

A charitable organization that meets the requirements of section 501(c)(3) of the Internal Revenue Code of 1986 (Public Law 99-514, 26 U.S.C. § 501 (c)(3)), as amended, may own or purchase life insurance on an insured who consents to the ownership or purchase of that insurance

Rhode Island - None

SOUTH CAROLINA CODE ANN. § 38-63-100

Notwithstanding any other provision of law, a bona fide charity or nonprofit corporation which is in compliance with the "Solicitation of Charitable Funds Act" (Chapter 55 of Title 33) has an insurable interest in the life of an insured under a policy in which the charity or corporation is irrevocably named as a beneficiary provided that the application for insurance is signed by the insured.

SOUTH DAKOTA CODIFIED LAWS §§ 58-10-4

Insurable interest in personal insurance defined. Insurable interest with reference to personal insurance includes only interests as follows:...(4) A charitable organization that meets the requirements of section 501(c)3 of the Internal Revenue Code of 1986, as amended to January 1, 1992, and owns or purchases life insurance on an insured who consents to the ownership or purchase of the insurance has an insurable interest in the life of the insured;

TENNESSEE CODE ANN. 56-7-314;

If an organization described in either § 170(c) or § 501(c)(3) of the Internal Revenue Code of 1986, codified in 26 U.S.C. §§ 170(c) and 501(c)(3), respectively, purchases or receives by assignment, before or after April 23, 1992, life insurance on an insured who consents in writing to the purchase or assignment, the organization is deemed to have or to have had an insurable interest in the insured person's life on the date of purchase or assignment.

TEXAS INS. CODE ANN. § 1103.005

A religious, educational, eleemosynary, charitable, or benevolent institution or undertaking may be designated as a beneficiary in a policy that insures the life of an individual.

UTAH CODE ANN. § 31A-21-104(7)

This section does not prevent an organization described under Section 501(c)(3), (e), or (f), Internal Revenue Code, as amended, and the regulations made under this section, and which is regulated under Title 13, Chapter 22, Charitable Solicitations Act, from soliciting and procuring, by assignment or designation as beneficiary, a gift or assignment of an interest in life insurance on the life of the donor or assignor or from enforcing payment of proceeds from that interest.

Vermont - None

VIRGINA CODE ANN. § 38.2-301(4)

In the case of an organization described in § 501 (c) of the Internal Revenue Code, the lawful and substantial economic interest required in subdivision 2 of this subsection shall be deemed to exist where (i) the insured or proposed insured has either assigned all or part of his ownership rights in a policy or contract to such an organization or has executed a written consent to the issuance of a policy or contract to such organization and (ii) such organization is named in the policy or contract as owner or as beneficiary.

WASHINGTON REV. CODE ANN. § 48.18.030

(d) Subject to rules adopted under subsection (4) of this section, upon joint application with a nonprofit organization for, or transfer to a nonprofit organization of, an insurance policy on the life of a person naming the organization as owner and beneficiary, a nonprofit organization's interest in the life of a person if:

(i) The nonprofit organization was established exclusively for religious, charitable, scientific, literary, or educational purposes, or to promote amateur athletic competition, to conduct testing for public safety, or to prevent cruelty to children or animals; and

(ii) The nonprofit organization: (A) Has existed for a minimum of five years; or (B) Has been issued a certificate of exemption to conduct a Charitable Gift Annuity business under RCW 48.38.010, or is authorized to conduct a Charitable Gift Annuity business under RCW 28B.10.485; or (C) Has been organized, and at all times has been operated, exclusively for benefit of, to perform the functions of, or to carry out the purposes of one or more nonprofit organizations described in (d)(ii)(A) or (B) of this subsection and is operated, supervised, or controlled by or in connection with one or more of those nonprofit organizations; and

(iii) For a joint application, the person is not an employee, officer, or director of the organization who receives significant compensation from the organization and who became affiliated with the organization in that capacity less than one year before the joint application.

(4) The commissioner may adopt rules governing joint applications for, and transfers of, life insurance under subsection (3)(d) of this section. The rules may include: (a) Standards for full and fair disclosure that set forth the manner, content, and required disclosure for the sale of life insurance issued under subsection (3)(d) of this section; and (b) For joint applications, a grace period of thirty days during which the insured person may direct the nonprofit organization to return the policy and the insurer to refund any premium paid to the party that, directly or indirectly, paid the premium; and (c) Standards for granting an exemption from the five-year existence requirement of subsection (3)(d)(ii)(A) of this section to a private foundation that files with the insurance commissioner documents, stipulations, and information as the insurance commissioner may require to carry out the purpose of subsection (3)(d) of this section.

WEST VIRGINA CODE § 33-6-2(c)4

(c) "Insurable interest" with reference to personal insurance includes only interests as follows:...(4) A charitable institution as defined under Sections 501(c)(3), 501(c)(6), 501(c)(8) and 501(c)(9) of the Internal Revenue Code of 1986, as amended.

WISCONSIN ADMIN. CODE INS. § 2.45

A charitable organization may be the applicant, owner or beneficiary of a life insurance policy issued on the life of any individual. A charitable organization is deemed to have an insurable interest in the individual.

WYOMING STAT. ANN. § 26-15-103

(a) Contracts of life insurance may be made and entered into in which the person paying the consideration for the insurance has no insurable interest in the life of the person insured, if charitable, benevolent, educational or religious institutions are designated irrevocably as a beneficiary but not necessarily the primary beneficiary thereof.

(b) In making a contract as specified in subsection (a) of this section, the person paying the premium shall make and sign the application therefor as owner and shall designate a charitable, benevolent, educational or religious institution irrevocably as the beneficiary or one (1) of the beneficiaries of the policy. The application also shall be signed by the person whose life is to be insured.

Even when it works, encouraging donors to make premium payments on life insurance will typically benefit the charity only after many years. During the intervening time, donors are making cash gifts year after year, but the charity has no gift income to spend. Depending upon the needs and desires of the charity, this may be a highly undesirable result even if, ultimately, the charity receives substantial gifts.

Another potential downside for the donor is that because the gift occurs only after the donor's death, the donor will never actually get to see the impact of his or her gift during life. Ultimately, the charity may be able to build a building, create a scholarship, or achieve any number of important charitable tasks, but the donor will never witness this. In contrast, if the donor were to take the premium payments and simply give them to the charity as a traditional donation, the impact would occur immediately. This is an important downside given that life insurance does not make the total gift bigger unless the donor dies earlier than expected. (If the donor lives to his or her life expectancy, a life insurance policy will not return more than simply investing the premium payment amounts.)

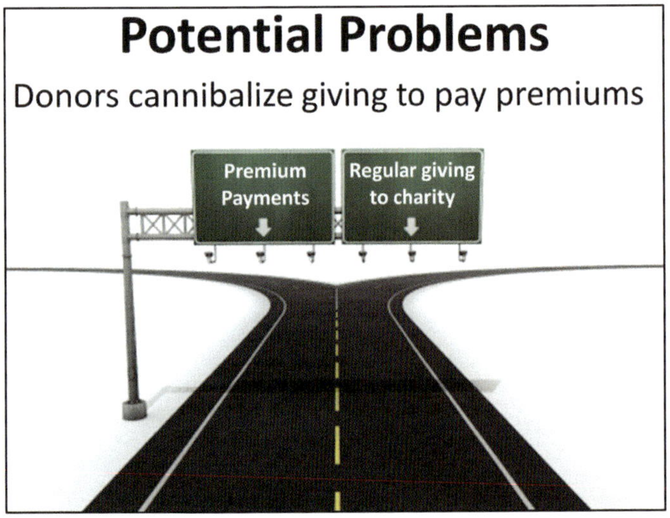

Some charities may take the approach that "something is better than nothing," meaning that any money raised by life insurance agents through the sale of charity owned life insurance is simply a bonus. This approach, however, ignores the possibility that the donor may be directing funds to premium payments that otherwise might have gone to the charity as simple donations. If the premium payments result in cannibalizing the donations that the donor would otherwise have made, then it is important for the charity to carefully weigh the value of using life insurance policies as a means to raise funds. Although these premium payments may indeed generate something for the charity, it is possible that the charity will also be losing something greater in the process.

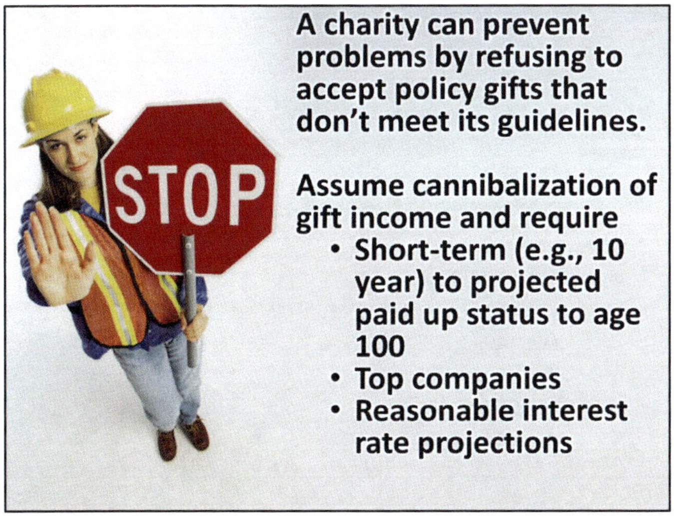

How can a charity influence a donor's decision to use life insurance to benefit the charity? Ultimately, the charity can refuse to accept the donation of a life insurance policy. If the charity does not accept ownership of the policy, then the donor cannot deduct premium payments as gifts to the charity. Given the potential for premium payments to cannibalize regular giving, it may be wise for a charity to establish guidelines for the types of newly-created insurance policies that it will accept. (Of course, transfers of long-term life insurance policies that have built up substantial cash surrender value are a different matter as discussed in the previous section.) These requirements can include accepting only policies that will reach paid-up status in a relatively short time. Paid-up status is the point at which no additional premium payments are necessary in order to keep the death benefit in force for the remainder of the insured's life (or up to, e.g., age 100). This paid-up status may depend upon the projected returns of underlying assets and the stability of the issuing company. Thus, these companies should be highly rated and the return projections should be reasonable to make sure that once a policy reaches paid up status the charity will, ultimately, receive the death benefit. Reaching paid-up status in a relatively short time (e.g., 10 years) is important for two reasons. First, it reduces the likelihood that the policy will lapse due to non-payment of premiums by the donor, resulting in no gift to the charity. Second, it provides a planned break in the premium obligation to allow for shifting the donor into an alternative campaign or gifting approach at that time.

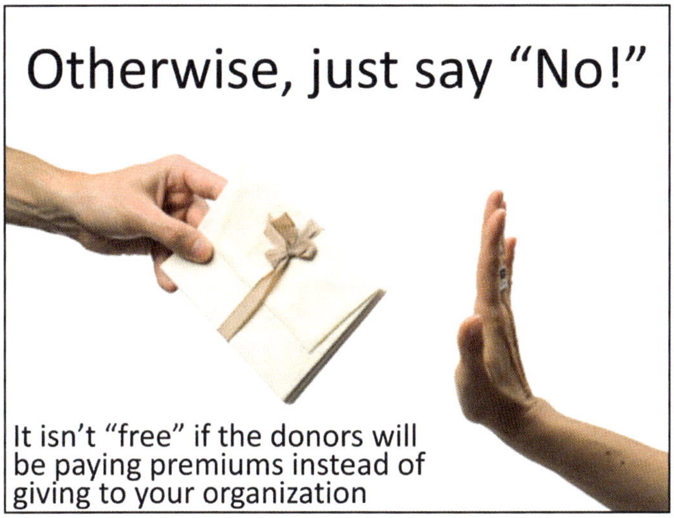

It may be counter-intuitive and even uncomfortable for a nonprofit organization to refuse a gift, especially one desired by the donor and the donor's insurance agent. But, the potential for the charity to receive nothing despite the donor's many contributions may suggest this unusual approach in cases where the policy does not meet the charity's guidelines. If the donor's regular gifting will be less because of the premium payments he or she is making on the charity owned life insurance policy, the charity should consider making a special effort to understand the value of the proposed insurance policy prior to accepting the gift.

Financial advisors and fundraisers can often help donors accomplish their charitable goals using life insurance in a variety of different ways. Life insurance can serve as tax-free wealth replacement for charitable estate gifts transferred to charity. Older life insurance policies may have built up significant value over time, making them potentially attractive sources for charitable transfers. New life insurance policies owned by a charity, with proper planning, can also be a beneficial strategy. Although the rules can be complex and the techniques may be appropriate only for certain circumstances, when life insurance is needed, it is important for advisors and fundraisers to be ready suggest these potentially attractive solutions.

15 DONATING RETIREMENT ASSETS

Donating retirement assets can be result in terrible tax consequences or fantastic tax consequences depending upon the timing and circumstances of the donor. Thus, it is especially important for advisors and fundraisers to have some familiarity with the tax rules associated with such gifts.

Given the inherent complexity in dealing with retirement assets, some might consider simply ignoring these assets as a source of charitable gifts. Rules for traditional IRAs, 401(k) accounts, 403(b) accounts, SIMPLE-IRAs, SEP-IRAs and so forth may seem intimidating. However, retirement assets should not be ignored. This is true in part because the client can experience significantly positive tax consequences from such gifts in certain circumstances.

Aside from these potential tax advantages, retirement assets cannot be ignored because they represent such a large share of all household wealth. More than a third of all household financial assets are held in the form of retirement assets. Thus, neither fundraisers nor advisors should ignore this substantial source of wealth holding.

Retirement assets can be donated during life or at death. The tax consequences are very different for each type of gift, so they will be covered separately. Gifts during life involve more complicated considerations and their advisability depends in part upon the "life stage" of the retirement account.

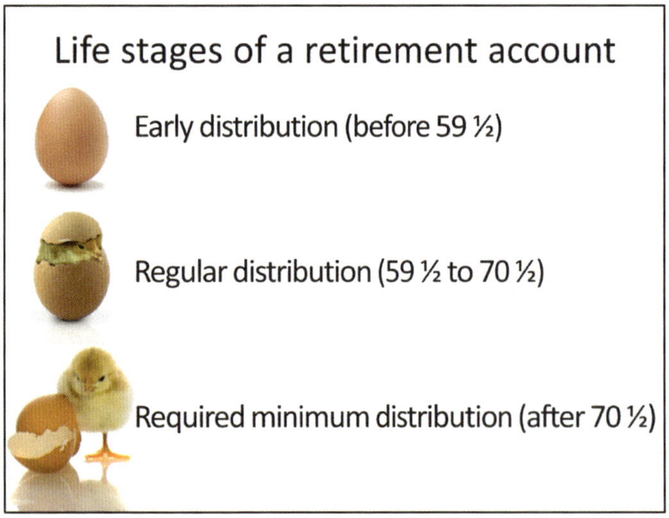

Retirement accounts such as traditional IRAs, 401(k) accounts, and 403(b) accounts have three different stages. Each stage corresponds to a different tax consequence resulting from gifting assets from the accounts. Before the account holder reaches age 59½, distributions will be considered early distributions, and are typically subject to penalties for withdrawal. When the account holder reaches age 59½, these penalties no longer apply. However, as with other distributions from the account, the account holder must pay taxes on these distributions, because the income was not taxed when initially put into the account. Finally, when the account holder reaches age 70½, he or she is required to take at least minimum distributions from the accounts each year. These distributions count as taxable income to the donor.

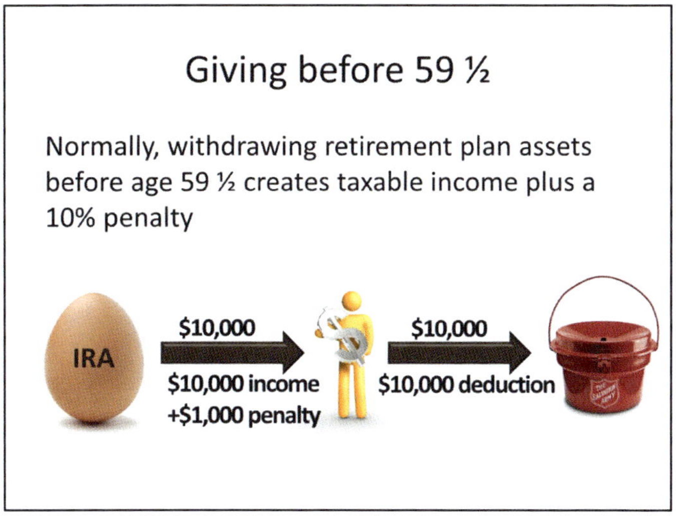

For donors younger than 59½, making gifts from a retirement plan is generally a bad idea. Not only will the withdrawal be considered income to the donor, and thus be subject to taxation, but the donor will also have to pay an additional 10% penalty. This penalty is charged because the donor is withdrawing assets from the account prior to age 59½. The donor may receive a charitable deduction from the gift. This deduction could offset the income charged to the donor as a result of withdrawing the funds. However, this charitable deduction will not offset the 10% penalty charged for early withdraw.

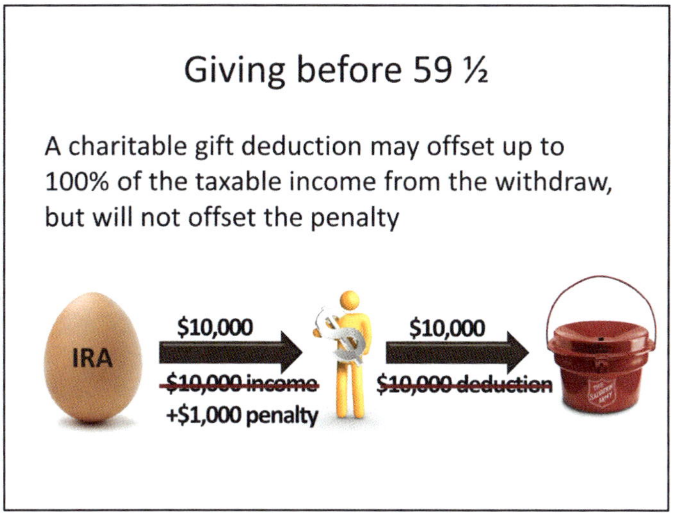

The charitable deduction resulting from the donation will not offset the 10% penalty for the early withdraw. Thus, even in a perfect situation, making a $10,000 gift by withdrawing funds from the retirement account will cost at least $11,000. Beyond this, it is often the case that the charitable deduction may not perfectly offset the effects of the increased income resulting from the withdraw of funds. For example, if the donor was not otherwise an itemizer, the charitable deduction for a $10,000 gift will not reduce income by the full $10,000. Or if the donor is in the range of income where Pease amendment rules result in a reduction of such deductions, the charitable deduction for a $10,000 gift will not reduce income by the full $10,000. Or, if the donor reaches the income limits for deducting charitable gifts, the deduction will be not be available until future years.

Further, the increase in income, even if offset by deductions, may generate other negative tax consequences because certain tax benefits are not available for those whose adjusted gross income falls above specific levels. For example:

- The personal exemption is reduced by 2% for each $2,500 that adjusted gross income exceeds threshold levels. (In 2014 the threshold was $254,200 for single taxpayers and $305,050 for married taxpayers filing jointly.)
- The earned income tax credit is reduced for income above certain thresholds. (In 2014 these thresholds were $8,110 for a childless single taxpayer, $17,830 for a single taxpayer with children, $13,540 for childless married taxpayers filing jointly, and $23,260 for married taxpayers with children filing jointly. In 2014 the credit phased out at 7.65% of income above the threshold for childless taxpayers, at 15.98% of income above the threshold for taxpayers with one child, and at 21.06% of

income above the threshold for taxpayers with more than one child.)

- The adoption credit ($13,190 in 2014) is reduced for those with modified adjusted gross income above the threshold level ($197,880 in 2014).
- The child tax credit ($1,000 for each qualifying child) is reduced by 0.5% for any modified adjusted gross income above the threshold level (in 2014 $75,000 for single taxpayers, $110,000 for married taxpayers filing jointly).
- Education tax benefits also phase out after certain income thresholds such as the American Opportunity Credit ($80,000 for single taxpayers, $160,000 for married taxpayers filing jointly), Lifetime Learning Credit ($54,000 for single taxpayers, $109,000 for married taxpayers filing jointly), and deductibility of qualifying student loan interest ($60,000 for single taxpayers, $125,000 for married taxpayers filing jointly).
- Eligibility to make Roth IRA contributions begins to phase out after certain income thresholds ($114,000 for single taxpayers, $188,000 for married taxpayers filing jointly), as does deductibility of IRA contributions ($60,000 for single taxpayers, $96,000 for married taxpayers filing jointly with participating spouse, $181,000 for married taxpayers filing jointly with non-participating spouse).

For taxpayers affected by these phase-out ranges, the negative tax consequence resulting from the increased income resulting from the retirement account withdraw will not be perfectly offset by the charitable income tax deduction. Additionally, if taxpayers are eligible for other income-based government benefits, the increase in income resulting from the retirement account withdraw may have additional negative consequences.

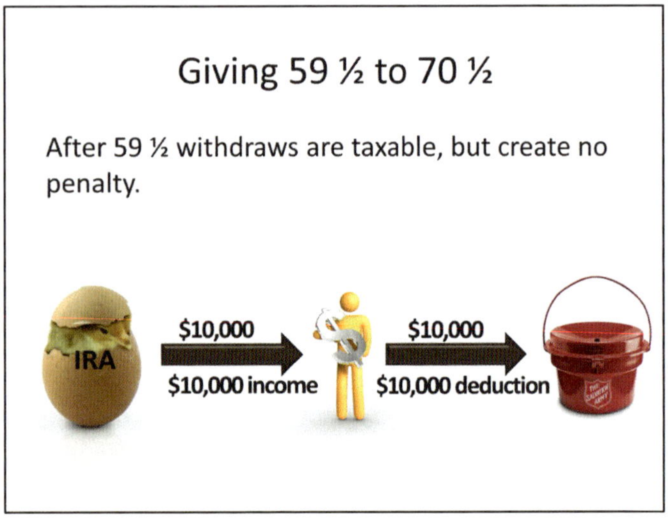

Withdraws made after age 59½ do not generate the 10% penalty as do those made before this age. Consequently, it is possible that the deduction generated by making a corresponding charitable gift could completely offset the effects of the increased income due to a withdraw from a retirement account. As before, the ability to completely offset the effects of the increased income with the charitable tax deduction depends upon a variety of factors such as the donor's itemization status, the income giving limitations, and whether or not the increased income will have negative effects for the donor in other areas such as income-based phase outs for various tax benefits.

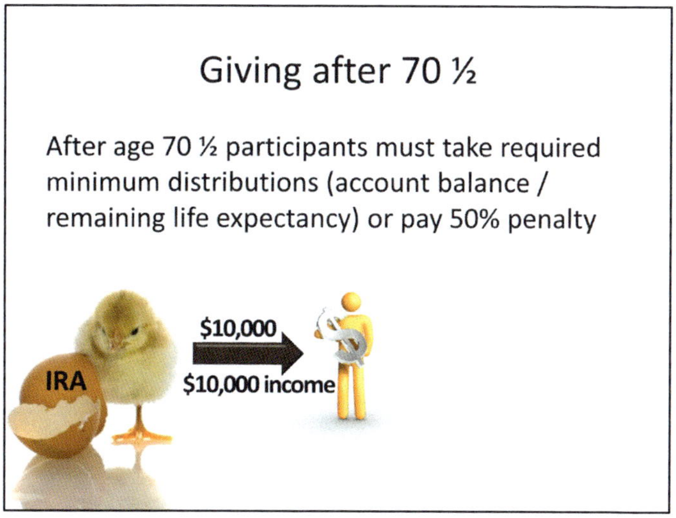

Withdraws after age 70½ receive the same tax treatment as those taken at any point after age 59½. The primary difference is that minimum withdraws are required beginning at age 70½. Thus, the account holder cannot simply choose not to take a withdraw. Instead the account holder must take a minimum withdraw in the amount of the account balance divided by the remaining years of life expectancy for a typical person of the account holder's age. If the account holder fails to take this withdraw, he or she will be taxed in the amount of 50% of the required minimum distribution.

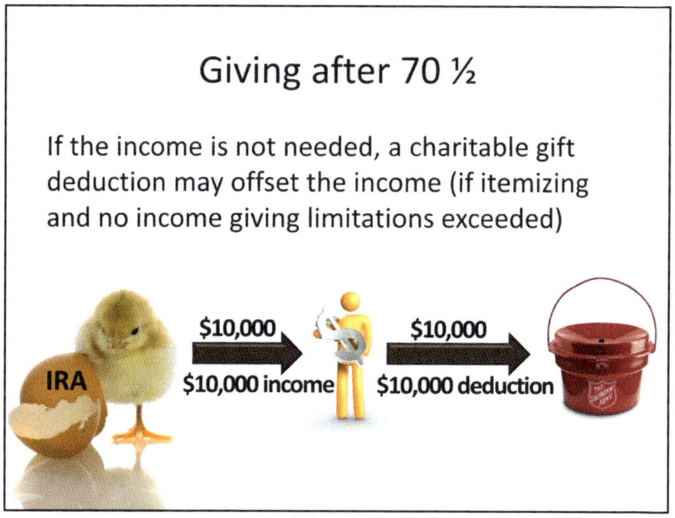

Because the taxpayer is forced to withdraw the required minimum distribution from the retirement account, the negative tax effects from increased income will occur regardless of whether or not a charitable gift is made. The taxpayer cannot simply choose not to take a withdraw. If the taxpayer is forced to withdraw the funds, but does not need them for consumption, a charitable gift may be an ideal use of these funds. The charitable deduction resulting from the gift may entirely (or at least partially) offset the negative tax affects resulting from the increased income due to the required distribution.

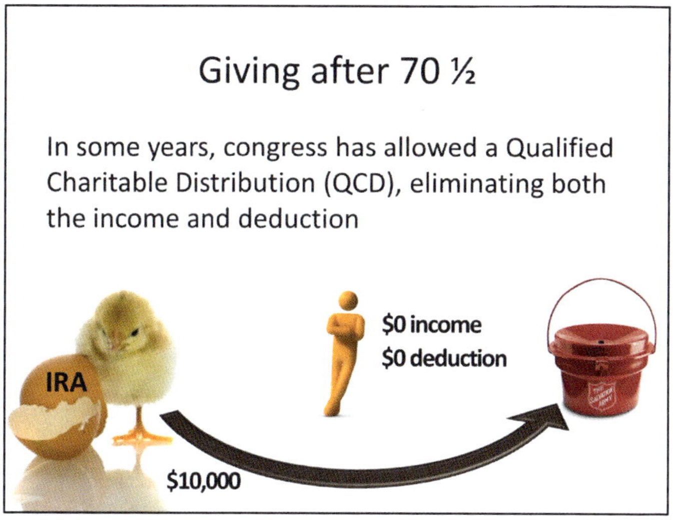

The ideal charitable distribution is a qualified charitable distribution (QCD). This arrangement is ideal because the donor is allowed to make a transfer directly from his or her retirement account to a charity. This transfer does not count as income to the donor, but *does* reduce the required minimum distribution from the account. The donor receives no deduction, but also has no increase in income. This perfect offset makes this transaction equivalent to the "perfect" withdraw and gift transaction with a 100% useable tax deduction and no negative effects from the increased income.

The qualified charitable distribution has

been approved by congress in many, but not all, years. Although it is not part of the permanent tax code, planning for qualified charitable distributions has become common because of the frequency with which congress has passed legislation temporarily authorizing such transactions.

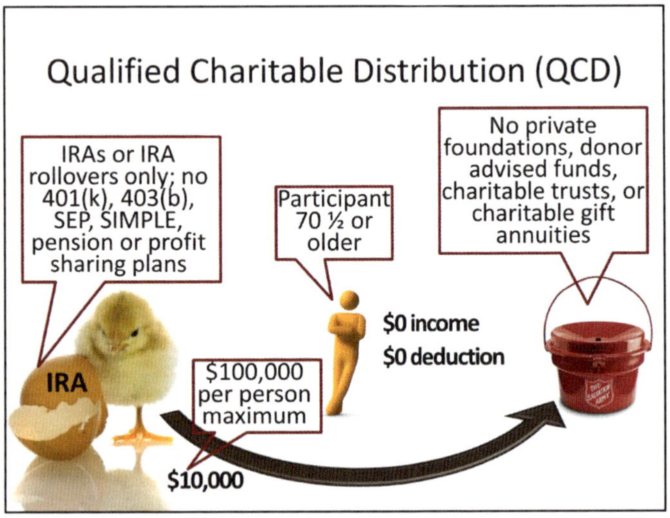

In years in which the qualified charitable distribution has been approved, the typical provisions include the following limitations. The participant must be 70 ½ or older (i.e., subject to required minimum distributions). The maximum transfer is limited to $100,000. The qualified charitable distributions must be from an IRA or IRA rollover. These are not allowed from 401(k), 403(b), SEP, SIMPLE, pension or profit sharing plans. However, the retired account holder with a 401(k), 403(b), 457 plan, SEP-IRA, or SIMPLE-IRA (assuming it is more than 2 years old) could consider rolling the account over into a traditional IRA rollover to allow for future qualified charitable distributions. However, this will work only for qualified charitable distributions in future years because any current required minimum distribution from the non-traditional IRA account must be distributed and cannot be rolled over into a traditional IRA.

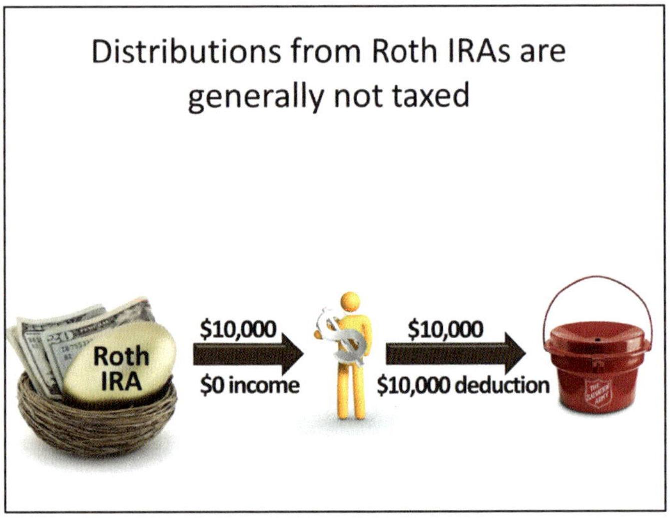

Distributions from Roth IRAs will be tax free in a number of circumstances. First, if the distribution is from the account holder's regular participant contributions to the Roth IRA, there is no taxation or penalties for withdrawing funds. The account holder has already paid taxes on this amount and its contribution into or withdraw from the Roth IRA does not generate any additional taxes or penalties. Any distributions from the Roth IRA are considered to be from the account holder's regular participant contributions until all of these have been distributed. Distributions in excess of the account holder's regular participant contributions will next be distributions of any IRA conversions. A conversion occurs when the account holder converts a retirement account such as a traditional IRA into a Roth account. This conversion requires the account holder to pay income taxes on the amount of the converted account. Thus, distributions of such conversions do not generate income taxes because the income taxes on this money have already been paid. However, if the account holder is younger than 59½ and the conversion was less than five years ago, the 10% penalty on early withdraw must still be paid for these conversion assets. (If this rule did not exist, the 10% penalty on early withdrawals from a traditional IRA could be completely avoided by simply converting it to a Roth IRA and taking the distribution.) Finally, all remaining distributions will be considered earnings. Distribution of earnings after age 59½ do not generate income taxes or penalties (assuming the distribution occurs at least five years after the account holder funded his first Roth IRA account). However, distributions of earnings after age 59½ typically generate both income taxes and penalties. (The 10% penalty could be avoided from either traditional or Roth IRA accounts if the funds are used for specific allowed purposes, but these do not include making charitable gifts.)

When distributions from Roth IRAs are tax free, they may make a desirable source for charitable gifts. However, this will result in reducing the amount of funds in the Roth IRA and may not correspond with the retirement tax planning strategies of the donor. For example, additional growth in the Roth IRA can be withdrawn without taxation (after age 59½) and reducing IRA assets through gifting eliminates this future tax-free growth on the gifted assets.

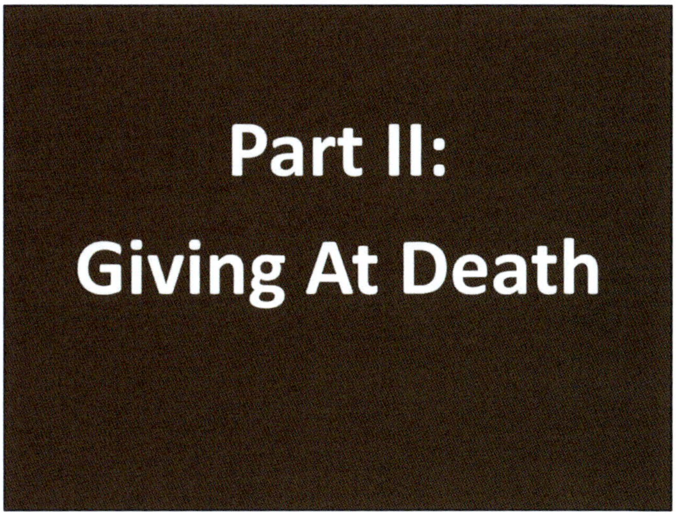

Giving from retirement accounts during life often may have negative tax consequences, but in some cases – such as a qualified charitable distribution – may have distinct tax advantages. Charitable giving from traditional retirement accounts at death, in contrast, is almost always more beneficial than giving other types of assets to charity at death.

Traditional retirement account assets are "tax heavy" for heirs. Not only are these assets subject to gift and estate taxation, but they are also subject to income taxation. The money in these traditional accounts has never had income taxes paid on it. Therefore, income taxes must be paid when the funds are withdrawn. This tax burden makes these "tax heavy" assets less desirable for heirs. But, it does not make these assets less desirable for tax-exempt organizations, because these organizations do not pay such taxes. Therefore, it is always to the heirs' advantage (and not to the disadvantage of charities) to make as much of the charitable share of estate assets as possible consist of traditional retirement accounts (i.e., qualified plan money).

Consider this simple example. A donor has only two assets, a $1 million IRA and a $1 million house. The donor wishes to leave half of her estate to a charity and half to her child. The child earns a high income and is a resident of California. Does it matter which asset the charity inherits and which asset the child inherits?

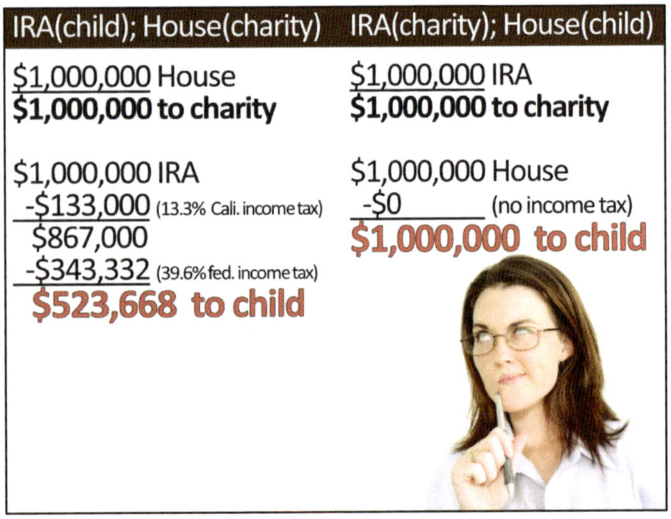

If the child inherits the home, the child will receive the $1,000,000 asset free from any taxation. (There are no estate taxes because the donor's estate is too small.) The child can sell the asset and spend the entire $1,000,000. The results are quite different if the child instead inherits the $1,000,000 traditional IRA. The assets in the IRA have never had income taxes paid on them. Thus, withdraws from the account will be treated as additional income to the child. Assuming the child is paying the highest income tax rates at both the state (California) and federal levels, this leaves slightly more than half of the money available to the child after paying income taxes. Notice that this massive difference in taxation occurs simply by the donor's selection of which asset to give to charity. The difference occurs even though the donor's estate is not subject to estate taxes. Although the difference would be less if the inheriting child were in a lower income tax bracket, it would still be substantial enough to warrant selecting the retirement assets instead of other assets for the charitable estate gift.

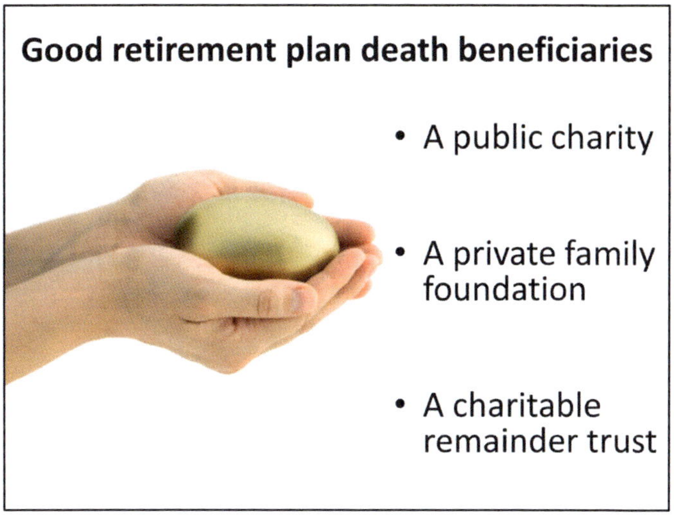

Retirement plan death beneficiaries are typically named in the beneficiary designation of the retirement account. In other words, the donor's will usually does not control the distribution of these assets. (In fact, the will is best thought of as a back-up document in general because it will not control any assets with beneficiary designations or owned in joint ownership with right of survivorship.) Good retirement plan beneficiaries include any public charity and any private foundation.

Charitable Remainder Trusts (which are also charitable entities) may also make good beneficiaries, but with some additional considerations. The unpaid income taxes on the retirement account funds will cause the retirement distribution to be considered "income in respect of a decedent", a.k.a., IRD. This IRD treatment is important in a Charitable Remainder Trust because it makes the retirement distribution funds ordinary income assets. Ordinary income assets must be paid out first (i.e., Tier 1), prior to paying out any capital gain, non-taxable income or return of principal. When paid out to non-charitable beneficiaries, the IRD will be taxable to the beneficiary as ordinary income. Thus, to the extent that the retirement assets are ultimately paid to non-charitable beneficiaries, the tax advantages of leaving these assets to a charity disappear. Another issue also arises regarding a potential income tax deduction. Typically, if a beneficiary inherits an IRD asset, such as an IRA account, the beneficiary is entitled to an itemized income tax deduction in the amount of any estate taxes paid as a result of the transfer of the IRD asset. For example, if Jane inherits a $100,000 IRA account which generated $40,000 of estate taxation (as compared to the estate taxes that would have been owed had the asset not existed), Jane will receive a $40,000 income tax deduction. The idea here is to avoid taxation of dollars that have already been taken by the IRS in estate taxes. In theory, this same deduction applies to the non-charitable portion of the Charitable Remainder Trust. The estate pays estate taxes on the taxable portion of the IRA transfer to the Charitable Remainder Trust (i.e., the present value of the share that will *not* be going to charity). These are estate taxes paid on an IRD and thus generate an income tax deduction. However, this tax deduction is treated as return of principal in the Charitable Remainder Trust, meaning that the deduction will not be distributed to the beneficiary unless all other ordinary income, capital gain income, and exempt income held in the trust is first paid out. The net effect of this is that the tax deduction will most likely be completely lost.

Problems can arise when naming a Charitable Lead Trust as beneficiary of a retirement account. The Charitable Lead Trust is not a tax-exempt entity, thus it must pay income taxes when receiving the retirement account funds, just as any other taxpayer would (although perhaps at higher rates due to the compressed tax schedule of complex trusts).

Naming the estate as beneficiary, even if the estate will make charitable distributions, could result in the estate having to pay the income taxes on the retirement account funds. This can arise if the account holder specifically names the estate as beneficiary or if no beneficiary is named, which will also cause the retirement account to pay to the account holder's estate. Typically, if the estate receives IRD (such as qualified plan money), the estate must pay the income taxes resulting from this IRD. However, this can be avoided if the estate transfers the right to receive the IRD to fulfill a bequest of that specific item or of a share of the remaining estate. In that case the recipient, not the estate, would owe the income taxes on the IRD. If the recipient is a charity, no taxes will be owed. This result is possible if the estate documents allow the executor to distribute assets on a non-pro rata basis (i.e., if the executor can send a disproportionate share of the IRD asset to the charitable beneficiary). However, if the assets are used to fulfill dollar amount charitable bequests (i.e., estate gifts of specific dollar amounts), the estate will still have to pay the income taxes due from the IRD/retirement account asset.

Finally, if the retirement account is to be divided between charitable and non-charitable beneficiaries, the non-charitable beneficiaries have until the end of the next year following the decedent's death to establish separate accounts for the charitable and non-charitable beneficiaries. This is not necessary if the charity's share is completely paid out prior to September 30 of the year following the decedent's death. Creating these separate accounts is important because if the charity is not paid off or separated out, it will reduce the maximum time allowed for the non-charitable beneficiaries to remove the funds (with income taxes being due at the time of removal). These separate accounts may not be possible if the amount designated for charity was listed as a dollar amount, rather than a percentage amount. However, such separation of accounts will not be needed if the administrator simply pays off the entire charitable portion prior to September 30 of the next year following the decedent's death. This complexity can also be avoided if the only other beneficiary is a spouse because the spouse can simply roll over his or her share into his or her separate IRA.

Naming someone other than the spouse as a beneficiary for an ERISA account, such as a 401(k), a SIMPLE IRA, a SEP IRA, an ESOP, or profit sharing plan, requires consent from the spouse. Thus a charity may not be named as a primary beneficiary without the consent of the account holder's spouse. Such consent is not required in a traditional IRA or Roth IRA unless the company managing the accounts decides to add such requirements.

Estate gifts of retirement account assets, of course, require that the accounts have value after the death of the account holder. Thus, traditional pension plans (i.e., defined benefit plans) are not directly relevant for charitable planning purposes because no valuable assets will survive the death of the participant (or, in some cases, the death of the participant and the participant's spouse).

Because of their creation and administrative expenses, Charitable Remainder Trusts are generally reserved for substantial transfers of assets. One way to conceptualize a qualified plan with a charitable beneficiary is like a mini-Charitable Remainder Trust with minimal administrative costs. In both instruments the charity receives the assets at the death of the donor. Both allow tax-free growth of assets and both can provide income to the donor. In the Charitable Remainder Trust the income is fixed for life, whereas the qualified plan provides income at the discretion of the donor (and without a 10% penalty after age 59 ½). The Charitable Remainder Trust reduces income by the share of the transfer representing the present value of the charitable interest. The qualified retirement plan reduces income by the entire amount of the transfer. Of course a retirement account can be funded only with cash and there are limits to the amount of funding allowed. The Charitable Remainder Trust can be of unlimited size and can be funded with appreciated assets and thereby postpone or eliminate the associated capital gains tax. In cases where a donor is attracted to the features of a Charitable Remainder Trust, but where the nature and size of the potential gift does not warrant its use, it may be helpful to consider marketing the naming of a charity as a qualified plan beneficiary as a mini-Charitable Remainder Trust substitute.

A final area where charitable planning can connect with retirement accounts is in managing the tax consequences of Roth IRA conversions. The goal here is to match a spike in income, caused by a Roth IRA conversion, with a simultaneous spike in charitable deductions.

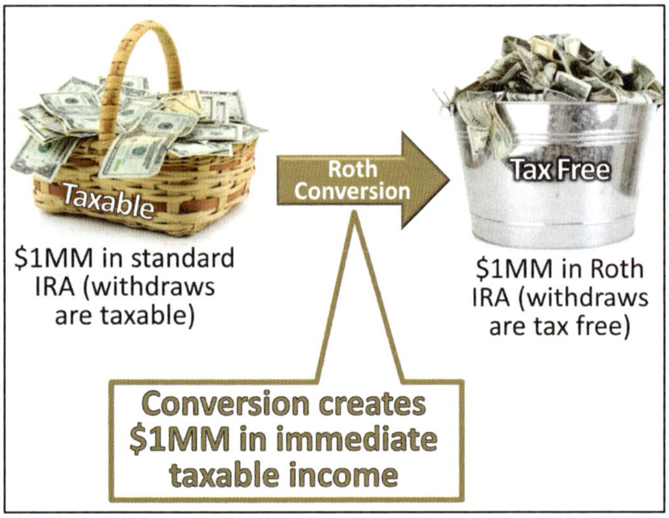

The idea of a Roth conversion is to change a traditional IRA into a Roth IRA. A traditional IRA grows tax free, but income taxes must be paid whenever distributions are taken from the account. In a Roth IRA, taxes were paid on the initial contributions, but no taxes need to be paid when qualified distributions are taken from the account, regardless of whether the distributions were of initial contributions or subsequent growth on those initial contributions. Converting a traditional IRA into a Roth IRA causes the account holder to be charged with income taxes on the amount of conversion less any basis in the traditional IRA. (Basis in a traditional IRA consists of amounts originally contributed with after tax funds, i.e., contributed with no deduction.) In exchange for this tax disadvantage, the account holder gains the ability to take future qualified distributions free from income taxes, whether those distributions are from the converted assets or from subsequent growth on those converted assets. Thus, the extra tax benefit is the income tax free receipt of future growth on the Roth IRA assets. Although acquiring the benefits from such a conversion may make perfect sense in the context of an overall retirement plan, it can generate a substantial immediate spike in taxable income. Because there are no limits on the amount of an IRA that can be converted to a Roth IRA, the amount of this spike in income can be dramatic relative to the account holder's normal income.

This spike in income may make the account holder particularly interested in generating income tax deductions. First, this may be true because the increased income resulting from the Roth IRA conversion may temporarily push the account holder into a higher income tax bracket. Thus, deductions taken in the year of the conversion will be more valuable than deductions taken in a later year. (The value of a deduction is the amount of the deduction multiplied by the taxpayer's marginal tax rate. Therefore a higher tax rate makes the deductions more valuable.) Additionally, the taxpayer may wish to pursue a larger conversion but may not have enough cash to pay for the resulting tax consequences. Deductions could reduce the costs of the tax consequences of the Roth conversion, allowing the cash-limited account holder to convert a larger amount into the Roth account.

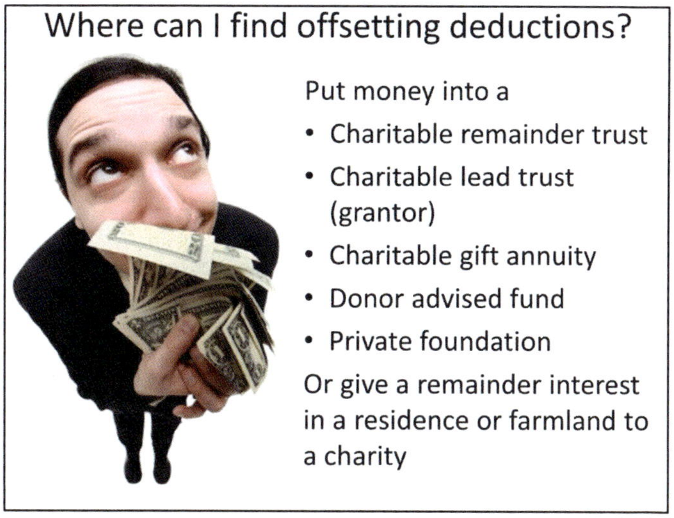

Of course, much of charitable planning is designed to provide creative ways to generate charitable income tax deductions, making charitable planning a natural fit with Roth IRA conversion. Thus, a donor might move assets or cash into a Charitable Remainder Trust, grantor Charitable Lead Trusts, Charitable Gift Annuity, donor advised fund or private foundation. Such charitable planning may permit a large immediate deduction even where the donor does not wish to sell the underlying asset (such as with a Charitable Remainder Trust, grantor Charitable Lead Trust, or Private Foundation), or where the donor wishes to receive income from the underlying asset (such as with a Charitable Remainder Trust, or Charitable Gift Annuity), or where the donor wishes to receive the asset back after a period of time (such as with a grantor Charitable Lead Trust). Finally, the donor who has neither the cash nor the desire to transfer assets in order to generate a charitable income tax deduction may consider gifting the remainder interest in a personal residence or farmland. This gifting of the inheritance rights to the property generates an immediate, potentially very large, deduction with no requirement for immediate cash or loss of income from or use of the underlying real estate.

Of course, the use of charitable deductions is not unlimited and depending on the gift type and the recipient type the deductions are limited to 20%, 30%, or 50% of income. Thus, charitable deductions cannot completely offset an spike in income of unlimited size. However, the ability to reduce taxable income by up to 50% is still a potentially powerful tool. When these income limitations are exceeded, charitable deductions can be carried forward into future years. However, after five additional years these deductions will expire.

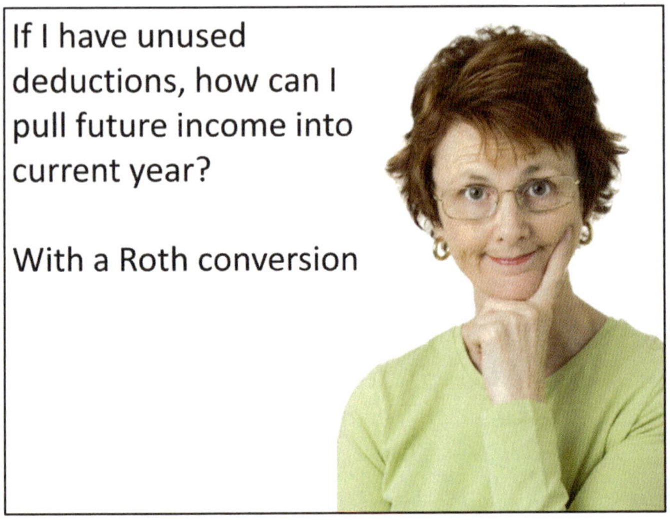

A donor may have substantial charitable deductions that, due perhaps to a large transfer of assets, exceed the income giving limitations for one year or even for all five carryover years. Especially in cases where these deductions would otherwise expire, there may be interest in pulling income back from future years, so that the deductions can be used.

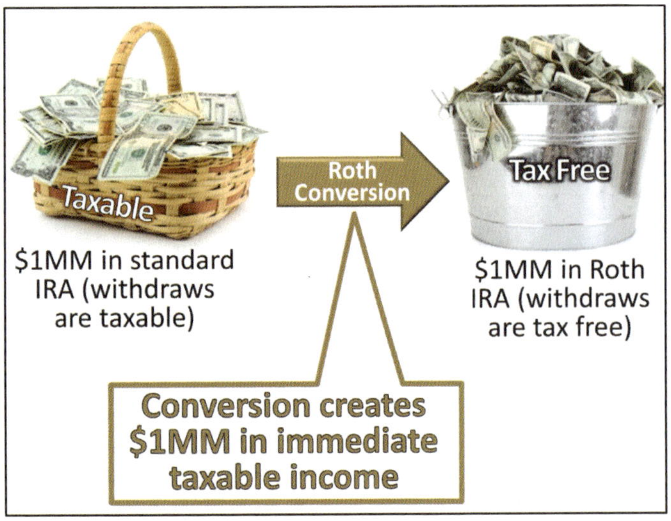

A perfect way to accomplish the task of pulling income back from future years is to convert some funds from a traditional IRA into a Roth IRA. The conversion does not create additional taxes, but does result in pre-paying taxes that would otherwise be due later and subsequently allows for tax-free growth following the conversion. Consequently, paying taxes for the conversion can be a wise investment. This investment is made all the more beneficial if it can be partially paid for with charitable tax deductions that, otherwise, would have expired unused.

In this way Roth conversions and charitable deductions can work together to help match income with deductions. When income is temporarily high, due to any cause including a Roth conversion, charitable deductions become temporarily more valuable due to higher marginal tax rates. The use of charitable deductions can reduce the immediate tax costs associated with a Roth conversion. When excessive charitable deductions might otherwise go unused due to income limitations, a Roth conversion can provide the temporary spike in income that allows for the deductions to be used.

Working with retirement assets is important simply because of the magnitude of household wealth held in such instruments. Additionally, it is useful to have a basic understanding of the options because the results from charitable giving from such funds can have tax consequences ranging from absolutely awful to absolutely wonderful. The well advised donor will successfully avoid the former and embrace the latter.

16 PRIVATE FOUNDATIONS
& DONOR ADVISED FUNDS

Some prior chapters covered topics, such as Charitable Gift Annuities, that are of interest mostly to nonprofits and nonprofit fundraisers. In contrast, private foundations and donor advised funds are more centrally important in the world of financial advisors. Financial advisors are naturally interested in these structures as they allow for compensated financial management and they contain the bulk of managed private charitable wealth. Private foundations are, by far, the largest sophisticated charitable planning instrument as measured by total assets and charitable distributions. Donor advised funds are, by far, the fastest growing charitable planning instrument. Both structures are covered in the same chapter as both share some common characteristics and, in many circumstances, are potential substitutes for each other.

The core purpose of both private foundations and donor advised funds is to hold wealth and distribute grants to public charities. They are, essentially, containers for wealth designated – at some point – to benefit charity. In this chapter, "private foundation" refers to a non-operating private foundation. The adjective "non-operating" points out that, although contributions to private foundations can generate charitable tax deductions, these organizations do not themselves conduct charitable activities. They simply hold wealth and distribute grants to charities that actually conduct charitable operations. Although not common, there are entities known as operating private foundations. These are more similar in function to regular public charitable organizations, are not typically used as a charitable planning vehicle, and will not be discussed in this chapter. Another relatively rare entity is called a "supporting organization." This entity functions similarly to a private foundation, but typically delivers support to a specific public charity. With the increased restrictions on supporting organizations brought about by the Pension Protection Act of 2006, these entities are relatively less attractive, less common, and, consequently, will not be covered in this chapter.

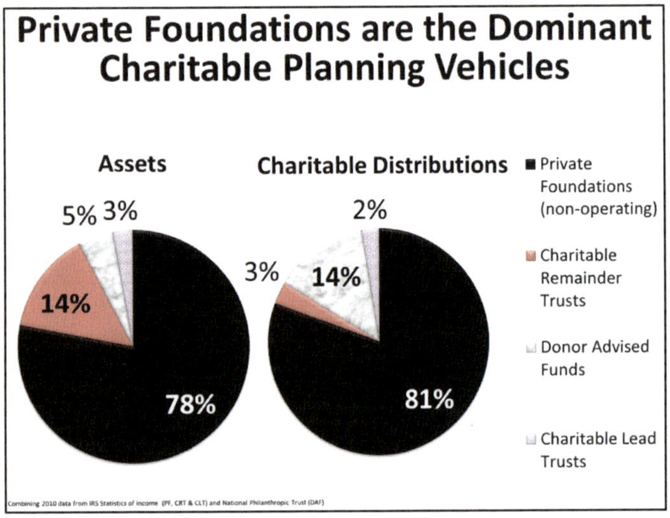

In terms of relative size, private foundations are the "Big Kahuna" of charitable planning. The accompanying chart demonstrates that. Private foundations hold more than four times the assets and make more than four times the charitable distributions of all Charitable Remainder Trusts, Charitable Lead Trusts, and donor advised funds combined. Despite the relatively small share of all assets held by donor advised funds (5%), these funds are responsible for an outsized portion of all charitable distributions (14%). This reflects the frequent use of such funds as a temporary pass-through mechanism, rather than an instrument for long-term wealth holding. Despite this common short-term use, donor advised funds can also be used for long-term, even multi-generational, holding of wealth.

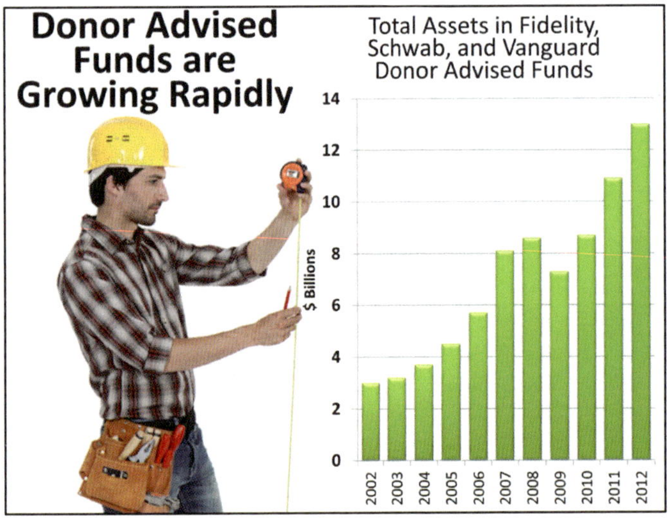

Another reason for interest in donor advised funds is their rapid growth. Donor advised funds have existed since the 1930's. Traditionally, they were operated by community foundations as a way to encourage giving that supported the local community. The dramatic growth in donor advised funds began with the creation of Fidelity Charitable Gift Fund in 1991. For the first time, this provided a nationally available means for donors to establish low-cost accounts where their financial advisors could continue to manage the funds and collect the associated management fees. This brought more financial advisors into the charitable planning arena than ever before. Since then, the dramatic growth in donor advised funds has been driven predominantly by growth in those funds affiliated with financial institutions. The accompanying chart shows the continued dramatic growth of the three largest financial-institution-affiliated donor advised funds.

Other charitable planning devices that hold wealth are typically designed to end after a few years or at the death of the donor. Charitable Gift Annuities, Charitable Remainder Trusts and Charitable Lead Trusts rarely exist much beyond the life of the donor, or perhaps the donor and the donor's spouse. Private foundations are different. These entities are often designed to last indefinitely and many have existed for numerous generations. In large part, private foundations are intended to be permanent entities.

The permanence of private foundations can make them particularly psychologically attractive to some donors. A branch of psychology, referred to as terror management theory, rigorously examines the effects of personal mortality reminders. Among other things, these reminders generate a psychological defense expressed as seeking symbolic immortality. Symbolic immortality is the idea that something important about one's self, e.g., one's name, impact, story, family, culture, community, or values, will live beyond one's death. This attraction towards symbolic immortality is particularly important in the context of charitable estate planning, when personal death reminders are particularly strong. (For a more extensive review of the psychology and neuroscience of charitable estate planning see the book, *Inside the Mind of the Bequest Donor: A visual presentation of the neuroscience and psychology of effective planned giving communication* by Russell James, ISBN 978-1484197837.)

The private foundation provides the ideal charitable structure for achieving this psychologically attractive symbolic immortality. The foundation typically bears the name of the founder or the founder's family. Unlike its mortal founder, the private foundation can live indefinitely. For generations after the death of the founding donor, the private foundation can continue to carry the founder's name and will be legally bound by the founder's values and desires, necessarily required to continue impacting the world within the parameters established by the founder. In this way, the private foundation can serve as a partial substitute for the deceased founder, indefinitely exhibiting to the public the positive and pro-social aspects of his or her character.

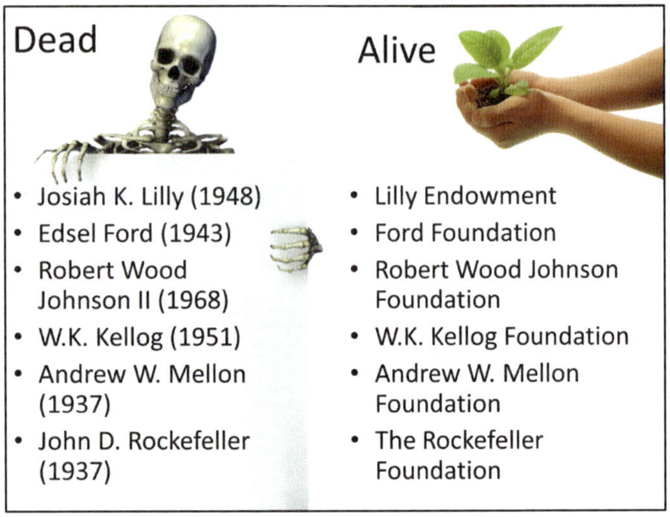

This continuation of the founder's name and ideals is not merely a theoretical idea, but one that can be readily seen in many of today's most important grant-making foundations. Although the founders of these famous foundations may have been deceased for many generations, their name and impact continues to this day. Such symbolic immortality becomes particularly attractive in an estate planning context as the client contemplates his or her personal mortality.

The private foundation's most attractive feature is its permanence. Not only can the foundation last indefinitely, but the rules established by the founding donor can also last indefinitely. Almost all other forms of transfers are subject to rapid dissipation in both finance and purpose. A wealthy business owner may leave behind an important company bearing his or her name, but the company can quickly change names and reject the values established by the founder. Leaving an inheritance to heirs is subject both to substantial taxation and to expenditures reflecting values contrary to the decedent's values. The private foundation offers a unique vehicle to preserve and protect the founder's wealth, name, and values.

Although a private foundation ultimately makes distributions to charitable organizations, it often involves the participation and substantial control of the founder's family both during and after the founder's life. The founder's family can be appointed to have the power to decide how the money will be invested and who (within the limits of the foundation guidelines) will receive distributions. In addition to controlling the wealth (largely undiluted by taxation either at transfer or on subsequent growth) within the parameters of the private foundation's purpose and guidelines, family members can receive benefits such as being reimbursed for their associated travel and expenses as well as being employed for reasonable compensation in some professional and managerial tasks necessary for operation of the foundation.

The private foundation can also serve as a way for the founder to transmit his or her values to later generations. These descendants may be appointed as trustees of the foundation and be given authority to make charitable distributions amongst the causes permitted by the founding donor. For example, a donor who wanted to pass along his love of nature might limit the charitable purposes to supporting nature organizations. Administration of such a foundation would likely increase trustees' involvement with the various related causes and organizations vying for the foundation's grants.

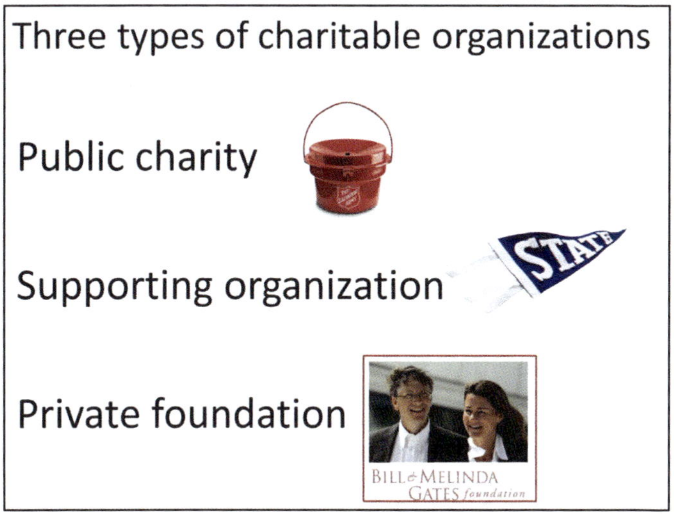

There are three large classes of charitable organizations that can generate charitable tax deductions for donors: public charities, supporting organizations, and private foundations. Due to the relatively rare creation of supporting organizations (wealth-holding entities designed to support a single or single set of public charities), this chapter will focus on public charities and private (non-operating) foundations. Public charities are typically the organizations that actually *do* charitable work. Private foundations simply hold wealth and distribute grants to these public charities.

In tax law a charitable organization is, by default, treated as a private foundation. All charitable organizations not meeting the guidelines for public charities (or supporting organizations) are automatically private foundations. Only if the charitable entity can *prove* it is a public charity (or supporting organization) will it be classified as such. The two ways in which an organization can prove it is a public charity is by showing that it actually engages in charitable operations (e.g., running a church, hospital, school, or homeless shelter) or by showing that it receives widespread financial support from the public. Although most public charities actually engage in charitable activity, it is possible for grant-making bodies to be public charities if they receive widespread financial support. For example, community foundations and united appeals (such as the United Way) can be public charities even if they only make grants to other public charities.

Most private foundations are quite similar. They are usually funded by a single person, family, or corporation. They don't *do* charitable work, but instead make grants to charities. Commonly their charitable expenditures are funded by financial returns on their invested assets. This idea of a pool of assets, set aside by one person, with charitable activity limited to issuing grants predominantly from investment income is the classic concept of the private foundation. The ways in which a charitable organization can avoid the default classification as a private foundation largely center on demonstrating a divergence from these classic elements of a private foundation. There are four approved pathways through which a charitable organization can qualify as a public charity.

Traditional charities qualify as public charities because they are primarily engaged in the day-to-day operation of delivering charitable services. In sharp contrast to a typical private foundation, these organizations do not simply make grants to others engaged in charitable operations. Churches, hospitals, schools, and other traditional operating charities qualify as public charities rather than private foundations due to the nature of their operations.

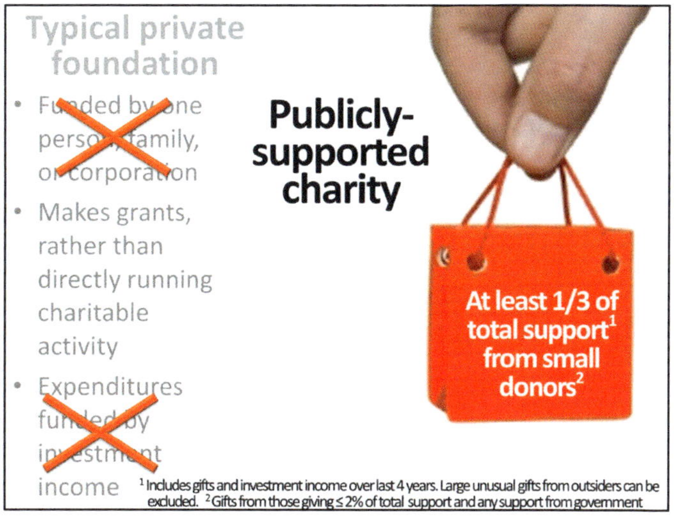

Another way that a charitable entity can be classified as a public charity is by having widespread financial support. Even if the charity is simply making grants and is not directly engaging in charitable operations, widespread financial support will cause it to be a public charity rather than a private foundation. In this first case, the concept of widespread financial support is a purely mathematically issue. The test is met if the support from those who individually give 2% or less of the total support (a.k.a. small donors) sums to at least one-third of all support given to the charity. In other words, if there are a lot of small donors who, combined, are financially important to the organization, then it isn't a private foundation. Instead, it is a public charity.

Suppose a grant-making charity received total support of $100,000. If 35 donors gave $1,000 a piece and the charity's founder gave $65,000, this charity would still pass the test for being a public charity, because more than 1/3 of all support came from small donors (those giving 2% or less of the total support).

There are two additions to this rule that prevent the charity from being disqualified due to financial support from government or an unusual large gift from an outside donor. Government support is treated as small donor support (i.e., less than 2% of total support), regardless of how large a share the government support actually constitutes. So, for example, if a non-operating, grant-making charity had $100,000 of total support consisting of a $65,000 gift from the charity founder and a $35,000 grant from government, the charity would qualify as a public charity. Additionally, unusual large gifts from an outside donor (i.e., not from the organization's founding donor, trustees, managers or their families) can be ignored. Suppose a non-operating, grant-making organization that otherwise would have had total support of $1,000 a piece from 35 donors and $65,000 from the founding donor received an additional one-time $100,000 gift from a wealthy donor unrelated to any of the organization's insiders. If this unusual gift were included in the calculation, it would disqualify the organization from being a public charity, because the small donor support of $35,000 would then constitute only 17.5% of total support. For this reason, such an unusual gift from an outsider can be excluded from the calculation.

A more subjective rule allows for small donor support (including government support) to constitute as little as 10% of the organization's total support. However, in order to take advantage of this lower limit, the charity must also fulfill two subjective requirements. First, the charity must be operated in such a way as to be intentionally attempting to attract new public or government support. In other words, the charity is not yet at the 1/3 level, but it is at 10% and appears to be working to grow that 10%. Finally, the "facts and circumstances" must suggest that it is appropriate to treat the organization as a public charity. In a sense, a charity (other than a traditional operating charity) with small donor (and government) support between 1/10 and 1/3 of total support is in a "maybe" zone for qualification as a public charity. This subjectivity allows for open consideration of any circumstances that might make the charity appear more like a classic private foundation or more like a public charity. Because of the subjectivity, it may be useful to think of this as a "smell" test asking, "Does this smell more like a private foundation or a public charity?"

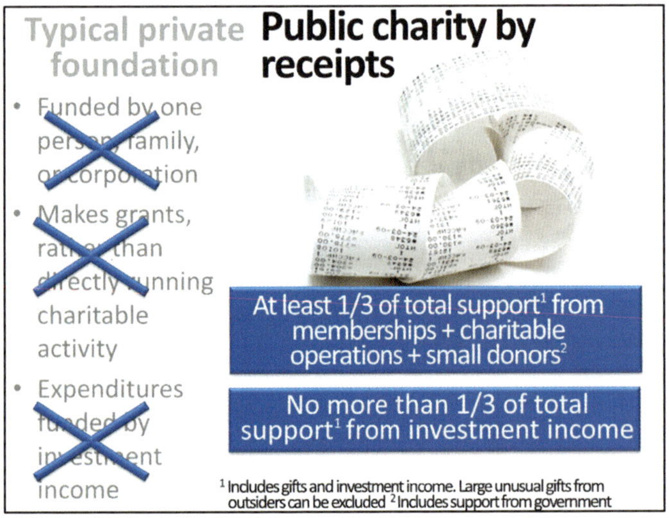

Finally, a charity can qualify as a public charity based upon not only its small donor support, but also its income memberships and any charitable operations. If these sum to at least 1/3 of total support and the charity receives no more than 1/3 of total support from investment income, then the charity will qualify as a public charity.

For example, if a local parent-teacher association received $10,000 in total income from $4,000 in memberships, $4,000 in bake sale profits, and $2,000 in investment returns, with no donations and no income from charitable operations, the organization would qualify as a public charity. This is because at least 1/3 of total support came from memberships ($4,000, which is 40% of total support), small donations ($0), and income from charitable operations ($0). Additionally, no more than 1/3 of total support came from investment income ($2,000, which is 20% of total support).

If instead, the organization received its $10,000 of total support from $4,000 in memberships and $6,000 in investment returns, then it would not qualify under this rule. This large investment income (more than 1/3 of all support) shades the organization more into the appearance of a private foundation.

A charitable organization can qualify as a public charity through any of these four rules. However, if the charitable organization does not qualify under these rules (nor under rules for supporting organizations), then the default classification as a private foundation remains.

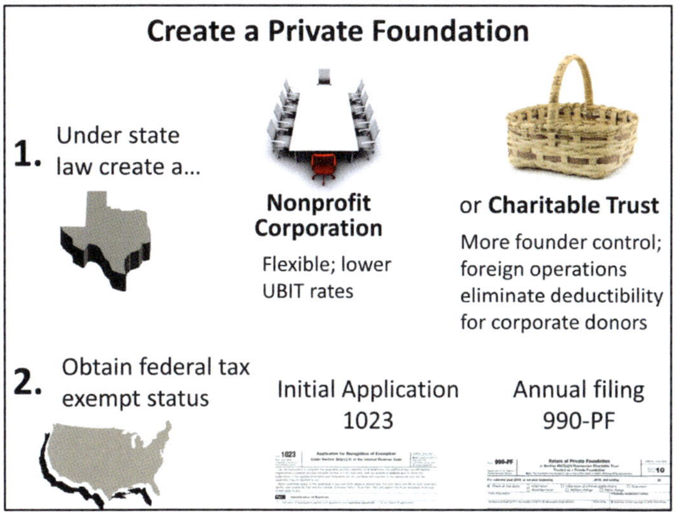

In order to receive tax treatment as a private foundation, the organization must first be brought into existence under state law. A private foundation can be structured as either a nonprofit corporation or a charitable trust. Charitable trusts allow for more founder control in that the trust document can be specific and restrictive as to the permitted activities of the trust. The corporate structure offers flexibility to future directors, allowing amendments that can alter the corporation's goals, structure, and operation. The corporate structure may offer some additional tax benefits, such as lower tax rates for unrelated business income. Additionally, gifts by corporations to a nonprofit trust that makes international grants are not deductible, but gifts by corporations to a nonprofit corporation that makes international grants are deductible. So, if the founder intends for the foundation to both receive gifts from corporations and make grants in other nations, the corporate form will be preferred over the trust form.

Once the foundation organization has been created under state law, it can then seek recognition as a tax-exempt organization for federal tax purposes. This begins with the filing of IRS Form 1023. Granting of this tax exempt status will be retroactive to the date the private foundation was created if Form 1023 is filed within 15 months of the creation date. Once granted, continuing tax exempt status requires the annual filing of IRS Form 990-PF. This process is similar to that required of all nonprofit organizations (except churches), which are required to annually file the IRS Form 990. States differ as to their requirements for getting recognition as a nonprofit organization for state tax purposes, with some accepting the federal recognition and others having their own separate processes.

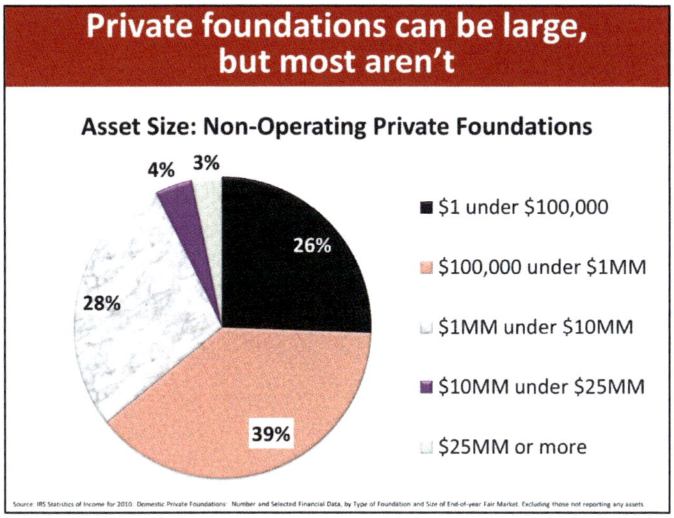

As stand-alone organizations private foundations require various forms of administration such as accounting, annual tax filings, recordkeeping, and, in the case of corporate foundations, regular annual meetings. Combining this with the cost of creating the initial organization suggests that the hassle might not be justified for relatively small amounts. Nevertheless, of the more than 83,000 non-operating private foundations holding assets in the year 2010, more than one-fourth held less than $100,000, and nearly two-thirds held assets less than one million dollars.

The board of the foundation, and the rules for adding or replacing board members, is typically selected by the founding donor. As a result, it is most common for the foundation creator to select like-minded individuals, usually family members. The selection of family members can serve several purposes. Involving family members in the operation of the board can help to transmit the founder's charitable values. Additionally, travel and expenses to attend board meetings or visit current or potential grantee sites can be paid for board members. Board members may also benefit from the prestige and influence that comes from being an important decision-maker regarding distribution of funds.

There is no set requirement for how a board must function. It is possible to have different voting rights and different terms for different types of board members. Rules for continuation as a board member, especially in the context of a charitable trust, may be as unique as each founder. Although minor children cannot make legal decisions that would bind the organization, they can serve on an advisory "junior board" that considers some types of grants or other issues. This junior board concept can be used to aid in the training of a younger generation of future board members and to justify reimbursement of the travel expenses of such junior members' travel to board meeting locations.

Once a private foundation has been successfully created, the primary guidelines for its operation come from federal tax law. Tax law affects private foundations indirectly, through the deductibility of gifts, and directly, through taxation of investment income and levying of penalties for violations of IRS rules.

Unlike other charitable entities, private foundations do pay taxes on net investment income and capital gains. However, this tax is relatively minimal, typically charged at the 2% rate. This 2% rate will drop to 1% if the foundation distributes charitable grants at least equal to its assets multiplied by its average percentage payout for the last five years (or less if the foundation is not that old) plus 1% of its net investment income. For a private foundation intending to distribute the same percentage of assets in charitable grants as it had done over the previous five years, this rule means that the 1% payment can go either to the IRS (by payment of the 2% standard excise tax) or to a public charity (thus reducing the IRS obligation by 1%). Although private foundations are not completely tax exempt, the burden of a 1% or 2% tax is relatively minimal.

This tax is paid on net investment income and net capital gains. However, the tax is not paid on any unrelated business income, which is taxed at different rates. Net investment income allows for the reduction of gross investment income by any ordinary and necessary expenses incurred in generating the income (such as investment management fees, real estate management fees, or the share of officer or employee compensation related to investment and investment management).

As discussed in the chapter on this topic, private foundations have lower income limitations for charitable deductions than public charities do. The highest (50%) limitation is never available for deductions from gifts to private foundations, which are instead limited to 30% or 20% of adjusted gross income (slightly modified) for individual taxpayers, and 10% of taxable income for corporations. Any deductions from charitable gifts in excess of the maximum percentage of the donor's income cannot be deducted in the year of the gift, but must instead be carried forward until such time as they can be used without causing the total deductions to exceed the relevant limitation. Carryover deductions that cannot be used in the five years following the year of the gift will expire.

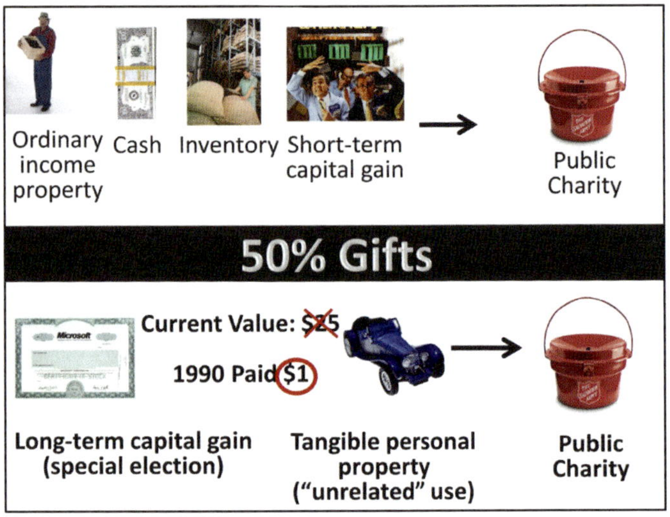

As discussed in a previous chapter, gifts that may be deducted up to 50% of income are all gifts to public charities.

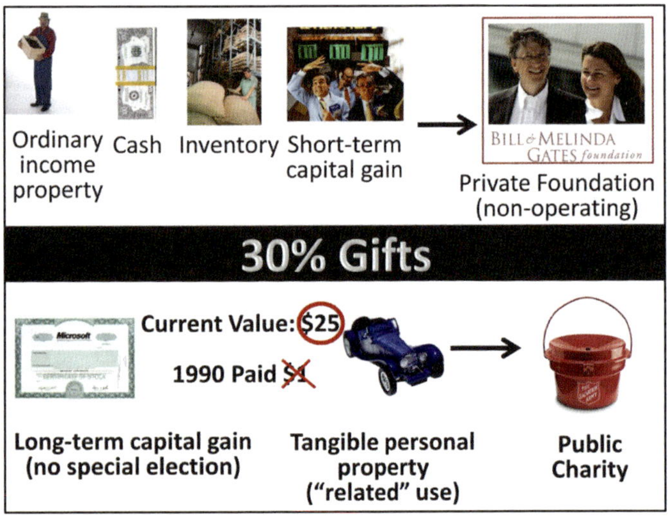

Gifts to private foundations of cash, inventory, short-term capital gain or ordinary income may be deducted up to 30% of the donor's income, with the remainder carried forward.

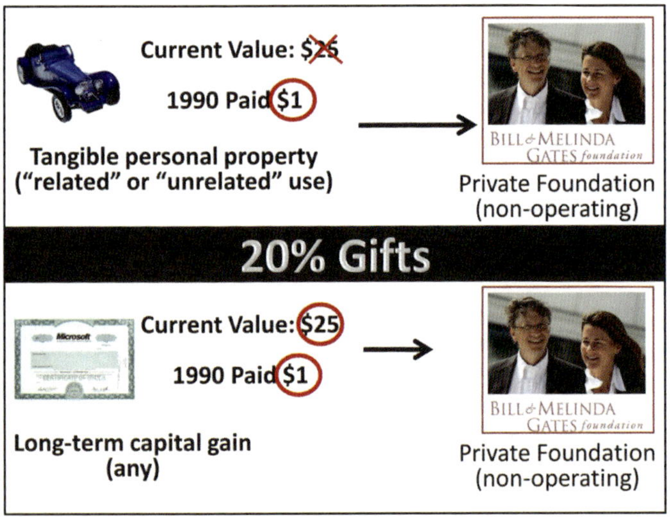

Any gifts of long-term capital gain to a private foundation may be deducted only up to 20% of the donor's income, with the rest carried forward into future years. This is true regardless of whether or not the gift can be valued at the greater of or the lower of basis or fair market value.

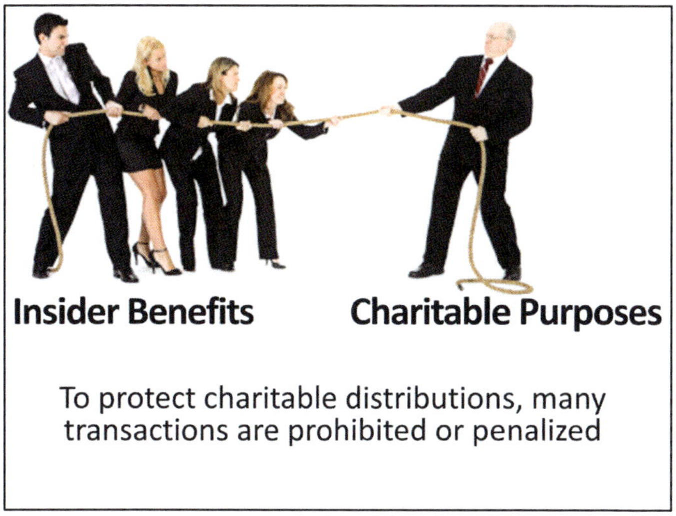

The underlying reason for many of the tax rules for private foundations is the desire to insure that the foundations appropriately pursue a charitable purpose and do not use their resources to provide benefits to insiders. Prior to the passage of these rules many private foundations were used in such a way as to provide excessive benefit to those who created and operated the foundations.

Private foundations receive highly favorable tax treatment for the purpose of encouraging charitable activity. The rules designed to prevent insider benefits and insure that the charitable purposes are being accomplished fall into the five categories of (1) self-dealing, (2) failure to distribute income, (3) excess business holding, (4) jeopardizing investments, and (5) taxable expenditures.

A range of penalties can arise for violating these tax rules, from an initial tax to additional taxes if the violation is not corrected to revocation of the exempt status of the foundation. Previous to this legislation the only penalty was revocation of the tax exempt status. Due to the harshness of the penalty, it was rarely enforced, leading to the need for the current system allowing for intermediate penalties.

As mentioned above, a wide range of rules protects against giving excess benefits to insiders. Enforcement of these rules requires a definition for who is and who is not an insider. The tax code uses the term "disqualified person" to designate a foundation insider.

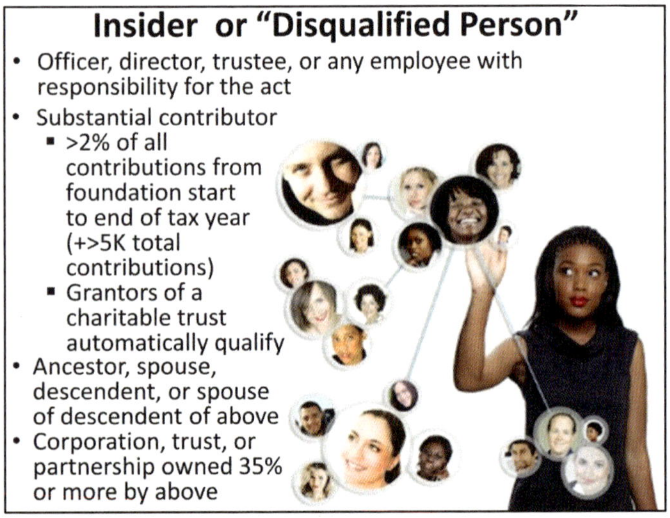

The definition of a disqualified person is, in most respects, extraordinarily broad. Naturally, the people running the foundation are insiders. This includes officers, directors, and trustees of the foundation. However, it can also include any employee of the foundation if the employee has responsibility for the act under consideration as a potential violation of the rules. In addition to those who run the foundation, those who create or significantly support the foundation are also insiders. The original founder (grantor) of a charitable trust is automatically an insider regardless of whether or not he or she is a substantial donor. Additionally, any donor who has given more than 2% of the total contributions ever given to the foundation is also an insider (assuming that the donor's contributions are greater than $5,000 in total).

The designation of "disqualified person" applies not only to these donors or managers, but also to all of their ancestors, descendants, spouses, or spouses of descendants. Curiously, this definition – although broad reaching – does not include the siblings of insiders. Additionally, organizations significantly controlled by disqualified persons are also disqualified persons. Specifically, any corporation, trust, or partnership that is owned or controlled 35% or more by *all disqualified persons combined* is also a disqualified person. For example if a corporation is owned 10% by the founding donor's grandson, 10% by the founding donor's grandson's wife and 15% by the mother of an unrelated foundation trustee, then the corporation is itself a disqualified person.

This first set of rules designed to limit insider benefits is a prohibition against self-dealing. Self-dealing rules prohibit most transactions between the private foundation and the disqualified person.

Self-dealing rules prohibit the private foundation from selling, exchanging, leasing, transferring or loaning money, goods, services, property or facilities to a disqualified person. Correspondingly, they also prohibit disqualified persons from selling, exchanging, leasing, transferring or loaning money, goods, services, property or facilities to the private foundation except when this occurs as a free gift. Rather than investigating the propriety of each individual transaction with disqualified persons, this rule simply prohibits all of them.

Prior legislation permitted self-dealing transactions if they were completed under reasonable terms comparable to an "arm's length" transaction. However, this previous rule made enforcement difficult and permitted substantial benefits to insiders. For example, a private foundation might purchase property from an insider for fair market value, but provide benefit by offering the insider a source for an immediate sale, whereas selling in the market could require much time. Or, a private foundation might offer a loan to an insider at market interest rates, but during a time when financial liquidity was tight and other sources of credit were unavailable. None of these transactions are permitted under the current rules, because their relative benefit to the foundation is now irrelevant. All such transactions are simply prohibited.

In addition to the prohibition against transactions with disqualified persons, this section also prohibits transactions with government officials – primarily those with a policymaking role. This rule relates to the core idea that private foundations should not be used for political purposes. Further, an insider could benefit through gaining political influence by using the foundation to influence government officials.

These transactions with disqualified persons are categorically prohibited and this prohibition does not depend upon the relative benefit given to the foundation. For example, a donor could sell a $200,000 property to a public charity for $10,000. Under the bargain sale rules, this would generate a $190,000 deductible charitable gift. However, if the donor completed the identical transaction with a private foundation for which the donor was a disqualified person the transaction would be a prohibited act of self-dealing. The fact that the private foundation received a $190,000 benefit is irrelevant; the exchange is still prohibited.

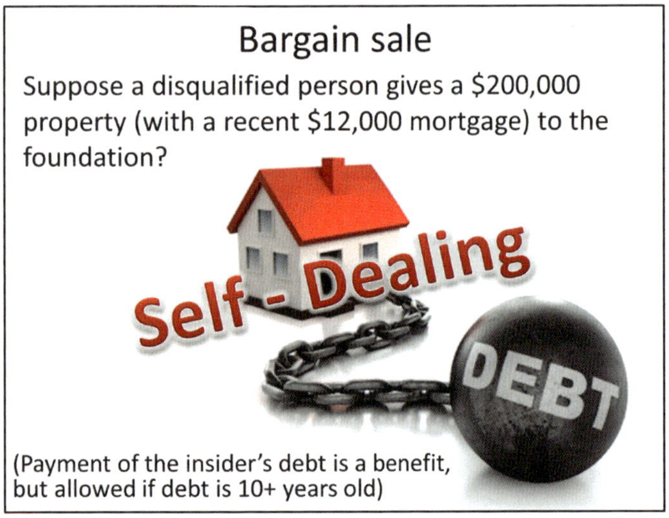

In an attempt to circumvent this rule against bargain sales, a disqualified person might be tempted to simply take out a mortgage, take the money, and then donate both the property and the mortgage to the private foundation. However, the private foundation's acceptance of the debt incurred by the insider is considered to be a benefit to the insider and, consequently, the transaction is prohibited. As before, this is true regardless of how beneficial the transaction is to the private foundation. Even if the mortgage is less than, say, 10% of the value of the property donated, it is still a prohibited act of self-dealing. This rule has one exception which permits the private foundation to accept a property that an insider has encumbered with debt if the debt is at least ten years old.

Self-dealing transactions generate a 10% penalty for the disqualified person and an additional 5% penalty for the foundation manager who knowingly participates in such a transaction. (Given the broad definition for disqualified persons, it is possible, for example, that the foundation manager was unaware that the person was a disqualified person.) In addition to this penalty, the transaction must be undone. This correction is required within 90 days of the IRS notice, otherwise the foundation is subject to an additional tax of 200% of the transaction amount, and the foundation manager is subject to an additional tax of 50% of the transaction amount. An excessive degree of self-dealing could, in extreme cases, also lead to the removal of the foundation's tax exempt status.

Despite this blanket prohibition on transactions with insiders, the rules do permit some exceptions. These permitted transactions include, obviously, the ability of disqualified persons to make gifts to the foundation. Thus free gifts (e.g., not bargain sales or debt-encumbered property) of money, property, or the use of money or property are allowed. However, these gifts cannot require the foundation to make any payments back to a disqualified person. For example, a disqualified person cannot give free rent of office space to the charity with the requirement that the foundation must pay the disqualified person for utilities, insurance, or maintenance. A gift of free rent is allowed if such payments are not made to the disqualified person, but are instead made to an outside utility company, insurance company, or maintenance company.

Despite this prohibition on self-dealing, some transactions with benefit to insiders are specifically allowed. In particular, a foundation can hire an insider to perform necessary professional and managerial services so long as the compensation is reasonable. The official term for these permitted services is "personal services," and it includes investment advice, legal services, accounting, tax services, banking, and administrative assistance. This does not include non-professional or non-managerial services such as janitorial work. The compensation for such services must be reasonable. In order to assist foundation managers in knowing and demonstrating what compensation is reasonable, The Council on Foundations publishes the *Foundation Management Report* giving compensation information for a variety of positions for foundations of different sizes. So long as the payments to insiders are for services necessary for the operation of the charity and fall within these reasonable guidelines, the foundation is allowed to hire these disqualified persons.

In addition to the ability of the foundation to hire and pay reasonable compensation to disqualified persons for necessary professional and managerial services, the foundation may also reimburse the reasonable travel expenses of insiders necessary for the operation of the foundation. For example, reimbursing travel and meal costs for board members to attend a board meeting of the foundation is a commonly accepted foundation expenditure. The foundation may not reimburse expenses for other family members to travel when those family members are not a necessary part of the foundation's activities. So, the travel expenses of a board member's spouse may not be reimbursed unless the spouse is also a board member (or is filling some other necessary function for the foundation). As discussed previously, a private foundation may have a junior board, including minors, which is allowed to make recommendations for grants and gradually learn about foundation management in potential preparation for a future appointment to the regular board. The use of such boards can make the travel of minor children to board meetings a reasonable and necessary expense. In addition to travel to board meetings, travel to investigate current or potential grant recipients is also a commonly accepted activity, and thus reimbursement of reasonable expenses are also appropriate. Some founders may employ these travel reimbursements for necessary board functions as a way to pay for family gatherings in attractive locations.

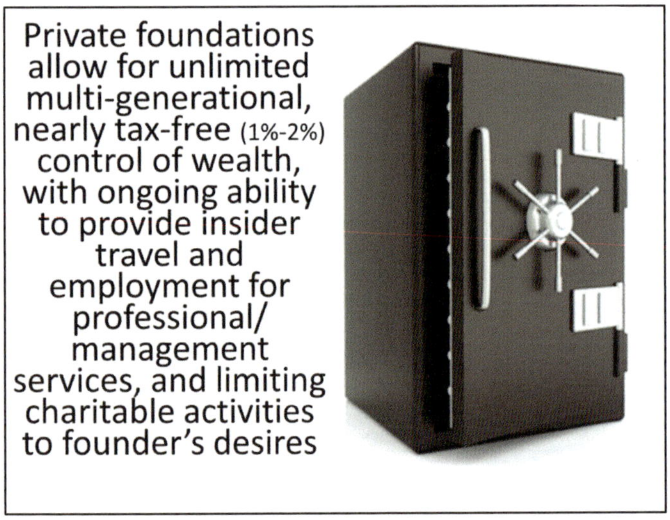

A wealthy donor may choose to ignore sophisticated planning and simply leave the estate to his or her children (perhaps with some donation to charity). This type of traditional inheritance typically results in dissipation of the family's wealth. The wealth is dissipated first by division among heirs at each generation, leaving smaller and smaller separate amounts. Additionally, the wealth is subject to 40% estate taxes at every generation, further reducing remaining wealth. Beyond this, investment returns in the intervening years are subject to constant annual taxation. All of this dissipation by division and taxation occurs even if every heir in every generation is completely responsible and consumes none of the original inheritance. The likelihood of a spendthrift heir – or one who is attracted to highly risky investments – dramatically increases the likelihood of rapid dissipation. (A recent national U.S. study shows that 1/3 of all heirs receiving inheritances spend their entire inheritance within a few months. In addition, among all heirs, about half of the typical inheritance has been spent within 12 months. See Zagorsky, J. L. (2012). Do people save or spend their inheritances? Understanding what happens to inherited wealth. *Journal of Family and Economic Issues*) The typical pattern of family wealth accumulation and dissipation has generated such common descriptions as "from shirtsleeves to shirtsleeves in three generations," to reflect its temporary nature.

In contrast, a private foundation can provide an excellent means to keep the family's wealth completely intact across many generations and still provide some attractive benefits to heirs. The use of the family foundation means that there is no dissipation by division at each generation, no estate taxes at each generation, no annual taxes on earning and gains (beyond the 1% or 2% excise tax), and no temptation for spendthrift heirs to benefit themselves by consuming all of the assets. Even excessively risky investments are prohibited by tax law. Although some transfers (discussed below) must be made to charitable organizations, these are typically less than the investment income generated by the foundation's assets. Heirs who are involved with the work of the foundation have the benefit of employment (assuming some professional or managerial skills) and travel. Additionally, those controlling significant distribution decisions often enjoy the less documented benefits of this financial power. Managers of recipient nonprofits may be more than happy to provide favors in order to build good relationships with those who make substantial funding decisions. Although such favors cannot be direct transfers to disqualified persons, the ability to subtly influence organizational decisions (including hiring decisions) of recipient nonprofit organizations may be indirectly valuable.

The private foundation offers a means by which a donor's wealth can remain intact, and growing, for indefinite generations serving only the causes the donor has selected and benefitting subsequent generations of managing heirs both directly and indirectly. The donor's financial managers can also benefit substantially by keeping the wealth intact, undivided, and largely untaxed across generations.

Private foundations are, of course, charitable entities. These entities do not engage in charitable activities directly, i.e., these are *non-operating* private foundations. The charitable nature of a private foundation depends entirely upon its distributions to operating charities. Consequently, a private foundation is required to make a minimum amount of distributions (i.e., gifts or grants) to public charities.

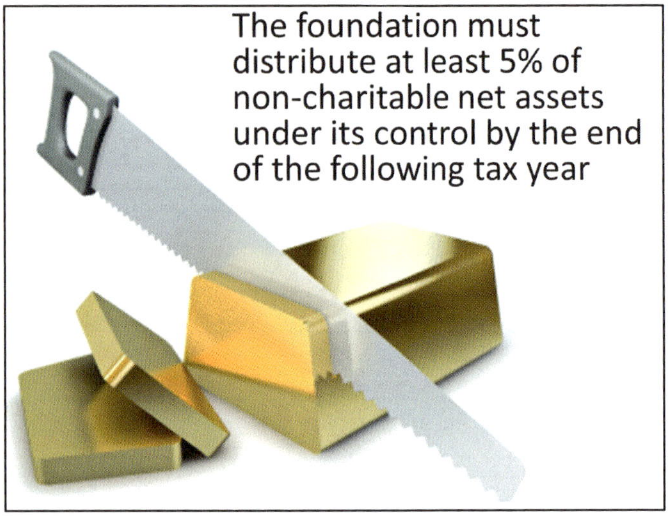

A private foundation is required to distribute at least 5% of all non-charitable net assets (i.e., investment assets) under its control at the end of the tax year. This distribution must be made by the end of the following tax year. Violating this requirement to make charitable distributions is sometimes referred to as a failure to distribute income, although the required distributable amount is based entirely upon the foundation's non-charitable assets. (In previous legislation distributions were based, in part, upon income.)

The value of non-charitable net assets is reduced by any debt used by the foundation to purchase investment assets. These assets do not include charitable assets, i.e., assets being used in a charitable operation such as a painting being loaned without charge to a public charity art gallery. This charitable exclusion also excludes assets being used by the foundation to carry out its own exempt purposes, but not those being used by the foundation for investment management purposes. (This distinction would require a foundation that owns the building in which it operates to allocate the value between charitable and other functions.) Non-charitable net assets excludes assets that, even though they are booked as assets, are not yet under the control of the foundation such as pledges to make a gift or a future interest in real estate.

The 5% required distributable amount is reduced by the taxes paid to the government either as the 1% or 2% net investment income tax or any unrelated business income tax paid by the foundation. There is, however, no reduction in the required distributable amount due to penalty taxes paid for violating any of the private foundation rules discussed in this chapter.

The 5% requirement does not mean that the entire 5% (less the unrelated business income tax and net investment income tax) must actually be distributed to charity. Any reasonable and necessary administrative expenses incurred for grant-making or fundraising are themselves considered to be charitable expenditures. Thus, the 5% would be reduced by reasonable and necessary expenses for administration costs related to soliciting and evaluating grant applications (such as travel to meet with grant applicants), supervising the use of funds granted (such as travel to review the use of funds), and general administration of the charitable functions of the foundation (such as employee salaries, office rent, utilities, IRS form 990-PF preparation fees, and legal fees related to charitable functions). These expenses do not include any expenses associated with managing the foundation's investments. Due to the reductions for expenses and taxes, the actual amount distributed to public charities may be far less than 5% of non-charitable assets held by the foundation. The only limitation is that these operational expenses must be reasonable and necessary to accomplish the charitable functions of the foundation.

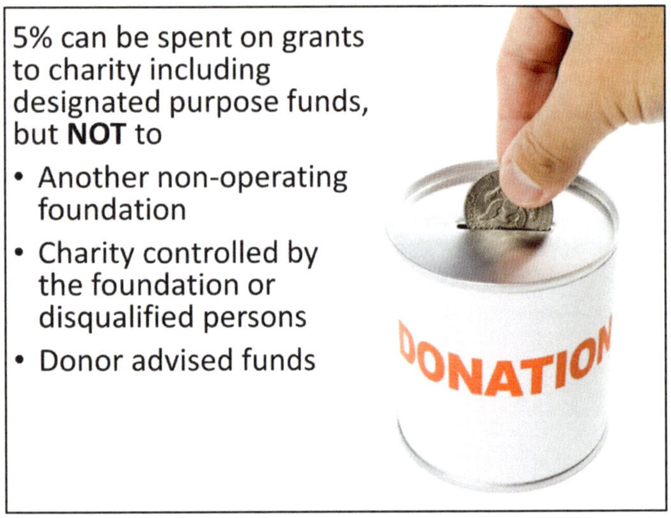

The point of the required distributable amount is to insure that some share of the foundation's assets is actually used in charitable operations. Consequently, distributions to other non-operating foundations do not qualify. This would simply be transferring funds from one holding area to another, rather than actually making funds available for charitable operations. For similar reasons, transfers to donor advised funds will not qualify. The charity receiving the funds cannot be controlled, either directly or indirectly, by the foundation or by any disqualified persons. In this case, control means that any combination of disqualified persons could, working together, require or prevent the recipient charity from making an expenditure. Although disqualified persons may not control the recipient charity, the private foundation is allowed to make a restricted gift which the recipient charity must use for the designated purposes.

The private foundation need not make transfers only as cash gifts to public charities, but may also purchase or improve assets used directly in charitable purposes. This could include assets transferred to a public charity, or assets used by the private foundation for charitable purposes. Thus, the purchase of a building to be used exclusively by the foundation in its charitable purposes (e.g., soliciting and evaluating grant applications and evaluating grant expenditures, but not investment management) is a qualifying distribution.

The general rule is that a nonoperating private foundations must make qualifying distributions of at least 5% (reduced by payments for net investment income tax or unrelated business income tax) of its net non-charitable investment assets. However, private foundations are allowed to accumulate funds instead of distributing them as a means of saving up for a later large qualifying distribution in certain cases.

Saving up these charitable distributions is referred to as a "set aside," following the idea that these funds are set aside for future qualifying distributions. This is permitted only if the project would be better accomplished through saving up these distributions than by making them immediately and if the qualifying distributions are made within 60 months of the first set aside. These sets asides are typically used for very large single purchases, such as the purchase or construction of a building.

Not only may a nonoperating private foundation save up qualifying distributions through a set aside plan, but it may also do the reverse and make a large qualifying distribution today which will reduce the requirement for future qualifying distributions. Thus, any amount paid by the private foundation in excess of the 5% minimum requirement can be carried over for up to 5 years. During this carry over period, the excess amount can be used to reduce any remaining required qualifying distributions not paid during any year. The carry forward amounts are used much like charitable tax deductions carried forward due to exceeding the income giving limitations in that transfers made during the tax year are counted first and only then can carry forward distributions be used with the oldest non-expired carry forward distributions being used first.

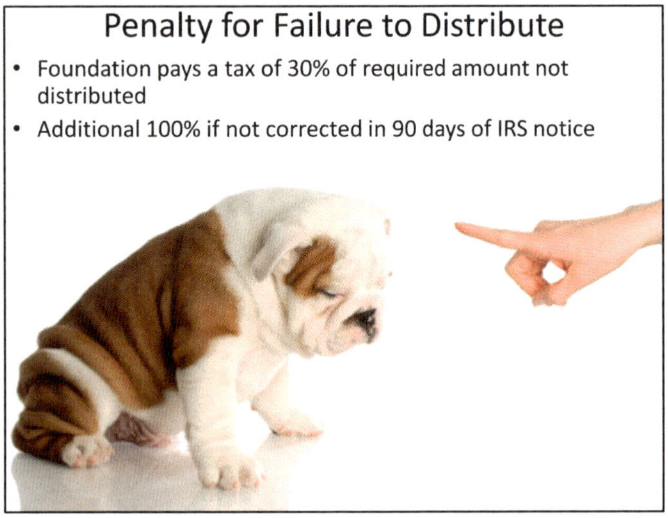

As with the other violations, failure to distribute the minimum required amount to charity results in a tax penalty. The penalty begins at 30% of the undistributed amount. An additional tax of 100% of the undistributed amount is charged if the distribution is not made within 90 days of the IRS notice of the violation. These taxes do not substitute for the payments to charity, and that obligation remains. Persistent failure to distribute could result in the revocation of the foundation's tax exempt status.

The next type of prohibited transactions is excess business holdings where the private foundation, combined with insiders, holds too large of a share of a business entity.

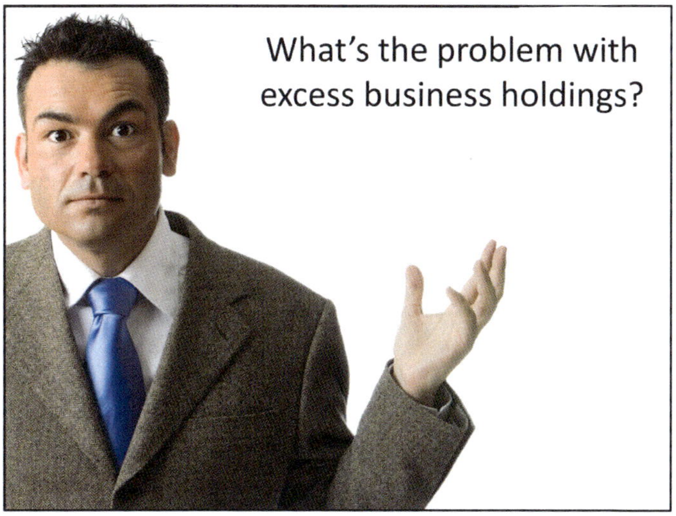

Prior to the legislation preventing excess business holdings an owner could transfer his or her business into the private foundation, take a tax deduction for the transfer, and still continue to control the business precisely as before with no functional changes. This level of control created a number of opportunities for abuse.

The problems with excessive business holdings come because the donor receives a tax deduction, but continues to control the business. This control means that the donor can decide if any profit is distributed to the foundation, which was particularly important under previous legislation where charitable distributions were based upon income rather than assets. Further, the donor – as controller of the business – would continue to control his own personal compensation as well as all other employees. A donor could thus transfer a business into a foundation, take a large tax deduction, and then extract the value out of the business through salaries paid to the donor and the donor's family members as employees of the business. This payment of salary (or, e.g., "sweetheart" deals benefitting others in exchange for reciprocal treatment in the donor's other non-charitably owned operations) could be used to cause the company to incur losses, reducing the value of the company, and thus reducing the foundation's required charitable grants based on the company's value. The various schemes for taking a large deduction at transfer and then subtly extracting the value from the company without benefitting the private foundation are nearly limitless, but all are predicated upon the donor being able to control the underlying business entity. Thus, the tax code was changed to eliminate the use of private foundations as a means to control an operating business.

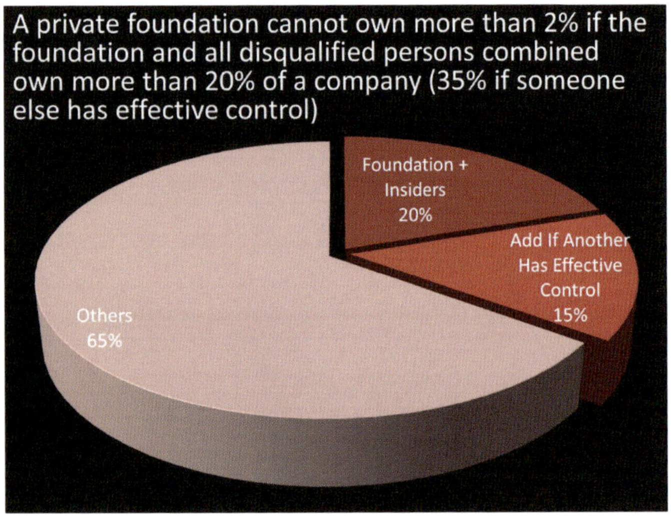

A private foundation is allowed to own up to 2% of a company regardless of the ownership interests of other insiders. Thus, a private foundation could own 2% of a corporation that was otherwise entirely owned by the founding donor. A private foundation may not own more than 2% of a business entity if the foundation and all insiders *combined* own more than 20% of a business entity. Ownership can refer to voting stock ownership in a corporation, beneficial interests in a trust, or profit interest in a partnership. (Thus, e.g., a private foundation may own 100% of non-voting shares in a corporation where it and all disqualified persons combined own fewer than 20% of the shares.) This permitted ownership percentage will increase to 35% where the foundation can demonstrate that an unrelated person or "cohesive group of third parties" does, in fact, exercise control over the business. In this case, the risk of abuse is likely reduced by the influence of an outside controlling person or group.

An exception to the prohibition against private foundations controlling a business is allowed when the business entity is engaged in activity directly related to the private foundation's charitable purposes, and not simply through earning profits for the foundation's use. Thus, a private foundation could have full control of a school or hospital and thereby further its charitable purposes in education or healthcare. Other allowed businesses include thrift shops selling donated items, a business operated by volunteers, or a business primarily for the convenience of the employees or customers of its charitable business, such as a hospital gift shop or museum cafeteria.

Additionally, a private foundation is allowed to have full ownership of a "passive" business entity that merely collects payments from assets such as dividends from stock holdings, interest from investments, royalties from intellectual property or rent from real estate. So long as this type of income constitutes at least 95% of the business entity's gross income, full ownership of the entity is allowed. Similar to the rules for unrelated business income, borrowing money to purchase real estate (i.e., leverage) will cause such investments to no longer be passive.

The private foundation finding itself in the circumstance of owning excess interest in a business must sell or transfer those interests. This sale must occur within 90 days if the foundation acquired the business interests by purchase or within five years if the foundation receives the business interests by gift. This five year limitation allows time for a business owner to transfer all or part of his or her business to his or her private foundation prior to a sale (thus avoiding the capital gains taxes that would otherwise be due at sale) and still have sufficient time to market and sell the asset, even in a difficult market. Indeed, if the five years is not sufficient to achieve and appropriate sale, the foundation may go through a procedure to request an extension of the time from the IRS, allowing for up to five additional years.

As with other violations, a private foundation having excess business holding is subject to tax penalties. The foundation must pay a tax of 10% of any excess holdings, based upon the highest excess business holdings occurring during the tax year. If the excess business holdings are not removed from the foundation within 90 days of the IRS notice of the violation an additional 200% penalty may be imposed.

In order to preserve the charitable function of the private foundation, the tax code prohibits the foundation from investing in jeopardizing (excessively risky) investments.

Without this restriction, there is a risk that the private foundation's assets could be squandered, thus eliminating any further charitable benefit. In such a case, the taxpayer would have received a large charitable tax deduction, but with no resulting charitable activity. Issuing charitable tax deductions in return for little or no charitable activity violates charitable tax policy principles and, consequently, such risky investments are prohibited.

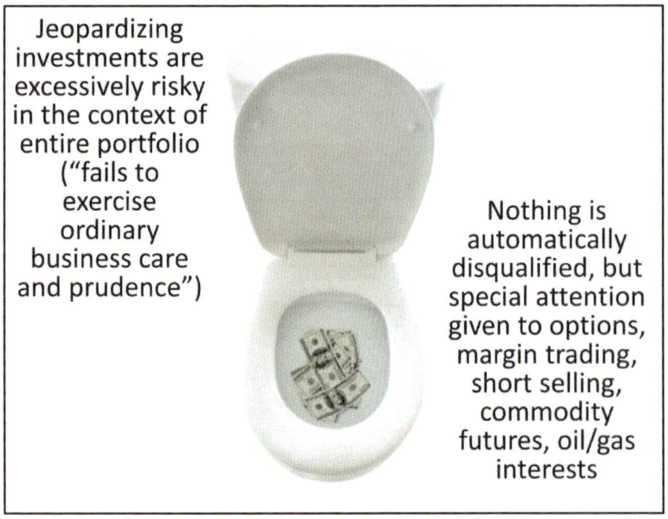

There is no "black and white" rule to determine what a jeopardizing investment is. Instead, it occurs when the manager "fails to exercise ordinary business care and prudence." Although a particular investment may be highly risky, it will be considered in the context of the entire portfolio. For example, the purchase of 60-day out-of-the-money options could be a reasonable part of a hedging strategy taken in the context of other asset holdings, but would clearly be a jeopardizing investment if such options constituted the foundation's entire investment portfolio. Because of the potential for excessive risk, the IRS will pay particular attention to investments in options, margin trading, short selling, commodity futures, and oil and gas interests. Nevertheless, each of these may be a perfectly appropriate investment in the context of the risk profile of the overall investment portfolio.

Because the purpose of the jeopardizing investment rule is to ensure that charitable activity will ultimately occur, rather than the assets being squandered, the rule will not apply to high risk investments that are primarily intended to advance charitable goals. Thus, investments in college loans for needy students or low-income housing may indeed by highly risky, but will not constitute jeopardizing investments. In this case even if the foundation loses its investment, the funds were still used to advance charitable purposes and so the underlying tax policy goals were not violated.

As a penalty for making a jeopardizing investment the foundation must pay a tax of 10% of the amount invested in the jeopardizing investment. Because the foundation manager is directly responsible for managing the foundation's assets, he or she will also be charged a penalty of 5% of the amount invested up to a $10,000 penalty if he or she willingly and knowingly participated in making the investment without any reasonable cause for doing so. As with other violations, an additional tax applies if the violation is not corrected within 90 days of the IRS notice of violation. If the foundation has not divested itself of the jeopardizing investment within this time, the foundation is subject to another tax of 25% of the amount invested in the jeopardizing investment, and the manager may pay an additional 5% of the amount invested up to an additional $20,000 penalty.

The final way in which the private foundation rules attempt to protect charitable purposes is to prohibit and penalize non-charitable grants from the foundation. These non-charitable grants are referred to as taxable expenditures.

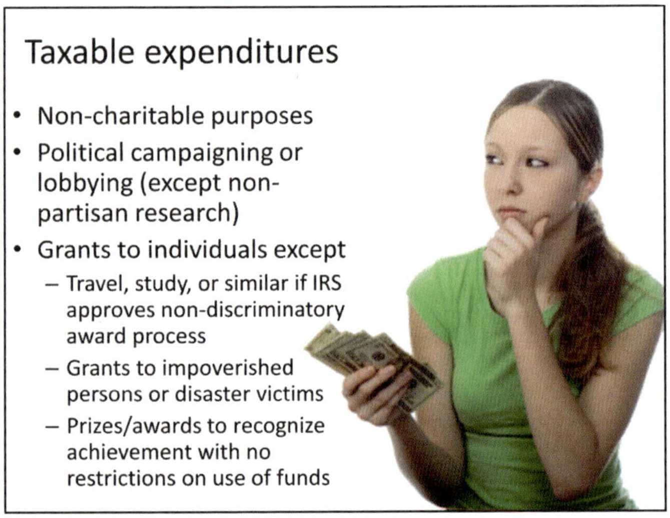

Any grant made by the foundation that does not qualify as an appropriate charitable grant is a prohibited taxable expenditure. This is not a problem for typical grants made to public charities. However, prior to the current law some private foundations were being used to further political campaigns, which is not a charitable purpose. Thus, the use of funds for campaigning and lobbying are now prohibited as taxable expenditures. Non-partisan research is allowed, but there is careful oversight of such activities. For example, support of voter registration drives is not allowed if such drives are limited to specific geographical regions as this may advantage one party or candidate.

Grants to individuals are not charitable gifts, because an individual is not a charity. However, in certain cases a private foundation may fund a grant to individuals for travel, study, or similar purposes. This may be done only with advanced approval of the granting procedures by the IRS. In seeking such approval, the foundation must show that the grant is (1) a scholarship to a nonprofit educational institution, (2) a prize made primarily in recognition of religious, charitable, scientific, educational, artistic, literary, or civic achievement, [note that these awards may be made without prior approval by the IRS if there are no restrictions on or expectations regarding the use of the prize money] or (3) the purpose of the grant is to achieve a specific objective, produce a report or other similar product, or improve or enhance a literary, artistic, musical, scientific, teaching, or other similar capacity, skill, or talent of the grantee. In addition to grants for travel, study, or similar purposes, the foundation may also make grants to impoverished individuals or those who experience catastrophic medical expenses or property loss. These poverty-relief or catastrophe grants do not require advanced approval from the IRS.

Grants made to most charitable entities other than 501(c)3 organizations, e.g., private foundations, labor unions, trade associations, fraternal orders, veterans groups, type III non-functionally integrated supporting organizations, or other supporting organizations controlled by a disqualified person, are taxable expenditures. The exception to this rule is that if the private foundation exercises "expenditure responsibility" on grants made to such organizations then the grant is permitted. Expenditure responsibility requires a variety of tasks including a written agreement of the specific charitable tasks the non-501(c)3 charity will accomplish, segregation of funds, regular reports from the recipient, and special reports to the IRS.

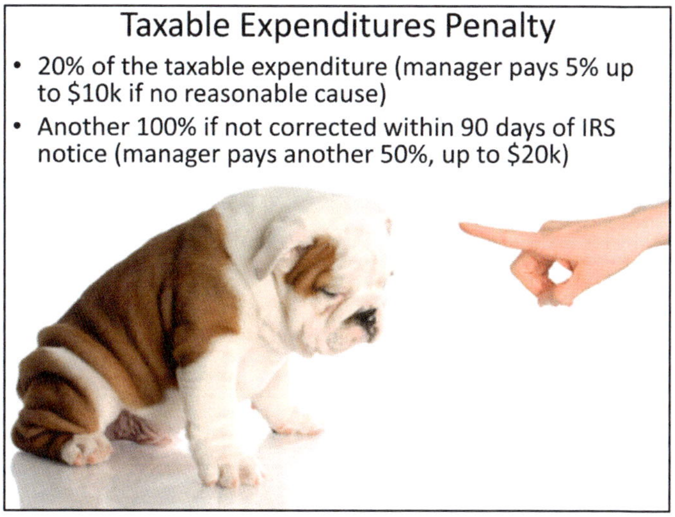

If a private foundation makes grants that do not qualify as appropriate charitable grants it will be penalized initially by 20% tax on the amount of the taxable expenditure. The foundation manager is subject to a 5% tax, up to $10,000 maximum, if there was no reasonable cause to believe the expenditure would be appropriate. The foundation must recover the expenditure or, where full recovery is not possible, the foundation must recover as much as possible and take any corrective action directed by the IRS within 90 days of the IRS notice of the violation or the foundation will receive an additional penalty of 100% of the taxable expenditure. Absent such timely correction, the foundation manager may also be penalized another 50% penalty, up to $20,000.

As briefly summarized above, the rules for establishing and managing a private foundation are extensive. There is, however, an alternative to a private foundation that is much cheaper and easier for the donor. This simple substitute for the private foundation is the donor advised fund.

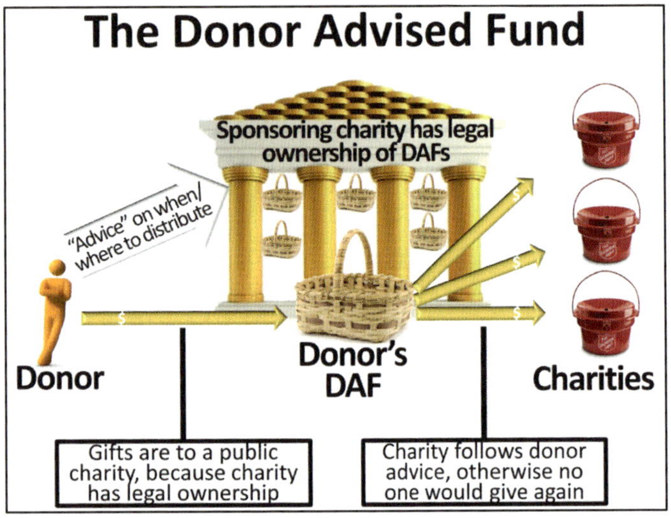

The simple concept of a donor advised fund is that the donor gives money to a public charity which the public charity sets aside in a separate account. The public charity then typically follows the advice of the donor regarding when and where to distribute those segregated funds to other public charities. The charity has legal control of all of the donor advised funds and could choose to ignore the donor's advice. This legal reality does not impact the practical reality that donor advised funds do follow donors' advice (so long as the advice is for legally permissible distributions), because failure to do so would discourage other donors from using the charity for their donor advised funds. Nevertheless, this legal control of the accounts by the public charity owning the donor advised funds means that the donor has made a completed gift to a public charity immediately upon transfer of funds or assets into the donor's account.

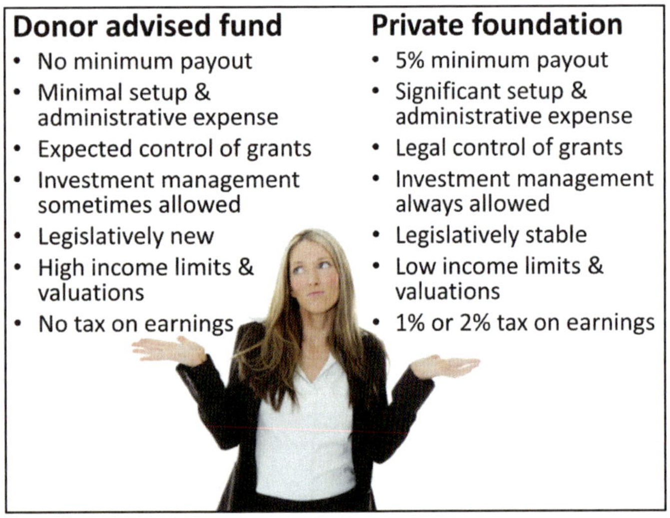

Whether the private foundation or donor advised fund is the best instrument will depend upon the gifts and goals of the donor. Donor advised funds are remarkably simple for the donor to establish. No legal documents need to be specially drafted and there are no annual meetings or required filings. Depending upon the organization, donor advised funds may be started with only $5,000. Annual costs vary with the size of the account, but typically range from 1% to 0.1% of the account value. Donor advised funds meeting certain minimum account sizes (e.g., $250,000), often permit management of assets by the donor's own qualified financial manager and allow for these managers to charge fees to the fund for this management. Large donor advised funds are often comfortable with accepting not just cash, but also complex assets such as privately-held C- and S-corporation stock, limited partnership interests, real estate, and even valuable personal property. Donor advised funds do not expire at the death of the donor. Managing charities typically allow for the appointment of new advisors at death. These new advisors can appoint others during life or at death, indefinitely continuing the passage of control. Further, there are currently no minimum payout requirements for these funds, meaning that no charitable distributions would ever have to occur. Donor advised funds have several tax advantages over private foundations. Gifts to public charities (such as donor advised funds) may have higher valuations and generate deductions that can be used up to a higher percentage of the donor's income than gifts to private foundations. Additionally, donor advised funds are not subject to the 2% excise tax on net investment income as are private foundations.

With all of these advantages of the donor advised fund, why would a donor ever use a private foundation? There are several reasons. Private foundations offer a much higher degree of multi-generational control of assets. The founding donor can create legally enforceable trust rules that limit the charitable purposes of the foundation, limit the trust expenditures, and dictate who may – and may not – be trustees and board members. The rules for private foundations are quite old and legislatively stable, suggesting a high likelihood for multi-generational stability. Although donor advised funds are not new, the massive growth of funds from charities affiliated with financial institutions is new, and consequently many of the rules have only been recently established. This legislative newness combined with the complete lack of any enforceable legal rights to control the funds in the donor advised account make donor advised funds a less certain option for long-term planning. Although convenient, donor advised funds lack the ability to directly benefit friends or family members through travel reimbursements and employment in professional and managerial tasks.

Donor advised funds have a much higher average payout rate than private foundations, reflecting their common use as a short-term place to park charitable funds. It often makes sense for donors to estimate their giving for the upcoming year and then transfer that money to a donor advised fund at the end of December. This allows for the charitable deductions to be taken earlier, even though the ultimate distributions to charities will not take place until the following tax year or later. This type of short-term planning corresponds perfectly with the convenience and simplicity of the donor advised fund, and avoids any potential limitations with regard to multi-generational planning.

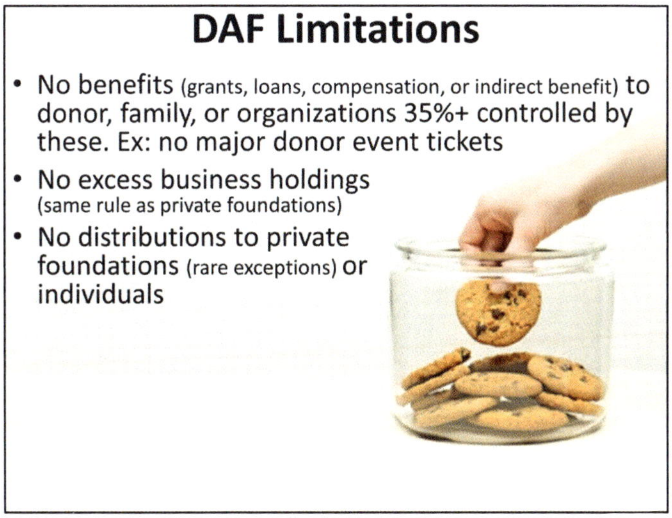

Many of the same type of limitations on private foundations also apply to donor advised funds. For example, there can be no benefits going to the donor, the donor's family, or organizations controlled by either. Grants from a donor advised fund cannot be used to fulfill the legally enforceable pledge by the donor to a charity. This would provide a benefit to the donor by reducing his or her legally-enforceable obligations. Similarly, grants from a donor advised fund cannot result in the charity giving benefits, such as donor event tickets, to the donor. Donor advised fund grants that generate such benefits are subject to a tax of 125% of the amount of the benefit payable by either the donor/advisor or the benefit recipient, and a 10% tax on the donor advised fund manager who knowingly made such a transfer (up to $10,000). Donor advised funds are also subject to the same rules preventing excess business holdings as private foundations are. Unlike private foundations, donor advised funds may make distributions to other donor advised funds. However, donor advised funds may not make distributions to individuals. Donor advised funds may not make distributions to private foundations, unless the managing charity follows the rules for "expenditure responsibility," and even then distributions to a private foundation controlled by the donor or donor's family may result in excess donor control leading to the fund be reclassified as a private foundation. Any distributions to private foundations may also create the opportunity for challenges to the higher deduction taken for a gift to a public charity upon transfer to the donor advised fund, rather than for a gift to a private foundation.

Private foundations and donor advised funds offer opportunities to take an immediate tax deduction for a transfer where the donor and donor's financial advisors can continue to manage the funds for the indefinite future. Once transferred, the funds can grow in a tax-free or tax-minimal environment. Although private foundations are typically used for long-term holding of more significant wealth, and donor advised funds are more commonly used for short-term holding of less significant wealth, finding the best fit will depend upon the specific values and goals of each particular donor.

QUIZ QUESTIONS, ANWERS, & EXPLANATIONS

CHAPTER 3: TIMING OF CHARITABLE DEDUCTIONS

1. Which of the following are completed deductible gifts?
   a) Donor delivers money or property to a charity with a limitation that it must be spent on a particular person specified by the donor
   b) Donor delivers valuable property to a charity, but keeps retained interests that are not specifically allowed by statute
   c) Donor gives money or property to the donor's agent with instructions to deliver the money or property to the charity
   d) Donor promises to deliver money or property to the charity in 3 days
   e) Donor delivers money or property to an agent representing the charity, but the agent will not actually transfer the money or property to the charity for another 30 days

2. In which of the following circumstances will the IRS permit an organization to deduct a charitable gift that is made after the close of the tax year?
   a) A C-corporation, s-corporation, or partnership passes a resolution authorizing the giving during the tax year, and then gifts within three months of the close of the tax year
   b) A C-corporation, using cash accounting, passes a resolution authorizing the giving during the tax year and then gifts within two months of the close of the tax year
   c) A C-corporation, using accrual accounting, passes a resolution six days after the close of the tax year authorizing charitable giving that is then carried out the following day
   d) A C-corporation using accrual accounting, passes a resolution authorizing the giving during the tax year, and then gifts within two and one-half months of the close of the tax year
   e) A C-corporation makes a gift 48 hours after the close of the tax year although no board resolution is involved

3. On which day was the gift completed for tax purposes?
   a) Day 1: I put cash into an envelope addressed to a charity
   b) Day 2: I put the envelope with proper postage in the U.S. mail
   c) Day 4: The cash arrives at the charity
   d) Day 5: The charity deposits the cash in its bank account
   e) There was no charitable gift

4. On which day was the gift completed for tax purposes?
   a) Day 1: I write a check to a charity
   b) Day 2: I put the check in the post office mailbox with proper address and postage
   c) Day 3: The charity receives the check
   d) Day 5: The charity's bank receives the funds and the charity is credited with the funds
   e) There was no deductible charitable gift

5. On which day was the gift completed for tax purposes?
   a) Day 1: I write a check to a charity
   b) Day 2: I put the check in the post office mailbox with proper address and postage
   c) Day 3: The charity receives the check

d) Day 5: The charity's bank receives notice of insufficient funds and the check is not honored
e) There was no deductible charitable gift

6. On which day was the gift completed for tax purposes?
   a) Dec 26: I put a check, post-dated for January 1, in the post office mailbox with proper address and postage
   b) Dec 31: The charity receives the check
   c) Jan 1: Nothing happens
   d) Jan 2: The charity deposits the check and is credited with the funds
   e) There was no deductible charitable gift

7. On which day was the gift completed for tax purposes?
   a) Dec 25: I sign a promise to donate to charity prior to the end of the year
   b) Dec 31: I make a donation by credit card and the charity is credited with the funds
   c) Jan 20: I receive a credit card statement noting the donation
   d) Jan 30: I pay my credit card bill in full
   e) There was no deductible charitable gift

8. On which day was the gift completed for tax purposes?
   a) Day 1: I earn $20 in rebates from my credit card company
   b) Day 2: I click online on my credit card company website to donate those rebates to a charity
   c) Day 9: The credit card company mails a check to the charity
   d) Day 10: The charity receives a check from the credit card company
   e) There was no deductible charitable gift

9. On which day was the gift completed for tax purposes?
   a) Dec. 1: I sign a legally enforceable contract (a pledge) to give $100,000 to the charity on August 1
   b) Dec. 5: The charity books this as an asset in their general ledger
   c) Dec. 10: The charity sells the rights to this pledge to an accounts receivable purchasing agency for $90,000
   d) Dec. 11: The charity spends the $90,000
   e) Aug. 1: I pay the $100,000 pledge to the charity

10. I give land worth $1 million to a public charity and retain a two year option to repurchase the land for $700,000. How much can I deduct today?
    a) $0
    b) $500,000
    c) $1. 5 Million
    d) $2 Million
    e) Only the rental value

11. I give land worth $2 million to a public charity and retain a two year option to repurchase for $500,000. After the option expires, how much can I deduct?
    a) $0
    b) $500,000
    c) $1. 5 Million
    d) $2 Million
    e) Only the rental value

12. Which of the following restrictions on a gift to a university will make the gift non-deductible?
    a) The university must use these funds for football scholarships
    b) The university must use these funds for a scholarship limited to female, international graduate students studying English literature
    c) The university must use these funds for to pay the tuition for Sarah P. Student, a person unrelated to the donor
    d) The university must use these funds to purchase a pipe organ for the music department
    e) None of the restrictions will make the gift non-deductible.

13. Jonathan donates $500 to a local bank for a family who lost their house in a mud slide. Feeling bad for the family, Jonathan also spends three full days (i.e., 8 hours per day) volunteering for the Red Cross, which is taking the lead on restoring their house. How much can Jonathan deduct for charitable donations? Jonathan's wage rate is $10 per hour, and he spent $25 on reasonable expenditures while donating his services.
    a) $0

b) $25
c) $240
d) $500
e) $765

ANSWERS

1/Answer: E. Explanation: The gift is completed when the donor delivers money or property to the charity or the charity's agent. The time delay imposed by the charity's agent is irrelevant as the gift is completed upon delivery to the charity's agent. However, delivery to the donor's agent does not make a completed gift, only delivery to the charity's agent. Also, promises to give are not completed gifts until the delivery actually occurs. Gifts where the donor retains an interest in the property are generally not allowed, unless they fall into one of the exceptions such as an undivided share in all rights of the donor in the property or a gift of a remainder interest in a farm or home. A gift with a restriction that it must be used for one particular person is not deductible.

2/Answer: D. Explanation: This exception applies only to C-corporations on an accrual basis and the resolution authorizing the future giving must be passed in the year of the deduction.

3/Answer: B. Explanation: A gift is complete when money is delivered to a charity or the charity's agent. The post office is considered to be the agent of the charity. When it receives a properly addressed and stamped letter, then the charity's agent has received it and the gift is complete.

4/ Answer: B. Explanation: A valid check is considered to be a valuable negotiable instrument even before it is converted into cash. As such when the charity or charity's agent receives the check, the gift has been completed. In this case, the post office is considered to be the agent of the charity. When the post office receives a properly addressed and stamped letter containing a valid check, then the charity's agent has received a valuable negotiable instrument and the gift is complete.

5/ Answer: E. Explanation: An invalid check was never money or valuable property. Therefore at no time was money or valuable property given to the charity or the charity's agent. As such, there was no deductible charitable gift.

6/ Answer: C. Explanation: A post-dated check is the equivalent of a promise to pay money in the future (specifically on the check's date). As such, it is treated like any other promise to pay money to the charity, meaning that there is no gift prior to the date on the check. However, at the point the check reaches its stated date, it becomes like any other valid check and is a valuable negotiable instrument at that point. Thus, on January 1, the valid check becomes a valuable negotiable instrument, and as the charity has already received the check, the gift is complete.

7/ Answer: B. Explanation: The charity received the funds on Dec. 31, and thus that is the date of the gift. The legitimate source of the money for the gift, whether from wages, borrowings, or gifts from another person, is irrelevant to the date of the completed gift. Thus, whatever date the debt related to a gift is paid (or even if it isn't) is irrelevant to the timing of the completed gift, which is the date on which the charity receives the funds.

8/ Answer: C. Explanation: When I click online to instruct the credit card company to make the donation, I am directing my agent (the credit card company) to make a gift. However, the gift is not completed until it is received by an agent OF THE CHARITY. Here the post office is treated as an agent of the charity, and thus the gift is completed on day 9.

9/ Answer: E. Explanation: A promise to pay a gift is not a completed gift until money or property is actually received by the charity or the charity's agent. It does not matter if the promise is legally enforceable; it is still a promise. The ability to sell the contractually guaranteed promise to a collection agency does not change the character of the contract as a promise, which generates no completed gift unless and until the promise is actually fulfilled.

10/ Answer: A. Explanation: A gift with a retained interest is not deductible unless it falls into one of the specific statutory exceptions such as a Charitable Remainder Trust, an undivided interest in all property interests owned by the donor, or a remainder interest in a home or farm. Thus, in this case the transfer generates no current tax deduction because of the donor's retention of the rights to repurchase.

11/ Answer: D. Explanation: The gift is not completed until the donor releases his or her retained interest. This occurs when the option expires. At that point, the gift is complete and the donor may deduct the value of the land

12/ Answer: C. Explanation: Although the gift has been given to the university, one of the restrictions requires that it be spent on an individual person. Limiting the gift to be spent by the charity on one particular person makes the gift non-deductible. It is permissible, however, to restrict the gift to benefit a particular type, class, or group of people such as football players or female, international graduate students. Further, the gift may be restricted to purchase a specific kind of asset without any damage to the deductibility of the gift (so long as the charity accepts the gift with the restriction).

13/ Answer: A. Explanation: Volunteering time is not a deductible gift. (This makes sense, because the net result on income is similar to when a person was paid and then gives the payment to a charity.) Donations that are restricted to a particular individual are not deductible. However, money spent on reasonable expenditures while serving on behalf of a charity can be deducted.

CHAPTER 4: DOCUMENTING CHARITABLE GIFTS

1. Dorcas donates a $200 hand-made robe, in very good condition, to a local public charity's thrift shop at an unattended clothing donation drop box. Because the donation drop box is unattended, she is not able to receive any receipt or other written recognition from the charity. Which statement is true?
   a) The gift cannot be deducted
   b) In order to deduct, she must somehow obtain a note from the charity indicating location & description of the property
   c) In order to deduct, she must somehow obtain a note from the charity indicating location & description of the property, the donor & the date with statement either that "No goods or services were provided in exchange for these gifts" or description and value of items provided
   d) In order to deduct, she only needs to have her own reliable records of value (and cost basis if relevant), charity, date & place of gift
   e) The gift is deductible without documentation as receiving a receipt was impractical

2. If an employee donates via payroll deduction such that he is giving $300 from each paycheck, how would he or she document the gift if the charitable contributions of employees are divided among many different charities and so there is no specific charity from which to get a receipt?
   a) The W-2 or paystub is sufficient
   b) The employee must write to each separate charity supported by the united appeal
   c) A pledge card indicating that no goods or services are given in exchange for the gift, along with the W-2 or paystub is sufficient
   d) A cancelled check or credit card statement is sufficient
   e) These gifts may not be deducted

The following options apply to all remaining questions for this chapter

I. Cancelled check, bank statement, or credit card statement
II. Note from charity indicating amount (or location & description if property), donor & date
III. Note from charity indicating amount (or location & description if property), donor & date with statement either that "No goods or services were provided in exchange for these gifts" or description and value of items provided
IV. Donor's own reliable records of value (and cost basis if relevant), charity, date & place of gift
V. IRS Form 8283 (Noncash Charitable Contributions)
VI. IRS Form 1098-C (Contributions of Motor Vehicles, Boats, & Airplanes) from charity 30 days after gift or sale
VII. A summary of a qualified appraisal attached to the tax return
VIII. A qualified appraisal attached to the tax return

3. Ann O. Nemus receives a large collection of ancient coins known as Leptons from her husband's estate. She gives this collection, worth $510, to her local synagogue. What items must she have in order to document this gift?
   a) I
   b) I or II
   c) I or II or III
   d) I or II or III or IV
   e) III, IV & V

4. In which of the following cases would a donor need III, IV, V, and VIII in order to properly document a charitable gift?
   a) Donor donates non-publicly traded stock valued at $600,000
   b) Donor donates publicly traded stock valued at $2,000,000
   c) A cash gift of $600,000 to a public charity
   d) Clothing in good condition valued at less than $400
   e) Donation of collectibles with a basis and fair market value of $4,000

5. Dorcas gives $2,000,000 in stock in Tabitha's Textile Manufacturing Corporation, a publicly traded corporation, to a local poverty

relief charity. What items must she have in order to document the gift?

a) III & IV
b) III, IV, and V
c) III, IV, V, and VII
d) III & V
e) III, IV, V, VII and VIII

6. James and John, joint owners as tenants in common of a fishing boat worth $11,000, give it to the local Boy Scouts of America. What items must they have in order to document the gift?

a) III & IV
b) III, IV, V, and VI
c) III, IV, and VI
d) IV and VI
e) III, IV, V, VI, and VII

7. Zebedee gives a small boat worth $400 to the local Boy Scouts of America to be used in their camping trips. What items must he have in order to document the gift?

a) III & IV
b) III, IV, V, and VI
c) III, IV, and VI
d) IV and VI
e) III, IV, V, VI, and VII

8. Jezebel purchases a vineyard at the estate sale of a deceased acquaintance named Naboth for $650,000. She then donates the vineyard to the Society Against Public Defamation, a public charity. What items would be sufficient to document this gift?

a) III
b) III & IV
c) III, IV, & V
d) III, IV, V, & VI
e) III, IV, V, & VIII

9. Herodias gives a slightly used silver platter, valued as artwork, to an art gallery for display in their collection. She deducts $25,000 for her gift. What items would be sufficient to document this gift?

a) III
b) III & IV
c) III, IV, & V
d) III, IV, V, & VII
e) III, IV, V, & VIII

10. Tamar gives an intricately carved walking staff with a fair market value of $1,100 to Planned Parenthood, a public charity. What items would be sufficient to document this gift?

a) I
b) III, IV & V
c) III, IV, V & VII
d) III
e) IV

11. Mary gives $35,000 worth of pure nard (an expensive perfume) for use by a charitable organization providing burial services to needy families. What items would be sufficient to document this gift?

a) I
b) III, IV & V
c) III, IV, V & VII
d) III, IV, V & VIII
e) IV

12. Rahab purchases $400 worth of red ribbon for a community charity to use in children's art projects. What items would be sufficient to document this gift?

a) I
b) III and IV
c) III, IV, and V

d) III
e) IV

13. Mary donor makes a gift by check of $200 at the morning services of her church. At the evening service on the same day, she makes another gift by check of $200. What items would be sufficient to document this gift?
a) I
b) II
c) III
d) I or III
e) I, II, and III

14. Mary donor makes a cash gift of $300 to her local church. What items would be sufficient to document this gift?
a) I or II
b) III
c) I and III
d) I, II, and IV
e) IV

ANSWERS

1/ Answer: D. Explanation: For property gifts under $250, a receipt or note from the charity is not required where it is impractical. However, the donor must have her own reliable documentation showing the value (and cost basis if relevant), charity, date & place of gift.

2/ C. Explanation: Because of the impracticality of receiving a receipt or acknowledgement from the charity in this circumstance, A pledge card indicating that no goods or services are given in exchange for the gift, along with the W-2 or paystub is sufficient documentation.

3/ Answer: E. Explanation: Although the items being given are coins, they are valued as an item of property rather than as a currency. As such, they must follow the rules for a gift of $510 of property, which require III, IV & V. IRS Form 8283 is required for any gifts of property worth more than $500 and so is required in this circumstance.

4/ Answer: A. Explanation: A qualified appraisal is not required to be attached to the tax return for any amount of cash or publicly traded securities, but would be required for property worth more than $500,000.

5/Answer: B. Explanation: Publicly traded securities do not require any appraisal, thus VII and VIII are unnecessary. Publicly traded securities are valued based upon the market price. However, because the gift is a gift of property over $500, Form 8283 must be included with the tax return. As with any other gift of property worth $250 or more, III and IV are both required.

6/ Answer: E. Explanation: As with any other gift of property worth $250 or more, III and IV are required. IRS Form 8283 is required for any gifts of property worth more than $500 and so is required in this circumstance. Because the property qualifies as a car, boat, or airplane worth over $500, Form 1098-C is also required. Finally, because the gift is $5,000 or more, but less than $500,000, a summary of a qualified appraisal is required.

7/ Answer: A. Explanation: The IRS Forms 8283 and 1098-C are required only for gifts of property over $500 in value and thus do not apply. Consequently, this gift is documented as any other gift of property worth $400, which is by III & IV.

8/Answer: E. Explanation: All property gifts of at least $250 require both III and IV. All gifts of property over $500 must have IRS Form 8283. Gifts of property worth more than $500,000 or gifts of artwork worth more than $20,000 must have a qualified appraisal attached to the tax return.

9/ Answer: E. Explanation: All property gifts of at least $250 require both III and IV. All gifts of property over $500 must have IRS Form 8283. Gifts of property worth more than $500,000 or gifts of artwork worth more than $20,000 must have a qualified appraisal attached to the tax return.

10/ Answer: B. Explanation: All property gifts of at least $250 require both III and IV. All gifts of property over $500 must have IRS Form 8283. No appraisal forms need be filed with the tax return as the gift is under $5,000

11/ Answer: C. Explanation: All property gifts of at least $250 require both III and IV. All gifts of property over $500 must have IRS Form 8283. Because the property gift is more than $5,000 a summary of a qualified appraisal must also accompany IRS Form 8283.

12/ Answer: B. Explanation: All property gifts of at least $250 require both III and IV (and some require more)

13/ Answer: A. Explanation: These gifts are both under the $250 limit, so the donor is not required to have option III as she would if she gave one gift of $400.

14/ Answer: C. Explanation: A cancelled check or credit card statement is insufficient documentation for gifts of $250 or more. These gifts require a note from the charity indicating amount and description of any goods or services provided in exchange that is delivered before the taxes are filed (or before taxes are due if not filed in a timely manner).

CHAPTER 5: VALUING CHARITABLE GIFTS OF PROPERTY

1. When can you deduct the portion of value of a gift of property that has previously been deducted as a depreciation deduction?
   a) Only when fair market valuation is permitted
   b) Only when cost basis valuation is permitted
   c) When either cost basis or fair market valuation is permitted
   d) Only when giving to a public charity
   e) Never

2. I give real estate to a public charity. I originally paid $10,000 for it 2 months ago. I have taken no depreciation deductions. Its current fair market value is $20,000. What is the maximum deductible amount of this gift?
   a) $0
   b) $5,000
   c) $10,000
   d) $15,000
   e) $20,000

3. I give real estate to a private (non-operating) foundation. I originally paid $10,000 for it 2 years ago. I have taken depreciation deductions for $5,000 of that original price. Its current fair market value is $20,000. What is the maximum deductible amount of this gift?
   a) $0
   b) $5,000
   c) $10,000
   d) $15,000
   e) $20,000

4. I give real estate to a public charity. I originally paid $10,000 for it 2 years ago. I have taken depreciation deductions for $5,000 of that original price. Its current fair market value is $20,000. What is the maximum deductible amount of this gift?
   a) $0
   b) $5,000
   c) $10,000
   d) $15,000
   e) $20,000

5. I give real estate to a public charity. I originally paid $10,000 for it 2 years ago. I have taken depreciation deductions for $5,000 of that original price. Its current fair market value is $20,000. I take a special election so that I can deduct long-term capital gain gifts up to 50% of my income. What is the maximum deductible amount of this gift?
   a) $0
   b) $5,000
   c) $10,000
   d) $15,000
   e) $20,000

6. I give furniture (not considered business inventory) from my home business to a public charity. I originally paid $10,000 for it 2 years ago. I have taken depreciation deductions for $5,000 of that original price. Its current fair market value is $20,000. The charity sells the furniture at its annual benefit auction. What is the maximum deductible amount of this gift?
   a) $0
   b) $5,000

c) $10,000
d) $15,000
e) $20,000

7. I give good quality furniture (not considered business inventory) from my home business to a public charity. I originally paid $10,000 for it 2 years ago. I have taken depreciation deductions for $5,000 of that original price. Its current fair market value is $20,000. The charity uses the furniture in its business office. What is the maximum deductible amount of this gift?
a) $0
b) $5,000
c) $10,000
d) $15,000
e) $20,000

8. I give shares of Microsoft Corporation to a private (non-operating) foundation. I originally paid $10,000 for it 2 years ago. Its current fair market value is $20,000. What is the maximum deductible amount of this gift?
a) $0
b) $5,000
c) $10,000
d) $15,000
e) $20,000

9. I give shares representing 20% ownership in a local locksmith business to a private (non-operating) foundation. I originally paid $10,000 for the shares 2 years ago. Their current fair market value is $20,000. What is the maximum deductible amount of this gift?
a) $0
b) $5,000
c) $10,000
d) $15,000
e) $20,000

10. I give several bags of clothing in poor condition to the local Salvation Army charity. Originally, I purchased the clothes for a total of $4,000 three years ago. I have a qualified appraisal that proves the total value of the clothes is $400. What is the maximum deductible amount of this gift?
a) $0
b) $400
c) $3,600
d) $4,000
e) $4,400

11. I give an automobile to a local public charity. I purchased the car for $5,000 three years ago. I have a qualified appraisal that proves the current value of the car is $6,000. After receiving the car, the charity sells it at a poorly attended benefit auction for $800. What is the maximum deductible amount of this gift?
a) $0
b) $500
c) $800
d) $5,000
e) $6,000

11. A newly formed local natural history museum (a public charity) puts out a request for donations of specimens of rare animals, such as the Komodo dragon. To do my civic duty I purchase a special lizard gun, fly to Indonesia, stay in a local village, track down a Komodo dragon, shoot it, pay to have it stuffed at a local taxidermist, attempt to take is as carry-on luggage, then have to pay an extra checked baggage fee at the gate, return home and donate the stuffed dragon to the natural history museum. The natural history museum uses the dragon in its display entitled "recently killed endangered animals." My expenses are travel=$2,000; meals & lodging =$1000; special lizard gun=$1,000; cost of taxidermy=$200. A qualified appraiser values the stuffed dragon at $6,000. What is the maximum deductible amount of this gift?
a) $0
b) $200
c) $3,200
d) $4,200

e) $6,000

13. I write a new book on the History of Ducks Unlimited. I donate the copyright for the book to Ducks Unlimited (a public charity). A qualified appraisal indicates that the copyright is worth $50,000. My cost basis in creating the book was only about $50 worth of paper and ink. How much can I deduct for this gift?
   a) $0
   b) $50
   c) $50,000
   d) $50 + a share of revenue from the copyright for the next 12 years
   e) $50,000 + a share of revenue from the copyright for the next 12 years

14. I create a piece of artwork involving my shredding, gluing, and painting hundred dollar bills to a canvass. My cost basis in creating the art is $10,000. The art is ugly and pointless and has a fair market value of $1. I give this art to a local art gallery (a public charity), and they place it in their quarterly public auction. How much can I deduct for my gift of art to the charity?
   a) $0
   b) $1
   c) $9,999
   d) $10,000
   e) $10,001

15. A local public charity for children puts out a request for new stuffed animals. I give 500 stuffed animals, each of which normally retails for $10 at local specialty shops ($10 X 500 = $5,000). I purchased the stuffed animals in an e-bay auction 15 months ago, where I was able to buy the entire lot for $2,000. When sold in lots of 500, these stuffed animals usually sell for $2,500 per lot today. The charity accepts the gift and uses the stuffed animals in its charitable operations. How much can I deduct for my gift?
   a) $0
   b) $2,000
   c) $2,500
   d) $3,000
   e) $5,000

16. Sarah donor takes her grandmother's antique solid gold tea set out of her attic. She has owned it for many years following the death of her grandmother. Sarah decides to give it to the local historical society (a public charity), and they use it as a regular part of one of their seasonal displays for visitors. Sarah investigates the value of the tea set by checking various auction sites and guesses it is worth about $200,000. She gets a qualified appraisal (at a price of $100) showing the value to be $200,000. She deducts the $200,000 and pays $40,000 less tax because of the deduction. After the deduction is taken, the IRS auditor uncovers that, in fact, this particular tea set was a reproduction, rather than an original, and its actual value was only $110,000, and that Sarah should have paid $18,000 more in taxes. In addition to correcting the valuation error and paying the taxes due, what additional penalties for the valuation error will the IRS charge?
   a) $0 to the taxpayer $125 to the appraiser
   b) $0 to the taxpayer $1000 to the appraiser
   c) $0 to the taxpayer $1,800 to the appraiser
   d) $3,600 to the taxpayer, $125 to the appraiser
   e) $7,200 to the taxpayer, $0 to the appraiser

ANSWERS

1/ Answer: E. Explanation: If the value of the property that had been previously depreciated (deducted as a depreciation deduction) were allowed to be deducted again as a charitable contribution, it would allow the taxpayer to deduct the same item twice, which is not permitted.

2/ Answer: C. Explanation: Deducting fair market value ($20,000) for real estate is allowed only for long-term capital gain property. Because this property was purchased 2 months ago, any gain is not long-term capital gain. (Long-term capital gain requires that the owner held the property for more than one year.) Consequently, only the basis can be deducted. The original price was $10,000, so original cost basis was $10,000. There have been no depreciation deductions, so no adjustments to the original basis have occurred, meaning the maximum deductible gift is $10,000.

3/Answer: B. Explanation: Because this property was purchased 2 years ago, it is long-term capital gain property. (Long-term capital gain requires that the owner held the property for more than one year.) However, gifts of long-term capital gain property to a private (non-operating) foundation do not qualify to be deducted at Fair Market Value (even though the same property, donated to a public charity, could qualify for a Fair Market Value deduction). Consequently, only the basis can be deducted. The original price was $10,000, so original cost basis was $10,000. Since that time $5,000 has been taken as depreciation deductions. Depreciation reduces the basis. (The idea is that depreciation is like a claim that something is "wearing out," so we can pretend that $5,000 of the original $10,000 of value has disappeared, and deduct this loss.) Consequently, the current adjusted basis is only $5,000 (calculated as the original $10,000 less the $5,000 of depreciation deduction). Thus, the maximum deductible gift is $5,000.

4/ Answer: D. Explanation: Because this property was purchased 2 years ago, it is long-term capital gain property. (Long-term capital gain requires that the owner held the property for more than one year.) Because the property is being given to a public charity, I can deduct the fair market value. However, for deduction purposes, fair market value is its current value less any depreciation deductions already taken, or $20,000-$5,000. This has to be the rule; otherwise, a taxpayer could deduct the same dollars twice. (E.g., if we didn't reduce the deduction by depreciation, I could pay $20,000 for property, deduct the full $20,000 as depreciation losses, then give it away and deduct the full $20,000 again!)

5/ Answer: B. Explanation: Taking the special election provides the benefit of deducting up to 50% of one's income, but it comes at the cost of being able to deduct only the basis in the property and not the fair market value. If I had not taken the "special election," I could have deducted this gift at fair market value. However, having taken the "special election" by deduction is limited to basis. My original cost basis was $10,000, from which I have deducted $5,000 as depreciation deductions, leaving an adjusted basis of $5,000. Thus, $5,000 is my maximum charitable deduction.

6/ Answer: B. Explanation: Because this property was purchased 2 years ago, it is long-term capital gain property. (Long-term capital gain requires that the owner held the property for more than one year.) However, gifts of unrelated use tangible personal property can be deducted only at cost basis (even though other types of long-term capital gain can be deducted at fair market value). This gift is personal property (furniture) and the charity is not using it for exempt purposes, but rather is simply selling it. Thus, this property is a gift of unrelated use tangible personal property. The original cost basis for this property was $10,000, but that amount has been reduced by the $5,000 of depreciation deductions already taken, leaving an adjusted basis of $5,000.

7/ Answer: D. Explanation: Because this property was purchased 2 years ago, it is long-term capital gain property. (Long-term capital gain requires that the owner held the property for more than one year.) Gifts of unrelated use tangible personal property can be deducted only at cost basis, but in this case the tangible personal property is *related* use tangible personal property, because the charity is using this personal property in its own office. Thus, we can deduct the fair market value ($20,000) less any depreciation deductions that have already been taken ($5,000), for a total of $15,000.

8/ Answer: E. Explanation: Long-term capital gain property given to a private foundation is normally deductible at cost basis. However, if the property giving is "qualified stock," the donor can take the fair market value deduction. This "qualified stock" exception requires that market quotations are available (i.e., it is publicly traded) and that not more than 10% of the company is given to the foundation. In this case, Microsoft stock is regularly traded, and $20,000 worth of stock would reflect less than 0.00001% of the total company value. Thus, this is a gift of "qualified stock" and can be deducted at Fair Market Value, which is $20,000.

9/ Answer: C. Explanation: Long-term capital gain property given to a private foundation is normally deductible at cost basis. However, if the property giving is "qualified stock," the donor can take the fair market value deduction. This "qualified stock" exception requires that market quotations are available (i.e., it is publicly traded) and that not more than 10% of the company is given to the foundation. In this case more than 10% of the company is being given, so the gift cannot be "qualified stock". (In addition to which, a local locksmith business would not have market quotations for its shares of stock.) Consequently, the "qualified stock" exception does not apply, and the normal rule must be followed, allowing a deduction of only the basis in the stock or $10,000.

10/ Answer: A. Explanation: No deduction is allowed for clothing and household items unless the items are in "good used condition or better" or the donor is giving more than $500 worth of clothes as shown by a qualified appraisal. Neither exception applies here as the clothes are in poor quality and the qualified appraisal indicates the total value is only $400. Thus, no deduction is allowed.

11/ Answer: C. Explanation: If the charity sells the automobile, rather than keeping it and using it in the conduct of their charitable purposes, the maximum deduction is the money actually received by the charity for selling the automobile ($800). Thus, in this case the basis of the car ($5,000) and the fair market value of the car ($6,000) become irrelevant because the charity actually received only $800 when the car was sold.

12/ Answer: B. Explanation: Because of special action by congress to prevent abuse, deductions for gifts of taxidermy are limited to the cost of stuffing the animal only and do not include any other expenses associated with obtaining the animal.

13/ Answer: D. Explanation: Because of the uncertainty in valuing intellectual property, there is a special rule for valuing charitable gifts of copyrights, patents, and trademarks. Under this rule, the donor may deduct the *lesser* of fair market value or cost basis. In addition, the donor may deduct a portion of any revenue that comes to the charity through the charity's ownership of the copyright.

The actual sliding scale for deductions in subsequent years is Year 1 - 100% Year 2 - 100% Year 3 - 90% Year 4 - 80% Year 5 - 70% Year 6 - 60% Year 7 - 50% Year 8 - 40% Year 9 - 30% Year 10 - 20% Year 11 - 10% Year 12 - 10%.

14/ Answer: B. Explanation: The cost basis in any property can be deducted only if it is less than fair market value. In no case can the cost basis be deducted if it is more than fair market value. In this case, cost basis ($10,000) exceeds fair market value ($1), so the deduction is for the fair market value of $1.

15/ Answer: C. Explanation: This is a gift of long-term capital gain property because it was purchased more than 12 months before the gift. It is not unrelated use tangible personal property because the charity is using the items in their charitable operation. Thus, the donor may deduct the fair market value of the donation. However, to arrive at the fair market value for gifts of large quantities, the items must be valued as a group, rather than multiplying the value of one individual item by the total number. In this case, the phrase, "when sold in lots of 500, these stuffed animals usually sell for $2,500 per lot today," indicates that the fair market value is $2,500.

16/ Answer: A. Explanation: Normally the taxpayer would have to pay a 20% penalty on the unpaid taxes of $18,000 (i.e., a penalty of $3,600) because the valuation was more than 1.5 times actual value and resulted in more than $5,000 of tax underpayment. However, because the valuation was based on a qualified appraisal, the donor made a good faith investigation of value, and the valuation was less than 2 times the actual value, there are no taxpayer penalties. The appraiser is penalized because the valuation was greater than 1.5 times the actual value. The appraiser's penalty is the greater of $1,000 or 10% of the tax payment up to 125% of the appraisal fee. The appraisal fee was $100, making the maximum penalty $125.

CHAPTER 6: INCOME LIMITATIONS ON CHARITABLE DEDUCTIONS

1. With regard to income limitations on deductible giving, all of the following property is treated similarly EXCEPT for
   a) Ordinary income property
   b) Short term capital gains
   c) Inventory
   d) Cash
   e) Long-term capital gains

1. What is the income limit for deductible giving of long-term capital gain property to a public charity deducted at current fair market value
   a) 50%
   b) 30%
   c) 20%
   d) 10%
   e) Either 30% or 50%

2. If I make a "special election" to increase the income percentage limit for long-term capital gain property gifts made to charity, what must I give up?
   a) I must give up the ability to deduct my cost basis
   b) I must give up the ability to deduct my appreciation
   c) I must give up the ability to deduct my depreciation
   d) I must give up the ability to deduct my long-term capital gain property gifts
   e) I must give up the ability to deduct my ordinary income gifts

3. What is the income limit for deductible giving for long-term capital gain property given to a private foundation by a C-corporation?
   a) 50%
   b) 30%
   c) 20%
   d) 10%
   e) Either 30% or 50% depending on the special election choice

4. Examples of property given "for the use of" charity thereby triggering a 30% income giving limitation includes the following
   a) Both paying premiums to a life insurance company for a charity owned policy AND putting money into a Charitable Lead Trust
   b) Both putting money into a Charitable Remainder Trust AND putting money into a charitable gift annuity

c) Both paying premiums to a life insurance company for a charity owned policy AND paying money to a charity with the instruction that the charity use the money to pay premiums on a charity owned policy
d) Loaning a charity $10,000 which you expect to be repaid without interest
e) Giving an automobile to a charity which its employees will drive while carrying out charitable efforts

5. An example of "related use" of a personal property item would be
a) Giving an automobile to a charity which its employees will drive while carrying out charitable efforts
b) Giving a famous modern art painting to a modern art museum which the museum then immediately trades with another museum in order to acquire two modern art sculptures
c) Giving a new guitar to the local public television station to be sold in the annual benefit auction
d) Giving farmland to an orphanage on which they immediately build a new orphanage
e) Giving cash to a charity which it uses to buy supplies

6. Which of the following is a gift subject to the 20% income limitation on deductible giving?
a) A gift of an item of appreciated personal property owned over 1 year for "related use" by a private non-operating foundation
b) A gift of an item of appreciated personal property owned over 1 year NOT for "related use" by a private non-operating foundation
c) A gift of appreciated publicly-traded stock (long-term capital gain) where less than 10% of the company is transferred to a private non-operating foundation
d) A gift of appreciated publicly-traded stock (long-term capital gain) of more than 10% of the company given to a private non-operating foundation
e) All of the above

7. A donor has carryover deductions from cash gifts made to public charities in both 2008 and 2009 and makes additional cash charitable gifts to public charities in 2010. In what order will these deductions and carryover deductions be used for a tax return in the 2010 tax year?
a) 1st-2008 gifts, 2nd-2009 gifts, 3rd-2010 gifts
b) 1st-2010 gifts, 2nd-2008 gifts, 3rd-2009 gifts
c) 1st-2010 gifts, 2nd-2009 gifts, 3rd-2008 gifts
d) 1st-2009 gifts, 2nd-2008 gifts, 3rd-2010 gifts
e) 1st-2008 gifts, 2nd-2010 gifts, 3rd-2009 gifts

8. Sam has an AGI of $100,000 and makes a gift of $30,000 of appreciated capital gain property to a public charity that he deducts at the fair market value of the property and a gift of $20,000 of appreciated capital gain property to a private (non-operating) foundation that he deducts at the fair market value of the property. Which of the following income limit categories are exceeded, if any?
a) The income limitation applicable to all gifts
b) The income limitation applicable to gifts of all capital gain property except "special election" property
c) The income limitation applicable to all gifts to private (non-operating) foundations
d) The income limitation applicable to gifts of capital gain property to private (non-operating) foundations
e) No gift limits are exceeded

9. Sam has an AGI of $100,000 and makes a gift of $10,000 of appreciated capital gain property to a public charity that he deducts at the fair market value of the property, a gift of $20,000 of capital gain property to a private (non-operating) foundation that he deducts at the fair market value of the property, a gift of $10,000 of cash to a private (non-operating) foundation, and a gift of $10,000 cash to a public charity. Which of the following income limit categories are exceeded, if any?
a) The income limitation applicable to all gifts
b) The income limitation applicable to gifts of all capital gain property except "special election" property
c) The income limitation applicable to all gifts to private (non-operating) foundations
d) The income limitation applicable to gifts of capital gain property to private (non-operating) foundations
e) No gift limits are exceeded

10. Sam has an AGI of $100,000 and makes a gift of $10,000 of capital gain property to a public charity that he deducts at the fair market value of the property, a gift of $20,000 of capital gain property to a private (non-operating) foundation that he deducts at the fair market value of the property, a gift of $10,000 of cash to a private (non-operating) foundation, and a gift of $20,000 cash to a public charity. Which of the following income limit categories are exceeded?
a) The income limitation applicable to all gifts
b) The income limitation applicable to gifts of all capital gain property except "special election" property
c) The income limitation applicable to all gifts to private (non-operating) foundations

d) The income limitation applicable to gifts of capital gain property to private (non-operating) foundations
e) No gift limits are exceeded

11. Sam has an AGI of $100,000 and makes a gift of $55,000 of capital gain property to a private (non-operating) foundation. Which of the following income limit categories are exceeded?
    a) The income limitation applicable to all gifts
    b) The income limitation applicable to gifts of all capital gain property except "special election" property
    c) The income limitation applicable to all gifts to private (non-operating) foundations
    d) The income limitation applicable to gifts of capital gain property to private (non-operating) foundations
    e) All of the above gift limits are exceeded

12. Which of the following types of gifts would be deducted first (i.e., carried over last), if the total gifts for the year exceed the limitations?
    a) cash to a public charity
    b) long-term capital gain property to a public charity (without special election)
    c) cash to a private (non-operating) foundation
    d) long-term capital gain property to a private (non-operating) foundation
    e) short-term capital gain property to a private (non-operating) foundation

ANSWERS

1/ Answer: E. Explanation: Income limitations differ depending on the type of property and the type of charitable recipient. In general ordinary income property, cash, short-term capital gains, and inventory are all treated similarly. Usually less favorable treatment (i.e., lower percentage limitations) are given to long-term capital gains.

2/ Answer: B. Explanation: The full 50% limit is not available because this is long-term capital gain property, which is somewhat disfavored as compared with cash or ordinary income property. However, because the gift is given to a public charity instead of a private non-operating foundation, the limit stays at the next highest level, which is 30%

3/ Answer: B. Explanation: A donor making a gift of long-term capital gain property to a public charity normally has an income limit of 30% for current year deductibility of charitable gifts. However, the donor may choose to elect the 50% limit for all such property during a year. Using such election requires the donor to deduct basis (typically the cost of the item) rather than fair market value. If the property has appreciated, i.e., if it is worth more than the donor originally paid for it, then the donor can deduct only the basis, but not the new, higher fair market value. Thus, the appreciation occurring since the donor acquired the property cannot be deducted if the donor chooses this special election.

4/ Answer: D. Explanation: This is a bit of a trick question as C-Corporations are always limited to 10% of their net income for deductible charitable gifts. This applies regardless of the type of property or charitable recipient. The differences based on property type and charitable recipient apply to individual taxpayers, but not to C-Corporations.

5/ Answer: A. Explanation: The only examples in which courts have applied the "for the use of" definition to change the income limit definitions are premiums paid to a life insurance company and money given to a Charitable Lead Trust. Note that, in both cases, the immediate recipient (the Charitable Lead Trust or the insurance company) is NOT a charitable entity, but is merely holding assets some of which will be used to benefit the charity. (Note that application of this rule for premium payments made to a life insurance on charity owned life insurance may be in doubt due to some recent decisions.)

6/ Answer: A. Explanation: Related use personal property is property that the charity actually uses in the conduct of its operations. This does not apply to personal property that is simply sold, rather than being used, with the proceeds from the sale being used in the conduct of the operations. Farmland is not personal property.

7/ Answer: E. Explanation: Gifts to private non-operating foundations of either long-term capital gain property or personal property are subject to the 20% income limitation on deductible giving. Only cash, ordinary income, short-term capital gains, and inventory are subject to the 30% limit when given to a private non-operating foundation.

8/ Answer: B. Explanation: Current year gifts are always counted before any carryover gifts are considered. After current year gifts are counted, then any gifts still being carried over from previous years are counted with the oldest gifts being counted first.

9/ Answer: B. Explanation: There are four relevant income percentage gift limitations. 1. No more than 50% for all gifts of any type. 2. No more than 30% for all gifts of capital gain property except "special election" capital gain property. 3. No more than 30% for all gifts to private (non-operating) foundations (and any "for the use of" public charities gifts through insurance premium payments or

Charitable Lead Trusts). 4. No more than 20% of capital gain property given to private non-operating foundations. Any gifts causing the donor to fail any one of the tests will be carried forward to future years.

In this case, all gifts total $50,000, which is not more than 50%. However all capital gain property totals $50,000, which is more than the 30% limit for all gifts of capital gain property except "special election" capital gain property. We know this is not "special election" capital gain property because it is appreciated property being deducted at fair market value and special election property limits the deduction to basis. (Because the property has appreciated, the fair market value is higher than the cost basis.) The total of all giving to private (non-operating) foundations is $20,000, which is less than the relevant 30% limit. The total giving of capital gain property to private (non-operating) foundations is $20,000, which is no more than the 20% limit.

10/ Answer: E. Explanation: There are four relevant income percentage gift limitations. 1. No more than 50% for all gifts of any type. 2. No more than 30% for all gifts of capital gain property except "special election" capital gain property. 3. No more than 30% for all gifts to private (non-operating) foundations (and any "for the use of" public charities gifts through insurance premium payments or Charitable Lead Trusts). 4. No more than 20% of capital gain property given to private non-operating foundations. Any gifts causing the donor to fail any one of the tests will be carried forward to future years.

In this case, all gifts total $50,000, which is not more than 50%. All capital gain property totals $30,000, which is not more than the 30% limit for all gifts of capital gain property except "special election" capital gain property. The total of all giving to private (non-operating) foundations is $30,000, which is not more than the relevant 30% limit. The total giving of capital gain property to private (non-operating) foundations is $20,000, which is no more than the 20% limit. Therefore, no gift limits are exceeded.

11/ Answer: A. Explanation: There are four relevant income percentage gift limitations. 1. No more than 50% for all gifts of any type. 2. No more than 30% for all gifts of capital gain property except "special election" capital gain property. 3. No more than 30% for all gifts to private (non-operating) foundations (and any "for the use of" public charities gifts through insurance premium payments or Charitable Lead Trusts). 4. No more than 20% of capital gain property given to private non-operating foundations. Any gifts causing the donor to fail any one of the tests will be carried forward to future years.

In this case, all gifts total $60,000, which is more than the 50% limitation applicable to all gifts, violating that limitation. All capital gain property totals $30,000, which is no more than the 30% limit for all gifts of capital gain property except "special election" capital gain property. The total of all giving to private (non-operating) foundations is $30,000, which is not more than the relevant 30% limit. The total giving of capital gain property to private (non-operating) foundations is $20,000, which is no more than the 20% limit. Therefore, only the first gift limit is exceeded.

12/ Answer: E. Explanation: In this case, all gifts total $55,000, which is more than the 50% limitation applicable to all gifts, violating that limitation. All capital gain property totals $55,000, which is more than the 30% limit for all gifts of capital gain property except "special election" capital gain property. (The special election cannot be used for gifts to private non-operating foundations, so it is not relevant for this question.) The total of all giving to private (non-operating) foundations is $55,000, which is more than the relevant 30% limit. The total giving of capital gain property to private (non-operating) foundations is $55,000, which is more than the 20% limit. Therefore, all four of the gift limits are exceeded.

13/ Answer: A. Explanation: In this case, more favored gifts are counted first. Gifts of cash (or inventory, ordinary income property, or short-term capital gains) are favored as compared with gifts of long-term capital gain. Additionally gifts to public charities are favored over gifts to private (non-operating) foundations. The most favored gift is thus a cash gift to a public charity.

CHAPTER 7: BARGAIN SALE CHARITABLE GIFTS

1. A bargain sale is
   a) The sale of an asset to a charity at less than fair market value
   b) When a percentage of the gross proceeds from the sale of an item are dedicated, in advance, to go to a charity
   c) When a percentage of the net proceeds from the sale of an item are dedicated, in advance to go to a charity
   d) When a donor finds an item needed by a charity available for sale at a discounted price, purchases the item, then gives the item to the charity
   e) When the charity sells an asset to a donor at less than fair market value

2. What is the general rule for how much of a charitable deduction a donor can claim as the result of a bargain sale when the donated item is valued at its fair market value?
   a) The donor may deduct the fair market value of the item given
   b) The donor may deduct the proceeds from the sale less the share of basis attributable to the sale portion of the transaction
   c) The donor may deduct only the cost basis of the item given
   d) The donor may deduct the value of the donation less the value of what the donor receives in return
   e) The donor may deduct up to 30% of his or her adjusted gross income

3. Which of the following transactions would result in a potential charitable deduction of $600,000?
   a) The donor gives land worth $1,000,000 to a charity in exchange for $400,000
   b) The donor gives a $1,200,000 house to a charity with a mortgage of $600,000
   c) The donor gives $900,000 in stock to a charity in exchange for a lifetime income with a present value of $300,000
   d) The donor makes a gift of appreciated artwork to a charity for display in the charity's art gallery. The artwork has a fair market value of $600,000
   e) All of the above

4. Several years ago, I purchased land for $200,000 in cash. It has since gone up in value to $1,000,000. The property is next to the campus of a small college (a public charity), and the college would like to have the land. In order to benefit the college, I sell the land to the college for $500,000. What is my charitable deduction?

5. Several years ago, I purchased land for $200,000 in cash. It has since gone up in value to $1,000,000. The property is next to the campus of a small college (a public charity), and the college would like to have the land. In order to benefit the college, I sell the land to the college for $500,000. How much of the original cost basis is attributable to the sale portion of the transaction for purposes of calculating the capital gain?
   a) $100,000 (50%)
   b) $200,000 (100%)
   c) $500,000 (50%)
   d) $1,000,000 (100%)
   e) $0 (0%)

6. Several years ago, I purchased land for $200,000 in cash. It has since gone up in value to $1,000,000. The property is next to the campus of a small college (a public charity), and the college would like to have the land. In order to benefit the college, I sell the land to the college for $500,000. What is the capital gain resulting from this transaction?
   a) $200,000
   b) $400,000
   c) $500,000
   d) $800,000
   e) $1,000,000

7. Several years ago, I purchased a quad-plex apartment building for $200,000 in cash. It has since gone up in value to $1,000,000. I have claimed depreciation deductions on the property of $50,000 and have make capital improvements to the property of $250,000. The property is next to the campus of a small college (a public charity), and the college would like to have the building. I sell the building to the college for $500,000. What is the capital gain resulting from this transaction?
   a) $200,000
   b) $300,000
   c) $400,000
   d) $500,000
   e) $600,000

8. What is the capital gain on a transaction where I sell a piece of property with a basis of $200,000, for its fair market value of $1,000,000 and then give $500,000 from that sale to a charity?
   a) $300,000
   b) $400,000
   c) $500,000
   d) $800,000
   e) $900,000

9. What is the capital gain on a transaction where I sell a piece of property, with a basis of $200,000, to a charity for $500,000 and the charity then immediately sells the property for its fair market value of $1,000,000?
   a) $300,000
   b) $400,000
   c) $500,000
   d) $800,000
   e) $900,000

10. I have a piece of property worth $600,000 with a basis of $100,000. I would like $300,000 of the value to go to charity and I would like to keep $300,000 of the value. What is the difference in the capital gain if I sell this property for $600,000 and give

$300,000 in cash to the charity ("sale then gift") as compared to selling the property to the charity for $300,000 ("bargain sale"), allowing the charity to then sell the property for $600,000?

a) The capital gain is the same
b) The capital gain from the "sale then gift" is $500,000, and the capital gain from the "bargain sale" is $200,000
c) The capital gain from the "sale then gift" is $500,000, and the capital gain from the "bargain sale" is $250,000
d) The capital gain from the "bargain sale" is $500,000, and the capital gain from the "sale then gift" is $250,000
e) The capital gain from the "bargain sale" is $500,000, and the capital gain from the "sale then gift" is $200,000

11. I have a piece of property worth $600,000 with a basis of $100,000. I would like $300,000 of the value to go to charity and I would like to keep $300,000 of the value. Ignoring non-tax related transaction costs, what is the difference in the net amount received by the charity if I sell this property for $600,000 and give $300,000 in cash to the charity ("sale then gift") as compared to selling the property to the charity for $300,000 ("bargain sale"), allowing the charity to then sell the property for $600,000?

a) The amount retained by the charity is less in the "bargain sale" because the charity must pay capital gains tax upon the sale of the property
b) The amount retained by the charity is less in the "sale then gift" because the charity must pay capital gains tax upon the sale of the property
c) The amount retained by the charity is less in the "bargain sale" because the donor must pay more capital gains tax
d) The amount retained by the charity is less in the "sale then gift" because the donor must pay more capital gains tax
e) The amount retained by the charity is the same in both transactions

12. I purchased stock several years ago for $500,000. Today it is worth $400,000. I give the shares to a charity for $200,000. What is my capital loss on the transaction?

a) $0
b) $50,000
c) $100,000
d) $200,000
e) $300,000

13. A donor owns three lots, each worth $100,000, each with a $10,000 cost basis, and each with $50,000 of debt. What is the capital gain if the donor gives two of these lots to a charity along with the mortgage debt?

a) $0
b) $20,000
c) $80,000
d) $90,000
e) $100,000

14. A donor owns three lots, each worth $100,000, each with a $10,000 cost basis, and each with $50,000 of debt. The donor works with a lender to shift the debt such that two lots each have $75,000 of debt and the third lot has no debt. What is the capital gain if the donor gives this third lot with no debt to a charity?

a) $0
b) $20,000
c) $80,000
d) $90,000
e) $100,000

15. Madolyn would like to donate some land to a public charity that builds parks in downtown areas. She acquired the land ten years ago for $100,000, and it is now worth $200,000. She still has an outstanding mortgage balance of $40,000 on the property. If she transfers the property to the charity subject to the mortgage, how much will she have to pay in capital gains taxes? (Assume her capital gains tax rate is 15%.)

a) $3,000
b) $6,000
c) $15,000
d) $20,000
e) $40,000

16. Grace would like to donate some land to a public charity, which will use it to provide hippotherapy opportunities for people with disabilities. She acquired the land twenty years ago for $50,000, and it is now worth $200,000. Grace wants to receive or retain $20,000 from the transaction. She is debating whether she should sell the property and give the proceeds above $20,000 ("sell and gift"), or simply give the land to the charity and have the charity pay her $20,000 ("bargain sale"). Grace would get the most tax advantages from

a) "Sell and gift" because of the difference in charitable tax deduction
b) "Sell and gift" because of the difference in capital gains taxes
c) "Bargain sale" because of the difference in charitable tax deduction
d) "Bargain sale" because of the difference in capital gains taxes
e) Both transactions are equally advantageous.

17. Mary has two lots, each worth $500,000. She plans to give one lot to charity and sell the other lot for her personal use. Seven years ago she originally purchased lot A for $100,000 and lot B for $400,000. Which transaction would give her the largest potential tax benefit?
    a) The tax consequences are the same regardless of which lot is given to charity.
    b) Giving lot A and selling lot B maximizes the tax benefits because of differences in both capital gain and the charitable deduction.
    c) Giving lot A and selling lot B maximizes the tax benefits because of differences in capital gain, even though the though the charitable deduction is the same regardless of which lot is given.
    d) Giving lot B and selling lot A maximizes the tax benefits because of differences in both capital gain and the charitable deduction.
    e) Giving lot B and selling lot A maximizes the tax benefits because of differences in capital gain, even though the though the charitable deduction is the same regardless of which lot is given.

ANSWERS

1/ Answer: A. Explanation: A bargain sale is when the donor sells an asset to a charity for less than its fair market value, thus constituting a part sale and part gift. A charity may not sell an asset to a donor at less than fair market value as this could be considered a violation of the rule against private inurement.

2/ Answer: D. Explanation: The general idea of a bargain sale is that the donor may deduct the value of what he or she gives less the value of what he or she receives. Whether fair market value or basis is used, or what income limits apply, is not dependent upon the existence of a bargain sale. Finally, the proceeds from the sale less the share of basis attributable to the sale portion of the transaction is the capital gain from the sale, not the charitable deduction.

3/ Answer: E. Explanation: All of the options would generate a potential charitable deduction of $600,000.

4/ Answer: $500,000. Explanation: The charitable deduction for a bargain sale is value of the item given less the value of any items received in return from the charity. In this case, the land had a current value of $1,000,000 and the charity paid $500,000. Thus, $1,000,000 - $500,000 = $500,000

5/ Answer: A. Explanation: The percentage of the property value sold is equal to the percentage of the cost basis allocated to the sale. In this case, 50% of the value of the property was sold ($500,000 price / $1,000,000 value). Consequently, 50% of the cost basis is allocated to the sale. The cost basis was the price paid of $200,000. (If the property had been depreciated or if it had capital improvements added to it, the basis would have changed and would be referred to as the adjusted basis however, the same *percentage* of the adjusted basis would still be applied to sale portion of the transaction.)

6/ Answer: B. Explanation: The capital gain is the price paid, $500,000 less the portion of the basis attributable to the sale part of the transaction. The percentage of the basis attributable to the sale part of the transaction is equal to the ratio of the money received ($500,000) to the value of the property ($1,000,000) or 50%. (You can also think of this as the percentage of the property value sold.) Thus, 50% of the basis (or $100,000 of the original $200,000 basis) may be applied to the sale portion of the transaction. This means the gain is the money received, $500,000, less the basis allocated to the sale, $100,000, for a difference of $400,000.

7/ Answer: B. Explanation: The capital gain is the price paid by the charity ($500,000) less the portion of the basis attributable to the sale part of the transaction. The percentage of the basis attributable to the sale part of the transaction is equal to the ratio of the money received ($500,000) to the value of the property ($1,000,000) or 50%. (You can also think of this as the percentage of the property value sold.) Thus 50% of the basis may be applied to the sale portion of the transaction. The original cost basis was $200,000. This original basis has been reduced by $50,000 of depreciation deductions, but it has also been increased by $150,000 of capital improvements, so the adjusted basis is now $400,000. This means the gain is the money received ($500,000) less the basis allocated to the sale ($200,000) for a difference of $300,000.

8/ Answer: D. Explanation: The fact that part of the money from the sale of the property is given to charity is irrelevant for calculating capital gain. Consequently, this is simply the sale of a $1,000,000 item of property with a basis of $200,000. The capital gain is the fair market value price received ($1,000,000) less the basis ($200,000), or $800,000

9/ Answer: B. Explanation: I received $500,000 in the transaction. From this, I subtract a portion of the basis. I can allocate the percentage of the basis to the sale part of this transaction that is equal to the percentage of the property value sold. In other words, I received $500,000 for a $1,000,000 value property, so I can use 50% ($500,000/$1,000,000) of the property's basis. The basis is $200,000, so I can use 50%, or $100,000, of that basis. The $500,000 I received less the $100,000 of basis I can use is $400,000.

10/ Answer: C. Explanation: The capital gain from selling then gifting is the $600,000 price less the $100,000 basis or $500,000. The capital gain from a bargain sale is the $300,000 price less the part of the basis allocable to the sale part of the transaction. The percentage of the basis allocated to the sale part of a bargain transaction is equal to percentage of the property value received or, in this case $300,000 / $600,000, or 50%. Thus 50% of the original $100,000 in basis can be used to offset the $300,000 price in the bargain sale. Thus, the gain from the bargain sale is the $300,000 price less $50,000 of the original basis, for a total gain of $250,000.

11/ Answer: E. Explanation: In both cases, the charity retains $300,000 (ignoring non-tax related transaction costs). Charities do not pay capital gains tax when selling property. The capital gains tax paid by the donor is irrelevant to the amount that the charity keeps in the transactions described.

12/ Answer: A. Explanation: Bargain sale transactions cannot generate capital losses for tax purposes.

13/ Answer: D. Explanation: If the charity receives property with debt, it is considered to be a bargain sale. The amount of debt taken over by the charity is considered to be an amount received by the donor. Thus, in this case the charity is taking on $100,000 of debt. The donor's capital gain is the $100,000 less the share of the original basis that can be allocated to the sale portion of the transaction. The percentage of the basis allocated to the sale part of a bargain transaction is equal to percentage of the property value received or, in this case $100,000 / $200,000, or 50%. Thus 50% of the original $20,000 in combined basis on the two properties (or $10,000) can be used to offset the $100,000 price in the bargain sale. Thus, the donor's capital gain is $90,000 ($100,000 relief of debt less $10,000 of basis).

14/ Answer: A. Explanation: This transaction is not a bargain sale as the donor received no relief of debt or other consideration from the charity. As a simple gift of appreciated property, there is no capital gain.

15/ Answer: A. Explanation: If she gifts the property subject to a $40,000 mortgage, she is deemed to have received $40,000. She can offset this with the percentage of the basis allocated to the sale part of a bargain transaction. The percentage of the $100,000 basis allocated to the sale part of a bargain transaction is equal to percentage of the property value received or, in this case $40,000 / $200,000, i.e., 20%. Thus the capital gain is $40,000 - $20,000 (20% of the $100,000 basis) which is a difference of $20,000. Her capital gains taxes are $20,000 * 15% = $3,000.

16/ Answer: D. Explanation: The adjusted basis allocated to the sale portion of the bargain sale is $5,000 (The $20,000 price is 10% of the $200,000 value. 10% of $50,000 basis is $5,000). In the bargain sale, she will recognize a gain of $15,000 ($20,000 - $5,000). In the "sell and gift" transaction her gain is the $200,000 value less the $50,000 basis or $150,000. Thus, the capital gain is much larger in the "sell and gift" making the "bargain sale" the more tax advantaged transaction. In either the "sell and gift" or "bargain sale" transactions the charitable deduction will be $180,000 ($200,000 - $20,000),

17/ Answer: C. Explanation: Because lot A is more highly appreciated (lower basis), selling it will result in a larger capital gain. Thus, the more beneficial transaction is to give lot A and sell lot B. There are no differences in the income tax charitable deduction regardless of which lot is sold.

CHAPTER 8: INTRODUCTION TO CHARITABLE GIFT ANNUITIES

1. If a donor purchases a gift annuity for $100,000, what is the minimum amount that must go to the charity?
   a) The charity must receive at least $10,000 at the donor's death
   b) The charity must receive at least $50,000 at the donor's death
   c) If the donor lives exactly as long as his or her life expectancy, the charity must receive greater than $10,000
   d) If the donor lives exactly as long as his or her life expectancy, the charity must receive at least $50,000
   e) If the donor lives exactly as long as his or her life expectancy, the charity must receive an amount with a present value (at the time of the initial transaction) greater than $10,000

2. Some common reasons to use a charitable gift annuity would include all of the following EXCEPT
   a) A donor wishes to make a large gift to a charity, but is concerned that she may outlive her assets and be left with no income
   b) A donor already plans to leave an estate gift to the charity, but would like to get an immediate income tax deduction
   c) A donor wishes to receive a fixed income stream that won't change or run out, even if market returns are poor

d) A donor wishes to receive income that is guaranteed by all of the assets of a large charitable institution
e) A donor wishes to gift appreciated property and completely avoid the payment of any capital gains taxes while receiving some income

3. Which of the following is an example of a requirement found in a state rule regulating charities issuing gift annuities in that particular state?
   a) The charity must maintain a reserve equal to their payment obligations in the gift annuities
   b) The charity must maintain a reserve equal to their payment obligations in the gift annuities plus a designated surplus
   c) The charity must have been in operation for a minimum number of years (such as three years) and must have a minimum amount of cash reserves (such as $300,000).
   d) The charity must meet no financial, reserve, or age requirements at all
   e) All of the above are examples of state rules regulating charities issuing gift annuities in at least one state

4. Which of the following is NOT a negative risk for a charitable organization that is issuing charitable gift annuities?
   a) The annuitants may, on average, live longer than their actuarial life expectancy
   b) The annuitants may, on average, live only to their life expectancy, but those with relatively large annuities live longer
   c) The annuitants may, on average, live only to their life expectancy, but those with relatively small annuities live shorter
   d) The annuitants may, on average, live only to their life expectancy, but those with relatively small annuities live longer
   e) The charity's investment returns may be less than those needed to fund the annuity payments

5. Appropriately licensed financial advisors can become involved in the charitable gift annuity process in all of the following ways except?
   a) Managing gift annuity assets pools for nonprofit organizations
   b) Selling commercial annuities as reinsurance for nonprofits issuing gift annuities
   c) Giving advice to clients regarding the financial strength and stability of a nonprofit organization issuing charitable gift annuities
   d) Selling charitable gift annuities on behalf of financial institutions
   e) Giving advice to clients regarding the financial results of a charitable gift annuity

6. Which of the following actions would NOT create any risk of losing the exemption from securities regulations normally given to the offering of charitable gift annuities?
   a) Paying a sales commission to fundraisers selling charitable gift annuities
   b) Marketing charitable gift annuities primarily as investments, rather than as a means to make a charitable gift
   c) Listing the rates available for donors as a percentages
   d) Comparing the gift annuity rates with CD rates as a comparison of "yields"
   e) Indicating that because gift annuity published rates are higher than other investment interest rates, they are therefore generating a higher "return"

7. Reinsuring gift annuities (where the charity purchases commercial annuities to match some or all of its annuity payment obligations) can offer the following benefits to a charitable organization operating a gift annuity program, EXCEPT
   a) Reinsurance can exactly match an income stream (from the annuity company) to the charity's obligation to pay annuity checks.
   b) Reinsurance removes the charity's legal obligation to make the annuity payments
   c) Reinsurance removes the risk from the charity that the annuitant may live much longer than expected.
   d) Reinsurance can be used to cover the risk associated with accepting a few very large gift annuities by allowing the charity to reinsure only those few annuities
   e) Reinsurance prevents the charity from being in the odd circumstance of wishing for the early death of its donor annuitants.

8. Why is a gift annuity that is actuarially projected to pay 75% of its original cost to an 80 year old annuitant (with a 9 year life expectancy) riskier for the issuing charity than a gift annuity that is actuarially projected to pay 75% of its original cost to a 40 year old annuitant (with a 42 year life expectancy)?
   a) An 80 year old annuitant is more likely to die
   b) A 40 year old annuitant is more likely to die
   c) An 80 year old annuitant is more likely to live 10 years past her original life expectancy
   d) A 40 year old annuitant is more likely to live 10 years past her original life expectancy
   e) An 80 year old annuitant is more likely to live to twice as long as her original life expectancy (thus resulting in 2 times the actuarially projected payout) than is a 40 year old annuitant.

9. Which of the following comparisons between charitable gift annuities and Charitable Remainder Trusts is incorrect?

a) A charitable gift annuity usually involves no costs charged directly to the donor for setup or administration, where a CRT may require both expenses
b) Charitable gift annuities can commonly be created even for transactions as small as five or ten thousand dollars, where a CRT is usually not practical unless much more money is involved.
c) A charitable gift annuity is a simple (often one page) document, where a CRT often involves many pages and greater legal expense.
d) A charitable gift annuity pays a fixed dollar amount to the donor, where a CRT is required to pay a percentage of all trust assets
e) A charitable gift annuity is issued by the charity itself, where a CRT is typically created by the donor.

10. All of the following are available options using some type of a charitable gift annuity EXCEPT:
a) The donor can name a different person as recipient of the annuity payments other than the donor himself or herself
b) The donor can select a fixed period annuity rather than a life annuity to receive larger payments over a shorter term
c) The donor could donate the remainder of the annuity if income payments from it are no longer needed
d) The donor could defer the payments of the annuity to increase the value of the remaining payments by purchasing a deferred charitable gift annuity
e) The donor could opt for a two life annuity in which the payments cease only after the death of both individuals

ANSWERS

1/ Answer: E. Explanation: The charity must receive a share with a present value that is actuarially worth more than $10,000 (i.e., more than 10%) at time of the charitable gift annuity transaction. In other words, the value of what the charity receives must be worth more than $10,000 today (on the day the gift annuity is purchased). If the charity is expected to have to wait many years (the donor's life expectancy) to receive $10,000, this is clearly worth less than $10,000 today. So, the charity must be entitled to receive some future amount that is worth something more than $10,000 today.

2/ Answer: E. Explanation: Although a charitable gift annuity can defer the payment of capital gains tax where the annuitant is also the donor, the charitable gift annuity does not avoid the payment of capital gains tax, as would be possible with a direct gift or sometimes possible with a Charitable Remainder Trust. The other desires can be met by a charitable gift annuity

3/ Answer: E. Explanation: State rules vary widely. Some states have absolutely no regulation while others require annual reports proving that reserve amounts including a surplus percentage are always on hand.

4/ Answer: D. Explanation: The charity is at risk if the investment returns are less than expected or if the annuitants – weighted by the relative size of their annuities – live longer than expected. If the annuitants, on average, live to their life expectancy, but those with relatively small annuities live longer, it means that those with relatively large annuities are living shorter than their life expectancies. This would result in a positive net effect to the charity. All of the other options would result in a negative effect to the charity.

5/ Answer: D. Explanation: A financial institution cannot offer a charitable gift annuity. Only charities can offer a charitable gift annuity. All other alternatives are open to financial advisors who are appropriately licensed (e.g., with a license to sell commercial annuities).

6/ Answer: C. Explanation: Listing the rates available for donors as percentages is not a risky practice and such rates are included in almost all brochures for charitable gift annuities. Paying sales commissions results in an automatic nullification of the exemption, and all other practices listed are risky according to existing case law.

7/ Answer: B. Explanation: Even if a charity purchases a matching commercial annuity, it still has a legal obligation to make the annuity payments. Although there appear to be no modern examples where the bankruptcy of an insurance company led to the reduction of annuity payments for annuity holders, it is theoretically possible. In such a circumstance, the charity would still be obligated to make the annuity payments for the remainder of the donor's life. All other examples are potential benefits of reinsurance.

8/ Answer: E. Explanation: The actuarial projected payout is based upon the annuitant's life expectancy. If the 80 year old annuitant lives to age 89, she would receive payments worth 75% of the initial amount paid for the charitable gift annuity. If, however, she lived to age 98, she would receive twice that many payments. In order for the 40 year old to receive twice as many checks as expected, she would have to live to age 122. The likelihood of a 40 year old reaching age 122 is less than the likelihood of an 80 year old reaching age 98. In other words, although the average (or expected) payout percentage is the same in both cases, the potential variance is much greater for the older annuitant because her payout is based upon a shorter life expectancy.

9/ Answer: D. Explanation: Charitable Remainder Trusts can pay a fixed dollar amount like a charitable gift annuity. These are called charitable remainder annuity trusts. Charitable remainder unitrusts pay a percentage of all trust assets. The other comparisons are accurate.

10/ Answer: B. Explanation: Charitable gift annuities must be for the life of the annuitant. They cannot be for a fixed number of years. All other options are available with certain types of charitable gift annuities.

CHAPTER 9: TAXATION OF CHARITABLE GIFT ANNUITIES

1. Which of the following tax consequences CANNOT be generated by a charitable gift annuity?
   a) Additions to taxable income
   b) Deductions from taxable income
   c) Postponement of capital gains tax
   d) Gift taxes
   e) All of the above can be generated by a charitable gift annuity

2. Which interest rate must be used to calculate the value of the annuity part of a charitable gift annuity?
   a) The §7520 rate for the month of the charitable gift annuity creation
   b) The §7520 rate for the month of the charitable gift annuity creation or either of the two previous months, selected at the discretion of the taxpayer
   c) The §7520 rate for the month of the charitable gift annuity creation or either of the two previous months, selected at the discretion of the IRS
   d) The §7520 rate for the month of the charitable gift annuity creation or either of the two previous months, selected at the discretion of the charity
   e) The applicable federal midterm rate for the month of the charitable gift annuity creation or either of the two previous months, selected at the discretion of the taxpayer

3. A donor purchases a charitable gift annuity in August when the §7520 rate is 3.0%. If the rates were 2.8% for July and 3.2% for June, what rate should the donor use to calculate his best tax deduction?
   a) The June rate, because a higher interest rate means that the value of the annuity is less.
   b) The June rate, because a higher interest rate means that the value of the annuity is more.
   c) The July rate, because a higher interest rate means that the value of the annuity is less.
   d) The July rate, because a higher interest rate means that the value of the annuity is more.
   e) The August rate, because that is the month in which the gift annuity was purchased.

4. A donor purchased a charitable gift annuity that pays her $10,000 per year. During the first year of the annuity, $4,000 of the annuity check was capital gain, $4,000 was return of investment, and $2,000 was earnings. What is the proper taxation of the $10,000 annuity check received in the second year following the end of the donor's life expectancy?
   a) $4,000 is tax free, $4,000 is taxed at the appropriate capital gain tax rate, & $2,000 is taxed at the relevant personal income tax rate.
   b) All $10,000 is taxed at the relevant personal income tax rate as ordinary income
   c) All $10,000 is tax free
   d) Only $2,000 is taxed at the relevant personal income tax rate as ordinary income, the rest is tax free
   e) $4,000 is taxed at the relevant personal income tax rate, $4,000 is taxed at the appropriate capital gain tax rate, & $2,000 is tax free

5. What is the appropriate tax rate for the portion of a charitable gift annuity check that is calculated to be return of investment?
   a) The applicable capital gains tax rate
   b) The applicable personal income tax rate
   c) The applicable ordinary income tax rate for passive investments
   d) The applicable personal gift tax rate
   e) Nothing (0%)

6. In a cash transaction, how are the tax consequences different for a donor who purchases a charitable gift annuity for $100,000 paying $5,000/year for life as compared with a donor who uses part of $100,000 to purchase a commercial annuity paying $5,000/year for life and gives the rest of the $100,000 directly to the charity?
   a) The tax consequences are always identical
   b) There is no charitable deduction for the second transaction

c) In the first transaction the charitable deduction is the $100,000 less the value of the annuity based upon IRS value principles, and in the second transaction the charitable deduction is for the $100,000 less the price of the commercial annuity
d) The charitable deduction for the commercial annuity transaction will be greater than for the gift annuity transaction
e) The charitable deduction for the commercial annuity will be calculated as a bargain sale, while the charitable deduction for the charitable gift annuity will be calculated as a direct gift

7. A donor with a 10-year life expectancy purchases a charitable gift annuity for $12,000. The immediate charitable tax deduction is $2,000. If the donor receives an annual annuity check for $1,250, how much of the first check is considered to be annual return of investment?
8. A donor with a 10-year life expectancy purchases a gift annuity for $12,000. The immediate charitable tax deduction is $2,000. If the donor receives an annual annuity check for $1,250, how much of the 14th check is considered to be annual return of investment?

9. What is the total capital gain if I purchase stock for $100,000, it increases in value to $200,000 and I give it to a charity in exchange for a gift annuity worth $160,000 paid to my nephew?

10. What is the total capital gain if I purchase stock for $10,000, it increases in value to $100,000, and I give it to a charity in exchange for a gift annuity worth $80,000 paid to my nephew?

11. What is the total capital gain if I purchase stock for $20,000, it increases in value to $200,000, and I give it to a charity in exchange for a gift annuity worth $100,000 paid to my nephew?

12. I purchase stock for $100,000, it increases in value to $200,000 and I give it to a charity in exchange for a gift annuity worth $160,000 paid to me for my life. At the time of purchase my life expectancy was 40 years. How much of each annual annuity check during my life expectancy will count as capital gain to me?

13. I purchase stock for $20,000, it increases in value to $200,000, and I give it to a charity in exchange for a gift annuity worth $100,000 paid to me for my life. At the time of purchase my life expectancy was 9 years. How much of each annual annuity check during my life expectancy will count as capital gain to me?

14. I purchase stock for $100,000, it increases in value to $200,000 and I give it to a charity in exchange for a gift annuity worth $160,000 paid to me for my life. At the time of purchase my life expectancy was 40 years. How much of each annual annuity check during my life expectancy will count as tax-free return of investment to me?

15. I purchase stock for $20,000, it increases in value to $200,000 and I give it to a charity in exchange for a gift annuity worth $100,000 paid to me for my life. At the time of purchase my life expectancy was 10 years. How much of each annual annuity check during my life expectancy will count as tax-free return of investment to me?

16. IRS Table S (Based on Life Table 2000CM) for interest at 2.8 Percent lists the following factors for a person age 80: Annuity = 7.0895, Life Estate = 0.19851, Remainder = 0.80149.
James, age 80, has $100,000 cash that he wants to use to establish a charitable gift annuity in October of 2010. Using the ACGA suggested payout rate of 7.2% and the IRS §7520 rate of 2.8%, James's income tax deduction for this donation would be:

ANSWERS

1/ Answer: E. Explanation: The charitable gift annuity creates additions to taxable income based upon the portion of the annuity payment that is ordinary income. It creates a charitable deduction from taxable income based upon the initial gift portion of the transaction. If the donor is also the person receiving the income (i.e., the annuitant), capital gains taxes are postponed and are recognized gradually over the life expectancy of the donor as he or she receives each annuity check. If someone other than the donor or the donor's spouse is the annuitant, creating a charitable gift annuity can increase gift taxes (although an immediate annuity is reduced by the annual gift exclusion for present interest gifts). Therefore, all of these consequences can result from the charitable gift annuity.

2/ Answer: B. Explanation: The taxpayer may select the §7520 rate for the month of the charitable gift annuity creation or either of the two previous months. The §7520 rate is 120% of the applicable federal midterm rate.

3/ Answer: A. Explanation: The higher interest rate causes the annuity to be valued at a lower amount. Because the charitable gift is the difference between the amount paid and the value of the annuity, a lower value for the annuity means that the charitable gift amount, and thus the deduction, is larger. The donor may choose from the §7520 rates during the month of the transaction or the two previous months.

4/ Answer: B. Explanation: After a donor outlives his or her life expectancy, all annuity checks are 100% taxable as ordinary income. By that point, the donor will have recognized all of his or her capital gain and will also have received back all of his or her original investment, thus leaving only ordinary income characterization for the entire amount of each subsequent annuity check.

5/ Answer: E. Explanation: There is no tax on receiving back your own money. Thus, the portion of an annuity check calculated to be return OF investment is not taxable.

6/ Answer: C. Explanation: The tax consequences for the two transactions are similar. However, the charitable gift in a charitable gift annuity is (using bargain sale rules) the difference between the price paid and the value of the annuity based upon IRS value principles. In the second transaction, the gift is the amount left over after paying the price of the commercial annuity. If the price of the commercial annuity were identical to the value of the annuity portion of the gift annuity based upon IRS value principles, then the tax consequences would be identical. (This would not be true for a transaction using appreciated property, but this is a cash transaction.)

7/ Answer: $1,000. Explanation: The annual return of investment during the donor's life expectancy is the non-charitable/sale portion (i.e., money attributed to buying the annuity payments in the contract) divided by the donor's life expectancy at the time of purchase. Because the charitable tax deduction was $2,000, this means that $10,000 of the gift annuity purchase price was used to purchase the annuity payments. The remaining $2,000 was used to make a gift to the charity, not to purchase the annuity. Thus, $10,000 divided by the donor's 10-year life expectancy is $1,000. $1,000 of each check during the donor's life expectancy will be return of the donor's original investment.

8/ Answer: $0. Explanation: A donor with a 10-year life expectancy would have already received back his or her original investment by the time of the 14th annual check. Thus, no part of any check received after the donor's life expectancy (i.e., after the 10th check) is return of investment.

9/ Answer: $80,000. Explanation: The annuity portion is worth 80% of the amount I gave (160,000/200,000=.80), thus I can use 80% of the original cost basis of $100,000, which is $80,000. I received something (the annuity) worth $160,000, and I can subtract $80,000 of my cost basis from that, leaving me with a capital gain of $80,000 ($160,000-$80,000). The capital gain would be $80,000 regardless of whether it was paid to me or to my nephew, but because it was paid to my nephew the entire capital gain will be recognized (i.e., taxed) immediately, rather than being paid out over my life expectancy as I receive each annuity check.

10/ Answer: $72,000. Explanation: The annuity portion is worth 80% of the amount I gave (80,000/100,000=.80), thus I can use 80% of the original cost basis of $10,000, which is $8,000. I received something (the annuity) worth $80,000, and I can subtract $8,000 of my cost basis from that, leaving me with a capital gain of $72,000 ($80,000-$8,000). The capital gain would be $72,000 regardless of whether it was paid to me or to my nephew, but because it was paid to my nephew the entire capital gain will be recognized (i.e., taxed) immediately, rather than being recognized in small portions as I receive each annuity check.

11/ Answer: $90,000. Explanation: The annuity portion is worth 50% of the amount I gave (200,000/100,000=.50), thus I can use 50% of the original cost basis of $20,000, which is $10,000. I received something (the annuity) worth $100,000, and I can subtract $10,000 of my cost basis from that, leaving me with a capital gain of $90,000 ($100,000-$10,000). The capital gain would be $90,000 regardless of whether it was paid to me or to my nephew, but because it was paid to my nephew the entire capital gain will be recognized (i.e., taxed) immediately, rather than being paid out as I receive each annuity check.

12/ Answer: $2,000. Explanation: The annuity portion is worth 80% of the amount I gave (160,000/200,000=.80), thus I can use 80% of the original cost basis of $100,000, which is $80,000. I received something (the annuity) worth $160,000, and I can subtract $80,000 of my cost basis from that, leaving me with a capital gain of $80,000 ($160,000-$80,000). The capital gain of $80,000 is recognized over the course of my 40-year life expectancy, thus $2,000 ($80,000/40 year life expectancy) per year will count as a capital gain to me.

13/ Answer: $10,000. Explanation: The annuity portion is worth 50% of the amount I gave (200,000/100,000=.50), thus I can use 50% of the original cost basis of $20,000, which is $10,000. I received something (the annuity) worth $100,000, and I can subtract $10,000 of my cost basis from that, leaving me with a capital gain of $90,000 ($100,000-$10,000). The capital gain of $90,000 would be recognized in equal portions over the course of my 9 year life expectancy, thus $10,000 ($90,000/9 year life expectancy) per year will count as a capital gain to me.

14/ Answer: $2,000. Explanation: The annuity portion is worth 80% of the amount I gave (160,000/200,000=.80), thus I can use 80% of the original cost basis of $100,000, which is $80,000. The basis used for the annuity of $80,000 is returned over the course of my 40-year life expectancy, thus $2,000 ($80,000/40 year life expectancy) per year will count as a tax free return of basis to me.

15/ Answer: $1,000. Explanation: The annuity portion is worth 50% of the amount I gave (100,000/200,000=.50), thus I can use 50% of the original cost basis of $20,000, which is $10,000. The basis used for the annuity of $10,000 is returned over the course of my 10-year life expectancy, thus $1,000 ($10,000/10 year life expectancy) per year will count as a tax free return of basis to me.

16/ Answer: $48,956. Explanation: To calculate John's income tax deduction, start by calculating his annual payment, which is $100,000 X 7.2% = $7,200. Next, calculate the value of his annuity, which is $7,200 X 7.0895 = $51,044. His income tax deduction is the part of his $100,000 that is not used for the annuity. Therefore, his income tax deduction is $100,000 - $51,044 = $48,956.

CHAPTER 10: GIFTS OF PARTIAL INTERESTS

1. Which of the following is an example of an immediately deductible charitable gift?
   a) I own a building and allow a charity to use it rent free
   b) I inherit a time share in a vacation rental property and I give all of it (all of my interests in the property) to a charity
   c) I own an automobile and sign a contract promising to give it to the charity in ten years
   d) I give land to a charity, but retain the mineral rights in the land
   e) I give the right to use a farm for 20 years to a charity, and retain the reversionary interest that directs that it will become owned by me again at the end of the 20 years

2. Which of the following would constitute a deductible gift of an undivided interest in an office building that I own?
   a) I give a charity a 10% ownership interest as a tenant in common including the right to 10% share of all net operating income
   b) I give a charity the right to use the top floor of the office building without charge
   c) I give a remainder interest in the property giving the charity a right to own the property after my death
   d) I give the charity the right to 10% of all profits from the building for a ten year period beginning in 12 months
   e) I give the charity the right to lease out any open office space to paying clients and receive half of all rent collected from those clients

3. What is the general rule for partial interest gifts where the donor retains some interest in the gifted property?
   a) They are deductible, but only up to 20% of adjusted gross income
   b) They are not deductible unless accompanied by a qualified appraisal
   c) They are not deductible unless the gift fits into one of the specific exceptions
   d) They are not deductible unless given to a qualified 501(c)3 organization
   e) They are generally deductible

4. What is the primary motivation behind the rule against deducting partial interest gifts?
   a) Partial interest gifts are unnecessarily complex, and this complexity suggests an attempt to defraud the IRS
   b) Charities must receive a minimum of 5% per year in benefits for the gift to qualify
   c) If a donor keeps part of the interests in a piece of property, it is often possible to manipulate the circumstances such that the donor receives a much higher share of the benefit than is reflected by the initial deduction
   d) The value of future interest gifts is not ascertainable until such time as the all intervening rights are removed and the charity is the sole owner
   e) Gifts of less than the entire ownership interest in a piece of property are inherently difficult to correctly value

5. An example of a non-deductible divided share gift would be
   a) Giving a wheel from a car that I own
   b) Giving 10 acres from a 1,000 acre farm that I own
   c) Giving the right to use my entire 1,000 acre farm for 10 years for free
   d) Giving a 10% ownership right as tenants-in-common in my 1,000 acre farm
   e) Giving one painting out of a collection of 200 that I own

The following options apply to the next 3 questions

I. A gift of farmland where the donor retains the right to later place a limited number of billboard signs or wind turbines on the property

II. An undivided 15% ownership in farmland given by a donor where the donor retains all underlying mineral rights to the farmland

III. An undivided 15% ownership right in a condominium owned by the donor where the donor has never resided, but has used exclusively as rental property

IV. A gift of the use of a time share interest for ten years

V. A gift of the reproduction rights to a work of art where the donor never owned any rights in the art other than the reproduction rights

6. Which of the options qualifies as a deductible gift that gives away only part of the donor's ownership interests?
   a) II
   b) III
   c) II & III
   d) III & IV
   e) None of the above

7. Which of the options are not deductible because of the retention of an ownership right by the donor?
   a) I, II, & IV
   b) I, II, III & IV
   c) I, II, & V
   d) II, III & IV
   e) I, I, IV & V

8. Which of the options describes a deductible gift where the donor gave up all of his or her rights in the property being donated?
   a) III & V
   b) I only
   c) I, IV, & V
   d) V only
   e) III and V

9. How many of the following charitable gifts could generate an income tax deductiblion?
   I. Donor gives a West Texas cotton farm, but keeps all mineral rights
   II. Donor gives a valuable painting to an art museum, but keeps all digital and reproduction rights
   III. Donor gives all ownership rights in a painting that he painted himself which, although it has great sentimental value, does not have any fair market value
   IV. Donor gives to charity the right to receive his automobile after his death
   V. Donor gives a local church the right to farm his highly productive land for the next 10 years without any rent charge
   a) 0
   b) 1
   c) 2
   d) 3
   e) 4

10. How many of the following charitable gifts could generate an income tax deductible?
   I. Donor gives a 5% interest as tenants in common in a West Texas cotton farm without the mineral rights because the donor never owned the mineral rights
   II. Donor gives a 10% interest as tenants in common in an Iowa corn farm where a billboard company (unrelated to the donor) owns the rights to place billboards on the farmland where the interstate highway adjoins the farmland.
   III. A donor pays for a ten year lease to the top floor of an office building in downtown Seattle. (The lease represents her only rights in the building.) She then gives the right to use the office building during the entire period of the ten year lease to a local charity at no charge to the charity.
   IV. A donor has a life estate giving her the right to use a vacation property for the remainder of her life. The donor gives an 11/12 interest in the life estate as tenants in common to the charity. The donor retains a 1/12 interest including the right to use the property for one month out of each year during the remainder of her life.
   V. Donor owns a cotton farm in West Texas including all mineral rights. Donor simultaneously gives half of the mineral rights to charity A, the other half of the mineral rights to charity B, the right to use the property for the next 5 years to charity C, the right to use the property for years 6-10 to charity D, and all remaining interests following the 10 year period one-half to charity E and one-half to charity F.
   a) 1
   b) 2
   c) 3
   d) 4
   e) 5

11. A donor gives a 1/12 undivided interest in all his rights in a painting to a public charity art museum (including the right to display the painting for one month per year). The donor gives an additional 1/12 undivided interest each year for 10 more years to the same art museum. The donor retains the final 1/12 interest to be kept by his family so that the art work can be displayed for one month out of the year in his family home. The painting is valued at $120,000 at the time of the initial 1/12 interest gift. Each year it increases by an additional $12,000 by the time of the transfer of each subsequent 1/12 interest gift. What is the total value of the deduction for this gift?
    a) $10,000 (year 1)+ $11,000 (year 2)+ $12,000 (year 3)+ $13,000 (year 4)+ $14,000 (year 5)+ $15,000 (year 5)+ $16,000 (year 6)+ $17,000 (year 7)+ $18,000 (year 8)+ $19,000 (year 9)+ $20,000 (year 10)+ $21,000 (year 11).
    b) $10,000 x 11
    c) $22,000 x 11
    d) $120,000
    e) $0 (or less depending upon interest and penalties)

12. A donor gives a 1/10 undivided interest in all his rights in a painting to a public charity art museum (including the right to display the painting for 1/10 of each year). The donor gives an additional 1/10 undivided interest each year for 9 more years to the same art museum, completing a gift of the entire work of art in 10 years. The painting is valued at $100,000 at the time of the initial 1/10 interest gift. Each year it increases in value by an additional $10,000 by the time of the transfer of each subsequent 1/10 interest gift. What is the total value of the deduction for this gift?
    a) $10,000 (year 1)+ $11,000 (year 2)+ $12,000 (year 3)+ $13,000 (year 4)+ $14,000 (year 5)+ $15,000 (year 5)+ $16,000 (year 6)+ $17,000 (year 7)+ $18,000 (year 8)+ $19,000 (year 9)+ $20,000 (year 10)
    b) $10,000 x 10
    c) $20,000 x 10
    d) $150,000
    e) $0 (or less depending upon interest and penalties)

13. A donor gives a 1/12 undivided interest in all his rights in a vacation home to a local charity (including the right to use or rent out the property for one month per year). The donor gives an additional 1/12 undivided interest each year for 10 more years to the same charity. The donor retains the final 1/12 interest to be kept by his family so that they can use the vacation home for one month out of each year. The property is valued at $120,000 at the time of the initial 1/12 interest gift. Each year it increases by an additional $12,000 by the time of the transfer of each subsequent 1/12 interest gift. What is the total value of the deduction for this gift?
    a) $10,000 (year 1)+ $11,000 (year 2)+ $12,000 (year 3)+ $13,000 (year 4)+ $14,000 (year 5)+ $15,000 (year 5)+ $16,000 (year 6)+ $17,000 (year 7)+ $18,000 (year 8)+ $19,000 (year 9)+ $20,000 (year 10)+ $21,000 (year 11)
    b) $10,000 x 11
    c) $22,000 x 11
    d) $120,000
    e) $0 (or less depending upon interest and penalties)

14. Which of the following gifts will NOT qualify for a current income tax deduction?
    a) Artie signed and delivered a deed conveying his beach house residence to the American Cancer Society.
    b) Benjamin executed a new will which gives 200 acres of his farm to the Boy Scouts of America for use as a campground.
    c) Carrie irrevocably transfers an undivided 1/3 interest as tenants in common in a rental house to the American Red Cross.
    d) All of these gifts qualify for a current income tax deduction
    e) None of these gifts qualify for a current income tax deduction

15. Alvin and Amy own a ski chalet outside of Taos, New Mexico. When the chalet is not being used by Alvin and Amy or their close friends and family, they rent the property through an agent and they earn $1,000 per week. This year, Alvin and Amy signed a written authorization for their minister to use the chalet for one month each year for three years to host a series of marriage retreats where young married couples would get away and recommit to each other and to God. The authorization letter was signed by Alvin and Amy and placed into the donation plate that was passed around the congregation during a Sunday service. Which of the following amounts is closest to the deduction that will be allowed this year?
    a) $12,000
    b) An amount between $4,001 and $11,999
    c) $4,000
    d) An amount between $0 and $3,999
    e) $0

16. Which is NOT an exception to rule that gifts of partial interests generate no income tax deduction
    a) a qualified conservation easement
    b) a "qualified percentage" of the donor's partial interest in property

c) an "undivided portion" of the donor's entire interest in property
d) an interest transferred in the form of a Charitable Lead Trust, charitable annuity trust, charitable remainder unit trust, or pooled income fund
e) a remainder interest deed in a personal residence or farm

17. Which one of the following qualifies for an income tax deduction:
a) Owner of a building allows a charity to use it rent free for 10 years
b) A painter giving his highly valued painting to charity but keeps the copyright interests
c) A donor puts his office building in an IRREVOCABLE trust that will transfer the land to the charity at his death.
d) A local art gallery receives a 1/12 interest in a painting owned by a donor. The donor never makes any other gifts of the remaining interest in the painting to any charity.
e) A person donates an office building to his church with the provision that all proceeds from rent for the first 10 years must be given to the Red Cross.

ANSWERS

1/ Answer: B. Explanation: Giving all of one's interest in the property will generally qualify for a charitable deduction (unless the donor has previously divided the interests for the purpose of defeating the tax rule against deducting partial interest gifts, which is not likely in a situation where the donor inherits and gives all of his inherited interest). All other examples are partial interest gifts that do not fall into one of the exceptions, thus making them non-deductible gifts. Note that the gift of the automobile in ten years may be deductible when it is actually transferred in ten years, but there is no immediate deduction based on the irrevocable, enforceable commitment to gift the property because of the donor's retained interest.

2/ Answer: A. Explanation: An ownership share as a tenant in common is considered to be an "undivided portion" of the donor's entire interest and is thus deductible. All other gifts are partial interest gifts that do not fall into any particular exception to the general rule against deducting partial interest gifts. Giving a remainder interest is not deductible because this property is not a farm or home. Giving the right to 10% of all profits is a non-deductible partial interest gift.

3/ Answer: C. Explanation: The general rule is that partial interest gifts where the donor retains some interest in the gifted property are not deductible. Exceptions to this rule include giving all or an undivided portion of one's entire interest, giving a remainder interest in a home or farm, giving by Charitable Remainder Trusts, Charitable Lead Trusts, or pooled income funds, or giving a qualified conservation easement. Unless the gift falls into one of these exceptions, giving with a qualified appraisal or to a 501(c)3 organization does not make the gift deductible.

4/ Answer: C. Explanation: The primary motivation for the general rule is that donors can manipulate the circumstances following the gift (and deduction) such that they will be able to receive a much greater share (and the charity receive a much smaller share) than was reflected in the deduction. The exceptions to the rule are circumstances in which this potential is much less because of the specific requirements of each exception. Gifts of future interests and partial interests are ascertainable and, in the case of the exceptions to the rule, are regularly ascertained. The complexity of the partial interest gifts is not the problem as the exceptions to the rule show that enormous complexity, in the form of charitable trusts, is welcome. The 5% rule does not apply to all exceptions of deducting partial interest gifts (e.g., remainder interests in homes or farms), and is thus not the motivation for the general rule.

5/ Answer: C. Explanation: A divided share gift occurs when the donor gives some ownership rights to a particular piece of property, but keeps some other ownership rights in the same piece of property. Physically separating property into different items, and giving one of those items is not a non-deductible divided share gift because the donor is keeping no ownership rights in the item of property that has been gifted. Consequently, giving a wheel from a car, 10 acres from a farm, or one painting from a collection is not a divided share gift as the donor is giving all ownership rights in the donated item of property. However, giving the use of one's farm does divide the ownership interests, and the donor does keep some ownership interests in the donated item of property. This makes it a non-deductible divided gift. Giving a 10% share in the farm as tenants-in-common is an "undivided share" as the charity has a share of all of the donor's rights, and there are no rights that the donor retains entirely for his own use.

6/ Answer: B. Explanation: Only III is a deductible gift of an undivided share, because it gives a 15% share of all of the donor's ownership interests to the charity. The fact that it is not a personal residence would prevent a deductible remainder interest gift, but this is not a remainder interest gift. In I, II, and IV the donor also gives away less than his or her entire interest, but in each of these cases the donor keeps some ownership rights entirely for himself or herself, so the charity does not have an undivided share in all ownership rights, and the gift is thus not deductible. In V the donor gives away all of the donor's ownership interests and so, although it is deductible, it does not meet the criteria for the question.

7/ Answer: A. Explanation: In all but V the donor retains some ownership interests. However, in III the donor retains only an undivided share in all property rights (and gives an undivided share in all property rights to the charity). Consequently, III is a deductible gift and thus does not meet the criteria for the question, leaving I, II, & IV.

8/ Answer: D. Explanation: The donor retains some interest in the property in all examples except V. In V, the donor did not own all of the property rights but the donor gave up all property rights which he did own. Giving up all rights that one owns to the charity makes the gift deductible.

9/ Answer: A. Explanation: In all cases except III, the donor retains a separate, divided ownership interest and the gift is consequently not deductible. In III the donor gives a piece of property with no fair market value thus generating no deduction.

10/ Answer: E. Explanation: All gifts described are deductible. In I, II, & IV the donor gives an undivided share of all of the donor's rights to an item of property. In II the donor gives all ownership rights that the donor owns in the building to the charity. In V the donor does give partial interests, but because he/she retains no ownership interests for himself or herself, but instead gives away all rights to various charities, the gifts are deductible.

11/ Answer: E. Explanation: This gift violates the rules for fractional shares in tangible personal property because all of the donor's rights must be given to charity with 10 years and this was not the case. As such, the gifts are not deductible and any deductions taken are subject to recapture includes interest and a 10% penalty. If this gift had not been a gift of tangible personal property, the special rule wouldn't apply and answer A would have been correct. Note that these rules apply only to gifts of fractional shares in tangible personal property and do not apply to gifts in other kinds of property.

12/ Answer: B. Explanation: This gift of fractional shares in personal property meets the rules of giving an undivided share in all of the donor's property rights and giving up all rights to the tangible personal property within ten years. As such it is deductible. However, the special rules for tangible personal property require that the deduction be limited to the lesser of the value during the first or later transfers. Consequently, each gift is valued at 1/10 of the initial $100,000 value, even though the tangible personal property grew in value each subsequent year. Note that these rules apply only to gifts of fractional shares in tangible personal property and do not apply to gifts of other kinds of property.

13/ Answer: A. Explanation: This is not tangible personal property so there are no requirements to transfer the entire ownership of the property within 10 years. Further, there is no requirement to value each fractional interest at the lesser of the value during the first or later transfers, as with a fractional share gift in tangible personal property. As such, each separate gift is valued as a share of the entire property, which must be valued at the time of each fractional interest gift. (Recognize that it is possible the IRS may require a reduction in valuation of the first gift based upon the cost of partitioning the property, because converting the ownership interest to cash by a forced sale would require some additional cost.)

14/ Answer: B. Explanation: A is incorrect since this is a direct gift of a piece of property. B is correct. Since Benjamin could revoke his will at any time and execute a new one that does not include the gift it is not deductible even though it involves an interest in a family farm. C is incorrect. Since this is a partial gift of an undivided interest, it qualifies for the exception to the partial interest rule and for the deduction.

15/ Answer: E. Explanation: A right to use property is a gift of a partial interest and is not deductible where the donor owns additional rights to the property.

16/ Answer: B. Explanation: B is not an exception.

17/ Answer: E. Explanation: The rent-free use of real or personal property is not deductible where the donor retains other interests in the property. The painter's gift is a divided share partial interest and because he retains interest in the property the gift does not qualify for a deduction. Although irrevocable, the gift of the office building in trust is not deductible for income tax purposes because it is a divided share partial interest gift. (In contrast, a remainder interest transferred by deed in a home or farm would be deductible because of a special exception.) The 1/12 interest in the painting is not deductible because fractional shares in tangible personal property are deductible only if the entire item is transferred to charity within ten years (or the donor's death if earlier). The final option is correct because, although the interests are divided, all interests in the building are going to charity while the donor keeps nothing.

CHAPTER 11: REMAINDER INTERESTS IN HOMES & FARMS

1. The tax code provides a special exception for charitable gifts of remainder interests in homes and farms. This is an exception from what general rule?
   a) Charitable gifts of partial interests, where the donor retains a portion of the property rights, may not normally be deducted.
   b) Charitable gifts of future interests must be valued based upon the current §7520 interest rate
   c) Valuation of gifts of future interests in houses must include a factor for the estimated depreciation of the property
   d) The gift of a home or farm to a charitable organization is not normally deductible
   e) The rental value of property given for the use of a charitable organization may not be deducted

2. A charitable gift of a partial interest may NOT be deducted if it is
   a) A remainder interest in a home
   b) An "undivided portion" of a property interest
   c) A Charitable Remainder Trust
   d) The direct gift of a farm where the donor retains the mineral rights
   e) A qualified conservation easement

3. Which of the following is a charitable gift that generates an income tax charitable deduction?
   a) I give a charity the right to use my home for one month
   b) I sign and deliver a deed giving a remainder interest in 100 acres of farmland to a charity which will transfer full ownership of the property at my death
   c) I leave my farm to a charity in my will
   d) I sign an irrevocable trust agreement (not a Charitable Remainder Trust) giving the cash equivalent of 100 acres of farmland to a charity effective at my death
   e) I give to charity a remainder interest in only the mineral rights to my farmland

4. Which of the following arrangements would not be considered a deductible remainder interest in a farm?
   a) Donor gifts by deed to charity the right to own the farm following donor's death
   b) Donor gifts by deed to charity the right to own the farm after 20 years
   c) Donor gifts by deed to charity the right to own the farm following the death of the donor and the donor's spouse
   d) Donor gifts by deed to charity the right to own the farm following the death of the donor's 4 year old grandson Bob.
   e) Donor gifts by deed to charity the right to use the farm until the donor's death

5. In what ways is a remainder interest in real estate similar to a will?
   a) A remainder is irrevocable
   b) A remainder creates an immediate property right in the named recipient
   c) A remainder can be immediately sold by the holder to another person
   d) A remainder can be recorded by a deed
   e) A remainder can be used to transfer real property to a charity at death

6. After recording a deed giving a remainder interest in my home, effective at my death, to a charity, I learn that my child would like to live in the home after my death. How do I alter the remainder interest gift so that my child can live in the home after my death?
   a) Add a codicil to my last will and testament directing that the home must not be sold unless agreed to by my child
   b) Record a life estate deed in favor of my child giving the right to the child to live in the home for the child's life
   c) Transfer my property ownership interest into a trust with instructions to the independent trustee to permit the child to live in the home after my death
   d) Revoke the remainder interest by recording a revocation in the recorder of deeds office
   e) Remainder interests are not revocable, so the gift cannot be altered

7. Which of the following would qualify as farmland for purposes of making a deductible remainder interest charitable gift?
   a) 20 acres of tillable land that the donor currently uses as an airport runway for private planes
   b) A 100 acre industrial park housing manufacturing and shipping companies
   c) A 100 acre dairy farm purchased by the donor 13 months ago that has been out of use for two years, but which can be placed back into agricultural production at any time
   d) A 10 acre segment from a 1,000 acre cotton farm where the 10 acres consists of land covered by an electric power line right-of-way, none of which can be used to raise crops or livestock
   e) A 10 acre segment consisting of pasture land and a dairy barn leased to a corporation that uses it to graze and milk cattle, where the 10-acre segment is part of a 1,000 acre farm.

8. Which of the following remainder interests in a farm would not be deductible if given to a charity?
   a) A remainder interest giving a 10 acre segment of pastureland taken from a 300 acre cattle ranch
   b) A remainder interest giving a right to use the property for 20 years following the death of the donor
   c) A remainder interest where, following the death of the donor, the charity will own a 20% undivided interest in the farm as a tenant in common with the donor's children
   d) A remainder interest in 10 acres of a solid rock shelf (without any dirt or vegetation) which has been used as a feedlot to raise hogs for several years
   e) A remainder interest in an operating farm where, after the death of the donor, the donor's children will receive the house, the barns, and all timber land and the charity will receive only 5 acres of pasture land

9. Mary Donor owns a 5,000 acre cotton farm in West Texas. Sarah Smith, an unrelated person, inherited the mineral rights to the farm many years ago. Both Mary and Sarah are interested in benefiting Texas Tech University. Which of the following would not generate a deductible charitable gift?
   a) Mary gives a remainder interest in the farm, without the mineral rights, to Texas Tech University
   b) Sarah gives a remainder interest in the mineral rights to Texas Tech University
   c) Mary purchases Sarah's mineral rights and gives a remainder interest in the farm, including mineral rights, to Texas Tech University
   d) Sarah purchases Mary's farm and gives a remainder interest in the farm, including mineral rights, to Texas Tech University
   e) Mary gives a remainder interest that will transfer the farm, without mineral rights, 50% to Texas Tech University and 50% to her son Joshua, to be held as tenants in common.

10. Calculating the deduction for a remainder interest in farmland following the donor's life estate would involve all of the following except
   a) Finding the applicable §7520 interest rate
   b) Identifying the donor's age
   c) Locating the remainder valuation percentage or ratio from IRS publication 1457
   d) Estimating the useful life of the farmland itself
   e) Estimating the current fair market value of the farmland

11. You hear the announcement that the §7520 rates are lower than they have ever been in history. The impact of this on the deduction value of a remainder interest charitable gift of a home is
   a) Negative as the deduction will now be lower due to the cheap availability of money
   b) Positive in that it decreases the mortgage costs for refinancing a home
   c) Positive as the value of charitable deductions for remainder interests varies inversely with interest rates (they move in opposite directions)
   d) Positive as the estimated life expectancy tables for donors will decrease, thus increasing the value of the charitable deduction
   e) Positive as the value of charitable deductions for remainder interests is positively correlated with interest rates (they move in the same direction)

12. The charitable deduction for a remainder interest gift in farmland (with retained life interest) made by a 59 year old donor when valued at the 2.0% §7520 rate of Oct 2010, as compared with the 11.6% rate of May 89 would increase by
   a) About 2%
   b) About 8-9%
   c) About 11. 6%
   d) About 100%
   e) About 400%

13. What are some potential advantages of leaving farmland to charity by a remainder interest instead of leaving farmland to charity in a will?
   a) The donor can receive a large income tax deduction when giving a remainder interest, but not when giving by will
   b) The donor can receive a large estate tax deduction when giving a remainder interest, but not when giving by will
   c) Prior to death, the donor can change which charity will receive the farmland after giving a remainder interest gift
   d) Deductible gifts of remainder interests can be completed by means of a simple contract agreement
   e) The donor can continue to use the farmland during his or her life after giving a remainder interest to charity

14. Which of the following is NOT a reason why a donor might choose to give separate remainder interests in portions of farmland over several years rather than making a single gift of a remainder interest in the entire farm immediately?
   a) Gifting in portions each year allows for larger deductions to the extent that the farmland has increased in value each year

b) Gifting in portions may allow the donor to avoid exceeding the income limit maximum thresholds for charitable giving in a particular year
c) Gifting in portions could allow the donor to gift only to the point where remaining income is taxed at a lower marginal tax bracket
d) Gifting in portions could avoid the risk of losing the carryover deduction at death if a carryover deduction would otherwise be created due to exceeding the income limitations on charitable giving
e) Gifting in portions allows the donor to take the charitable income tax deduction earlier than making a single gift of the remainder interest in the entire farm

15. Why might a child benefit from a wealthy parent who gives a remainder interest in a farm to a charity and uses the value of the tax benefit to pay for life insurance in an Irrevocable Life Insurance Trust (ILIT) instead of simply leaving a gift to the charity in the will?
a) Life insurance from an ILIT passes to the children estate tax free, but the farm would not
b) The family farm will pass to the child estate tax free
c) Life insurance will always appreciate faster than farmland
d) With a remainder interest, but not a will, the farm will pass to the charity estate tax free
e) Farmland will always appreciate faster than life insurance

16. Which of the following would NOT qualify for a deductible charitable gift of a remainder interest in a personal residence?
a) A boat with bathroom, cooking, and sleeping facilities where the donor resides two weeks per year
b) A second home on a lake where the donor live four weeks per year
c) A vacation home in the mountains owned by the donor and used only by the donor's children six weeks per year
d) A condominium owned by the donor that is her primary residence
e) A co-op apartment home owned by the donor in New York City where the donor resides every other weekend

17. A 59 year old donor is considering giving the remainder interest (and retaining the life estate) in $200,000 of unimproved farmland or in her $200,000 personal residence to her favorite charity. Which of the following is true?
a) The remainder interest gift in the farmland will generate a greater deduction because it has fewer depreciable elements
b) The remainder interest gift in the farmland will generate a greater deduction because it has more depreciable elements
c) The remainder interest gift in the farmland will generate a deduction equal to the remainder interest gift in the house
d) The remainder interest gift in the house will generate a greater deduction because it has fewer depreciable elements
e) The remainder interest gift in the house will generate a greater deduction because it has more depreciable elements

18. In calculating the useful life of a personal residence for purposes of estimating depreciation, which of the following is probably NOT a reasonable approach?
a) Use a qualified appraiser to estimate the useful life of the house
b) Use a qualified structural engineer to estimate the useful life of the house
c) Use the IRS example of 45 year life span for a personal residence if the home is new
d) Use the IRS depreciation tables for residential rental property indicating a useful life of 27.5 years
e) Use examples of antebellum homes to show the residential property can last over two centuries if properly maintained and assume a similar future for the personal residence at issue

19. A 59 year old donor is giving a life estate in his $100,000 of farmland to a charity while retaining the remainder interest which he plans to distribute to his children (his life is the measuring life). Assuming a §7520 interest rate of 2.4%, IRS Table S reflects the following numbers for age 59: Annuity = 16.4213, Life Estate = .39411, Remainder = .60589. What is the correct charitable deduction for this gift?
a) $0
b) $39,411
c) $60,589
d) $100,000
e) $160,000

20. Which of the following would not be an available option for the donor and the nonprofit if she gives a remainder interest in her home to a charitable organization and later decides to leave the home?
a) Rent the property
b) Sell the life estate to an investor or property manager
c) Agree with the charity to a joint sale and divide the proceeds
d) Give the life estate to the charity in exchange for a gift annuity
e) Complete a bargain sale where the charity sells the remainder interest back to the donor for 50% of its current value, thereby allowing the donor to sell the property with a fee simple title.

21. Which of the following is NOT a common law requirement that a donor who gives a remainder interest in a home, but retains the life estate, is required to follow?
    a) The donor ("life tenant") must maintain the home
    b) The donor ("life tenant") must insure the home
    c) The donor ("life tenant") must pay taxes the home
    d) The donor ("life tenant") must improve the home
    e) The donor ("life tenant") must have leaks in the roof of the home repaired

22. Which of the following is an expense that the donor could deduct a portion of as a charitable gift after making a transfer of a remainder interest in a home to a charitable organization?
    a) Payments for fire insurance on the home
    b) Payments for local property taxes on the home
    c) Payments for fixing a leak in the roof
    d) Payments for building an additional bedroom onto the home
    e) Payments to insure the home against wind damage

ANSWERS

1/ Answer: A. Explanation: Charitable gifts of remainder interests in homes and farms may be deducted, even though partial interest gifts are generally not deductible. However, these gifts must still be valued using the § 7520 rate and accounting for depreciation in houses. Direct gifts of homes and farms are deductible. The transfer of a remainder interest does not relate to deducting rental value for the use of property.

2/ Answer: D. Explanation: Giving a farm outright but retaining the mineral rights is a classic example of a retained interest gift and may not be deducted. The other choices are all exceptions to the general rule against deducting partial interest charitable gifts.

3/ Answer: B. Explanation: There is no deduction for giving a charity rent free use of property owned by the donor. Leaving the farm to a charity in a will does not generate an income tax deduction, although it does generate an estate tax deduction. Usually remainder interests are deductible only if transferred by deed not by trust (and in the rare exceptions to this, the charity must retain the right to take the property itself if desired). Mineral rights do not qualify as farmland because they are not used to raise agricultural products or livestock, and so a remainder interest is not deductible. A remainder interest in farmland conveyed by a deed is deductible.

4/ Answer: E. Explanation: The right to use property is not a deductible charitable gift, even if given in the form of a life estate. Remainder interest gifts can transfer the property after a period of years or after the death of any person or persons. Of course, the value of the remainder interest gift will change depending upon the period of time or life expectancy of the person or persons used.

5/ Answer: E. Explanation: Transferring a remainder interest in real estate is accomplished by recording a deed. At the point of transfer, the recipient immediately owns an irrevocable property interest, namely the right to receive the property at the death of the named person. This property interest can be immediately sold, and the new purchaser will then have the right to the property at the death of the named person. A will, however, can be changed at any point, and thus creates no property right. However, both can be used to transfer real property to a charity at death.

6/ Answer: E. Explanation: Remainder interests cannot be revoked. All of the proposed changes will be ineffective as the transfer of the remainder interest has already taken place.

7/ Answer: E. Explanation: A farm is any land and improvements used (even by a tenant) to raise crops or livestock. The fact that a land could potentially be used to raise crops or livestock is not sufficient. It must actually be used for that purpose to qualify as a farm. Therefore property used as a runway or industrial park does not qualify, nor does land that is out of use or could not be used to raise crops or livestock.

8/ Answer: B. Explanation: The charity must become the owner of land (or an undivided share of the land) at the conclusion of the life estate. It is not enough for the charity to have a right to use the property.

9/ Answer: B. Explanation: A remainder interest in mineral rights does not qualify as a farm and would thus not be deductible. However, if the donor gives a remainder interest in a farm, it can include the mineral rights. If the donor doesn't own the mineral rights, the remainder gift of the farm is still deductible. A remainder interest where an undivided share of the farm goes to the charity is also deductible.

10/ Answer: D. Explanation: Estimating the useful life of the farmland itself is not necessary as land is not considered depreciable (i.e., it doesn't wear out). If the farm included improvements or attachments such as a barn or corral, those items would need to be depreciated, but not the farmland itself. All other components are necessary to estimate the value of a remainder interest in farmland.

11/ Answer: C. Explanation: As interest rates decrease, the value of a remainder interest increases, thus increasing the deduction for a gift of a remainder in a home or farm to a charitable organization. All other statements are false. The cheap availability of money (lower interest rates) increases the charitable deduction. The mortgage refinancing costs do not impact the deduction value and interest rates are unconnected with the IRS life expectancy tables.

12/ Answer: E. Explanation: The dollar value of the gift would change from $15,684 (per $100,000 of farmland fair market value) to $65,553 (per $100,000 of farmland fair market value), an increase of 418%

13/ Answer: A. Explanation: Only a remainder interest gift allows the donor to take an immediate income tax deduction. This is because the remainder interest, once transferred, is irrevocable and cannot be changed. Thus, the donor may not change which charity will receive the farmland after a transfer of a remainder interest is made. A gift to charity by either a will or remainder interest can generate an estate tax deduction. Deductible gifts of remainder interests must generally be completed by deed, rather than by a contract or trust (an exception has arisen where local law allowed the charity to take the property directly after death, however generally the transfer must be by deed). Although the donor can continue to use the farmland during his or her life after giving a remainder interest, this is not an advantage over a will as the same is true for a gift in a will.

14/ Answer: E. Explanation: Gifting in portions delays the taking of deductions, although this may at times be beneficial for various reasons such as increasing value of the underlying gifted asset and avoiding deduction carryover due to income limitations on charitable deductions.

15/ Answer: A. Explanation: The advantage is that life insurance from an ILIT passes to the children estate tax free. The other statements are false.

16/ Answer: C. Explanation: In order to qualify, the home must be a personal residence of the donor, although it need not be the primary residence of the donor. Therefore the vacation home used only by the donor's children would not qualify.

17/ Answer: A. Explanation: Depreciable elements reduce the size of the deduction because the estimated value of what is left after the death of the donor is lower. Depreciable elements are things that wear out and are consequently of less value over time. Land is not depreciable. It is assumed not to wear out. However the building components of a personal residence (aside from their salvage value) are depreciable because they can wear out. Thus, a remainder interest in the $100,000 residence is calculated as being worth less, because the depreciable elements are assumed to be more likely to wear out.

18/ Answer: E. Explanation: It is not reasonable to assume that the home should be depreciated on a 200+ year time horizon. The other four approaches all fall within the realm of a potentially reasonable approach.

19/ Answer: A. Explanation: There is no deduction for giving a life estate to a charitable organization while retaining the remainder interest. This is a partial interest gift, which are generally not deductible, and it does not come under the exception for remainder interest gift in farmland because it is a gift of a life estate, not a remainder interest.

20/ Answer: E. Explanation: A charity may not sell a property interest for 50% of its current value to a donor (although a donor could do so for a charity) as this may be a form of "private inurement" meaning that the charity is being used to benefit a particular donor or manager rather than using its resources to accomplish its charitable purposes. All other options are available.

21/ Answer: D. Explanation: Life tenants are not required to improve the property, only to keep it in its original condition. All other items are required under the MIT duties of Maintain, Insure, and Pay Taxes.

22/ Answer: D. Explanation: The donor can deduct the remainder value of major improvements as additional gifts. Only the bedroom addition would qualify as a major improvement. The other expenditures are required of the life tenant by common law under the MIT requirements of Maintanence, Insurance, and Taxes

CHAPTER 12: CHARITABLE REMAINDER TRUSTS

1. Which of the following are NOT allowable for the current payout benefit of a Charitable Remainder Trust?
   a) Providing annual fixed payments to a friend, relative, or the donor for their life or lives
   b) Providing annual fixed payments to a friend, relative, or the donor for 25 years
   c) Providing 5% of the trust assets to a friend, relative, or the donor for their life or lives
   d) Providing 45% of the trust assets to a friend, relative, or the donor for 2 years
   e) Providing 10% of the trust assets, or the total income from the trust, whichever is less, to a friend, relative, or the donor

2. Which of the following are allowable for the ongoing payout benefit of a Charitable Remainder Trust?
   I. Providing payments of the lesser of the net income of the trust or 4% of trust assets
   II. Providing payments of 20% of trust assets or all trust income, whichever is less, with the provision that anytime payments are less than 20% they should later be made up whenever income exceeds 20%
   III. Providing payments of 60% of trust assets for two years
   IV. Providing payments of the net income of the trust, not to exceed 8% of all trust assets, until the sale of a piece of real estate by the trust, after which time the trust must pay 8% of all trust assets, regardless of the net income of the trust
   V. Providing a payment of 5% of all trust assets, with the payment to be divided equally between the donor and a charitable organization
   VI. Providing payouts of between 5% and 10% of trust assets, with the donor retaining the right to choose the payout rate on an annual basis
   a) Only II is allowed
   b) Only II, IV & V are allowed
   c) Only I, II, IV, & V are allowed
   d) Only II, III, IV, & V are allowed
   e) Only II, IV, V, & VI are allowed

3. If a trust is drafted to allow it, a donor that sets up a CRT is allowed to do all of the following except
   a) Act as the trustee of the CRT and continue to manage the trust assets
   b) Choose his friend, the charity, or a trust company as the CRT trustee
   c) Change which charity will receive the remainder interest
   d) Give all of his rights in future payments to the charity that is the remainder beneficiary, which would result in the CRT terminating and all assets being immediately delivered to the charity if the donor is the only income beneficiary
   e) Modify the original rules of a Charitable Remainder Trust after it is established

4. Which of the following planning goals could NOT be accomplished using a Charitable Remainder Trust?
   a) "I want to control my own investments and spend about 5% of my assets each year. After death I want it all to go to charity."
   b) "I would like to use $50,000 per year from my assets. The rest, I want to go to my favorite charity."
   c) "I want to retire today, but my pension doesn't start paying for 9 more years. I want to give assets to charity, but I still need $65,000 per year for the next 9 years."
   d) "I want to leave my assets to charity at death. Prior to my death I think I will want 10% of the value of the assets each year, unless I or one of my family members has unexpected medical expenses, in which case I need to have access to enough of the trust principal to pay for reasonable and necessary medical expenses."
   e) "I have a $1,000,000 asset from which I would like to provide an income of $50,000 per year for my nephew – assuming he submits to and passes random drug tests, and the rest, I want to go to my favorite charity."

5. A donor with $1,000,000 in developable raw land with a basis of $100,000 plans to sell the land, invest in income producing securities, spend 8% of the remaining value each year for the rest of her life, and leave the rest to charity. Which of the following is NOT a potential tax advantage of doing this through a Charitable Remainder Trust as compared with keeping the assets and giving to charity through her will?
   a) The donor can receive an immediate income tax deduction for the present value of the projected remainder interest that will go to charity at death with the CRT.
   b) No capital gains tax will be due at the sale of the land if the property is sold by the CRT
   c) The donor will not need to pay income taxes on any income earned by the CRT beyond the 8% being taken annually to the donor.
   d) The donor will receive a charitable estate tax deduction for the value of any property that is transferred to the charity.
   e) Because the donor pays no capital gains tax, the entire $1,000,000 value can be invested to generate income rather than only the amount left over after paying taxes on the $900,000 of gain.

6. Abimelek has developable raw land with a basis of $100,000. He sells the land for $1,000,000 and invests in income producing securities. If the Abimelek pays capital gains tax at a 20% rate, how much will be left to invest after paying all capital gains taxes?
   a) $900,000
   b) $1,000,000
   c) $800,000
   d) $820,000
   e) $860,000

7. Asher has developable raw land with a basis of $100,000. He gives the land to a Charitable Remainder Unitrust paying him 8% of all trust assets per year for life. The Charitable Remainder Trust sells the land for $1,000,000 and invests in income producing securities. If the Asher pays capital gains tax at a 20% rate, how much will be left to invest after paying all capital gains taxes?
   a) $900,000
   b) $1,000,000
   c) $800,000
   d) $820,000
   e) $860,000

8. Jael owns a historically important archeological artifact in the form of an ancient hammer and slightly used matching wooden peg that she expects to sell as a set to one of the top international museums for about $500,000. She has no basis in the property and she would like to place it in a Charitable Remainder Trust before it sells. However, it is likely that such a sale may take up to three years to complete because of the difficulties and delays involved in such transactions. During this period of time, there will be no other assets in the trust, and the artifact will generate no income. Which of the following would NOT likely be a reasonable planning approach?
   a) She can place the artifact in an 8% NICRUT. Before the artifact sells, the CRUT will not need to make payments because payments are limited to 8% of trust assets or net income, whichever is lower.
   b) She can place the artifact in an 8% NIMCRUT. Before the artifact sells, the CRUT will not need to make payments because payments are limited to 8% of trust assets or net income, whichever is lower. After the artifact sells, whenever trust income exceeds 8% these funds can be used to make-up the previous 8% payments that were not paid due to lack of income
   c) She can place the artifact in a FlipCRUT that changes from an 8% NICRUT to an 8% CRUT upon the sale of the artifact. Before the artifact sells, the CRUT will not need to make payments because payments are limited to 8% of trust assets or net income, whichever is lower. After the artifact sells, the trust will be required to pay 8% of net assets, even in years when income was lower than 8%
   d) She can place the artifact in an 8% CRUT. Before the artifact sells, the CRUT can borrow money against the artifact to make the annual payments. After the sale, the CRUT can use the proceeds to pay off the loan.
   e) All of the approaches are reasonable planning approaches for this asset.

9. In what circumstances will there be a difference in payments between an 8% Net Income Charitable Remainder Unitrust (NICRUT) and an 8% Net Income Makeup Charitable Remainder Unitrust (NIMCRUT) over the course of the life of the trust?
   a) If net income always exceeds 8% of trust assets
   b) If net income never exceeds 8% of trust assets
   c) If net income is 9% of trust assets in odd years and 7% of trust assets in even years
   d) If net income is always 7% of trust assets
   e) If net income is always 9% of trust assets

10. Which of the following is a potential advantage of a Charitable Gift Annuity over a Charitable Remainder Trust?
    a) Donor can receive rights to a fixed amount of annual income for life
    b) Donor can benefit a charity at his death, but receive a current income tax deduction
    c) Donor can transfer highly appreciated property and avoid paying capital gains tax at the time of the sale of the property
    d) Donor can receive income, some part of which may be tax-free return of capital.
    e) The donor will receive payments regardless of his or her life span or the returns on the original money invested so long as the charity does not go bankrupt

11. Which of the following is a NOT a potential advantage of a Charitable Remainder Trust over a typical Charitable Gift Annuity?
    a) The donor can choose an unlimited number of income beneficiaries
    b) The donor can receive rights to income for the life of the donor and the donor's spouse
    c) The donor can retain the ability to change the charitable beneficiary
    d) The donor can choose income payments for a fixed number of years, rather than for life
    e) The donor can require that the income payments be made to a child, but will be paid to another beneficiary if the child drops out of school before obtaining a college degree

12. A donor transfers $100,000 to a Charitable Remainder Unitrust scheduled to last for 10 years. It will pay equal shares to all 12 grandchildren of the donor for 10 years. However, if one of the children drops out of school before completing a college degree, their share will be given to the other grandchildren. The charity is projected to receive $10,000 when the trust terminates at the end of 10 years. Why is this trust disqualified such that the donor will receive no income tax deduction for the transfer?
    a) This trust will violate the rule that there must be no greater than a 5% chance that the charity will receive no charitable gift at the termination of the trust
    b) This trust will violate the rules for Generation Skipping Transfer Tax because of the transfers to grandchildren, thus causing disqualification of the trust
    c) This trust will violate the "10% rule" where the present value of the projected amount going to charity must be at least 10% of the transfer
    d) This trust violates public policy by penalizing a beneficiary for his educational/career choices
    e) This trust will violate the trust distribution rules because the income beneficiaries are not irrevocably determined at the beginning of the trust, but could change over time

13. A donor completes his charitable transfer when market returns and interest rates averaged 15%, after which market returns and interest rates averaged only 2%. In which of the following circumstances is the donor MOST likely to permanently stop receiving any payments during his life?
    a) The donor placed $100,000 in a CRUT paying 10% of all trust assets for life to the donor
    b) The donor placed $100,000 in a NICRUT paying 10% of all trust assets for life to the donor
    c) The donor placed $100,000 in a NIMCRUT paying 10% of all trust assets for life to the donor
    d) The donor placed $100,000 in a CRAT paying $10,000 of all trust assets for life to the donor
    e) The donor placed $100,000 in a CGA from Yale University paying $10,000 of all trust assets for life to the donor

14. Sheerah gives $100,000 of stock (she originally paid $95,000 for it) to her Charitable Remainder Unitrust. The trustee immediately sells the stock for $100,000 and invests half in corporate bonds that pay $2,000 of annual ordinary interest income and half in municipal bonds that pay $1,000 of annual tax exempt interest income. At the end of the first year, Sheerah receives her annual payment from the unitrust. What is the smallest of the following annual payments that would result in part of her payment being tax-free return of principal?
    a) $1
    b) $2,001
    c) $3,001
    d) $7,001
    e) $8,001

15. Salome gives $100,000 of stock (she originally paid $95,000 for it) to her Charitable Remainder Unitrust. The trustee immediately sells the stock for $100,000 and invests half in corporate bonds that pay $2,000 of annual ordinary interest income and half in municipal bonds that pay $1,000 of annual tax exempt interest income. At the end of the first year, Salome receives her annual payment from the unitrust. What is the smallest of the following annual payments that will result in part of her payment being tax-exempt income?
    a) $1
    b) $2,001
    c) $3,001
    d) $7,001
    e) $8,001

16. Serah gives $100,000 of stock (she originally paid $95,000 for it) to her Charitable Remainder Unitrust. The trustee immediately sells the stock for $100,000 and invests half in corporate bonds that pay $2,000 of annual ordinary interest income and half in municipal bonds that pay $1,000 of annual tax exempt interest income. At the end of the first year, Serah receives her annual payment from the unitrust. What is the smallest of the following annual payments that will result in part of her payment being capital gain income?
    a) $1
    b) $2,001
    c) $3,001
    d) $7,001
    e) $8,001

17. Many years ago, Drusilla purchased shares of a publicly traded company for $100,000 that today are worth $1,100,000. She places these shares into her Charitable Remainder Annuity Trust that pays her $50,000 per year for 20 years. Her trustee sells the shares and spends the proceeds to purchase a 30 year corporate bond with a face value of $1,100,000 paying exactly $50,000 per

year in interest. Over the course of twenty years, if the relevant capital gains tax rate was 20%, how much capital gains tax is paid on this initial transaction and the subsequent income payments?
a) $0
b) $8,000
c) $16,000
d) $160,000
e) $200,000

18. Which of the following assets can be held by a Charitable Remainder Trust and create no accompanying tax problems?
a) A 5% share of a profitable dog-grooming business held as subchapter S corporation shares
b) A 5% share of a profitable dog-grooming business held as a general partnership
c) A 100% share of a profitable dog-grooming business held as a sole proprietorship
d) A 5% share of a profitable dog-grooming business held as shares in a standard C-corporation
e) A $150,000 building with a $50,000 mortgage rented to a dog grooming business for $1,000 per month.

19. Cozbi and Zimri, a married couple, transfer their $1,000,000 house with a $100,000 basis into a charitable remainder annuity trust paying them $50,000 at the end of each twelve month period as long as either one of them is alive. The trustee borrows $100,000 against the house to make improvements to the house in preparation for sale. Within three months of the establishment of the CRT, the house is sold for $1,200,000 and the $100,000 loan is paid off with the proceeds of the sale. After receiving two $50,000 annual payments, Cozbi and Zimri are both stabbed to death by an assailant. Assuming that the proceeds from the sale were held in a non-interest bearing savings account subsequent to the sale, how much money will be available for the charity at their death.
a) $0
b) $100,000
c) $1,000,000
d) $1,100,000
e) $1,200,000

ANSWERS

1/ Answer: B. Explanation: Charitable Remainder Trusts cannot offer payments for a fixed period of more than 20 years, although they may pay for a life or lives that are projected to live far more than 20 years. All other payout scenarios are allowable in a Charitable Remainder Trust. Providing 10% of the trust assets, or the total income from the trust, whichever is less, is a form of Charitable Remainder Trust known as the Net Income Charitable Remainder Trust.

2/ Answer: B. Explanation: Answers I and III are not allowed because CRUTs must payout between 5% and 50% of all assets. Answer VI is not allowed because the payout rate must be fixed, either as a fixed dollar amount in a CRAT or a fixed percentage of trust assets in a CRUT. The only exception is that trusts may restrict that payment may not be made from principal, as in a NICRUT (Net Income Charitable Remainder Unitrust) or NIMCRUT (Net Income Makeup Charitable Remainder Unitrust). II is allowed and is referred to as a NIMCRUT. IV is allowed and is referred to as a FlipCRUT. V is allowed, so long as at least one non-charitable beneficiary remains.

3/ Answer: E. Explanation: A CRT is irrevocable and the original rules may not be changed after it is established. However, if the original rules permit it, the donor may act as trustee or select someone else to act as trustee. It is quite common for the donor to retain the right to change which charity will receive the remainder interest. If the donor retains the only rights to income, he or she can terminate the trust by giving those rights to the remainder beneficiary charity. In that case the charity would hold both the life interest and remainder interest in the trust property, making it sole owner, and the trust could be dissolved.

4/ Answer: D. Explanation: A Charitable Remainder Trust does not allow the donor, or anyone else, to invade principal beyond the fixed payment level, even if it is for a good reason such as unexpected medical expenses. All other arrangements are allowed for Charitable Remainder Trusts.

5/ Answer: D. Explanation: The donor will receive a charitable estate tax deduction for the value of any property that is transferred to the charity regardless of whether the transfer happens through a will or through a Charitable Remainder Trust. All other tax benefits are available only by use of a Charitable Remainder Trust and will not be available if the donor continues to own the property herself and makes her charitable gift through a will.

6/ Answer: D. Explanation: Capital gains tax is paid on the difference between basis and the sale price. Basis is normally what you paid for the asset, but can sometimes be adjusted upward for later expenditures on asset improvements, or downward for depreciation deductions taken in intervening years. In this case the gain (sale price – basis) is $900,000 ($1,000,000 sale price - $100,000 gain). Because the tax rate is 20%, Abimelek pays $180,000 in capital gains tax ($900,000 gain X 20% tax). After paying the $180,000 tax, he will have $820,000 left to invest.

7/ Answer: B. Explanation: Because the Charitable Remainder Trust is a tax exempt entity, it pays no taxes. As such, when the CRT sells the land, no capital gains taxes are due, leaving the trust with the entire $1,000,000 left to invest.

8/ Answer: D. Explanation: When the trust borrows money against the asset it becomes debt-financed property. The sale of debt-financed property generates unrelated business income, which is taxed at a 100% rate. Thus, the entire value of the artifact (less the payments previously made) would be lost. Thus, this is not a reasonable planning approach. All other examples are common approaches for dealing with non-income produces assets in a Charitable Remainder Trust.

9/ Answer: C. Explanation: The NIMCRUT will pay more than the NICRUT if net income is 9% of trust assets in odd years and 7% of trust assets in even years. This is because during the years when income is 7% of trust assets, the NIMCRUT will record an "IOU" for the 1% that was not paid out, and will then pay out more than 8% during the later years when returns are 9% of trust assets. If net income is always greater than 8% (for example if it is always 9%), both trusts will payout the same 8% unitrust rate. If net income is always less than 8% (for example if it is always 7%), then the NIMCRUT will record the "IOUs" for the missed payments, but it will never have any additional net income above the 8% to pay any of these "IOUs," meaning that the payout levels will be identical to a NICRUT.

10/ Answer: E. Explanation: The first four items are potentially available with either a Charitable Gift Annuity or a Charitable Remainder Trust. The last item is available only with a Charitable Gift Annuity. If the CRT experiences investment losses or the donor lives much longer than expected, it is possible for the CRT assets to exhaust and no funds will be left for charitable payments.

11/ Answer: B. Explanation: Either a CRT or a CGA can provide an income for life to the donor and the donor's spouse. However, the typical CGA will not permit the other options listed.

12/ Answer: C. Explanation: This trust violates the "10% rule" where the present value of the projected amount going to charity must be at least 10% of the transfer. Although the charity does receive 10% of the initial value of the property, it has to wait 10 years to receive that amount. Because it has to wait 10 years to get the $10,000, this gift is worth less than the value of $10,000 received today. Thus, the present value of the charity's share is worth less than 10% of the initial gift amount. This would be true regardless of whether the §7520 rate was .01% or 10%, because any positive interest rate would make the present value of the gift portion of this trust worth less than $10,000. The rule insuring no greater than a 5% chance that the charity will receive no charitable gift at the termination of the trust applies only to CRATs, not to CRUTs. The generation skipping transfer may be relevant for those tax purposes, but not for income tax purposes. Making income payments contingent on the recipient's behavior is perfectly acceptable, as long as the trust does not encourage behavior that is illegal or against public policy.

13/ Answer: D. Explanation: The Charitable Remainder Annuity Trust (CRAT) is most likely to completely exhaust because the trust must keep paying $10,000 regardless of the poor market returns. Once the trust runs out of money, no further payments can be made. The Charitable Gift Annuity (CGA) will not exhaust because the charity is responsible for making payment, even if the original amount and all subsequent returns have been completely spent. A CRUT is less likely to completely run out of funds, because as the trust becomes smaller, the payments will also become smaller. The NICRUT and NIMCRUT do not permit payments out of principal, thus making it highly unlikely for these trusts to run out of money.

14/ Answer: E. Explanation: For income tax purposes, the trust is considered to be paying out all of its ordinary income first, then all of its capital gain income, then all of its exempt income, then all of its return of principal. (This is sometimes referred to as WIFO, worst in first out, because the income type with the worst tax rates is paid out first.) In this case, the trust first pays out all if its ordinary income, which is the $2,000 of ordinary income earnings from the corporate bonds. Second, it pays out all capital gain, which is the $5,000 of capital gain (difference between the original $95,000 cost of the stocks and the $100,000 sale price of the stocks). Third, it pays out all tax exempt income, which is the $1,000 of municipal bond income. Finally, it pays out return of capital. In order for the trust to pay out any return of capital the payment must be larger than the ordinary income ($2,000) + the capital gain ($5,000) + the tax exempt income ($1,000). In other words, the payment must be larger than $8000.

15/ Answer: D. Explanation: For income tax purposes, the trust is considered to be paying out all of its ordinary income first, then all of its capital gain income, then all of its exempt income, then all of its return of principal. (This is sometimes referred to as WIFO, worst in first out, because the income type with the worst tax rates is paid out first.) In this case, the trust first pays out all if its ordinary income, which is the $2,000 of ordinary income earnings from the corporate bonds. Second, it pays out all capital gain, which is the $5,000 of capital gain (difference between the original $95,000 cost of the stocks and the $100,000 sale price of the stocks). Third, it pays out all tax exempt income, which is the $1,000 of municipal bond income. Finally, it pays out return of capital.

In order for the trust to pay out any tax exempt income the payment must be larger than the ordinary income ($2,000) + the capital gain ($5,000). In other words, the payment must be larger than $7000. The smallest annual payment meeting this qualification listed is $7001.

16/ Answer: B. Explanation: For income tax purposes, the trust is considered to be paying out all of its ordinary income first, then all of its capital gain income, then all of its exempt income, then all of its return of principal. (This is sometimes referred to as WIFO, worst in first out, because the income type with the worst tax rates is paid out first.) In this case, the trust first pays out all if its ordinary income, which is the $2,000 of ordinary income earnings from the corporate bonds. Second, it pays out all capital gain, which is the $5,000 of capital gain (difference between the original $95,000 cost of the stocks and the $100,000 sale price of the stocks). Third, it pays out all tax exempt income, which is the $1,000 of municipal bond income. Finally, it pays out return of capital. In order for the trust to pay out any capital gain income the payment must be larger than the ordinary income ($2,000). In other words, the payment must be larger than $2000. The smallest annual payment meeting this qualification listed is $2001.

17/ Answer: A. Explanation: There are no capital gains taxes paid at any point. There is no capital gains tax paid when Drusilla transfers the property to the CRAT. Because the CRAT is a tax exempt entity, it pays no capital gains taxes when the property is sold. Each year, Drusilla receives $50,000. However, because the trust earns $50,000 of ordinary income from the corporate bond, all of this income is considered to be ordinary income. None of the payments are considered capital gain, and thus no capital gains tax is ever paid.

18/ Answer: D. Explanation: Charitable Remainder Trusts are not permitted to hold subchapter S corporation shares. If the CRT owns a business as a sole proprietor or a general partner it is treated as if it is directly managing the company itself. This direct management ownership would cause the net income from the business to be treated as unrelated business taxable income, which generates a 100% excise tax. Similarly, rent from debt-financed property is considered to be unrelated business taxable income. Shares owned as a C-corporation are considered to be a passive investment and any dividends or capital gains will not generate unrelated business taxable income so long as the shares are not debt-financed. Therefore, the C-corporation shares are the only assets that can be held by the CRT and create no accompanying tax problems.

19/ Answer: A. Explanation: Because the trustee took out a mortgage on the property, it became debt-financed property. Income from debt-financed property, including capital gain income, is unrelated business taxable income in a CRT and is taxed at a 100% excise tax. Thus the entire $1,000,000 of capital gain will be taken in taxes. This leaves only the $100,000 of original basis, which was paid out in the two $50,000 annual payments. Because no other interest was earned during this time, there is nothing left for the charity. Similarly, had the couple survived beyond two years, there would have been no funds left to make any additional annuity payments.

CHAPTER 13: CHARITABLE LEAD TRUSTS

1. The distributions from a CLT are similar to the distributions from a CRT where the charitable and non-charitable beneficiaries have switched places. True or False?

2. Neither CLTs nor CRTs can make payments for a fixed period of more than 20 years. True or False?

3. CLTs and CRTs must both pay from 5% to 50% of initial trust assets (CRAT or CLAT) or ongoing trust assets (CRUT or CLUT). True or False?

4. CLTs and CRTs are both tax exempt entities. True or False?

5. On average, CLTs will hold significantly more assets than a CRT. True or False?

6. There are more CRTs than CLTs and all CRTs combined hold more assets than all CLTs combined. True or False?

7. CLTs are much more likely than CRTs to be set up for a "public benefit" charity rather for a specific cause charity such as those focused on the arts, education, environment, or religion. True or False?

8. Grantor CLTs often pay the remainder interest back to the donor, but Non-Grantor CLTs do not. True or False?

9. When a Grantor CLT earns income it is taxed to the donor, but when a Non-Grantor CLT earns income it is taxed to the trust itself. True or False?

10. When a donor creates a Non-Grantor CLT he receives an immediate income tax deduction for the present value of all future distributions to the charity, but he receives no income tax deduction for gifts made to a Grantor CLT. True or False?

11. If the donor dies while the CLT is still in existence, the donor's estate will include the value of the CLT if it is a Grantor CLT, but not if it is a Non-Grantor CLT. True or False?

12. The consequences of a CLT having significant amounts of unrelated business taxable income are much less serious than the consequences of a CRT having significant amounts of unrelated business taxable income. True or False?

13. Jochebed regularly makes $10,000 annual gifts to her favorite charity. She plans to continue making such gifts for the next 10 years. She would like to take an immediate tax deduction for the present value of these 10 years of future gifts that she plans to make. Which of the following methods will allow her to do so?
    I. Funding a Grantor Charitable Lead Trust paying $10,000 per year for 10 years to the charity
    II. Funding a Non-Grantor Charitable Lead Trust paying $10,000 per year for 10 years to the charity
    III. Signing a legally enforceable contract with the charity promising to deliver $10,000 each year for the next ten years
    IV. Simply deducting the present value of all ten years worth of future gifting on her tax return this year, so long as she actually makes the gifts and doesn't deduct those contributions in future years
    a) I only
    b) II only
    c) I or II
    d) I, II, or III
    e) I, II, III, or IV

14. Rhoda establishes a Grantor Charitable Lead Annuity Trust (CLAT) paying $10,000 per year for 10 years to her local church and a Non-Grantor Charitable Lead Annuity Trust (CLAT) paying $10,000 per year for 10 years to The Unopened Door, a local 501(c)3 religious charity. How will the §7520 rate affect her current charitable income tax deduction received for establishing these two CLATs?
    a) A low §7520 rate will increase the size of her charitable deduction for both CLATs
    b) A low §7520 rate will increase the size of her charitable deduction for the Grantor CLAT, but not the Non-Grantor CLAT
    c) A high §7520 rate will increase the size of her charitable deduction for both CLATs
    d) A high §7520 rate will increase the size of her charitable deduction for the Grantor CLAT, but not the Non-Grantor CLAT
    e) The §7520 rate will not affect the size of her charitable deduction

15. Chloe is a wealthy retiree who regularly makes large charitable gifts out of her assets. Her accountant informs her that, as in past years, she is continuing to exceed the maximum deductible contributions allowed for her level of income. In fact, even if she stopped making gifts, her expected income still would not allow her to deduct all of the charitable deductions she will be carrying over for the next 5 years. Ultimately, she would like her estate to go to her children, not to charity. Chloe is frustrated because she has to pay taxes on her investment income, but then can't deduct when she gives that income to charity because of her past gifts. Assuming her investments generate 5% per year, which of the following arrangements would allow Chloe to avoid paying taxes on the income generated by her assets if that income is given to charity, but still preserves the ability for her children to inherit her assets?
    a) Chloe transfers assets to a Non-Grantor Charitable Lead Trust paying 5% of trust assets to charity each year for her life with remainder to her children
    b) Chloe transfers assets to a Grantor Charitable Lead Trust paying 5% of trust assets each year to charity each year for her life with remainder to her estate
    c) Chloe writes a check for all of the income earned from the assets to charity each year
    d) Chloe transfers assets to a Charitable Remainder Trust paying 5% of trust assets to charity each year with remainder to her children
    e) None of these arrangements can accomplish her stated goals

16. Abishag married a very wealthy older man when she was young. He passed away and she is now very wealthy. She doesn't want to leave a gift to charity at death, but would like to give money while she is alive, so she can actually see the impact of her giving. She would also like transfer wealth to her children while avoiding estate taxes. Currently the §7520 rate is at 2%, but many of her assets will grow at 8%. Which of the following techniques best fits her goals?
    a) Transfer the fast growing assets to a non-grantor Charitable Lead Trust, with a fixed annuity paid to charity and remainder to her children
    b) Transfer the fast growing assets to a grantor Charitable Lead Trust, with a fixed annuity paid to charity and remainder to her children
    c) Transfer the fast growing assets to a Charitable Remainder Trust, with a fixed annuity paid to her children for her lifetime and remainder to charity

d) Hold the assets in her name, write annual checks to the charity, and then leave her estate to her children in her will
e) Transfer the fast growing assets to a charity in exchange for a charitable gift annuity payable to her children

17. Ada transfers $10 million to a 15 year Non-Grantor CLT with the remainder going to her two children Jabal and Jubal. Using the §7520 rate on the date of transfer, the present value of the remainder going to her children is $100,000. During the 15 year period of the Non-Grantor CLT, the assets increase in value much faster than the initial §7520 rate. Consequently, the children actually receive $8 million in assets at the end of the trust period. Assuming Ada is still alive at the end of the trust period, on what amount does she pay gift taxes?
a) $0
b) $74,000 ($100,000 less two $13,000 per year annual present interest gift exclusions)
c) $100,000
d) $8,000,000
e) $8,100,000

18. Naomi, a widow, learns that her son's 30-year-old wife Orpah has contracted a largely untreatable form of cancer. The doctors indicate that she is expected to live for 2 years. Upon hearing this, Naomi sees a potential opportunity to reduce estate taxes. She places $10 million in a Non-Grantor Charitable Lead Trust paying $300,000 per year to a charity for the life of Orpah, with the remainder to her son. Using current §7520 rates, and the life expectancy of a healthy 30 year old female, the projected remainder value is $1. Orpah dies 18 ½ months later, after the trust has paid $450,000 to the charity. Due to good investment returns during the 18 months, her son receives $10.2 million dollars. Assuming Naomi is still alive, on what amount will she have to pay gift taxes?
a) $0
b) $1
c) $10,000,000
d) $10,200,000
e) The remainder value of $10 million CLT calculated based upon a 24 month life expectancy

19. Which of the following rules applies to which kind of charitable trust with regards to holding S-corporation stock?
I. Holding S-corporation stock is always allowed.
II. Holding S-corporation stock is never allowed.
III. Holding S-corporation stock is allowed only if the trust makes a special ESBT election that eliminates its ability to take future charitable deductions
a) Grantor CLT (rule I), Non-Grantor CLT (rule III), CRT (rule II)
b) Grantor CLT (rule II), Non-Grantor CLT (rule III), CRT (rule II)
c) Grantor CLT (rule III), Non-Grantor CLT (rule I), CRT (rule II)
d) Grantor CLT (rule I), Non-Grantor CLT (rule II), CRT (rule III)
e) Grantor CLT (rule I), Non-Grantor CLT (rule II), CRT (rule I)

20. The CLT "Defective Grantor Trust" (a.k.a., "Super Trust") attempts to produce a trust that is
a) A Non-Grantor CLT for income tax purposes and a Grantor CLT for estate tax purposes
b) A Grantor CLT for income tax purposes and a Non-Grantor CLT for estate tax purposes
c) A Non-Grantor CLT for income tax purposes and a Grantor CLT for capital gains tax purposes
d) A Grantor CLT for income tax purposes and a Non-Grantor CLT for capital gains tax purposes
e) A CLT for income tax purposes and a CRT for estate tax purposes

ANSWERS

1/ Answer: True. Explanation: Although many characteristics are different between the two kinds of trusts, the essential distribution difference is that in a CLT the charity is the current beneficiary and the non-charitable beneficiary is the remainder beneficiary whereas in the CRT the non-charitable beneficiary is the current beneficiary and the charity is the remainder beneficiary.

2/ Answer: False. Explanation: CRTs are limited to a maximum of 20 years for fixed period payments, but CLTs are not.

3/ Answer: False. Explanation: CRTs are bound by this rule, but CLTs are not.

4/ Answer: False. Explanation: CRTs are tax exempt. CLTs are not. Ongoing income taxes from income generated by a CLT must be paid either by the donor (grantor CLT) or the trust itself (non-grantor CLT).

5/ Answer: True. Explanation: In a 2007 IRS study, the average CLT had $2,930,990 in assets while the average CRT had $840,640 in assets.

6/ Answer: True. Explanation: Although CRTs are, on average, smaller than CLTs, there are far more CRTs. A 2007 IRS study showed 115,754 CRTs in existence and only 6,377 CLTs in existence. Consequently, all CRTs combined hold far more assets ($97.3 billion) than all CLTs combined ($18.7 billion).

7/ Answer: True. Explanation: This is likely because of the increased propensity to have family foundations (which are rarely cause specific entities) as the charitable beneficiary for a CLT. Family foundations are much more common among the very wealthy as are non-grantor CLTs.

8/ Answer: True. Explanation: The idea of a grantor CLT is that the grantor/donor keeps enough rights in the trust that the trust is treated for many tax purposes as if the donor still owned the property. One example of a right that will cause this treatment is where a donor keeps the right to get the remainder of the property at the end of the term of the CLT.

9/ Answer: True. Explanation: The idea of a grantor CLT is that the grantor/donor keeps enough rights in the trust that the trust is treated for many tax purposes as if the donor still owned the property. (One example of a right that will cause this treatment is where a donor keeps the right to get the remainder of the property at the end of the term of the CLT.) Because of the retention of these rights, any income earned by the Grantor CLT is taxed as if it were earned by the donor himself or herself. The Non-Grantor CLT is treated as a separate taxpayer. Because of this, the Non-Grantor CLT trust itself pays income taxes on any income earned by the trust.

10/ Answer: False. Explanation: When a donor creates a Grantor CLT he receives an immediate income tax deduction for the present value of all future distributions to the charity, but he receives no income tax deduction for gifts made to a Non-Grantor CLT. Instead, the Non-Grantor trust is treated as a separate taxpayer and it deducts each ongoing charitable transfer in the year in which the payment to charity is actually made.

11/ Answer: True. Explanation: The idea of a grantor CLT is that the grantor/donor keeps enough rights in the trust that the trust is treated for many tax purposes as if the donor still owned the property. This includes estate taxes, which treat the donor as if he still owns the property in the CLT.

12/ Answer: True. Explanation: Unrelated business taxable income in a Grantor CLT is treated like any other form of income and taxed to the donor. (The assets of the trust are still treated as the donor's assets for income tax purposes.) A non-grantor CLT with unrelated business taxable income cannot deduct the income if given to charity beyond the income deduction limits applied to regular taxpayers. A CRT with unrelated business taxable income will have all of that income taken by means of a 100% excise tax.

13/ Answer: A. Explanation: Only a grantor Charitable Lead Trust allows the donor to take an immediate charitable income tax deduction for the present value of 10 years of future gifting at $10,000 per year. The non-grantor Charitable Lead Trust allows no deduction (although the trust itself can deduct when the payments to charity are actually made). Signing a legally enforceable contract with the charity promising to deliver $10,000 each year for the next ten years is the same thing as a pledge to charity. Although the charity must record a charitable pledge as current asset, like an account receivable, there is no deduction to the donor until he actually makes the gift.

14/ Answer: B. Explanation: Only a Grantor CLAT will create a charitable deduction for the donor. This deduction will grow larger as the interest rate used to calculate the deduction moves lower. In essence, the deduction is equal to the amount we would have to set aside today that would be large enough to pay these future gifts, assuming the money grew at the §7520 rate. If the money is assumed to grow at a high rate, then we have to set aside less money at the beginning to meet the obligation of paying $10,000 per year for 10 years. If it is assumed the money won't grow much at all, then we have to set aside a larger amount at the beginning to pay $10,000 to the charity each year for 10 years.

15/ Answer: A. Explanation: The non-grantor CLT is considered a separate taxpayer. Chloe would receive no tax deduction for making the transfer to the non-grantor CLT. That creates no disadvantage in this case because Chloe is already over the limit for deducting charitable gifts anyway. However, the non-grantor CLT can deduct the payments made to charity from its earnings and it is not bound by the income limitations of human taxpayers (so long as the CLT isn't generating unrelated business taxable income). If the trust earns 5% each year, the trust can deduct all of the earnings when they are paid to the charity. Writing checks or using a Grantor CLT is not helpful, because the deductions would go to Chloe personally, and she cannot use them because she is already over the limit for deducting charitable gifts. Finally, CRTs do not allow the remainder to go to children, and require at least one non-charitable current beneficiary.

16/ Answer: A. Explanation: By transferring the fast growing assets to a non-grantor Charitable Lead Trust with a fixed annuity paid to charity and remainder to her children, she can pay a low gift tax based upon what the children would receive if the assets grew at 2%, but the children will actually receive much more because the assets will grow at 8%. The charity receives money while she is alive (either for her life or a fixed term), so she gets to see the impact of her gifts. Transferring assets to a grantor CLT is not as helpful because she will still be treated as the owner for estate tax purposes, and thus she will pay estate taxes on the entire amount that is eventually transferred to her children. Neither the CRT nor CGA meets her desires because the charity will likely not use the funds until after her death, and the children do not benefit from the additional growth because their share is a fixed annual annuity. Finally, holding the assets in her name provides no estate or gift tax benefits unlike the non-grantor CLT.

17/ Answer: C. Explanation: Gift taxes are paid based upon the present value of the expected remainder using the §7520 rate. Thus, Ada would pay gift taxes on $100,000 at the creation of the trust. The $8,000,000 amount actually transferred to the children is irrelevant for gift tax calculations. This $100,000 initial gift does not qualify for the annual present interest gift exclusion, because it is a future interest, not a present interest.

18/ Answer: B. Explanation: Gift taxes are paid based upon the present value of the expected remainder using the §7520 rate and, if the charitable payment is to be made for life, the standard life tables provided by the IRS. These tables may not be used if there is at least a 50 percent probability that the individual used as the measuring life will die within one year unless the person actually lives at least 18 months. Because Orpah was the spouse of a remainder beneficiary, and she lived for 18 months, there is no prohibition against using her life as a measuring life. Thus, the estimated remainder value of $1 is valid and Naomi will pay gift taxes on the $1 transfer even though her son ultimately received $10,200,000.

19/ Answer: A. Explanation: CRTs are not qualified to hold subchapter S-corporation shares. Grantor CLTs are qualified because they are treated as if the donor/grantor still owns all of the assets. Non-Grantor CLTs are not normally qualified to hold S-corporation stock but can make a special ESBT election to become qualified, although this is rarely done because it eliminates the ability to take future charitable deductions.

20/ Answer: B. Explanation: The CLT "Defective Grantor Trust" (a.k.a., "Super Trust") attempts to produce a trust that is a Grantor CLT for income tax purposes and a Non-Grantor CLT for estate tax purposes. The goal is to create a CLT where the donor can deduct the present value of the charitable gift from his or her income taxes, as in a Grantor CLT, but not be treated as the owner of the assets for estate tax purposes. There are existing private letter rulings suggesting that this arrangement may work, but no definitive authority on the question.

CHAPTER 14: USING LIFE INSURANCE IN CHARITABLE PLANNING

1. Common uses for life insurance involving charitable giving include all of the following EXCEPT:
   a) Giving an existing policy to charity
   b) Creating a new policy to give to charity with charity as sole death beneficiary, where future donations will be made to the charity, allowing the charity to make future premium payments
   c) Replacing wealth for heirs who were initially disadvantaged by the use of a charitable planning technique
   d) Creating a new policy to give to charity where future premium payments (deductible as charitable gifts) on the policy owned by the charity will be made by the donor to the insurance company, and where the charity will receive all death benefits of the policy
   e) Creating a new policy to give to charity where future premium payments (deductible as charitable gifts) on the policy owned by the charity will be made by the donor to the insurance company, and where some of the death benefit of the policy will be given to the donor's children.

2. John Smith has enough wealth to have a taxable estate for estate tax purposes. In which of the following cases will a $1,000,000 death benefit life insurance policy on the life of John Smith where his child, Mary Smith, is named as the beneficiary, pass $1,000,000 to Mary, but generate no estate taxes?
   I. If Mary Smith owns the policy and has owned it for more than three years
   II. If an Irrevocable Life Insurance Trust, managed by ABC Trust Company, has owned the policy since the creation of the life insurance policy
   III. If John Smith owns the policy
   IV. If John Smith and Mary Smith own the policy jointly
   V. If the John Smith revocable living trust, with John Smith as the trustee, owns the policy
   a) I & II
   b) I, II & IV
   c) I, II & V

d) III only
e) III, IV, & V

3. All of the following are reasons why a Charitable Remainder Trust funded with highly appreciated property might work well in combination with creating an Irrevocable Life Insurance Trust owned life insurance policy benefitting the donor's heirs, EXCEPT
   a) Because the Charitable Remainder Trust produces a stream of income that can be used to pay for life insurance premiums
   b) Because the Charitable Remainder Trust produces an initial charitable tax deduction, the value of which could help to pay for life insurance premiums
   c) Because the Charitable Remainder Trust leaves its principal to charity at death, excluding the heirs, and life insurance naming the heirs can help to mitigate this loss of inheritance
   d) Because the ILIT owned life insurance can pass estate tax free to heirs, whereas the assets transferred to the Charitable Remainder Trust may have been heavily taxed if left to the heirs
   e) Because the Irrevocable Life Insurance Trust is a charitable entity preventing the payment of income taxes on the appreciation of the underlying life insurance policy

4. Priscilla, who has a taxable estate, wants to sell a $1,000,000 non-income producing zero-basis asset then spend the interest income of 5% while leaving the principal at death for her heirs and a charitable organization. What taxes might she reduce or avoid if she accomplishes this goal through a CRT-ILIT combination rather than simply selling the asset and dividing the property at her death by will?
   a) Capital gains taxes
   b) Estate taxes
   c) Income taxes due to a charitable deduction
   d) All of the above
   e) None of the above

5. How can giving a remainder interest to charity in farmland generate an immediate financial benefit that can be used to fund the purchase of life insurance?
   a) Because the remainder interest generates lifetime income
   b) Because the remainder interest avoids the payment of capital gain tax if the donor's remaining interest is sold at a profit
   c) Because the gift of a remainder interest in farmland to charity generates an immediate income tax deduction
   d) Because the gift of a remainder interest is a partial interest gift, and thus not deductible for income tax purpose
   e) Because the gift of a remainder interest in farmland to charity reduces the payment of estate taxes due to the charitable deduction

6. Why might an heir be happier to be the death beneficiary of a $5,000,000 life insurance policy held by an Irrevocable Life Insurance Trust, instead of being named to receive shares of stock valued at $5,000,000 from the decedent's estate?
   a) Because, unlike the ILIT, the shares of stock will create capital gains tax liability at death
   b) Because, unlike the ILIT, the shares of stock will create income tax liability at death
   c) Because the ILIT life insurance death benefit can pass to the heir without the payment of estate taxes
   d) Because the ILIT can be funded without consideration of gift tax implications
   e) Because the potential post-death appreciation is higher for the ILIT distribution

7. Which of the following would not be a reason to consider giving an existing life insurance policy to charity?
   a) If the donor bought too much insurance for actual or current needs
   b) If the donor bought insurance for children who are no longer dependent
   c) If the donor is terminally ill and knows the charity will surrender the policy for its cash value
   d) If the donor bought insurance for a buy-sell agreement that is no longer needed
   e) If the donor does not need the cash value in the life insurance policy

8. The valuation rules for determining fair market value and basis of charitable gifts of typical life insurance policies are somewhat in transition due to Rev. Rul. 2009-13 and the emergence of the life settlement market. However, for newly issued policies and paid-up policies the rules for determining fair market value are
   a) Use the first premium paid for fair market value of a paid up policy and replacement cost for the value of a newly-issued policy.
   b) Use the interpolated terminal reserve plus the unused part of the last premium for fair market value of a paid-up policy and the first premium paid for the value of a newly-issued policy.
   c) Use the interpolated terminal reserve plus the unused part of the last premium for fair market value of a newly-issued policy and the first premium paid for the value of a paid-up policy.
   d) Use the first premium paid for fair market value of a newly-issued policy and replacement cost for the value of a paid up

policy.
e) Use the replacement cost for the fair market value of a newly-issued policy and the interpolated terminal reserve plus the unused part of the last premium for fair market value of a paid-up policy

9. All of the following would be required to document a gift of a life insurance policy worth $5,000 EXCEPT
   a) IRS Form 8283 Noncash Charitable Contributions
   b) A statement from the life insurance company or agent indicating the fair market value of the policy
   c) A note from the charity before taxes are filed or due indicating the date, location, and description of the property and that "no goods or services were provided in exchange for these gifts"
   d) Summary of a qualified appraisal attached to the tax return
   e) The donor's own reliable records of the gift, the charity, the date, the place, and fair market value

10. Mary donates a policy with a fair market value of $100,000 to a public charity. She had previously taken out a loan of $2,000 against the policy and never paid it back. What is the net deductible amount for her charitable gift?
    a) $0
    b) $2,000
    c) $98,000
    d) $100,000
    e) $102,000

11. After a charity receives a policy, it could reasonably choose to do any of the following except
    a) Ask the donor to continue to pay premiums
    b) Surrender it for cash value
    c) Pay premiums from the charity's funds if this maximizes the expected net return from the policy
    d) Sell the policy in the life settlement market
    e) Ask the donor to continue to pay premiums in exchange for leaving the donor's children as beneficiaries of the policy

12. A typical arrangement to create a new policy for the charity might include any of the following EXCEPT
    a) The donor creates a new policy owned by the charity
    b) The donor makes gifts to the charity which the charity can use to make premium payments
    c) The donor makes payments to the insurance company to pay the premiums on the policy owned by the charity
    d) The death benefit on the policy is payable to the charity
    e) The death benefit on the policy is payable half to the charity and half to the donor's child

13. A donor wishes to create a new policy for a charity and fund future premium payments with appreciated stock, thereby avoiding any capital gain tax on the stock. All of the following might be included in such a transaction EXCEPT
    a) The donor creates a new policy owned by the charity
    b) The donor makes gifts to the charity which the charity can use to make premium payments
    c) The donor makes payments to the insurance company to pay the premiums on the policy owned by the charity
    d) The death benefit on the policy is payable to the charity
    e) The charity provides receipts to the donor reflecting the gifts given to pay for the policy premiums

14. All of the following are plausible reasons why a charity might not want to encourage donors to give by creating and paying the premiums on new life insurance policies owned by the charity, EXCEPT
    a) Donors may give less in current gifts to the charity because they are also making premium payments (i.e., current giving is cannibalized)
    b) In very rare cases, the charity may not, under state law, have an insurable interest sufficient to justify a new policy of the intended size
    c) Depending on policy structure, the donor may give for years, and charity receives nothing due to later policy lapse
    d) The charity may prefer to have current gifts today, rather than waiting to receive a benefit at the death of the donor
    e) Premium payments made by the donor directly to the life insurance company will not result in ongoing charitable deductions for the donor

15. All of the following are policy characteristics that a charity might want to insist on in order to prevent a donor giving premium payments for many years and the charity later receiving nothing due to subsequent policy lapse, EXCEPT
    a) Require policies with a relatively short-term before they are projected to no longer need additional premium payments
    b) Require policies from highly rated insurance companies
    c) Require that policy projections on reaching the point where additional premium payments are no longer needed must be based upon reasonable interest rates
    d) Require that the donor give money for term life insurance policies only

e) Require that policy projections on reaching the point where additional premium payments are no longer needed must be based upon the donor living to age 100, rather than a younger age such as 80

ANSWERS

1/ Answer: E. Explanation: The first four techniques are common uses of life insurance in charitable planning. E is a form of a "Charitable Split-Dollar" plan. Charitable deductions are no longer given to any such plans, and consequently such plans are no longer in use.

2/ Answer: A. Explanation: In III, IV, & V, John Smith is retaining some ownership rights or control in the policy. As such, the policy, and the death benefit, will be included in his estate. In I & II, John Smith retains no rights or control over the policy. If he originally had owned the policy and then transferred it, the policy would still be included in his estate unless it had been more than three years since the policy was transferred. However, this does not cause a problem in scenarios I or II, because in I, Mary has owned the policy for more than three years and in II, the ILIT has owned the policy since the creation of the policy.

3/ Answer: E. Explanation: The irrevocable life insurance trust is not a charitable entity. However, all other reasons are examples of why these two planning techniques (CRTs and ILITs) can work well together.

4/ Answer: D. Explanation: The capital gains taxes are avoided because the CRT, a charitable entity, sells the asset and pays no taxes on the capital gain. Estate taxes are avoided because the property in the CRT goes to charity (and is thus deductible for estate tax purpose), and the ILIT owned life insurance is not in Priscilla's estate because she does not own it. Income taxes are reduced because placing property into an CRT generates an immediate income tax charitable deduction.

5/ Answer: C. Explanation: Giving a remainder interest in farmland to charity generates an immediate income tax deduction. As such it creates immediate financial benefit. Although such a gift will also avoid estate taxes for the underlying property because of the estate tax charitable deduction, this does not generate any immediate financial benefit. The remainder interest does not generate income, it is simply the right, owned by the charity, to receive the property at death. If the donor's remaining interest, called a life estate, is sold at a profit (or gain), capital gains taxes would be due.

6/ Answer: C. Explanation: The major benefit of an ILIT is that the death benefit can pass to beneficiaries without estate taxes. Neither gift would create capital gains tax (due to stepped up basis) or income tax at death. Funding of an ILIT does create the need to consider gift taxes, although often substantial funding can be accomplished using the present interest gift annual exclusion (currently at $13,000 per year per recipient per donor). Presumably, the post-death appreciation would not be higher for the ILIT distribution, because it is simply cash. The $5,000,000 of stocks can always be sold for $5,000,000 and converted to cash if post-death appreciation of cash would be higher.

7/ Answer: C. Explanation: If a donor was terminally ill, the policy would be much more valuable than the cash surrender value. Giving such a policy knowing that the charity would surrender the policy for its cash value would not be a good idea. Instead, the donor might consider selling the policy on the life settlement market for a larger amount and donating this to the charity. All other listed explanations are valid reasons to consider giving an existing life insurance policy.

8/ Answer: D. Explanation: The fair market value of a newly-issued policy is the first premium payment. The value of a paid up policy is the cost to replace it with another paid up policy. Note that very few policies are truly paid up, meaning that no future payments will be due under any circumstances. This is different than a policy that projects no future payments will be due depending upon the investment returns of a policy.

9/ Answer: B. Explanation: The life insurance company or agent may not prepare the appraisal (estimate of fair market value) because they are parties to the transaction and are thus disqualified. Consequently this statement would not be required to document the gift. All other items would be needed.

10/ Answer: A. Explanation: Under the new charitable split-dollar life insurance rules the deduction for the gift will be entirely lost. This is because Mary is giving a policy and, in return, getting a personal benefit. The personal benefit here is the relief of the loan. Under normal bargain sale rules the charitable deduction would be $98,000 (the value of what she gave less the value of what she received), but the charitable split-dollar rules completely disallow the deduction.

11/ Answer: E. Explanation: The first four options are reasonable approaches for the charity, depending upon what produces the most cash for the charity. The last option is not reasonable as such arrangements violate the charitable split-dollar rules (because the donor's family is receiving benefit) resulting in negative tax consequences and because the children, rather than the charity, would receive any benefit at death.

12/ Answer: E. Explanation: Typically, the donor creates a new policy owned by the charity and makes premium payments either directly to the insurance company or gives sufficient amounts to the charity so that it can make the premium payments. The death benefit on the policy is payable to the charity. The death benefit would not typically go to the donor's child due in part to the new charitable split-dollar rules that will eliminate any charitable deductions.

13/ Answer: C. Explanation: One advantage of making gifts to the charity that the charity can then use to pay policy premiums is that the donor can make gifts of appreciated property, such as appreciated stock. When the charity sells these appreciated shares of stock, the charity pays no capital gains tax because it is a tax exempt entity. If the donor is paying the premiums directly to the insurance company, the donor must pay with cash, and cannot avoid capital gains by paying with appreciated stock.

14/ Answer: E. Explanation: Premium payments made by the donor directly to the life insurance company on a policy owned by the charity will generate charitable deductions, so this is not a disadvantage. All other reasons listed might prevent a charity from wanting to encourage such gifts.

15/ Answer: D. Explanation: In order to prevent a situation where the donor gives premium payments for many years and the charity later receives nothing due to subsequent policy lapse, the charity will want the donor to be able to achieve a status in the policy where no future premiums are due. Once reaching that stage, the charity can normally expect that they will eventually receive the death benefit and the policy will not lapse. However, some projections can show a policy reaching a point where no future premiums would be due, but the projections may become invalid due to donor longevity or interest rate changes. In order to limit this risk, the charity can insist on illustrations that use reasonable interest rates and assume the donor will live to a very old age. Term policies never reach a stage where future premiums would not be due, so there would never be a point, prior to the death of the donor, where the charity would not be at risk of the donor giving premium payments for many years and the charity later receiving nothing due to subsequent policy lapse.

CHAPTER 15: DONATING RETIREMENT ASSETS

1. Which of the following is NOT an important reason why fundraisers would likely be interested in learning about charitable giving and retirement plan assets?
   a) Because such a large share of wealth is held in retirement plan assets
   b) Because retirement plan assets left at death to non-charities can be heavily taxed, making bequests to charities relatively inexpensive
   c) Because current gifts from IRAs are particularly attractive for living donors under age 59 ½
   d) Because donors over 70½ must make withdraws from standard IRAs even if they don't need the money, potentially opening up the possibility for charitable giving
   e) Because Roth conversions may cause large spikes in income that donors will want to offset with charitable, or other, deductions

2. According to a 2010 publication by the Investment Company Institute, about what percentage of all household financial assets are held in the form of retirement assets?
   a) 5%
   b) 10%
   c) 36%
   d) 51%
   e) 75%

3. The participant ages that separate the life stages of a standard IRA account between early distributions, regular distributions, and required minimum distributions are
   a) 49 ½ and 70 ½
   b) 59 ½ and 69 ½
   c) 59 ½ and 70 ½
   d) 70 ½ and 79 ½
   e) 55 ½ and 70 ½

4. All of the following are possible reasons why withdrawing money from an IRA to make a charitable gift during life may generate net tax costs, EXCEPT

a) If the donor is not yet itemizing deductions, the donor will not receive the full value of the resulting charitable deduction due to the loss of the standard deduction
b) If the donor has already made charitable gifts beyond the income giving limitations, the donor will not receive the full value of the resulting charitable deduction in the current year
c) If the donor is under age 59 ½, withdrawals from the IRA will generate a 10% penalty that will not be offset by the charitable deduction
d) Because the withdrawal will count as income to the donor, the donor's increased income level may disqualify him or her for other tax deductions that are phased out at specified income levels.
e) In certain years Congress has allowed those over age 70 ½ to make qualified charitable distributions (QCD), and donors using these provisions may lose the value of the deduction due to increased levels of reported income and/or loss of the standard deduction

5. What is the number one most obvious reason why withdrawing money from an IRA before age 59 ½ in order to make a charitable gift is NOT tax efficient?
a) Because such withdraws generate at 10% penalty
b) Because withdraws count as taxable income to the participant
c) Because taking a charitable deduction requires itemization
d) Because there are limits on the amount of deductible charitable gifts that a person can make each year
e) Because required minimum distributions do not start until age 70 ½

6. A person of the following age can make a withdrawal from his or her IRA, give it to charity, and potentially have all taxes and penalties completely offset by the charitable deduction:
a) 40
b) 45
c) 50
d) 55
e) 60

7. What happens if a person does not take the required minimum distribution from an IRA after reaching age 70"½?
a) Nothing
b) The principal of the IRA becomes fully taxable
c) The taxpayer is taxed on the value of the Required Minimum Distribution, regardless of whether he actually withdraws it or not
d) The IRS charges a 50% penalty for the amount that should have been withdrawn but was not
e) The IRS charges a 10% penalty for not withdrawing, mirroring the 10% penalty charged for withdraws before age 59 ½

8. In years in which the Qualified Charitable Distribution has been allowed by congress, which of the following charitable transfers might have been considered a Qualified Charitable Distribution?
a) A transfer of $10,000 from a 401(k), 403(b), pension, or profit sharing plan by a person aged 72
b) A transfer of $10,000 from an IRA by a person aged 65
c) A transfer of $10,000 from an IRA to a private foundation by a person aged 80
d) A transfer of $100,000 to a public charity from an IRA by a person aged 73
e) A transfer from an IRA to a Charitable Remainder Trust of $50,000 by a person aged 74

9. Which of the following transactions would normally result in a charitable deduction in the year of transaction greater than any income reported as the result of the transaction?
a) Withdrawing $10,000 of direct contributions made to a Roth IRA and giving the money to a public charity
b) Transferring $10,000 directly from an IRA to a public charity through a Qualified Charitable Distribution in a year in which such transactions were permitted
c) Withdrawing $10,000 from an IRA and giving the money to a public charity when the donor was age 50.
d) Withdrawing $10,000 from an IRA and giving the money to a public charity when the donor was age 65.
e) Withdrawing $10,000 from an IRA and giving the money to a public charity when the donor was age 75 and the $10,000 was a required minimum distribution.

10. Why is it more advantageous to give retirement plan assets, rather than other types of assets, to charity at death?
a) Retirement plan assets receive no step-up in basis if given to non-charitable beneficiaries
b) Retirement plan assets are subject to both gift and estate taxes if given to non-charitable beneficiaries
c) Retirement plan assets are subject to both income taxes and estate taxes if given to non-charitable beneficiaries
d) Retirement plan assets accumulate tax free, making them a larger part of the overall estate

e) Retirement plan assets are more difficult to sell in the subsequent estate administration if given to non-charitable beneficiaries

11. Which of the following would not be a good way to name a charity on a beneficiary form in order to transfer retirement assets to the charitable entity?
   a) 100% of a $1,000,000 IRA to a public charity
   b) 100% of a $1,000,000 IRA to a private foundation
   c) 100% of a $1,000,000 IRA to a private foundation managed by my surviving children and grandchildren
   d) 100% of a $1,000,000 IRA to the decedent's estate where his will directs that $1,000,000 shall be paid to a public charity
   e) 100% of a $1,000,000 IRA to a public charity's donor advised fund with the decedent's daughter as the named advisor

12. John Donor is the participant in a defined benefit pension plan that will pay him $50,000 per year for life (a.k.a., an annuity with no term certain). What are possible tax advantages if John bequeaths this asset to a charity in his will?
   a) John's estate will receive a charitable estate tax deduction
   b) John's estate will receive a charitable income tax deduction to offset the income taxes associated with an IRD asset
   c) John's estate will receive both a charitable estate tax deduction and avoid paying income taxes from the IRD asset
   d) The charity will receive more money than if he had engaged in lifetime giving
   e) There are no tax advantages

13. Steve is a graduate of Texas Tech University. His wife Mary is a graduate of a rival school, Texas A& M University. Steve makes gifts to Texas Tech out of his separate bank account, because Mary hates the school. Steve plans to name Texas Tech University as a 10% death beneficiary of his 401(k) account and Mary as a 90% death beneficiary. Why might he not be able to do this?
   a) Because it is impossible to name more than one death beneficiary on a 401(k) account
   b) Because beneficiaries must share equally, it is not possible to list Texas Tech University as a 10% beneficiary
   c) Because the spouse, if she survives, must be the sole beneficiary of a 401(k) account
   d) Because if Mary splits the 401(k) with someone else, the transfer will no longer qualify for the marital deduction
   e) Because Mary must give her permission for Texas Tech University to be named as a death beneficiary and she hates the school

14. John dies leaving a $1,000,000 IRA to his wife Mary. Mary rolls the IRA into her own account. Over time the account grows to $2,000,000. Mary dies at age 69 having never made a withdrawal from this account. She leaves the account to her favorite public charity. If Mary and John were both in a 40% estate tax bracket at both of their deaths and both had a 40% combined state and federal income tax bracket, how much tax will all of these transactions generate in total?

15. An IRA with a charity listed as the death beneficiary is similar to a Charitable Remainder Trust in that the account can be used during life, but goes to charity at death. Which of the following is NOT an advantage to the donor of an IRA with a charitable beneficiary as compared with a Charitable Remainder Trust?
   a) With an IRA, the donor has the freedom to change his or her mind and later decide not to leave the funds in the IRA to any charity
   b) With an IRA, the donor may take any amount of money in the account out (subject to taxes and penalties) at any time and is not limited to fixed dollar or fixed percentage payouts
   c) With an IRA, the donor receives a 100% tax deduction for all funds placed into the IRA, whereas the Charitable Remainder Trust provides a deduction for only the share of funds representing the present value of the charity's projected remainder interest
   d) With an IRA, the donor incurs almost no administration costs, whereas with a Charitable Remainder Trust there are significant ongoing administration costs, including the requirement to annually file a tax return on behalf of the Charitable Remainder Trust
   e) The donor can place more money into an IRA than into a Charitable Remainder Trust

16. Roth conversions and charitable planning are often complementary. All of the following are examples of that complementarity EXCEPT
   a) By giving a remainder interest in a home or farmland to charity, the taxpayer can generate a significant deduction to offset the taxable income created by the Roth conversion even without having cash available to make a direct charitable gift
   b) By use of a grantor Charitable Lead Trust, the donor can take an immediate deduction for his next ten years worth of charitable giving (assuming sufficient assets are shifted into the CLT to fund the future charitable contributions), helping to immediately offset the taxable income created by the Roth conversion
   c) By naming a charitable organization as the death beneficiary of the new Roth IRA resulting from the Roth conversion, the donor can avoid the income taxes that would have to be paid at death by his or her heirs due to these assets being considered Income in Respect of a Decedent (IRD)

d) For a donor who has given in excess of the income giving limitations and has carryover charitable deductions that are about to expire, a Roth conversion can generate the taxable income needed to claim these deductions by allowing the donor to pay taxes in advance on future withdrawals from the retirement account.
e) By use of a donor advised fund, the donor can take an immediate deduction for future charitable grants by placing money into the donor advised fund that will, in the future, be paid out to other charities, helping to offset the taxable income created by the Roth conversion

17. Roth conversions and charitable planning can work together largely by helping to balance
a) Gifts and Deductions
b) Income and Deductions
c) Income taxes and Estate taxes
d) IRD and Charitable Deductions
e) Taxes and Retirement Withdrawals

ANSWERS

1/ Answer: C. Explanation: Current gifts are not particularly attractive for living donors under age 59 ½, because then withdrawals from traditional IRAs are subject to a 10% penalty in addition to the withdrawal being taxable as income. All other reasons given would be valid reasons why a fundraiser would want to know about the possible interaction of charitable giving and retirement plans.

2/ Answer: C. Explanation: According to the publication, about $16.5 trillion, or 36% of all household financial assets, were held in the form of retirement assets in 2010.

3/ Answer: C. Explanation: Distributions taken before age 59 ½ are early and are usually subject to a 10% penalty. After age 70 ½, participants are required to take minimum distributions from the IRA, regardless of their desire or need for the funds.

4/ Answer: E. Explanation: Qualified charitable distributions (QCD), when allowed by congress, result in no income and no deduction for the donor. Thus, the donors cannot be disadvantaged by either an increased income or the need to itemize deductions.

5/ Answer: A. Explanation: The most obvious reason why making such withdrawals for charitable gifting are not tax efficient is the 10% penalty on withdrawals before age 59 ½. The withdrawals do count as taxable income, but that does not necessarily create a problem, as it is possible for the resulting charitable deduction to offset this taxable income. Charitable deductions do require itemization, but many taxpayers are itemizing deductions already (most commonly to take the mortgage interest deduction), so this is not an obvious disadvantage. There are limits on the amount of deductible charitable gifts that a person can make each year, but this applies to all forms of giving and doesn't explain why making withdraws from an IRA account prior to age 59 ½ is particularly disadvantageous. Similarly, although it is true that required minimum distributions do not start until age 70 ½, this does not explain why it would be disadvantageous to make a withdrawal prior to age 59 ½.

6/ Answer: E. Explanation: Before age 59 ½ withdrawing money from an IRA typically generates a 10% penalty that will not be offset by the charitable deduction.

7/ Answer: D. Explanation: Failing to take a required minimum distribution results in a 50% penalty for the amount that should have been withdrawn but was not

8/ Answer: D. Explanation: When congress has allowed the Qualified Charitable Distributions from IRAs to charities (permitting the transaction to generate no income or deduction) such QCDs have been limited to IRA or IRA rollovers by participants age 70 ½ or older only to public charities and in a maximum amount of $100,000

9/ Answer: A. Explanation: Withdrawing funds from the Roth IRA generally generates no taxable income and the subsequent gift creates a charitable deduction, thus resulting in a transaction that generates more deduction than income. A Qualified Charitable Distribution generates no income and no deduction. IRA withdrawals after age 59 ½ can, at best, result in a deduction as large as the reported income. Prior to age 59 ½, such withdrawals typically generate an additional 10% penalty.

10/ Answer: C. Explanation: Whenever possible, testamentary charitable gifts should be made from retirement plan assets because such assets are subject to both income taxes and estate taxes. Because no income taxes have yet been paid on the assets they are considered Income in Respect of a Decedent (IRD), and income taxes will be due on them. However, when received by a charity, no income or estate taxes are due because the charity is a tax exempt entity. Thus, non-charitable beneficiaries are much better off if they receive other assets, which do not generate income tax liability, than if they receive IRD assets – like retirement plan assets – that do generate income tax liability.

11/ Answer: D. Explanation: Paying the IRA to the estate and using those funds to fulfill the specific dollar (pecuniary) bequest to a charity will cause the estate to pay the income taxes on the IRA. No income taxes would have to be paid if the IRA were paid directly to a public charity or private foundation.

12/ Answer: E. Explanation: A defined benefit pension plan paying $50,000 for life has no residual value after the death of the participant. Thus, at John's death there is no retirement asset remaining. Attempting to bequeath the asset has no effect.

13/ Answer: E. Explanation: Nothing prevents a 401(k) account from naming multiple death beneficiaries in equal or unequal shares. However, the participant's spouse must approve the beneficiary for any retirement accounts covered by ERISA, and 401(k) accounts, unlike IRAs, are covered by ERISA.

14/ Answer: $0. Explanation: There are no income taxes due on the money placed into the IRA. There are no income or capital gains taxes on the growth of the money inside the IRA. There are no estate taxes when transferring the IRA from John to Mary because of the unlimited marital deduction. There are no estate taxes when transferring the IRA from Mary to the charity because of the charitable deduction. Mary pays no income taxes because she never withdrew any money from the IRA. Her estate pays no income taxes as it never owned the IRA. The charity pays no income taxes because it is a tax exempt entity. Thus, $0 of taxes are generated by this series of transactions.

15/ Answer: E. Explanation: The two primary disadvantages of the IRA with charitable death beneficiary is that only a limited amount of funds can be placed into the IRA and that the IRA cannot avoid capital gains tax by accepting transfers of appreciated property. Because of these limitations, the donor would not normally be able to place more money into the IRA than into a Charitable Remainder Trust. All other examples are advantages to the donor of the IRA with charitable death beneficiary over the Charitable Remainder Trust.

16/ Answer: C. Explanation: Roth IRAs do not generate IRD (Income in Respect of a Decedent) because unlike traditional IRAs, the income taxes have already been paid. All other examples are valid ways in which Roth conversions and charitable planning can work together.

17/ Answer: B. Explanation: Roth conversions generate taxable income and charitable planning generates charitable deductions. When used alone it is possible for charitable planning to generate too many deductions for the donor's income level. Similarly, a Roth conversion can generate too much taxable income creating the need to offset such income with large deductions such as those that can be created by charitable planning.

ABOUT THE AUTHOR

Russell James, J.D., Ph.D., CFP® is a professor in the Department of Personal Financial Planning at Texas Tech University. He holds the CH Foundation Chair in Personal Financial Planning and directs the on-campus and online graduate program in Charitable Financial Planning. Additionally, he is an adjunct professor at the Texas Tech University School of Law where he teaches Charitable Gift Planning. He graduated, cum laude, from the University of Missouri School of Law where he was a member of the Missouri Law Review. While in law school he received the United Missouri Bank Award for Most Outstanding Work in Gift and Estate Taxation and Planning. He also holds a Ph.D. in consumer economics from the University of Missouri, where his dissertation was on charitable giving.

Prior to his career as an academic researcher, Dr. James worked as the Director of Planned Giving for Central Christian College in Moberly, Missouri for 6 years and later served as president of the college for more than 5 years, where he had direct and supervisory responsibility for all fundraising. During his presidency the college successfully completed two major capital campaigns, built several new debt-free buildings, and more than tripled enrollment.

Dr. James has over 150 publications in academic journals, conference proceedings, and books. These predominantly focus on statistical analysis and experimental research related to gifts, estates, and property. He has been quoted on charitable and financial issues in a variety of news sources including The New York Times, The Wall Street Journal, CNN, MSNBC, CNBC, ABC News, U.S. News & World Report, USA Today, the Associated Press, Bloomberg News and the Chronicle of Philanthropy.

Proof

27585169R00244

Made in the USA
Charleston, SC
13 March 2014